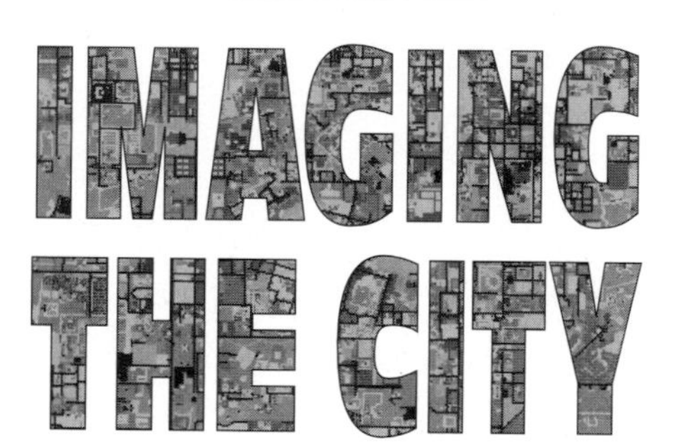
IMAGING
THE CITY

CONTINUING STRUGGLES AND NEW DIRECTIONS

Edited by
Lawrence J. Vale and **Sam Bass Warner Jr.**

CENTER FOR URBAN POLICY RESEARCH
EDWARD J. BLOUSTEIN SCHOOL OF PLANNING AND PUBLIC POLICY
RUTGERS, THE STATE UNIVERSITY OF NEW JERSEY
NEW BRUNSWICK, NEW JERSEY

Published by the Center for Urban Policy Research
Edward J. Bloustein School of Planning and Public Policy
Civic Square • 33 Livingston Avenue
New Brunswick, New Jersey 08901-1982

Printed in the United States of America

Cover and Interior Design: Helene Berinsky

Library of Congress Cataloging-in-Publication Data

Imaging the city : continuing struggles and new directions / edited by Lawrence J. Vale and Sam Bass Warner Jr.
p. cm.
Includes bibliographical references and index.
ISBN 0-88285-169-1 (cloth : alk. paper) — ISBN 0-88285-170-5 (pbk. : alk. paper)
1. City planning—History—20th century. 2. City planning—Social aspects. 3. Cities and towns in mass media. I. Vale, Lawrence J., 1959– II. Warner, Sam Bass, 1928–

NA9095 .I46 2001
711'.4'09—dc21

00-060111

The authors and publisher have made extensive efforts to contact and credit copyright holders of the illustrations reprinted in this book. If copyright proprietorship can be established for any illustration not specifically attributed in the Credits section of this book, please contact Editor, Center for Urban Policy Research.

The publisher wishes to express special thanks to Activeworlds.com, Inc., of Newburyport, Massachusetts, for use of a portion of its Alphaworld map on the dust jacket of this book, as a design element throughout the book, and on pages 294–95. © Activeworlds.com.

Cover photo: View of New York City in Miniland, Legoland (Carlsbad), California, opening weekend, March 1999. Photo © L. J. Vale.

To the memory of Kevin Lynch

ABOUT THE EDITORS

LAWRENCE J. VALE is associate professor and associate head of the Department of Urban Studies and Planning at the Massachusetts Institute of Technology. His research is devoted to interpreting the history, politics, and sociology of urban design. He is the author of three books and numerous articles examining government-sponsored environments, including *Architecture, Power, and National Identity* (1992) and *From the Puritans to the Projects: Public Housing and Public Neighbors* (2000). His work has been recognized with the Spiro Kostof Book Award for Architecture and Urbanism (1994), a Guggenheim Fellowship (1995), the Chester Rapkin Award from the Association of Collegiate Schools of Planning (1997), a Place Research Award from the Environmental Design Research Association and the journal *Places* (1999), and the Best Book in Urban Affairs prize from the Urban Affairs Association (2000).

SAM BASS WARNER JR. is an urban historian best known for his writing on the history of American urban development: *The Urban Wilderness: A History of the American City*; *The Private City: Philadelphia in Three Periods of Its Growth* (winner of the Bancroft Prize in 1968); and *Streetcar Suburbs: The Process of Growth in Boston 1870–1900*. He is currently a visiting professor at the Massachusetts Institute of Technology in the Department of Urban Studies and Planning and was formerly William Edwards Huntington Professor of History at Boston University and Jack Meyerhoff Professor of Environmental Studies at Brandeis University. He is also past president of the Urban History Association. His most recent book is *Greater Boston: Adapting Regional Traditions to the Present* (University of Pennsylvania Press, 2001).

CONTENTS

ACKNOWLEDGMENTS

The editors are grateful to Bish Sanyal, head of the MIT Department of Urban Studies and Planning (DUSP), and William Mitchell, dean of the MIT School of Architecture and Planning, for providing the intellectual and financial support that enabled this book project to take place. Most of the chapters originated as papers commissioned for a DUSP Faculty Colloquium held in late 1998. We particularly appreciate the commentary on colloquium papers provided by Eran Ben-Joseph, James Buzard, Bernard Frieden, Langley Keyes, David Laws, Tunney Lee, Leo Marx, William Mitchell, Lisa Peattie, Karen Polenske, Terry Szold, and Krzysztof Wodiczko. Although, for various reasons, we were not able to include their papers in this book, we also greatly value the colloquium presentations made by Dolores Hayden, David Lowenthal, Alex MacLean, and Richard Sennett, as well as the post-colloquium symposium contributions by Tridib Banerjee, Christine Boyer, Gary Hack, and Michael Southworth.

Anne Beamish helped coordinate the colloquium with grace and efficiency, assisted by T. Luke Young. Jennifer Villemure Czysz aided us with illustrations, as did photographer John Cook. As always, we remain indebted to Margaret de Popolo and the staff of MIT's Rotch Library and Rotch Visual Collections.

At CUPR Press, we are enormously grateful for the editorial skills of Arlene Pashman, who artfully shepherded two editors, nineteen authors, and hundreds of illustrations. Robert Lake provided significant encouragement for the project. Our gratitude also to Helene Berinsky, the book's designer.

Finally, we wish to acknowledge the invaluable contributions of the MIT students who participated in our "Imaging the City" seminar: Dulcy Anderson, Fabio Carrera, Rachel Gakenheimer, Francisca Ortiz, Brent Ryan, Ben Schonberger, Jeff Shumaker, Domenic Vitiello, and T. Luke Young. Their sustained engagement with the issues explored in class and their trenchant assessments of the colloquium presentations have greatly improved this book.

Cities, Media, and Imaging

Sam Bass Warner Jr. and Lawrence J. Vale

IMAGING CITIES

Urban projects today, at whatever scale or ambition—whether they be vast highway or water constructions or the placement of a neighborhood infill house—proceed amid a blizzard of visual and verbal images. There is nothing new about this; urban life has always been lived among the play of social knowledge, stereotypes, sharp observations, and metaphorical pictures. Today's image climate, however, has two new elements. First, the mix of the visual and the verbal has changed: Visual image-making has exploded at an exponential rate, so that fused images of pictures and words are commonplace. Second, the invention and popularization of these fused images has spawned a vast industry of advertisers and public relations propagators as well as sustained the older professions of artists, writers and architects. Out of this blizzard, city planning must now forge ahead.

The chapters that follow are our attempt to clarify the situation and to help urban planners function in the new climate. Planners have always faced a difficult and controversial task because their professional role requires them to be the spokespersons for the public interest. In such a welter of conflicting pictures and voices, how might the public interest be discovered? And once identified, how might it be expressed so that competing publics might attend to it? As generations of city planners have learned from practice, there are no easy answers to such questions, but the experience of planners today does suggest both successful ways of working and innovations of considerable promise. The essays that follow set these forth in a perspective from the long tradition of city marketing to the latest experiments with building communities via the Internet.

The focus on planning practice led the editors toward images that are now at work in our cities. We pose these questions: What images are being advanced, and who is proposing them? What happens when images come into conflict? Urban form and design did not command our entire attention; rather, we also concentrated on institutional practice and on how institutions implement urban visions. In this, we join in the call for what Kevin Lynch termed "true city design." Skeptical of large building complexes masquerading as "urban design," Lynch instead favored a process of city design and development, one in which designers would "[deal] directly with the ongoing sensed environment of the city in collaboration with the people who sense it."[1]

For us, all city design, all constructions of the city, offer material that people may include in their images of their environment. The built and building city are a part of the experience of all city dwellers; thus, it is theirs to incorporate, interpret, or ignore. All urban imagery, however, is not a product of the built city. Social experience, historical events, human knowledge of all kinds are powerful influences, and they play upon the imagery of places. The discussions that follow trace this interplay between the physical stuff of planners and architects and the social experience and outlooks of image makers and their audiences.

The word *image* has many meanings. An image can be a mental representation conjured up by reading a text or by listening to words or music. Images can arise even from particularly evocative smells and, especially for the visually impaired, from tactile contact of all sorts. An image can also be a physical likeness that is consciously produced by designers of diverse stripes—from architects and urban designers to location managers and set designers of television and film to designers of Web site interfaces. Sometimes an image is more of a symbolic and metaphorical embodiment, as when concepts such as "democratic" or "fascistic" are associated with particular places; more prosaically, image is what fosters the ambience that constitutes "brand identity."

Today, however, the very term "image" has become a verb as well as a noun. To a greater extent than ever before, places no longer simply *have images;* they are continually *being imaged* (and re-imaged), often in ways that are highly self-conscious and highly contentious.

The term *imaging* as it is understood here involves actors and actions concerned with transforming all of these kinds of meanings. As Kenneth Boulding put it, "The meaning of a message is the change which it produces in the image."[2] City imaging, in this sense, is the process of constructing visually based narratives about the potential of places. It is what occurred, for example, when urban designers broke the impasse over developing Manhattan's West Side Highway by reconceptualizing that urban edge as a "park" rather than a "highway."[3] City design, if understood like this, is a process of brokering the best metaphor, in ways that will shift or consolidate public sensibilities and invent the possibility for new kinds of place attachments.

This media-enriched image-building process involves not only place-based and form-based visions but also strategies for economic opportunity and environmental stewardship. Place promotion transcends economics-grounded efforts to attract new investment; it is also a strategy for reinforcing (or reconstructing) city image. As such, it always matters who builds these images, for which reasons, and for whom.

Many of the contributors to this volume are faculty members at the Massachusetts Institute of Technology who still keenly feel the intellectual presence of long-time colleague Kevin Lynch (1918–1984). The chapters of this book were written forty years after the publication of his pathbreaking book, *The Image of the City.*[4] That slim volume most famously connected the words "image" and "city" and helped educate two generations of students and practitioners about the form of urban places. We are all admirers of his work and have been influenced by his concern for the public perception of urban imagery. Even today we find the criteria and metacriteria of city design that he set forth in his last major book, *Good City Form*, to be useful.[5] We particularly share his concern for assessing the benefits and injuries of urban projects, the metacriterion he called "justice." His is a voice that still should be heard.

Yet we must now extract the Lynchian call out of a more complex cacophony. For Lynch—and for those he interviewed during the late 1950s—it was still possible to see cities in terms of the direct sensory appreciation of their qualities and to assess the structure and identity of places based strictly on the physicality of their "paths, edges, nodes, landmarks, and districts."[6] Lynch's seminal work was translated into several languages, and his investigations of city image were replicated and extended with gratifying degrees of confirmation on six continents. Yet such studies rarely probed *how* city dwellers gained the knowledge about their cities or questioned whether their ways of knowing differed in relation to the distance their mental maps traveled from their places of most frequent direct experience. For Lynch, and for most who followed him, it was enough to stress that some areas of the city were less "imageable" than others and, thus, appeared as blank spots when people were asked to draw mental maps of their cities.

What mental maps miss, however, are the multiple other ways that citizens learn about places, especially—though not exclusively—about places that are more distant from the precincts of their own direct experience. More often than not, evocation of a neighborhood or city name yields not a mental blank spot but a clearly imaged stereotype about a never-visited place, based entirely on what has been seen and heard through various forms of media.

IMAGING AND MEDIA TECHNOLOGIES

Although it can certainly be argued that all media help construct the ways that people interpret cities and other places, certain kinds of media seem to have a greater current impact on city design and development. This impact takes both direct and indirect forms.

First, there are media—graphic design, drawings, some computer software, and the full range of public relations techniques—that play a direct role in the design and development process, either by facilitating the testing and representation of design possibilities or by contributing to the efforts needed to establish sufficient consensus to permit implementation of urban transformations. Ever since the development of the first city maps and perspectival views, designers have been able to project graphically a range of potential future directions for urban places. Over the last three decades, however, technologies for representation have multiplied and gone digital, enabling increasingly sophisticated forms of computer simulation.

In addition to visualization technologies, there is a second type of direct media influence on cities. Some forms of media—such as advertising signage and public art installations—have become a constituent part of the visual and auditory landscape of cities and roadsides. In places like Times Square or the Las Vegas strip, visual media themselves become the principal environmental stimuli.

Finally, there are media—especially television, film, and software—that depict cities and affect city design and development more indirectly, simply by virtue of widespread distribution and repeated exposure. These media have the power to help set the agenda for how broad segments of the public think about cities.

IMAGING: CONTINUING STRUGGLES AND NEW DIRECTIONS

Lynch began his career before the proliferation of television and computers, and his observations were rooted in a pedestrian's focus. His writings did not confront the enormous explosion of visual imagery that today permeates everything. Today, people unconsciously parrot the lines of television newscasters; "Have a good day!" is repeated ad nauseum. They gesture in imitation of characters in situation comedies. Across the nation, pictures of cities, neighborhoods, buildings, and people make and remake popular images of urban living. This is not a Lynchian climate of individual citizens with their cognitive maps; rather, it is a climate of clashing values and visions. The chapters that follow offer a variety of suggestions about how a planner might find a bearing in such confusion.

The arrangement of the chapters reflects what the editors have learned from the academics and practitioners who participated in a fall 1998 faculty seminar at MIT. First of all, much is known about how this world works and how a planner might deal with it. There are active promoters, there are visible conflicts, and there are deep anonymous cultural movements and societal attitudes that must be clearly identified and dealt with. The discovery and the elucidation of the public interest among these actors and their conflicting values and images constitutes the art of city planning and the central challenge of city design. We have gathered these chapters together under the thematic heading, "Struggles over City Images."

A second aspect of the current image climate lacks clarity, as it always has. Its images are polarized between those of fascination with the city and those seeking a pastoral antithesis. All the images in this cluster draw their shape and power from a perception of the city as a force, a powerful energized entity of some kind that shapes human lives for better or for worse. The scale of these images is usually metropolitan; these image makers try to grasp the city as a totality or, conversely, present quarters of the city as total environments. We have gathered these accounts under the heading "Responses to the Overwhelming City."

Not all who shape city images see the process as a struggle or as a wrenching choice between total celebratory congestion or anti-urban escape. A third group of essayists has explored innovative ways of image-making and brought to the fore a set of new or previously overlooked image makers. The innovations and innovators range from the cities of children's television and their professional creators to amateurs logging on to the Internet seeking virtual citizenship in a cybercity. They include volunteer performers in urban festivals as well as city designers who seek to nurture environments that afford a myriad of ways to confront personal and collective heritage. There is special promise in each of the different kinds of urban image-making, and each encompasses a range of suggestions for the art of city planning. We have gathered these essays under the heading "New Images and New Image Makers."

In such a collection of essays many interpretations are possible. Our arrangement, however, is structured to lead forward toward new possibilities for image-making and productive new roles for planners and city designers. Part One, "Struggles over City Images," tells of the long continuity and slow evolution of municipally sponsored image-making. Today's city guide, featuring its prominent buildings and ranked attractions, bears a startling resemblance to the "books of praise" used to attract pilgrims to the medieval cities described by Julian Beinart (ch. 1). Briavel Holcomb also stresses continuity in the marketing of cities, even as formulaic city promotion materials—paeans to capitalist potential—have recently added scenes of residential felicity and emphasized sports and other cultural facilities (ch. 2).

Image conflict, an essential element of democratic planning, appears in two dramatic examples: Eugenie Birch's account of efforts to revive the devastated physical fabric and economic collapse of New York's South Bronx (ch. 3) and the contested fight to spruce up downtown Cleveland, explored by Patricia Burgess, Ruth Durack, and Edward Hill (ch. 4). The Bronx case admonishes all planners to attend early on to the visions and images held by the residents of an area slated for redevelopment; to ignore such images is to court injustice and failure. The Cleveland case raises the interesting issue of how a downtown renewal program of high-profile entertainment and tourist attractions might sustain itself without a substantial residential component; the problem is further complicated by the lack of residents to work with. Both the Bronx and the Cleveland studies review issues that lie at the core of today's American urban planning practice.

Most often, image competition occurs within a single city or region, but sometimes the struggle over city image takes on an international dimension. Larry Ford shows how the projection of new skyscrapers in Asian cities continues an image battle once confined to New York and Chicago. From Kuala Lumpur to Shanghai, city leaders have used "signature" buildings to seek or affirm new international status as players in the global economy (ch. 5).

The last essay in this section calls attention to the force of vernacular culture. The struggle over images is displaced onto the home front. Judith Martin and Sam Bass Warner Jr. (ch. 6) review commonplace urban and suburban neighborhoods in the Twin Cities of Minneapolis and St. Paul, where they find evidence of the compelling power of the vernacular. First, the popularly held images of the neighborhoods—inner city, post-World War II suburb, new outer suburb—presuppose a reputation that departs from the social reality of the three areas. Second, the strong elements of greenery—the trees, the lawns, the lot layouts common to all three—reveal a popular consensus about what constitutes a good urban neighborhood. Here, the battle over urban images is waged between the visual environment (with its surprising continuity) and the social environment (full of divergent stereotypes about who will live in each kind of place). Thus, the Martin/Warner essay reminds planners that beneath the images of whatever may be in conflict over a particular intervention, there may lie a strong value consensus.

Part Two, "Responses to the Overwhelming City," reveals a deep current of ambivalence among some image producers. At least since the poet Wordsworth, images of the city have been seen in antithesis to imagined pastorals. Henry Jenkins (ch. 7) reviews some classic films to demonstrate that those who view the modern city as an active force, either in its entirety or as a neighborhood, see it as an overwhelming presence. It is not difficult, when reading these essays, to hear the voices of the past. Even in Sandy Isenstadt's essay that discusses the urban theories of contemporary urbanists Leon Krier and Rem Koolhaas (ch. 8), the voices of the past intrude. Krier's image-making echoes William Morris in *News from Nowhere* and Theodore Dreiser in *Sister Carrie*, while Koolhaas's fascination with the possibilities of urban flow might have been drawn from William Dean Howells's imaginings of Grand Central Station in *A Hazard of New Fortunes* or H. G. Wells's science fiction.[7] Thomas Campanella's essay examining the cultural roots of current urban imagery on the Internet continues these themes (ch. 9). These essays remind us that American planning and urban image-making ride the rolling waves of Western culture in perpetuity.

Part Three, "New Images and New Image Makers," suggests that many alternatives lie in wait for city planners. Some are trends to watch; some are activities planners might join or encourage. The good news from these essays is that planners may do much more than cope with public hearings at which neighbors shout about zoning and traffic; they can also participate proactively in new forms of image-making.

Dennis Frenchman (ch. 10), a designer of heritage areas, points out that the new approach in his field is not to feature a didactic message but instead to create settings in places, and with artifacts, that allow visitors the freedom of their own interpretations. In these new heritage places, visitors are expected to mentally merge the given materials with their own previous experience to create a personal history. In the future, as Frenchman demonstrates, city designers will increasingly use the built world in combination with new kinds of virtual spaces.

The Internet is surely a phenomenon to be respected. As Anne Beamish (ch. 11) shows, at present its urban imagery puts forth simplistic versions of vast city configurations, or arid suburbia. Both images are perpetrated within the context of urban pastoral ambivalence that Campanella identifies. The communitarian aspects of the "Net," the chat rooms and the games, and some of the interest-group communities suggest that, as the Internet matures from its infancy, it might become an important source of new urban images and new social constructions.

The current urban imagery of children's television, as described by Lawrence Vale and Julia Dobrow, demonstrates a playful manipulation of both traditional big city and suburban elements (ch. 12). The empowerment of children is the hopeful theme of these urban places, a significant contrast to other television presentations of cities. Moreover, the authors offer an analysis of these imaginary places in Lynchian terms.

Deborah Karasov (ch. 13) continues this empowerment theme by reviewing the recent history of public artists who wish to give expression to aspects of urban life that are omitted or slighted by the commercial mass media. Her essay concludes with a discussion of an exact parallel to the planner's situation. If an urban mural or public work is to be displayed in a given neighborhood, by what process should such a work of art be made? What should the artist's relationship be to the neighbors, and how should the neighborhood be engaged?

Mark Schuster reviews a wide range of urban performances—programmed "ephemera" (ch. 14)—that take place in contemporary cities and that are largely disregarded by planners. Some of these events and temporary transformations have municipal or corporate sponsorship, some do not. Some are elaborate, some small and local presentations. The variety and richness of the imagery projected earns these ephemera their rightful place in the planner's lexicon.

Next, John de Monchaux (ch. 15) raises a serious planning issue, outcome evaluation, vis-à-vis the current fashion of publishing city rankings in the popular press. He finds that the methods of the rankers are deeply flawed and argues that the outcomes should not be taken seriously; nevertheless, rankings are used by municipalities to proclaim their special virtues. The question of whether a substantial city planning program succeeds in improving the life of that city remains a vital question, one for which little systematic evaluation has been hazarded.

Ultimately, city designers and planners need a framework for taking action in a media-saturated environment. The volume concludes with Lawrence Vale's attempt to sketch out a new set of avenues for planners to traverse in conceptualizing and contributing to the "public realm" in urban and regional environments (ch. 16). The essay identifies four emerging forms of public realm-making, which he calls Corridors, Traces, Watches, and Ways. Each of these place-types cuts across multiple neighborhood and political jurisdictions, permitting city designers to operate on a broader canvas than that of the urban pedestrian whose world is so well captured by Lynch's celebrated quintet of paths, edges, nodes, landmarks, and districts.

Current American city planning practice not only has its established ways of working within the blizzard of proliferating imagery, but it also possesses deep chords of tradition. Lynch's enduring concern with the consensus image of places thus remains central but must now be embedded in more conscious political and artistic processes. City designers and planners need not merely stand by and watch the parade of images pass by, nor need they become paralyzed by the overwhelming polar tension between congested engagement and nostalgic escape. Instead, such design professionals can participate effectively in re-energizing cities by using new city-imaging techniques proactively.

Those who care about the future of cities must confront a salient reality: Cities are no longer just built; they are imaged. City designers, like others who observe the metropolis, image and re-image cities through the calculated use of media. Every classic urban proposal that has engaged the public imagination in the last century—Ebenezer Howard's Garden City, Le Corbusier's Ville Radieuse, Frank Lloyd Wright's Broadacre City—has done so through the careful use and marketing of images. Deft contemporary imagist–urbanists from Robert Venturi to Leon Krier to Rem Koolhaas provide compelling evidence that such methods endure. At base, this book seeks to help city designers and planners explore positive ways to capitalize on the image-making phenomenon.

PART 

Struggles over City Images

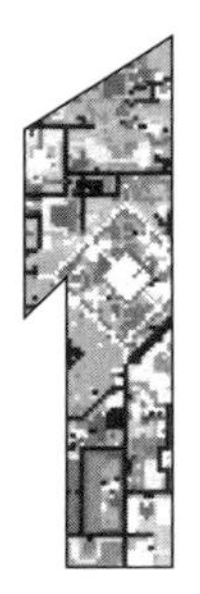

Image Construction in Premodern Cities

Julian Beinart

■ EDITORS' OVERVIEW

A significant push in economic development offices these days is devoted to luring tourists. Architect/urbanist Julian Beinart reveals that this is, in one form or other, a two-thousand-year-old tradition, although throughout most of history the effort has been to attract pilgrims, not tourists.

Before the era of the printing press, before books were available to the masses, the earliest Jewish, Christian, and Muslim guides and city eulogies had to be read aloud to their audiences. Yet, much of the content would be familiar to a listener of today: wondrous public buildings, extraordinary past events, notable families, booster statistics, and fabulous landscapes. In this tradition, Beinart especially examines the elaboration of the Cult of St. James by French and Spanish bishops to strengthen their competition with Rome. It was a corporate effort complete with a logo for all travelers (the scallop shell) and an accompanying book of miracles and tips on the best pathways to Santiago de Compostela.

In his conclusion, Beinart raises the core ethical and design question that bedevils image promoters. What if the images of the campaign differ substantially from the later experience of the visitors or the images of the residents? He doubts whether a good city can long sustain such a disjunction.

INSIDER AND OUTSIDER IMAGES

Just after July 4, 1998, *Time* magazine, no doubt wanting to associate local identity and national patriotism, invited its readers to "come visit seven places that do something better than anyone else does. They tend not to brag much, so we'll do it for them." One of the *Time* seven is Clinton, Montana, home of an annual Testicle Festival, where the previous September fifteen thousand people came to eat Rocky Mountain Oysters (delicately defined by *Time* as "the business part of the bull"). The Festival's founder, a retired school superintendent, now a bar owner, says "A bar has to have a signature event. . . . I don't care if it's maggot races." *Time* concluded that "a town needs an identity, or it doesn't exist."[1]

Time's conclusion, if somewhat abrupt, is nevertheless one of a few general propositions that emerges in research about image construction in premodern cities. Inevitably, there are two sets of images of a town: one, the mental images carried by its citizens; the other, those held by outsiders. Both images are manipulable. Kevin Lynch focused on the former; this book probes both. *Time*'s argument is that only when you manufacture a salable external image do you have identity (and presumably wealth). But identity is inescapable: nature mandates it. And naming something increases the intrinsic difference of identity. "We must never forget the importance of a name: giving a name to a city is giving it the very being of the name it bears."[2] So Jacques Ellul emphasizes the significance of Cain, the exiled murderer and founder of the first city in the Bible, giving his city the same name, Enoch, as he does to his son. According to *Time*'s philosophy, neutrality of image—that is, doing very little to distinguish yourself—means no identity; therefore, "you don't exist." Of course, this is literally untrue. Towns, like individuals or firms, while inevitably different, are also different in their drive to externalize themselves.

There are places, although probably not too many, that advertise in order to repel. In 1973, a pamphlet entitled *Guida Turistica di Controinformazione* appeared in the small northern

Fig. 1.1: ***Guida Turistica di Controinformazione*****, a 1973 publicity poster to dissuade people from being attracted to Bergamo.**

Italy town of Bergamo (fig. 1.1). To ward off outsiders, especially those from nearby Milan looking to purchase second homes in the town, this document focused on twenty-four horrible sites within the town. In the Corsarolo area, for instance, it warned that you can sleep only three or four hours a night because of traffic noise. The town cinema is open only two days a week. The Teatro Sociale, a significant Lombardian neoclassical theater and the mayor's pride, has had unrepaired holes in the roof for a decade. In any case, the pamphlet concludes, three-quarters of the city is owned by the church.[3] (In contrast, the *Liber Pergaminus,* the first of the twelfth-century city "praise" books, has only good things to say about Bergamo some eight hundred years earlier: "a quiet hill-town whose squares serve equally well as play-grounds for the children and for the trying out of the war horses."[4])

Just because you tell people how bad things are does not mean they won't come. This is apparently the message of the film *Crazy People*, in which a group of mental patients produce slogans such as "Come To New York: It's Not As Filthy As You Think," or "Come To New York: There Were Fewer Murders Last Year,"[5] to market New York City. By contrast, sometimes you advertise what you think will attract, only to find that it turns off outsiders. I recall seeing a publicity brochure for the city of Lagos, Nigeria, that showed a traffic jam as evidence of how modern it is.

In many cases, the images created for external purposes and those designed to nourish the city's own inhabitants are congruent. "I Love New York," a slogan created to magnetize visitors, implies that New Yorkers themselves love their city. Bringing important ephemeral events to a city often involves binary image construction as well. So, when Hitler propagandized the Teutonic bond between ancient Athens and Nazi Germany at the 1936 Olympic Games, he did so both to distract the outside world (while there were detention camps on the outskirts of Berlin) as well as to manifest the eternity of the new Reich to his own citizens.[6] In less demonic circumstances, cities continue to justify hosting the Games both for their external value (foreign attention, trade and tourism) as well as for their boosting of local morale, health, and infrastructure.[7] Another connection between outside promotion and internal condition can be seen in a letter written by Duke Ercole I of Este to the Jewish families expelled from Spain in 1492, then temporarily resident in Genoa. The letter sets out the terms that presumably will attract the Jews to Ferrara, where the Duke believes that "We are certain that every next day they will be more happy to have chosen to come here."[8] Marketing Ferrara to the Jews in 1492 came at a time when the city was "very open and dynamic," and municipal optimism was evidenced in the implementation of a new city plan.[9]

The frescoes painted more than a century earlier by Ambrosio Lorenzetti in a hall of the Palazzo Pubblico of Siena, however, are images created entirely for internal purposes. Commissioned by a governing group of nine merchants and bankers whose regime had been threatened more than once by the city's nobles, the *Buon Governo/Mal Governo* murals were, in the words of Chiara Frugoni, "intended as a propaganda man-

Fig. 1.2: Ambrosio Lorenzetti, *Good Government, the Effects in the City,* fresco, 1338–1339. Siena, Palazzo Pubblico, Sale della Pace.

Fig. 1.3: Ambrosio Lorenzetti, *Good Government, the Effects in the Country,* fresco, 1338–1339. Siena, Palazzo Pubblico, Sale della Pace.

ifesto . . . providing reassurance of its beneficial effects, and a warning to all who thought of attempting to replace it."[10] In the Good Government fresco, the benign authority of the ruling Nine is represented by a white-haired old man who supervises over the common wealth (*comune*) of the city. The form of the well-governed city is splendidly displayed: there are palaces, large-windowed buildings, towers and landscape, people working and maidens dancing and singing, even a grid of good stone roads leading to the city (figs. 1.2 and 1.3). Siena is to be read as a well-cared-for place, a "convincing picture, as if it might be an exact reproduction of reality."[11] While Lorenzetti's images of Siena clearly were aimed at locals, such image-making is part of a long tradition of efforts to promote the distinctive advantages of particular cities to outsiders as well.

THE PILGRIMAGE NETWORK

Very early in *The City in History,* Mumford proposes the primacy of flow over settlement in explaining the origin of cities. "The magnet comes before the container" is one of his most resonant metaphors: "this ability to attract non-residents to (the city) for intercourse and spiritual stimulus no less than trade. . . . The first germ of the city, then, is the ceremonial meeting place that serves as the goal for pilgrimage."[12]

The construction and transmission of images to attract pilgrims of three major religions to premodern holy cities is the primary focus of this chapter. As mentioned before, there will be images made for visitors ("the magnet") as well as those created for the cities' own inhabitants ("the container"). While most of the material will be about the encouragement of movement for religious purposes ("spiritual stimulus"), there will also be examples of commercial attraction ("trade"). These were seldom separate in medieval life. "The religious impulse was so all-pervading an element of medieval life that even the entire economic structure depended on it," writes von Simson in his book on the Gothic cathedral.[13]

Religion and commerce were responsible for the spatial network along which people moved in medieval times. Pre-Islamic Mecca lay on an overland trade route from suppliers in the East to purchasers around the Mediterranean; in the seventh century, Islamic Mecca suddenly became a center no longer only of regional goods transfer but of international religion as well.[14] Traders and pilgrims traveled long distances, and danger and mutual benefit caused both traders and pilgrims to travel in groups. Pirenne suggests that even late medieval merchants traveled in caravan-like fashion.[15] In the prologue to *The Canterbury Tales*, Chaucer's pilgrim describes the society of some twenty-seven fellow pilgrims in his group.[16] The great German pilgrimage of 1064 to Jerusalem consisted of anywhere from seven to twelve thousand people;[17] and the *hajj* of the African king Mansa Musa brought fifteen thousand to Mecca in 1325.[18]

Pilgrimage travel was dangerous and protection expensive. It has been pointed out that the word *travel* comes from *travail*, which derives from the Latin word *tripalium*, an instrument of torture that tears the body apart.[19] Pilgrims had to be housed, fed, and cared for at their shrine destinations and along their travel routes. The four main travel routes to the shrine of St. James in Compostela in northern Spain traversed France, setting up scores of overnight hostels, taverns, and secondary shrines profitable to the French, in whose interest it was to promote European pilgrimage to Compostela rather than to Rome (fig. 1.4). Pilgrimage covered large distances and took time: two or three years to Mecca was not uncommon. A pedestrian or donkey-borne pilgrim from Eastern Europe traveled more than three thousand kilometers to Compostela; an Englishman's trip to Jerusalem meant a painful crossing of the Mediterranean. In holy cities, secondary services for pilgrims meant large local incomes and, in some cases, even the genesis of special retail districts. The *Mishna*, for instance, requires Jewish pilgrims to Jerusalem to pay a secondary tithe for their commercial needs.[20] Peters describes the situation in Mecca as follows:

> Mecca offered all the commercial services that might be expected in the context of the *hajj*. Bedouin sold the pilgrims sheep and goats at highly inflated prices for the sacrifice at Mina. The town itself had an abundant supply of barbers to shave or clip the pilgrims' heads; camel brokers to provide transportation to and from Arafat; loan sharks for the impecunious, pawnbrokers for the improvident, and prostitutes for the incontinent.[21]

Pilgrim traffic was large. According to Flavius Josephus, a census in the first century counted more than two and one-half

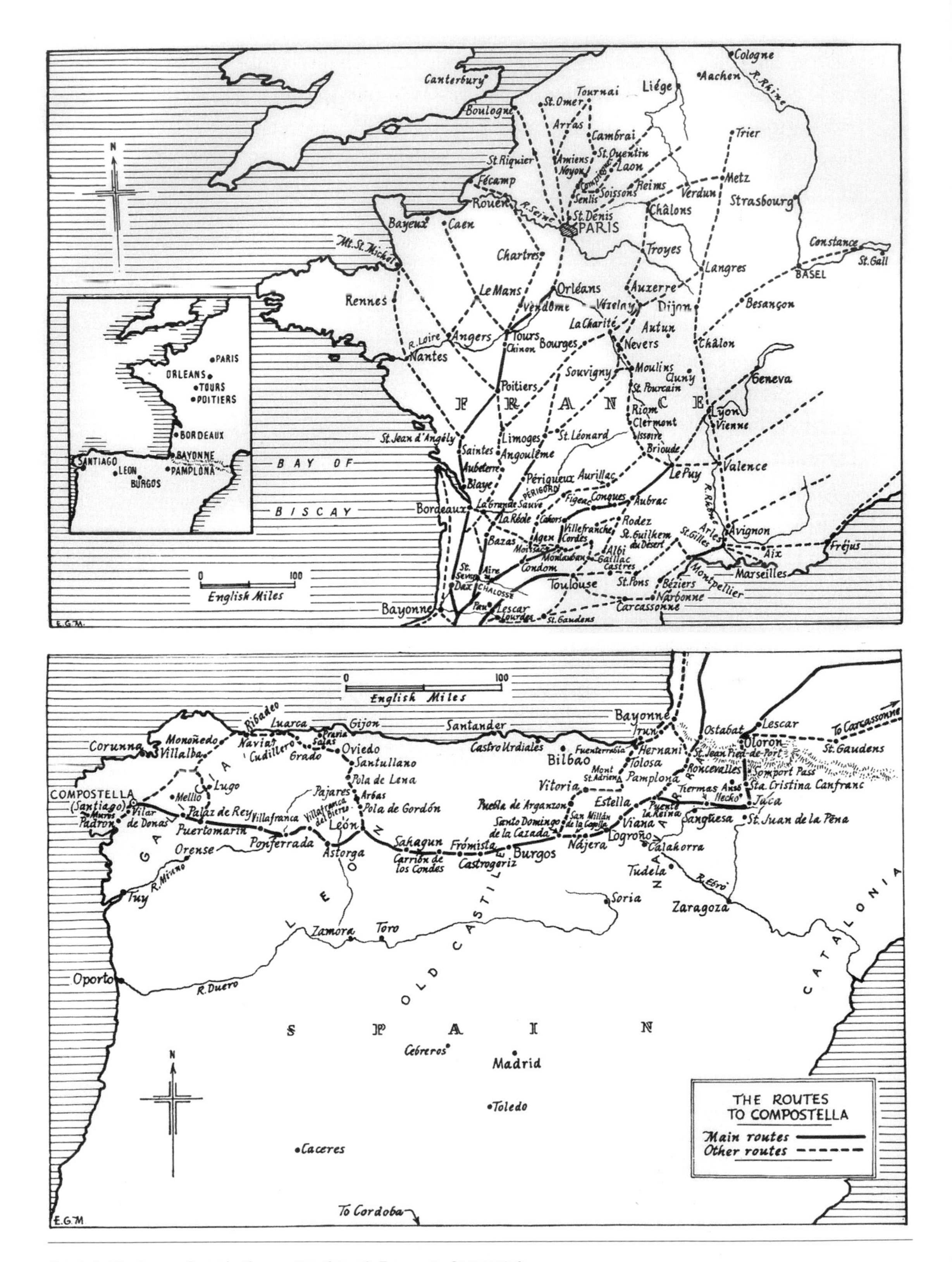

Fig. 1.4: The four main and other routes through France to Compostela.

million pilgrims in Jerusalem at the time of the Passover festival.[22] Another source claims that, in Chaucer's time, with the population of England no more than two million people, more than two hundred thousand pilgrims visited the shrine of St. Thomas of Canterbury each year.[23]

The spatial geography of pilgrimage varied by religion. For the Jews, there was no other spiritual center but Jerusalem, both the earthly city and the heavenly city, from which the messianic predictions of Isaiah and Micah claimed the world would be redeemed. Whenever allowed, they returned regularly from the diaspora for festivals. When prevented, they lived in what has been described as a "psychic empire" with Jerusalem as their "metropolis of the mind" and their "capital of memory." Their religious manuals prescribed that they pray toward Jerusalem three times a day: "Return in mercy to your city Jerusalem and dwell in it as you have promised; rebuild it soon, in our own days."[24]

The religious space of the Muslim world also was unicentric, vectored toward Mecca by the ritual obligation of daily prayers and the annual *hajj.* This made Mecca, in the words of the Turners, a "mandalalike center of normative communitas."[25] Medina and Jerusalem have always been major second-tier shrines, and Jerusalem in particular has fluctuated in importance as an Islamic pilgrimage site. Unlike both Judaism and Islam, however, the spiritual landscape of medieval Christianity was not shaped by single destinations.

Among the reasons for the decentralization of Christian holy places, two seem pertinent. While the papal bureaucracy and justice system were centered in Rome, a great deal of authority was allowed to local dioceses where bishops were responsible for screening the visions, miracles, and apparitions that attracted pilgrims. Since stature and income accrued to the site of such events, bishops tended to support claims. A second factor is the distribution of relics. Nowhere was competition between potential pilgrimage shrines fiercer than in the search for religious relics.

The essential components of pilgrimage were not only travel (what Brown calls the "therapy of distance")[26] but also "praesentia"—being in the presence of the holy—and touching something venerated as a relic. Together, these constituted the transfer of the sacred, for which procedure a relic was indispensable: "Pilgrimage and relic are the two sides of the same coin . . . the essential mobility of the pilgrimage is a function of the essential immobility of the relic; and the fixedness of the latter is predicated upon the mobility of the latter."[27]

With the development of the "cult of the cross" in Jerusalem in the fourth century, the search for relics ransacked the churches of Jerusalem and other sites.[28] Thousands of churches and shrines were built in Europe on the basis of the speculative relic economy. For many pilgrims to Jerusalem, part of the point of the journey was returning with some relic. Bishops and royalty sent envoys to find religious material: the agents of one ex-Queen brought back a fragment of the cross and the finger of a saint.[29] Muslims were not immune to collecting relics of their own faith,[30] but this was minor compared to the Christian display of spurious curios, among which, for example, the following:

> As many as fourteen foreskins of Christ were on view in various European churches in Poitiers, Coulombs, Chavraux, Hildesheim, Le Puy-en-Velay, Antwerp, and Rome. Calvin cynically recorded the large number of phials ostensibly filled with the virgin's milk and observed that even if she had been a cow she could not have produced such an enormous quantity.[31]

IMAGE CONSTRUCTION AND DISTRIBUTION

Already by the third century B.C., large crowds of Jewish pilgrims traveled to Jerusalem from the Mediterranean and the Near East. Even before the birth of the Prophet in the sixth century, pilgrims journeyed to Mecca. The eleventh century saw the mass pilgrimage of Christians to sites all around the Mediterranean: the movement to Compostela in Galicia, for instance, was so great that it was compared to the stars of the

Milky Way by Dante: "the white circle which the common people call, Way of St. James."[32] With no newspapers or magazines, no widely circulated books or telephones, no radio or television, no photography or developed techniques for drawing cities, how did so many people, often a very long distance from holy cities, know about them?

Little research deals directly and comprehensively with the ways images of cities were created and disseminated during this time. From a wide variety of sources, however, it is possible to put together a very general picture of how cities informed the world about themselves and how this information was spread. To this end, three aspects stand out: (1) oral societies, (2) books, and (3) campaigns and incentives.

■ ORAL SOCIETIES

> St. Brendan the holy man was a monk of Ireland . . . And there came to him a holy abbot named Beryne . . . and Beryne began to tell of many wonders that he had seen in diverse places . . . And then St. Brendan purposed soon after to seek that place.
>
> R. BRANTL, *Medieval Culture*[33]

Pilgrimage eroded the localism of medieval life. Large numbers of people who otherwise never would have met exchanged news and ideas, stories and songs. Together they built up and passed on a body of experience, some real, some embellished or imagined in the forms of legend, lore, or myth. Of pilgrims it was said that "if they be half a month out in their pilgrimages many of them become, half a year later, great jugglers, storytellers and liars."[34] Pilgrims were a familiar sight as they traveled in groups through the European countryside. Because many of the pilgrims were known to be making the journey for the remission of sins sometimes as grave as murder, onlookers, sinners themselves, sympathized and helped them. The many oral societies formed by pilgrimage, so random and interactive in nature, were responsible for much of the news transmission about holy venues.

The circularity of pilgrimage involved departures, sanctioned and ritually celebrated, as well as returns. Homecoming was another opportunity to add to the word-of-mouth system about places. But the role of the Christian church, given its enormous superintendency, cannot be diminished. Holy sites were constantly in competition with one another and, particularly as pilgrimage became an increasingly popular means for the absolution of sins, so confessors advised in favor of their own private selections. In the eighth century, when manuals—the *Poenitentialia*—appeared to recommend penance through pilgrimage, no destinations were included, this being left to verbal interaction with the confessor.[35] Sermons were also powerful vehicles of spoken influence over the mass of illiterate listeners.

Miraculous cures, apparitions, and visions were other occasions for the Catholic Church to wield influence, as the sites of their occurrence held much promise for power and money. Such events had usually been kept private, but the church urged greater display to advertise them, so that they were "now deliberately made public: files are kept, the healed stand up and show themselves to the congregation." Augustine writes in the fourth century about his annoyance on hearing that the recipient of a cure, an important lady in Carthage, had not publicized her healing in the city.[36] (Protagonism by the church for giving publicity to the sites of visions continues strongly to present times as attested to by the widely told stories of the two young children in Ezkioga, Spain, in 1931,[37] and three in Fatima, Portugal, in 1917.[38])

The church also played an important part in pilgrim organization, another tool for influencing the venues of pilgrimages. On Christmas Eve in 1326, a treaty allocated three hundred Flemish pilgrims equally to shrines in Spain and France.[39] After the First Crusade, the Hospitallers of St. John of Jerusalem and the Templars, having entered the pilgrimage travel business, became "the great banking agency whose branches in the European capitals, in Jerusalem, and in the majority of Eastern centers handled all manner of exchange transactions with enormous profits from the pilgrim service."[40] The Templars accumulated such a vast fortune that Philip IV of France confiscated it and dissolved the order in 1312.

■ TRAVEL BOOKS

Written accounts of travelers' and pilgrims' experiences, as well as guides that explained routes and places, increased knowledge about cities and whetted the appetite to visit them. Although only relatively few copies of these documents seem to have been made (presumably since few could read them), they found their way abroad. The first Christian to inscribe his experience as a pilgrim to Jerusalem came from Bordeaux in the fourth century. Three hundred years later, the Abbot Adomnan addressed his book to "those who live far away from the places where the Patriarchs and Apostles used to be, and can only know the holy places through what they learn from books." The book was presented to King Aldfrith "through whose generosity it was handed on to be read by lesser people."[41]

The few early Christian guidebooks to Jerusalem, such as Theodosius's *The Topography of the Holy Land,* were geographies of the holy monuments and the surroundings of Jerusalem. These guides often were very short, easily carried, and, because of their brevity, used as broadsheets by shipping companies advertising for pilgrim travelers.[42] There were far more pilgrim travelogues, however, especially after the Crusades, than guidebooks. However vast the Jerusalem Christian travel literature of the time, it pales in comparison with later times: In England alone, in the nineteenth century, an estimated sixteen hundred such books were published in forty years.

Conversely, Muslim accounts of Jerusalem are from travelers rather than from pilgrims. The Persian Nasir-i-Khusrau, who visited the city on his travels in the eleventh century, found as many as twenty thousand Muslims in Jerusalem during the holy month.[43] Mecca itself was known through the writings of many Muslim travelers. Typical of these travel diaries is al-Harawi's twelfth-century *Pilgrimages,* which includes descriptions of other religious centers of Islam as well. Mecca also had a body of histories of the city, which formed an unbroken line from the writings of Azraqi, who begins with the pre-Islamic history of the city, to Qutb al-Din in early Ottoman times.[44]

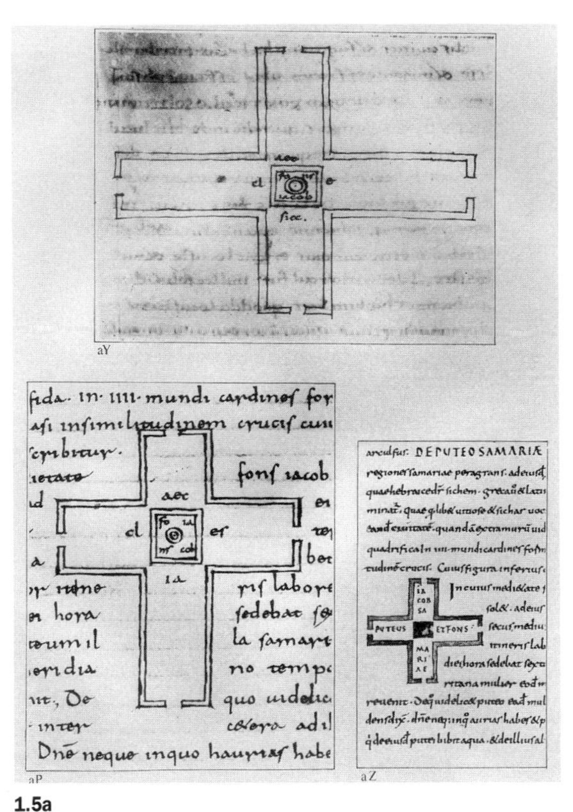

1.5a

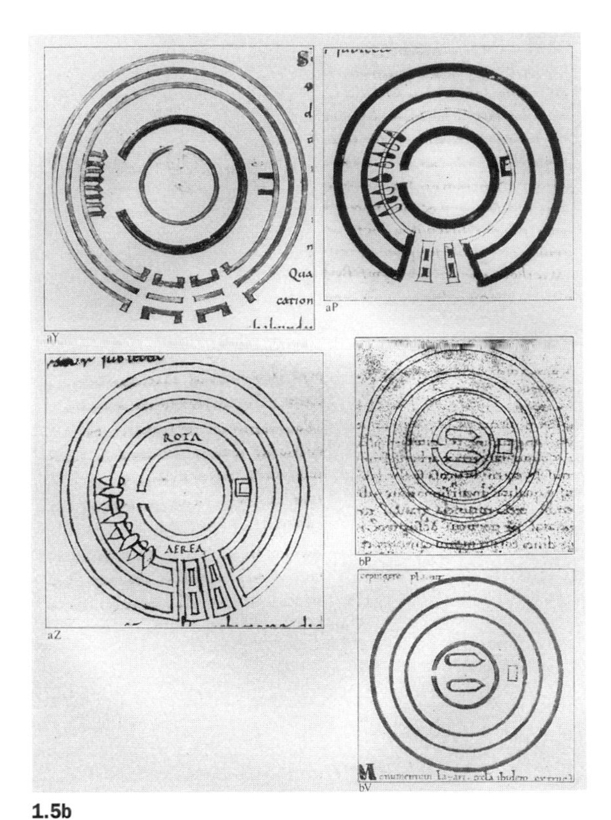

1.5b

Fig. 1.5: Versions of four church plans in Jerusalem from the Abbot Adomnan's seventh-century guidebook.

1.5a: The church at Jacob's Well, spreading out as a cross toward the cardinal points of the world around a center where Jesus spoke with the Samaritan woman.

1.5b: The Ascension, a "great round church" open to the sky in the middle, set up around a patch of dust with Jesus' footprints.

1.5c: The Great Basilica on Mount Sion, a "landscape"-shaped oblong with an entrance on the south.

1.5d: The Round Church on Golgotha, made of three circular stone walls divided from each other by the width of a street.

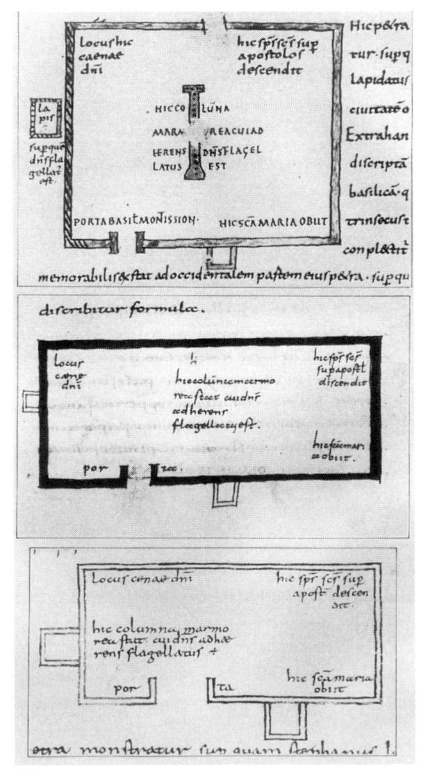

1.5c

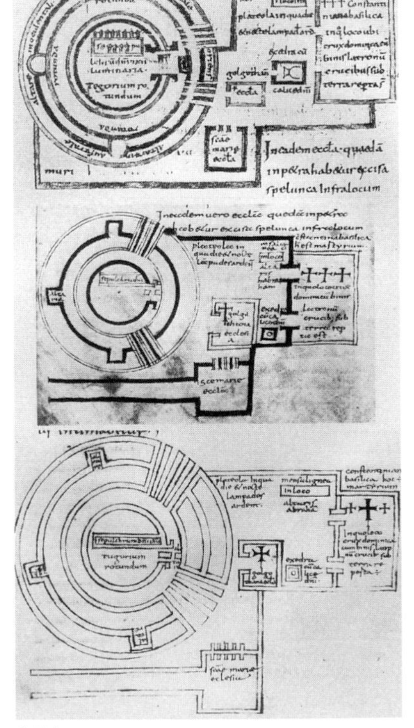

1.5d

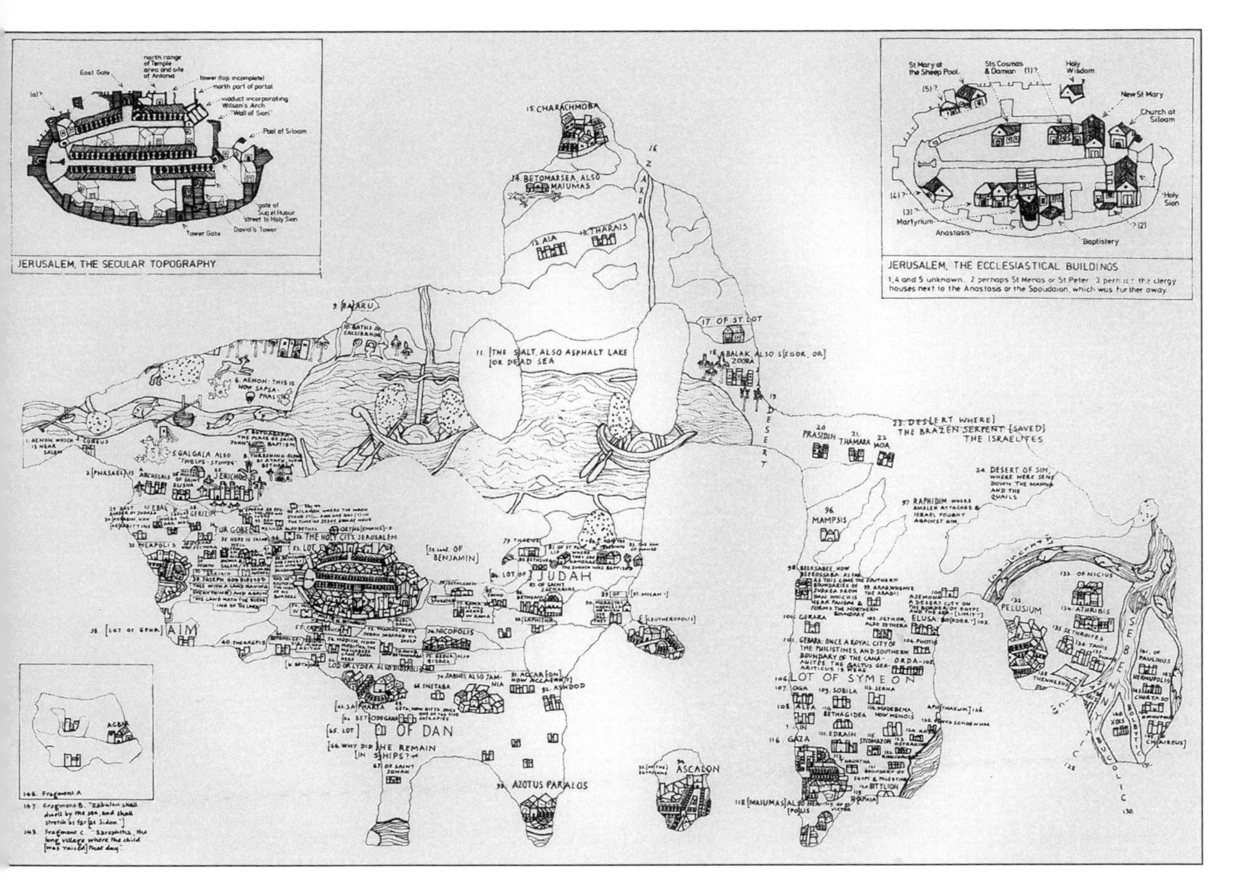

Fig. 1.6: The sixth-century Madaba mosaic map, including the secular and ecclesiastical topography of Jerusalem.

There is also a tradition of travel writing among Jews which, according to Adler, began in the ninth century. Notable among these is the written itinerary of the French rabbi, Samuel ben Samson, who recorded his visit to the sites of the holy land in the early thirteenth century and obtained from the King of Jerusalem a letter inviting Jews to visit Palestine—an invitation that led to the pilgrimage of three hundred French and English rabbis to Jerusalem soon after.[45]

These travelogues and guidebooks never contained drawn images of cities or buildings. The one exception is Adomnan's seventh-century guidebook, *On the Holy Places*, mentioned above, in which there are indeed plans of churches in Jerusalem (figs. 1.5a–d), though these are probably the only such plans until the sixteenth century.[46] The so-called Madaba map, a mosaic laid out on the floor of a church in Jordan in about A.D. 600, including a bird's-eye view of Jerusalem from the west, is equally

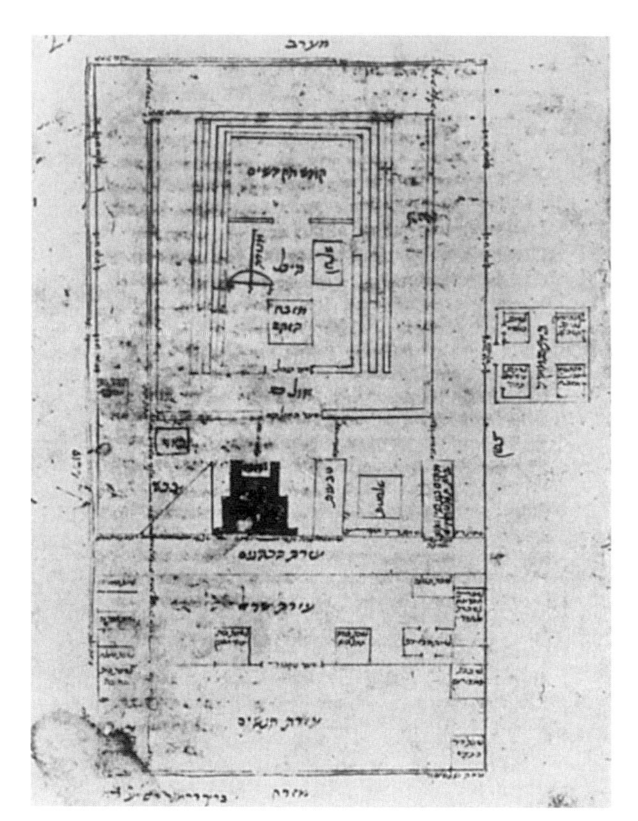

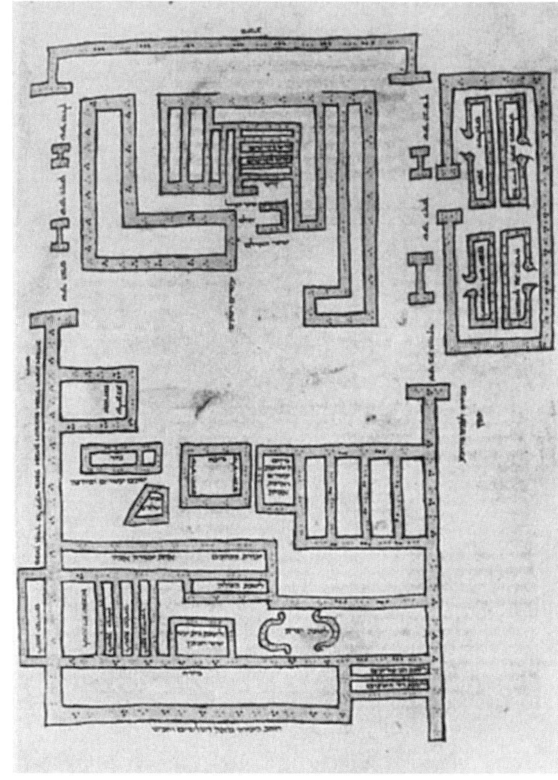

Fig. 1.7: Twelfth-century drawings of the Temple by Maimonides.

unique[47] (fig. 1.6). The first known record of an architectural drawing by a Jew is considered to be that of the sage, Rashi, who included a primitive plan of the Temple in his eleventh-century text, *Responsa*. In the next century, Maimonides also made drawings of the Temple to accompany the text in his *Mishna Commentary*[48] (fig. 1.7). Although written descriptions of the architecture of Jerusalem were the only sources available to potential visitors to the city, the memory of its religious buildings could be maintained by the building of replicas. Stanford Anderson uses the example of the many emulations of the Holy Sepulchre all over Europe in constructing the idea that architecture aids memory in society.[49] There are many examples of "vicarious" Jerusalems all over the world.[50] One is the twelfth-century city of Lalibala in Ethiopia, complete with a river Jordan, seven olive trees in a garden of Gethsemane, and replicas of the churches of the Holy Sepulchre and Golgotha.[51]

■ BOOKS OF PRAISE

Although travel books spread knowledge about cities to places where they were unknown, their contents were relatively superficial. However, the genre of books dating from the eighth century, written mostly to describe Italian cities, while still formulaic in character, is much richer. These books were authored not by visitors but by local residents who sought to bring their cities to the attention of outsiders and thus to compete directly with other cities. In a twelfth-century text, two cities compete for relics and argue over who has the greater claim:

> On the one hand, Mantua says she is an *urbs* and not simply an *arx*, encircled as she is by a river furrowed with ships; but she is immediately taunted (by Canossa) with being an *urbs* in name only, with not being encircled by solid walls, with having a humid and unhealthy climate, being short of wine, meat and grain. Mantua then replies that it is *she* who possesses relics, in the church to which her rival is constrained to travel; Canossa retorts that *she* is a direct dependency of the Pope and not of the patriarch, and attempts to dismantle the myth that Virgil was Mantuan.[52]

There are many praise books written about Milan. In the most famous, Bonvesin della Riva, a thirteenth-century language teacher and poet, explains in his introduction to his book *De Magnalibus Urbis Mediolanis* that it is intended for foreigners and for those of his fellow citizens ignorant of the city's greatness. He glorifies Milan as without equal anywhere and contests Rome as the Pope's best location: "(Milan) is not only worthy to be called a second Rome . . . it would be right and proper in my judgment that the seat of the papacy and the other dignitaries should all be transferred here from there."[53]

Although it is unclear how many copies of praise books were made, they are known to have influenced one another. An early poem about Verona, *Laudes Veronensis,* was inspired by an earlier one about Milan; the Franciscan who wrote a praise book of Lodi also had read previous works about Milan.[54] The descrip-

Fig. 1.8: ***The City of Verona,*** **ninth- to tenth-century illumination of the city.**

tion of Verona is accompanied by a large illustration, an elevation of the city showing its Roman monuments and current buildings (fig. 1.8). This visual portrayal is an exception to the rule of the praise books of this time which were, by and large, written descriptions of infrastructure, monuments, churches, the natural setting of the city, population statistics, local saints and relics, important citizens, wealth, and the legal framework of the city. The best known and most influential of these praise books, the twelfth-century *Mirabilia Urbis Romae*, includes only some of these elements.[55] Nevertheless, its "mixture of fact and fantasy proved highly acceptable to the flood of pilgrim and visitors and, carried by some of them back to their homes, was no doubt read by many who had never set foot in the Eternal City."[56] Only later, as Baron argues, in works such as Bruni's laudatory writing about Florence, are these rather practical and segmented descriptions of earlier medieval time superseded by more intellectually integrated "humanistic eulogies."[57]

There is a parallel in the Arabic tradition of books of "merit" or *fada'il* treatises composed to eulogize cities in the Islamic world. Mecca, Medina, and Jerusalem had such merit books, but so did less holy places. Between the tenth and fifteenth centuries, Cairo, for instance, had at least twenty texts extolling its virtues. Like their European counterparts, these laudatory texts seemed to be both media for attracting pilgrims and travelers as well as documents affirming local patriotism. So, typically, a *fada'il* book would include descriptions of monuments, the topography of the city, the reasons for its buildings, stories about famous kings, lists of Muslim and non-Muslim saints, recantings of miracles, dreams and divinations, and many volumes about religious scholars who visited or lived or died in the city.

In early Islam, Moslems, like Jews, said their prayers facing Jerusalem. Later, Jerusalem was relegated to the position of third-holiest city in Islam, but there was nevertheless a large amount of writing praising the city. This literature took various forms. One is the *hadiths* or oral sayings associated with the prophet Mohamed, such as "Whoever makes the pilgrimage to Jerusalem, counting upon merit, Allah will give him the reward of a thousand martyrs."[58] Another is the acclamatory writings of geographers, the most celebrated of which is that of the tenth-century Jerusalemite, al-Muqadassi, whose book *Descriptions of the Muslim Empire* tells this story of praise:

> Once, in a gathering in al-Basra . . . when I was asked: Which, in your opinion, is the most illustrious country? I answered "Our country" [meaning Jerusalem and Palestine]. Then I was asked: Which is the most pleasant country? and I answered "Our country." Then I was asked: Which country is the best? I said, "Ours." The audience was amazed.[59]

Other than the *fada'il* literature, the *ziyarat* (the equivalent of Christian pilgrim manuals) and the singing of mystic and devotional poetry are also forms of idealization. There are three *fada'il* treatises on Jerusalem before the Crusades, about ten during the tenth and eleventh centuries, and many more afterwards. In the earliest of these, the author al-Wasiti reluctantly recognizes that Mecca is more central to Islam than Jerusalem: a prayer in Jerusalem is worth fifty thousand prayers, as is one in Medina; but one in Mecca is worth one hundred thousand, he admits.[60] There was more than religious value to glorifying Jerusalem, however. At times there was political benefit to stressing Jerusalem's centrality to Islam—and, to be sure, great economic profit as well if the rich pilgrim caravans on the *hajj* to Mecca could be persuaded to stop in Jerusalem en route.

■ CAMPAIGNS AND INCENTIVES

The oral network and travel and praise literature, powerful instruments of diffusion as they were, do not convey the sense of corporate publicity and product marketing of modern city governments and chambers of commerce. The closest case in early medieval times may be that of the contrivance of a religious product, the Cult of St. James, and its directed distribution throughout Europe, and later, South America. The beheaded body relic of St. James was magically discovered by a hermit in a cave in Galicia at the beginning of the ninth century. After a conscious and aggressive campaign to elevate the importance of the saint and his supposed final resting place, Compostela overtook Jerusalem and Rome as a pilgrim venue and became the "Christian Mecca," a term used by Christian and Muslim writers alike.

In the hierarchy of Christian saints, James ranks as one of the inner circle of Christ's apostles. The tombs of Peter and Paul were preserved in Rome, leaving James as the most unretrieved of relics. Beheaded by Herod in A.D. 42, there is an extensive mythology explaining his putative missionary work in Spain and the metaphysical translation of his body from the Holy Land to the site of the discovery of his body some eight hundred years later (fig. 1.9). Spain needed an important saint, particularly to galvanize the military reconquest of that part of its land in Islamic hands since the eighth century. The discovery at Compostela came at a time when the Christian political fortunes in the land were at their lowest ebb, and a "religious–national figure of apostolic grandeur" was a dire need.[61] Compostela was under threat from Muslims; like Jerusalem, it had to be recovered by a crusade.

Without French aid, Spain could not be retrieved from the hands of the "misbelievers." For France, collaboration under the military flag of St. James would secure important economic, political, and religious penetration into Spain. For the French bishops, support for Santiago de Compostela would weaken the influence of the Roman church bureaucracy. By boosting the status of Compostela, Rome and Jerusalem would suffer as pilgrim centers and, not incidentally, France would collect the income from the mass pilgrimage routes that all European pilgrims would be forced to follow to Compostela. A dream appearing to the emperor Charlemagne was marvelous material for the marketing of Compostela:

Fig. 1.9: ***The Embarkation of the Body of St. James,*** by an anonymous Spanish painter.

> In his dream he sees the Milky Way whose ultimate meaning, however, he fails to understand. At that point the Apostle Santiago appears to him and explains to the astonished monarch the significance of the road to the stars: it is the road to the saint's tomb presently impassable for being overrun by the infidels. Before the end of the vision, the apostle spurs Charlemagne to deliver the lands invaded by the Saracens and thereby to open up the pilgrimage to his holy tomb.[62]

Fig. 1.10: The Standard of St. James, the Moorslayer, with the Saint on horseback.

Another item in the advertising of Santiago de Compostela was a twelfth-century book called the *Codex Calixtinus*, named for Pope Calixtus II who, conveniently, as a French archbishop, had been a close friend of the archbishop of Compostela. The *Codex* was a compilation of publicity for the city, a "manual of propaganda to boost the pilgrimage to the tomb of St. James . . . (which) introduced the golden age of the cult of Santiago."[63] The first book contained liturgical texts, including a sermon by Calixtus exalting pilgrimage to Compostela. The second book recounted twenty-two miracles by St. James, eighteen of which apparently were collected by Calixtus. The third book glorified the Cult of St. James and the medical benefits of scallop shells, the cult's corporate logo that was worn by pilgrims on their trips; Coquille St. Jacques may be the culinary contribution of the cult. The fourth book detailed the exploits of French heroes like Roland and Charlemagne in Spain, while the fifth book was a kind of *Guide Michelin* to the mainly French places that a pilgrim would encounter on his journey to Compostela.

Fig. 1.11: St. James and attendants wearing scallop shells.

The battles and passions of St. James found another outlet for advertising in the Romanesque iconography of the twelfth century. In one typology, St. James is shown on a galloping horse slaying the Moors (fig. 1.10). In another, he is depicted as a pilgrim on his way either to or from Santiago wearing a scallop shell, at times distinguished from other pilgrims by a halo over his head (fig. 1.11). The most complete portrayal of the episodes of St. James is in a fifteenth-century Hungarian panel-painting cycle, evidence of the distant spread of his story and of the long journeys that pilgrims were willing to make to bask in his presence.

St. James went everywhere the Spaniards went. There are seven Santiagos in Latin America and a San Diego in this country. When Cortes, on his way to Montezuma, was attacked by Indians, he shouted "the war-cry, '*Santiago y a ellos*' ["St. James and at 'em"], and with the help of the Apostle the Indians were driven back with great slaughter."[64] St. James, in quite another sense, was spread widely. According to the Reverend Stone, his body is also claimed to be in Toulouse and Milan. Two of his heads are in Venice. Another is in Valencia, another in Amalfi, a third in Artois, and a part of his head in Pistoia. A piece of his skull and some blood are in Rome. And

there are bones, hands, and arms in Sicily, Capri, Pavia, Liège, Cologne, Bavaria, and elsewhere.[65] Compostela's advantages over such competitors testify to the dimensions of its public relations effort, which, if not availing itself of the same technology, could well be considered a successful modern campaign.

After the success of Compostela, Rome, in an effort to restore its share of the pilgrimage market, resorted to new enticements. Pope Boniface VIII (fig. 1.12) introduced two radical changes to the incentive system: (1) the granting of the plenary remission of sins (indulgences) to any penitent visiting Rome, and (2) the specification of a time zone during which such indulgences could be achieved. Indulgences were periods of relief from the stay in purgatory and could be obtained only

Fig. 1.12: Pope Boniface VIII.

Fig. 1.13: Pontifical blessing given from St. Peter's in the Jubilee Year of 1575.

through first confessing and then fulfilling the tasks of repentance set by a confessor. Boniface's indulgences were complete delivery from the "pains of purgatory . . . where, it is said, for every mortal sin one must remain ten years.[66] Such relief had previously been available only to Crusaders. All Boniface required was that the visitor be penitent and spend fifteen days visiting the basilicas of St. Peter and St. Paul (fig. 1.13). Visits to St. John Lateran and St. Mary Major were added by subsequent popes.

Like today's frequent flyer mileage bonuses, indulgences could be obtained only during certain prescribed periods known as Jubilee years. Boniface established the year 1300 as the first Jubilee, and contemporary observers estimated that at any given period during that year some two hundred thousand pilgrims were in Rome to claim indulgences, with some two million there at Christmas time.[67] As late as 1900, the idea of the Jubilee year still prevailed in Rome, and a century later, Rome was again the site of a holy year and the offering of indulgences (fig. 1.14).

Indulgence incentives impacted Rome in a number of ways. The city needed to respond to huge crowds requiring food, lodging, and medicine. Traffic had to be regulated and temporary bridges built across the Tiber. Over time, however, the Jubilee, like the contemporary Olympic Games, became a source of permanent urban renewal. In the second half of the fifteenth century, for example, Jubilees were the impetus for the old Roman bridge of the Janiculum to be completely rebuilt, a major aqueduct to be cleared out and lengthened to the Fountain of Trevi, and the road now known as the *Borgo Nuovo* to be widened and paved to the Vatican. Jubilee years brought money to the private Roman economy as they did

SALIENT FACTS: PAPAL INDULGENCES

Roman Holiday

In celebration of the millennium, a long-forgotten tradition is due for a (second) renaissance.

INDULGENCES? SOUNDS LIKE A DISTANT MEMORY FROM HISTORY CLASS
That's because they were most notorious in the 16th century — or about halfway through the second semester. They're meant as a way for Catholics to reduce their debt to God, which people build up through sin (and which they otherwise must work off through penance or, later, in Purgatory). To earn these indulgences, worshipers had to perform special prayers, make pilgrimages or undertake acts of personal sacrifice.

DIDN'T THEY CAUSE A WHOLE MESS OF TROUBLE THE LAST TIME AROUND?
During the Renaissance, the Catholic Church started actually selling indulgences, for cash, to wealthy patrons. That move didn't go over very well with critics like Martin Luther, who called them frauds of the faithful. In fact, they were a big part of what caused him to break with the Church — and thereby launch the Protestant Reformation.

THEN WHY DOES THE VATICAN WANT TO BRING THEM BACK?
To celebrate the millennium. Selling them was forbidden in 1563, but indulgences themselves — though increasingly marginalized — were never officially disallowed. In celebration of the year 2000, which has been declared a holy year, the Vatican has chosen to promote them once again.

SO WILL LOURDES BE THE NEXT HOT SPOT?
It's not out of the question. After all, medieval religious rituals have become surprisingly fashionable — most notably cabalistic Judaism, the darling of movie stars and models. And in a move that will make this arcane tradition more appealing, the requirements have been updated — even "abstaining for at least one whole day from unnecessary consumption (e.g. from smoking or alcohol)" is said to lessen your stay in Purgatory if you donate your drink money to charity.

SO YOU CAN GET TO HEAVEN MORE QUICKLY BY GIVING UP SMOKING?
And you thought it would get you there more slowly. Religious folk of every stripe are trying to make devotion more relevant to everyday life, and the Catholic Church is no exception. In this case, however, some people think the project might be going a bit too far. "Offering indulgences for giving up smoking," says the Rev. Richard McBrien of the University of Notre Dame, "is like offering indulgences for not drinking poison." — **Andrew Santella**

Fig. 1.14: Commentary on the Jubilee Year of 2000.
© 1999 Andrew Santella. Courtesy *The New York Times.*

to the church. One visitor to the first Jubilee writes that he saw clerics raking in money day and night by the altar of St. Paul's.[68] Defenders of the church claim that these were only small coins and that the church needed this income to maintain its churches and other properties. But the indulgence economy, no matter how pietistic its essence, became a system for the pervasive sale of salvation. Already in the late twelfth century, the drive to raise money for the construction of a church in Canterbury to honor St. Thomas offered to those who contributed money annually a one-third reduction in all penances.[69] By the end of the fifteenth century, Pope Innocent VII founded a bank in Rome for the sale of indulgences.[70] And if the sin book of rates published in the seventeenth century by the reformed Confessor-General of Ireland is to be believed, the Catholic Church would pardon any act of murder for the payment of a sum of no less than one and no more than fifty pounds sterling.[71]

MEANING, IDENTITY, AND STRUCTURE

To many, the construction and marketing of a city's image is a by-product of modern times. Yet the material of the research for this chapter suggests that, in many fundamental respects, the identity of cities has always (and one might say inevitably) been at issue, and, like today, differs in the degree to which it is promoted. In the face of contemporary advertising professionals, marketing sciences, media technologies, and diffusion systems, there certainly have been changes in content and technique, many of which are illustrated in this book. Nevertheless, the diachronic view of city-image construction offers much to those whose business it is to design cities.

For one, the tradition of orienting similar images of the city to its own citizens as to outsiders, as in the books of praise, creates not only a sense of civic pride but also an awareness of the value of a good environment. Realizing that a well-formed city is its own best advertisement may diminish the need to manufacture city image artificially. And a well-informed city may also be one where the quality of design is highest.

Understanding cities as continuous over time engenders in designers the habit of observation and adjustment rather than the constant obligation to invent anew. For many of the activities of premodern life described in this chapter still endure. Tourists and merchants journey more than before, use more guidebooks, and read more travel literature than ever. Three and one-half million pilgrims went to Lourdes in 1972, and Saudi Arabia was recently forced to limit pilgrimage to Mecca by its citizens to once in five years. Only now, those wishing to light a candle at Lourdes may also consult its Web site at *http://www.candela-lourdes.com/en/main-en.htm,* or those destined for Mecca its site at *http://www.ummah.org.uk/hajj/.*

Changes in the mode of communicating city images from premodern spoken and written words to contemporary drawings, photographs, film, and computer graphics have changed the context within which designers work. It is not completely clear which cultural factors adequately explain why drawings of buildings and cities are almost entirely absent from the material discussed in this chapter, though presumably the absence of the art of mechanical printing and the expense of hand-copying contributed mightily. Beyond these key factors, Nasser Rabbat[72] argues that differences in social status between those who used words, such as scribes and others of high aura, and the lower order of craftsmen who drew and built, account for the premium placed on writing. Today, the advertising of cities is almost entirely visual, and designers work in a world suffused with pictorial representation.

Architecture, however, has always been a medium that identified cities despite the fact that buildings were only spoken or written about. Solomon's and Herod's temples were widely held in awe. Four hundred years later, the Greek poet, Pindar, said that Agrigento was "the most beautiful the mortals had ever built."[73] Would a postcard suffice today? And how well would those of us who have never been to Sydney know it had we only heard or read about its opera house? For that matter, would we even know of Bilbao but for its museum?

To know of places, especially in our expanded world, we must trust those who inform us. Premodern oral tales and books often exaggerated what had been seen. Do visual media prevari-

Fig. 1.15: Boston as seen on "Cheers."
© 2001 Wm. Hoest Enterprises. Reprinted courtesy Bunny Hoest and *Parade*.

cate less? Architects have long known how to show their buildings in the best light, often not in the way they are experienced. Photographers are similarly skilled. But the opportunity to manipulate visual images today is of a much higher order than ever before. Take Boston's "Cheers" bar, one of the city's largest tourist venues (fig. 1.15). The only actual image of Boston that appeared in the television sitcom was the Beacon Street entrance to the bar. The interior of the bar visited by tourists is not the "real" bar, the one they saw when watching the television comedy. That bar is a Hollywood set. This may be merely the abstraction required of synthetic presentation, but it may also presage a scale of adulterated vicarious experience of places that dwarfs that of premodern times.

These differences in media aside, one comes back to the pervasive similarities of city-image construction over the past few thousand years. How does the story of Compostela, Galicia, differ from that of Clinton, Montana? A moral position may well distinguish between the value of religious belief as opposed to scatological entertainment, between the serious and the frivolous. But the identities of both of these far-off places were deliberately and consciously created to attract visitors who had the opportunity to go elsewhere. Both offered rewards, the one heavenly and painful, the other earthly and pleasurable. In Compostela they built an august and permanent cathedral manifest to the profound purposes of pilgrimage (fig. 1.16); in Clinton they eat and drink beer in the open (fig. 1.17). For designers, these are only programmatic distinctions.

The research for this chapter causes us to reflect again on the triad of *structure*, *identity*, and *meaning* that Lynch put forth in *The Image of the City* as the essential components of an environmental image.[74] Three observations come to mind. The first is about the important role that meaning and identity, rather than structure, plays in advertising cities. Clearly, as Lynch warns us, it is difficult to separate these components; yet the tasks involved in publicizing cities are primarily about crystallizing many meanings into recognizable and transferable packages of identity. So, the Cult of St. James is a set of

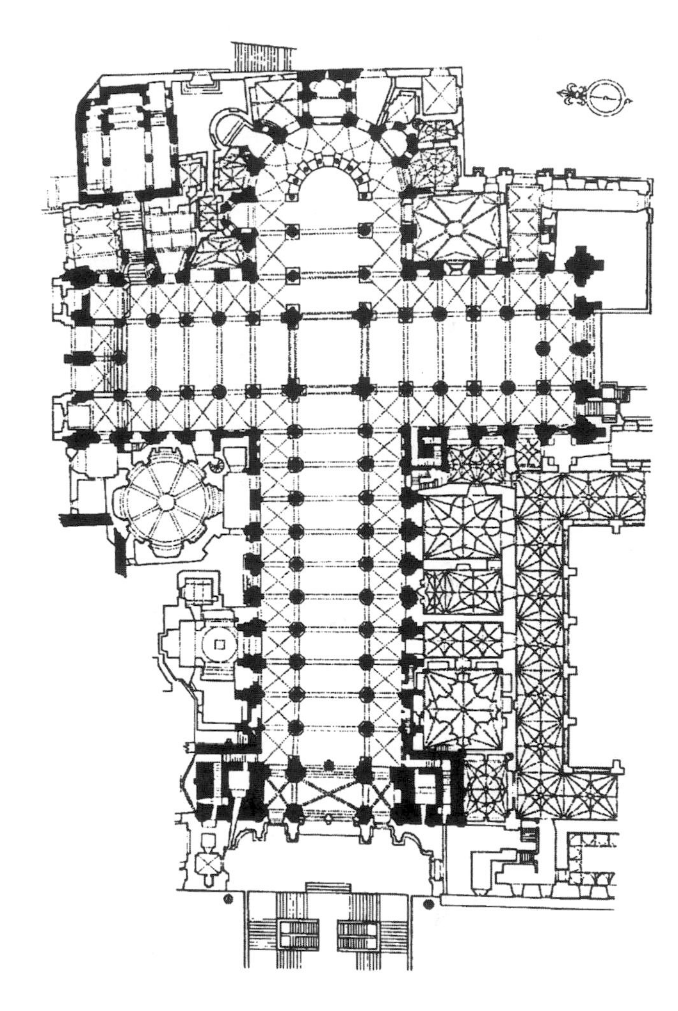

Fig. 1.16: Floor plan of the Cathedral of Santiago in Compostela.
Courtesy Tourist Office of Spain

Fig. 1.17: Rocky Mountain Oyster Capital.
© Chip Simons

meanings compressed into a quickly identifiable item, as is its relic, its scallop logo, and its *Codex*. And this process of meaning and identity construction is in the hands of agents, then bishops, now professional public relations consultants.

A second observation concerns the meaning of *meaning*. Sometimes the meaning of a place may reside in a quite personal and individualized response to a building or piece of a city. In other instances, city officials try to communicate meaning more proactively, by erecting street signs or distributing maps and plans intended to encourage common reference. We may regard the act and product of city promotion—be it a story, book, or drawing—as involving this sort of designative meaning. Yet only if there is an intersubjective agreement between experiential meaning and promotional meaning is the meaning of a city truly *shared*.[75] For prospective visitors to a town, there can be as yet no shared meaning. Only if there is an honest and accurate fit between the promotion and the experience does *shared meaning*, arguably the highest form, come into play.

This leads to a third reflection. What distinguishes the experience of a city's own inhabitants from that of outsiders is the access that citizens have to "shared" meaning. And it is this understanding that city designers need to tap into in crafting city form, something that Lynch argued for so strongly in his best work. City designers may have little to do with the way cities promote themselves. It may not even matter. What is their obligation, however, is to use their skill, together with that of their fellow citizens, to nurture and resolve the many and often conflicting meanings of their own cities so that identity is, most importantly, a locally constructed and understood quality of good city life. This having been achieved, the making and marketing of externally oriented images may well be left to professional and political persuaders.

Place Marketing: Using Media to Promote Cities

Briavel Holcomb

■ EDITORS' OVERVIEW

Geographer Briavel Holcomb carries the tradition of urban image making to its present manifestations. At the outset, she notes that the promotional landscape of the United States is composed of fifteen thousand separate offices, and despite their various labels, they are most often engaged in image selling, not information gathering.

In an expert summary she ticks off the formulas of the contemporary promotional packages: the brand new parts of town; the promising future times; the clean, green, and vibrant lifestyles; the abundance of high and popular arts; the notable sports teams, dramatic buildings, and quaint old streets; all illustrated by snapshots of well-to-do professionals with a small supporting cast of smiling minorities, women, and children. Lest a reader discard all this as inconsequential puffery, she points out that often parts of modern cities, like Glasgow, are reworked to resemble the brochures.

Like Beinart, she raises the question of images for export versus images derived from the experiences of residents, and she tells of some cases of conflict between the two. In the end, she asks the reader to attend to the question of who in a given city benefits from these image campaigns.

> Changing the image of a locality is . . . seen as a central component of entrepreneurial governance and, as such, it is perhaps best to consider the entrepreneurial city as an imaginary city, constituted through a plethora of images and representations.
>
> T. Hall and P. Hubbard, *The Entrepreneurial City*[1]

INTRODUCTION

This chapter explores the role of interplace competition for economic growth in producing new urban images. I argue that the increasing emphasis on, and professionalization of, economic development is changing both the material and the mental city and that the disjunctions between the two are growing. Long before postmodernism and deconstruction undermined our faith in a stable text, Kenneth Boulding argued that, for society to function, there must be some shared image of reality. Without that, communication is impossible. Today, most of us would accept the suggestion that the text of the city is polysemic—that the same material reality is understood differently. The goal of the city marketer, however, is to convey a particular version of the city's image—a version that often has little congruence with material reality. While Kevin Lynch and Boulding sought to understand people's mental images, city marketers seek to change them and, in doing so, to change behavior.[2]

FROM BOOSTERISM TO ENTREPRENEURIALISM: ECONOMIC DEVELOPMENT GROWS UP

The radical changes that have accompanied the shift from a manufacturing to a service economy in much of the developed world, as well as the increasing mobility of capital in a globalizing economic system, have received much attention. In the United States, employment in agriculture and manufacturing declined between 1970 and 1994 (to three million and twenty-one million, respectively); employment in services more than doubled, from twenty million in 1970 to forty-three million in 1994.[3] Britain lost 45 percent of its manufacturing jobs between 1974 and 1994.[4] The old locational criteria of accessibility to raw materials, labor supply, and transportation have been largely superseded by quality of life and workforce issues. Technological advances in communications have homogenized information space, and telecommuters have replaced suburban commuters. As jobs leave the United States for cheaper labor elsewhere, and as capital disinvests from deteriorated urban centers, local governments have reacted by becoming increasingly entrepreneurial.[5]

This period has coincided with a rapid rise in economic development as a profession. Boosterism has a long history in the United States.[6] Even the reports of early exploratory voyages "usually stressed the economic plenitude of the new settlement, the excellence of its climate, the healthiness of its situation, and the gentleness of the natives."[7] Indeed, Boorstin claims that the continent's settlement pattern is better explained by the boostering businessmen, eager editors, and enterprising entrepreneurs than by such "natural" locational advantages as fall-line or river confluence. Although "amateur" boosters have been augmented (not replaced) by chambers of commerce and official departments of economic development in the twentieth century, there has been a rapid growth of, and increasing specialization in, locality economic development. Boyle reported that there were fifteen thousand economic development organizations in the United States by 1990, and Bingham and Mier summarized the recent evolution of economic development as a profession.[8]

Obviously, economic developers have many tasks, some of which involve "rational planning models" such as data gathering, analysis, and policy making. But Levy's survey of directors of local economic development agencies found that they see "sales (as opposed to 'rational model' activities) as the most important, the most time consuming, and the most productive aspects of their work." "Sales"—or marketing—included such activities as "calls on firms, speeches to Rotary Clubs, public relations, advertising, writing and dissemination of brochures, attendance at trade shows and other events, and 'networking,'" a list to which attention to Web sites must now certainly be added.[9] In brief, most governmental agencies engaged in economic development spend more time marketing the locality than planning and implementing physical changes to it.

City marketing is by no means confined to the local economic development department. City governments in general have become increasingly entrepreneurial in their pursuit of jobs and investments.[10] Regime theory, which seeks explanations of who has the power to act and why, suggests a version of the golden rule: Whoever has the gold makes the rules. In an urban context, this may mean that although city governments have official powers as elected representatives of the people, scarce public revenues limit the power to act. As an adaptation, many cities have formed public–private partnerships to combine the formal authority of government with the capital power of business. The implications of such partnerships are numerous but beyond the scope of this chapter.[11] Suffice it to say that the "public" in the partnerships are often elected and appointed officials, not "ordinary citizens," and the "private" are business elites not acting as "private citizens." While Eisenschitz and Gough argue that the entrepreneurial strategy can appeal to both right and left of the political spectrum by promoting business growth, local pride, and solidarity[12]—and presumably a "bigger pie to be divided"—others, myself included, are less sanguine. The pie may be larger, but income and wealth inequalities are also growing as the pie is increasingly unequally divided. Public resources devoted to marketing efforts may be diverted from social welfare functions. From Atlanta to Glasgow, from Tampa to Detroit, and from Birmingham to Baltimore, critics have shown that entrepreneurial strategies often have socially regressive consequences with little improvement in the quality of life for those at the bottom of the economic strata.[13]

Numerous other groups and individuals play roles in urban marketing image creation. Competition for tourist visitors involves marketing on the part of local tourist boards, tourist establishments such as hotels and theme parks, local tour operators, transportation companies, and others.[14] Urban images designed to lure visitors are myriad in travel sections of newspapers; in upscale, in-flight, and specialist magazines; on television and the Web; and on posters and travel brochures. Imagery to attract new residents is found in real estate sections and agency brochures as well as regional and city magazines. Publications directed toward niche markets (such as the elderly or sports fans) or trades (such as filmmaking or interactive technology) often include advertisements or articles on cities as good places to live or work.

The newest and already most prolific source of place-marketing imagery is the Internet. Cities of all sizes in the United States and major cities in much of the rest of the world maintain Web sites to lure visitors, business, and, to a lesser extent, new residents. Web sites constitute a relatively low-cost means to reach a worldwide market, and although they are "visited" only by potential "customers" rather than arriving unrequested as do, for example, mailed brochures, nevertheless they presumably reach the most important part of the market. City Web sites vary from the relatively primitive, containing little other than text with basic data, to the highly sophisticated, with moving visual images, sound, and links to local attractions. The home page usually has links to sites providing information for businesses (e.g., tax rates, loan availability, and other economic development information), visitors (local attractions and events), and residents (schools, affordable housing). When visual images are used, the city's skyline and local landmarks are commonly incorporated. In general, Web sites are more factual and less hyperbolic than other forms of marketing material, though "negative information" such as crime rates or substandard housing are rarely included.

THE CITY, THE IMAGE, AND IMAGINEERING

In thinking about the relationships between the material and mental worlds, it can be useful to consider the mutual influences that the material city of the built environment and its inhabitants have on both the mental images in which Lynch was interested and the "imagineered" images of the place marketer (fig 2.1). I

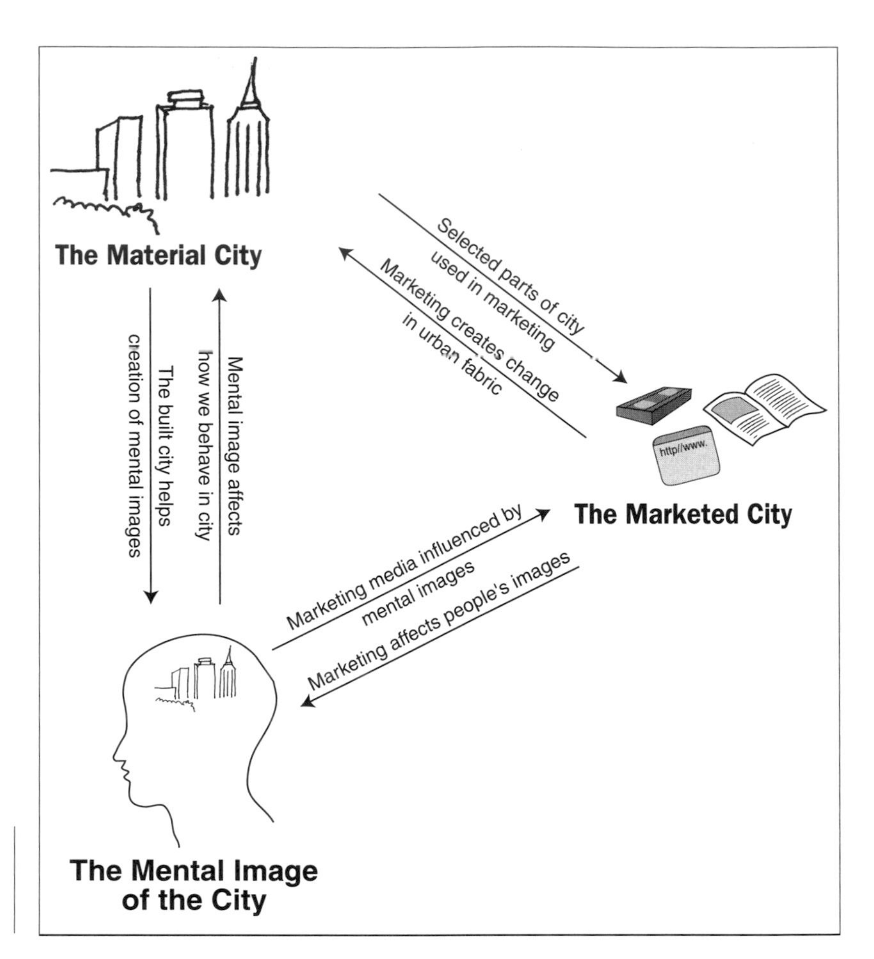

Fig. 2.1: Mutual influences among the material, imaged, and imagineered cities

assume that the derivation of the neologism "imagineered"—a term applied to, and perhaps invented by, Disney—implies the engineering of images. This is the central task of the place marketer. The goal is to create and effectively convey positive images of the city to current and potential investors, employers, residents, and visitors. Using a panoply of media and strategies, marketers seek to affect positive change in people's mental images to influence their behaviors toward, as well as in, the city. Reciprocally, presumed existing mental images guide marketers in their choice of imagineering as already positive images are reinforced and negative images counteracted.

There are also mutual influences between the material city and the imagineered city. The imagineered city is a highly selective version of its material counterpart, typically incorporating only the more spectacular, iconic, historic, and status-enhancing elements of the physical and social environments. But the material city is often "re-engineered" itself in the interests of marketing. "As image assumes ever greater importance . . . it becomes increasingly apparent that the actual shaping and production of urban landscapes are reflecting the imperatives of the necessity for cities to present positive images of themselves in the outside world."[15] It should be remembered, too, that the success or failure of the marketer's imagineering will have impacts on the well-being of the material city. A successful campaign can be the catalyst in transforming the urban landscape.

Finally, as Lynch first discussed, there are mutual influences between the material and mental cities. Our mental maps are constructed from features in the urban landscape, but, equally, our mental images strongly influence our behavior in that landscape.[16] Mental images affect which parts of the city we frequent and which we avoid, where we live, shop, work, and play. They have, therefore, great consequences for the spatial patterns of potential profitability and resultant investment. Significantly, mental images are not only the product of place-based experience; indeed, most of us have images of cities we have never visited, images derived from many sources, including the marketer's media. Giddens, Baudrillard, and others have suggested that increasing immersion in media has created a condition in which more of our images are now derived from hyper-reality than from unmediated experience.[17] Those vicariously acquired images affect the range of places considered in decisions about investment, choice of residence, or vacation destination.

MARKETED IMAGES OF THE CITY

I and others have discussed the characteristics of urban images created by marketers.[18] As one might expect, the components of the typical marketed city image are positive. Ironically, while many cities claim to be unique (one of the most overused words these days), their marketed images are much more generic than

Fig. 2.2: A "pop-up" promotional card from the New Brunswick Development Corporation (in New Jersey) with the message "There's even more popping up on the horizon for 1999."

their material realities. As Ward notes in his analysis of the marketing of older industrial cities, their "primary inspiration came not from the distinctive qualities of the place they were promoting but from what their competitors were doing."[19] More recently, the "cloning" of such landscape features as festival markets, convention centers, and pedestrian malls, along with the ubiquity of chain retail outlets ranging from The Gap to McDonalds, has increasingly made the redeveloped parts of cities in the same country relatively indistinguishable one from another. As Ward remarks, "the post-industrial city has already begun, unknowingly, to caricature itself."[20] But it is the newer parts of town that are usually featured in marketing materials (fig 2.2). The older, more idiosyncratic parts are included only if they are sufficiently sanitized.

■ LOCATION

It is ironic that, although advances in communication and transportation technologies have made places much more uniformly accessible, a physically "central" location is claimed even by quite peripheral places such as Sunrise (Florida), Cuero

(Texas), or Hempstead (New York). Atlanta, which considered among many suggested slogans for its Olympic bid the "World's Next Great City" (presumably challenging New York, London, Tokyo, and like cities), urged readers in an advertisement in *Expansion Management*, a publication for business relocation and expansion, to "Put your Business in the Center of the World"—meaning Atlanta. Although technological advances have bestowed cyber-centrality on remote locations, places remain sensitive to the images of their place on the map.

■ TIME

While the location of the imaged city is central, its time is future. Anchorage (Alaska) invites us to "Come North to the Future"; Nashville is becoming "a prototype of America's future"; and New Milford (Connecticut) has a "Great Past, and a Greater Future" (but no present?). Cities claim to be forward-looking, dynamic, progressing into a bright tomorrow and the best place to be in the future. Illustrations of the material city typically focus on the newest, most up-to-date parts of the urban fabric, on the redeveloped waterfront, the new corporate headquarters, the festival marketplace. Exceptions to these generalizations are images of a glorious past captured in historically preserved neighborhoods and heritage sites. Absent are the residential suburbs, industrial districts, and outdated retail areas built in the twentieth century (prior to its last decade) that comprise the greatest proportion of the built environment of a typical sprawling North American city. Figure 2.3a shows a digitally enhanced, carefully cropped photograph of new (but Federal-style) housing and office blocks contrasting with a historic church, images that appeared in a marketing brochure. In contrast, the same view from a quarter of a mile away reveals the sea of parking lots and highways in which this scene is actually embedded (fig. 2.3b). Lynch argued that "a desirable image [of time] is one that celebrates and enlarges the present while making connections with past and future."[21] If large tracts of the present city are absent from the marketers' imagery, it would be difficult

Fig. 2.3a (*left*): A digitally enhanced photograph from a New Brunswick (New Jersey) promotional brochure.

Fig. 2.3b (*right*): The same scene photographed from a distance.

to satisfy Lynch's criterion for a desirable image—at least temporally. The time of imaged cities diurnally is, not surprisingly, usually daytime though, as Ward points out, often sunset or sunrise when special lighting mellows the scene.[22] The paucity of night views is presumably explained by optimal photographic conditions (although many promotional packages include a shot or two of sunset scenes or twinkling stars above floodlit skyscrapers), but it may also disguise the absence of available nightlife opportunities. Interestingly, the "speed" of a city—its passage through time—is marketed as both fast (the dynamic, quickly moving, get-ahead place bustling with activity) and slow (where time stands still, where you can step back to quieter times), yet it rarely conveys the mundane pace of everyday life.

Marking the Millennium

Occasionally, cities even use time in their marketing strategies. Britain's Millennium Commission, funded largely through the National Lottery, made major grants to various urban projects designed to enhance the images of cities. The Science Edutainment Center, named *@Bristol,* is described as a "landmark project for the South West"; the Wales Millennium Centre in Cardiff is a "building of international status"; the National Space Centre in Leicester aimed to "provide the nation with an exciting and unique education and leisure facility based on space science"; and The Earth Centre in Doncaster was intended as a "state of the art world centre for environmental research and sustainable technology."[23]

The largest project, of course, was London's Millennium Dome, completed in time to host millions of visitors from January 1 through December 31, 2000. The Dome, which cost $1.24 billion, is the world's largest, with a circumference of a kilometer and a height the same as Nelson's Column (fig 2.4). Built on the Greenwich Peninsula Meridian Line, "which marks the beginning of all time and space on earth," according to the Old Royal Observatory's visitor's leaflet, the Dome's promoters sought to increase the visibility of not just Greenwich or London

Fig. 2.4: The Millennium Dome, Greenwich, UK.
Chorley Handford/Hayes Davidson

but Britain as a whole. As a 1997 *Millennium Experience* poster put it, "The Millennium Experience is changing the face of London. A once-derelict and polluted area is being transformed into one of the great public arenas of the world. A nation . . . proud of its past but fully engaged with the future [but no mention of the present] . . . is inviting the world to share in the Millennium Experience. In the year 2000 the eyes of the world will turn to Britain. . . . Placing the nation on the world map as a place of excitement, innovation, inspiration and optimism, the Millennium Experience is set to make a real difference to our country." Whether or not the project has had the desired effect remains highly controversial.[24] The *New York Times* editorialized that, whether the Dome succeeds or fails, "something truly unique will have been added to the London skyline—an immortal monument to 1999."[25] When the Dome closed on December 31, 2000, the millennium attraction had drawn fewer than 6 million paying visitors—half the number projected—and had been repeatedly bailed out financially. It received a flood of criticism in the media, and its impact on London's image is ambiguous at best.

■ QUALITY OF LIFE

Not surprisingly, the images created by marketers vary somewhat depending on the potential target audience. Images directed at traditional manufacturing firms are more likely to emphasize such positives as cheap labor—not usually expressed that way but by more polite euphemisms like "realistic wage levels" (in Decatur, Illinois) or a "value-for-money workforce" (in Nottingham, U.K.)—as well as low taxes and land costs, good infrastructure, and "helpful" regulations (one-stop-permitting and right-to-work legislation). Images designed to attract high-tech research and development sectors or service businesses more frequently emphasize quality of life. This somewhat nebulous, all-encompassing term is shorthand for conditions ranging from recreational opportunities to health care facilities, from cultural events to climatic conditions, and from cost of living to commutation times. There is widespread agreement, however, that quality of life is becoming increasingly critical in locational decision making by both labor and capital, though there is less agreement about which components of that quality are more influential. It has been suggested that "a 'well-developed community spirit' may be the greatest factor in the attraction and retention of business and community residents,"[26] though community spirit is as equally amorphous a term as quality of life.

Quality of life is conveyed by city marketers through visual, verbal, and auditory images. Visually, the marketed city is clean and green. Unlike its smokestack-chasing predecessors, its air is unpolluted, its streets unlittered, and its open spaces wide and well maintained. It is rich in amenities ranging from verdant golf courses to elegant symphony halls, from well-equipped schools to state-of the-art medical facilities, from sports stadia with retracting roofs to churches with soaring spires. Its architecture is distinguished, harmonious, and contemporary. Should the material city not altogether conform to the desired image, photomontages, collages, paintings, or drawings can do the trick (see fig. 2.2). Whether the visual images are conveyed in print or on video, they portray a city with all the amenities a body, mind, and soul could desire with no congestion, crowding, or crime.

Likewise, the texts that accompany visual images describe cities rich with amenities: Abilene, Texas, has cultural opportunities that "range from chili cook-offs to the symphony"; Pittsburgh has "nature trails where intrepid joggers, hikers and bikers can be spotted year round"; Paterson, New Jersey—whose promotional booklet is ambiguously entitled "A Quality of Life"—claims to be a microcosm of the world, boasting of "a top-rated Italian restaurant frequented by New Yorkers and neighborhood residents alike." Verbal texts abound in superlatives and hyperbole, riddled with words such as *greatest*, *best*, *most*, *abundant*, *top*, and *excellent*. Guess which city in America is "uniquely poised to prosper in the new global economy" (Anchorage); which has "perhaps the cleanest, most vibrant downtown in America" (Cincinnati); which is becoming "the nation's inner citadel of quality" (Nashville); which is blessed more than any other American city with "a generous choice of elegant, comfortable and safe suburbs" (Cleveland).

While I cannot claim to have listened to many marketing videos or TV and radio place advertisements, those that I have heard typically feature an upbeat, fast narration accompanied by background music often with an insistent disco beat. For example, oddly enough, the background music in promotional videos for Swansea, Wales, is reminiscent of that for Wilmington, Delaware. One assumes that the fast-paced music of place promotion enhances the image of a vibrant, active city.

■ THE CULTURED IMAGE

One of the most critical components of quality of life for marketing purposes is the presence of "culture" in the city. While the real, everyday quality of life for most residents probably depends more on such issues as garbage pickup or crime rates, and a relatively small proportion of local residents actually attend symphonic concerts or art exhibits, such amenities are vital to the image of the marketed city. It is not only that cultural facilities attract visitors (consumers) to town but, just as important, they help produce an image of a civilized, upscale place. Old and new "palaces of culture" enhance the material and imaged city. In the United States, cities as diverse as Charleston, West Virginia; Fort Lauderdale, Florida; Kansas City, Kansas; Newark, New Jersey; and San Jose, California have each made recent major investments in edifices for the arts.[27] In Britain, there are significant new art galleries in Dundee, Gateshead, Liverpool, Salford, and Wallsall, as well as new or expanded galleries in London (British Museum, Dulwich Picture Gallery, National Portrait Gallery, Somerset House and the Gilbert Collection, Tate Modern and the Wallace Collection).[28] Newark, New Jersey's $180 million Performing Arts Center (fig. 2.5), which opened in 1997, attracted a half-million people to its events in the first season; it has already been credited with stimulating investment in nearby properties and perhaps marking the reversal of Newark's long decline.[29] The image of Newark as a serious challenger to New York's Lincoln Center as a mecca for the performing arts may seem like hubris, but the association of Newark with great per-

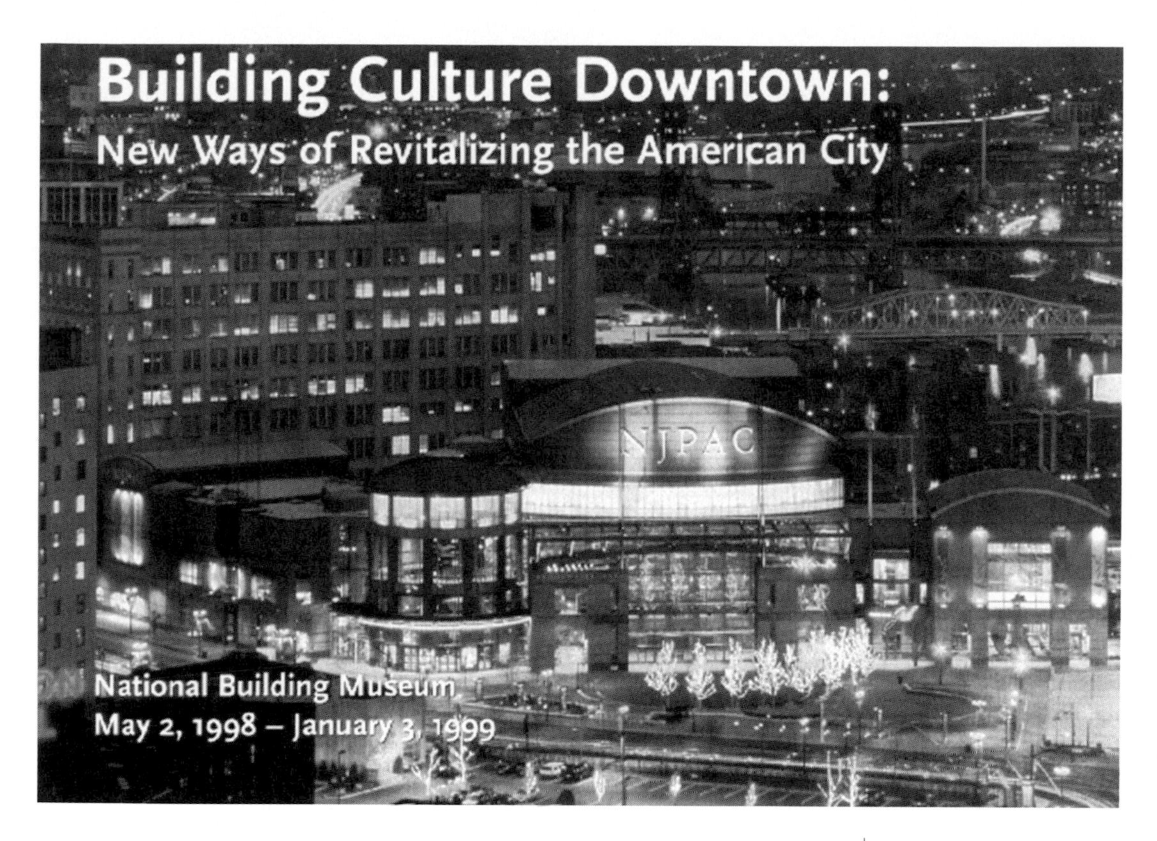

Fig. 2.5: The New Jersey Performing Arts Center, Newark.

formances of ballet, jazz, and symphonies is certainly a change from earlier associations with car theft, crack cocaine, and corruption. Visually, the brightly lit glass atrium of the brick Performing Arts Center building is intended to be open to the city around it, even though the press package for the Center contained photographs of the architectural model divorced from its urban context (which included a soup kitchen across the street).

The "high" arts of the earlier part of the twentieth century have been democratized to include popular forms of culture and ethnic festivals that more accurately reflect cities' diverse populations. Summer in New Brunswick, New Jersey, celebrates Puerto Rican and Hungarian heritages at separate weekend festivals. Mardi Gras in New Orleans not only attracts many tourists but reinforces the city's international image as the home of jazz and Cajun cooking. Cincinnati is one of many cities whose Oktoberfest not only celebrates German culture but provides a large market for designer beers. Nevertheless, the more elite forms of art associated with the Spoleto Festival in Charleston (South Carolina), the Wagner Festival in Seattle (Washington), or the Aspen (Colorado) Music Festival have all helped communicate images of cities whose residents are as cultured as their visitors.

These images of cultured cities are not always uncontested. Perhaps the most controversial case is that of Glasgow, which won the competition to host the *European City of Culture* program in 1990.[30] In a city that had experienced decades of severe decline as its shipbuilding and metallurgical industries closed, the local authority recognized the necessity of changing the city's image in order to attract new investment. To many, Glasgow was seen as "the City of mean streets and mean people, razor gangs, the Gorbals slums, of smoke, grime, and fog, of drunks, impenetrable accents and communists."[31] A concerted campaign using the slogan "Glasgow's Miles Better" (or was it "Glasgow Smiles Better"?) went head-to-head with that of "Edinburgh: Slightly Superior." Eventually, Glasgow beat out the other metropolis in the Silicon Glen to win the City of Culture designation. However, as Boyle and Hughes argue, the new marketed image was not one "sedimented down the years as Glaswegian consciousness but one which encourages thinking about Glasgow in new terms, i.e., without having direct reference back to any external reality."[32] The new image was resented and resisted by various working-class groups; blue-collar residents of the city replaced the Saatchi and Saatchi slogan, "There's a lot Glasgowing on in 1990," with "There's a lot of con going on in 1990."[33] Nevertheless, the urban fabric of parts of the city was transformed as the Gorbals (slum tenements) were torn down, Victorian downtown stores sandblasted, city parks replanted, and the town draped with artful banners. The marketer's image produced a new material landscape that is now pictured in the revised images of both residents and promoters and helped Glasgow win designation of the European Union's 1999 City of Architecture.[34] The poor and working-class neighborhoods are still there; they are just less visible. Council (public) housing was relegated to peripheral sites/sights. The jobs that replaced the steady, unionized shipbuilders' jobs are now often low-wage, tourist-sector slots. Glasgow's proud tradition of shipbuilding was portrayed during the City of Culture year by a nightly theatrical reenactment of a ship launching on the River Clyde, a spectacle that drew crowds to the docks where no great ship had been built for years. Nevertheless, competition for proclamation as the European City of Culture is intense—so much so that, for the 2000 observance, the selection committee designated ten exemplary cities to share the honor and the funding. Despite Glasgow's claims, Edinburgh's annual International Festival makes it Scotland's cultural capital in most minds.

■ THAT SPORTING CITY

In the United States, sports rival culture in enhancing the image of livability of a city—possibly more so, since they appeal to a wider range of consumers. The value to image making for promotional purposes of a winning NFL team, a state-of-the-art stadium, or a major sporting event such as the NCAA finals, the World Cup or—that grand prize—the Olympic Games, is ultimately incalculable but is regarded as "priceless"—the playing card used to justify public expenditures on bids (and perhaps bribes), infrastructure, and major facility construction. Winning teams, major events, and new facilities can put the host city on the mental map of potential investors and visitors nationally and even internationally. As important, such sporting triumphs are assumed to build local pride and community spirit. When the Oakland Raiders considered a move to Los Angeles in the early 1980s, local officials claimed that the team not only provided positive role models for youth (keeping them from crime and drugs) but that worker productivity declined when the Raiders lost a game. (Fortunately, although they did leave town, the Raiders later returned.) The potential peregrinations of New York Yankees owner George Steinbrenner keep New Yorkers on tenterhooks as political leaders in that and adjacent states vie for the privilege of providing a stadium fit for the Yankees of the new millennium. Meanwhile, the taxpayers of Connecticut offered deep subsidies to the owner of the New England Patriots to lure that team out of Massachusetts. Numerous studies have concluded that the economic benefits of public investment in stadia construction do not cover the fiscal costs, but local governments continue to subsidize sports, rationalizing that the intangible image enhancement justifies the expenditure—and no politician wants to be known for losing the home team.[35] As McMenemy wrote, "A city facing budget cuts will only impact small groups of constituents with the cuts. But losing a pro-franchise is visible to all voters. It is a sign of weakness, a lack of machismo. . . ."[36]—and who would want that! So stadium building continues unabated, with eighty-five such venues opening since 1990, sixteen under construction, and eighteen on the drawing board as of 1998.[37]

The Grand Prize for cities, of course, is the right to host the Olympic Games. I have written elsewhere about the pros and cons of entering this quadrennial global competition, but there is certainly no shortage of cities willing to commit large financial and organization resources to the goal of landing the Olympics.[38] Before the 1999 International Olympic Commission bribing scandals, the consensus seemed to be that even entering the competition, and especially winning the right to be the nation's entry, was worth the effort. Law argued that even if the bid was unsuccessful, as most are, perhaps "of greatest importance is the element of unity which the bid engenders. Politicians of different parties, leaders of the private sector, and voluntary groups are able to come together around a bid and perhaps agree not only on the proposal itself, but also on the general direction the city should be moving . . . and how the city should be marketed."[39] Despite the fact that this unity may be more illusory than the media suggest, and that the image of unity may serve to consolidate the power of elites and stifle dissent (as Rutheiser suggests was the case in Atlanta during the 1996 Olympics[40]), it can nevertheless be a powerful marketing tool. As of the time of writing, it is premature to assess the impact on Sydney of the 2000 Olympics, but the controversy generated by Germany's choice over South Africa for the 2004 games is indicative of the importance attached to winning the site-selection competition.[41]

■ THE GAY GAMES

The Gay Games, held every four years since it was first staged in San Francisco in 1982, is another event that combines athletic with cultural events. Appealing to a group with above-average disposable income, the Gay Games and associated celebrations of gay culture in New York in 1994 attracted a million visitors who accounted for more spending than that related to the World Cup soccer tournament the same week in the same metropolitan area.[42] The 1998 Gay Games in Amsterdam attracted 13,300 participants from sixty-six countries—one and one-half times that of the Atlanta Olympics—and was marketed as the largest multiple-sport tournament ever held in Europe. With Dutch government subsidies and corporate sponsors, this was the first gay event to receive funding from the European Union. Although the Games were projected to bring $75 million in associated spending, they were not without controversy: Some corporations (e.g., Heineken—the domestic beer market leader) declined sponsorship, causing others to question the desirability of continuing the Games.[43] Obviously, only large cities with a reasonably visible gay population are likely to compete for the Gay Games. Smaller, conservative, and less tolerant places would avoid such possible "threats" to their images.[44]

TROPHY ARCHITECTURE AND URBAN IMAGERY

> There is probably no greater advert for cities than their own landscape.
>
> T. HALL AND P. HUBBARD, *The Entrepreneurial City*[45]

It is now widely accepted that trophy architecture—large, impressive, and distinctive new buildings—is an effective conveyor of revised urban images.[46] Whether palace of culture or an arena of sport, or a corporate edifice such as San Francisco's Transamerica pyramid or Pittsburgh's PPG tower, highly conspicuous buildings become distinguishing landmarks that locate and define a city on our mental maps. If the Transamerica pyramid were not already an icon, its appearance in the first "pop-up" advertisement published in *Time* in 1986 ensured its landmark status.[47] While in times past the most prominent building in town was the Gothic cathedral (in Europe) or the State House/Courthouse (in the United States), these icons are now dwarfed by the temples of Mammon and Muse. The triumph of capitalism is marked by a landscape of consumption, and the skyscrapers reach upward not to heaven but in competition to be the tallest in town, just as Larry Ford suggests in chapter 5 in this volume.

The use of architecture to sell cities is not new, of course. The city of Melbourne, Australia, held a competition in the 1970s offering a $100,000 prize for the best idea for a landmark that would compete with Sydney's Opera House and make Melbourne "famous around the world."[48] Yet despite the premium, the city remains without a signature structure to match its rival. In the ensuing decades, however, many other cities have built megastructures in the hope of replicating the same sort of image marker as the Eiffel Tower, Gateway Arch, Astrodome, or Inner Harbor (which most people can associate with the correct city). While sometimes the emphasis is on distinctiveness, too often the primary criterion is size. As the president of Detroit's Renaissance Center explained in the 1970s, "We wanted to build something with the kind of critical mass that would make people say, 'Something's really happening in Detroit.'"[49] Megaprojects have arisen in many cities, with mixed success.[50] Few have failed economically in as spectacular a manner as the Renaissance Center, but the Ren Cen did succeed as a very visible marker in that still-distressed city, a notoriety renewed by its recent transformation into a home for General Motors. Such megaprojects too often become "white elephants" which, like the animals that the kings of Siam bestowed upon their enemies because they were relatively useless but required much upkeep, necessitate continued expenditure even as they age less than gracefully. The message is clear: even if they are financial failures, their image may continue to be useful for city promotion.

PEOPLING THE IMAGINEERED CITY

The people depicted in marketing images of cities are overwhelmingly not poor, not old, not minority, and not unhappy. Rather, they are well dressed, smiling as they walk vigorously through safe streets or chat with coworkers in well appointed offices. They are disproportionately professional in occupation—more brain surgeons than garbage collectors, more symphony conductors than assembly-line workers. There are few African Americans depicted even in cities where they constitute a significant portion of the population and, when they do appear, they are often children or jazz musicians. As an example, the New Brunswick (New Jersey) Development Corporation's 1998 annual report was illustrated with local scenes and portraits that included twenty-six white men, nine white women, two African American men, and no African American women, even though half the city's population is black or Hispanic, and more than half are female. The one politically correct multicultural photo is of four smiling children. In fairness it should be added that New Brunswick's Web site[51] is much more representative of the city's population, including photographs of the "diverse population [which] can trace its origins to countries in Europe, Africa, South America, Central America, and Asia." A few cities, most notably Atlanta, are exceptions: "Imagery deriving directly from African-American culture has also found an important, if still rather cautiously expressed, place in Atlanta's tourism promotion."[52]

Some cities prepare promotional materials targeted to particular segments of the population. The New Cleveland Campaign produced a pamphlet entitled "Cleveland Woman," which included articles about how well dual-career couples cope in that city and the services available there to assist women's careers. Cincinnati's "Views from Young Professionals" pamphlet is illustrated profusely with photos of glamorous yuppies and boasts "the sexiest zoo in the nation."

Place marketers also frequently target the elderly, at least those who are retired. Municipalities vie for retired residents who bring with them capital, income, and spending power, who have low crime rates and no need for schools, but who pay property taxes. Advertisements for retirement communities appear in many media depicting safe (often gated), amenity-rich neighborhoods replete with golf courses and community centers. Their occupants are invariably healthy and happy looking, and, unlike real life, are rarely overweight or bald.

Children are seen, if not heard, in urban marketing images. They are happily learning in well-equipped classrooms, visiting the zoo, and playing in spacious parks. They, of course, represent the city's future and, as Mitchell argues, "also embody a sense of historical rootedness, of tradition and stability and familial ties."[53] While they are typically more racially diverse than their parents' generation, none seem neglected, underprivileged, or sad.

CONCLUSION: LYNCH, LACUNAE, AND THE MARKETED CITY IMAGE

> The predominant forms of urban representation now revolve around the marketing of the city.
>
> J. SHORT AND Y. KIM, "Urban Crisis/Urban Representations"[54]

In *The Image of the City*, Lynch wrote of parts of the city that were "invisible" or absent from the mental maps of his subjects.[55] Lacunae lay beyond the "edges," and locations dropped off the map. So too, the images used to market cities are highly selective and omit districts, people, and even landscape features that are not only prominent in the material city but may also play a central role in the Lynchian maps of the city's inhabitants. The marketed images, produced by the elite of the entrepreneurial city, influence the production of social and material space in the city, even though they may be resisted by oppositional groups. Kenny, in particular, has shown how blue-collar workers and black inner-city representatives contested the marketed imagery of Milwaukee, disrupting the calm surface of public relations.[56] Croucher demonstrated how an image of ethnic harmony was created in Toronto even as ethnic conflict prevailed.[57] Deakin and Edwards examined four inner-city cases in Britain, remarking that even "a cursory glance at inner-city brochures . . . is all that is required to see that there has been a strong presentational element in the way in which policy information is conveyed. These are not long policy statements so much as hortatory notices of progress and intent. Their style allows of no debate or dissension any more than the sales brochures of property developers."[58] And, moreover, they found that even successful economic regeneration stimulated by the entrepreneurial inner city has not coincided with improvements in the welfare of local residents.

A goal of Lynch's research was to make the city more legible—more comprehensible—to its inhabitants. The goal of city image makers today is to hide the real city behind rose-colored glasses, to obscure the flaws, and to highlight the presumed successes. Lynch sought illumination. Today's marketers seek obfuscation. Perhaps this can be justified if marketing imagery is successful in attracting new investments, employment, residents, and visitors—but only if the fruits of this economic growth are equitably divided among the citizens in such a way that benefits accrue to those most in need.

From Flames to Flowers

The Role of Planning in Re-Imaging the South Bronx

Eugenie Ladner Birch

■ EDITORS' OVERVIEW

City planning historian Eugenie Birch carries the issue of urban imagery deep into the specifics of planning in one of America's most dramatized areas, the Bronx borough of New York City. Built as a vast expanse of exemplary turn-of-the-century apartments and supported by thousands of jobs and generous public amenities, its former middle-class and working-class residents recall it as "The Beautiful Bronx." By 1970, however, much of the borough, especially the South Bronx, had become the national stereotype for urban unemployment, poverty, crime, drugs, abandoned young mothers and child neglect, and landlord arson. Yet, by 1997, the Bronx boasted a new image, having won an All-American City award for its revitalization efforts.

Birch follows the parallel pathways of images and city planning by documenting the politics of both. The story begins by documenting policies of Robert Moses and downtown planners' neglect of the social and economic changes that were transforming New York and other American cities. The political explosions of the 1960s altered the city's formal structure of planning, ultimately granting a good deal of power to the borough presidents and to community groups.

The ensuing initiatives and conflicts allow Birch to pinpoint the links between land-use technicalities and image. Local politicians, planners, and residents repeatedly attacked the planning fashions of the 1980s and 1990s—inner-city ranch houses, town houses, and

urban parks—because they retained images of the historical fabric of their area as they had come to value it through the decades of loss and abandonment. Some, particularly a church coalition, wanted tiny minimal row houses suitable for starter homes for families emerging from public housing. Public agencies, in turn, favored mid-rise condominiums so that they could use middle-class tenants to support their larger economic development schemes. Slowly, out of such a yeasty land-use and image politics, a newly rebuilt Bronx is emerging.

INTRODUCTION

The Yankees were burning up the Dodgers' pitching during the 1978 World Series. Bucky Dent and Brian Doyle hit for .417 and .438, respectively. But the Yankees' bats weren't the only things from the Bronx that were smoking. Slowly, a television camera in the Goodyear blimp swung away from the diamond, and thousands of viewers turned their attention from the Yankee victory to a horrifying scene flashing in front of them—the world just outside the stadium. Through a smoke-filled haze, the landscape passed by, and screaming sirens wailed above the cheering fans. The announcer breathlessly counted out: "One, two, three...no, seven, eight, nine, ten . . . buildings were in flames. . . ." (figs. 3.1a, 3.1b). The Yanks may have been winning, but the Bronx was burning.[1]

Figs. 3.1a, 3.1b: When Ted Koppel featured the South Bronx on *Nightline* in 1996, he replayed the 1978 World Series tape showing Yankee Stadium and the splashes of light surrounding it (*left*, fig. 3.1b). A close-up of the illuminated points revealed their true nature: out-of-control fires (*right*, fig. 3.1b).
American Broadcasting Company

Fig. 3.2: In Fall 1998, Fernando Ferrer released his vision for a rehabilitated Yankee Stadium that featured an upgraded playing field and supporting activities.

Flashing forward to 1997, Bronx Borough President Fernando Ferrer steps up to the podium at the annual meeting of the National Civic League. He is there to accept the group's prestigious All-American City award. At about the same time, the *New York Times* declares with uncharacteristic enthusiasm: "The unmistakable transformation [in the Bronx] is nothing short of a miracle." *Business Week* echoes the sentiment: "The South Bronx is 'what's in.'"[2] Riding this crest, the Bronx hits the headlines again when, in the fall of 1998, Ferrer unveils his plan for "Yankee Village," featuring a modern stadium and a glittering restaurant–retail complex interconnected by shimmering

Fig. 3.3: By the late 1970s, rubble-strewn lots dominated the South Bronx landscape.
Photograph by Camillo Vegara. Courtesy of Office of the Borough President, Bronx, New York.

glass walkways that also link to the region's far-flung transportation system[3] (fig. 3.2). Light and flowers abound. And by February 14, 1999, the lead article in the *New York Times* Real Estate section would herald: "A South Bronx Very Different from the Cliché."[4]

Back in 1978, the Bronx provided a vivid image of America—at least part of America, urban America. Its visual representations featured once-grand buildings now crumbled and rubble-strewn lots populated by a stray dog, a zombie-like drug addict, or a wretched mother with several children clutching her legs (fig. 3.3). The accompanying captions screamed "shame of the nation," "out of control," "devastated."

The terms "South Bronx" or "Bronx" had become code for "slum." They symbolized the wide-scale depopulation, housing abandonment, and invasion and succession (the replacement of one population by another) that transformed many cities in the post–World War II period. Between 1970 and 1990, the Bronx suffered a 20 percent population decrease, dropping from 1.5 million to 1.2 million people. It lost thousands of dwelling units to abandonment and arson. In a single generation, one South Bronx neighborhood saw its 198,000 residents dwindle to 54,000 and its 40,000 dwellings reduced to 15,300, about half of them in public housing built between 1956 and 1965. The most precipitous fall occurred in the 1970s when the community experienced a 65 percent loss in the number of inhabitants.[5] In other neighborhoods, vacant land and buildings would constitute more than 60 percent of the total area.[6]

But the *New York Times*–cited miracle of 1997 referred to a new image for the Bronx, one where population had increased (2 percent) and new housing was on line (thirty thousand new and rehabilitated housing units). The Bronx was witnessing other significant new construction (valued at about $25 billion since 1990, including a regional shopping center complete with a twelve-screen multiplex cinema and a Home Depot, the borough's first big-box store). More than $50 million of investment capital flowed into the area from Small Business Administration and Empowerment Zone subsidies. A laudatory article in a 1997 issue of the *Smithsonian* that began "Welcome to the good-news Bronx" underscored these dramatic changes in what had been reputed to be the nation's worst inner-city district.[7]

This chapter explores a single question: How did one image—"shame of the nation" (1978), become another—"All-American City" (1997)? It uses the concept of "image" to engage issues of the definition of a place in thought and reality and probe the interactions between public policies, changing municipal government arrangements, individual actions of elected officials, planning and design professionals, citizens and media observers.[8] Finally, it argues that images develop incrementally: When one image seemingly dominates, it is already in a state of change.

In fact, the Bronx story illustrates the dynamic, politicized surroundings in which urban images emerge. It reveals the fluidity of a history where, increasingly, multiple players vie for and clash over the right to determine the destiny of a place. The case develops in a changing environment for planning, one featuring evolving roles for government, civic groups, and individuals. While it highlights specific personalities and events, its general theme—that image is a result of the interplay of policy, structure, and people—applies to most planning scenarios and provides important lessons for planners and urban designers.

Evidence found in written plans and supporting narrative descriptions derived from newspaper accounts, interviews, government and civic association reports, and media portrayals documents the Bronx's movement from the "shame of the nation" to the "All-American City." These references not only capture the images in words and pictures but also help explain the processes that created them. Table 3.1 summarizes the critical items and sequence of events.

Table 3.1

THE EVOLUTION OF SOUTH BRONX IMAGES, 1930s–1990s

Period	Image	Source	Author/Actors
1930s–1950s	The Beautiful Bronx	Memory, histories	L. Ultan and G. Hermalyn (1998), *Beautiful Bronx: 1920–1950* (New York: Crown) K. Simon (1983), *Bronx Primitive: Portraits in a Childhood* (New York: HarperCollins)
1960s	Corridor of Misery	*Plan for New York City*	Municipal government
1970s–1980s	Shame of the Nation	*New York Times*	Presidential declaration
		With Love and Affection: A Study of Building Abandonment	Civic groups and municipal government
		T. Wolfe (1987), *The Bonfire of the Vanities* (New York, NY: Farrar, Straus and Giroux)	Media
1980s	Phoenix rising	Charlotte Street	Economic development organizations
		Mayor's Ten Year Housing Plan	Municipal government
1990s	All-American City	*New Directions, Bronx Center, Melrose Commons, Site 404, Yankee Village*	Borough government, civic groups, citizens, municipal government

Note: Additional bibliographic data is contained in the endnotes.

THE "BEAUTIFUL BRONX" AND ITS EROSION

Any discussion of the Bronx must begin with a recognition of its transformation from farmland to thriving metropolis and an appreciation of the strength of memories held by its pre–World War II residents, often first- and second-generation immigrants who viewed their lives in the borough as an exciting step in social mobility.[9] In 1950, the Bronx's forty-three square miles, once the agricultural hinterland for Manhattan and later consolidated into New York City in the 1890s, housed 20 percent of the Big Apple's population (fig. 3.4). In the early twentieth century, subways had linked it to downtown, enabling German, Italian, and Jewish families to occupy what many perceived as the city's best housing stock.[10] New Law tenements, six-story apartment buildings built at a density of about 275 to 300 dwelling units per acre, predominated. Industry and retail followed. Called "The Beautiful Bronx" for its amenities and layout, there was a general belief that Bronx residents, whatever their ethnic origin, were middle class either in actuality or aspiration. Nuclear families with clearly defined gender roles were the norm. Historian Lloyd Ultan captures these dimensions:

> [D]ifferences between Bronxites were real, but in a larger sense they were not substantial. In many ways the people were very much alike. Rich or poor, Catholic, Protestant or Jew, living on a farm, in a small house or in an apartment . . . they were all middle class and embodied middle-class values.[11]

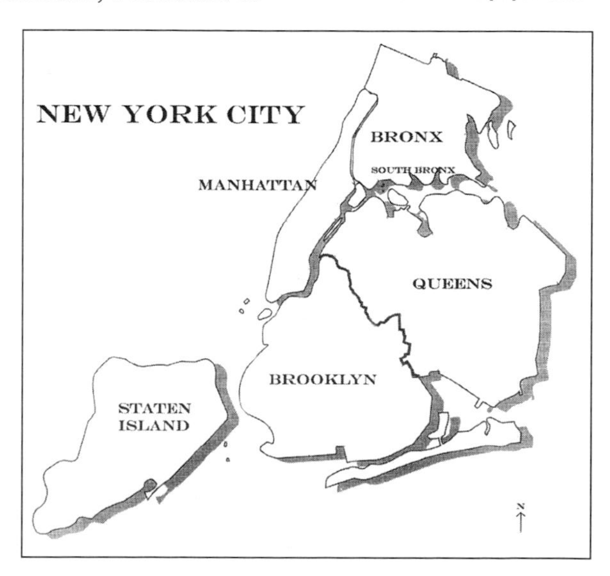

Fig. 3.4: By 1950, the Bronx's forty-three square miles housed 20 percent of New York's population.

New Deal and postwar public policy—federal, state, and local—for housing, transportation, and urban renewal, well-intended programs based on contemporary images of a better life for Americans, would have enormous implications for the Bronx, ultimately spawning the "shame of the nation" image. Under the National Housing Act (1934), banks and their insurers, primarily the Federal Housing Administration, developed financing practices that featured widespread redlining of large areas of the South Bronx, disqualifying the property within the boundaries for inexpensive mortgages or other loans. Federally funded public housing programs, authorized under the 1937 Wagner-Steagall Housing Act and subsequent legislation, deposited more than 28,000 housing units in the Bronx, concentrated in high-rise buildings and often built on cleared sites.[12] State-subsidized efforts on greenfields sites located two enormous middle-income projects, Parkchester (1932) with 40,000 units and Co-op City (1968) with 15,000 units, in the north, draining population from the south. Furthermore, New York City's rent control (1943) and rent stabilization (1947) laws, which in 1981 covered 70 percent of all occupied units in the South Bronx, ultimately led to landlord disinvestment because

Fig. 3.5: As the Interstate Highway System grew, four routes would impinge on the South Bronx (upper center): the Major Deegan Expressway, Cross Bronx Expressway, Sheridan Expressway, and Bruckner Expressway.

regulated rents could be, on average, 15 percent lower than market prices.[13] Federally mandated code enforcement programs that coupled punitive rent reductions to noncompliance tended to increase the owner's assessed valuations after compliance, thereby creating a problem in an area where artificial or market conditions limited the income potential of the units.[14]

After passage of the Federal-Aid Highway Act of 1956, transportation programs left the borough riddled with interstate highways—the Bruckner Boulevard to the east, the Cross Bronx Expressway to the north, and the Major Deegan Expressway to the west (fig. 3.5). Their construction wreaked havoc with many well-established neighborhoods, as demonstrated by Robert Caro's case study of the seven-mile Cross Bronx Expressway built between 1952 and 1963. This road bisected the 60,000-resident East Tremont section, directly dislocating five thousand people who lived in the right-of-way. Discouraged by the destruction of the area's strong informal and formal institutions—clubs, the Young Men's Hebrew Association, shopping patterns, and friendships—another ten thousand residents would move away within a few years.[15]

Urban renewal impacted the Bronx by causing major population dislocations throughout the city. Under the aggressive leadership of Robert Moses, New York City would capture half of the funding authorized for the program. By 1969 the city had more than fifteen large-scale urban renewal sites in Manhattan alone. It cleared entire neighborhoods to make way for performing arts halls at Lincoln Center, housing and hospital space for New York University, a new Penn Station and associated office buildings, middle-income housing in Kips Bay, and a mixed-income neighborhood on the Upper West Side. While these projects helped New York retain its world-city status, they also contributed to a growing crisis among the displaced who tended to be poor and, desperate for shelter, often resorted to doubling up in the limited housing in the neighboring boroughs, especially the South Bronx.[16]

These programs hastened a socioeconomic process already under way in the South Bronx: the departure of white, nuclear families and their replacement by poorer, minority families whose numbers would become increasingly dominated by female-headed households. (In 1950, the minority population in the city was 13 percent; by 1980, it was 43 percent.[17]) In the South Bronx this demographic shift was even more pronounced: in 1980, minorities constituted 83 percent of the area's population. The newcomers had a lower average household income (more than half were below the poverty level), higher rates of transience (contemporary surveys indicated that the majority had moved into the South Bronx within the past five years), and higher rates of dependency (about 40 percent were receiving welfare).[18] Thus, in the years following World War II, the "Beautiful Bronx" was slowly changing, especially the southern sector, where large-scale clearance and construction of highways and housing, discriminatory financing practices, and other policies tore neighborhoods asunder. The federal, state, and city government officials who conceived and implemented these programs operated in a system that neither favored maintenance or conservation of inner-city neighborhoods nor allowed local residents to participate in the decision-making processes revolving around the policies.

■ THE "CORRIDOR OF MISERY," PRECURSOR TO THE "SHAME OF THE NATION"

Against this background of demographic and physical change in the Bronx, in 1969 the city approved its first master plan, *Plan for New York City.*[19] The plan established the contemporary official image for the Bronx. Issued as a set of six 17-inch by 17-inch volumes, one was a summary and the others focused on the boroughs. Each borough volume contained comprehensive inventories of census and land-use data, a rough analysis of problems, and simple responses.

Many, including some members of the City Planning Commission, criticized the plan as a "top-down document."[20] The chair of the City Planning Commission and his staff had determined its outlook with little local consultation. Although the approval process included public hearings, the sessions occurred after the document had been published, depriving citizens of meaningful input.[21]

The authors were extremely conscious of the plan's sensitive political nature.[22] They wrote it during some of the most turbulent times in the city's history, a period characterized by civil disorder and struggles for community empowerment.[23] The school system was in the midst of battles over local control while various municipal departments were fighting about the meaning of the "maximum feasible citizen participation" language incorporated in the War on Poverty and Model Cities legislation. Poor relations between city professionals and locally elected citizens' committees led to stalemates and confusion, with the city often caught between warring elements within communities.[24]

The plan had a single goal: to maintain the Big Apple as a national center. Its recommendations focused on achieving this objective and emphasized strengthening Manhattan's central business district. The volume for the Bronx exhibited neither a clear vision of the Bronx's place with regard to maintaining the city as a national center nor any particular message defining any other role for the borough. From beginning to end, the analysis revealed a helpless and insensitive city administration faced with alarming socioeconomic trends. The first paragraph illustrates the dilemma:

> The Bronx is a paradox. It is the home of some of the City's wealthiest and most notable citizens, as well as of hordes of its poorest and most anonymous. Some of the City's finest and most spacious parks are here, yet there are crowded districts that boast little or no open space and junk-strewn vacant lots. . . . Fine neighborhoods, like Riverdale and Williamsbridge, are found in the borough's northern and eastern fringes. A central corridor of decay, including Morrisania, the South Bronx and Hunts Point, now threatens to engulf adjoining neighborhoods such as the Grand Concourse and Tremont. . . . Where the corridor of misery touches more stable communities, the competition for decent, affordable homes is compounded by a polarization of race.[25]

The racial change and economic decline of the Bronx had been made imageable, not just a collection of statistics. It was a "corridor of misery."

Fig. 3.6: View of Co-op City, the new town with 15,000 dwelling units, stores, schools, and recreation.

To address this plight the plan offered the following solutions. Model Cities efforts, supplemented with code enforcement and incentive programs for rehabilitation, would quickly eliminate blight. Construction of low-income housing in homogeneous residential enclaves interlaced with vest-pocket parks—all built on existing, underutilized larger parks—would cure crowding. Completing Co-op City, a quasi "new town" for fifty-five thousand residents housed in thirty-five high-rise apartment buildings and serviced with three shopping centers, an educational park, a fire department, and a heating plant, would provide an escape from the creeping "corridor of misery" (fig. 3.6).

The vision embodied current theories about the proper arrangement of cities drawn from Garden City advocates, progressive social reformers, and the Chicago School of sociologists. Its tenets were to separate classes into homogeneous neighborhoods and to clear and rebuild slums with low-cost housing in large-scale developments. In practice, these ideas merely reinforced emerging Bronx settlement patterns: concentrations of the poor in the south and middle-income citizens in the north.

The plan's treatment of transportation also reflected the

limited attention afforded the Bronx. Calling for the dismantling of the elevated subway (the "El") and the completion of an additional line from downtown Manhattan to the Bronx, it ignored the land-use implications of these recommendations. It was silent on the redevelopment of the blighted areas surrounding the El or the siting issues of the new line. For vehicular congestion, the expansion of parkway capacity would suffice. More parking spaces on the main thoroughfare, Fordham Road, would support commerce.[26]

These ideas sustained an image of a Bronx that prevailed for the ensuing decade, informing public policy and resource allocation. Through the early 1970s Model Cities and successor programs would pump money into the area, but there was never enough. The El came down, but the new subway did not materialize. Furthermore, New York, like other large Rust Belt cities, experienced crushing losses in its industrial base: After 1970, seven hundred thousand factory jobs vanished, a phenomenon that contributed to the relentless downward spiral in the South Bronx.

"THE SHAME OF THE NATION" EMERGES

The "corridor of misery" image soon turned more lethal. Housing abandonment, often associated with arson, accelerated in the 1970s, as did social disintegration, indicated by the rise of violent crime, drug use, and high rates of unemployment. A contemporary description of conditions related:

> Between 1970 and 1975 there were 68,456 fires in the Bronx, more than thirty-three each night. . . . People burned their own apartments because they would be relocated then to new public housing projects. . . . Junkies then systematically stripped buildings of copper pipes . . . making rehabilitation almost impossible. . . . There is also abundant evidence that, in order to collect insurance payments, landlords hired professional "torches" to incinerate apartment buildings that had lost their profitability.[27]

Fig. 3.7: On October 5, 1977, President Jimmy Carter (center), accompanied by Patricia Harris, Secretary, U.S. Department of Housing and Urban Development, and Abraham Beame, Mayor, New York City, toured South Bronx devastated neighborhoods around Charlotte Street.
Courtesy Jimmy Carter Library

The police reported assaults rising from 998 in 1960 to 4,256 ten years later; burglaries went from 1,765 to 29,276 in the same time span.[28]

By 1976 these problems were beginning to overwhelm local government officials. The Department of Housing Preservation and Development became the owner of a growing stock of derelict, tax-delinquent properties—twelve thousand dwellings in the Bronx alone.[29] Housing Commissioner Roger Starr gained local attention when he advocated "planned shrinkage," an approach that called for concentrating existing residents in pocket neighborhoods and triaging the remaining land and buildings. Implementing this policy was easy, he argued, because as the distressed area's largest landlord, the government could use public housing or strategically located repossessed holdings as anchors.[30]

A year later, President Jimmy Carter paid a surprise visit to a devastated block on the Bronx's Charlotte Street, where, surrounded by an entourage of reporters and photographers, he walked among the weeds and piles of rubble vowing to redress the deplorable conditions. In 1980, attacking Carter's domestic policy in a well-publicized campaign speech on the same site, Ronald Reagan declared that he had "not seen anything that looked like this since London after the Blitz." He labeled the place the "shame of the nation"[31] (fig. 3.7).

By 1987, this image was so familiar that novelist Tom Wolfe would use the Bronx as the backdrop in his best-selling *The Bonfire of the Vanities*, the plot of which revolves around tense racial encounters. Wolfe needed few words to describe the environment. For one scene he observed:

> The housing project . . . was now a huge cluster of grimy brick towers set in a slab of cinders and stomped dirt. . . . The ebb and flow of the city, caused by the human tides of labor, didn't cause a ripple at the Edgar Allan Poe Towers, where the unemployment rate was at least 75 percent. A small pack of male teenagers scurr[ied] past the graffiti at thc base of the buildings. The graffiti looked half-hearted. The grimy brick, with all its mortar gulleys, depressed even the spray-can juvies.[32]

In another, he provided a harsh description of an image shift in the heart of the Bronx:

> Before him rose the great bowl of Yankee Stadium. Beyond the stadium were the corroding hulks of the Bronx. . . . He looked up—and for an instant he could see the old Bronx in all its glory. At the top of the hill where 161st Street crossed the Grand Concourse, the sun had broken through and had lit the limestone face of the Concourse Plaza Hotel. . . . The Yankee ballplayers used to live there during the season, the ones who could afford to, the stars. . . . The Grand Hotel . . . was now a welfare hotel.[33]

The "shame of the nation" image embodied widespread physical and social deterioration. Its defining characteristics were an abundance of abandoned buildings and vacant lots,

Figs. 3.8a, 3.8b: The City cleared the sites (*left*, fig. 3.8a), and later grassy fields (*right*, fig. 3.8b) grew over the vacant lots in the South Bronx.
Photographs © E. L. Birch

islands of rundown public housing, and concentrations of socially dysfunctional poor in shattered neighborhoods. Eventually the city cleared the sites, and grassy fields covered the vacant land (figs. 3.8a, 3.8b). Any new image would have to counteract these features.

PHOENIX RISING AND RECONSTRUCTION

In the early 1980s, a new image for the Bronx began to emerge, jump-started by two initiatives. For the first, reformers, led by South Bronx Development Organization president Edward J. Logue, used massive subsidies to transform the site of the two presidential visits into Charlotte Gardens, a middle-income sub-

Figs. 3.9a, 3.9b: Charlotte Gardens featured single-family homes on 6,800-square-feet lots, a density of six units per acre.
Photographs © E. L. Birch

Figs. 3.10a, 3.10b: Mayor Ed Koch's Ten-Year Housing Program dedicated $5.1 billion for rehabilitating abandoned city-owned apartment buildings such as the South Bronx example above. The "before" view (*left*, fig. 3.10a) features evidence of an earlier policy, using window decals to simulate occupancy. The "after" view (*right*, fig. 3.10b) shows the restored, fully occupied building.

Photographs by Camillo Vegara. Courtesy of Office of the Borough President, Bronx, New York.

division. It featured ninety single-family, ranch-style houses on 6,800-square-feet lots at a density of six units per acre (figs. 3.9a, 3.9b). They anticipated that the project, like a phoenix rising from ashes, would spur recovery of nearby retail strips.[34] For the second, Mayor Ed Koch fashioned an enormous shelter effort, "The Mayor's Ten-Year Housing Program," focusing $5.1 billion on housing rehabilitation and construction in the city's most desolate neighborhoods: Central Harlem, Washington Heights, Bedford Stuyvesant, and the South Bronx.[35]

By most accounts, both programs were enormously successful. In 1985, bombed-out Charlotte Street looked like the American Dream. In the late 1980s, blocks of formerly boarded-up apartment buildings were restored and occupied (figs. 3.10a, 3.10b).

While these efforts contributed to the creation of a new image for the Bronx, there were flaws. Planners soon realized that successful inner-city revitalization depended on development of heterogeneous, mixed-income neighborhoods built at sufficient density to sustain local commercial activities and social institutions while reducing the concentration of the poor.[36] New York's experiments on Charlotte Street and in the Mayor's Program did not conform to the theories. The Charlotte Street model (followed shortly by many other projects at somewhat increased densities) was too small-scale. It left the existing infrastructure, such as subways and schools, severely underutilized and did little to reduce the concentrated poverty.[37] Furthermore, its low densities did not

Figs. 3.11a, 3.11b: The low densities of Charlotte Street (*left*, fig. 3.11a) and later, more-compact development (*right*, fig. 3.11b), would not support hoped-for retail and institutional revitalization.
Photographs by Camillo Vegara. Courtesy of Office of the Borough President, Bronx, New York.

provide enough population to support hoped-for retail and institutional revitalization (figs. 3.11a, 3.11b).

The Ten-Year Housing Program also had its limits. The city had mixed purposes for the program; specifically, it aimed to link housing rehabilitation with provision of permanent shelter for homeless families. (At the time, more than 24,000 people were in homeless shelters; of these, 63 percent were families.[38]) The authorities gave this group preference when allocating the rehabbed units. Homeless families soon dominated their new neighborhoods.[39] This situation fostered extreme resentment among the older South Bronx residents, who believed that the invasion of ill-prepared families into their already weak neighborhoods was just another indication of the low regard with which the city held them. Moreover, it did little to change the social features of the "shame of the city" image, as the newcomers had the following profile:

> A typical family consists of a young, minority female, with a very young child, who receives public assistance. . . . Analysis of possible service needs based on mental health, drug abuse and employability problems . . . suggests that (1) 42 percent of the families appear to have either a mental health or drug abuse problem; and (2) a quarter (23 percent) have a serious employability problem with no indications of either mental health or drug abuse problem[s].[40]

ROOTS OF THE "ALL-AMERICAN CITY" IMAGE

This scene was unfolding when a 37-year-old Bronxite, Fernando Ferrer, assumed the borough presidency in 1988. One of the few Hispanics to hold public office in the city, Ferrer had studied public administration at New York University and Baruch College. His previous experience as a city councilman (1982–87) and as Bronx's Director of Housing (1979–82) had sensitized him to the area's politics and needs. As a legislator, he had sponsored an important amendment to the city's tax abatement law, one that required a substantial contribution to affordable housing by the developers of luxury units employing the device.

Ferrer was a beneficiary of a vastly changed planning environment, a phenomenon that began in the early 1960s and peaked just as he came into office. While institutional city planning dated from the 1930s, it had evolved substantially over the years. Originally focused on the efficient management of capital resources, it later aimed to broaden participation in the land-use decision making. When Mayor Fiorello LaGuardia appointed the first seven-member city planning commission in 1938,[41] it had a charter mandate to produce a master plan, devise the capital budget, and oversee the zoning ordinance.[42]

A 1975 charter revision redefined the city's planning operations. It moved responsibility for the capital budget to the New York Office of Management and Budget. It designated that fifty-nine local community boards would have specific project review functions embodied in a legal format called the Uniform Land Use Review Process (ULURP).[43] By 1989, an additional charter revision led to major changes in the planning framework. It expanded the planning commission to thirteen members, retaining seven appointments for the mayor and adding one for each of the borough presidents and one for the city council president, thereby making the group more representative but also subject to larger power struggles. It strengthened the role of the borough presidents in the ULURP process, enabling them to override planning commission decisions under certain conditions. It also gave them control over 5 percent of the city's capital budget, encouraging them to augment their own planning and development offices and hire professional staff to oversee their interests. The charter revision also allowed communities or other groups to submit general plans (known as "197a plans," after the provision in the charter) for commission and city council approval, providing a way for locally generated alternative images to gain higher visibility in centralized decision making.[44]

These changes meant that borough presidents and community boards gained a louder voice in the planning process. Not only were they to be regularly consulted prior to the completion of decision making, they also had resources to utilize in forming and implementing policy. Frequently, these new conditions would create difficulties among groups with differing views about an area's destiny.

■ ONWARD TO THE "ALL-AMERICAN CITY"

Borough President Ferrer seized upon planning as the hallmark of his administration. He was not only genuinely interested in the challenge the borough presented; he also knew that the person who turned the devastated Bronx around would have a bright political future. As he focused on reversing the area's negative image, one that prevailed despite the reconstruction efforts of the early 1980s, he immediately took two important actions. First, he geared up his planning staff, hiring a seasoned professional, Bernd Zimmerman, to head his Office of Planning and Development. Second, he contracted with the Regional Plan Association (RPA), a well-regarded nonprofit enterprise with a sixty-year record of excellent planning work, to undertake a plan for the Bronx.

Zimmerman was a logical choice for the borough's chief planner. Having served as the Director of the Bronx Office of the Department of City Planning for four years prior to his appointment, he knew the borough intimately and had thought deeply about its needs. Before coming to the Bronx, he had held a series of responsible departmental positions including head of the Office of Midtown Planning, a post that made him acutely aware of the web of support and interrelationships necessary for a healthy, vibrant central business district. He had received his training in city planning at Hunter College at a time when social science research, including Herbert Gans's work, and professional practice, including Paul Davidoff's invention of advocacy planning, were transforming the field with their revisionist approaches.[45] Finally, like Ferrer, Zimmerman was a strong-minded and savvy fighter, able to pursue an objective with determination and focus.

By 1989 the RPA, in conjunction with Ferrer and Zimmerman, had fashioned the new image, issued in its report, *New Directions for the Bronx* (fig. 3.12), which was widely distributed as a newspaper supplement. *New Directions* articulated the image in four principal recommendations directly challenging the city's approaches.

First, it called for a reexamination of city attitudes regarding abandonment, noting that vacant land was a precious and limited resource whose disposition should be carefully considered in conjunction with a comprehensive plan. This philosophy ran counter to current municipal practices of opportunistically selling properties without reference to an overall strategy, or casually transferring the land for needed but often-disruptive agency functions (transfer stations, sanitation maintenance facilities, drug treatment centers, juvenile detention homes, and other locally unwanted land uses).

Second, it questioned the city's residential density policies, calling for new construction to be built at levels two to four times greater than existing practices (i.e., at sixty to one hundred units per acre, not fifteen to thirty units per acre). In conjunction with this recommendation, it called for increasing home-ownership and economic diversity in subsidized shelter programs. It also maintained that new housing projects should include such neighborhood amenities as open space, commercial enterprises, and community facilities. Current city practices focused either on single-purpose rehabilitation projects or on lower-density construction efforts, with little regard for community building.

Third, it called for the development of a comprehensive plan for the Bronx Center, a 300-block area encompassing the borough's civic and commercial heart, casting it as the borough's economic engine. It also envisioned appropriate linkages of nearby residential and industrial areas to this downtown. Previously, the city had no strategy related to this concept.

Fourth, it stressed the importance of including meaningful citizen participation in the planning process. It argued that coordination of city agencies around the consensual plans was an essential ingredient in all redevelopment efforts.[46]

Taken together, these "New Directions" envisioned a South Bronx that would be residentially denser, economically centered, community sensitive, and comprehensively planned.

Immediately, Ferrer engaged a good-government group, the Urban Assembly, under the leadership of Richard Kahan, onetime chief of the New York State Urban Development Corporation and later its spin-off agency, the Battery Park City Corporation, to flesh out the Bronx Center concept through an intense community-based planning process. Kahan was politically adept and well-connected to the citywide civic, union, and corporate groups concerned with urban issues. He formerly headed the Riverside South Corporation, which had successfully managed to revise and shepherd an extraordinarily complex and controversial Donald Trump plan through the city's approval process. For the Bronx project, he garnered substantial financial support from several sources, including the New York City Economic Development Corporation and the New York State Urban Development Corporation; he

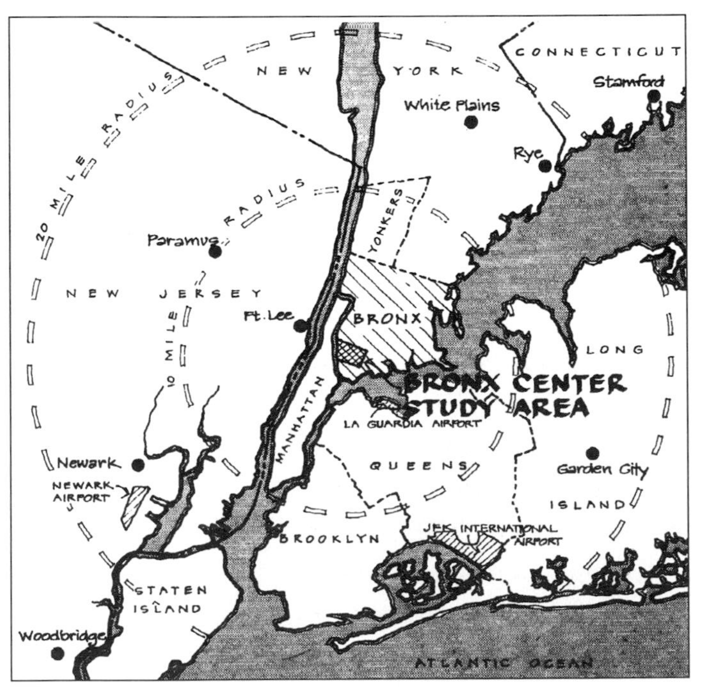

Fig. 3.12: ***New Directions for the Bronx*** **(1989) identified 300 blocks as the Bronx Center, an area that would serve as the heart of the borough's activities.**

arranged technical assistance from the New York State Urban Development Corporation, the Municipal Art Society's Planning Center, and the Pratt Center for Community and Environmental Development, experienced advocate planners. He pulled together a steering committee consisting of the borough president's planning staff, community representatives, and city-based civic associations and business members who labored ten months to create *Bronx Center*, a comprehensive plan for the heart of the borough.[47] They disseminated the preliminary results to five thousand people and community groups via a newsletter, *Bronx Center News*; held a series of public forums for more than six hundred attendees; and revised their proposals in accordance with the feedback. By May 1993, they produced a final report. This document detailed the Bronx's new image by filling in its economic development, housing, open space and urban design, health and human services, education and culture, and transportation components. Its underlying thesis was to rebuild the area's "economic engine" as the centerpiece of the "All-American City" image (fig. 3.13).[48]

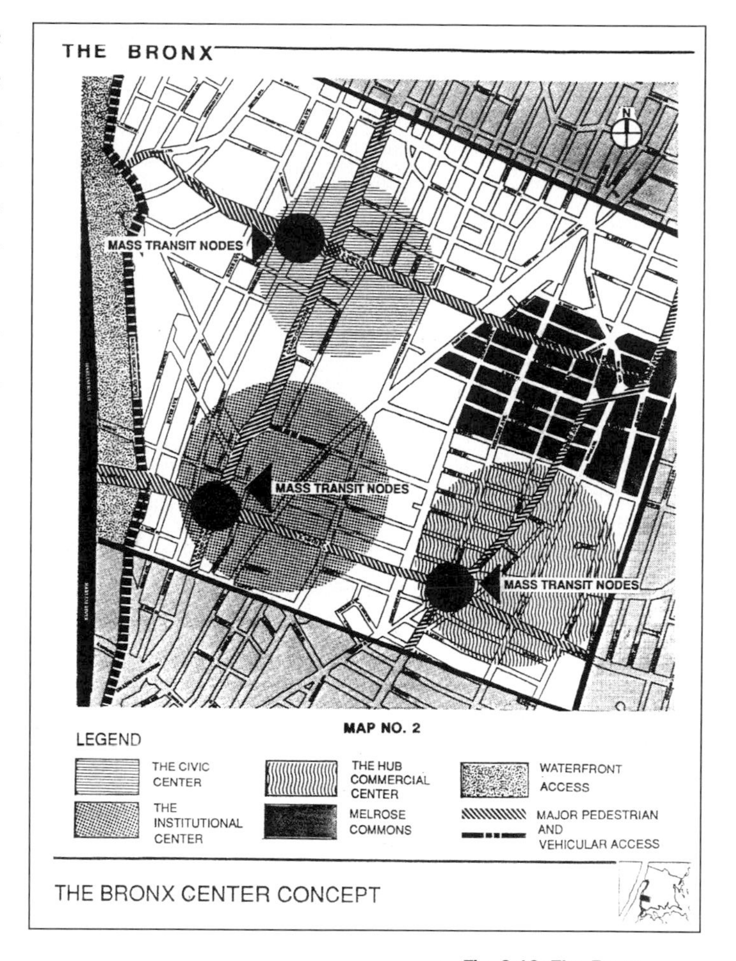

Fig. 3.13: The *Bronx Center* plan encompassed three nodes—civic, institutional, and commercial—and showed the proximity of the area's last large urban renewal site, Melrose Commons, to them.

For implementation, the document incorporated anticipated public works investment (a city police academy and new state and federal court facilities); focused funding from the existing budget allocations (especially health, housing, and education) and private initiatives (Yankee Stadium and the Bronx Terminal Market); retail strategies in an older commercial center

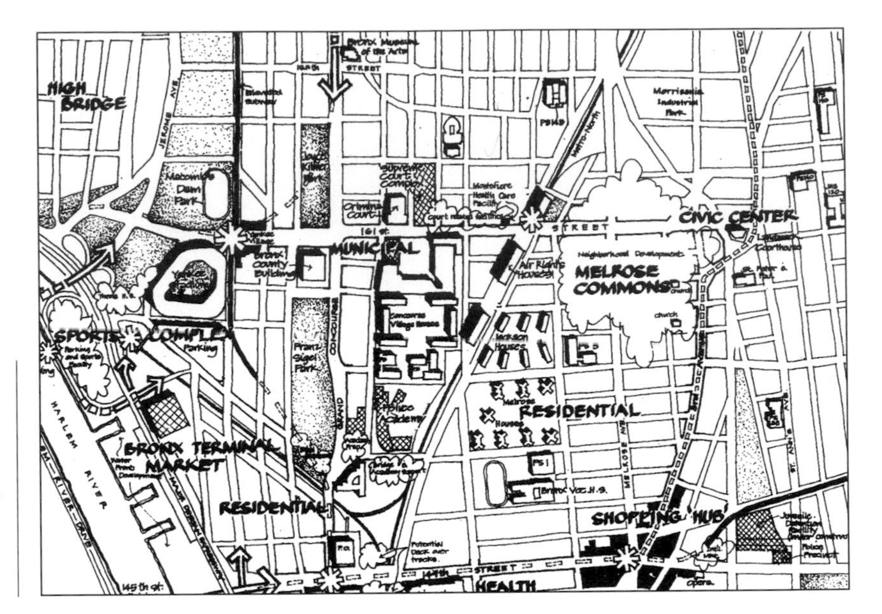

Fig. 3.14: A detailed scheme laid out anticipated public and private initiatives to forge a modern services- and entertainment-oriented downtown and adjacent high-density residential development.

(the Hub); and the enhancement of cultural facilities (the Bronx Museum of the Arts). The vision would forge a modern services- and entertainment-oriented downtown programmed to meet the needs of the borough's current and future residents and to attract others to the borough from elsewhere in the region (fig. 3.14). The new Bronxites would live in reclaimed areas, notably Melrose Commons, a 36-acre urban renewal area that was one of the largest assemblages in the city, and on other large development sites built at densities high enough to sustain the new activities.

Comprehensive, practical, and focused, the plan could easily be achieved if all the relevant decision makers were in agreement; that is, in a perfect world, this rational plan would secure the new image. In 1997, with the All-American City designation, Bronx planners gained a major symbolic victory. As of 1999 its achievements in terms of actual physical development remained mixed. The police academy was on hold; the courts were either built or under construction. Prospects for Yankee Stadium were looking hopeful, with the governor sweetening the deal with financial support to keep Yankee Stadium in the Bronx. The Hub and the Bronx Museum were holding their own.

Competing Plans Emerge within the "All-American City"

While the borough president developed the Bronx Center concept, other institutions also undertook their own planning efforts for the South Bronx. The Departments of City Planning (DCP) and Housing Preservation and Development (HPD) drew up the urban renewal plan for Melrose Commons. Community Board Three, which covered about a fifth of the South Bronx, prepared a 197a plan, entitled *Partnership for the Future*.[49] The city's Department of Sanitation developed a citywide solid waste disposal plan in anticipation of the closing of New York's only remaining landfill in Staten Island, targeting South Bronx sites for recycled-material transfer stations. Other agencies—the Human Resources Administration, the Department of General Services, and the Department of Transportation—earmarked Bronx land for their operations, which included methadone clinics, juvenile group homes, revenue-generating auctions of city-owned property, and maintenance garages. Finally, various nonprofit housing groups eyed specific sites for development, especially a particularly desirable four-acre parcel, Site 404, adjacent to Melrose Commons. All had their own images of the South Bronx and its future; some were in accord with Ferrer's image, many were not. The Melrose Commons plan and the Site 404 case are illustrative. Their development demonstrates divergent images and reveals Ferrer's methods for resolving conflicts while promoting the "All-American City" image.

Contending Images for Melrose Commons

By the late 1980s, the Melrose Commons area—a district whose population had plummeted from twenty-one thousand in 1970 to three thousand a decade later—had been under scrutiny for at least two decades.[50] The city owned about 60 percent of the property, and the Bronx DCP envisioned construction of three thousand middle-income units in attached houses, intended to create a residential anchor for an improved retail strip that would extend more than two miles from Melrose across the Grand Concourse to Yankee Stadium. After discussion with the Bronx Center planning group in 1992, DCP

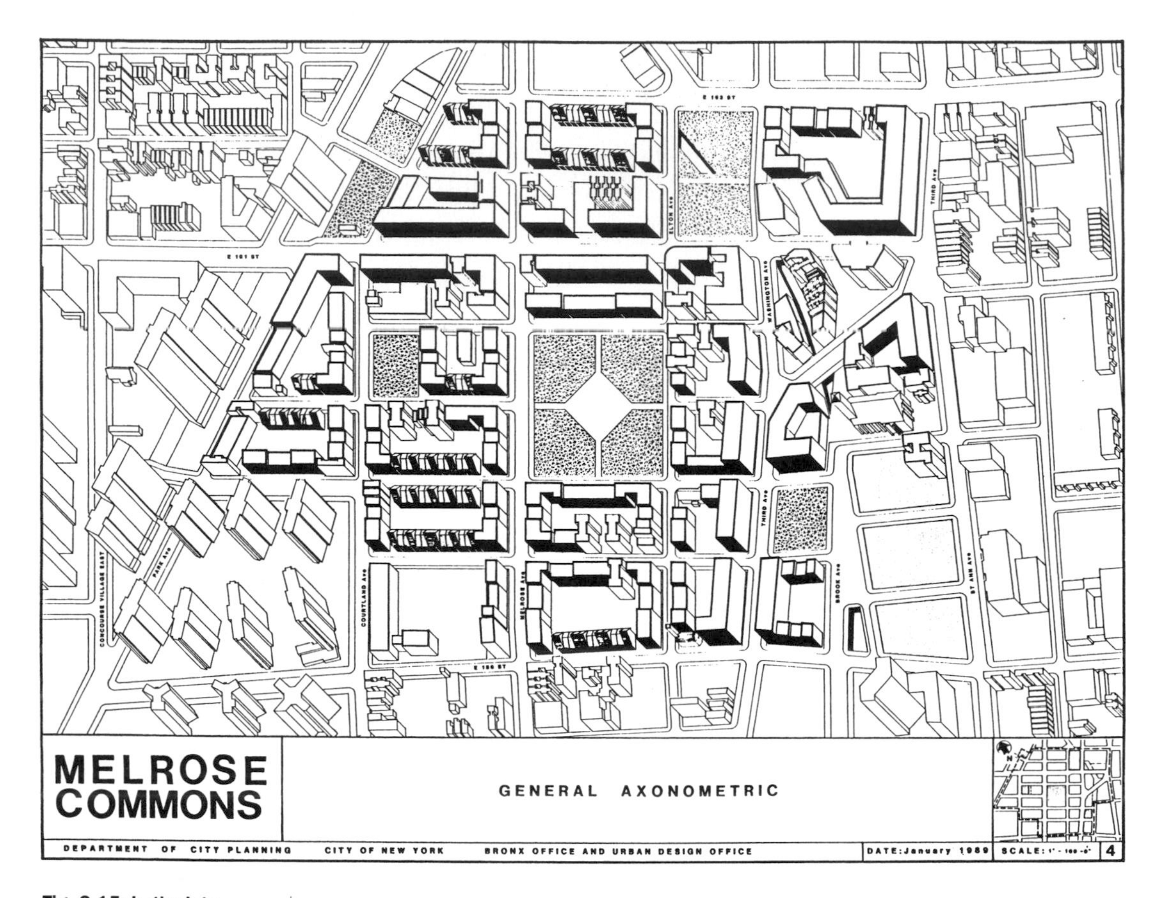

Fig. 3.15: In the late 1980s, the New York City Department of City Planning envisioned Melrose Commons as having 3,000 middle-income dwellings and a four-acre central park.

reduced the number to 2,600 dwellings arranged in two-, four- and six-story buildings. The department also programmed a four-acre central park with two satellite open spaces, a realigned street network, and strengthened retail corridors along 161st Street and Third Avenue (fig. 3.15).

This scheme required the relocation of two hundred sixty households and eighty-eight businesses and community facilities—more than a quarter of the existing households and 70 percent of the commercial and nonprofit firms—and almost 40 percent of the area's jobs.[51] Despite the high level of dislocation, Ferrer, Zimmerman, and Kahan were in complete agreement with the plan. They thought the displacement unfortunate but necessary for the realization of their primary goal—the introduction of middle-income housing at higher densities (about 70 units per acre in this plan). By the spring of 1992, the plan was in the first stages of the city's ULURP process.

The plan's supporters were in for a rude surprise. In June

1992, a Melrose resident happened upon a city worker taking notes in the neighborhood, who alerted her to the proposal. As word spread rapidly, irate residents, led by Yolanda Garcia, a long-time resident and owner of Garcia's Floor Coverings, one of the area's larger employers, organized a protest group called *Nos Quedamos* ("We Stay"). Bearing placards with a slashed-circle overlay on the plan, they attended Bronx Center meetings, interrupting them with loud complaints, insisting that "those who stayed in the neighborhood through the hard times, who had kept it going through the decay and crime and the difficulties, should be part of the progress"[52] (fig. 3.16). Up to this time, the Bronx Borough President and the Bronx Center Steering group had been in full agreement with the city's plan: The Bronx Center plan had even included the DCP–HPD schematics for Melrose Commons.[53] Now, confronted by Nos Quedamos, they retracted their endorsement.

Ferrer successfully badgered the chair of the planning commission and the housing commissioner to grant a several-month pause in the ULURP process to allow community review—a wholly unprecedented action.[54] Kahan, who had been taken by surprise by the vehement community opposition, reported "It was not that anything jumped out at us as a terrible idea."[55]

Later, Ferrer recounted how his reversal occurred during a meeting with Nos Quedamos. The group consensus was that "Melrose Commons . . . had been designed without their knowledge, involvement, or approval. To area homeowners and their families these changes meant an end to their status as property owners and their identification with the neighborhood which, in some cases, spanned over thirty years."[56]

It was not only the high level of dislocation that specifically irked residents; it was also the image conjured up by the proposed centrally located park. Locals believed the area could not

Fig. 3.16: "We Stay/Nos Quedamos" read the placards citizens bore to the community meetings that convinced Borough President Fernando Ferrer to support a major revision of the Melrose Commons plan.

WE STAY/NOS QUEDAMOS COMMITTEE

WE STAY

MELROSE COMMONS

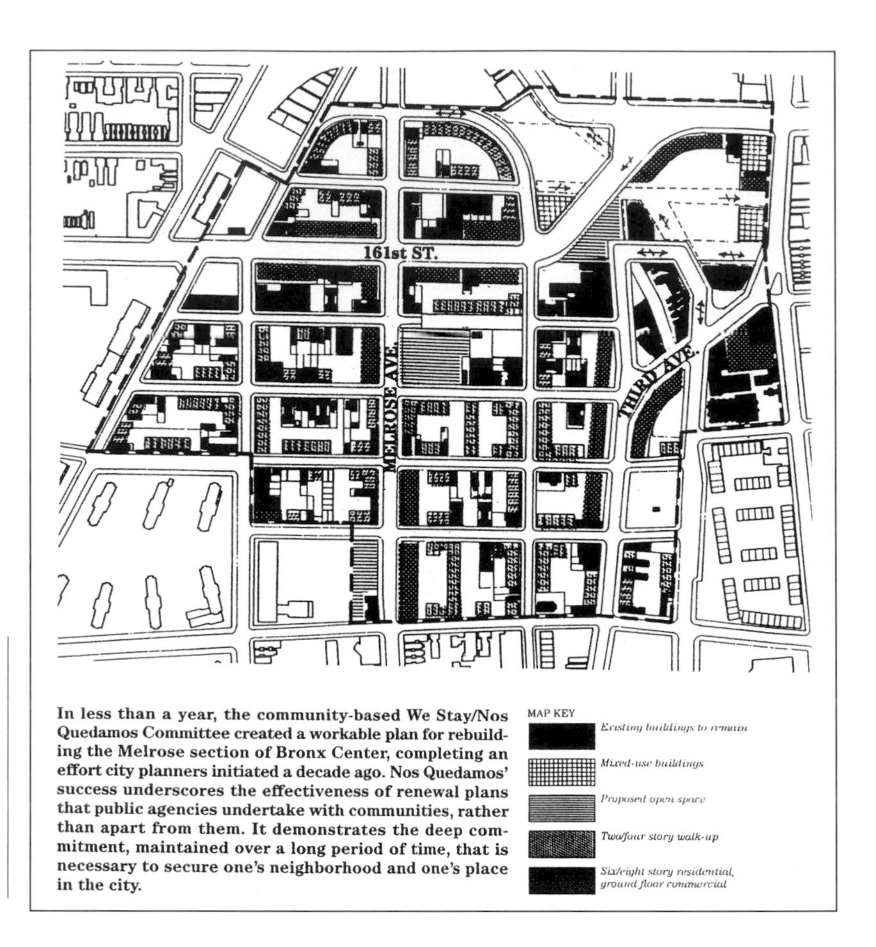

Fig. 3.17: The new Melrose Commons plan called for less displacement, redistributed open space, a community center supported by reconfigured streets amenable to pedestrians, and strict urban-design guidelines.

be properly supervised and would become a haven for drug dealers, the last element they wanted in their new community. Kahan recruited two community organizers and two architects to work on revising the scheme. For the next few months, representatives from Nos Quedamos, officials from the city's planning, housing, parks, and transportation agencies, the architects, and other volunteer planners met weekly, modifying the plan block by block.[57]

Their proposal reduced displacement to fifty-five households and fifty-three businesses and community facilities, cutting the original losses by one-third. To achieve this target, they reduced the number of dwelling units to 1,700; the gross density fell to fifty, although some individual sites had higher density. They replaced the large central park with highly visible smaller parks convenient to housing and schools. They also proposed reviving an abandoned landmark courthouse to serve as a community base and help create a real town center; it would have space for a planning center, neighborhood services, and an exhibition gallery.[58] They reconfigured the street plan with pedestrian and vehicular paths to emphasize the town center. Finally, they developed strict urban design guidelines to secure their image for the area since reconstruction would be undertaken by different developers over a long period of time. Their directives designated building heights and street walls and eliminated curb cuts within the blocks (fig. 3.17). The intent was to use regulation incorporated in an approved urban renewal plan to ensure development compatible with the neighborhood's historic fabric.[59] These features counteracted the typical affordable housing project site plan by placing vehicular parking in the back, accessed through an alley. By eliminating the repetitive curb cuts on each block and moving the buildings to the sidewalk, the designers hoped to restore the denser urbanism that had once prevailed in the area.

At the same time, however, designers tried to take into account the cultural preferences of a new generation of residents. In 1994, the community engaged the Environmental Simulation Lab, headed by planner Michael Kwartler, to detail these elements in a digital modeling exercise. He overlaid the proposed buildings with elements from a "kit of parts," trellises, stoops, entryways, sidewalks, and terraces "rooted in vernacular architecture specifically that of the Caribbean."[60] In reflecting on this experience, Kwartler observed that the process embodied "the tension between a place's present condition and its future hopes. In the best case, this tension leads to community involvement and activism. In the worst, it may promote frustration with the unavoidably slow pace of physical construction."[61]

In summarizing the roles of planners and architects in this process, Kahan's assistant, Catherine Cary, executive vice president of the Urban Assembly, related:

> We helped the community shape a plan simply by talking and listening. . . . We realized that planning can work only if the community feels it is involved from the beginning. . . . Pieced together issue by issue, block by block, the new

> Melrose plan is a coherent response by a justifiably shocked and outraged community. Nos Quedamos has given us more, a new measure of a neighborhood's health—not bricks and mortar . . . but . . . that social infrastructure [that] is the conceptual framework that the physical urban design process must embrace.[62]

In the end, Nos Quedamos offered one of the clearest statements about its role in helping develop the area's image. In addition to "physical characteristics," it is the "human dimension" that "defines the 'sense of place.'"[63]

As the plan wended its way through the ULURP review process, however, an alternative image for residential development emerged. The new views came from two sources, the real estate developers and the Department of Housing Preservation and Development. They objected to the precision of the design guidelines as well as to the urban renewal plan modification process. They believed that the design guidelines precluded the development of lower-density housing, specifically the attached row houses and two- or three-family town houses that were currently being constructed by the city's principal affordable housing providers, whose densities of eighteen to thirty units per acre were well below the goal articulated by the Bronx borough president, the *New Directions*, Bronx Center, and Melrose Commons plans. I. D. Robbins, the brains behind one group, argued that restoring the former six-story appearance of the Bronx would cost three times as much as low-rise building and would be excessively difficult to manage and maintain: "Low land values do not require high density as in Manhattan. . . . The Melrose area is largely . . . degenerated beyond redemption. . . . It is an ideal location for . . . single-family row housing. . . . Strip stores are failing all over the United States. People want centrally located magnet supermarkets that charge fair prices, not bodegas at high prices."[64]

For its part, the Department of Housing Preservation and Development also wanted more flexibility and discretion than the plan allowed but did not want the changes to trigger a full

ULURP review process.[65] A bitter debate among members of the planning commission ensued. The commission chair, the housing agency, the developers, the Bronx Borough President's office, the Bronx Center group, Nos Quedamos, and individual citizens lobbied intensely. In an emotional special meeting, the commission approved the plan with the housing agency's modifications in a split vote: seven in favor and six abstentions.[66]

Plan implementation moved slowly and featured a major setback as well as some progress. The hardest blow was the city's decision to auction the abandoned landmark courthouse, the building slated for the community center, aborting nearly completed negotiations for its lease to the Bronx Overall Economic Development Corporation.[67] Then newly elected Mayor Rudy Giuliani won out, but the editorial pages had the last word: "There are those who feel that Mayor Giuliani's rush to sell the building which has been vacant for almost twenty years is fueled by a desire to foreclose the possibility of its eventually becoming a showcase in the South Bronx, which could reflect favorably on Borough President Fernando Ferrer."[68]

On the positive side, Phase I of the Melrose plan broke ground in late 1998 with more than two hundred dwellings and supportive uses in the eight-block area. Bronx leaders also launched a capital improvement fund and created a planning activities committee.[69]

More Conflicting Images: Site 404

In the late 1980s, a rectangular parcel in the Melrose area, called Site 404, was ripe for development. Cleared for an urban renewal housing project that never happened, its 4.4 acres were highly desirable for their location near mass transit and the Hub, the commercial center. It was one of the few large ready-to-go sites left in the South Bronx. In 1987, the city detached the parcel from the urban renewal site and down-zoned the land, permitting only a half million square feet of new construction. HPD envisioned the site as supporting three hundred fifty dwelling units built at a density of about eighty per acre.

But before the agency could issue a request for proposals, a newly formed group, South Bronx Churches (SBC), proposed eighty Nehemiah-style houses[70] at a density of twenty dwellings per acre. It premised the scheme on gaining considerable concessions: a low site-acquisition cost, building department permission for a single sewer hookup (a real cost saver, avoiding individual lines to each house), real estate tax abatements for fifteen years, and a $15,000 per-unit grant. Thus, a house costing $71,000 to build could carry a discounted price tag of $56,000, affordable to a family earning $26,000 annually. The discussions centered on housing finance but, as before, the underlying issue was driven by image. And again, one group's image of desirable housing proved distinctly different from that of another key player.

Thirty congregations joined together to found SBC in February 1987 after two years of weekly prayer meetings and planning, having raised $3 million from two wealthy Manhattan churches; national offices of the Roman Catholic, Lutheran and Jewish denominations; and their own tithes. SBC aimed for "the accrual and exercise of power to make changes consistent with civic and religious values." At its first general meeting, attended by two thousand people, "the lay and clergy leadership stood together to announce a new force in the South Bronx . . . organized for the long haul."[71] SBC focused on housing as a symbol of its strength and accomplishment. The organization's goal was construction of fifteen hundred new units. Securing Site 404 for the group's first project became a holy cause, a political objective, tightly bound to its mission.[72] One participant later observed, "The Nehemiah project became . . . a kind of burning bush, reminding them of God's promises, calling them to take a prophetic stance in the face of repressive city policies and providing encouragement when things got rough."[73]

Even as SBC was pressing for the property, HPD circulated a request for proposals to develop the site for higher-density housing, working through the New York City Housing Partnership.[74] Fourteen companies responded (SBC did not submit anything), and HPD awarded the site to a local developer, Procida Construction, a family-run business. Procida's project,

Melrose Court, had 256 units designed at eighty-five units per acre. In contrast to the SBC plan for subsidized houses that would carry a discounted price tag of $56,000 (affordable to a family earning $26,000 annually), the Procida project's units would sell for $75,000.[75] In response, an outraged SBC staged a 5,000-participant protest with mayoral hopeful Giuliani in attendance. HPD offered SBC fifteen other sites within a five-block radius of Site 404. SBC refused to negotiate and attacked the plan as elitist. Countering this charge, Borough President Ferrer threw $4.5 million into Procida's $21 million development package, bringing the purchase price down to $60,000, comparable to the Nehemiah units.[76]

In the end, the city held fast to its position, and by 1999 the first residents moved into Melrose Court. SBC opened negotiations with the city, ultimately obtaining sufficient land for five hundred homes, which were completed rapidly. One observer assessed SBC accomplishments: "SBC's Nehemiah project has reclaimed thirty-five square blocks for single-family homes. . . . Gardens now bloom where once was rubble"[77] (figs. 3.18a, 3.18b).

Figs. 3.18a, 3.18b: In contrast to Charlotte Gardens, built two decades earlier, Melrose Court has a density of eighty-five units per acre (*below,* fig. 3.18a) and provides for open space integrated in inner courtyards (*right,* fig. 3.18b). Photos © E. L. Birch

CONCLUSIONS

This discussion of the South Bronx has documented how images, defined as the definitions of a place in thought and reality, develop over time. It has covered five images: "Beautiful Bronx," "corridor of misery," "shame of the nation," "phoenix rising" and "All-American City," and five decades, while highlighting the complications of moving from a negative image to a positive one.

Two types of players contributed to and interpreted the area's negative postwar images, the "corridor of misery" and the "shame of the nation." The first were citywide elected or appointed officials implementing housing, transportation, and urban renewal policies. Their single-minded pursuit of center-city development, clearance, and new construction ignored and damaged existing communities. Their posture related, in part, to the authoritarian nature of contemporary public administration and, in part, to an inability to recognize and address large socioeconomic trends playing out in cities and suburbs. In fact, their well-intentioned albeit ultimately wrongheaded public policies helped fuel many of these trends. The second were nonlocal politicians, exemplified by Jimmy Carter and Ronald Reagan, and media figures, represented by Tom Wolfe. The former sought to promote their own domestic policies; the latter dramatized racial division and economic contrast in American society.

Together, these two groups solidified the negative images of the South Bronx. To be sure, these images reflected current conditions. Further, they seemed even more tragic in contrast to their predecessor "Beautiful Bronx" image as perpetuated by the nostalgic memories of earlier inhabitants. These images camouflaged others existing below the surface.

Recognition that the "shame of the nation" image was neither permanent nor wholly accurate slowly emerged. Community-oriented and advocacy-planning challenges came from many sides, given fuller expression by structural changes in planning, public policy development, and resource allocation. Specifically, New York City amended land use, service delivery, and budget procedures, empowered community boards, and developed a consultative project review process (ULURP). It also redefined the power of borough presidents. The new system dramatically altered the playing field and its rules. Local political leaders, professionals, foundations, a battery of inside-the-community and outside-the-community civic associations and individual citizens—all having some direct interest in the outcome—now engaged in articulating images, sometimes deeply contrasting, for the South Bronx.

As the environment for planning and decision making became more participatory, crafting a new image involved more players and encompassed a greater number of geographic scales. City commissioners, the borough president, city and borough planning directors, affordable housing providers, civic associations, community board members, and activist citizens contributed their views. They spoke out on citywide management issues pertaining to urban renewal plan modifications, areawide visions incorporated in the *New Directions* and Bronx Center documents, neighborhood plans for Melrose Commons, and development details for Site 404.

The bold strokes of creating Charlotte Gardens and reclaiming the abandoned buildings and properties through the Mayor's Ten-Year Housing Plan began the turnaround. Borough President Fernando Ferrer's leadership—characterized by vision, wit, cunning, courage, attention to detail, and commitment—was a key ingredient. A beneficiary of the changed planning environment and the shift in municipal government arrangements, he took over at a time when numerous redevelopment initiatives were in place. Nonetheless, he seized the opportunity to package the "raw materials" of a new Bronx. With assistance from an array of players, he formulated a "marketable" image, negotiated its expression among newly emerging groups, and maneuvered in the chess game of city politics.

Working with Ferrer were two professionals, Bernd Zimmerman, his director of planning, and Richard Kahan, head of the Urban Assembly. Their presence was fortuitous. Zimmerman's depth of experience in citywide and borough planning efforts, his ability to address citizen complaints, and his resolve in promoting a clear and rational image were valuable assets for Ferrer. Kahan's close connections with just about every important group in the city—civic, foundation, business and labor, which he enlisted in the effort, bringing their ideas and resources to the table—were equally valuable to Ferrer. Their primary achievement was stimulating the *New Directions* and Bronx Center concepts.

Finally, the self-confident persistence of the residents of Bronx communities fighting for recognition of their rights also helped form the new image. They were especially active in formulating the neighborhood redevelopment piece.

Together, these players forged the "shame of the nation" into the "All-American City," an image of a healthy urban community with a strong economic engine and flourishing mixed-income neighborhoods. Although they split over how to organize local public and private spaces, they worked out their differences. They struggled bitterly over the issue of appropriate densities on specific sites yet also resolved the fight.

Overall, the argument about densities was probably the hardest part of the discussion. The seemingly dry and technical debate enfolded important economic and social issues. Although the area would never achieve the three hundred-units-per-acre density of the "Beautiful Bronx," the choices reflected substantial differences. Each housing type either targeted different populations through pricing and its sponsorship or presented a development scenario that had desirable or less desirable implications for the rest of the plan. Charlotte Gardens' six-units-per-acre (single-family detached) dwellings equated to the densities of suburbia. Although Charlotte Gardens served its purpose in offering proof that the South Bronx was redeemable, it could not support such other desired activities as commercial revitalization. Two hundred units per acre (high-rise towers) evoked the image of public housing, a shelter icon that no one desired. The fifty- to eighty-units-per-acre program (two- and three-family-attached row houses) symbolized the middle class—the group some hoped to attract back to the South Bronx. Finally, twenty units per acre (attached single-family houses) was associated with the working class, providing dwellings primarily for residents already in the area—probably those moving out of public housing into their first homes.

As this chapter has related, the Bronx's move to the "All-American City" image emanated from the interplay among public officials, planning and design professionals, citizens, and media observers. This story holds lessons for planners and designers seeking to refashion negative images in disadvantaged communities. First, it underscores the necessity of developing a planning structure that combines wide participation with able leadership and technical expertise. All actors in the process must be deeply committed to the area; such an alliance is essential in crafting a comprehensive vision that incorporates identifiable components for strategic public and private investment. Second, this chapter illuminates the need to understand development-scenario details, especially the design and placement of public space and the perceptions created by differing residential densities. Technical knowledge is essential for community-building and fleshes out social science models for revitalization. Third, the lessons learned from the Bronx experience reiterate a continuing theme of planning history: the highly political nature of land-use decision making. Ultimately, the story of the South Bronx illustrates the need for re-imaging efforts to combine strong visual marketing statements with genuine evidence of physical and social change.

Re-Imaging the Rust Belt

Can Cleveland Sustain the Renaissance?

Patricia Burgess, Ruth Durack, and Edward W. (Ned) Hill

EDITORS' OVERVIEW

A team of Clevelanders—historian Patricia Burgess, urban designer Ruth Durack, and economist Edward Hill—continues the evaluation of the fused politics of image-making and land-use planning. In the 1970s, Cleveland, like the Bronx, suffered a national reputation as a dying city. Re-imaging the whole city was the new goal, and rebuilding its downtown was the heart of the undertaking. Downtown renewal, however, called into play a different set of actors than the efforts to revive a residential district. Like the Bronx, however, the nature of the planning process itself exerted a powerful force upon both the image sought and the building that followed.

In Cleveland, private foundations and downtown business groups initiated the campaign. They funded economic development studies in 1979 that led to an ever-widening circle of involvement. In time the *Civic Vision 2000* plan attracted downtown corporate officers and their law and accounting firms, the mayor and his planning staffs, county officers, and the state and federal representatives of the region. Because plans for development proceeded in a climate of decreasing federal urban aid, progress toward realization depended on elaborating public–private partnerships. From such a process there emerged a downtown plan of multiple elements for new office

construction, sports facilities, a retail mall, and an entertainment quarter, as well as some housing. The authors see the image of "The New Cleveland," a dynamic—not a dying—city, to be the result of the broad base of the coalition planning process.

They then contrast the success of the first plan with the 1998 *Civic Vision 2000 and Beyond* proposal, which they argue was organized by a few downtown groups without much public or political consultation. The plan is entertainment-focused, designed to add the tourist business to the existing downtown mix. The authors question the wisdom of this specialization since it will not rest within the existing fabric of the city, as do successful themed city areas elsewhere.

INTRODUCTION: THE "COMEBACK CITY"[1]

From a present-day perspective it is difficult to "image" the Cleveland of the late 1970s. Everything seemed to be falling apart. Then mayor Dennis Kucinich survived a recall election by 236 votes. Randy Newman's hit song "Burn On, Big River, Burn On" declared the region's greatest natural assets—the Cuyahoga River and Lake Erie—ecologically dead. The city defaulted on its debt. From 1979 to 1983, corporate headquarters and plant closings cost the four-county Cleveland Primary Metropolitan Statistical area 30 percent of its manufacturing employment. Both residential and downtown office construction ceased.[2]

Now, heralded as the "comeback city," Cleveland has won five All-American City awards. In 1989 Fortune magazine featured it as the place where corporate leadership saved a sick city. NBC newsman Tom Brokaw showcased Cleveland's renaissance by anchoring the evening news from Public Square.[3] Chamber of Commerce–sponsored delegations, corporate not-for-profit groups, and community foundations visit Cleveland to observe its development model; to examine the use of tax credits in stimulating moderate-income, inner-city housing development; and to learn how the Cleveland and Gund Foundations helped facilitate the city's revival.

With Cleveland's new image seemingly intact, it is time for the next act of Cleveland's comeback. But those portions of the next act revealed so far seem to belong to a different play, and it is not clear that they can sustain the renaissance. Cleveland re-imaged itself in the 1980s and early 1990s through a public–private partnership. The re-imaging began as an economic development strategy and expanded to include a physical plan, in part because economic development takes place in real space. The primary goal of the strategy was to strengthen Cleveland for its citizens and for the region. The initial projects are done. The big ones—Tower City and Playhouse Square, the BP America and Key Bank headquarters office towers, the Gateway complex of the Cleveland Indians' Jacobs Field and the Cleveland Cavaliers' Gund Arena—all contribute to Cleveland's image as a comeback city. There has been genuine economic growth as well. Now, the issue is how to sustain it and whether a new downtown plan, conceived through a very different process, can do so.

For twenty years, planning activity in downtown Cleveland has had a consistent goal of increasing the economic viability of the city, its neighborhoods, and the region. This would secure not only an important source of wage and property tax revenue but also a unifying symbol for the region. Achieving that goal meant developing strategies that would find commercially viable uses for downtown land and buildings, uses that could both provide employment and support an active street and commercial life. The new plan, however, reveals a different focus and seems to imply a different goal.

Although there are elements of the larger saga of Cleveland's comeback that involve neighborhood businesses, housing, and the region, the focus of this chapter is on downtown.

PLANNING THE RENAISSANCE

The saga of Cleveland's revival has been told from different vantage points and thus consists of several stories. One involves the role of business elites who led the city's and region's cultural change.[4] Another is about public–private partnerships and the creation of a complex civic infrastructure housed mainly in a web of nongovernmental organizations.[5] An alternative view is that a ruling oligarchy slapped down rowdy populist politicians, then structured downtown development politics to boost their firm and personal profits.[6] There is also the regional economic story.[7] And, of course, there is the tale of physical rebuilding—the big, shiny, new buildings that house offices, hotels, museums, and stadiums for professional sports teams that the public associates with the "new" Cleveland, as well as many smaller, less publicized projects in the neighborhoods. Which story is most convincing or important depends in part on one's own point of view and faith in the teller; and the full story is more complex than any single interpretation can accurately portray. All the interpretations contain common elements, though, for all reveal a carefully crafted strategy to rejuvenate the city and its economy; further, all note that multiple players, representing different interests and constituencies, worked together. Most also see downtown development as the most visible evidence of Cleveland's re-imaging.

■ STRATEGY

Overlaying the stories of Cleveland's rebirth is a template of strategy and organization that became the Cleveland development model. Initially, economic development in Cleveland consisted of opportunistic actions taken within a strategic framework,[8] but there is no one place to find the development goals and strategies that evolved in the formative years between 1979 and 1983. No one organization owned the strategy because it was a consensus among many government, private, and nonprofit players that the region's residents generally accepted.[9] This consensus presented a sharp contrast to the contentious and adversarial relations that had characterized the 1960s and 1970s.[10] By the late 1970s, a group of business and political leaders, with the support of the Cleveland and Gund Foundations, began working to forge the consensus that developed the economic development strategy of Cleveland's rebirth. Three reports, released over a dozen years and all initiated by Cleveland Tomorrow (an organization of the fifty largest corporations in Cleveland), illustrate the strategy's evolution.[11]

The first was a 1981 McKinsey and Co. report. Cleveland Tomorrow's predecessor organization had contracted with McKinsey to study and help develop a strategy to revive the local economy. The report made five issues clear:

1. Cleveland had lost its competitive position in the world economy.
2. Manufacturing was declining faster regionally than it was nationally.
3. The economy was not replacing lost manufacturing jobs with jobs in new companies.
4. Labor–management relations needed to be improved.
5. New companies needed to be formed from a research base that existed in the region's universities, hospitals, and federal laboratories.

A year later, a Rand Corporation report added that the region needed to develop its own economic research capability to carry out its agenda effectively and to continue moving the process forward. It also stated that the strategizers needed to consider physical development along with economic revival. The issues raised by McKinsey and Co., to which physical development considerations were added, formed Cleveland Tomorrow's initial agenda.[12] Reports by Cleveland Tomorrow[13] illustrate how the strategy was refined over time and how it was implemented.

Concurrently with the work of Cleveland Tomorrow and the McKinsey and Rand studies, the City of Cleveland was also examining development issues. Early in his administration, Mayor George Voinovich hired a new planning director for the city. Within a couple of years he had reorganized city government so that the three departments that dealt with development—City Planning, Economic Development, and Community Development—would coordinate their efforts.[14] A 1983 report of the Department of Economic Development indicated that its mission was "to provide leadership to capitalize on Cleveland's strengths to build a stronger City and regional economy."[15] The director of Economic Development viewed "capacity building" as one of his highest priorities. This included (1) creating a "consensus and commitment" within the private sector and (2) developing and promoting grassroots support for development projects throughout the city. Given that Voinovich had run for mayor partly in response to requests from business leaders and that he enjoyed their support, and because Cleveland Tomorrow was already engaged in developing an economic development strategy, the groundwork for multiparty consensus was in place.[16]

Others joined Cleveland Tomorrow and the city in the effort to rejuvenate Cleveland and the region. The Greater Cleveland Growth Association, the Cleveland and Gund Foundations, the county commissioners and state government, members of the state and federal legislative delegations, and a host of not-for-profit organizations provided staff support, financial support, and/or expertise. Collectively, their efforts framed a three-pronged development goal: (1) to provide an economically viable rationale for Cleveland's downtown; (2) to stabilize and expand the region's employment base; and (3) to stabilize the middle-class base of Cleveland's neighborhoods. Separate strategies and plans would be developed for each element of the larger goal, but the comprehensive goal remained constant from the early 1980s. If achieved, it would help fulfill Cleveland Tomorrow's stated mission: to "help Greater Cleveland become known as the preeminent business and professional center between New York and Chicago."[17]

Of the three elements, the strategy for downtown was no more important to the goal than the others. However, the projects it involved were highly visible, and they proved to be a major factor in the re-imaging of Cleveland. They are also evidence of the consensus because, with one major exception, the projects were public–private partnerships involving the agreement or participation of many parties. The first ones were Tower City, Playhouse Square, and the BP America (then Sohio) headquarters building. The second round of projects began with the State of Ohio's initial investment in the basin that became known as North Coast Harbor, followed by foundation, County, and other funding. Key Tower (then Society Tower), which incorporated both the historic Society for Savings building and a new Marriott hotel, was next, followed shortly by Gateway, the complex housing Jacobs Field and the Gund Arena (where the Cleveland Indians and Cavaliers, respectively, play). Development along North Coast Harbor—the Rock and Roll Hall of Fame and the Great Lakes Science Center—completed this round.[18] The BP America building was the only major project funded solely with private money. The others combined private-sector dollars with funds from one or more of the following sources: county or state capital budgets, state economic development monies, County Port Authority bonds, or federal UDAG or transportation grants.[19] Indeed, state and county funds were often key elements, so it was important to have support of elected and appointed members of state government and of the county commissioners (who needed to "sell" bond issues to voters who might work in the city but generally do not live there).[20] Some projects also used historic preservation or other tax credits and abatements. In addition, grants from corporations and foundations helped by providing financial assistance to some of the not-for-profit organizations involved.[21] Clearly, packaging the financing and development of each of these projects was complex and required agreement among the participants on both the particulars of the project involved and the larger economic development goal it was to serve.

These big downtown projects most likely contributed to the city's economic well-being in two ways. First, they may have encouraged a second tier of downtown development investment. This involved mostly small-scale or individual projects to convert structures in the Warehouse District to a mix of apartments, shops, restaurants, and offices, and to develop the "Flats" along the Cuyahoga River as a restaurant and entertainment area. While not as visible as the big downtown projects, these endeavors have contributed to the economic vitality of the city's core.

Second, the major downtown projects very likely secured the financial health of city government because approximately 40 percent of the city's general operating budget comes from suburbanites who work in Cleveland.[22] If the city lost its downtown employment base (which includes businesses housed in Tower City, Key Tower, and the BP America building, among others), Cleveland's finances would deteriorate markedly.

The big downtown projects also seem to indicate a subtle shift in strategy that would be reflected in the new *Civic Vision 2000 and Beyond* plan for downtown, revealed in preliminary form in February 1998. Although it was never articulated as such, the initial strategy for achieving the downtown portion of the larger economic development goal focused on corporate headquarters, retailing, and financial services employment as the anchor of the central business district (CBD)—hence the inclusion of Tower City, the BP America headquarters building, and Key Tower in the early rounds. If it succeeded, this strategy would solidify downtown as a place of employment, strengthen the downtown real estate market, and create a visible symbol of the region's revitalization. However, the next round of projects—Gateway, the Rock and Roll Hall of Fame, and the Great Lakes Science Center—were a result of a shift in strategy. This change is documented in Cleveland Tomorrow's 1988 and 1993 strategic reports.[23]

While preserving existing office employment and pursuing more, there was now an emphasis on developing a destination tourist industry to complement the CBD's function as a regional entertainment district.[24] The 1988 Cleveland Tomorrow report called for reshaping Cleveland into a "major regional destination for work, entertainment, and recreation. This thrust also entailed shifting focus from our industrial past to a new city sustained by water—the Cuyahoga River and Lake Erie." A graphic on the same page called for a development partnership of corporations, developers, and government dedicated to creating hotels, commercial enterprises, housing, and recreational facilities. The organization's 1993 report furthered the theme: "The visitor industry is the most promising of the service sectors for substantial job growth." A fundamental element of the 1993 strategic plan called for support for a critical mass of linked visitor attractions by undertaking three planning efforts to "foster a visitor economy":

1. Create an amenities master plan emphasizing items that tie attractions in Northeast Ohio together.
2. Underwrite a regional marketing program.
3. Build community support for investment in the visitor destination industry.[25]

Another essential element of the same strategic plan aimed at stimulating market-driven neighborhoods through a public–private organization, Neighborhood Progress, Inc. This effort, in conjunction with the City of Cleveland's residential tax abatement program, proved quite successful.

■ ORGANIZATION

As it evolved, the Cleveland model of redevelopment became almost a six-part formula.

1. The formula starts as a "bricks-and-mortar" project with "doable" funding (i.e., an identifiable base that serves as the investment capital or very patient debt).
2. The project must fit into a broad development strategy to become part of Cleveland's "redevelopment story," championed by a stakeholder who could build a coalition to include the primary investor (often a unit of government), the corporate community, and city and county government.
3. The project then must be adopted by the civic infrastructure, who could staff the project—either by supporting the private developer or through a not-for-profit organization (which was often created for a specific purpose).
4. The project needed some broad appeal to gain the necessary electoral support on funding issues.[26]

There were two necessary conditions for projects to be successful in Cleveland, and they complete the formula:

5. A knowledge base in the community to staff and complete complicated projects.
6. An understanding of the process by all of the players—the corporate community, developers, banks, not-for-profit organizations, and state, county, and city governments (as well as the legislative delegations).

Projects that did not follow the formula were unlikely to develop.

The knowledge base in the community of how to package, staff, and complete a project applied to economic development projects in the neighborhoods as well as to the large projects downtown and was an implicit (if not explicit) extension of a model that had evolved in the 1970s.[27] In that era, an extensive network of neighborhood-based nonprofit community development organizations evolved. The foundations and churches (particularly the Catholic Diocese of Cleveland) provided some of their support, and through the city they gained access to Community Development Block Grant (CDBG) funds. As they conducted their activities and completed their projects, their staffs became increasingly professional and proficient. These organizations were not part of either government or the business sector but developed the capacity to build coalitions around specific projects.[28] A decade later their political and technical skills would help supply the knowledge base of the civic infrastructure. As for the other critical element, all of the players understood the process and subscribed to the original Voinovich dictum: "Together we can do it." Consensus and shared goals without credit-claiming produced cooperation. An overarching agenda hatched by a small cabal of downtown development interests did not exist. Indeed, the Gund Foundation's Robert Jaquay noted that there were "a handful of agendas" that came together in the strategy for the region's revival.[29]

The big downtown projects were only one—albeit the most visible—element in the overall economic development strategy. Those that succeeded followed the formula and reflect the model;

proposed projects that did not develop during the 1980s and early 1990s provide further evidence of the model's success. Projects that did not reach fruition include a rail transit line to connect the University Circle area to downtown along Euclid Avenue; an early Cleveland Tomorrow–staffed attempt to build a new baseball park without a public partner;[30] the City of Cleveland's initial attempts to provide a new home for the Cleveland Browns football team; and the Cleveland Foundation and City of Cleveland's proposal for a lakefront aquarium. A broad-based coalition of private, public, and not-for-profit interests did not coalesce around any of these proposals. The aquarium was proposed for the waterfront at the same time as the Great Lakes Science Center but was perceived as a purely public project and consequently was not built. The science museum, which followed the proven Cleveland model outlined above, was.

■ PHYSICAL PLANNING

Economic development did not occur in a vacuum. In the mid-1980s, Planning Director Hunter Morrison and Economic Development Director Gary Conley recrafted a proposal for a new master plan for Cleveland. Funders had rejected an earlier proposal, but they responded positively to the new one, the work plan of which included "(1) A Citywide Development Strategy; (2) Research and Analytic Capacity; (3) Land-Use Analysis and Development Plans for the Eight Neighborhood Regions; (4) Downtown/Central Business District Development Plan."[31] Thus began the development of *Civic Vision 2000.*

Working in committee with the private-sector funders, Morrison settled on an approach for carrying out the process. The *Civic Vision 2000* master plan would be divided into two equal components: (1) a downtown plan, and (2) a citywide plan that included the neighborhoods—each with its own steering committee and individual in charge within the city planning department. The downtown plan steering committee included several elected and appointed city officials and several representatives from different elements of the downtown business community. The citywide plan steering committee had fewer city officials and many more representatives from the not-for-profit sector and neighborhood groups; it also included some members of the business community.[32] This approach thus reinforced the consensus- and coalition-building already under way for the larger economic development strategy. Development of each half of the plan also included extensive opportunity for input from the general public, the neighborhoods, and the not-for-profit sector. Through this broad-based process, *Civic Vision 2000* was able to incorporate the actual projects of the larger economic development strategy into the appropriate physical plan (i.e., the citywide plan or the downtown plan). *Civic Vision 2000* was also able to consider design issues of the major individual projects and to look at both downtown and the city as a whole from a larger urban-design perspective. Raising the level of urban design in Cleveland had been a goal of Morrison since his arrival as the city's planning director.[33]

■ RESULTS

The original Cleveland model appears to have worked very well, if a comparison of the fiscal and physical city of the 1970s with its 1990s counterpart is any guide. The physical evidence abounds, especially downtown. Employment figures show that between 1989 and 1996 employment increased by 6,269, which matched the growth rate for the metropolitan area. Downtown's employment growth outpaced that for the rest of Cuyahoga County, where growth was nearly stagnant.[34] If the central business district is expanded to include the strip of businesses and hospital facilities that stretches east to University Circle, the scenario is repeated. Between 1994 and 1998 employment in this larger area grew by 2,200, while Ohio's other two largest cities experienced stagnation in their central business districts. Columbus added sixty jobs over that time, while Cincinnati lost 2,200 jobs.[35]

By the end of the 1990s, however, the original Cleveland model was under stress, a victim, perhaps, of its own success. That Cleveland is a very different city is apparent to long-time residents, newcomers, and visitors alike. Still, continuing the momentum of the years between 1985 and 2000 takes a great deal of energy, particularly if some players believe the city has recovered. Changes in the city and development environment may also be a factor. The years 1994 to 1996 seemed to mark a transition. Leadership changed in both the Greater Cleveland Growth Association and Cleveland Tomorrow. Many of the original downtown construction projects were completed. Meanwhile, the politics of constructing a dual sports complex (Gateway, with baseball and basketball), the Rock and Roll Hall of Fame, and the Science Museum dominated discourse in the same way that the projects themselves dominated the downtown development scene. Then, questions about retaining the Cleveland Browns—and building them a new stadium as well—were thrown into the mix.

Equally important, these highly politicized large, later projects were of a very different type than the early ones and were less likely to develop the same sort of consensus and public support. The office and retail development of Tower City, the BP America building, and Key Tower were easily seen as integral to the economic health of the city. The service sector would meet the needs of downtown businesses whose employees would patronize the restaurants and retail establishments. Sports stadiums and museums seemed more oriented to visitors and tourists. Moreover, from a larger perspective, there appeared to be a danger that these large, later projects, along with those suggested in the new *Civic Vision 2000 and Beyond,* could make downtown an opportunistic collection of architectural icons isolated from the fabric of buildings, shops, housing, open space, and street-level activities that promote a vibrant streetscape—the very elements that make downtowns competitive with suburban shopping malls and office parks, and the elements that could make downtown a community.

CIVIC VISION 2000—AND BEYOND

Examination of the two *Civic Vision* plans reveals a shift in Cleveland's direction. Both seek to strengthen the city, but the first was broad and comprehensive and the second very narrow.

As noted previously, *Civic Vision 2000* consisted of two roughly equal elements—a citywide plan and a downtown plan—that resulted from a broad-based public process. Both plans were prepared simultaneously, to be complementary and integrated as a comprehensive pattern for strengthening the city and its role in the region. Both the citywide and downtown plans conceived downtown as a regional center, with housing, retail, and office commercial activity as well as entertainment opportunities. Neither the citywide nor the downtown plan was an urban design plan per se, but both focused on land use as a key element in economic rejuvenation and included design considerations by visually illustrating proposed projects and changes.

The citywide plan provided some background on development, economics, and population, and it outlined the city's goals and policies. It divided the city into eight subareas (one of which included downtown) and presented information and illustrations of land use, housing, commercial and industrial facilities, transportation, and other major aspects of development. Each section discussed present conditions and potential opportunities as well as how that potential might be achieved. *Civic Vision 2000: Downtown Plan*[36] provided much more detailed information on downtown Cleveland. Detailed sections discussing every major aspect of development (e.g., land use, infrastructure, preservation) followed the "Introduction" and "Goals" sections. A separate section addressed implementation.

The primary goal for downtown was to strengthen the core, creating a high-quality center for commerce, with public space along the city's river and lakefronts, housing for downtown employees, and retail and entertainment opportunities for downtown employees, residents, and visitors. While retaining as much downtown industrial capacity as possible, the plan sought to increase the office and service sectors. Much of the housing suggested was geared to either twenty-five to forty-year-old white-collar workers or to "empty nesters." Overall, the plan was well balanced, with complementary elements intended to have a synergistic effect. The increased service-sector and office employment would draw employees to live downtown; they, in turn, would stimulate the retail and entertainment sectors that would provide a second tier of downtown employment. Non-downtown residents attending events at Playhouse Square or Gateway, or coming to conventions, would have places to go as well. But the downtown plan's most distinguishing trait was its cohesiveness, with residential, office, retail, and entertainment uses all stimulating and supporting each other. The plan's structure implied a recognition that any one element by itself probably would not suffice. Except for the housing component (which did not result from one or two large projects but rather from an array of smaller dispersed ones), the major projects discussed earlier in this chapter and encompassed by *Civic Vision 2000* reflect the broad comprehensive goal outlined in the plan and expressed in the city's economic development strategy.

Civic Vision 2000 and Beyond is different.[37] As with the earlier plans, the goal is still an economically viable downtown Cleveland, but there is a three-part strategy:

1. Creation of a number of destination activities along the lakefront to attract visitors.
2. Development of downtown housing, especially along Euclid Avenue. Although presented as an objective of the plan, this strategy stems from the need to transform 1.5 million square feet of nonviable office space into housing rather than from the desire to create a people-centered, complex, urban neighborhood for those employed downtown.
3. Construction of a new convention center with an attendant hotel and transit mall.

The outcome of the plan reflects its beginnings. Joseph Roman, executive director of Cleveland Tomorrow, the organization that developed *Civic Vision 2000 and Beyond*, stated that the organization acted at Mayor Michael White's request. Steven Strnisha, who actually directed the current *Civic Vision* project for Cleveland Tomorrow, said that Mayor White initially asked Cleveland Tomorrow to undertake planning for the aquarium that was backburnered over efforts associated with the Cleveland Browns football team and stadium. Cleveland Tomorrow instead suggested that the mayor work on developing a comprehensive plan linking all of the waterfront tourist destination activities.[38] Simultaneously—but not initially as part of the planning process—Downtown Development Coordinators (a not-for-profit group) was working on a plan with property owners along derelict Euclid Avenue to convert outmoded office space into hotel and residential properties. Both that effort and the third element of the plan—the new, midsized convention center, which also began independently—were then brought into the framework for *Civic Vision 2000 and Beyond.*

Civic Vision 2000 and Beyond was released for public comment in May 1998. Major elements of the proposal called for more attractions and activities to join the Rock and Roll Hall of Fame and Science Center at North Coast Harbor; a new, larger convention center and associated hotel complex, whose placement would join the lakefront to downtown; and a revitalized Euclid Avenue. Among the attractions proposed for North Coast Harbor are a visitors center, a transportation and industry museum, an aquarium (resurrected from *Civic Vision*'s previous incarnation), an indoor sports center (for tennis, skating, and swimming, among other activities), a retail village, two hotels, expanded marina slips, a passenger ferry terminal, and a seasonal retail site. Associated with these proposals are major transportation changes: converting the Shoreway into a boulevard; extending the Waterfront line of RTA's light rail transit system to form a loop around downtown, which would also provide access to the lakefront attractions; and constructing a multimodal transportation hub near the new convention center and North Coast. The plan for Euclid Avenue would renovate and convert 1.5 million square feet of office space in existing buildings to produce 2,000 housing units, 700 hotel rooms, and 600,000 square feet of retail space. The plan also supports widened sidewalks, fewer traffic lanes, and dedicated bus lanes along the avenue. Additional for-sale and rental housing in or near several downtown locations is also recommended.

Of the three major plan elements, revitalization of Euclid Avenue is probably the most critical to creating a viable downtown residential neighborhood that can sustain eighteen to twenty hours of activity per day in the city's core. In its present form, though, even the plan's representation of the revitalized Euclid Avenue is almost a caricature of urbanity. The presentation of the proposed housing does not suggest a neighborhood. Equally important, this element of *Civic Vision 2000 and Beyond* receives less attention than other elements of the plan.

Unlike its predecessor, the current plan does not provide a cohesive vision for the future of downtown Cleveland. Rather, there is one plan to devote the six acres of available lakefront to tourism and a second, separate plan to convert Euclid Avenue to a mix of restaurants and hotels, with some housing. The convention center neither quite connects to the other development components nor connects them to each other. The vitality of the city as a business center, and arguably the attractiveness of downtown Cleveland to visitors, would be better served if the plan's major elements were more coherently integrated. Development of the remaining waterfront as an amenity that supports a downtown residential community could provide that coherence.

Civic Vision 2000 and Beyond, however, presents development of the lakefront and a new convention center as the most effective actions to attract visitors and stimulate the downtown economy. It concentrates visitor attractions around a vibrant, mixed-use waterfront, which has proved to be a successful formula in cities around the country. But it stretches that formula to encompass every component of waterfront revitalization used since the development of Baltimore's Inner Harbor in 1963. The plan has something to appeal to just about every segment of the tourist public but little of real value to potential downtown residents. What is missing in the consideration of the lakefront is the way it could help to build the nascent neighborhood on Euclid Avenue. The lake and riverfronts are potential recreational amenities that could relate to downtown residential development and reinforce an urban fabric that would appeal to a more sustaining source of tourism: one built on urban living.

The plan uses the new convention center (its third major element) to bridge the sixty-foot drop, railroad tracks, and Shoreway that separate downtown from its lakefront. The roof of the new facility becomes an eleven-acre park, linking the northeast corner of the Mall to public plazas adjacent to the Rock and Roll Hall of Fame, the Great Lakes Science Center, and the new Browns Stadium. Supplementing these waterfront attractions are several parcels labeled "retail/attraction," "hotel/residential," and "commercial opportunity," most concentrated on a mere six acres. Curiously, the historic steamship *William G. Mather,* now a maritime museum, has disappeared from its current berth in North Coast Harbor.

Renderings of the proposed waterfront complex show crowds of pleasure seekers and impart an air of festivity. As illustrated in the proposals, the attractions and festivity are all but hidden from downtown, as is the lakefront itself. The proposed park over the convention center will provide an excellent panorama of the lakefront area, but this new open space is shown surrounded on its downtown sides by convention center facilities, a new hotel, and the existing parking garage north of City Hall. None of the buildings in *Civic Vision 2000 and Beyond*'s aerial view of the lakefront has been designed in any detail, contributing to the overall impression of a disconnected jumble of new development where the level of activity is equated with public enjoyment, and commercial success substitutes for civic vision.

The original *Civic Vision 2000* provided a physical setting for an economic development strategy based on a cohesive synergy in which downtown housing, office employment, and retail and entertainment activities would support and stimulate one another. The overarching goal of that plan and strategy was an economically viable downtown. The overall goal of the new plan remains the same as that of its predecessor. However, with office development no longer an element, the strategy now is to market downtown Cleveland as a destination for out-of-town visitors by developing a series of attractions at the lakefront while separately promoting housing and hotel development on Euclid Avenue.

An alternative strategy framed around the Euclid Avenue residential component could provide the synergy and coherence of the original approach. One of Cleveland's most valuable resources is the remaining land around North Coast Harbor. Developing a downtown neighborhood around upper Euclid Avenue, with access to the waterfront as part of downtown's package of amenities, may be the key to stabilizing downtown as an office and commercial marketplace. A residential neighborhood proximate to existing attractions can provide street activity for about eighteen hours a day. A residential neighborhood can also provide an anchor for downtown's fastest employment generator, the business and financial services industry.

This alternative vision is not only more cohesive, it is more fiscally feasible. Residential development can maximize the city's most effective development tool—tax abatement—in conjunction with capital subsidies. But a new convention center, conversion of the Shoreway into a boulevard, or improvements to downtown public transit circulation, as proposed in *Civic Vision 2000 and Beyond,* can be accomplished only if federal mass transit monies can be shifted, if funds from the state's capital budget are forthcoming, and if the Port Authority's bond rating holds up. *Civic Vision 2000 and Beyond* contains no clear implementation strategy. However, the fiscal reality is that the plans contained in it are highly dependent on subsidy at a time when federal programs are closed, when there is increasing reluctance in the state capital to open up the budget for more projects in the downtowns of Ohio's three largest cities, and when the coalitions that came together in the past to promote projects no longer exist. Attempting to take downtown to the next step of its revitalization using the approach presented in *Civic Vision 2000 and Beyond* may hold the future hostage either to a mega-development that fills in what is left of the waterfront or to subsidy from highly speculative sources of finance. On the other hand, creation of a vibrant downtown neighborhood with lakefront recreational access can serve as a stronger visitor attraction than additional gated destination activities.

PLANS AND PROCESS

That *Civic Vision 2000* and *Civic Vision 2000 and Beyond* are two very different plans is quite evident. Although both seek to strengthen downtown and its economy, the former plan incorporates economic development as one goal in a larger initiative to strengthen the entire city and the region, whereas the latter plan focuses solely on the downtown. The two plans, as well as the projects they propose, reflect different approaches to achieving their downtown goal as well. The 1989 *Civic Vision 2000* illustrates a multifaceted approach that includes office and retail development and downtown housing along with tourist attractions and entertainment venues to appeal to both tourists and residents (e.g., Jacobs Field and the theaters of Playhouse Square). The preliminary version of *Civic Vision 2000 and Beyond* unveiled in February 1998 focuses on the lakefront tourist attractions and convention center.

The other key difference between the two plans is the process by which they were developed. Under the mayoral administration of George Voinovich, development of *Civic Vision 2000* was coordinated with the economic development strategy then being crafted by what was essentially a coalition of government, private sector, and not-for-profit entities. Moreover, there was broad consensus throughout the city on both the larger economic development strategy and the projects in the plan. The City Planning Department increased its staff and conducted dozens of meetings with neighborhood groups, community development corporations, and special interest organizations to involve the public in the planning process. There was greater participation in the neighborhoods with respect to the citywide plan than for the downtown plan, but even downtown there was ample opportunity for public input while the plan was in preparation. Limited staff required the city to employ consultants in plan preparation, but the city used them judiciously, merging their findings with public input.[39]

Civic Vision 2000 and Beyond grew out of a very different process. It was not part of a larger coordinated strategic effort to strengthen the city and region. Indeed, it seems that the final projects of the first plan developed a momentum of their own that drove the project-based, tourist-attraction–oriented approach of the second. And there was no public process. Between the city's November 1996 announcement that Joseph Gorman (CEO of TRW, Inc., and an officer of Cleveland Tomorrow) would chair a steering committee to update the downtown plan and the February 1998 unveiling of the preliminary plan, there were no public meetings or other opportunities for public input. Moreover there was almost no mention in the press of the work in progress.[40] This was not a participatory consensus-based process. *Civic Vision 2000 and Beyond* lacked the consensus that underlay the earlier plan, thus breaking the Cleveland development model forged in the Voinovich administration and the first White administration.

THE EVOLVING IMAGE

Cleveland has indeed re-imaged itself. The renaissance is real if not yet complete. Places to dine and shop complement office towers, hotels, theaters, and sports venues that blend new construction with sensitive historic preservation. There is life downtown, even on weekends and evenings; moreover, people now reside downtown. However, there are still vacant storefronts and derelict office suites; the synergy envisioned in both the original development model and *Civic Vision 2000* has not fully developed. Will the next step in the evolution of downtown continue the process that has achieved positive change so far, eventually producing a self-sustaining central city where people live, work, and play, and where their activity begets more activity?

Or will it change the course, perhaps effecting a different kind of vitality but stopping short of its full measure of success?

Civic Vision 2000 and Beyond elicited a mixed reaction at its unveiling.[41] Public hearings were held in June 1998, and the following spring the city requested proposals for North Coast Harbor from thirty teams of developers; only four responded. All proposed variations of the concentrated activity and attractions initially suggested in *Civic Vision 2000 and Beyond.*[42] One commentator noted that "the Mayor's goal is to lure more visitors, keep them longer."[43] Another called the proposals a "Disney-style theme park."[44] The plans that brought about Cleveland's rebirth would not have inspired such comments.

The goal of the new plan may be the same as before, but questions about the techniques proposed to achieve it linger. Tourism and entertainment are known to be the most erratic and unpredictable of industries, as evidenced by failed attractions and faltering theme parks around the world. While there have been some notable successes, the recently published *Fantasy City: Pleasure and Profit in the Postmodern Metropolis* urges policymakers to exercise caution and not be too quick to jump on the theme-park bandwagon.[45] With the possible exception of Disney's own creations, "attraction"-based destinations command a notoriously mercurial share of the tourist market. And ironically, the most successful and enduring urban tourism destinations—whether cities such as Florence or Munich in Europe, or Boston, San Francisco, and Santa Fe in the United States—were not designed as tourist attractions. Their appeal derives from a natural and built environment that reveals the social and cultural blending of unique past and present lives. The "entertainment" a sidewalk cafe provides is watching ordinary people going about their daily lives. These great tourist cities are, first and foremost, good places for those ordinary people to live.

By focusing on a "package" of attractions rather than a comprehensive mix of developments, Cleveland is failing to capitalize on some of its most important assets: a dramatic natural setting; a vibrant industrial past; and a compact, walkable downtown with magnificent late-nineteenth- and early-twentieth-century commercial architecture. More importantly, the new proposals do not build on Cleveland's success as "comeback" city of the Rust Belt. People may come to see and participate in a community rebuilding itself. Whether they will come for a carnival of diversions similar to those found in many other cities is open to question. In Cleveland, the Rust Belt has been re-imaged. Now, can Cleveland sustain the renaissance?

Skyscraper Competition in Asia

New City Images and New City Form

Larry R. Ford

■ EDITORS' OVERVIEW

A seeming uniformity of economic function and civic advertisement has lured geographer Larry Ford to take a closer look at the new image-making skyscrapers in Asian cities. These towers are of recent origin, proliferating only since the 1970s. They are located in the largest Asian cities, those that recently have become financial service centers. The designs of these buildings are borrowed from the work of world-renowned architects. Although some of the skyscrapers are decorated with local motifs, most resemble the office towers and megastructures found elsewhere in the world. What might such an architectural parade mean in terms of a city's image and its form?

Professor Ford seeks to answer this question by comparing what might be called export meanings with local experience meanings. On the export side, the skyscrapers are both the business suits of the world financial community and very practical buildings whose sites in the downtown or in midtown expansion areas are determined according to the land forms of their host cities. These office clusters, along with their associated hotels and shopping centers, tell foreign businessmen that they will be working in a familiar setting. They also tell tourists that they will enjoy all the comforts of the Western cities they are accustomed to.

The meaning of the skyscrapers locally is more difficult to gauge. Professor Ford suggests that these dense buildings may well be the most suitable form for the Asian habit of face-to-face business transactions. He also stresses the local desire to succeed in the game of international image competition among cities, a sport well known to Americans. The variations in local living styles in such places as Singapore, Hong Kong, and Jakarta are reflected in the design of street connections and street use and the public circulation within the lower-floor malls and spaces. Customs in some cities support sidewalk business, others make use of bits and pieces of the megastructures as public space, while many buildings' lower levels function just as American malls do. These local adaptations to a standard structure suggest that the images held by a building's users and neighbors may be very different from the postcard exteriors these skyscrapers present to the outside world.

INTRODUCTION: GLOBALIZING TOWERS

During the past few decades, a vast literature has appeared on the topic of globalization and the emergence of world cities.[1] After many years of concern about deindustrialization, deurbanization, and suburbanization, we are suddenly confronted with the fact that some cities are reemerging as control points in the new world economy. Cities such as New York, London, Paris, Tokyo, and Zurich are now widely regarded as well-wired centers where decisions are made that impact the entire world economy. In such cities, there is often a reconcentration of important decision makers in centrally located, prime downtown office space. After years of recession, the costs of doing business in Midtown Manhattan, for example, have once again soared, as has the demand for well-located space. While back-office activities can take place in the suburbs, and at least some employees can be part of the much-publicized telecommuting revolution, centrally located office space is still vital in the new global cities. This is particularly true in the up-and-coming financial capitals of Asia.

The production of downtown space, however, has not been the focus in most of the literature on globalization. The majority of authors have dealt primarily with such things as capital flows, communication networks, and the total volume of business transactions in particular cities. Much of the literature ignores the fact that businesses must be *housed*, for the most part in increasingly sophisticated buildings, and that high-level decision making in the new global economy must take place in particular types of settings, not just in vaguely defined megacities.[2] There is, however, a growing discussion of this topic in popular and architectural publications.[3]

The focus of this chapter is on the production of new office buildings and business districts in several Asian cities and the impact they are having on urban form, city images, and the spatial organization of metropolitan areas. In particular, the emphasis is on the meanings (in the Lynchian sense) attributed to the new office towers and how those meanings vary in different contexts. Sophisticated office buildings have been around for a long time in the traditional business centers of London, New York, and Tokyo (although newer, better-wired buildings continually make older structures obsolete for some of the most important activities). They are a relatively new phenomenon, however, in most of the cities of Asia. Even Hong Kong, one of the first Asian cities to have a skyline of business buildings, began to construct modern office buildings only during the late 1960s and early 1970s. In spite of a serious economic crisis, considerable building activity is still occurring in many of the newer business centers of the Pacific Rim, especially those in East and Southeast Asia. Cities such as Hong Kong, Singapore, Kuala Lumpur, and Shanghai have just recently begun to expand their foci to include, and even to specialize in, financial activities in addition to the traditional industrial and trading sectors. To accomplish this transition, these cities have had to build a lot of high-quality office space quickly.[4]

The new financial cities of Asia increasingly are exporting shipbuilding, oil refining, manufacturing, and trade to lower-cost locations in their hinterlands. Hong Kong, for example, finds itself with unused industrial space in its recently completed new towns, as much manufacturing has moved to special economic zones further inside China.[5] Similarly, industrial parks have been constructed in Malaysia and on the Indonesian islands of Batam and Bintan, in close proximity to Singapore. In Shanghai, the percentage of gross domestic product (GDP) resulting from tertiary activities rose from 18 percent in 1978 to 40 percent in 1994.[6] In each of these cities, there has been an incredible boom in the construction of office space, retail facilities, hotels, and convention centers. These booms have been expensive and controversial and have recently contributed to some serious economic problems, as vast amounts of capital have gone into the property market—at one point, 43 percent of all investment in Thailand. It is estimated that at least $600 billion in "bad loans" were made in Asian countries, much of them in property, a factor leading directly to the 1997 to 1999 economic crisis.[7] On the other hand, if Asian cities are to succeed as important centers in the global economy, their landscapes must change. The remainder of this chapter examines some of the pros and cons of the current explosion in architectural megaprojects and speculates about its impact on city structure. The focus will be primarily on Hong Kong, Singapore, Kuala Lumpur, Jakarta, and Shanghai.

For a variety of reasons, most of the major cities on the Asian side of the Pacific Rim have chosen to use signature skyscrapers to house the majority of their newly constructed office space as well as related hotel and convention facilities. The result has been the emergence of impressive skylines surpassed only by those of some of the larger corporate centers of North America. This building trend in the new financial centers of Asia has had both symbolic and pragmatic dimensions. The pragmatic—the simple need for lots of new space—is the easiest and most straightforward to discuss, but it is completely intertwined with the symbolic. Cities need major office buildings, first-class hotels, and modern shopping facilities, as well as improved infrastructure and housing; in addition, there is also a fascination in Asia with having the newest, fanciest, tallest, largest, and most modern and innovative buildings and landscapes in the world.[8] The reasons for this are many and complex, including perhaps the response to colonial subjugation coupled with a strong work

Fig. 5.1a *(left)*: Children sketching the Hong Kong skyline.

Fig. 5.1b *(below)*: Hong Kong skyline.

Fig. 5.2: Singapore skyline.

ethic and the perceived need to symbolically join the global economy. The full story may be beyond the scope of this brief essay. I will, however, make an attempt to explore the topic.

For a long time, the quest for a skyline was an uphill battle. Sukarno, for example, a former student of architecture before becoming the leader of the new nation of Indonesia, built grand boulevards through Jakarta that he wanted to line with impressive towers. It did not happen during his tenure. Indonesia had neither the demand for space, the capital, or the engineering expertise to build skyscrapers until the oil boom of the 1970s. Significantly, the urge to build high preceded Suharto's turn toward capitalism after 1967. The demand for skyscrapers crosses party lines.

The story of hyperdevelopment began in the relatively investment-friendly colonial cities of Hong Kong and Singapore. Even here, however, development has blossomed only recently. As late as 1960, the skyline of Hong Kong's business district consisted of two twelve- to fifteen-story art deco buildings from the 1950s; Singapore had only one such building. Office and hotel construction accelerated during the mid-1960s, but the real boom did not occur until the 1970s. By the late 1970s, both Hong Kong (figs. 5.1a, 5.1b) and Singapore (fig. 5.2) each had one building more than fifty stories tall, and downtown skylines were beginning to loom large in the depiction of these cities on postcards and travel brochures. Intercity competition also emerged in the 1970s, particularly between Singapore and Kuala Lumpur, the capitals of two countries that had split in a bitter dispute in 1965.

THE REACH FOR THE SKY: NORTH AMERICAN PRECEDENTS

The competition between Singapore and Kuala Lumpur is particularly interesting because it replicates, fifty years later, the kind of intercity skyscraper competition that emerged in the United States during the building boom of the 1920s.[9] The skyscraper office building, although technically invented in Chicago during the 1880s, first began to take the form of outrageously tall signature towers in New York City during the early years of the twentieth century. The Singer Building (1906), for example, rose to 612 feet at a time when few other buildings were half as high. It was meant to be an advertising symbol, giving assurance to those buying sewing machines around the country that the company was strong and highly visible. But the skyscraper was not the domain of private businesses alone. The New York City Municipal Building (1915), which at more than five hundred feet tall gave symbolic power and authority to the municipality, paved the way for governments as well as businesses to create impressive skylines. For more than a decade, such landmark buildings were confined largely to New York City, but by the booming twenties, dozens of American cities were ready to compete for skyline supremacy in their own states or regions. Rational need had little to do with it. The Empire State Building, for example, was built by a consortium headed by former New York governor Al Smith; the group simply wanted to erect the tallest tower in the world. Completed in 1931, the famous icon remained partly empty for much of the Depression. Still, many other cities were joining in the game.

While Chicago had on-again, off-again height limits during the early decades of the twentieth century, other cities gained the lead in emulating the New York skyline. An insurance company in Cincinnati made that city the first in Ohio with a tower five hundred feet tall, but Columbus soon followed. The American Insurance Union "citadel" was erected in Columbus in 1927 and, at 556 feet, was meant to be six inches taller than the Washington Monument. At its gala opening, hundreds of secretaries paraded down the street singing "Ode to the Citadel" as biplanes showered the new building with flower petals. Clearly there was more to all of this than "bottom line" business decisions. By the time the dust had settled in 1930, Cleveland had constructed the Terminal Tower, which, at 708 feet tall and with over two million square feet of space, remained the tallest and largest complex outside of New York City for forty years. It also served to reorganize the spatial layout of downtown Cleveland. In every case, the new towers provided not only symbolic centers for their respective downtowns but functional centers as well. Were these skyscrapers needed in the sense that market forces required very high densities? The answer is, probably not.

Similar competitions took place in other parts of the country; they illustrate the varying roles of business and government in creating skyscrapers and skylines. Shortly after the 433-foot Russ Building was unveiled in San Francisco, work began on the 450-foot Los Angeles City Hall (1928). While the former was a private office building in the center of a financial district with very high land values, the latter was designed as an isolated tower in a city with strict twelve-story height limits. Clearly, the Los Angeles City Hall, which later became a national icon when featured on the popular television show *Dragnet*, was primarily intended to establish an appropriate urban image for Los Angeles in its competition with San Francisco. While market forces were for the most part responsible for the San Francisco skyline, such was not the case in Los Angeles.

While there are many contenders for the distinction, perhaps the best example of a purely symbolic skyscraper built during the early decades of the century is the Louisiana State Capitol (1932). At thirty-four stories and 450 feet, this tower set in a park remained the tallest building in the Southeast for several decades. It was built by Huey "The Kingfish" Long, the governor and populist leader of Louisiana, and it was there that he was later assassinated. The bullet holes remain in the main corridor, making the tower a sort of political pilgrimage site for some.

Clearly, American skyscrapers have been capable of carrying a mélange of messages—civic, heroic, corporate, and functional. The motivation for building them has always involved some combination of a real need for space and the desire to display power, authority, and a sense of place identity. The American story, although best illustrated by the towers of the 1920s, is far from over. New supertowers in cities such as Cleveland and Charlotte serve to announce both urban revitalization and movement up the urban hierarchy.

Given the complexities involved in understanding the evolution of skyscrapers and skylines in the American context, there is no reason to expect that there will be simple explanations for what is currently happening in Asia. Indeed, understanding the production and use of skyscrapers in Asia requires attention to trends toward both global homogenization and global hybridization.

SKYSCRAPER COMPETITION IN ASIA

In 1966, Jean Gottmann posed the question, "Why the skyscraper?"[10] That question seems to be a very important one for this discussion. For example, whereas the current trend in many American cities is for corporations to head for the woods and locate in edge cities or greenfield sites, this may not be possible or desirable in most Asian cities. In Hong Kong, for example, it is the satellite towns that are having the most trouble, as high-order business seeks the cozy connections of the central district while mass production heads further into China. The Asian reliance on personal interaction and handshakes over a brandy makes the isolated telecommuting world so often hyped in the United States seem wildly inappropriate. There are also physical constraints. In Singapore, suburban office parks are unlikely due to the small size of the country and a serious lack of space. Indeed, Singapore plans to double the size of its present very compact downtown by filling in the adjacent harbor.[11]

Even in more spacious cities, cultural traditions, congestion, lower rates of automobile ownership, and a whole range of differences in the spatial organization mean that corporate headquarters "out in the woods" are not really an option. For such cities, skyscraper megaprojects may be the best response to the need for high-quality space. Sprawl and isolation are not often options in either the relatively poor hinterlands of Chinese cities or the wealthy but train-dependent edges of Japanese cities. Scholars must be careful, therefore, not to assume too quickly that skyscrapers built in cities and/or districts with low land values and little congestion are merely symbolic. Asian skyscrapers may be evidence of a continuing demand for the kind of face-to-face contact and intense personal relationships that no longer characterize North American business dealings. Asian skylines may well reflect the old combination of functional and symbolic motivations, but in new and different ways.

Many of the stories about North American skyline competitions are now being retold, with variations, in the cities of Asia. For more than thirty years, for example, since the breakup of the former state of Malaya, there has been an intense rivalry between Singapore and Kuala Lumpur. Singapore was the first to create an impressive urban skyline, in part because of the very real need for concentrated activity in the tiny city-state. Today, Singapore has a very Western-style central business district that seems more akin to Toronto than to a traditional Asian metropolis. While the compact downtown bristles with towers, mostly built by banks and other private financial institutions, there is no dominant theme building that gives a unique identity to the city. Indeed, strict planning guidelines have resulted in the three tallest buildings being exactly the same height (an impressive 919 feet). Still, the skyline has played a very important role in the image of the city in business- and tourist-oriented promotional literature over the past two decades. Skyscrapers are used to convey a dual message: First, Singapore is open for business; second, although it has exotic elements, it is basically a clean, modern tourist destination with all the comforts of home.

Kuala Lumpur is a very different kind of city. While the old downtown is somewhat constrained by topography, the city has sprawled over many square miles, and new business centers have arisen in outlying areas. Although it has been necessary to construct large amounts of office space for the new global economy, there is no obvious need for skyscrapers and other megastructures. The fact that Singapore has an impressive skyline, however, requires that Kuala Lumpur have one too. The twin Petronas Towers of Kuala Lumpur (at present the tallest twin buildings in the world at 1,483 feet) provide perhaps the best example of using the skyscraper as both a symbol of participation in the new global economy and a symbol of a unique cultural identity.[12] When Petronas (the national oil company that

Fig. 5.3: The twin Petronas Towers in Kuala Lumpur.

occupies one of the towers) announced the design competition for its new headquarters, there were two requirements to be met—the building(s) had to be the tallest in the world, and the project had to include Islamic (preferably Malaysian Islamic) design elements (fig. 5.3). The twin towers of the winning American architect, Cesar Pelli, succeed on both counts. They are very tall, and they display a modern yet Islamic motif that makes them immediately unique and recognizable. Designed by an Argentine-born American and constructed by Japanese and Korean firms using American materials, Malaysian supervisors, and a great many Indonesian and Bangladeshi laborers, they also epitomize the globalization of landscape production. Think globally, build locally.

The towers, each with nearly two million square feet of space, are the theme buildings for a much grander scheme called Kuala Lumpur City Center (KLCC). The creation of KLCC involves converting a former racetrack into a central park and lake surrounded by dozens of new skyscrapers. The base of the Petronas Towers includes a huge horizontal structure that houses a cultural complex complete with a symphony hall and art gallery, as well as a mix of retail and recreational uses. Modern hotels and luxury condominiums are being built nearby. When completed, the new City Center, along with the nearby Golden Triangle, will be the new downtown for the Malaysian capital. As in American cities seventy years ago, towers are being used symbolically to anchor and provide a powerful image for a new node of activity. They may also provide the close and cozy internal arrangements and cultural embellishments necessary for business dealings in Islamic Asia. For example, there are prayer rooms throughout the building, an amenity that might not be available in other business settings.

■ THE IRONY OF CHINA

The cities of China offer perhaps the most ironic and interesting examples of the changing urban landscapes of Asia. Clearly, the city to emulate is Hong Kong.

In cities where land is in short supply, usually it is in the best interest of local governments to find and/or create spaces for megaprojects in order to increase the tax base. In Hong Kong, existing policies make land availability an even more crucial matter. For example, taxes are generally low (and it is argued that many get out of paying taxes altogether). At the same time, Hong Kong relies on the construction and maintenance of one of the most expensive urban infrastructures in the world—

including subway and highway tunnels under the harbor and a new airport. Much of the funding comes from land leases, especially from the creation of fill land that can be used for monumental skyscrapers and other megaprojects in highly desirable locations. Since the 1970s, one-fourth of Hong Kong's harbor has been reclaimed. The landfill projects that are in greatest demand are those closest to the traditional central area. In addition, land has been created seaward of the Wanchai District (an old tenement area associated with the popular book and movie *The World of Suzie Wong*) only a mile or so from the core of the city. This "midtown" district is now home to a massive new convention center, luxury hotel facilities, and the city's tallest skyscraper. In many ways, it is a second downtown—and one that has meant profits for local government (fig. 5.4).

Fig. 5.4: Hong Kong street scene.

Hong Kong now has not only some of the tallest skyscrapers in the world (two above 1,200 feet) but more very tall buildings than any city outside of North America. It is the only city in Asia with a large and dense clustering of towers à la Manhattan. In spite of recent economic problems, it is very likely that, when it comes to building, the sky is the limit. For example, the old airport at Kai Tak, which closed in July 1998, will be redeveloped as a new midtown in Kowloon. The area will no longer have height restrictions, so the impressive skyline of Victoria may well be matched by a competing center across the harbor. Hong Kong Harbor may be reduced to a narrow canyon.

Just as Kuala Lumpur has sought to emulate (and surpass) Singapore, so too have some of the cities of China sought to be new and improved versions of Hong Kong. First among these is Shanghai. By the 1930s, Shanghai had one of the first downtown business skylines outside of North America. The mini-skyscrapers constructed by Victor Sassoon along the Bund represented the arrival of the Western city in mainland China and were used extensively as symbols for a city that had relatively little in the way of traditional Chinese architectural monuments. After three decades of Maoist anti-urban ideology, during which time Shanghai was condemned as bourgeois and passé, the city is once again developing a world-class skyline.[13] From a practical point of view, there is little doubt that a massive amount of new office space is needed. As recently as 1990, for example, both Beijing and Shanghai had only about as much office space as downtown Dayton, Ohio, and much of that was nearly obsolete. Communist China was to be a land of rural agriculture and industry, and the urban infrastructure was largely ignored. But global cities cannot consist of hovels, and international financiers do not operate out of sheds, so something had to be done.

There is some irony in the adoption of what many have described as the quintessential symbol of American capitalism—the skyscraper—by the still technically communist Chinese government. After all, the traditional aesthetic of China was essentially horizontal, with few structures over two stories. It was this aesthetic that Chairman Mao used extensively in expanding Beijing's Tiananmen Square. The rise of the Shanghai skyline represents more than a practical necessity; it is a very important ideological leap. Given a combination of huge population, thirst for international investment, and single-minded purposefulness in creating a new symbolic landscape, China may one day become the skyscraper capital of the world.

There are other cultural–symbolic issues as well. While Hong Kong, Singapore, and the cities of China have largely opted for modern (and postmodern) towers, cultural factors are sometimes important. For example, Feng Shui elements cannot be ignored in China, and there is a strong preference for certain numbers—eighty-eight stories is an ideal height for a major tower (Petronas Towers, Jin Mao Tower), whereas forty-four is to be avoided. In addition, Asian cities have sometimes sought a unique cultural identity through architecture. This has involved exploring connections to both the future and the past. In Japan, for example, designers have tended to push the envelope when it comes to new and wildly original shapes and forms. From the older Ginza to the new Teleport Town, Tokyo bristles with unusual buildings that have come to be associated with a "Japanese look." At the other extreme, many of the cities of Indonesia have experimented with oversized versions of traditional house types for use by banks, government offices, and especially hotels. Malaysia currently occupies a middle position, with many buildings referencing either traditional culture or a tropical setting in rooflines, shading patterns, and materials. The vast majority of new buildings everywhere, however, are simply modern. Both large corporations and government agencies tend to prefer skyscrapers that symbolize their competitiveness with New York and Chicago rather than local traditions and sense of place.

■ MIDTOWNS, MEGAPROJECTS, AND CITY STRUCTURE

When it comes to choosing locations to build spaces to house the new global economy, most Asian cities have two choices—the existing downtown or nearby convenient "midtowns." Until recently, building downtown has been relatively easy in most cities. Nearly every area, with the exception of Beijing's Forbidden City, was underbuilt, with rustic villages and small "shop houses" predominating. Ignoring for a moment the issues of historic preservation and sense of place, it was not hard to argue that older structures should be replaced. They were small, easy to tear down, and could not be renovated easily for prime space in the way that turn-of-the-century buildings in Europe or

America might be. The central areas of Hong Kong and Singapore changed overnight. To some degree, construction is still going on downtown, as even taller buildings, such as the 1,207-foot Bank of China in Hong Kong, are being flanked with new towers. But this will soon end as the larger cities fill up with buildings too big and expensive to replace easily. In most cities, midtowns, or centrally located subdistricts, are the answer.

Shanghai is a case in point. Given the existing urban fabric, population density, infrastructure, and congestion of the downtown Shanghai Bund, there was little choice but to move across the river to develop an entirely new urban core, the Pudong Redevelopment District (fig. 5.5a). Architects, planners, engineers, and other experts who

Fig. 5.5a (*above*): Pudong skyline, Shanghai.

Fig. 5.5b (*right*): Sketch depicting midtown configurations: landmarks, nodes, districts, paths.
Nina Veregge

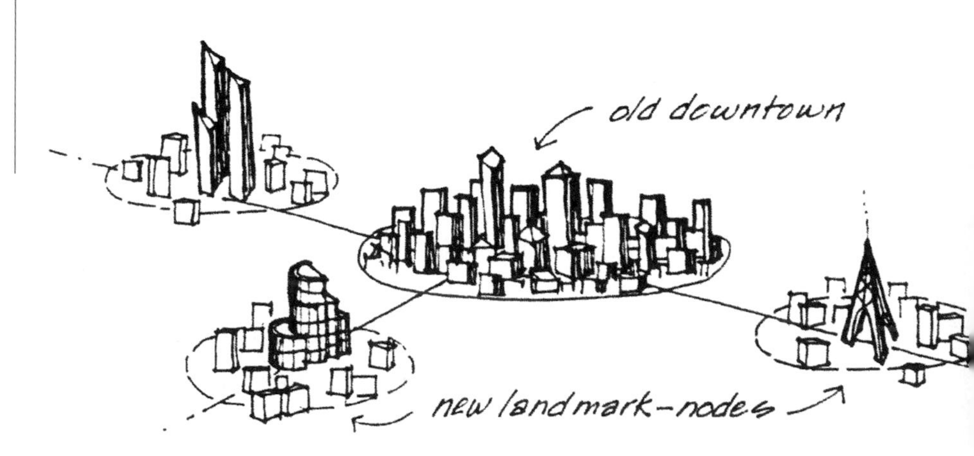

had worked on other new midtowns such as La Défense in Paris and Docklands in London were brought in to help plan the new area. Midtowns are nothing new. They normally are upscale areas close to and/or well connected by mass transit to the existing downtown business district, and are characterized more by pleasant housing, parks, and government buildings than by port facilities, industries, and slums. The most famous example is Midtown Manhattan, but similar districts can be found in cities such as London, Paris, Vienna, Mexico City, Boston, and Atlanta. Indeed, many of the areas identified by Joel Garreau as American edge cities, such as Rosslyn, Virginia, or the West Side of Los Angeles, are really best described as midtowns (fig. 5.5b).[14] In Asian cities, midtowns abound, and there are more in the making. They loom large in the imagery of the new cities of the Pacific Rim.

There are basically two types of midtowns in Asian cities, although there are many variations on the theme. Midtowns are typically either reclaimed and/or sanitized waterfront zones or close-in, formerly residential/commercial areas. They have become the location of some of the biggest and most impressive architectural projects in the world. In addition to the lack of suburban options characterizing most Asian cities, the majority of the land (85 percent in Singapore) is owned by the state.[15] Even in times of economic recession, the government managed to amass huge reserves, in part due to its involvement in the property market. By making land in midtown areas (such as the old European Town, across the river from the traditional business district) and adjacent reclaimed land available for projects such as Portman's four-million-square-foot Marina Square mixed-use development, Singapore not only makes money for other, less-profitable projects but enhances its highly salable image as a dynamic new tropical city for the twenty-first century. Big-name architects and signature buildings play an important role in this.[16]

There is much more to making midtowns than building signature skyscrapers, however. In most cities, massive upgrading of the infrastructure is vital. The issue of infrastructure brings up a number of questions that are beyond the scope of this chapter. For example, skyscrapers and other megabuildings must be thought of as part of a much larger urban design issue. As entirely new districts, such as Pudong in Shanghai or Teleport Town in Tokyo, are opened up for development, vast improvements must be made in the urban infrastructure. New bridges, highways, monorail and subway systems, water supplies, and power generators must be constructed. Towering office blocks and retail emporia are perhaps the most symbolic elements in the changing images of major Asian cities, but there are many other projects that will involve massive amounts of foreign investment, expertise, and planning. The new skyscrapers and skylines are really just the tip of the iceberg. Nowhere else in the world have cities gone from traditional villages to gleaming metropoli so rapidly. Changing the image of a city (and a country) involves much that is belowground, as well as that which is above and visible. The exporting of advice and other services will continue to be a major part of the global economy despite periodic economic recessions.

■ INTERNATIONAL FIRMS AND PASSPORT ARCHITECTS

The construction of skyscrapers has nearly always involved the use of imported talent. This diffusion of architectural and engineering expertise occurred during the original skyscraper competitions in the United States, as architectural firms from bigger cities worked in smaller, high-aspiration towns. Similarly, many of the projects associated with the creation of the skylines of the emerging financial centers of Asia involve the use of foreign architects and designers. Cities seeking notable buildings that will put them "on the map" in the global economy often retain world-famous architects and internationally known firms in order to obtain not only the best possible building but also a vast amount of publicity in the international press and architectural journals as the project progresses. There is nothing new about architects working abroad. Throughout the nineteenth century, the British brought in designers from home to construct colonial headquarters and railroad stations from New Delhi to Kuala Lumpur. The scale of activity, however, has changed considerably as various combinations of foreign architects, engineers, surveyors, investors, and laborers are now likely to join together for major projects all over the world.

At least until the economic downturn of 1997, a large number of American architectural firms did a significant percentage (between 30 and 50 percent for many San Francisco Bay Area firms) of their work in Asia.[17] Architectural expertise is an excellent example of the "export of services" component of the world economy, as the "advanced" nations increasingly deal in advice as frequently as in products. British, Canadian, Australian, French, German, and Japanese firms are also highly international, and it is likely that the import-of-talent trend will grow as cities seek foreign landscapes to emulate and foreign experts to build them. In the face of these global connections, is it possible that Asian cities will be able to create unique, place-specific skylines?

In most of the new global cities of Asia, it is now possible to find the work of such architects as Cesar Pelli, I. M. Pei, John Portman, Norman Foster, Kenzo Tange, Kevin Roche, Hugh Stubbins, and Helmut Jahn, as well as involvement by firms such as HOK (Hellmuth, Obata & Kassabaum), SOM (Skidmore, Owings & Merrill), and RTKL.[18] While some of these projects are reflective of local desires and concerns (like the Petronas Towers), others are very similar to buildings in America or Britain. Portman's Pan Pacific Hotel in Singapore, for example, is basically a taller version of his atrium-and-glass-elevator projects in Atlanta and San Francisco. Still, the diffusion of architectural expertise is by no means leading to simple global homogenization. Even when the pieces are similar, the whole remains subject to local exigencies, traditions, political contexts, and the constraints of physical site. From a distance, the buildings and skylines look similar, but at the microlevel, there are significant differences.

■ THE SPACES BETWEEN BUILDINGS AS SETTINGS FOR DAILY LIFE

It is tempting to critique the new internalized spaces of the Asian megaprojects using the same criteria and theoretical/political stances that have applied to North American cities. Indeed, the charge that real public space has been eliminated in favor of an almost total reliance on the private, or at best semiprivate, spaces of malls, entertainment centers, and theme districts is even more true in most Asian cities than elsewhere. In much of Kuala Lumpur, for example, there are not only no sidewalk cafés, but no sidewalks. The ballet of the street is rapidly being replaced by the ballet of the mall (and the car) (figs. 5.6a, 5.6b). In Singapore, rules for proper behavior are strict even in public space, and fines can be levied for spitting or chewing gum. At first glance, it would seem that Western social critics could have a field day critiquing the urban landscapes of Asia in terms of the usual list of concerns—private space, dress codes, surveillance, excessive rules, and so on. I am not sure, however, that such critiques are appropriate. The political, cultural, historical, and aesthetic traditions are different.

The scruffy, individualistic rabble-rousers so often portrayed by Western academia as people sure to be expelled from the private space of the shopping mall are relatively rare in East Asia. Even in the homeless camps of Tokyo, residents tend to dress neatly and rake their compounds as though they were Shinto shrines. Those exhibiting unruly or "crazy" behavior either have never existed in Singapore or they were all locked up by about 1970. Conservative Islamic-influenced dress codes keep nearly everyone, but especially women, looking clean in Malaysia and Indonesia. Even rioters tend to dress uniformly. The desire to stand out and "be yourself" is not as strong in Asia as it is in the West. To some extent, corporate landscapes in East Asia may be used to reinforce the already popular idea of behavioral conformity.

Neither has civic space generally played a significant role in political processes in East Asia. While large demonstrations and celebrations have occurred occasionally, as in Singapore during the mid-1950s, Hong Kong in 1997, and Jakarta in 1998, they are

Fig. 5.6a (*left*): A road in Kuala Lumpur.

Fig. 5.6b (*below*): Street scene, Kuala Lumpur.

not events strongly associated with particular kinds of public space. Indeed, there is concern in Hong Kong that discussions of urban design and environmental issues focusing on the need for public space are too often dominated by foreigners and Euro-Chinese. Tiananmen Square may be the exception rather than the rule. The street life that we associate with Paris, Rome, New York, and Buenos Aires is different in Hong Kong, where people are likely to work until nine or ten in the evening and then rush home. As we critique urban form, therefore, the meaning of the landmarks, districts, and nodes may vary in both expected and unexpected ways.[19]

The purpose of the above discussion is to introduce the idea that modern megastructures may be more appropriate for Asian cities than we, as Westerners, might think. As in the West, malls have become the de facto streets of the city, especially where the real streets have become clogged with automobiles and motorbikes. Although there are significant variations from place to place, in general people tend to congregate and talk (and photograph each other) where megaprojects have carved out some pedestrian-friendly space. Young men sit on the steps and plazas surrounding bank towers, and musicians gather in the open lobbies of skyscraper office buildings. In most cities, there are few options, and these spaces seem to work as well as any that have existed previously. The courthouse square and plaza mayor traditionally have played less-important roles in the civic life of Asian cities than in those of the West.

The most important question has to do with economic opportunities in the new landscape, especially given the entrepreneurial proclivities of the stereotypical East Asian. Here the issue of reliance on megastructures is not so easily dismissed. The nooks and crannies that provide space for small-time entrepreneurs in many cities are now largely missing from Hong Kong's central district and are rapidly disappearing in the neighborhoods nearby. If Kowloon fills with megastructures as expected, the opportunities for small businesses seeking a good location will decline substantially. Individual districts may still have recognizable names and landmarks, but they will be increasingly uniform in function and social class.

■ IDENTITY, ACCESS, AND PERSONALIZATION

At the macrolevel, urban skylines seem to be popular in most of the cities of Asia. They are featured on postcards and T-shirts, and art classes full of small children visit sites that enable them to view, sketch, and color the towers of the town. In spite of what seems to be a kind of uniform pride in the progress and prosperity symbolized by the new buildings, it is likely that there are some real differences in perceptions of the negative aspects of skyline development. In Singapore, for example, the skyline is generally seen as benign, especially now that neighboring districts are protected by strict historic preservation ordinances; it is coherent, controlled, and confined. Strict zoning keeps the towers "in their place," protecting residential areas. In Jakarta, on the other hand, skyscrapers have been built along major thoroughfares adjacent to low- and middle-income *kampungs.* The towers there often represent increasing congestion, rising land values, and eventual displacement of residential populations.

Displacement is also a very real threat in Hong Kong and Kuala Lumpur as new skyscraper districts are carved out of former low-income neighborhoods. In Hong Kong, some of the highest towers are residential buildings and symbolize the capturing of central-city living space for the elite.

But these problems are found in dynamic cities all over the world. The really interesting variations in skyscraper use occur in the spaces between buildings at street level. The relative political calm and social conformity of Singapore, for example, facilitate access to the lobbies and plazas around the towers for social and civic events (figs. 5.7a, 5.7b). Downtown Singapore has sidewalks, food hawker stalls, and a plentiful supply of small green

Fig. 5.7a (*above*): A lobby in Singapore.

Fig. 5.7b (*left*): Open plazas in Singapore are the locus for social and civic events: Here, groups of Girl Guides meet.

spaces and trees. The skyscrapers may exude power and authority from a distance, but at street level, they are comparatively friendly. While strict zoning guidelines make it difficult to personalize these spaces with makeshift commercial or social paraphernalia, they are heavily used by a variety of people. The plazas and stairways in front of towers are used for everything from wedding pictures to Girl Guide meetings.

In Hong Kong, there are extreme variations from district to district. In the central district, a network of highways separates the Bank of China and its neighbors from the livelier districts nearby. On the other hand, in the Wanchai district, a new "Times Square" has been created and linked to nearby market stalls and alleys. There, skyscrapers have served to create functional as well as visual nodes. In Jakarta, the landscape is more problematic. For physical (swampy soil) and political reasons, many of the skyscrapers are spaced far apart and are surrounded by large plazas with driveways, fountains, and parking. There is little interface between the buildings and the street. Sometimes the compounds are gated, or at least guarded, and access by "the masses" is difficult. Here, skyscrapers suggest "keep away," and design reinforces the power relations inherent in the close juxtapositioning of towers and shanties. While street vendors may try to locate as close as possible to the buildings so as to serve the occupants as they emerge, they are usually forced by the setback designs to keep their distance. Sidewalks tend to be narrow and poorly maintained, as the elite arrive by car. For most residents of a city, street-level design and usage have more meaning than the architectural symbolism and sheer height of the tower.

■ HISTORIC PRESERVATION: MORE GLOBAL ARCHITECTURE OR LOCAL SENSE OF PLACE?

Given the massive changes afoot in the major cities of Asia, the region would seem ripe for public outcries about the loss of historically and socially significant settings. There have been few. Of all the major cities of Asia, only a handful of places, such as Kyoto and Singapore, have anything resembling a comprehensive preservation program. In the case of Singapore, preservation (referred to as conservation) programs began only during the 1980s as a direct result of declining tourism revenues. Since tourists apparently were beginning to resist the idea of Singapore as a financial district and shopping mall, the government began to invest in rehabilitation programs for Chinatown, Little India, Arab Street, and the conversion of an old downtown market to a Victorian food hawker center. In addition, the old waterfront boat quay was turned into a picturesque restaurant row, and a former industrial area known as Clarke Quay was redesigned by the American firm Elbasani and Logan to become Singapore's version of Quincy Market. Tourist brochures now depict both the charming old and the magnificent new. Most of the preservation efforts have been geared for tourists rather than locals. Many of the rehabilitated storefronts along commercial streets remain empty as locals flock to the malls. The "history" that is so appealing to the residents of London, Boston, and San Francisco appears to be less salable in Asia. Spatial organization may be a contributing factor. One of the most popular preservation projects in Singapore has been the conversion of an old church and school into a series of shops and restaurants known as Chjimes. The complex occupies an entire block; most of the action is in an interior courtyard, away from the street. It thus serves as a sort of outside mall. Still, there seems to be a strong landscape preference for the modern and the big in Asia, and the preservation of the premodern (especially the colonial) past does not seem to be a high priority for most people.

To a very real degree, historic preservation may be just one more example of landscape globalization as different types of attractions are developed. Big-name international architects increasingly have become involved in preservation and rehabilitation efforts, especially in Singapore. These are not small projects. Tourist-related conservation efforts usually involve doing an entire block at once or large assemblages of structures, as in Clarke Quay. If Asian cities are to be major players in the world economy, the quality of life there must be enhanced. If businesspeople want more than a quick meal in the hotel café, there must be places to go and things to do. Singapore is currently planning an Entertainment Walk, with nods to Las Vegas and Ginza. Hong Kong and Singapore each now have a major shopping and entertainment district known as Times Square. In the global economy, quintessential nodes become universal.

CONCLUSION: SKYSCRAPERS AND THE IMAGE OF THE ASIAN CITY

Building has slowed a bit in Asia, but the processes leading to the creation of global landscapes will not remain dormant for long. Yet, it seems the more things change, the more they remain the same. I feel at home in Asia. Jon Jerde, the architect who designed Horton Plaza in San Diego, created a somewhat similar project in Fukuoka, Japan. Altoon Porter Limited remodeled Fashion Valley Shopping Center in San Diego and is now doing a mall in Hong Kong. The towers of Cesar Pelli can be seen in Cleveland, Charlotte, Kuala Lumpur, and Hong Kong, and all of them are within sight of a McDonald's. Yet these cities are not all the same; they are not becoming homogenized. Global trends are being played out in a number of local ways, and curious hybrids abound.

The images of the cities are changing as well. Large Asian cities are no longer widely perceived as anachronistic and backward places teeming with peasants and animal-drawn carts. In spite of recent economic crises, the gleaming skylines of Asia are forcing the world to take notice. Locally, the new towers are giving identity to recently developed midtown districts that did not exist only a few years ago. Places such as Pudong, Kai Tak, and Kuala Lumpur City Center are joining Midtown Manhattan and Boston's Back Bay as new districts defined by towering icons. It is too soon to say just what long-term impacts these buildings and districts will have on the ways local residents see and use the city, but it is clear that there are some new hybrids in the making.

The Images of Commonplace Living in Modern City-Regions

Judith A. Martin and Sam Bass Warner Jr.

■ EDITORS' OVERVIEW

The vast expanse of the typical American city does not provide many sharply defined images, except perhaps for its highways and malls. Modest structures built according to the fashions of their day carpet the metropolis. Most of the land is covered by residential streets. What can be said of this vernacular cityscape? What accounts for the difference between how residents and nonresidents experience these images?

Judith Martin, a geographer, and Sam Bass Warner Jr., a historian, document such imagery by selecting three typical neighborhoods in the Twin Cities of Minnesota: an inner-city neighborhood built between 1880 and 1930, a first-ring suburb built between 1950 and 1980, and a new outer suburb started after 1970. Such residential areas can be found throughout the Midwest, and districts closely resembling them appear across the nation.

To capture the local experience, Martin and Warner follow the usual pathways of the residents: the journeys to work and the journeys to shopping. Although their photographs reveal style changes, they also document a strong continuity of image presentation. An American consensus clearly exists. It calls for tree-lined streets, detached homes, and well-tended lawns. Indeed, this domestic

standard has become so ingrained over the years that in the new industrial parks, suburban apartment clusters, and municipal campuses, the land and buildings conform to this norm.

Such continuity of image does not mean uniformity of reputation, however. Inner-city blocks are commonly perceived as dangerous, and older sections in the suburbs are thought to be less-desirable places for children, regardless of their amenities and services. To a startling degree, for the outside viewer, geographical location becomes merely a position in the socially constructed map of the region, regardless of the actual images presented.

PROLOGUE

> A clear and comprehensive image of the entire metropolitan region is a fundamental requirement for the future. . . . Large-scale imageable environments are rare today. Yet the spatial organization of contemporary life, the speed of movement, and the speed and scale of new construction, all make it possible and necessary to construct such by conscious design.
>
> K. LYNCH, *The Image of the City*[1]

Commonly held images of urban life do not reflect the lived reality of most contemporary metropolitan residents or visitors.[2] We see parts of any region, not the whole. Familiar themes recur decade after decade. Even as critics argue that all cities are coming to resemble one another, the Manhattan skyline holds a permanent place in urban imagery, perhaps epitomizing "the city" more than any other skyline view (fig. 6.1). Jacob Riis's century-old images of immigrant slums still convey something about impoverished urban life that current visuals of south-central Los Angeles do not. The old images are firmly rooted in American culture,

Fig. 6.1

while contemporary images of daily life dissipate (figs. 6.2, 6.3).

This chapter seeks to redress the imbalance between long-accepted images of the city and those we experience every day—to attempt to "make our images commensurate with our experiences," as Lynch proposed.[3] What follows is an examination of ordinary urban images as most of us commonly experience them: from a moving vehicle. Although this specific analysis is of a midwestern region, we believe that these images represent much of what is familiar in the domestic American landscape, beyond the dense northeastern corridor.

Fig. 6.2

Fig. 6.3

COMMONPLACE IMAGES

City-regions in America today are gatherings of people and goods in motion, characterized by movement back and forth, in and out, around and across; and movement as change—change here, there, and everywhere. This is the essence of our contemporary urban existence across the entire country. The economy of any city-region requires the continuous flow of goods, energy, and people for its sustenance, as do urban dwellers for theirs. Thus, we wish to focus on the images that a city-region presents of people and property in motion.

That motion and the associated images examined here address four inescapable activities of human life: finding a home, going to work, gathering food, and acquiring the consumer products we need or desire. Having closely examined three areas in the Minneapolis-St. Paul Metropolitan Statistical Area (5,051 square miles; 1990 population of 2,460,000; metropolitan growth of 15.5 percent from 1980 to 1990), five characteristics of these associated images stand out:

1. The images of commonplace urban living are fairly similar across the entire city-region.
2. Although some of these images are encountered in settings where many people are present—in traffic, in parking lots, in stores—most of the time the images are experienced by an individual moving about alone, rather than by a group of people as a whole.
3. Spatially, the Twin Cities MSA bounds the daily journey to work, as well as errands for food and clothing, but many of the regionwide images are made up of national packages, not inventions specific to the Twin Cities region.
4. The pace of change in real estate is rapid. There is a great deal of turnover in five years' time. But unlike other images of common living, the real estate market is highly fragmented. Agents know only one or two localities well, and buyers typically have only partial knowledge of the offerings across the entire city-region.
5. The activities and the imagery of home and of neighborhood appear in many locations across the Twin Cities' five thousand square miles, but houses are presented in terms of localized uniqueness. Thus, the region remains an abstraction to most of those living within it.

TWIN CITIES CASE STUDIES

To present our material, we selected three residential neighborhoods that illustrate the contemporary urban typologies of central city, inner-ring suburb, and outer-ring suburb (fig. 6.4). It is important to note that none of our examples are places in crisis.

Relatively few locations within the Twin Cities metropolitan area are especially troubled, given the area's robust economy and low (less than 2 percent) unemployment rate during much of the late 1990s.

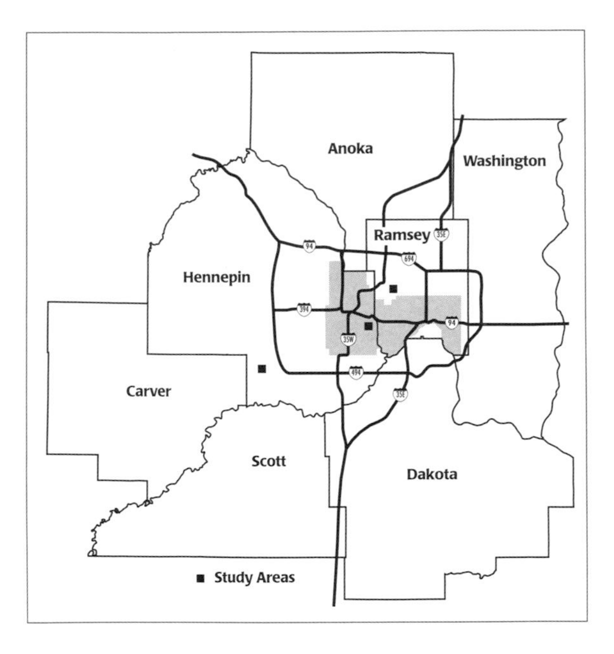

Fig. 6.4: Study areas within the Twin Cities region.

In using these familiar labels, we explicitly object to the careless tendency to equate "inner city" with "slum," because, as we all know, inner-city neighborhoods—although often lower in income—vary in style and social standing. These three, in their ordinariness, represent the Twin Cities MSA very well. Each encapsulates a style of living characterized by a low-density midwestern urban form. Nearly everyone has some access to a car, and public transit is limited.

For each case study, we chose a "modal block" as the point of origin for the household movements described. These modal blocks typify many blocks in each of the larger community areas we chose as a focus; they were selected on the basis of informant interviews and one author's extensive knowledge of the metropolitan area. The image pathways are those that are essential to the activities of everyday metropolitan life: commuting to work and shopping for groceries and other family needs. In each case, the routes described lead to the largest nearby shopping centers (including grocery stores) and are also the most obvious access routes to metro-area employment opportunities.

The central-city neighborhood, Seward, is located two miles from downtown Minneapolis. Seward was built up between 1880 and 1930. Some of its blocks were altered significantly by urban renewal efforts in the 1960s and 1970s; some changed only slightly, some not at all. Seward is now a modest, well-tended neighborhood of seven thousand people (1990) in 1.6 square miles. The inner-ring suburb, Roseville, was established immediately north of St. Paul, primarily between 1950 and 1980. It is centrally located between the two downtowns—five to six miles from each. Roseville comprises an area of 13.2 square miles, now all built out. Its 1990 population was 33,000. The outer suburb, Eden Prairie, is located approximately twenty miles from downtown Minneapolis. It began to boom in the 1970s and is now nearing completion. Its 1990 population of 39,000 was scattered over 32.4 square miles, with limited vacant land remain-

Table 6.1: Physical, Social, and Economic Profile of the Three Areas

	Seward	Roseville	Eden Prairie
Area (sq. mi.)	1.6	13.2	32.4
Density (people/sq.mi.)	4,564	2,500	1,204
Population	7,302	33,485	39,311
White (%)	89	96	97
Households	3,522	13,591	14,758
Median Income (1989)	$15,000–$32,000	$37,862	$52,956
Public Assistance (%)	7	3	2
Age Structure (%)			
Birth–4	7	5	10
5–15	11	12	17
16–20	5	7	4
21–64	61	60	65
65+	16	16	4
Educational Attainment (18 yrs. and older) (%)			
Not a High School Graduate	17	11	3
High School Grad	22	27	18
Some College	32	27	33
Bachelor's Degree	17	22	36
Graduate Degree	12	13	10
Occupation (16 yrs. & older, employed) (%)			
Management/Professional	37	38	41
Tech, Sales, Clerical	30	37	40
Services	17	11	7
Precision Crafts, Repair	5	7	6
Operative, Laborer	11	7	6

Source: 1990 Census of Population and Housing, Summary Tape File 3 ing for future development. (See table 6.1 for a profile of these three areas.)

As in the Twin Cities region as a whole, the populations of each of these case study areas are predominantly white. There are small proportions of Native Americans and African-Americans in the city neighborhood and modest numbers of Asian-Americans or Asian immigrants in the suburbs. The principal social differences between the three larger communities are found in the categories of household income, homeownership, and the ages of residents. In the four census tracts that comprise the Seward neighborhood, the median household income in 1989 ranged from lows of $15,000 and $19,000 (tracts 64/74) to highs of $27,000 and $32,000 (tracts 75/76). In Roseville, the median household income was $38,000; in Eden Prairie, $53,000.

These ranges accurately reflect the Twin Cities' economic diversity. The age of housing units and their location within the city-region were reflected in housing tenure data. Owners occupied 49 percent of Seward's units, 65 percent of Roseville's, and 73 percent of Eden Prairie's. Seward and Roseville shared the adult age profiles of long-settled communities, while Eden Prairie, a place of newer homes and families, abounded in young children and had few residents over sixty-five years of age. At the same time, we observe similar educational attainment and occupational distribution across the three communities. This suggests that the differing appearance of houses and the differing sizes of residential lots in the three places were less the product of class differences than of the history of fashions in the building process.

Census reports on transportation and housing confirm our observation that a contemporary city-region is a place of people and goods in motion. In the Twin Cities, in contrast to older and denser metropolitan areas, nearly everyone drives to work in a private automobile, even residents of the inner-city neighborhood. In Seward, 59 percent drove alone, while 11 percent joined a carpool. In Roseville, 79 percent drove alone; in Eden Prairie, 87 percent (table 6.2). Carpooling in the suburbs exceeded bus ridership, and the number of people walking often approached the number of those using public transit. Drivers traveled all over the region, but their destinations reflected their

Table 6.2: Housing, Work, and Travel Profile of the Three Areas

	Seward	Roseville	Eden Prairie
Means of Transportation (%)			
Drive Alone	59	79	87
Carpool	11	10	7
Bus	14	3	2
Walk	9	4	1
Other	4	1	<1
Work at Home	3	3	3
Travel Time (minutes one way)	18.6–21.3	17.9	20.6
Place of Work (%)			
Central City	79	45	30
Remainder of MSA	20	54	69
Elsewhere	1	1	1
Housing Units			
Total Units	3,624	14,216	14,447
% Owner Occupied	49	65	73
% Rental	45	30	27
Residence (%)			
Same House since 1985	53	58	36
Moved within MSA	34	28	41
From Elsewhere	13	14	23

Source: 1990 Census of Population and Housing, Summary Tape File 3A

home locations. Central-city workers were more likely to live in inner-city neighborhoods and close-in suburbs rather than farther out. In Eden Prairie, twenty miles from downtown Minneapolis, only 30 percent of commuters traveled into some part of the central city. The resulting regionwide pattern of movement no longer exemplifies the exponentially increasing traffic concentrations of fifty years ago. The pattern is instead a tilting surface of traffic densities that slopes away from the Twin Cities' dual downtowns and from regional centers like Roseville.

Daily rounds of work and errands are by no means the only

urban flows of significance. The census also records people's residential persistence—or lack thereof. Forty-seven percent of Seward's 1990 residents had moved in from somewhere else during the previous five years. Forty-two percent of Roseville and 64 percent of Eden Prairie were new residents (see table 6.2). New areas like Eden Prairie may distort the metropolitan averages of housing relocation. It might be best to say that half the residents of the Twin Cities remained in their homes at the end of the five-year period, and half had relocated. Residential persistence is thus a catchall variable—a proxy for the consequences of job seeking and for life-cycle events such as marriage, the birth of children, divorce, old age, and infirmity. But whatever the causes of change, the consequence is that even a stable neighborhood like Roseville achieves its stability amid waves of newcomers. Thus, the pace of movement in real property, although not as swift as that of retailing, is a fast one.

■ SEWARD

The officially designated Seward neighborhood consists of 1.6 square miles of houses, stores, and a large concentration of industrial buildings on one edge (fig. 6.5). Seward has neither Minneapolis's worst living conditions nor its most concentrated nonwhite population, but it is typical of most inner-city neighborhoods of the Twin Cities in its age, class, and stock of housing. It is bounded on the north by Interstate 94; on the south by

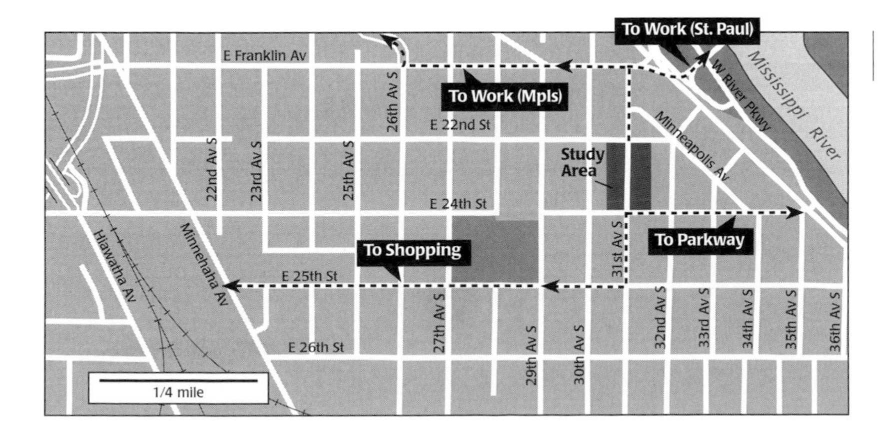

Fig. 6.5: Seward neighborhood, Minneapolis.

Fig. 6.6

the Canadian Pacific Railroad tracks; on the east by the Mississippi River, with its park and parkway; and on the west by an industrial park and a main artery, Hiawatha Avenue. Although Seward's fortunes waxed and waned during the past century, it has now achieved a measure of stability.

The neighborhood grew from west to east from 1870 to the 1920s, so the city's first zoning regulations (1924) merely confirmed what already stood on the ground. Engineering standards called for wide grid streets (thirty to thirty-six feet from curb to curb), house lots 40 x 125 feet, with twelve-foot paved alleys down the center of every block. Every street has sidewalks. Street trees have been planted between the curbs and sidewalks, and lawns and some gardens front houses that sit about twenty feet back from the sidewalks. Many old stores and industrial buildings abut the sidewalk edges. The rear yards of the houses are small and are further reduced by the alley garages; thus, this is a fairly dense neighborhood of small houses on small lots.

To provide a sense of the images such a neighborhood offers, we have imagined three alternative pathways for a journey to work. The paths commence in a block central to the neighborhood: 31st Avenue South, between East 22nd Street and East 24th Street (fig. 6.6). They proceed north to the I-94 entrances, or east toward St. Paul, or west toward Hiawatha Avenue. In the following scenarios, we imagine a person leaving home in the morning, walking out the kitchen door and through the backyard to either an alley garage or a parking bay.

Going North to the Interstate

The concrete-paved alley behind the house is lined with garages. Older garages face the alley, while newer ones parallel it and are accessed via small driveways. The newer garages are two-car units; many of the old ones are singles, forcing two-car families to park one vehicle on the street. Some residents have planted flowers along the alley, and an occasional basketball hoop faces a paved alley parking spot (fig. 6.7). Moving up 31st Avenue, the driver observes strips of parked cars, remnant arches of American elms and new locust trees, lawns, and rows of single and double houses typifying the styles of the period from 1890 to 1920. All are modest, well-tended homes. At the traffic light at East Franklin Avenue, our commuter confronts the modern reworking of a former streetcar commercial strip: a large, awkward apartment of the 1960s genre.

Fig. 6.7

The commuter turns left, down Franklin Avenue. Here, three scattered 1960s apartment towers, originally built for low-income senior citizens, punctuate the usual two-story commercial landscape. Between these towers are fragments of the past and present. A 1970s branch bank of giant Wells Fargo and its large parking lot anchor a community gateway (fig. 6.8). An early-twentieth-century commercial building abuts the sidewalk; it now houses an auto parts store and a Thai restaurant. Nearby is a local grocery store, small by chain standards; an old, narrow-fronted retail building with a lively mural on its long side; and another sizable parking lot. There is a liquor store behind a street-front parking lot, an example of the newer commercial ways. A few blocks away, a Standard Oil gas station stands near the freeway entrance.

Fig. 6.8

Our commuter now turns right, passes a small playground and the upper edge of the extensive Mississippi River parkway, and continues on to the I-94 entrances. At this interchange there is a Perkins, part of a metropolitan chain of restaurants. Just ahead is the huge Fairview-University Hospital complex. I-94 crosses high above the Mississippi River here. The river is a tremendous physical presence through much of the Twin Cities region; however, the highway has a solid concrete barrier next to its right lane, so the river and its valley are completely hidden from view.

Going East to St. Paul

If our commuter heads to St. Paul but eschews the freeway, the other choice is a journey through tree-lined residential blocks to a parkway. Along the way, only one old storefront recalls the years before exclusive residential zoning. At West River Parkway, East 24th Street joins a boulevard maintained by the Minneapolis Park Board (fig. 6.9). This picturesque two-lane parkway follows the crown of the river bluff. On the right (heading south), the green strip is planted with fine old oaks, their limbs partially concealing the bordering neighborhood houses. On the left, a well-used pedestrian path and separate bikeway parallel the road. From May to October, trees and brush conceal the river valley from motorist and jogger, but in the winter it is in full view.

Fig. 6.9

Going Southwest to Local Shopping

This journey reveals the neighborhood's variety and some of its history. Our commuter begins by heading south on South 31st Avenue, past an occasional large corner house of the late nineteenth century or a small 1970s ranch house. These reminders of the past are the result of spot clearance during Seward's modest urban renewal phase. This house-by-house and block-by-block rehabilitation continues today under the city's Neighborhood Revitalization Program (NRP). At East 26th Street, the driver turns right to follow an old Minneapolis-St. Paul streetcar line, now replaced by the Metro Transit bus service. Houses alternate with stores and small industrial buildings. On the left stands a popular local restaurant, the Birchwood Cafe, whose staff maintains a garden strip between the curb and the sidewalk in the best practice of the neighborhood. Tables and chairs are set out in summer for outdoor dining (fig. 6.10).

Fig. 6.10

As the driver heads farther west, the large Matthews Park comes into view. The neighborhood primary school, Seward, was rebuilt during the 1970s at the north end of this old two-block park (fig. 6.11). The homes here are older and more modest, reflecting their origin as housing for railroad men who worked in the yards nearby. An abandoned house lot has been turned into the Hub of Heaven Community Gardens (fig. 6.12). Across the way, there is a large sports bar and liquor store. When the driver turns left onto South 26th Avenue, heading south once more, the car travels through the

Fig. 6.11

Fig. 6.12

Fig. 6.13

Fig. 6.14

Fig. 6.15

core of the area's industrial redevelopment of the former railroad yards (fig. 6.13). Low industrial buildings and an occasional store line the street, punctuated here and there by the few remaining houses.

Now our driver is in a familiar suburban-style commercial landscape. On the right is the large Target parking lot, rimmed by a few service stores. This was the first inner-city location of the Twin Cities–based nationwide Target chain. Here shoppers can find a large selection of modestly priced clothing, as well as household goods, small appliances, and seasonal merchandise of all kinds. Sharing the same big parking lot is Cub, a large, metro-wide, warehouse-style grocery store (fig. 6.14). To the left, at the entrance to the giant Rainbow food store's parking lot, are two old buildings, the Schooner Tavern and a shoe repair shop. Rainbow is another Twin Cities food store chain (fig. 6.15).

The collective images of Seward's pathways are overwhelmingly particular and local. The specific mix of houses on each block and their varied configurations of trees, lawns, and gardens are the most frequent and perhaps the most powerful images. Most stores and industrial building signs hold little of either metropolitan or national symbolism. The exceptions to this rule are few: the Metro buses, the well-known Rainbow and Cub food chains, and the nationally recognized signage of Target and the Standard Oil gas station. There is little in this city neighborhood that fits neatly into the stereotypical categories of "center city," "suburb," or "metropolis."

■ ROSEVILLE

When popular journalism began to take notice of suburbs, it was places like Roseville that it focused on, with its streets of lawns, single-story ranch houses, and plenty of picture windows. Roseville's ten square miles of gently rolling land punctuated by lakes and marshes typify east-central Minnesota. A former farm area and truck terminal fringe of St. Paul, Roseville incorporated in 1948 and was built up with houses over the next two decades. It was an easy extension of St. Paul, because that city's main north-south streets, Snelling, Hamline, Lexington, Dale, and Rice, extend through Roseville. Indeed, the city fathers continued the St. Paul house numbering scheme on through the Roseville grids (fig. 6.16).

Today Roseville is much more than a bedroom suburb. Two branches of the Twin Cities' north-south interstate freeway (I-35) bracket the community, and a limited-access state highway

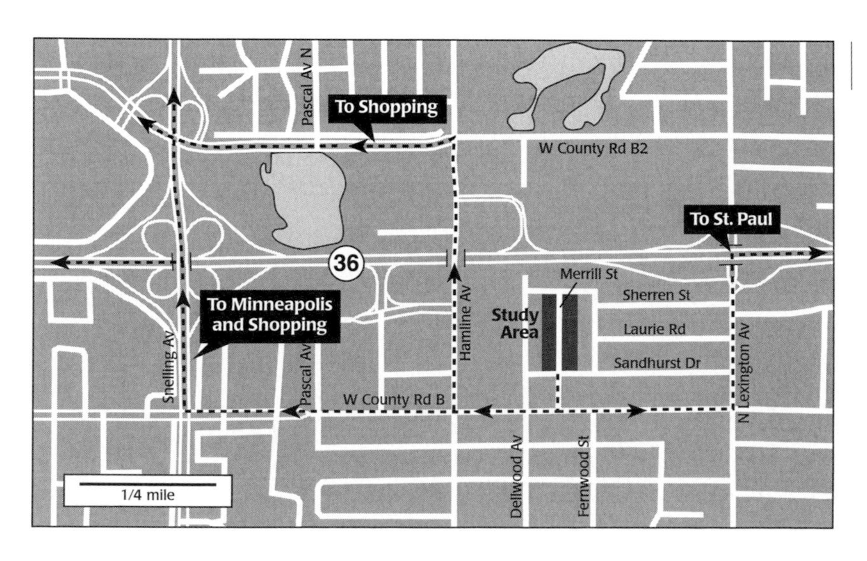

Fig. 6.16: Neighborhood in Roseville, Minnesota.

Fig. 6.17

(MN-36) runs through the lower third of Roseville, east to west, linking the two interstate roads. Easily reached by car, Roseville is conveniently located, and it is a commercial center for the northern quadrant of the whole metro region. It owes its importance to the automobile.

During the 1950s, one of the Twin Cities' earliest big strip malls was built on Snelling Avenue, an old streetcar route through St. Paul. At the start, HarMar featured a supermarket, a hardware store, and some small service stores. It has now evolved into a destination retail center, anchored by an eleven-screen theater and a large Barnes and Noble bookstore. A bit farther north on Snelling, abutting the Highway 36 interchange, the Dayton Corporation built a large regional shopping mall, Rosedale, in the early 1970s (fig. 6.17). (Target is now the parent company of the Dayton-Hudson department store chain, which built four "dales" in major quadrants of the Twin Cities MSA: Southdale to the southwest, Brookdale to the northwest, Rosedale to the north, and Ridgedale to the west.) The former Dayton Corporation also began its successful discount retail operation, the Target Stores, with a prototype in this same Snelling–Route 36 cluster. Today Roseville has at its geographical center a huge gathering of retail stores of every type and every price, from discount to luxury. This same highway node has also fostered a modest development of office and industrial buildings.

The Roseville Civic Center, a municipal campus, modestly mirrors the regional functions of this early suburb. Here the city brought together its municipal offices, police station, public works, and an impressive recreational facility in a sprawling quarter-section campus of lawns, parking, and low brick buildings (fig. 6.18). The regional draw is a large indoor ice-skating rink and an outsized outdoor rink, The Oval, that is kept frozen from November 1 through March 15. Boys' and girls' hockey teams and speed racers come to compete from schools all over

Fig. 6.18

Fig. 6.19

the Twin Cities region. It is also one of the very few Bandy rinks in the country. (Bandy is a noncontact hockey played with a rubber ball.) In warmer weather, The Oval is transformed with the platforms and ramps used for aggressive in-line skating; it also serves as an exhibition site. Now, reflecting the pattern of long-term settlement in Roseville, a fitness room for senior citizens is being added to the campus. This growing collection of activities constitutes an evolving "one stop" recreation center of the type now popular in Midwest municipalities. Nearby is another component of the civic center complex: the Roseville public library, with its interior coffee shop (fig. 6.19).

The modal Roseville block is 2190–2260 North Merrill Street, between Sandhurst Drive and Sherren Street (1250 West). This block features one- and one-and-a-half-story 1950s and 1960s ranch houses, all set back about forty feet from the curb by front lawns. The lots, eighty feet on the front and 130 feet deep, are arranged on a grid of thirty-two-foot streets (fig. 6.20). There are no sidewalks or alleys, and curbside parking is rare, since most cars are parked on wide driveways fronting one- and two-car garages. Some garages are attached, some are freestanding, but all are approached via a straight driveway at right angles to the street.

Fig. 6.20

Fig. 6.21

Going South to St. Paul

A local commuter walks out the kitchen door either directly into an attached garage or onto the driveway, then gets in his car and heads out Merrill Street to County Road B. Merrill Street has kept some of its 1950s appearance—the shaded look of most of St. Paul and Minneapolis is absent here because there are no long rows of trees. County Road B is a two-lane concrete east-west artery lined with ranch houses and lawns.

The first change in the residential street imagery appears as the car approaches Snelling Avenue and the edge of the HarMar mall. This intersection is a standard suburban commercial roadscape. A turn south on Snelling puts the car on a four-lane arterial with left-turn lanes at the traffic lights. The first segment of this journey carries the driver through a familiar mall landscape: the big Barnes and Noble store, a movie theater complex, Ground Round restaurant, video rental store, and so on (fig. 6.21). Our driver begins to pass ranch houses on the left and, on the right, between fences and hedges, will glimpse some of the impressive homes of successful 1950s suburbanites. The commuter soon leaves Roseville and enters St. Paul.

Going toward the East Metro

Another Merrill Street commuter might travel east on the highways to St. Paul or other suburbs. In this case, County Road B is again a pathway, and as the driver travels east, the same ranch house streetscape presents itself. At Lexington Avenue, the crossroads offer a new set of images: a drive-in bank, a city park, two gas stations, and, a bit down the block, Lexington Courts, a cluster of three-story 1960s brick garden apartments (fig. 6.22).

From here the trip on Route 36 takes the driver through the sort of grass and deciduous forest border that edges America's highways wherever twenty or more inches of rain fall each year.

There is no foreground, save the highway itself and the traffic. An occasional overpass carries the old north–south streets of St. Paul, and now and then a break in the trees offers glimpses of new condominium clusters. Gas stations occupy the corners at the exit ramps.

Fig. 6.22

Going to Minneapolis

The journey toward Minneapolis offers the same sort of images as the journey east: residential streetscapes followed by limited-access highway views. In this case, however, the westbound segment of Highway 36 is not bordered by forest and grass, but rather by strip mall retail buildings, suburban office buildings, and bits and pieces of the warehouse, trucking, and light industrial fabric of western Roseville. On the left, at the far edge of town, the highway is bordered by a tall sound barrier intended to screen an adjacent neighborhood.

Shopping

Roseville residents are literally surrounded by shopping opportunities, all reasonably close by. We imagine our driver to be seeking upscale goods on this trip—clothing from Dayton's large Rosedale department store and food from the high-end Byerly's supermarket. Both establishments are Twin Cities names, and both purvey nationally labeled and packaged goods. There are few Minneapolis-St. Paul goods offered for sale here, and surely few are marketed as such.

Fig. 6.23

Once the car turns north on Snelling Avenue, the driver is within the Roseville cluster of parking lots, shopping malls, and shopping strips (fig. 6.23). A bit farther north, a half-mile apart on the west side of Snelling, are both Dayton's (in Rosedale) and Byerly's.

The images of Roseville are something new, something cities never had before mass automobile ownership. The residential streetscape comprises many of the same elements as the older Seward city neighborhood—forty-foot streets set in a grid; lawns; small, set-back houses; trees—but only the scale is the same. In Roseville, the mix is quite different: square lots, low houses that place their long sides to the street, few front gardens or front plantings, automobiles and garages as part of the front yard. All these characteristics make for a significant change from the city image. The machine is not next to the garden as it is in Seward; in Roseville the machine is firmly planted in the garden. Here the residential streetscape announces that you cannot move about without a car.

The nonresidential landscape represents a break in scale from the measures of the old city. Seward accommodated commercial and industrial buildings, some within residential blocks, because many of the structures were not much taller than the houses. Here in Roseville, the four-lane arterial and the freeway have split the urban fabric in two: one scale for residential areas and another for the highway, shopping, offices, and industry. The commonplace highway elements are now at the scale of the very largest structures in the old city railroad era—the grain elevators, the rail yards, and the big factories. The images of these Roseville buildings are very much a newer type, neither residential nor suggestive of the region as a whole. They are something in between. Only the freeways possess a truly regional scale, but they are not designed to help motorists comprehend either the landforms or this particular part of the city-region.

■ EDEN PRAIRIE

Roseville was the typical new American city in the 1950s and 1960s. Eden Prairie is the city of the 1980s and 1990s. Now home to more than 40,000, its residents are scattered over 32.4 square miles, an area more than half the size of the city of Boston.

Situated twenty miles southwest of downtown Minneapolis, nothing here resembles either the farm or the rural factory town. Life in Eden Prairie is resolutely suburban, but it is a new form that has evolved out of former tendencies and patterns (fig. 6.24).

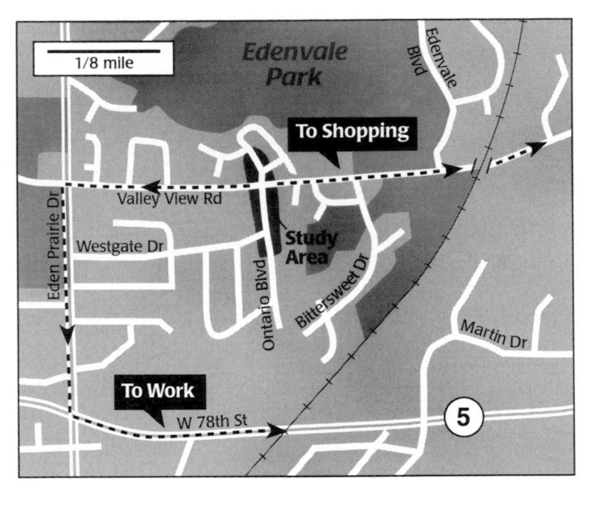

Fig. 6.24: Neighborhood in Eden Prairie, Minnesota.

Eden Prairie lies in the path of glacial moraines, so its land undulates with marshes, lakes and ponds, ridges and hills (fig. 6.25). It is pretty green land where farmers in past years stripped away most of the forest. At first, development followed the high ground, being situated along the main roads in curving circles and broken grids. This is not simply cul-de-sac development, however. Apartments and houses on the ridges often have handsome views of the small valleys below. It is ideal country for golf courses, and three have been built so far. Eden Prairie maintains one sizable park, Round Lake, and two smaller ones, but the only large public open spaces are Bryant Lake Regional Park, a Hennepin County facility, and the wetland of Purgatory Creek. There is also an airport, Flying Cloud, for small planes. The apparent abundance of open land belies the fact that Eden Prairie is now almost fully developed.

Hilly green farmland at the outer edge of a metropolitan region is hardly news—such land is found everywhere in the United States east of Colorado (fig. 6.26). Rather, Eden Prairie is

Fig. 6.25

Fig. 6.26

noteworthy because of the subtle but consistent townwide practice of stretching things out and lowering them down. Imagine, for a moment, that Frank Lloyd Wright's prairie house rooflines had been used as a measure to set the height limits for Eden Prairie, so that houses, schools, factories, offices, apartments, and municipal buildings all lay close to the land. "Big-box retail" here doesn't look like a case of wine, it looks more like the flat box the department store puts jackets in. The overall effect is to spread everything out on the land, to make buildings low, and to demand that there be space between everything.

Eden Prairie, thus, is aptly named. It is a prairielike setting—a curious creation for a gathering of office and industrial workers who must live by the automobile. Eden Prairie is dependent upon a circumferential highway, in this case I-494, just like so many other cities. Completed in the 1970s, this highway accounted for about 250,000 new jobs (two-thirds of the metro total) during the 1980s. Highway I-494 and its tributary roads are dotted with corporate headquarters, back offices, distribution warehouses, and factories—a more expansive version of comparable settings in Roseville and, more modestly, in Seward. Eden Prairie itself is peppered with new-style employers: Eaton Hydraulics, Vertical Systems, MTS, Minnesota Plastics, and so on. Such a mix makes for good jobs, albeit not fancy ones.

Eden Prairie is prosperous, but it is not simply a gathering of the wealthy. Everyone here must commute, most to the new highway clusters. Thirty percent still commute daily to Minneapolis or closer-in workplaces. To spread out to such an extent under these circumstances clearly adds unnecessary miles to everyone's day. In this sprawled landscape, a subtle mix of altered suburban elements have come together to mold an industrial–office–residential suburb into the image of a country club development for all its residents.

We chose two adjacent settings to illustrate the images of Eden Prairie, both sites on Ontario Boulevard on opposite sides of Valley View Road, approximately 7400–7500 south and 15600 west. The cluster on the south side of Valley View Road is a stretched-out 1980s version of earlier suburban styles. The cluster on the north side might aptly be called Seaside on the Prairie.

Fig. 6.27

The southern site lies on old farm fields, at the edge of a precipice overlooking the Purgatory Creek valley. Big cottonwoods and oaks have been preserved by the home builders, so even without the planting of street trees, the houses are shaded. The structures themselves are very conventional 1980s split-level ranches with attached garages. The lots are large and the homes are set so far back from the street that all mailboxes are on poles beside the road. There is no sidewalk (fig. 6.27).

Fig. 6.28

As a driver travels up the slight hill and along Superior Terrace, the remnant trees disappear while driveways, boats on trailers, lawns, and small front-yard gardens become the distinguishing features. The overall effect is not rural, although there would be plenty of land for ponies, chickens, or a family pig, none of which municipal rules allow. With all this land for homeowners to care for, it is surely no accident that there is a nursery and garden center two blocks away on Eden Prairie Road.

The northern site on Ontario Boulevard, a tasteful version of the New Urbanism, is a very self-conscious departure from the expanded suburb. The subdivision is a loop road with several cul-de-sacs running off to the sides. The houses are historically influenced, perhaps "New Englandy." They are situated on small lots without fences or hedges between them (fig. 6.28). The

Fig. 6.29

garage is not always the most dominant architectural element—it is sometimes turned so that its entrance is not even seen from the street. The street itself is narrow, twenty-eight feet, with a sidewalk on one side. Utilities are buried. Part of the development abuts the Purgatory Creek conservation land (fig. 6.29).

Commuting to I-494 and the Region

The growth of Eden Prairie and other nearby suburbs has forced the state highway department to widen old roads and incorporate traffic-light intersections into highway interchanges. In the summer of 1998, major highway construction made it likely that commuters from Ontario Boulevard would go west a few blocks to Eden Prairie Road and then south to Highway 5 to reach the road that would take them to I-494.

Eden Prairie Road is bordered on the west by the town's large Round Lake Park and its tennis courts and on the east by a modest strip of services: a post office, a bank, a gas station, and a nursery and garden center. Farther down toward Highway 5 is a slightly larger strip mall, with a good-sized grocery store, a bank, gas station, cleaners, and other necessary components of modern life. Ontario Road residents might well accomplish

Fig. 6.30

Fig. 6.31

most family errands here (fig. 6.30). Across the way, at the intersection, is a three-story apartment complex (fig. 6.31).

State Highway 5, which connects Eden Prairie to the airport, offers views of green wetlands and undeveloped farmlands as well as factories and warehouses that appear to be set in industrial campuses. To the east, at the intersection of Prairie Center Drive, a glacial moraine was removed to make room for a new interchange. As one approaches the entrance ramps to I-494, glimpses of retail appear: Bachman's Nursery, Wal-Mart, and a large commercial sports facility and day care center, the Flagship Club.

Commuting to Minneapolis

Commuters bound for Minneapolis would travel toward I-494 on Highway 5, but instead of entering the circumferential highway, they would pass beneath it on combined Highway 5 and U.S. 212 to reach I-35W. The images viewed by the passerby would mirror those of any other commute until one approached the city (fig. 6.32).

Fig. 6.32

Shopping for Food

Traveling from Ontario Boulevard to the big Rainbow supermarket on Prairie Center Drive entails a two-mile journey through the characteristic images of Eden Prairie. At the beginning of the trip, Valley View Road (heading east) is a wooded strip running down to the open wetlands of Purgatory Creek. Like other main local roads, the street is bordered by a paved bicycle and walking path. Many of these trails link together to form a subregional system. There is also a Southwest Metro Transit (a commuter line into Minneapolis) bus stop and signs, but there are no shelters for riders. Continuing on Valley View Road, a driver soon encounters areas of development, including a number of large new houses under construction,

Fig. 6.33

Fig. 6.34

closely spaced on small lots, their backs turned toward the road (fig. 6.33).

Next, the golf course associated with Quail Ridge "luxury" apartments appears, followed by a three-story brick apartment complex, Edendale Apartments, that stretches on for several blocks. On the other side of the street are gray wooden apartments with a two-level concrete parking structure. The next landmark is the Edenvale Corporate Park, which features a modest entrance to the road, a circle of parking lots and lawns, and widely spaced low brick buildings in the contemporary commercial style (fig. 6.34). At the traffic light, the driver turns right onto Prairie Center Drive and continues a short way to the large Rainbow Foods supermarket and the corral of service stores edging its parking lot.

Shopping for Clothes

Eden Prairie residents would continue on Prairie Center Drive, across Highway 5, and through the wide wetlands that surround Purgatory Creek in order to shop for clothes. As the road curves around to the east, the land rises to reveal a full panoply of modern suburban retailing (fig. 6.35). Just like Rosedale, Eden Prairie Center features a ring road of small stores and restaurants bordering a vast parking lot. In the center of the parking lot is the mall: Kohl's Department Store, a regional chain; Sears; Mervyn's of California; and Target—the latter two sharing local corporate ownership. These are all midprice retailers. For luxury goods the Eden Prairie resident would have to travel five miles farther east on Highway 5 (the Crosstown Highway) to the Southdale Mall in Edina (fig. 6.36).

Fig. 6.35

Fig. 6.36

Today Eden Prairie resembles a modern Arcadia, a mix of green nature, the new urban economy, and contemporary ways of urban living. Perhaps when fully built out, with all its dry land covered with houses and businesses, Eden Prairie will resemble the old suburbs more than it does now. A good deal of its future look will depend on how determined residents are in defending the wetlands and their low, spread-out architecture. At the present time, however, the real estate boom is offering a kind of country club landscape for everyone.

Throughout Eden Prairie, one can find apartments located next to a golf club, as they would be in any other planned-unit development (PUD) in the United States. Some houses, even modest ones, are scattered throughout the remnant forest on large lots, much as they might be in a fancy suburban development in the Northeast. Large and small houses alike are tastefully situated on carpets of lawn. The prevailing style consensus forces retailers, warehouses, and factories to be tidy and to maintain their open spaces as manicured green lawns. Here in Eden Prairie, the abundance of land seems to impact many facets of life. For individual homeowners, green space presents an opportunity for the intersection of gardening and domesticity. For Eden Prairie as a community, the green serves as a kind of uniform that expresses a common desire for order and harmony. In the city—and even in the older suburbs—bricks, pillars, and façades bespoke urbanity, wealth, and power. Here, life is expressed in the green ornaments of the college campus and the country club.

CONCLUSION

In terms of the images they present, there are more similarities among our three case studies than one might expect—particularly with respect to their commercial landscapes featuring identical retailers. Where differences do occur, they are largely a matter of scale. Thus, two possible lines of thought derive from these cases. One concerns the world of images and their relationship to real life. The other involves opportunities for design innovation.

In the Twin Cities, as in many midwestern and western urban areas, our mobility governs our imagery. Overall images are organized primarily by the interstate freeway system, perhaps even more than by the area's physiographic character. Lakes and parks may stand out on a regional map, but people race across the Mississippi and Minnesota Rivers daily at sixty to seventy miles per hour or more, scarcely noting the landscape. The rivers and lakes are present, but most often they are just features to be gotten around. Unlike Native Americans, the original residents here, few Twin Cities residents navigate the region by waterway, except for pleasure.

We have presented here what people see as they move about each day. The green, tree-lined streets of our case study communities epitomize the domestic imagery employed in standard promotional literature. Twin Cities residents connect these visual images to their mental map of metropolitan place reputation. Within the larger Twin Cities metropolitan area, social geography is hard at work, misrepresenting as well as representing reality. Most people have strong impressions of what it means to be north versus south of the Minnesota River, for example, or east versus west of downtown Minneapolis. Because Twin Cities residents, like most Americans, seldom stray from familiar paths in their daily journeys, these impressions solidify into belief systems.

These three cases underscore the complexity of the image/reality continuum in contemporary metropolitan life. Although one can find close approximations of the same house type in all three areas, one need only examine classified real estate ads to understand that very similar houses are valued very differently. Marketing and house pricing are closely associated with perception. Thus Seward, if known at all apart from Minneapolis, is an inner-city place, perhaps associated with where one's grandparents might have lived. Roseville is considered an older, close-in extension of St. Paul's ordinary northern end—and it is also in what historically has been the less-prosperous side of the region. To most, Eden Prairie equates with "new," and it is also squarely in the path of recent economic growth. These evaluations of community reputation are the active ingredients in the unfolding dramas of our case studies and in the rest of the region.

This cultural coherence and the histories of the three places described above suggest real opportunities for urban designers. The pace of change revealed here constitutes an opportunity in itself. Although much is made from concrete in American city-regions, there is little concrete that lasts for long unless it adapts to the tides of change. The direction of change in our three urban places has oscillated between two poles. On the one end, residential areas have accommodated themselves to the varying ways of business. At the same time, the practices of business have been adapted to fit homeowners' tastes and demands.

In our inner-city example, Seward, a neighborhood of the 1880 to 1930 era, the railroad and the streetcar set the transportation geometry. The alleys and their garages, however, are evidence of the neighborhood's response to the new opportunities of automobility. More than this adjustment to new times, even in the years before zoning, business and home accommodations went forward. Small industrial and commercial activities sprang up within the residential blocks, while the large railroad yards and warehouses and factory buildings located just beyond the residential fringes.

In Roseville, the automobile shifted the development from the old north–south streets of St. Paul to the new interstates.

Simultaneously, the interstates made the regional shopping center possible, creating a gathering of dozens of stores and services. The automobile encouraged, perhaps even demanded, new relationships in the design of homes. The linking of kitchen, yard, and garage shifted from the rear of the house to the side. The retail structure of the mall, offices, and factories also adapted to the new residential standards. The neat, clean, neutral-tone box for large stores and the tidy brick façade became the norm for commerce, thereby fitting commercial real estate more closely to the standards of the home lot. The public cleanliness and orderliness of land found in 1960s and 1970s industrial neighborhoods differed greatly from the manner in which pre–World War II industrial development met its neighbors.

In Eden Prairie, the tendency for domestic amenity to impact commercial and industrial standards has continued with the multiplication of domestic landscaping: the mowed edges of the interstates, the lawn spaces next to the parking lot, the store- and factory-front landscaping, and the municipal campus.

A review of these three Twin Cities neighborhoods underscores the degree to which urban land and buildings imagery has moved strongly toward using greening, lawn, shrubs, flowers, and trees as a standard for good urban practice. The five- and ten-story factory and department store, the pillared school and city hall—these are no longer the images of pride. Modest, clean, and a fit to a green setting have become the image goal. To a large extent, this image improvement has already been achieved with respect to signage, which is modest in all three communities (other than in the immediate freeway fringe). If this trend toward greening can be taken as representative of national tendencies, what does it say to designers? Where does opportunity for advancement lie?

Opportunity for improvement lies where it always has. The houses and buildings that cover the urban landscape are by no means the safest or most suitable to their tasks and activities, nor the most comfortable that ingenuity can devise. Neither the split-level ranch nor the New Urbanist cottages are all that they could be, even at current prices.

Moreover, the new suburbs, like the old city before them, have not yet achieved the "fitness" they could to the natural systems of the city-region. The streetscape needs renovation in order to meet modern environmental aspirations: Its paving, its trees, its lawns, as well as its houses, need upgrading. So do the vast, impermeable acres of unshaded parking lots that appear everywhere in inner city and in outer suburb. Given the fast pace of retail change, perhaps the mall and the shopping center are at a point of transformation. The open spaces in office and industrial parks have the great advantage of flexibility—all the land is not yet built upon; however, the windowless, air-conditioned warehouse and factory are neither the last nor the best answer to either human or machine work. Surely, whether urban or suburban, office towers, with their interior "landscapes" of cubicles, cannot be the ultimate answer in human suitability.

The commonplace images projected by these structures and their assembly in city and suburb suggest opportunities for urban change. They suggest as well the possibilities of design improvement at every level. If we read these images correctly, they have been moving steadily in the direction of making urban elements safer, cleaner, and more in conformity to the standards Americans have sought in their domestic lives. The overall trend seems to have been toward ever-higher residential standards. There is a green consensus. There is very active social valuation, which influences politics and the development strategies of the region. Within these trends, there is surely room for a world of design innovations in the best tradition of Kevin Lynch.

PART 

Responses to the Overwhelming City

Tales of Manhattan

Mapping the Urban Imagination Through Hollywood Film

Henry Jenkins

7

■ Editors' Overview

The city presents a chaos of images. A city like New York is so vast that there is always more to be seen than what meets the eye. Such a city is always building and rebuilding, erasing memory. Ever in motion, its portrait must be a motion picture; the origins and destinations of its people are so varied that their intentions cannot be grasped. Henry Jenkins, a film scholar, seeks order in this chaos through the study of films of New York and other large cities, retracing Kevin Lynch's steps and adding some steps of his own. He examines the various filmic interpretations of the city by becoming part of the audience and seeing what they see.

At the outset he warns that filmmakers do not observe as Lynch did; theirs is not an orderly progress down a street of fixed facades. The random, the fragmented, the simultaneous, and the unexpected qualities of the city are what the cinematographer captures. Yet filmmakers have employed many ordering devices. Jenkins reviews each in turn, making references to particular films.

The panoramic view, the city seen from afar or from above, transforms multiplicity into monumental forms, much as the praise books of medieval Italy did, or as today's postcards make the city into a massive landscape. When the filmmaker posts himself on the sidewalk, positions in space seem contested and the movements of people appear unpredictable. One group of filmmakers, the city symphony

group, placed themselves at a middle distance in order to find the rhythms of the chaotic flows. Another filmmaker follows a single individual in order to capture the sequenced movement of a person's tour of the city. Still others have structured their plots around contrasts between the impersonal mechanized city and the organic connections of imagined neighborhoods. Romantic comedies have used their magic wands to turn chance encounters of strangers in a city into passionate interludes. Finally, Jenkins presents films that portray the city as a vast, incomprehensible maze.

Throughout his essay, Jenkins traces the conflict between the means of abstraction and the means of particularity. He concludes with a passage from Lynch, allowing them to speculate together that the city might be presented as a hypertext whereby each viewer could find his or her own pattern of movement, rhythm, and order.

FALSE STARTS

The first chords of Gershwin's "Rhapsody in Blue" are heard. The sun glistens over the Manhattan skyline. The black-and-white images possess the sheen of old Hollywood glamour photographs. Woody Allen stammers the opening lines: "Chapter one. He adored New York City. He idealized it all out of proportion." Then, he stops, corrects himself, substitutes "romanticized" for "idealized," and continues, "To him, no matter what the season, this was still a town that existed in black and white and pulsated to the great tunes of George Gershwin."

"Ah, no. Let me start this all over."

In the opening montage of Woody Allen's *Manhattan* (1979), Allen's hesitations, revisions, and contradictions reflect his ambivalence toward New York. Sometimes Allen emphasizes glamour and romance, sometimes aggravation and self-doubt. In one passage, he "thrives on the hustle and bustle of the crowds and the traffic." In another, he is "desensitized by drugs, loud music, television, crime, garbage." Searching for a consistent vantage point from which to capture the totality of Manhattan in a single paragraph, he is, of course, doomed to fail.

Allen's ambivalence is reinforced by the images and music. The still photographs, which borrow from classic representations of the city, are only loosely linked to the narration (fig. 7.1). The Souvlaki King and the Empire Diner are treated with the same reverence as Times Square and the Guggenheim. A young couple kiss on a penthouse balcony; two black teenagers shoot baskets in the projects. Allen's narration suggests that the Gershwin sound track expresses the protagonist's romanticism, yet "Rhapsody in Blue" also uses jarring bursts of percussion, unanticipated fanfares, and syncopation to express the clashing and contradictory qualities of urban life. Allen makes no effort to coordinate the image to its rhythm. Only in the final moments do sound and image come together: Fireworks burst over the Manhattan skyline and Gershwin's music explodes into a crescendo of clashing cymbals and pounding drumbeats.

Fig. 7.1: Woody Allen's *Manhattan* borrows from earlier photographic representations to create a lushly romantic image of New York City.

IMAGES OF THE CINEMATIC CITY

In his classic study, *The Image of the City,* Kevin Lynch sought to bring to city design an appreciation of the aesthetics of urban experience as a "temporal art," recognizing that our perceptions of the city change and unfold over time. The book opens with an acknowledgment of the complexity and multiplicity of urban life, suggesting that the city can never be reduced to a single stable image but can be understood only in kinetic and dynamic terms:

> At every instant, there is more than the eye can see, more than the ear can hear, a setting or a view waiting to be explored. Nothing is experienced by itself, but always in relation to its surroundings, the sequence of events leading up to it, the memory of past experiences. . . . Every citizen has had long associations with some part of his city, and his

> image is soaked in meanings and memories. . . . Most often, our perception of the city is not sustained, but rather partial, fragmentary, mixed with other concerns. Nearly every sense is in operation, and the image is the composite of them all. . . . Not only is the city an object which is perceived (and perhaps enjoyed) by millions of people of widely diverse class and character, but it is the product of many builders who are constantly modifying the structure for reasons of their own. While it may be stable in general outlines for some time, it is ever changing in detail.[1]

Lynch sought to bring greater clarity and sensuality to our "images" of our native cities and to design urban spaces with more striking features that would enable a more coherent cognitive mapping of their basic parameters. At the same time, he recognized that city dwellers needed to be taught to perceive their cities in new ways. Lynch saw urban studies as a way of building a more educated and appreciative audience for city design. He recognized that our images of cities are shaped partially by formal properties of the cities themselves and partially by the process of perception and interpretation through which we construct mental representations of those properties. In *The Image of the City,* Lynch is interested primarily in the experiential process by which city dwellers develop a sense of their native turf. However, our mental maps of familiar cities incorporate not only memories of direct encounters but also secondhand experiences gained through mediated interactions with various representations of those cities—paintings, photographs, written descriptions, films, television programs, and the like.

In an oft-cited passage from *America,* Jean Baudrillard argues that in a European city the urban environment seems to be a "reflection of the paintings" one has just scrutinized in the galleries, while Manhattan "seems to have stepped right out of the movies."[2] This impression of Manhattan as a cinematic city is not surprising when one considers that a recent filmography of feature-length movies set in New York City listed more than five hundred titles.[3] In many cases, New York simply provides the setting for these films, a convenient and familiar backdrop for the narrative action, but this essay will be more centrally concerned with those instances where filmmakers sought to make movies about Manhattan, trying to give aesthetic shape to their own particular perceptions of America's most famous city.[4] Such an essay can not, of course, exhaust the full range of urban images that circulate in the American cinema; my goal is to focus attention on a set of aesthetic and ideological problems at the heart of representing the "cinematic city."

For Lynch, the "legibility" of a city image was what enabled it to become such a powerful basis for affective associations and metaphoric meanings: "The image of the Manhattan skyline may stand for vitality, power, decadence, mystery, congestion, greatness, or what you will, but in each case that sharp picture crystallizes and reinforces the meaning." The image of a city, for Lynch, must remain "plastic to the perceptions and purposes of its citizens."[5] The city image in film, however, already comes to us as interpreted through the powerful creative intelligence of an artist who wants us to see that skyline in a certain way. When Lynch writes about the "image of the city," then, he is primarily interested in formal features that make it harder or easier for us to grasp the city's essential structures, but when we discuss the cinematic image of the city, we are entering a space where formal and ideological issues merge.

Reading Lynch from the perspective of someone who studies cinema and not cities, what I find most striking is that he discusses urban form in a vocabulary that closely parallels the ideals of the classically constructed narrative. Lynch, for example, speaks of a "melodic" structuring of landmarks and regions along a succession of paths, which he suggested might follow a "classical introduction-development-climax-conclusion" pattern. Yet, Lynch is acutely aware of the various factors that prevent the city from achieving such a classical narrative form, that disrupt or break down its coherent development or fragment our perceptions of it. An ill-considered development deal may mar the urban landscape, blocking our ability to see important landmarks or to move fluidly between nodes. In one sense, the cinema would seem to be the perfect form to express the dynamic properties of the city, since like city design itself, cinema is a "temporal art form"; but the cinema brings its own expectations about what a classically constructed story looks like—expectations that urban-based stories are often unable to satisfy. Classically constructed stories remain focused on particular characters, their motives, their goals, their memories, and their experiences. The challenge for the filmmaker is to create a story that situates the individual in relation to the city in such a way that the film preserves what is distinctive about the metropolis—congestion, simultaneity, heterogeneity, randomness, fragmentation . . . in short, incoherence.

SPATIAL STORIES

Cultures, Michel de Certeau tells us, construct stories to explain and justify their occupation of geographic spaces, to describe and record their collective journeys and migrations, and to map the boundaries between known and unknown territories. Telling a story is an act of clarification that bestows coherence on ambiguous or ambivalent relationships between people and places. "Every story is a travel story," de Certeau writes, and often, the stories themselves circulate beyond their original cultures, justifying one community to another.[6]

The cinema emerged in the midst of a period of dramatic transformation within American culture. The urban population of the United States quadrupled in the forty years between 1870 and 1910.[7] The cinema helped the United States negotiate the tensions and uncertainties surrounding its transition from a predominantly pastoral society to a predominantly urban and suburban one. From the start, the American cinema was closely associated with the urban experience. The earliest films often documented a moment in time at a specific location, facilitating a process of virtual tourism. In Europe, such films typically linked colonial powers with the far-flung reaches of their empires. In the United States, cinema brought images of the emerging American metropolis to the hinterlands.

Exhibition was the central economic force behind the vertically integrated studio system that dominated American film production from the 1920s until the late 1940s. The primary exhibition revenue for the five major studios came from the urban hubs where they owned almost all of the theaters.[8] Rural and hinterland audiences were secondary markets. Urban markets determined what films would be made and what aesthetic sensibilities would dominate the American film industry. Consequently, a majority of Hollywood films of the studio era centered on the urban experience, albeit with a certain nostalgia for America's pastoral history. The Hollywood cinema explained to city dwellers the nature of their own experience and transmitted traces of that experience to a broader population that gradually was being absorbed into urban areas. Such films spoke to both immigrants from other countries who were hoping to better understand their new life in America and migrants from rural areas who were hoping to acclimate themselves to their new urban homes.

This is not to say that the American cinema offered a coherent or totally accurate picture of urban life. Urbanization provoked highly charged and often deeply ambivalent feelings even for—or perhaps especially for—those who lived in New York or Los Angeles. Many were horrified by mass culture, given the prevailing ideology of rugged individualism. Often, they came to the city seeking a social mobility and personal freedom they could not enjoy in the villages where their families had lived for generations. However, they also feared the alienation and isolation of inhabiting a world of strangers, and they felt buffeted by the rapid pace and fragmented nature of modernity. Hollywood's spatial stories gave expression to both these utopian and dystopian impulses, seeking to reconcile them through a more totalizing account of the city.

Though our contemporary relationships to the city are dramatically different from those that shaped these earlier spatial stories, the genre conventions that emerged during this important transitional period continue to exert a powerful influence over subsequent representations. Contemporary artists give new form to their perceptions of urban life, but often they do so in dialogue with these earlier representations. They quote them, as Allen does in *Manhattan* when he evokes a succession of classic photographs representing the New York skyline, or they rewrite them, as we will see in the example of *Dark City,* which merges the visual vocabulary of the film noir tradition with more contemporary science fiction trappings. For those reasons, any attempt to understand the contemporary cinematic city must always position those representations in relation to earlier images.

PANORAMIC PERSPECTIVES

Early writers emphasized the fragmentation and constant sensory bombardment of city life, traits that they felt resulted in perpetual disorientation and confusion. The cinema was the ideal apparatus for recording the diversity of urban experience. Cinema was an art form based on sequencing and juxtaposing image fragments to construct a more meaningful whole. Cinema could give shape to collective experience, while retaining the particularity of individual narratives.

Margaret Cohen has argued that the cinema's synthesizing function was prefigured by a nineteenth-century French genre of popular writings, which she calls "panoramic literature." Rather than telling a single story about fictional characters and their experiences, such works sought to tell the collective story of the city. Panoramic works create a composite account that combines written descriptions and narratives with various graphic representations, including maps, charts, cartoons, etchings, and photographs. Panoramic literature sought to record and classify all aspects of everyday experience. Cohen notes, "Panoramic texts evince a characteristic narrational mode: They are composed of micronarratives with no direct continuity from plot to plot."[9] Often, panoramic works had multiple authors, each writing in different genres with different styles and tones.

The cinema absorbed many of these panoramic impulses,

constructing a moving record of everyday life. Many early films were literally panoramas, offering views from the windows of streetcars, views of busy intersections, views from rooftops. These films encourage a pleasure in scanning the image and observing ordinary interactions. An evening's entertainment at the movies, which might include short comedies, dramas, documentaries, travel films, and the like, was itself a composite picture of turn-of-the-century life, though gradually, the feature film with its classically constructed narrative replaced "the cinema of attractions." Some later American films still adopted this panoramic approach, bringing together stories by multiple authors through some unifying structure based on thematic associations or movements through space. *Tales of Manhattan* (Julien Duvivier, 1942) uses the improbable circulation of a dress coat to link a series of short stories by some of the period's top screenwriters (including Ben Hecht, Donald Ogden Stewart, Alan Campbell, and Lamar Trotti). The coat takes us from the arts world (worn by Charles Laughton as a struggling concert conductor or Charles Boyer as a successful Broadway star) to the shantytown inhabited by a group of black sharecroppers.[10] The stories range from the broadly comic (W. C. Fields as a charlatan temperance lecturer) to the tragic (Edward G. Robinson as a down-and-out man who dresses up to attend his college reunion).

■ FROM THE 110TH FLOOR

Of course, the use of the term "panoramic" is misleading. These works were less panoramas than collages, composite pictures taken from multiple perspectives in which each element maintains some degree of separation from the others. Such works value diversity rather than coherence. A panorama, on the other hand, creates a totalizing perspective that integrates a wide array of elements into a single vista. What often gets lost in a panorama is the particularity of individual experiences.

In his essay, "Walking in the City," Michel De Certeau describes the experience of observing Manhattan from atop the World Trade Center. New York City unfolds around him like a panorama. His vantage point flattens the city into geometric patterns devoid of human activity:

> Beneath the haze stirred up by the winds, the urban island, a sea in the middle of a sea, lifts up the skyscrapers over Wall Street, sinks down at Greenwich, then rises again to the crests of Midtown, quietly passes over Central Park and finally undulates off into the distance beyond Harlem. A wave of verticals. Its agitation is momentarily arrested by vision. The giant mass is immobilized before the eyes.[11]

De Certeau is fascinated with the false sense of totality ("seeing the whole") created by this panoramic perspective: "To be lifted to the summit of the World Trade Center is to be lifted out of the city's grasp."[12] We build our modern Towers of Babel not to reach the sun, he suggests, but rather to see and know the urban world below us. One of the ways that this desire is fed is through the production and circulation of picture postcards that reproduce this "celestial" view of the city and make it available to many who have never visited the top of the World Trade Center.

Architectural critic Alvin Boyarsky has examined picture postcards as a conventional system for representing urban life, suggesting that they adopt a pictorial vocabulary that has remained relatively unchanged for more than sixty years and that varies only minimally from city to city.[13] The postcard embraces an ideology of urban progress, celebrating the man-built environment. Each postcard offers an emblematic image of the city, encapsulating the visit and allowing its transmission to those back home. The postcard, thus, depends on monumentalism, translating the cluttered urban environment into sights that can be isolated and recorded, dropped in the mail or plastered in scrapbooks. Typical New York City postcards feature civic landmarks photographed from a low-angle position, the skyline itself viewed from a boat in the harbor or across one of the bridges, or the aerial perspective, looking down on the city streets. The focus is mostly on architecture, not people (except as parts of crowds).

Fig. 7.2, Fig. 7.3: The opening of *West Side Story* looks down on the city from a "celestial" perspective before pulling us down to a more human vantage point of the street action.

The art of the cinema is not the art of the postcard. Cinema's focus is on movement, juxtaposition, and narrative, not static, emblematic, or monumental images. The cinema cannot remain in the clouds if it wants to tell the stories of those who walk below. Yet the opening montage in *Manhattan* draws liberally on the postcard's visual repertoire. Allen situates his actors against the backdrops of familiar New York landmarks—Diane Keaton and Woody Allen watch the sun rise over the Brooklyn Bridge; they have a spat amid the planetarium's alien moonscape.

A more complex play between "celestial" and earthly perspectives can be found in Jerome Robbins and Robert Wise's *West Side Story* (1961), one of the first Hollywood musicals to make extensive use of location shooting. The film opens with a sequence of spectacular views from a helicopter of the island of Manhattan (fig. 7.2). From such heights, we can see cars and buildings, but no people. However, we hear faint echoes of whistling and snapping fingers. A series of shots brings the camera closer to the ground to show us a group of teenagers loitering in a vacant lot (fig. 7.3). The scale of the film has shifted. We are now on ground level, inhabiting turf contested by the Jets and the Sharks. The camera toys with the spectator, making dramatic shifts in shot scale, swish panning from location to location, often racking focus or zooming out midshot to show unanticipated aspects of the image. The moment one side dominates a shot, the other appears from off-camera, moving in from the left and the right, or even from above and below the original framing, and the power dynamic shifts. In a few moments, the filmmaker moves us from the skies to the streets; it is this shift that enables the story to begin. The shift also represents a move from a conception of the city as unified to one that sees the urban sidewalks as a space being actively contested between recent immigrants and longer-term residents, one segregated by race, class, gender and nationality as well as a borderland where different communities come together.

■ FROM THE SIDEWALK

West Side Story prefigures de Certeau's own shift in focus. If the viewer standing atop the World Trade Center remains alien to the inhabited world below, those who walk the streets become active participants. Though individually "illegible," the aggregate of many such movements constitutes the story of urban life:

> The networks of these moving, intersecting writings compose a manifold story that has neither author nor spectator, shaped out of fragments of trajectories and alterations of spaces: in relation to representations, it remains daily and indefinitely other.[14]

Such uncoordinated movements, de Certeau argues, cannot be adequately expressed through abstractions, whether those of the artist or the urban planner:

> Their story begins on ground level, with footsteps. They are myriad, but do not compose a series. They cannot be counted because each unit has a qualitative character: a style of tactile apprehension and kinesthetic appropriation. Their swarming mass is an innumerable collection of singularities.[15]

De Certeau argues for a sociology that respects these singularities rather than searching for a totalizing account.[16]

The opening of Charles Lane's *Sidewalk Stories* (1989) explores these qualitative differences in ways of moving through the city, representing Manhattan from a pedestrian's perspective. An initial montage shows the morning migrations of urban office workers, a mass of people pushing their way down the sidewalk, pouring out of the subway or waving frantically for taxicabs. Three men arrive at the same cab seconds apart. They each grab at the door and try to push the others away. When one of them gets into the backseat, the others seize him by his legs and yank him out again. The rapid cutting between different images and the monumental music express the stress and tension of rush-hour traffic. Here, Lane self-consciously echoes a justly famous montage sequence from Charles Chaplin's *Modern Times* (1936), which compared the crowds shoving onto the subway to a flock of sheep being herded into the stockyards.

Fig. 7.4: Charles Lane's *Sidewalk Stories* shows a fascination with the different ways of moving through the city streets.

The rhythms of Lane's cutting and music shift as we pick up the trajectory of an aged street person pushing a shopping cart full of belongings (fig. 7.4). The takes become longer, preserving the slower pace of his footsteps. Deep-focus compositions position him against other unfolding narratives as he moves past bodies sleeping on the streets and people rummaging through trash cans. Our eye strays to observe a series of street performers, lingering long enough to appreciate their acts, before the tracking shot takes us a little further through Washington Square. In each case, the music shifts tone and genre to reflect the performers' individual sensibilities. Lane constructs a powerful class-based contrast between the urban environment as experienced by those who move with purpose and those who wander because they have no home and no job. As de Certeau suggests, the pedestrian's movements are unpredictable and shadowy, following no fixed trajectory, indifferent to the intended flow of traffic or the desired use of space. "To walk," de Certeau asserts, "is to lack a place." Lane builds his contemporary silent comedy, in the tradition of Chaplin, around such local acts of appropriation and disruption, seeing the homeless as the protagonists of their own stories living in the shadows of the great public drama of work life.

■ FROM A LOWER BALCONY

Between the streets and the skies are many other perspectives that offer a middle ground between alien abstraction and intimate involvement. The choice de Certeau poses for us—between voyeurs and walkers—is, in some sense, a false one (though as we will see, middle-level generalizations are often difficult to convert into spatial stories). In "Seen from the Window," Henri Lefebvre describes what he observes from his lower balcony. Lefebvre's perch is much closer to the street than de Certeau's, allowing him some distance from individual pedestrians yet enabling him to focus on the rhythms and patterns of collective movement. He has not lost touch with human scale, experiencing the city not as a static spectacle but as a series of intersecting narratives. From the opening paragraphs, Lefebvre is interested in the process of perception and interpretation:

> Noise. Noises. Rumors. When rhythms are lived and blend into another, they are difficult to make out. Noise, when chaotic, has no rhythm. Yet, the alert ear begins to separate, to identify sources, bringing them together, perceiving interactions. . . . Over there, the one walking in the street is immersed into the multiplicity of noises, rumors, rhythms. . . . But from the window noises are distinguishable, fluxes separate themselves, rhythms answer each other.[17]

He wants to document different durations of time, ranging from the intervals between green and red lights to the cyclical shifts from morning to night, as they influence the activity in the streets. Lefebvre's essay ends with the suggestion that the rhythms of the city are "much more varied than in music; no camera, no image or sequence of images can show these rhythms. One needs equally attentive eyes and ears, a head, a memory, a heart."[18] Lefebvre sees perception and interpretation as active processes that cannot be readily separated from their contexts.

A similar fascination sparked a genre of documentary films known as "city symphonies."[19] As that designation suggests, the central metaphors running through *Manhatta* (Paul Strand, 1921), *Berlin: Symphony of a Great City* (Walter Ruttman, 1927), or *Man With a Movie Camera* (Dziga Vertov, 1929) are musical; these films orchestrate the rhythms of urban experience. Often, like Lefebvre, these filmmakers were fascinated with the cyclical quality of a day in the life of a great city, starting at dawn and ending after dark, showing patterns of collective movement often invisible to individuals focused only on personal goals and activities. Empty streets come to life, fill with people, and then empty again at the end of the day. Berlin and the other city symphonies represent collective patterns of work, eating, recreation, and rest, built up from single images that express individual or particularized experiences. These images purposely cut across class distinctions, bring together many different occupational groups, mix and match men and women.

Godfrey Reggio's *Koyaanisqatsi* (1983) is a contemporary city symphony, set to Philip Glass's minimalist music. Koyaanisqatsi contrasts the gradual rhythms of the natural world with the frantic pace of modernity, seeing urban life as "crazy life . . . life in turmoil . . . life out of balance . . . life disintegrating." Reggio uses stop-motion photography to accelerate the action. A huge pile of newspapers evaporates in a matter of seconds. Subways become hives of insects as mobs of people flit from place to place (fig. 7.5). The flow of traffic becomes a throbbing pattern of

Fig. 7.5: In *Koyaanisqatsi*, the subway is represented as a hive of bustling activity, hopelessly out of touch with the rhythms of the natural world.

Fig. 7.6: When the camera in *Koyaanisqatsi* stops to observe individuals, they often look startled and confused.

light surging through urban arteries. Strategic juxtapositions create a succession of analogies between the population flow along crowded sidewalks and the flow of hot dogs down a conveyer belt. The pixilated images involve a play with perception as we struggle to focus on individuals, to sort out specific actions from the pulsating rhythms of the mass. Periodically, Reggio slows down the motion to offer portraits of individuals, looking like squirrels caught in headlights (fig. 7.6). In the film's final moments, a shot of the city taken from outer space is compared with the microscopic surface of a computer circuit, each indecipherable and yet clearly structured. The film wants us to perceive this acceleration of modern perceptual experience as horrific. Yet, there is a haunting beauty about Reggio's images, such as a giant moon floating rapidly across the nighttime sky or the glistening lights of cars whizzing along the freeway. We are fascinated by the city's ordered but relentless rhythms.

■ FROM THE PAGES OF A GUIDEBOOK

City symphonies existed on the fringes of the narrative cinema. Their abstraction from individual human experience meant that they did not fit comfortably within the character-centered storytelling associated with classical Hollywood cinema. How do we move from large-scale structures focused on collective activity to more personal stories that still express something of the complexity and heterogeneity of urban life? One common structure for spatial stories centers around the tour. Looking at the city through a visitor's eyes helps us to recognize distinguishing characteristics that we ignore in our daily lives. We underestimate the cities where we live, never able to see them with the wonderment that a tourist experiences. One function of spatial stories is to transform the city from a mundane space into a fantastic one, but the tour structure carries its own dangers. Tour guides lead us around by the nose and often do not leave us open to spontaneous discoveries or personal experiences. They prescribe where we should look and what we will see. They reduce the city to its landmarks.

"What can happen in one day?" a construction worker asks the trio of sailor boys on leave in *On the Town* (Stanley Donen and Gene Kelly, 1949), and as if to answer that question, the next number—"New York, New York"—compresses an entire tour of the city into a three-minute segment. Each shot shows a different location and a different mode of transportation as the boys race each other across the Brooklyn Bridge, ride horse-drawn carriages, take the ferry to the Statue of Liberty, point at the sites through the roofs of taxicabs, take the subway, gallop on horseback, and whiz by on bikes (fig. 7.7).

As the story unfolds, we learn that Chip (Frank Sinatra), who has never before been out of Peoria, has structured the whole day—in fifteen-minute increments—according to his grandfather's 1905 guidebook. The guidebook represents one way of organizing the eclectic experiences of the Metropolis, designating a series of sights particularly worthy of notice (because, as de Certeau suggests, they are "believable," "memorable," or "primitive") and structuring a route between them that lends coherence and purpose to the day. The guidebook fails Chip in two important ways. First, it does not capture the protean quality of the city. Many of the landmarks he hopes to see—the Hippodrome, the Floradora Girls—have been displaced by more contemporary attractions. As the female taxicab driver explains, "A big city changes all the time." Instead, she offers him "the one thing that doesn't change"—the experience of love and romance. He

Fig. 7.7: The sailors in *On the Town* tour the city's many memorable sites, following a route mapped for them by Chip's archaic guidebook.

wants to see the Flatiron Building and she wants to get him back to her place. And this suggests the other way that the guidebook fails him—displacing the personal, particularized narratives of individuals with totalizing, abstracted representations of the city. In disgust, she protests in a later scene, "Whisper sweet nothings in my ear, like the population of the Bronx or how many hotdogs were sold in the last fiscal year at Yankee Stadium." Only when Chip tosses his dated guidebook off the ledge of the Empire State Building does he enjoy Manhattan's real pleasures.

Long before Chip rejects his guidebook, *On the Town* abandons his itinerary for another route through New York City—one determined by Gabey (Gene Kelly) and his search for the girl of his dreams. The musical personifies the city's heterogeneity in the composite figure of Miss Turnstiles, the current month's poster girl for the subway system: "She's a home-loving girl but she loves high society's whirl. She loves the army but her heart belongs to the navy. She's studying painting at the museum and dancing at Symphonic Hall." And she has the one trait that allows her to embody Manhattan perfectly—she wasn't born there. In fact, she comes from Gabey's own hometown, Meadowville. Despite his friends' protestations that it would be impossible to find one girl among the multitudes, Gabey keeps running into her, then losing her again. His pursuit takes him through the city's museums, concert halls, high-rises, and nightclubs. Here, the shared experience of the guidebook tour gives way to the particularized goal of the search. Both scenarios offer stories that center around movements through space, but one focuses on the individual experience and the other on the collective. Both depend on the act of looking: one an act of looking at, the other an act of looking for.

■ FROM THE COUNTRYSIDE

Not surprisingly, a large percentage of Hollywood's spatial stories center around visitors who come to the city from regional cities like Peoria, small towns like Meadowville *(On the*

Town), Mapletown *(The Clock),* or Glenwood Falls *(The Out-of-Towners),* or from the countryside. Often, such films build a thematic opposition between town and city that is closely modeled on Ferdinand Tonnies's classic distinction between *Gemeinschaft* (community) and *Gesellschaft* (society). Philip Kasinitz provides a useful summary of these concepts:

> For Tonnies, *Gemeinschaft* is a type [of] social solidarity based on intimate bonds of sentiment, a common sense of place (social as well as physical), and a common sense of purpose. *Gemeinschafts,* he argues, are characterized by a high degree of face-to-face interaction in a common locality among people who have generally had common experiences. . . . In a *Gesellschaft,* in contrast, relationships between people tend to be impersonal, superficial and calculating, and self-interest is the prevailing motive for human action. Social solidarity is maintained by formal authority, contracts and laws.[20]

These differences surface especially powerfully in the silent cinema, popular in an era when the American people were still adjusting to the new centrality of urban life to their national culture. For example, such a distinction structures F. W. Murnau's *Sunrise* (1927). A woman from the city comes to the country on vacation and unsettles the relationship between a farmer and his wife. The city woman is depicted as operating outside the shared moral norms of the rural community. She has little respect for the institutions that hold the community together. She is soon the subject of gossip, one of the mechanisms Tonnies argues help enforce the stability of the *Gemeinschaft* by creating sanctions against the violation of its norms. The seductive and socially fragmenting force of the city is vividly represented in one of the film's key moments as the city woman urges the farmer to murder his wife and run away with her. She writhes in her slinky black dress as she describes to him the temptations and sensations of the city, and images of urban nightlife (city skylines, bright lights, jazz bands) appear behind her almost as if pro-

Fig. 7.8: The seductive city woman in *Sunrise* tells the farmer about the sensations of the urban environment.

jected on a movie screen (fig. 7.8). Murnau uses camera movements, superimposition, and layered images to convey something of the heterogeneity, intensity, and fragmentation of the *Gesellschaft.* The farmer's wife, by contrast, is a plain, simple woman who loves her husband and remains faithful to him despite his infidelities. When she visits the city, she is drawn to its simple pleasures—watching the church wedding of a young couple or getting a photograph taken with her spouse. She is suspicious of the easy, informal social relations of the city, anxiously eyeing the manicurist who trims her husband's nails. The city is full of threats and seductions that can destroy a marriage; they both are eager to return home to the country.

The story is a familiar one—the farm couple comes to the city, takes in its sights, then returns home where they belong. In Neil Simon's *The Out-of-Towners* (1970), George (Jack Lemmon), a small-town businessman, comes to New York City with his wife, Gwen (Sandy Dennis), for a job interview. George and Gwen have big plans to enjoy a night on the town, but all of their plans go awry. Before the night is over, George and Gwen stand shivering, starving, and desperate in a New York police station (fig. 7.9). "We were in a holdup. We might have been killed," Gwen proclaims, but they have great difficulty commanding the attention of the police officer on duty. The sanitation strike that left the city piled high with garbage has at last been settled, they are told, but now the milkmen have gone out. A horde of people press toward the desk, each with a story of crime, woe, and distress, each interrupting with their own demands for resolution and assistance. Gwen is distracted, worrying about everyone else's problems: "I know what you're going through," she explains, which is, of course, true. George and Gwen's troubles stem from their assumption that their experiences matter when, in fact, the city operates on the basis of statistics, not individuals.

One missed train, one lost piece of luggage, one mislaid hotel reservation, one stolen wallet, one important business transaction amount to little. There are too many people, too many problems, for city services to respond to any of them. George reacts by trying to order the events in preparation for a lawsuit, taking down names, making a list of grievances, as if the whole experience were one great conspiracy against him. He screams to the skies, "You're just a city. Well, I'm a person and a person is stronger than a city. You're not getting away with anything. I have all your names and addresses." In the end, the couple realizes they have no place in the city and they go back home to the Midwest, a region with a stronger sense of human proportion.

Fig. 7.9: George and Gwen confront an indifferent police officer in *The Out-of-Towners.*

■ ON A STREET CORNER

Gemeinschaft, as Tonnies describes it, has many of the familiar features of a classically constructed narrative—a unity of time and place, a consistency of viewpoint, a shared goal, a relatively limited cast of characters. In fact, to illustrate the social relations that arise in such a culture, Tonnies evokes plots that have long been building blocks of the western storytelling tradition—stories of the relationship between generations, between father and son, between siblings, between husbands and wives, between neighbors.[21] In such a world, relationships are defined through their continuity and reciprocity, the intensity and permanence of the emotional investments we make in other community members. Relationships within a *Gesellschaft* culture, on the other hand, are "transitory and superficial." People have many more social encounters in such a world, but they do not cohere into a consistent narrative because they do not demand the same emotional investments and thus do not leave lasting imprints.

Fig. 7.10: The early sequences of *Street Scene* capture the random interactions of the residents of a Lower East Side tenement house.

Street Scene (King Vidor, 1931), which is based on a stage play by Elmer Rice, was a bold experiment in narrative form because it attempted to create a plot structure appropriate for a *Gesellschaft* culture. Set on a tenement block, the film's opening scenes have little or no consistent focus. Children play in the streets. Neighbors linger on their stoops, shout from window to window, come and go along the sidewalks. Their conversations shift from topic to topic. They get into arguments that reflect their conflicting moral codes. Vidor captures the seeming randomness of Rice's plot with fluid camera movements that sweep the space, following dialogue from window to window or tracking down the street with one character and then pivoting and tracking back with another (fig. 7.10). These early scenes depict many potential plots—a woman cheating on her husband, a young couple awaiting a birth, a family about to be evicted because they can no longer pay their bills, a sister worried about her brother. In one shot, the camera pans across adjacent windows, revealing residents shaving, dressing, stretching and exercising, bouncing their babies, hanging the laundry, applying makeup. Each neighbor seems totally unselfconscious about the close proximity of the others.

Only late in the film does a single plotline dominate: A husband returns home unexpectedly and catches his wife in the arms of her lover; he murders her and the entire community is drawn into the investigation and its aftermath. *Street Scene* signals its sudden shift in plot structure by altering its editing style—from long-takes and camera movements to close-ups and rapid editing. A succession of reaction shots shows the startled and alarmed people as they witness the acts of violence or run down the street to see what has happened (fig. 7.11). Then, finally, the camera pulls back to show the entire city block mobbed with people. The multiplicity of urban life coheres into a narrative only when disaster occurs. Even then, coherence is provisional. Soon, attention will be drawn elsewhere.

Fig. 7.11: A montage sequence shows the reactions of various community members to the murder in *Street Scene.*

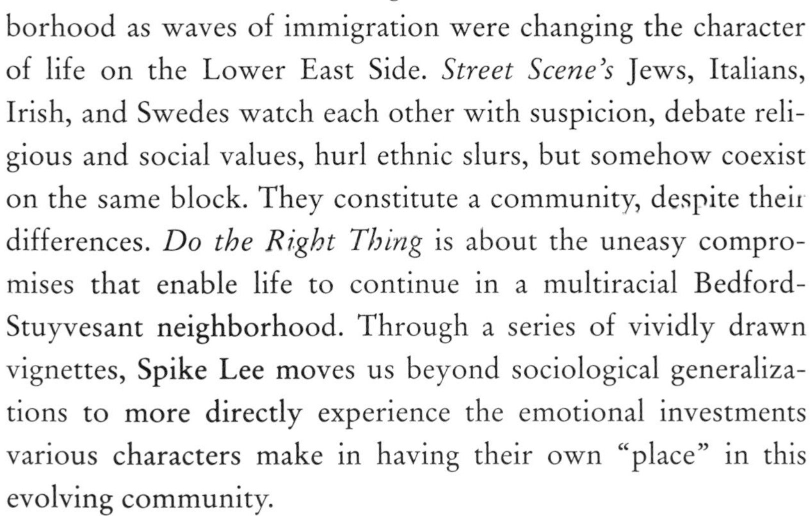

Spike Lee's *Do the Right Thing* (1989) might be viewed as an attempt to update *Street Scene.* Rice and Vidor documented the cultural conflicts that arose within a multicultural neighborhood as waves of immigration were changing the character of life on the Lower East Side. *Street Scene's* Jews, Italians, Irish, and Swedes watch each other with suspicion, debate religious and social values, hurl ethnic slurs, but somehow coexist on the same block. They constitute a community, despite their differences. *Do the Right Thing* is about the uneasy compromises that enable life to continue in a multiracial Bedford-Stuyvesant neighborhood. Through a series of vividly drawn vignettes, Spike Lee moves us beyond sociological generalizations to more directly experience the emotional investments various characters make in having their own "place" in this evolving community.

Who speaks for this community? The hot-tempered Buggin' Out, the sputtering Smiley with his photocopied images of great black leaders, the dignified but drunk "mayor," the fast-talking disc jockey Senior Love Daddy, the wise crone Mother Sister, or the pragmatic and unreliable Mookie? Each has a chance to articulate Bed-Stuy's values, but Spike Lee offers us little way of reconciling their contradictory assumptions. The neighborhood seems to be continually on the verge of racial conflict, as Sal's son resents having to work on "the planet of the apes," Buggin' Out demands that there should be pictures of "brothers" on the restaurant's wall of fame, the old black men who sit on the street corner sputter with rage over Korean immigrants buying up businesses in their neighborhood, Radio Rasheim tries to drown

Fig. 7.12: Many scenes in *Do the Right Thing* center around contested space along the borderlands between different racial communities.

out his Hispanic neighbor's salsa with his rapping boom box, and the locals feud with a Boston Celtics supporter who has invested in an old brownstone on their block (fig. 7.12). In one dramatic scene, the story stops altogether as Lee shows us one character after another hurling racial epithets directly into the camera in a montage sequence that traces the cycle of hate and bigotry. As individuals, these people can form friendships, make moral and personal distinctions, find ways to relate to each other, even parent children together. But as representatives of their own racial communities, they can only fight for space and seethe over historic injustices.

Lee's film, no less than *Street Scene,* depends upon a nostalgia for an organic community whose ties extend across generations and beyond cultural boundaries. Sal evokes such a vision of Bed-Stuy when he describes the experience of owning his own restaurant there for decades: "I watch the little kids grow old and the old people grow older. . . . They grow up on my food." Lee calls attention to the affection that Sal has for Mookie and his sister and the friendship between Mookie and Sal's younger son. He depicts Sal as someone who has learned to compromise to avoid conflict and who respects the hierarchy of the community. Yet, Lee has little faith that these kinds of sentimental attachments can transcend societywide racial conflicts, which are evoked moments later by a camera shot of graffiti scrawled on the side of the wall, "Tawana told the truth," or by the images of Malcolm X and Martin Luther King that Smiley peddles in the street. When violence erupts, the incidents are pulled into the history of police brutality against black defendants. There is an eerie familiarity to the moment when the firemen turn their hoses away from the blaze and toward the community members who have gathered to watch Sal's place burn to the ground.

No less than Rice and Vidor, Lee wants to use this street corner society as a microcosm to speak about the larger history of urban America. Much as in *Street Scene,* the opening moments of *Do The Right Thing* are episodic, with their focus shifting from one vivid character to another, until we know our way around Lee's fully drawn and richly populated milieu. And much like *Street Scene,* the film builds toward a moment of violence when all of the various characters and their stories come together. The violence in *Street Scene* was personal—a jealous husband murders his wife—though in the tightly woven communities of the Lower East Side, it is impossible to extract yourself fully from your neighbor's business. The violence in *Do the Right Thing* is collective and political. No one can remain neutral, as becomes clear when the spiritual Mother Sister shouts for her neighbors to "burn it down" and then, moments later, cries with horror at the destruction that has been unleashed. In the end, personal loyalties matter little. Mookie, who Sal described as being like a son, smashes a trash can through the pizzeria window. But racial loyalties are of vital importance; the Korean grocer shouts over and over, "I no white. You, me, the same," trying to close ranks against the Italians while preserving his own precarious status in the neighborhood. All social ties are temporary, unstable. The story of the city is being renegotiated along the borderlands, where different racial groups come together or break apart.

■ AT THE TRAIN STATION

Train stations are narrative nexuses where paths cross and new relationships are formed. What happens within such spaces depends heavily upon chance, upon the random ebb and flow of urban traffic. People are brought together and they are separated. Yet in the hands of an artist, such flux can become meaningful. The risk, of course, is that the characters will be swamped by the bustle surrounding them. A train pulls into Penn Station at the opening of Vincente Minelli's *The Clock* (1945) and a mob of people disembark. Among them is Joe (Robert Walker), a serviceman on leave. When he stops beside

Fig. 7.13: The young lovers in *The Clock* are pushed apart by the momentum of the crowd at Grand Central Station.

Fig. 7.14: By the closing moments of *The Clock,* Penn Station seems ordered as we encounter couples preparing for wartime separations.

an escalator to read his newspaper, Alice (Judy Garland), an attractive office worker, trips over him and breaks the heel of her shoe. It's love at first sight. Later, the couple gets separated at Grand Central Station. Pushing through an indifferent mob, Alice gets on a subway train and Joe doesn't (fig. 7.13). They still don't know the other's name and have no way of finding each other again. When Alice seeks advice at the local USO club or when Joe asks a newspaper stand owner whether he saw a girl get off a train, they are met with incredulity: "I see a thousand girls get off trains." All girls look alike to the man who sells the papers, but only one girl will do for the soldier in love.

Yet, despite all the odds, they do find each other again, and the closing moments of the film bring them back to Penn Station once more—now a young married couple separating for the first time. The camera pans slowly past the people awaiting their trains. A father clutches his newborn baby. Elderly mothers hold on to their servicemen sons (fig. 7.14). A husband discusses last-minute details of family business. An old officer bids farewell to his wife, a young black man to his father, and young lovers kiss one last time. But in each cluster there is at least one person who is serving his country, and all of them are saying good-bye.

What brings the young lovers together again is not so much chance as predestination. From its beginnings, the classical Hollywood cinema was suspicious of the arbitrariness of chance and coincidence. Ideally, its stories were structured around well-motivated causal-event chains. Conventions mandated that each event should be linked, logically and inextricably, to all those that come before and all of those that follow it. In romantic comedy, however, causality often gives way to predestination. Some couples are made for each other and will be united, one way or another. The more daunting the obstacles in True Love's path, the more inevitable the coupling seems. Consequently, the city becomes the ideal setting for romantic comedy—one that translates chance encounters into inevitable romances, provides appropriate backdrops for courtship, and contrasts the intimacy between the lovers with the alienation of urban culture. Though the enormity of Manhattan constantly threatens to engulf them, their love story stands out against the hurried backdrop of New York's various terminals.

But this "city of strangers" can just as readily lend itself to erotic nightmares. In Martin Scorsese's black comedy *After Hours* (1985), a young adventurer encounters a mysterious woman at an all-night Laundromat and gets taken in by her story, venturing into Soho during the wee hours of the morning. However, nothing coheres or makes much sense in this farce about contemporary urban alienation. As one character warns him, "Different rules apply when it gets this late." A series of random encounters with eccentric women strips him step by step of all the trappings of his identity—his wallet, his car keys, his clothing, even his hair (punk rockers threaten to give him a Mohawk) (fig. 7.15). An emblem of the role of happenstance in the film, the twenty-dollar bill he is clutching blows out the window of the fast-moving cab, leaving him no way to pay his tab and no way to get back home. Later in the film, the bill is seen plastered on a sculpture he encounters in his rambles.

Fig. 7.15: ***After Hours*** **depicts urban life as an erotic nightmare as the male antagonist experiences a series of disorienting encounters with eccentric women.**

Everything seems connected to everything else, but not in predictable ways. Everything that happens is subject to multiple interpretations, and our protagonist usually misunderstands what is happening to him. He spots a group of Hispanic men struggling with a television set, which he assumes must be stolen. When he screams, they drop it and run away, convincing him that he has foiled a crime in progress. It turns out that both men are criminals, but they have actually bought this set: "See what happens when you pay for stuff?" As the night unfolds, he finds himself under suspicion for local break-ins and is chased through the streets by an angry mob. An artist's sketch of his face is pasted on every telephone pole. Robbed of his identity, he has no way of freeing himself from these unjust suspicions. Lost in a strange neighborhood, he has no friends or family he can call on for support or assistance.

■ THROUGH THE REARVIEW MIRROR

Hollywood's spatial stories repeatedly tell us that we are a product of the spaces we inhabit. As we move through the city, we do not remain separate from it; the city becomes a part of us, alters our behavior, redefines our identities. In *Taxi Driver* (1976), Travis Bickle's eyes peer intently into the rearview mirror (fig. 7.16). Rain splatters on the windshield, and the wipers swish it away. The street outside is a neon blur. Red and blue flashing lights illuminate the human figures that bob in slow motion

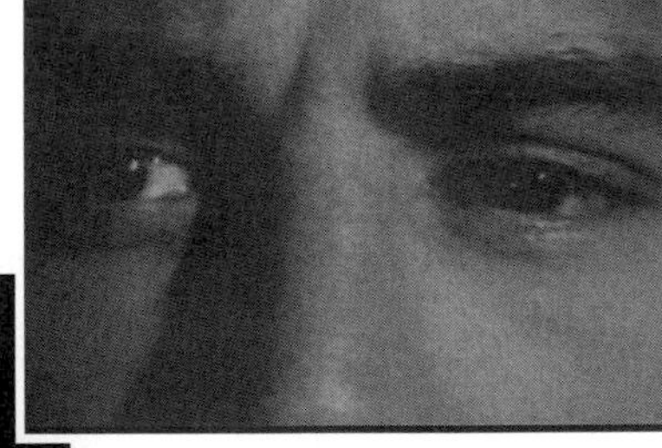

Fig. 7.16: *(Above)* Travis Bickle's eyes stare intently into the rearview mirror in *Taxi Driver.*

Fig. 7.17: *(Left)* Times Square seems lurid and abstract when seen through the rear window of Bickle's cab in *Taxi Driver.*

along steamy streets. And the taxicab scurries about the city, picking up passengers and dropping them off (fig. 7.17).

Martin Scorsese's *Taxi Driver* risks incoherence in trying to tell the story of a man who sees everything and understands little, who is constantly in movement and yet moves without purpose. "I go all over," he tells us. "It doesn't make any difference to me." The world as seen from the mirror of Bickle's cab is a lonely place full of lonely people, and he holds it in horror and contempt: "All of the animals come out at night. . . ." He imagines the approaching apocalypse: "Some day a real rain will come and wash the scum off the streets."

Bickle becomes, in Scorsese's film, the personification of New York—sometimes romantic, sometimes brutally violent. Bickle embodies the random events and unstable social relations of urban culture, constantly shifting his goals and tactics. The parts come together only retrospectively, when his violent impulses are redirected from his plans to assassinate a presidential candidate and toward the task of rescuing a young prostitute. He shoots his way into the brothel, leaving a path of bloody bodies, sitting in a dazed and confused state until the police arrive to take him away. None of this makes any sense. For the newspapers, however, Bickle has become a hero. The eyes of New York are upon him.

By the film's closing images, all coherence has broken down into a fragmented, almost cubist, image that recalls the stylized and subjective representations of New York that Joseph Stella created in the 1920s and 1930s. We see the world partly through his front windshield, partially through his rearview mirror. The scene is almost abstract, flashes of light and color which sometimes take shape into something we recognize but which, more often, remain blurry and indistinct.

ANTICLIMAX

Hollywood's spatial stories struggle to balance their utopian and dystopian conceptions of the city, their belief in urban progress, and their anxiety about the collapse of old social institutions. The film artists try to reconcile their focus on the totality of the urban environment and their fascination with the complex interplay between multiple experiences. Such tensions run through our attempts to theorize the city and to give it aesthetic form. The forces shaping urban experience are complex, multidirectional, transient, and often totally invisible. Nevertheless, we imagine urban life as controlled by secret societies, hidden forces, conspiracies, smoke-filled rooms. The current popularity of conspiracy theories in popular culture suggests our compelling need to personify the governing forces behind urban life and our fear that they may not be directly observed or readily mapped.

Dark City (Alex Proyas, 1997) offers a noirish vision of the postmodern city, depicting urban space as an incomprehensible maze. The city is mutating before our eyes. Nothing remains the same; nothing matters. Yet, Proyas suggests, the city follows a secret logic; its citizens are manipulated by hidden forces. The *Dark City* is not New York, not any place in particular. It has been, we are told, "fashioned on stolen memories, different eras, different pasts, all rolled into one." *Dark City* makes stunning use of morphing to literally restructure the city before our eyes. We watch new buildings rise from the concrete. Old buildings grow window ledges, expand into domes. While the city sleeps, dark hooded figures creep among us, changing our clothes, imprinting new memories, moving us from place to place, so that when we awake we are enmeshed in a different life, become part of an alternative narrative. Our memories are distilled, "mixed like paints," and then reinjected into us, offering no reliable way of understanding who we are and what is happening to us. As one of the characters explains, "They steal people's memories and swap them between us—back and forth, back and forth—until nobody knows who he is anymore." The protagonist awakens, naked and without any memories, conscious while others sleep, observing but not fully comprehending other people's behavior as he peers through their windows.

His search for an explanation is mirrored by the detectives and their serial murder investigation (which may or may not lead back to him). In a classic noir, the detective was a lone individual who understood better than anyone else the code of the city. His search for truth promised to untangle the web of relationships that link the story's various characters. In the neo-noir *Dark City,* the detectives do not have a clue; they have no hope of finding answers. One detective has been driven mad by the complexity of this city, scrawling endless spirals and scribbling cryptic words on his apartment walls. "I've been spending time in the subway, riding in circles, thinking in circles. There's no way out. I've been over every inch of the city." Though he never understands what he has discovered, his circles do contain the pattern that holds all of this together, linking an early shot of rats being run through a circular maze with the great clock that controls the waking and sleeping of the citizens and with our final image of the city—a spiral of skyscrapers arranged on a flat surface floating in the vast emptiness of space.

But there is a conspiratorial logic here. The city is controlled by the Strangers, who personify de Certeau's "alien" or "celestial" perspective (fig. 7.18). They are hooded figures with featureless faces and bald heads; they are interchangeable, sharing a collective memory. They are the very embodiment of urban experience as a totality, of a deterministic logic that allows little or no room for particular experience. Through a process of experimentation, they hope to understand the individuality that makes us human. They are the ones who move the hands of the clock, who set the rhythms of urban experience. If there is, in the end, a story of the city, they are its authors and its architects. They alone enjoy absolute mobility—they dwell in secret places beneath the city; they can walk among us without being seen; they can hover over the city streets, peering down at the pedestrians.

Fig. 7.18: The Strangers are the secret conspiracy of aliens who make and remake the urban environment in *Dark City.*

Dark City, thus, uses the struggle against the Strangers to personify the core conflicts that have run through this essay—the conflict between abstraction and particularity, between the city understood as a totality or as heterogeneity, between the urban environment experienced as ordered or as random and chaotic. What this chapter has described is the struggle to give shape and form to urban experience, to find its rhythms, map its labyrinthine streets, record its protean activities, and give it a cohesive identity. This task has inspired—and, arguably, defeated—the imagination of America's greatest filmmakers. The story of the city can't be told—at least not as a totality. There is no structure, no coherence, only simultaneous activities, people walking down sidewalks, pushing their way onto subway trains, standing in their windows, waiting impatiently at police stations, wandering aimlessly through museums, pursuing their own particular paths without regard for each other. There is no single vision that can express and contain our complex and contradictory feelings toward the American metropolis. There are only ways of seeing, only provisional vantage points that offer a succession of near-perfect images of urban life.

Kevin Lynch arrived at almost the same place. There is a curious passage near the end of *The Image of the City* where Lynch tries to imagine an alternative form that might preserve his own sense of the multiplicity of urban meanings and experiences while achieving the legibility and clarity that was central to his aesthetic conception of the city. For a few paragraphs, Lynch imagines the city as given ideal expression in a multilineal and polysequential form. Though Lynch would not have had access to the analogy in 1959, he imagines something akin to hypertext:

> Intuitively, one could imagine that there might be a way of creating a whole pattern, a pattern that would only gradually be sensed and developed by sequential experiences, reversed and interrupted as they might be. Although felt as a whole, it would not need to be a highly unified pattern with a single center or an isolating boundary. The principal quality might be sequential continuity in which each part flows from the next—a sense of interconnectedness at any level or in any direction. There would be particular zones that for any one individual might be more intensely felt or organized, but the region would be continuous, mentally traversable in any order. This possibility is a highly speculative one: no satisfactory concrete examples come to mind.[22]

Lynch seems to suggest that the city itself might be structured as a hypertext, but suppose that the hypertext gave us a more perfect representation of the city precisely because it was multilineal and interactive. Suppose a future artist were to construct such a hypertext, one in which the four million stories that O. Henry imagined in New York City were all recorded and viewers could traverse the narratives and observe their points of intersection and digression. Suppose we could represent at once the abstract patterns of movement and the particular journeys, searches, and tours that motivated individual experience. Suppose the structuring elements of this hypertext were Lynch's various paths, edges, districts, nodes, and landmarks, the features around which so many spatial stories arise and play themselves out. Suppose this artist were to construct the perfect model of the urban experience, one that was truly totalizing in its perspective. Could we as spectators comprehend such a story? Would we have the time or interest to experience the complex interweaving of its various plot strands? Could we feel its rhythms and witness the unfolding of random chance, romantic predestination, and urban indifference? Could we stand over the sum total of human experience as if it were a panorama or a picture postcard? This would be a truly celestial—and inhuman—perspective.

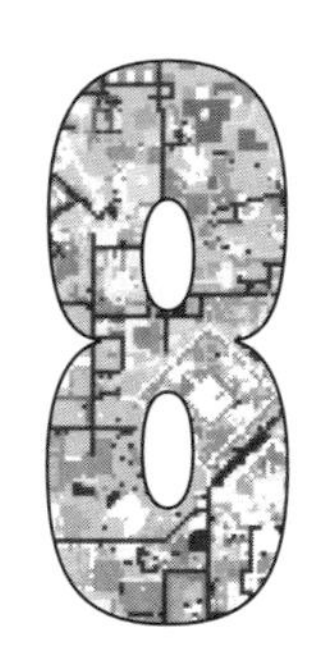

IMAGE RENEWAL

POLEMIC AND PRESENTATION IN THE URBAN THEORY OF REM KOOLHAAS AND LEON KRIER

Sandy Isenstadt

■ EDITORS' OVERVIEW

Architectural critic Sandy Isenstadt asks readers to join him and authors Rem Koolhaas and Leon Krier in imagining the contemporary city as being composed entirely of images. This approach is the result of his observation that the modern media have exponentially multiplied the volume of visual images and accelerated the speed and reach of their dissemination. At the same time, the circulation of words has been so infused with pictorial material that the contemporary city is populated by these visual hybrids. In such an atmosphere, two leading urban polemicists have proposed contradictory goals for urban design.

Krier and Koolhaas agree that the city as an embodiment of modernism, with its functional buildings and specialized land use, has been a terrible mistake. Both are also masters of the media image climate and take direction from its qualities.

Over the course of the past twenty-odd years, Krier has developed a series of pictorial texts that simultaneously express his criticism of the modern city and present his alternative goals. The means are artful drawings, carefully simplified so that they contrast nicely with contemporary cartoons and photography. They are old-fashioned, somewhat like children's illustrations where you can envision the peaceable kingdom from the posture of the animals. Krier places people in neoclassical settings where civility and community can be read directly from the imagery.

His idealized urban quarters are bastions of recovered *Gemeinschaft* and a key prototype for today's New Urbanist sensibility.

Koolhaas also has classical roots, but he is racing away from them. The ideograph for the city, the crossroads in the circle, represents his core understanding. The city is a place where strangers come to exchange. But Koolhaas does not want Krier's leisurely market square, he wants to accelerate exchange and invention. For him the modern functional city is too clumsy, too confining, an obstacle to maximum information flow. The grid could be his diagram; it is a design that allows movement in every direction, and mobility itself is his measure of a good city. In such a place, the role of the architect is to invent images that both facilitate and control flows.

INTRODUCTION: VISUAL CITIES

Architects have long considered visualization skills the backbone of their profession, recognizing early on that images encompass social philosophies as well as arrangements of rooms and that they build careers as much as they guide masons. At least two things are new, however. First is the ever-increasing circulation of images and what might be termed the velocity of visualization: Modern media have caused the production, distribution, and subsequent absorption of images to be both sweeping and swift. Second, images are deeply discursive—that is to say, they are embedded in texts. Word-image relations are, of course, an ancient preoccupation, but the speed with which they morph changes irrevocably how they are understood. Constant contact with a complex and ephemeral visual landscape has bred a population remarkably adept at navigating those complexities casually, indifferently. Whole academic fields, from public relations to visual studies programs, have emerged to examine and control the verbal-visual amalgam that makes up much of the texture of everyday life.[1]

Even those architects who do not draw explicitly from the media flood, or who resist or remain indifferent to it, are subject to the circulation of images of materials, building products, contemporary design work, and, perhaps most importantly, a clientele increasingly expert at symbolic reckoning. These new citizens of spectacle look upon even traditional images and traditional media with the powers and shortcomings of their capacity to evaluate and absorb streaming imagery. MTV and Michelangelo are both part of a perpetual circulation of images. The reception of architecture is likewise conditioned by modern media. Embedded today within wider contexts of portrayal, architects compete with each other for the media's attention, whereas buildings compete with media for the public's attention. Architectural relevance, in turn, means mastery—to some extent—of the circulation of images.

Rem Koolhaas and Leon Krier are two contemporary masters of media. Although occupying—or, rather, defining—opposite sides of an ideological divide regarding contemporary urbanism, both architects have made drawing and graphic design central to the formulation of their positions. In so doing, they have put forth urban visions that stick to the memory like a television jingle. In the process, both have advanced their polemics and their careers considerably. Negotiating the modern world of global communication, Krier and Koolhaas both understand that their work will be experienced by most observers as images, or "image texts," and that the strength of their arguments—their agendas for urban form—depends on the clarity and power of those images. As in any polemic, and especially for audiences with notably short attention spans, those images must be so much sharper or more fractious to ensure that their profiles will remain sharp thousands of miles or different languages away. This essay considers these two publicist-polemicists in terms of how their images advance their arguments regarding the direction for urban change.

SPENT CITY: THE USES OF URBAN EXHAUSTION

Modernism suffered some bad spin in 1978. Three publications—Maurice Culot and Leon Krier's "The Only Path for

Architecture," Rem Koolhaas's *Delirious New York*, and Colin Rowe and Fred Koetter's *Collage City*—all appeared that year to dismantle and bury modern architecture and urbanism.[2] The authors did not have to work very hard to make their cases. Kevin Lynch had already refocused attention from the monumental visions of architects and planners to the urban perceptions of taxi drivers, and Jane Jacobs's landmark indictment of modernism had been standing nearly twenty years. With rebuilding programs in postwar Europe and urban renewal projects in the United States, the technocratic mandate and blank face of modernist urbanism were already an all too familiar part of everyday city landscapes. The dust from the destroyed Penn Station settled in 1963 to reveal a band of citizens railing against the willful and unrestrained desecration of civic treasures for short-term profit; events like the razing of Boston's West End after 1958 added malice and misery, while the demolition of Pruitt-Igoe that commenced in 1972 concluded the story with irony. It was, in fact, only after its end that the story of rise and decline could be told so cogently in three memorable and much-reproduced images: Le Corbusier's utopian cities of the 1920s, their implementation in postwar projects such as Stuyvesant Town and Peter Cooper Village in New York, and the implosion of Pruitt-Igoe.

The issue in 1978, then, was less the death of modernist urbanism than what would be taking its place. More than just a matter of competing historical perspectives, each text, and its accompanying images, set the stage, in logical terms, for what should come next. The critique of modernism became the first step in new directions for urban change; where we have been is one way to determine where to go. Krier and Culot suggested we find our way back to history, believing that modernism, rather than being a decisive leap forward, was a stumble, a brier patch mistaken for a broad path. Industrialization was a necessary historical step, but the subsequent fetishization of industry through modernist architecture and urbanism was a categorical mistake of historic proportions. The only alternative was to resume the straight-and-narrow path so perilously abandoned: "Only the traditional urban fabric can lead to satisfactory counter-measures to the social and physical disintegration of the city."[3] Koolhaas was more oblique. In *Delirious New York,* modernist urbanism, in the form of Le Corbusier's Radiant City, appears reactive and sober, a post hoc attempt to represent modernity better than New York had already been doing. Rather than being revealed in modernist icons, the monuments of modernism were artfully hidden in public, in places like Rockefeller Center and Coney Island. Modernism's actual entrance into Manhattan, occasioned by the city's self-revelation, was the start of its decline: New York, Koolhaas wrote, "had no defense mechanism against the virulence of any explicit ideology." Consequently, Koolhaas advocated developing the previously unspoken mechanisms of Manhattan's "culture of congestion" into "an explicit doctrine that can transcend the island of its origins to claim its place among contemporary urbanisms."[4]

Fig. 8.1: "The Houses in front of the Station/The Evocative Meeting," 1978. Leaving the railway station, Leon Krier is astonished at the plain good sense exercised in the reconstruction of "the center of Brussels after its dismemberment by the construction of the Nord-Midi railway link." Letting fall his baggage and eyeglasses, this imaginary encounter with his friend Maurice Culot and a somehow familiar Brussels will be unmediated by such paraphernalia. Just as spontaneously, "an active level of social interaction has replaced the former desolation resulting from a 'modern' urbanism based on the principle of unbridled individual mobility."

Collage City appears in retrospect to be the more balanced work. New and old coexist within collage, a rubric that is plural at its core; it endows the stitching together of disparate pieces with both aesthetic authority and functional inevitability. Borrowing from Levi-Strauss, the authors counterposed the scientistic leanings of modernism with the finite horizons and limited means of the *bricoleur,* a figure possessing individual facility rather than professional training, whose contingent form-making both questions and complements the "engineer," modernism's iconic figure. Where Rowe and Koetter normalize a once avant-garde representational technique to counterbalance custom and invention, Koolhaas presents Manhattan as a model of total, nearly manic invention, while Krier and Culot excoriate modernism's unreasoning hunger for progress and, in thirteen evocative drawings that illustrate their text, imagine that older urban customs can be recovered (fig. 8.1). Where Rowe and Koetter theorize internal strategies for urban design but hesitate to point them in a direction, Krier and Culot and Koolhaas focus precisely on those social energies formalists hoped to evade.

Perhaps for these reasons, the proposals of Krier and Culot, on the one hand, and Koolhaas, on the other, have remained the more vivid and turned out to be the more influential over time. Notwithstanding the sophistication of *Collage City,* the other works are edgier, more sharply drawn. They risk nuance for the clarity of their visual destination. They seek compact and memorable claims that sink quickly and deeply into the reader's consciousness. They invent visual stories to make what was unseen or forgotten or not spoken seem somehow familiar, self-evident. Both pieces, and the work that has followed from each camp, recognize the role of effective, even preemptive imaging as a way to advance architectural and urban theories.

URBAN HISTORY FOR BEGINNERS

Although the hazards of criticizing modernism today are few, no one has done so more succinctly than Krier. In a series of diagrams developed since the late seventies, he has captured, codified, and caricatured many of the complaints leveled against modern ideas of planning (figs. 8.2, 8.3).[5] Most prominent of these ideas is, for Krier, the zoning of urban districts by function. Zoning is no more than a misguided effort to extend and replicate the industrial revolution's specialization of labor in the workplace into the compartmentalization of all dimensions of social life. It results in monocultures: one environment to work in, one in which to shop; a place for family, a place for recreation, a place to be entertained—all linked by cars. With each place designed around a single function, a distinct and inevitably exclusive interpersonal culture is built. As individuals circulate daily through these environments, they subtly shift their behavior to be in accord with them. The cumulative result is that in shifting their place-based personae, they eventually lose track of

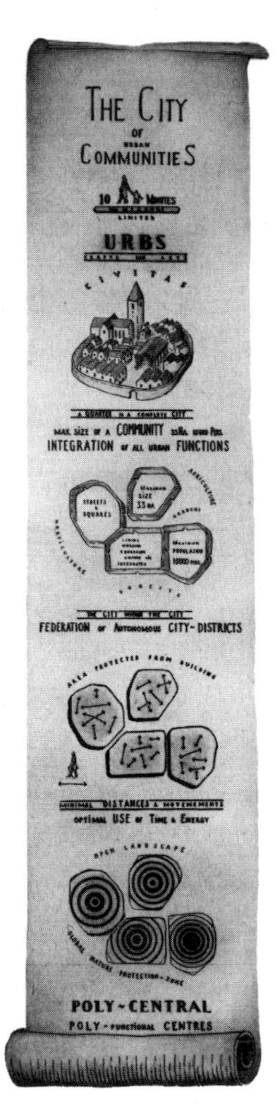

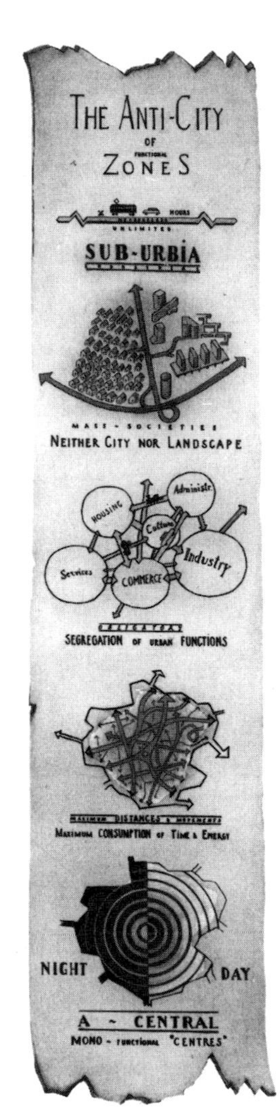

Fig. 8.2 ***(left)*****: City vs. Anti-City, 1978–1984. Two scrolls tell the story of longstanding antagonists. Neither city nor landscape, the "anti-city" is characterized by arrows aiming elsewhere, suggesting this urban form is somehow insufficient, an acid rebuke to its functional rationale. Time itself has left the ends of its scroll-story ragged. The city of communities is multifaceted, integrated, and complete in itself.**

Fig. 8.3 ***(below)*****: "Res Publica, Res (Economica) Privata, Civitas." 1 + 1 = 2, a simple sum that modernism's new math disallowed.**

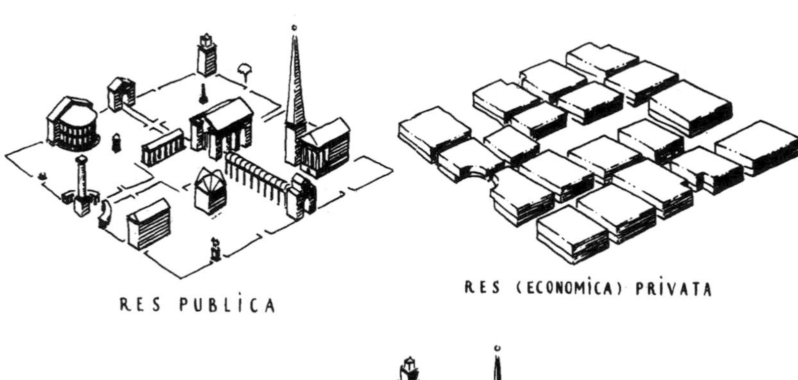

who they really are. Alienation of self, concludes Krier, historically has been a result of zoning.

Krier's diagrams counterpose the modern to the traditional city: The terms are clearly stated, the opposition well established and visibly balanced, the conclusion inescapable (fig. 8.4). Functional zoning has atomized society into an aggregate of one-dimensional activity settings, in contrast to the traditional city's functional chiaroscuro. Dependence on the car has emptied cities of human form and alienated the body from distance, once the key to an understanding of both space and time. Modern cities express new technologies of material production; traditional cities reproduce social values. Modern cities grow by hypertrophy, getting ever larger until they collapse from their monstrous violation of natural law; traditional cities grow as families grow, organically, not only in accord with nature, but in a way that allows for the passing of knowledge from generation to generation. Zoning also leads to megastructures, where the alternatives are either monotony or meaningless difference between otherwise identical parts. Having explained current urban degradation by reference to traditional cities, the obvious next step in reversing the process is to reclaim the city's birthright, a common architectural and urban language.

Much is left out of Krier's diagrams. Industry, for instance, appears only in the modern city; in the traditional city, "industry," "services," and "administration" become integrated as "working." We have to read elsewhere to learn that Krier advocates an economy based on artisanal production. Did traditional cities, with preindustrial sanitation, support other sorts of alienation? Athenian democracy surely had its high points, but what about Athenian health care or food distribution? Such questions are

Fig. 8.4: Two Forms of Growth, 1983. "Multiplication," where families grow the way nature intended, with two human beings first mating and then making room for others; and "Obesity," where excessive consumption leads to a couple's monstrous growth: crowding the frame and discharging some unidentifiable substance, there is no indication of intimate relations.

lost, since the diagrams traffic exclusively in answers. And this is their strength: They are complete in their own terms. Lucid self-evidence that transcends niggling questions is their currency. Even to raise questions, a critic must step outside the oppositions put forth by the diagrams. Criticisms require alternative representations to introduce terms beyond those chiseled in Krier's diagrams. It is this air of having been stripped to essentials, upon which a balanced comparison can be made, that gives them their power. They share in the efficacy of caricature: Traits are exaggerated but they are distinctive, belonging decisively to either one city or the other. The vital inheritance versus the modernist mutation: The solution to urban decline is as apparent as the diagram of the traditional city is legible.

While the comparisons of modern and traditional are diagrammatic and the drawings themselves are simple, we know Krier is a sophisticated critic. We know this because he is so obviously in control of the references he makes in these diagrams. They reflect various traditions, those he is aligned with and those he is set against. His "spoken" position—that is, his argument—is against functional zoning. He makes the case at one point with a diagram taken from Ebenezer Howard, an early advocate of the separation of urban functions. Krier is fond as well of biplanes, a direct homage to Le Corbusier, who figures prominently for Krier as modernism's most beguiling villain. He uses the format of modernist drawings and draws in the style of key modernists to argue against modernism. He caricatures modernism's own rejection of history to reject modernism. His unabashed promotion of classicism is entirely beholden to the self-righteousness of modernism's own earlier self-promotion. He learns from a cartoonist like Jacques Martin even as he castigates depraved forms of middle-class culture, which, one imagines, includes comics. He represents, in other words, not just places but representation itself. Krier's unspoken position, then, is more complex than his apparent frankness; the diagrams may be dismissed for their willful disregard of complicating issues, but Krier, so much in command of modernism's rhetorical forms, cannot be so easily dismissed. Frank and ironic, direct and coy, serious and playful, earnest and nonchalant, ambitious and self-effacing, Krier's oeuvre is paradigmatically postmodern. His images invite us to settle in a world of depth, a preoptical time before our present-day preoccupation with images.

Certainly, his critics are most comfortable with this Krier: an artist who comments on the condition of art in his age. Recognizing his intelligence and cogent positions, but unable to embrace his traditional planning solutions, critics often focus on his drawings precisely as images. In a telling moment captured in *The Charlottesville Tapes,* for instance, his critics and friends—who had vehemently rejected his arguments until this point—suddenly notice the beauty of his drawings and dote on his technique. Thus, they sidestep the content of his proposals. It is easier for them to accept his work as an image rather than as a concrete proposal. Most curious is that this recurrent drift is not one that Krier himself seems eager to inhibit. It allows him, perhaps, to smuggle polemical content underneath the mantle of rhetorical mastery.[6]

BEGINNINGS OF FUTURE URBANISM

Krier's proposals for urban form likewise aim for a sense of direct, unmediated representation. They rely on line drawings, simply presented perspectives, distinct frames, singular sources of light and unambiguous shadows, scale figures, and narrative captions (fig. 8.5). They often include an "establishing shot," an overview that provides a spatial and temporal framework enclosing the action to follow. Here, the urban order is laid out and already accommodating activities both public and private; the urban edge is certain and shows respect for the lightly farmed landscape beyond. Proposing a legible place and a navigable territory, the overview is a cognitive key that opens the door to the terms by which the larger landscape may be said to be moral. The drawings often also include what might be called a "telling detail," a detail that, by being both specific and irrelevant to the overall subject, indicates the irreducible manifold of lived experience; it convinces us of the authenticity of the scene. The detail's superfluity demonstrates the "unconstructed"

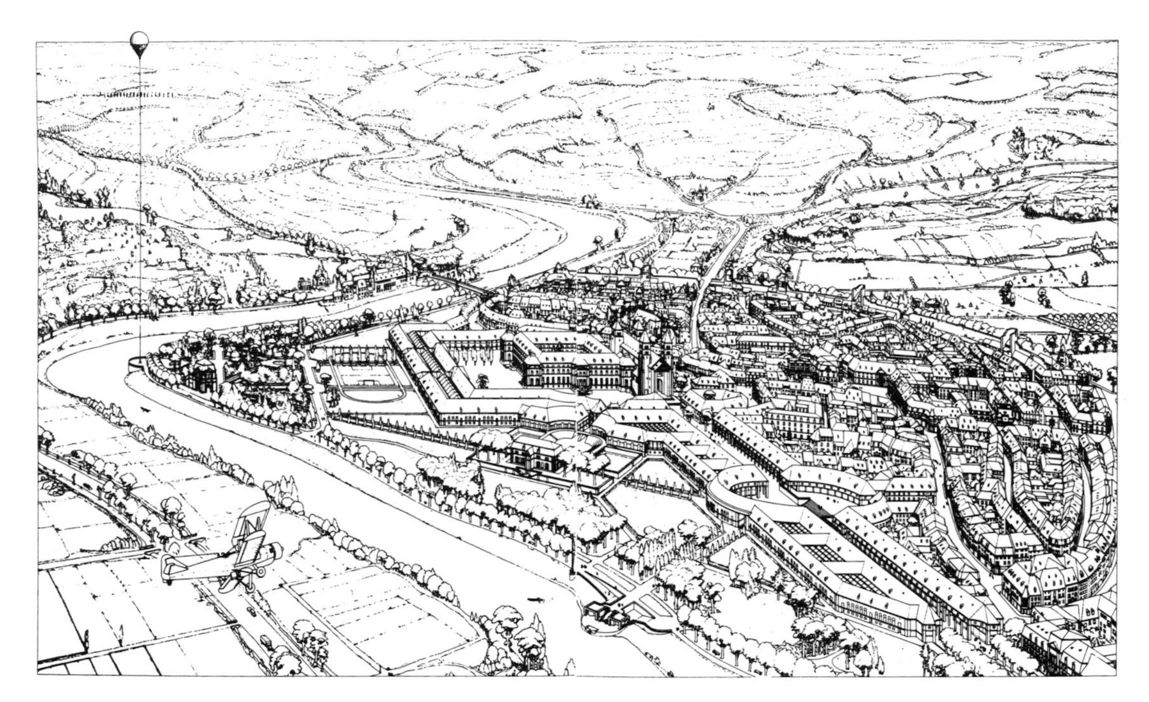

Fig. 8.5: Extension to the St. Willibrord Abbey, Echternach, 1970. A moment of transition for Krier, this project threw his "last remains of modernist thinking into terminal crisis." The bird's-eye view format, however, continues to appear in his work and usually includes well-marked urban boundaries, signs of everyday life that manage not to overshadow the architecture, a well-composed detail such as the balloon which, here, emphasizes the frame by breaking it in a precise fashion, and a biplane. Other drawings echo the wavy lines and 1920s roadsters of Le Corbusier. The façade of Le Corbusier's Planeix house appears five doors in from the right center edge, as well as, Krier tells us, "remnants of the 1968 student revolts."

nature of the image, making it, in terms of genre, a depiction rather than a polemic. Its ephemerality emphasizes, by contrast, the stability of the setting.

The drawings propose a reality much more legible, in fact, than the actual visual field which, as perceptual psychologists have demonstrated, is laced with movement, moments of inattention, and mental constructs that bridge the inevitable aporia of our limited perceptual equipment. In these drawings, such difficulties are not represented. It is a privilege of images, of course, to select parts of worlds, real and imagined, and to reconfigure them into idealized presentations. In Krier's case, however, the ease of reading such drawings combines with a cultural awareness of the forms presented to create almost an intimacy with those forms, as if, indeed, classicism were not a time-bound cultural expression but a formal pattern already resonant with the very tools of perception of those who might occupy it.

Like the figures within his scenes, Krier's images are working, but the labor comes easily. In a post-Levi's world, workers wear sweaters and vests, waiters wear tails, men perambulate—their canes tell us so—while togas rub up against jackets and ties. A laborer finds time to admire a sculpture; work in this place is

Fig. 8.6: Spitalsfields Market, 1986. An ordered architecture furnishes the theater of leisure and legibility, literally.

neither so sweaty nor atomized that it precludes beauty. The occasional isolated figure, the solitary self for whom the world has been ordered, pauses in reverie to take it all in. In general the scenes are lightly populated, which increases our attention to the setting (fig. 8.6). A hint of the theatrical, as in the cities of de Chirico or Serlio and in contrast with modernism's strident staginess, raises expectations of a narrative that can be fulfilled only by the architecture itself. Taken together, the comfort and generosity within which human interaction is accommodated in Krier's urban visions, along with notions of a harmonious society based on crafts, respect, and kindness as a foil to modernist anomie, make it hard to recall what is really so controversial about his proposals.

A NEW YORK MINUTE

In *Delirious New York,* Rem Koolhaas rewound and then rebroadcast, at high speed, the history of New York: Rockefeller Center, "the greatest urban complex of the twentieth century," was finished in an animated half-hour and not a decade; in fifty-odd postcard pages the sun rose and set thousands of times on the rise and decline of Coney Island; Le Corbusier and Dali departed under clouds of criticism just paragraphs after they had arrived; and, throughout, New York architects' voices were hurried, high, and hilarious. The book called attention to, historically analyzed, codified, reveled in, and attempted to compound the "culture of congestion" that Manhattan produces like few other places on earth. As New York temporarily changes a visitor's perception, irretrievably so for its residents, Koolhaas changed his readers' understanding of the city.

At the core of Koolhaas's intellectual agenda is the city as the locus of experience. In keeping with a long tradition of urban observation, often dated to Baudelaire, Koolhaas considers the city pleasingly neurotic, surrealistic and mentally stimulating, and inadvertently critical in its unplanned convergences of dissimilarities; it keeps you guessing. *Delirious New York* made clear that the lesson of time-lapse photography lies as much in the possibility of changing our relationship with time, and whatever happens in time, as it does in the forms and patterns revealed by seeing fast. Seeing the already known anew was akin to newly making the world. Having compressed time enough to reveal the form of urban growth—that is, to bring change within the limited horizons of human perspective—*Delirious New York* suggested a new raw material for architects and planners to shape.

In considering New York's built landscape, Koolhaas did not focus on its economic or political forces, as nearly every other urban history does. Instead, he reflected on the fantasies, the "human obsessions," behind the forces that undergird these urban developments. The city appears as a nearly autonomous force, its unspoken goal the triumph of the artificial, a place where every corner is marked by human desire, hope, vertigo, or amusement. Le Corbusier saw something modern there, but, as Koolhaas tells it, the very idea of Manhattan so dwarfed his own urban visions that he had to deny New York in order to appropriate it, surreptitiously and beneath the level of his own

Fig. 8.7: Needle and Sphere. "The most voluminous building ever proposed in the history of mankind, [the Globe Tower] combines in a single Gestalt the opposites—needle and sphere—that have been the extremes of Manhattan's formal vocabulary ever since the Latting Observatory and the balloon of the Crystal Palace were juxtaposed in 1853. It is impossible for a globe to be a tower." Is it delirious even to imagine such a thing?

comprehension. Of course, no one at the time could possibly have acknowledged marshaling millions for private fantasies, in part because only the passage of time has allowed for this perspective. This is the reason for Koolhaas's own description of his book as a "retroactive manifesto," the script that appears only after the performance is done. This is also a key to understanding how the book works and what the implications are for future urbanisms.

The text is built on a field of paradoxes: Logically opposed at one level, paradoxes manifest their truths in other planes of abstraction. Hindsight raised to the level of foresight, "retroactive manifesto" is only the first of many. Numerous phrases set in oppositional terms—"intuitive cartography" is a random instance—underpin more-developed paradoxes, like the recurring encounter of needle and sphere (fig. 8.7). These loom large at points and then are lost, like an orienting landmark eclipsed by the close at hand. Taken together, puzzles both trifling and profound pull at the cognitive categories that keep otherwise unquestioned conventions in place. Koolhaas's most significant contradiction involves the gap between building exteriors, informed by historicist ornament, and their interiors, preoccupied entirely by the expedient accommodation of function. Without ado, architects widened this gap as buildings grew bigger, unintentionally ratcheting the radically new into the comfortably familiar. This architectural invention, which Koolhaas calls "lobotomy" and "schism," incrementalizes the introduction of social change at the same time that it removes limits to change, precisely by disconnecting the standards of one realm from another. With judgment relativized, lobotomy implies the impossibility of a "moral" architecture.

Krier, by contrast, bases his explicit claims for a moral architecture on the clear markings of his moral compass: One term in each of his conceptual oppositions is made subordinate to its counterpart. Koolhaas, on the other hand, keeps his terms equal: Wholly incommensurate, they somehow exist in the same place. An epigraph from F. Scott Fitzgerald captures the direction of Koolhaas's thinking: "The test of a first-rate intelligence is the ability to hold two opposite ideas in the mind at the same time, and still retain the ability to function."[7] In contrast, modernism's ideal of an exterior generated from the interior and wholly transparent to function appears rather dim.

The city's grid, for Koolhaas, is what prevents urban lobotomy from becoming dysfunctional (fig. 8.8). It is a completely rationalized device that enfranchises fantasy, gives it a place, and makes it safe for the everyday. The grid makes space for isolated urban gestures and, in so doing, creates a community of inde-

Fig. 8.8: The City of the Captive Globe, 1972. Separate plinths facilitate the development of variant architectures and rival theories. The earth itself is bred from the growth, competition, and death of these disparate academies.

pendent values. A fluid order, a crystallized chaos, a medium for facilitating and relating differences, the grid institutionalizes nonconformity. It is to the city what collage is to the graphic arts. Claiming the book is itself structured like a grid, less a narrative than independent blocks of meaning, Koolhaas reenacts the myriad paradoxes, large and small, sweet and lethal, that are both ground and climax of Manhattan.

SIZE MATTERS

In an epilogue for his La Villette project, Koolhaas states that Manhattan has remained for him and his office an enduring obsession. The La Villette scheme is imagined as a skyscraper on its side: Just like identical floors stacked to the sky, a series of programmatic bands across the site separate and consolidate distinct activities (fig. 8.9). Other organizational devices are laid over the bands: point grids, access paths, singular elements. These demarcate programs but also increase unplanned encounters, which is where social energy is generated. It is not so much a design, Koolhaas argues, as a *framework* for perpetual changes that will exceed any *architecture* that might be designed for the site. Here, the grid figures as one part of this larger framework.[8]

The oblique intersections that result from overlapping rationalities become a common strategy in the architectural and urban design work of Koolhaas's office, OMA (Office for Metropolitan Architecture). This strategy is also employed in *S, M, L, XL,* a catalog of OMA's work through 1995, produced in collaboration with graphic designer Bruce Mau. Rather than a chronology reinforced by index, table of contents, and narrative, *S, M, L, XL* is ordered by several means, most notably, by size. The child's first system of classification—"How big?"—orders the presentation of sophisticated architectural designs; the consumer logic of ready-to-wear clothing underpins a practice based exclusively on custom design. The firm's design work is also described in dictionary form, an alphabetical (arbitrary) exposition of content. Comprised mostly of quotes from other people, it sets out in comprehensive fashion (A to Z) the integers of Koolhaas's urban theories, but without rules for their combination. At a finer level, certain themes, sometimes typographic, sometimes photographic, sometimes topical, create a kind of local topography in the book. All the while, a thread of digits tenaciously holds the bottom outside corner of each page. Each device organizes content, but partially, like a point of view. Each, moreover, is legible as a system, since the reader may observe its organizing capacities through the lens of some other system. When a simple chronology of the firm's work finally appears at the end of the book—that is, toward its higher numerals—it seems as arbitrary and as admirable a classification system as size.

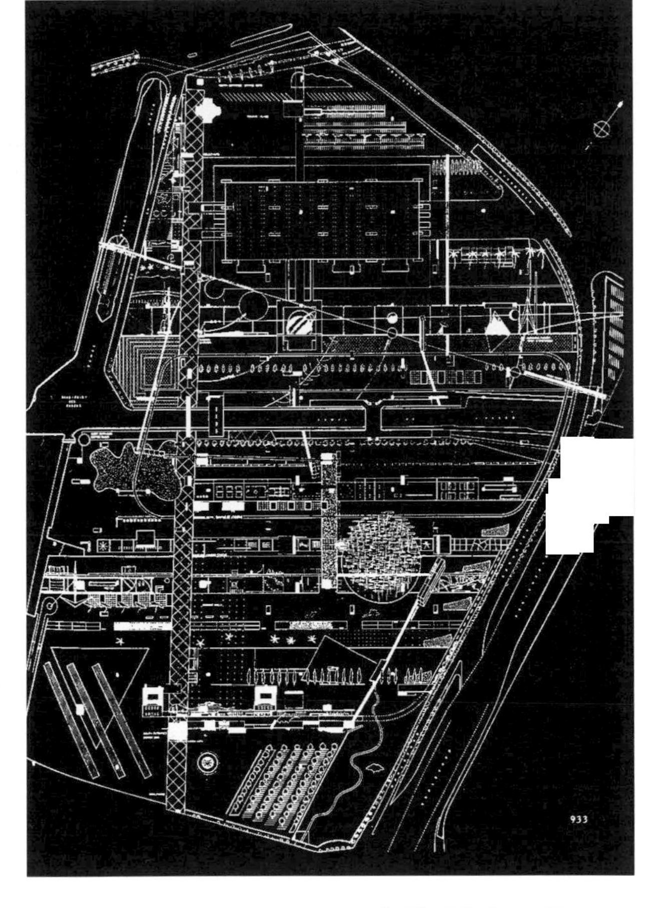

Fig. 8.9: Competition entry for Parc de la Villette, Paris, 1982. "We insist that at no time have we presumed to have produced a designed landscape," only programmatic bands running from east to west (left to right); point grids distributed in staccato rhythm "established mathematically on the basis of their desirable frequency"; access via a north–south boulevard; unique elements layered on top. Urban complexity cannot help but ensue. The strategy is likened to that employed in the design of Manhattan's Downtown Athletic Club.

While self-consciously unconventional, the book is both personal and navigable. One traverses the book rather than reads it, like some experimental novel, according to one's own inclination, yet still within parameters set by the author. Size is, in fact, a useful way to think about architecture: After all, architectural firms not only organize teams by project size, they often position themselves in the marketplace in terms of "how big." "Not big enough" was Le Corbusier's honestly dissembling pronouncement on New York's skyscrapers. But then, randomness also has its uses, in architecture and in life. The clear intention is to create a textual analog to the city, a space crossed by intersecting rationalities, multiple routes, each of which may, through effort and serendipity, lead to destinations both familiar and strange, like jump cuts in film or multiple focal lengths on split screens, or like discovering an imperial vista at the end of a crooked alley.

WHAT PACE IS THIS PLACE?

While contrary in their solutions, both Koolhaas and Krier respond to a shared diagnosis of contemporary urbanism. It is characterized by a mobility of people and things that for Koolhaas is both exhilarating and intoxicating and for Krier takes one step further into cultural madness. Krier's "city of stone" is counterposed to mobility; Koolhaas pushes total mobility to its conclusive "culture of congestion." Too much in flux; not enough.

In writing on what he calls "the space of flows," urban theorist Manuel Castells describes the functional logic that structures networks of exchanges. He goes on to suggest that this logic is already receiving cultural elaboration and that the space of flows will soon replace the space of places both as economic reality and social ideology. Similar to the structure of computer networks, Castells's "information-generating units" will be dispersed physically but connected by means variously indifferent to place, to topography, to territory, all of which reflect mankind's past, but may not be part of its future.[9] As media increasingly are part of the environment, space becomes more communicative and capable of participating in the flow of capital, of goods, of people, of images. Distributive processing will be the new organizing principle of human geography. From this perspective, both Koolhaas and Krier attempt to reterritorialize the space of flows.

In rejecting the current urban order, Krier does not pretend that the information age has yet to arrive. He simply refuses to allow it to be all there is. A psychological need and a human desire for legible communities are as much a part of the present condition as are new communication technologies or global corporations. In his paper at the 1998 MIT colloquium on which this book is based, Richard Sennett took this a step further, arguing that the two extremes are linked: Neotraditional New Urbanist residential communities offer appealingly nostalgic "images of restitution" that can represent the lone source of stability in an economy where lifetime attachment to single employers has become increasingly rare.[10]

Societies are not forced, but choose whether flexible workplaces or legible communities shall be the basis for an urban civilization; Castells's replacement of place with flow is in this sense not destiny but rather a prediction based on an expected failure to choose. Krier chooses to design a city to fit its inhabitants, not their tools; to make humankind the measure of building and not the machines used to build. That technology has led to new velocities in communication and distribution does not at all limit human philosophy to a consideration of speed.

Krier emphasizes instead destinations, places. The most convincing aspect of his work lies, as suggested above, in his ability to evoke a place. His drawings, moreover, provide various markers that suggest arrival, a cycle completed. Occasional vestiges of an industrial past, for instance, suggest a mentality molded by concerns for preservation as well as the charm of industrial architecture after it has been dismantled. It is a postnegotiation place: after the self-interest of private property has melted away, after manufacturers have decentralized all production, after the spontaneous realignment of opinion. We have moved beyond the relativizing, paralyzing effects of flux and are being rewarded for having chosen good architecture over bad. This quality of closure, of having already arrived, is what lends Krier's images a sense of having been removed from time. The passing pleasures of its pictured inhabitants emphasize the geological pace of urban change, like flowering brush on the face of a mountain. Krier's project is utopian in that he images a destination but slights the steps necessary to arrive there.[11] Without elaborating the means to achieve this utopia, based on artisanal production and proximate relations, Krier's drawn cities stand in for a social destination. He depicts the city to express civility. The goal is the good society, which already knows, and doesn't need to learn, how to build for its own well-being.

However, insisting on direct relations between an image and what it represents can, in cultural elaborations of capitalist logic, have an effect opposite that intended. Krier seeks to reinstate an urban order interrupted by industrialization. He recognizes, though, that modern citizens require images of good architecture and stories of moral behavior (presented obliquely through critiques of amoral modernism) in order to read classical environments properly; we must know them well enough to want them spontaneously. This is possible, Krier argues, because a sufficient level of cultural memory is embodied in classically inspired architecture and urbanism; people already prefer classically styled buildings over modern ones, all else being equal. Accustomed to facile readings of visual material, however, we need Krier's career's worth of image texts to understand this particular set of images as not just images but social and moral imperatives.

In other words, a classical vocabulary retains enough meaning to make it significant once employed, but it is not so specific in meaning that it can't be appropriated. In fact, a classical vocabulary is particularly well suited for appropriation. It is, today, a vocabulary without a grammar, perfect for people whose primary mode of assimilation is pastiche. It is an attitude that assumes the past is as accessible a source of urban form-making as the present. Recent popular success of communities based on principles of New Urbanism (including Poundbury, the English town designed by Krier) depends upon the fact that people do not have an attachment to specific places but require signs of place to locate them, to repeat to them their values. A promotional brochure for Kentlands, Maryland,[12] for instance, pictures those physical elements that capture a sense of small-town community: time-worn ironwork, casual conversations across picket fences, a newspaper and pot of geraniums casting long morning shadows across the front steps, porches, chance meetings of mothers on sidewalks, not to mention the housing styles that emphasize places—a dormer, a stair landing window, a half-open door, a sidelight—where an individual can look on the world with satisfaction and with privacy: grains of ready-made meaning in the solvent of commercial culture.

For Koolhaas, on the other hand, there is no destination: The trip, mobility itself, is the objective. Indeed, Koolhaas argued in *Delirious New York* that it was an explicit theory—that is, knowledge of a destination—that led to the demise of Manhattan's original promise. The city's builders had to con-

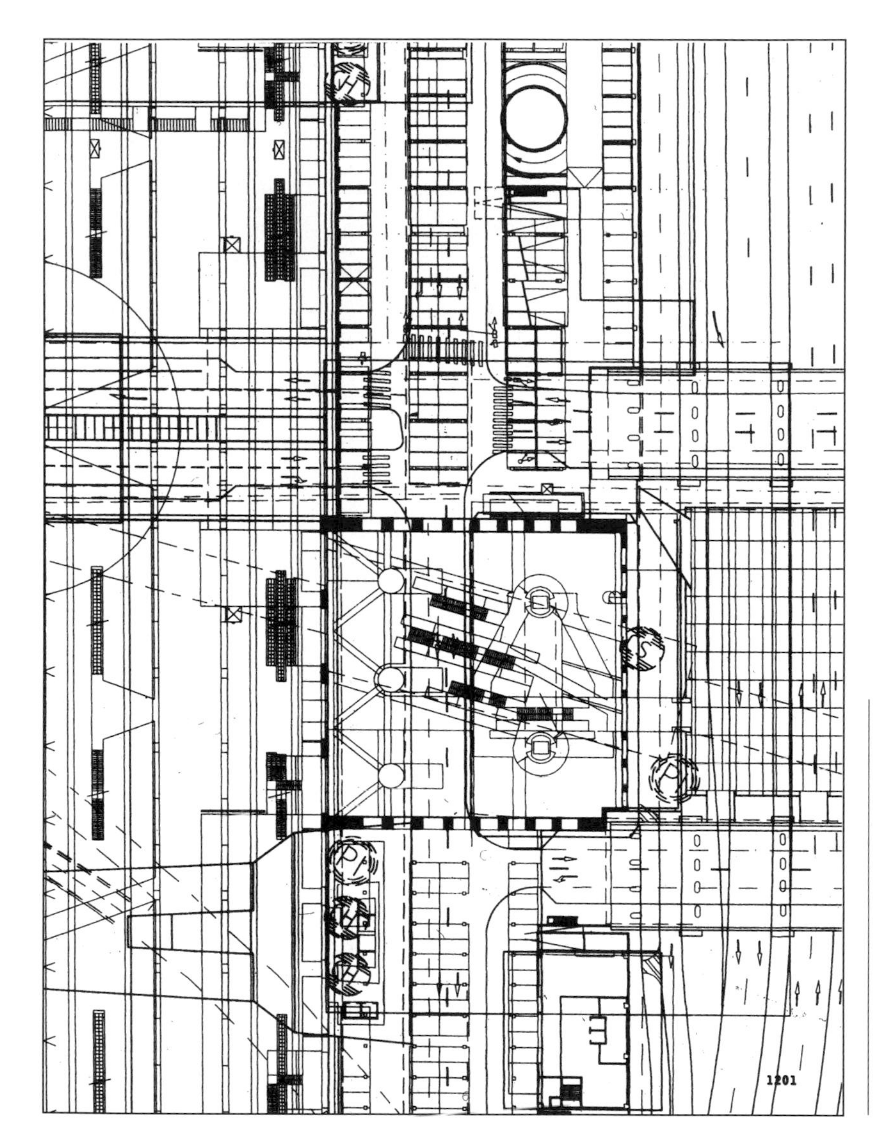

Fig. 8.10: Euralille, Centre International d'Affaires, Phase I, 1994. The Espace Piranesien is OMA's only direct formal proposal. Mostly a hole, it reveals the various forces in their typical habitat and at their typical rate as they cross the site. Flows—media, services, goods, rails, automobiles, and people—take a form here.

sciously forswear a goal in order to arrive at it. OMA's Euralille project, a master plan for 800,000 square meters of transit service and urban support, is premised on this notion: "What is important about this place is not where it is but where it leads, and how quickly"[13] (fig. 8.10). The speed of Lille's connections to other places, not its location, is what puts it on the map of newly integrated Europe; it is not the only path for social flows, just the fastest. Movement and the regional perspective that emerges from rapid transportation are the basis of Euralille's formal palette, which is flush with long, arcing lines, with high-tech materials, with sweeps of flat surfaces, and with sudden formal shifts that echo the instantaneous transgression of national boundaries. OMA felt compelled to design in detail only "the point of greatest infrastructural density," where different rates of movement exist side by side. They called it "Espace Piranesian," presumably for its vision of alternately swelling and receding ways of getting places, without an end in sight.

Both Krier's and Koolhaas's responses to flow have their implications. In one of the designed serendipities of *S, M, L, XL,* for instance, the following definition of "stupid" appears during the description of Euralille. It characterizes stupid by reference to tourism, a kind of travel undertaken to demonstrate that one has traveled. "Tourism is the march of stupidity. . . . There is nothing to think about but the next shapeless event." Euralille, as the jumping-off point for countless excursions, would seem to be very stupid. Coney Island, as described in *Delirious New York,* with its themed rides attracting day tourists, can be no better. The thrill of moving fast overshadows the fact that you're not going anywhere. The tourist moves past richly imagined places just as the city, with its differential rates of change, moves around its citizens. Koolhaas attempts to maximize this quality, to superimpose programs and channeled space: to "restore both density and continuity—the return of complexity as a sign of the urban." One of Koolhaas's goals is the elimination of goals, the "staging of uncertainty." Koolhaas explicitly argues that arrival can never be marked: "The access protocol of telematics replaces that of the doorway." But, in abandoning destinations for possibilities, in allowing for partial points of view, in favoring "free" over "better," Koolhaas's relativizing strategy allows for the distinct possibility that citizens will be ushered unwittingly, even gladly, into regimes of subordination.[14]

At the same time that global flows relativize all values, a project like Euralille manages to relate the global to a specific point on the globe. It does so in two key ways. First, it gathers flows in a place, creating a node. Each flow must negotiate the local even as it pulses through it, like a stream rushing around stones. Flows are figured—that is, given figures as they come into contact with one another. The inevitable interconnections make each component more valuable, as with a computer network, but they are also the place where the system is most likely to unravel. In giving form to these discontinuities, or changes in rate, Koolhaas makes imageable what previously was not. Where they emerge in form, such global flows may, for a moment at least, be accountable. This will not stop flows but might, like "lobotomy," incrementalize them. Unexpectedly, then, Koolhaas's strategy seems poised to localize the flow of global goods and services, things and people. By catching up with the velocity of modern life, he is able to punctuate it, to have it resonate with the materials and places it passes through. Like *S, M, L, XL,* there is no privileged epistemological promontory, but there are many negotiations with partial knowledge. Locating his practice at the intersection of physical and virtual geographies, Koolhaas speculates that it is in the modulation of global flows over certain terrains that we will recognize the human.

GOODNESS AND FREEDOM IN FLUX

An image is a device to control flows, whether sacred images that direct divine energies or, more recently, media images of cities meant to attract investment. A primary vehicle of urban design discourse today, images of cities channel our knowledge of them. I had hoped when starting this project that considering two influential but antithetical producers of urban image texts would establish a spectrum of possible positions to occupy between them or at least suggest a place for consensus and compromise amid the conflicting stakes and scales of image construction. It did not. Krier's position does not at root allow compromise, and Koolhaas's does not allow Krier. Reviewing their work has, however, made it clear that anyone wanting to enter the mediated forum of public debate must understand how ideas are positioned, and how cities and stories of cities are imaged.

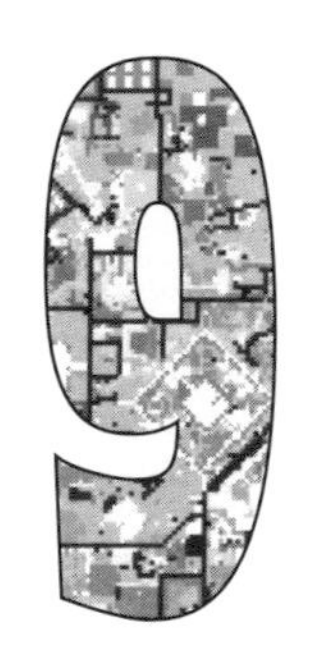

Anti-Urbanist City Images and New Media Culture

Thomas J. Campanella

■ EDITORS' OVERVIEW

Old images, commonly held and passed down from generation to generation, can direct new possibilities for urban life. Thus, the cultural geographer Thomas Campanella examines the tradition of American pastoralism as it manifests itself in the image world of the Internet. This communication system was devised to eliminate the hierarchies of space, the vulnerability of military information concentrated at big-city hubs. Now its civilian version offers space-free access to information: Everything can go everywhere. Campanella considers how the urban imagery is moving.

A long and deeply entrenched American tradition encourages the vision of an "engaged retreat," a life in a green setting that is also actively engaged in the quotidian world. Internet enthusiasts suggest that every Montana rancher who might wish to can imitate Jefferson's life at Monticello because the Net affords instant, world-wide communication. Campanella reminds us that this is not the first time such an idyllic vision has resulted from new technologies. The railroad and the automobile allowed for the realization of the suburban retreats of the twentieth century.

This same pastoralism carries with it a fearful anti-urbanism. Jefferson's fright at the Paris mobs, Poe's exploration of the evil city, and the parade of writers from Emerson to Frank Lloyd Wright repeatedly reinforced anti-urbanism. Their themes of barbarism, crime, and dereliction are now carried into computer games. Computer fiction

also nourishes its imagination with such fare. Perhaps the most dramatic example of the penetration of the pastoral into the world of the Internet came with the revival of millennialism. This time, instead of the end of the world in 1848 as calculated from biblical passages, problems with computers' clocks were expected to bring on the Apocalypse as the year 2000 dawned.

INTRODUCTION: ENGAGED RETREAT

This chapter examines an emerging dialectic in the relationship between new media technology and the city. It argues that our new digital "instruments of instant artificial adjacency"[1]—specifically the Internet—have been used to achieve an age-old American dream of pastoral retreat from the city. Against the larger backdrop of historical anti-urbanism in America, the essay explores the spatial affordances of this new technology and some representations of cities and urban life in digital media culture—in advertising, computer games, futurist literature, and the Y2K survivalist movement. Not only are these city images frequently negative, but the technology of the Net itself has made possible "engaged retreat" from urban life—gaining physical distance from the city while maintaining informational proximity and access to its many resources.

ANTI-URBANISM AND AMERICAN PASTORALISM

Americans have long expressed ambivalence—often outright hostility—toward the city. Even as great urban centers emerged in nineteenth-century America, many of the country's most influential political and intellectual leaders remained skeptical of the city's place or value in the nation's future. Thomas Jefferson, Ralph Waldo Emerson, Henry David Thoreau, Herman Melville, William Jennings Bryan, and Frank Lloyd Wright are among the many American intellectuals who considered the city a social, political, economic, and even moral liability.[2] Moreover, such thinkers concurred with a majority of Americans in favoring the pastoral countryside as the most propitious site for the American project.

The origins of American anti-urbanism are complex but may be traced first to the predominantly rural, agricultural character of the nation in its formative years; as late as 1860, more than 75 percent of the American population lived outside cities. Jefferson considered this largely agrarian population critical to the success of American democracy. His deep faith in the moral superiority of agriculture supplied "uncontested philosophical justification"[3] for the anti-urbanist pastoralism that, in time, would become a leitmotif of American history. Jefferson believed that cities were inherently corrupt; their mobs, he wrote in *Notes on the State of Virginia,* "added just so much to the support of pure government, as sores do to the strength of the human body."[4] In a letter to Benjamin Rush, written on the occasion of a yellow fever outbreak in several coastal cities, Jefferson argued that the disease, however lamentable, would perhaps discourage the growth of major urban centers. To him, the cities—rather than the disease—were a greater threat to "the morals, the health and the liberties of man."[5]

Bolstered by victory against the British in the War of 1812, America grew confident as a nation in the early decades of the nineteenth century. The country's expanding economic and military power during the Jacksonian period brought a new sense of nationalist pride and a new longing for a native source of national identity—something that would distinguish the young country in the eyes of the world. Americans believed, correctly, that their literary and artistic achievements paled in comparison to those of Europe and Asia. The nation did possess, however, an asset believed unmatched anywhere on earth: its rich and unspoiled natural landscape. Landscape was thus embraced, by the 1840s, as a core element of American national identity. The Hudson River, Niagara Falls, the White Mountains, and the elm-tossed vales of the Connecticut River were offered as collateral to the artifactual and cultural riches of the Old World. The deification of landscape shifted the locus of national identity away from cities and toward nature.

In the same period, European Romanticism, channeled through writers such as William Cullen Bryant, Emerson, Thoreau, and the Concord transcendentalists, introduced a spiritual dimension to nature. Influential "tastemakers" such as Andrew Jackson Downing, Susan Fenimore Cooper, and Nathaniel Parker Willis popularized a belief in the intrinsic superiority of rural and suburban environments—and by implication condemned the city as morally deficient. In the latter half of the nineteenth century, meteoric urban growth did little, paradoxically, to diminish root-level hostility toward cities—among either the clerisy or the population at large. As immigration increased, anti-urbanism took on a strongly nativist tone. Newcomers from Ireland, Italy, and Eastern Europe settled, for the most part, in large urban centers, further alienating the largely Anglo-Saxon rural majority.

As Leo Marx claimed, American anti-urbanist pastoralism manifested itself in both the rarefied precincts of literature and philosophy and in popular culture more generally.[6] One of the ironies here is that even as the city was condemned as a moral liability, Americans flocked to it in ever-increasing numbers. Between 1860 and 1900, America's urban population quadrupled, while dozens of rural communities in New England were being abandoned.[7] But the new urbanites were no less smitten by the charms of rural life; indeed, pastoralism, shorn of its less romantic aspects, increased in appeal with distance from the farm. In the 1850s, even as cities such as New York and Boston were gaining in density and population, the metropolitan envelope began crawling back out into the countryside. Seeking a mythic "middle landscape," shady respite from the chaos of industrial urbanization, Americans began building suburbia.

TECHNOLOGY AS THE ENABLER OF PASTORAL RETREAT

It is one of the central paradoxes in American landscape history that technology, the fruit of modern, urban civilization, became the primary means by which to escape the city and regain the "lost" pastoral life of an earlier age. The horse-drawn omnibus, the steam locomotive, the electric trolley, and, later, the automobile were each used to situate life farther from the city and closer to nature. The development of the streetcar enabled urbanites to settle semirural outlying districts yet remain within an easy commute of the city. Because streetcar lines all converged at the city center, the impact of this technology was to simultaneously expand the metropolis into the countryside while preserving the primacy of the center. The locomotive also caused suburban development to occur far from the city center; however, as the central station lay in the heart of town, this technology, too, did little to diminish the spatial authority of the city.

The automobile had a very different impact on the landscape, triggering extensive, free-form suburban development. The car also enabled people to take weekend jaunts out into the countryside, and as early as 1915 automobiles were being used for "autocamping" by thousands of middle-class Americans.[8] The Bronx River Parkway and the Westchester County park system were among the first infrastructural environments to celebrate the automobile as a means of urban escape and pastoral retreat.[9] The automobile became an essential part of "getting back to nature." The neopastoral counterculture movement of the 1960s chose an automobile as one of its definitive icons. We still associate the Volkswagen Beetle—a product of the Nazi-era German military-industrial machine—with flower children dancing on Yasgur's farm and singing ". . . we got to get ourselves / Back to the garden."[10] Marketing experts are well aware of the automobile's sustained appeal as an agent of the back-to-nature trend. The typical sport utility vehicle advertisement, for example, features unspoiled natural scenes in which well-heeled urban professionals enjoy a weekend romp in God's country.[11]

Indeed, ambivalence toward the city—and outright anti-urbanism—is still a fixture in the American psyche; and technology more than ever serves as its agent. In recent years, numerous writers have commented on the escalation of fear and loathing of the city, and a consequent withdrawal from urban public life.[12] This has occurred in spite of dramatic and well-publicized decreases in violent crime in most American cities. The increasing privatization of public space, the proliferation of gated communities, the rise of private police forces and electronic surveillance, and the popularity of aggressive, hulking sport utility vehicles all point to a rejection of the civitas. Rather than confront urban problems with social activism and government programs, we appear increasingly willing to turn our backs to the city and crawl into a safe shell of privatism. As Nan Ellin has written, one response to "postmodern insecurity" has been escapism—"characterized either by a retreat from the larger community (privatism) or a flight into collective or personal fantasy worlds that actively disregard the problems of real life."[13] In this country, nature has long been identified as a site of such escapism, and more recently, so has the cyberspace of the computer.

Digital media technology—particularly that of the networked personal computer—has aided and abetted the retreatist impulse. It has done so in at least two ways. First, the Internet has provided a whole new cultural space in which to pursue the very kinds of social interaction that once took place in the city, expanding "urbanness" without the bricks and mortar, or what Mel Webber referred to as "the non-place urban realm."[14] Secondly, the Net owes no allegiance to geography or place. It is, as William Mitchell has put it, a "fundamentally and profoundly *antispatial*" technology.[15] As a result, many historically "urban" functions, amenities, and sources of information have been displaced—detached from the built city and freed to relocate almost anywhere.

"ACTION AT A DISTANCE"

The inherent antispatiality of the Net counterpoints the most fundamental truth about cities: Cities are profoundly spatial, place-bound entities. Limitations on mobility and communications in the past required centralization. Physical proximity was essential to communication in the premodern "walking city," and as more and more individuals and organizations sought propinquity, the density of the city increased. But successive innovations in technology broke down the old spatial order. The trolley, locomotive, and automobile each expanded the time-space envelope of the city, allowing urban dwellers to live far from downtown. Successive advances in communications technology increasingly liberated human intercourse from the requirements of propinquity. As Lewis Mumford wrote in *Technics and Civilization*:

> With the invention of the telegraph a series of inventions began to bridge the gap in time between communication and response despite the handicaps of space: first the telegraph, then the telephone, then the wireless telegraph, then the wireless telephone, and finally, television. As a result, communication is now on the point of returning, with the aid of mechanical devices, to that instantaneous reaction of person to person with which it all began; but the possibilities of this immediate meeting, instead of being limited by space and time, will be limited only by the amount of energy available and the mechanical perfection and accessibility of the apparatus.[16]

More recent developments in communications and information sharing, most notably the Internet, have further diminished the limitations of space and time. In effect, this globe-spanning apparatus has permitted city-based, knowledge-intensive activities to break entirely free of the city's gravitational pull, and to recombine with a range of alternative geographies—including the rural countryside.

Along with related technologies such as cellular telephony, wireless data networks, broadband cable, and other innovations, the Net enables us to be informationally present from almost any location.[17] We can function as productive urban citizens from a rural retreat in Vermont, jacked into much of the same data flow that pours through the fiber optics of a Manhattan office building. Webber saw this coming a generation ago: "For the first time in history," he wrote, "it might be possible to locate on a mountain top and maintain intimate, real-time and realistic contact with business or other associates. All persons tapped into the global communications net would have ties approximating those used today in a given metropolitan region."[18] Anyone familiar with the World Wide Web can use it from any location to conduct library research, sample and purchase CDs and books, shop for groceries, arrange to test-drive a new car, make airline reservations, renew a driver's license, take a college course, meet a mate, and scan headlines from city dailies around the world—all activities that generally required urban presence not long ago. We can even observe, in synchronous real time (or close to it), cityscapes around the world via an expanding network of Web cameras.

The disengagement of information from place is a core part of the Internet's birthright. It evolved from a Cold War–era Defense Department initiative known as ARPANET. Developed in the late 1960s to enable defense researchers to share access to powerful mainframe computers, ARPANET was a multinodal knowledge organism that existed everywhere and nowhere at once. Its purpose was to assure that strategic intelligence remained in a state of perpetual suspension, thus assuring its security in the event of a military strike to any constituent site in the system. Many of the military research nodes joined by ARPANET were located in major urban areas, which had long been feared vulnerable to Soviet missile attack. Throughout the Cold War, urbanists such as Tracy Augur urged the diffusion of urban centers for precisely this reason, arguing that strategic resources (and population) should be distributed to a network of hinterland cities far from hot, glowing targets like New York and Washington.[19] ARPANET insulated intelligence from sabotage by disengaging it from the place and geography, in the process creating the invisible metageography we have come to call cyberspace.

By displacing information from the old context of place—particularly urban place—digital telecommunications technology is serving as an equalizer of geographies. Access to information is closing the information gap that once set the metropolis apart from the data-impoverished small town, or even the rural farm. The citizen in a rural New England community who taps in to the bit stream via cable modem is bypassing and, in effect, short-circuiting the information monopoly once possessed by the city. Marshall McLuhan captured the paradox therein: Media technology, fruit of modern industrial civilization, could well bring about a return of the nonurban, village-based life of the preindustrial age. He expressed this in what has become one of the most repeated mantras of the Information Age: "I think now of the city," he wrote in 1970, "as the planet itself, the urban village or global village." Indeed, with electronics, McLuhan observed, "any marginal area can become center." Or, put a slightly different way, "there are no remote places."[20]

The affordances of new media technology have given new life to the perennial American quest for pastoral retreat from urban life. If earlier technologies made the landscape more accessible to the city, the networked computer has effectively made the city more accessible to the landscape. We can have our city served to us in the garden, via a steady stream of bits. For the anti-urbanist, digital technology thus places within reach one of the holy grails of pastoralism—that is, the dream of *engaged retreat.* It enables us to connect to the great world of ideas and information—in a word, society—but from a remote, bucolic setting far from the city. This is, in effect, the ultimate resolution of what Thomas Jefferson sought at Monticello—retreat in a lovely mountain setting, yet engagement with the worlds of politics, diplomacy, and ideas from which he drew sustenance. Jefferson achieved the latter, asynchronously of course, primarily through books and assiduous letter writing to correspondents around the world.

The prospect of engaged retreat partly explains the appeal of telecommuting. While by no means as universal a phenomenon as was predicted several years ago, telecommuting nonetheless remains a real and attractive option for many of the professional elite—the very group historically most likely to seek respite in suburbia. Much of the discourse on telecommuting has focused on its potential to renew family and community life, or has emphasized the environmental benefits to be gained with the end of massive diurnal commuting.[21] But for many people, telecommuting's root-level appeal derives from the seductive promise of simultaneous retreat from the physical city and engagement with the world of ideas and information that the city represents.

The dream of engaged retreat by means of electronics is not so new. A 1914 *Scientific American* article entitled "Action at a Distance" essentially prophesied telecommuting and described an apparatus remarkably similar to the World Wide Web. The article's anonymous author lamented the "congestion of individuals crowding from one part of a city to another and interfering with each other both physically and mentally." The problem, he argued, "seems to be the idea that it is necessary for individuals to come into close proximity to each other if they are to transact business or to exchange ideas." Face-to-face exchange of knowledge was "crude and primitive," given the affordances of new technologies such as the telephone. Every day, people spend hours "crowding, hustling, and jamming together to get to each other, when what they really only want is to get their ideas phrased in words or arranged in plans without the real necessity of their persons being within reach at all."

> It is evident, therefore, that if some means of sending thoughts to a distance in such a shape that they could be co-ordinated perhaps by several, instead of by a single conversation at a time . . . and could receive such intelligent responses as one would expect to get if one were face to face with the speaker, it would be unnecessary for many people to travel to and from their work at all.

With the aid of rapid document transport (the writer suggested pneumatic tubes), such persons could "carry out the entire day's work without moving from their homes." The transmission of "intelligence and material" rather than bodies would eliminate "the great crush and crowding back and forth in our great cities" and, in the end, enable workers to "lead happier and more healthful lives" out in the rural countryside.[22]

ANTI-URBAN IMAGES IN ADVERTISING

The seductiveness of this techno-pastoral vision and the root-level longing to retreat from the city toward nature have not been lost on companies seeking to sell services or merchandise to the media-savvy middle class. Advertisements often appeal directly to the anti-urbanist proclivities of this group. In a 1997 AT&T Universal Card television advertisement produced by Young & Rubicam, a woman is shown clicking her way through offerings of shoes and clothing; she is window shopping in cyberspace (fig. 9.1). The implicit message is that the quintessential urban activity of shopping is now best carried out from the sanctuary of home, far from the civic space of the city. The former site of this activity is evoked romantically by the ad's soundtrack, which features the 1964 hit song "Downtown" by British pop star Petula Clark.

A far more disturbing chimera of latent American anti-urbanism is a 1996 television spot produced for the Packard Bell computer company by the New York advertising agency M&C Saatchi, Inc. The advertisement is both a shameless exploitation of urban fears and an affirmation of the pastoral landscape as the preferable site of life. The one-minute film packs enough apoca-

Fig. 9.1: A 1997 television commercial by Young & Rubicam extols the ease of shopping in cyberspace using AT&T's Universal Master Card.

Figs. 9.2, 9.3, 9.4: A 1996 television commercial produced for Packard Bell by M&C Saatchi takes the viewer on a visual journey from the threatening city through the pastoral countryside and into the sanctuary of the telecommuter's home.

lyptic imagery to upstage Ridley Scott: Chain gangs lug decrepit automobiles toward the city gates (a reference to commuting); aging patrons shuffle through a dreary banking hall; and the public library (where a child hides behind an ancient copy of *Paradise Lost*) is patrolled by neo-Nazi troops. Then, in a swift sequence of frames, the viewer is swept skyward past skull-studded parapets (fig. 9.2) and off to the green hills of Eden. The clouds break and the sun comes out, shining brightly on a single-family home surrounded by a picket fence (fig. 9.3). Away from the city, close to nature, life is good again. "Wouldn't you rather be at home?" the voice-over asks (fig. 9.4). The Packard Bell advertisement evokes a high-tech version of an age-old pastoral design, whose "ruling motive," writes Leo Marx, is "to withdraw from the great world and begin a new life in a fresh, green landscape."[23]

But blame for negative imaging of the city in new media culture cannot be laid wholly at the door of corporate America. The science of marketing is about gauging—and assuaging—existing societal attitudes. The marketing expert estimates potential appeal for a product or service, and then devises innovative ways to transform that appeal into sales. Advertisers rarely expend capital on messaging that flies in the face of popular trends. Therefore, advertising strategies such as those of Packard Bell and AT&T should be seen as savvy appeals to deeply embedded cultural trends. More obviously, the imagery and references in such ads are designed to attract that segment of the market most likely to have the resources and inclination to purchase the product being sold—sophisticated computer equipment or secure on-line shopping services. This cohort is largely white, affluent, and suburban. Imagery that blasts the city and coddles the suburban impulse both reaffirms the lifestyle choice of those who have made it and encourages those who aspire to it.

MEAN STREETS

Representations of cities in many interactive gaming environments also reveal a certain degree of anti-urbanism. While many computer games feature positive images of cities, many others utilize post-apocalyptic urban settings.[24] Often, the corpses of Los Angeles, New York, and other cities serve as a backdrop, with scenes of deserted streets, broken glass, and burned-out buildings. The social component is no less dysfunctional. In Tribal Rage, bikers and cyborgs do battle from trucks that, not surprisingly, resemble sport utility vehicles. On these streets, "We can't all just get along," noted *Computer Games* magazine, making the irresistible reference to the Rodney King incident.[25] Soldiers at War enables the suburban child to "fight fierce house-to-house battles in blasted cities like Anzio and Dresden"; Postal, one of the most violent games on the market, unfolds in a variety of urban settings where "real-time 3D characters rage against beautifully hand-painted 2D killing fields"—a dreary landscape of gas stations, all-night convenience stores, and a triple X–rated "desiplex."[26]

FUTURISTS AGAINST THE CITY

Ambivalence toward the city also exists in more rarefied, intellectual spheres. Some of the most influential futurists have expressed deeply skeptical—if not outright hostile—attitudes toward the city and urban life. Marshall McLuhan, patron saint of the *digerati,* repeatedly announced the coming obsolescence of the metropolis. In *Verbi-Voco-Visual Explorations*, McLuhan claimed that "THE CITY no longer exists, except as a cultural ghost for tourists," for "the metropolis is OBSOLETE."[27] Elsewhere, McLuhan proclaimed that "The cities, corporate extensions of our physical organs, are withering and being translated along with all other such extensions into information systems, as television and the jet—by compressing time and space—make all the world one village and destroy the old city–country dichotomy." He added: "New York, Chicago, Los Angeles—all will disappear like the dinosaur."[28]

Other futurists have more actively championed a nonurban future, a return to a world in which Jefferson's yeoman farmer—now armed with a cell phone and laptop—again rules the day. Conservative futurist George Gilder has claimed that "we are headed for the death of cities" and that cities are little more than "leftover baggage from the industrial era." In his best-selling *Third Wave*, Alvin Toffler argued that the coming "de-urbanization of production" and the return to home-based work would solve a wide range of social, environmental, and cultural problems. Toffler's barely concealed subtext is that the city—big, centralized, energy-hungry, and riven with pathologies—is something the digitized third wave will happily leave in its wake. "Our biggest factories and office towers may, within our lifetimes, stand half empty, reduced to use as ghostly warehouses or converted into living space," while "ultrahigh-abstraction workers"—the new cognoscenti—indulge "the new allure . . . of rural life" and rediscover the virtues of "the home as the center of society."[29]

DIGITAL DICKENSIA

Evocative of Dickens's portrayal of London, the cyberpunk literary genre often uses dystopic images of the city to draw a bead on the inequities, injustices, and alienation embedded in our machines. The future worlds evoked by novelists such as William Gibson and Neal Stephenson commonly describe urban landscapes fractured by race, class, and access to information. In the cyberpunk future, a digital cognoscenti oppresses an analog hoi polloi. The genre is not itself anti-urban, but rather offers a compelling, radical glimpse into a future where fear and loathing of the city have been permitted to flourish. Cyberpunk implicitly celebrates technology, but it also expresses a deep skepticism about its fair and equitable deployment.

In William Gibson's *Virtual Light,* the protagonist works for the "residential armed response branch" of a Singapore-based security force called IntenSecure, whose specialty is guarding American gated communities and "stealth houses" with armored Land Rovers. Urban crime has become voyeuristic entertainment for the suburban elite, and law enforcement is just another Hollywood specialty (security teams are always accompanied by cop show film crews, who often direct the action). In *Virtual Light,* the civic landscape has been abandoned: Trash fires burn in the Tenderloin, the L. A. Design Center has become a discount mall, and the Bay Bridge is home to an anarchistic array of betting shops, sushi bars, unlicensed pawnbrokers, barbers, and tattoo parlors ("illuminated by Christmas bulbs, by recycled neon, by torchlight, it possesses a queer medieval energy").[30]

In Stephenson's *Snow Crash,* Hiro Protagonist, a.k.a. the Deliverator, blasts along privatized California freeways to deliver pizza to white, middle-class, Type A occupants of Apartheid Burbclaves—gated communities with names like Gila Highlands, White Columns (marked with a "big ornate sign over the main gate: WHITE PEOPLE ONLY, NON-CAUCASIANS MUST BE PROCESSED") and The Mews at Windsor Heights, a standardized burbclave model that has been built "from Fairbanks to Yaroslavl to the Shenzhen special economic zone." Hiro himself lives in the city, hard by a "franchise ghetto," in a complex of converted storage sheds: "These are slum housing," he explains, "where Yanoama tribespersons cook beans and parboil fistfuls of cocoa leaves over heaps of burning lottery tickets." But though Hiro's body is in the city, his mind dwells in a virtual metropolis known as the Metaverse—a sparkling urban world through which runs a hundred-meter-wide boulevard known as the Street: "Garish and brilliant," the Street "does not really exist. But right now, millions of people are walking up and down it." Metaverse is a glowing virtual metropolis, with a downtown like "a dozen Manhattans, embroidered with neon and stacked on top of each other."[31] The city of bricks is now a corpse, but it lives on in the ether.

THE END OF THE (URBAN) WORLD AS WE KNOW IT

Perhaps the most extreme example of anti-urbanism in the culture of digital technology is the so-called TEOTWAWKI,[32] or Y2K survivalist movement, which persists despite the apparently successful arrival of the year 2000. Its adherents, a loose confederation of high-tech fundamentalists, had been convinced that the Y2K "millennium bug" would bring about urban apocalypse. They argued that, with widespread computer malfunction triggered by processors unable to cope with the number 2000, many of the essential functions of modern urban society would collapse—the power grid chief among them. Once electricity failed, looting would follow, food would perish, and within weeks anarchy and mob rule would set in. The metropolitan landscape would become a battle zone, torn apart by warring bands of hungry citizens. To the TEOTWAWKI movement, survival was predicated on moving as far away as possible from cities and their mobs. As the *New York Times* reported in 1998, Y2K survivalists "are moving to rural areas, drilling wells, setting up generators and even buying guns to fend off the hordes they fear will come from the broken cities in search of food."[33] Even though city life remained intact after the calendar changed to 2000, many doomsayers remained in active retreat.

The Y2K scare blended neatly with millennial anxiety and spawned dozens of "intentional communities" in Montana, Idaho, New Mexico, Oklahoma, and elsewhere in rural America. Such groups, often fundamentalist Christian, pooled resources to acquire remote land on which to "bunker" and await the collapse of the cities and the disintegration of urban society. God's

Wilderness is one such community in Finland, Minnesota; its promoters offer a plot of land equipped with a cabin, well, greenhouse, and outhouse. Stockpiling millennialists created tremendous demand for provisions and equipment such as solar cells and power generators. The Good Earth Market in Billings, Montana, for example, has attributed unprecedented sales of beans, grains, and other bulk items to survivalists, some of whom have squirreled away provisions to last for years. Walton Feed, an Idaho company, markets a product prized among Y2K survivalists—a sealed, oxygen-free drum full of food, its contents safe from spoilage and vermin.[34]

Perhaps the greatest irony of the survivalist movement is that the very source of fear, the computer, also serves as the chief enabler of the TEOTWAWKI community. The Internet has become central to this millennial community, with hundreds of Web sites and mail lists that distribute information on every facet of the retreatist project. Some of the most vocal advocates of the TEOTWAWKI movement have in fact been former crack programmers, including ones hired to solve the Y2K problem itself.[35] In this seeming paradox, the perennial American ambivalence regarding technology and the garden is revealed yet again. The computer, arguably the most sophisticated product of modern urban society, becomes an agent of retreat into nature on the eve of a city-born Armageddon.

CONCLUSION

Throughout American history, the city and the countryside have often been viewed as irreconcilable opposites. Both, however, have contributed equally to the development of national culture. Americans have built great cities and are today a predominantly urban people; however, the nation's rural past has been romanticized and still holds an important place in the American imagination. This duality of engagement and retreat manifests itself in literature, music, film, and other forms of cultural expression, and has also shaped the ways we have responded to technological innovation—particularly in the fields of transportation and communication.

Technology is not culturally independent. It is often seen as deterministic, although it is in fact deeply informed by the past. Before the potential of a new technology is fully understood, it is often first employed to achieve age-old dreams. The networked computer has given new life to the perennial American quest for retreat from urban life and the city. As with technological innovations in the past, it has begun to mirror our dreams, desires, and fears, thereby reflecting the complexity of life itself.

PART 

New Images and New Image Makers

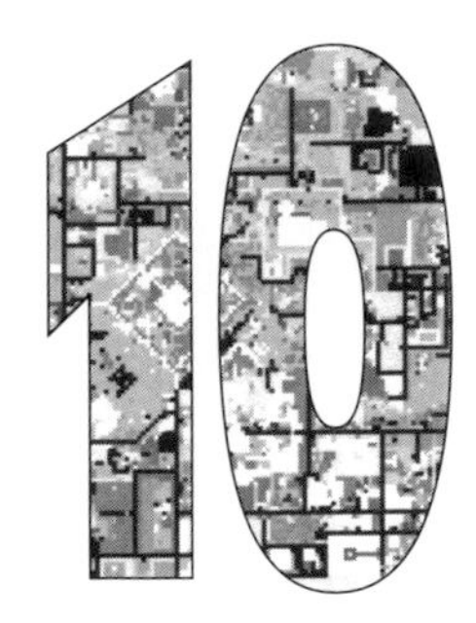

Narrative Places and the New Practice of Urban Design

Dennis Frenchman

■ EDITORS' OVERVIEW

Urban designer Dennis Frenchman wants to animate the spaces and structures of cities by making the stories associated with them available to residents and visitors. He sees such a goal as part of a larger process of cultural enrichment that he identifies as emerging from the new role of cities as centers of our information economy. Thus, as cities devote more and more of their energies to the management of information, their public spaces could be made to come alive with their pasts—not one past, but the multiplicity of stories of people and events that formerly inhabited the city.

To support this new direction, Frenchman observes that heritage places—spaces with narratives attached to them—today represent some of the most valued real estate, and that they attract all manner of activities as well as tourists. At the moment there are close to 100 state and nationally designated heritage areas under improvement in the United States and more than one million individual buildings, sites, and districts on the National Register of Historic Places. Given all this activity, it seems reasonable to expect that these places will come to be linked with each other, some as with the Freedom Trail in Boston, others in intercity networks.

Such a future calls for a new kind of city design practice, one that links archaeology, history, museums, and modern media to form

interpretive landscapes within cities. Frenchman illustrates the possibilities of such landscapes in a review of two projects now under way, the first at Pennsylvania's Gettysburg Battlefield and the second at Virginia's Jamestown settlement. In Gettysburg the interpretation has long been that of a Northern general, and plans by the National Park Service to offer multiple narratives of the battle experience have met opposition. In Jamestown all manner of devices are being considered to examine what is known and what is not known, so that each visitor can be his or her own interpreter. Frenchman's goal is to make the past speak to the present with all of its variety and richness.

INTRODUCTION

This chapter explores the opportunities and challenges that heritage interpretation raises for city design, particularly through the development of what I call "narrative places." The following three observations summarize my thinking:

1. Heritage development is an aspect of the information economy and the new technologies that support it. From this perspective, the growth of heritage is not being pushed by a yearning for the past, as critics have argued, but pulled by forces that are creating the future.

2. The information economy is leading to shifts in the way physical places are formed and experienced and in what we expect of them. There are increasing demands that public spaces be not only convivial but also *communicative*—of history and other narratives, requiring the incorporation of media into the environment.

3. The demand for "mediated environments" is raising important challenges for designers not only in terms of how to physically construct such places but also in

deciding what messages they should carry. The response is leading to what I see as a new practice of city design.

INFORMATION AND HERITAGE

The connection between urban places and information was raised by Kevin Lynch in *The Image of the City.* He argued that our understanding of the city is "the result of a two-way process between the observer and his environment. The environment suggests distinctions and relations, and the observer selects, organizes and endows with meaning what he sees."[1] Lynch argued that good places were those that were *legible* and *remembered*, poor places were *confusing* and *forgotten.* To find out which were which, he asked people to draw maps of their city, from which he deduced the famous five elements of a legible urban system: nodes, edges, paths, districts, and landmarks. These elements conveyed information enabling people to form a mental image of a city and to find their place within its complex fabric.

Lynch recognized that this information had both physical and cultural aspects; however, in the world of 1960, it was the physical attributes that most caught his attention. He researched the book while the West End of Boston was being demolished under the urban renewal program and other areas were being threatened. Such vast, cleared sites allowed designers to consider new schemes of urban form, free of the past and its cultural baggage. Lynch's set of elements provided some guiding principles by which city designers could organize their abstract compositions, an approach appropriate in its time. On the other hand—and of greater importance to Lynch—the idea that the formal qualities of a good city could be understood by talking to its inhabitants, rather than derived from a scientific or bureaucratic analysis, pointed the way to a more humane formulation of city design that eventually led to the demise of urban renewal a decade later. It is of interest that among the places considered most legible by participants in Lynch's study of Boston were those with strong historical associations, such as the State House and Beacon Hill, or those with high information and experiential content, like the entertainment district of old Scollay Square.

■ INDUSTRY TO INFORMATION

In the forty years since Lynch's book was written, American cities (and many elsewhere in the world) have undergone a remarkable transformation. They are no longer dependent upon the manufacturing and distribution of physical goods but focus instead on the creation and processing of information and services. Culture, entertainment, tourism, education, recreational experiences, and similar activities provide income to cities as well as an attraction for people going there. It follows that these activities have become a primary motivation for making and using urban places.

The information economy has been made possible by an explosion in media technology, which can provide information in many forms to many places. Communication by telephone from virtually any inhabited spot on earth is now taken for granted. We have come to not only appreciate but expect this level of accessibility to information. Without it we feel our ability to experience the world is somehow lacking. This applies as well to information about places. Our experience of the environment—and in turn its legibility—is shaped by what we know about it and what we can learn from it.

Expectations for information in the environment have been fueled by the fact that we move in so many more unfamiliar places. In chapter 1 of this volume, Julian Beinart points out that religious pilgrims needed information about places even in medieval times. It is also interesting to note that their travel destinations—the churches and holy places—were filled with graphic and narrative content. But in the past, pilgrims (at least those that traveled any distance) were a tiny fraction of society. Today tourism is one of the world's largest industries—and we are all pilgrims.[2] This has created endless demands by prospective visitors for place information and led to the development of informative places to receive them when they arrive.

■ VALUE IN THE ENVIRONMENT

Indeed, for many cities, the most valuable places in their environments are those that are most informative—where content is readily available and easily consumed. Historic and culturally significant places are particularly powerful sources of information, because by definition they are associated with stories and events. When these places and their narratives are interpreted through media, they become more accessible, or in Lynch's terms "legible and readable," and in turn, stronger attractions for visitors and local residents. It is no wonder that cities and the private sector have invested heavily in historical areas, not only as museum settings but to serve a wide variety of functions from retail shopping to affordable housing. In the process, the stories and places of the city have become more sharply defined and the city overall more *imageable*. One need only compare Boston's Faneuil Hall Marketplace area in Lynch's time, which "while distinctive acted only as a chaotic barrier zone,"[3] to the widely recognized attraction it is today—an icon drawing millions of people each year.

The economic potentials of historic places are being tapped to resuscitate declining cities and districts, particularly former *industrial* districts. Ironically, industrial environments are a powerful source of raw information material because they are so much a part of our shared national experience. Beginning with Lowell, Massachusetts, in the late 1970s, heritage revitalization projects have involved steel and textile mills, canals and railroads, oil fields, coal and iron mining areas, shipyards, and ports throughout the United States. There are nearly 100 state and federally designated heritage-area development projects now under way in this country, most involving industrial resources and multiple communities and most located in the eastern United States. A similar phenomenon is occurring in Britain following the precedent of the Iron Bridge Gorge

Museum and the rebirth of the British canal system for visitor use, as well as in other industrialized nations. Note that although virtually all of these countries aspire to tourism, in many cases it adds little of direct economic value. The real value and impact are in the improved image of the place and its ability to attract people, investment, and jobs, many not related to heritage at all.

The total scope of the heritage development effort is difficult to document. One measure is the National Register of Historic Places, which records elements of the built environment significant to the history of the United States. Established in 1966, the Register now includes more than one million individual resources—buildings, sites, districts, structures, and objects—including more than 80,000 individual places and tens of thousands of historic districts. The Register does not count locally recognized historic landmarks and districts (typically protected by zoning), which could easily double the above figures, or the myriad of private initiatives to identify, record, and protect historic places. Two aspects of the National Register of Historic Places cataloging deserve notice. First, each of these places is documented by a narrative history of the structure and people associated with it and an analysis of its current condition. In many cases, detailed drawings and photographs are included. Second, many of the sites are the subject of interpretation or information communicated to the public in a variety of media, from simple brochures to elaborate living-history presentations. The totality of these preservation documentation efforts represents an unprecedented reservoir of information connected to the built environment.

So, as Lynch anticipated, legibility of the environment is critical. While cities are seeking ways to develop a unique identity and message, citizens of the information age are seeking experiences that "entertain, educate, and inform." Historic places lie at the intersection of these forces. They are often distinctive physical environments with great presence, but just as important, they are associated with stories—narratives—that have been documented and can be communicated.

COMMUNICATIVE PLACES

Kevin Lynch saw legibility as a function of the physical form of the city, rather than its narrative content. In fact he deliberately eschewed content, saying that a good city form would provide a scaffold upon which content and meaning could be hung. But it can be argued that the city is experienced by its users as a system of meanings and narratives as well as of physical forms, and these narratives are as significant in determining the legibility of a city to its inhabitants and visitors. After all, the Old North Church in Boston would be inconsequential as a landmark, and probably would have been demolished by now, if it were not for the story of Paul Revere and Longfellow's poem. And Filene's Basement is a major landmark in the city, even though it has no physical presence at all.

Just as the form of a city can shape the stories that unfold there, stories can be used to shape urban form. In the latter case, good urban form is what helps to communicate these stories and ideas to the users of an environment. But how do we design such places? How can we make them speak? What is the medium? And what is the content? These questions are new to urban designers, and to answer them well it is important that we begin to sort out in a more systematic way the relationships between the ideas of narrative and place.

One way of understanding these relationships is illustrated in figure 10.1, which compares aspects of *literary culture,* involv-

Fig. 10.1
NARRATIVE AND PLACE: THE ROLE OF MEDIA

	Folkways	Scholarship
Literary Culture	Story (Narrative)	History (Documented Narrative)
	Media	
Material Culture	Place (Narrative + Form)	Heritage (Documented Narrative + Documented Form)

ing printed words and language, to parallel notions of *material culture,* involving objects, physical forms, and spaces. The products of both cultures can be divided into those relating to *folkways,* the common wisdom and activities shared by a particular group, and *scholarship*, involving the documentation of knowledge and critical reflection. Within the literary realm, *stories* are narratives shared by a particular group; *history* consists of documented narratives. Within the material realm, place is created when narratives are joined with form. This is an important connection and can be understood in opposition to *space,* which is physical form in the absence of narrative. The central challenge for contemporary city designers is to create places. Finally, *heritage* refers to the combination of documented narratives and documented forms (or places) inherited by each generation from its predecessor.

This schema illuminates several issues associated with the development and design of narrative places. First, it helps to put into context the criticism of heritage places, which have been characterized as sloppy history—a version of the past constructed in service of the present. By understanding that heritage is an aspect of *material culture,* we can appreciate the discomfort of historians who judge heritage using the standards of *literary culture.* Historians have the luxury of dealing in the medium of the printed word, where they are in control of the sequence of facts being revealed and can claim the undivided attention of a single person. They can therefore divulge with intimate delicacy and detachment the documented past. By contrast, an encounter with the material environment of the past is "in your face," encountered all at once, involving multiple dimensions and senses, where the current world is ever present and intruding. It is also, by nature, a communal experience—we cannot sweep most places free of other people to have a studied contemplation, nor can we ignore the fact that bathrooms must be provided. Walking through a historic environment with a family at lunchtime is a vastly different experience from sitting back with a good history book by yourself in the middle of the night.

Second, the matrix highlights the critical role of media in providing a bridge between the literary and material worlds.

After all, words that are related to thoughts are wholly different from physical forms, which are related to the senses. To experience these simultaneously requires incorporating communication and translation devices within the environment.

■ THE ROLE OF MEDIA

Incorporating communications media and narrative content into the built environment is an ancient idea. Signs, symbols, words, and pictures have always been a part of architecture. The study of *semiotics,* which reached its peak in the late 1970s, attempts to understand, for example, how we recognize the symbolic meaning of a door or a roof and which aspects of such form-language are universally shared and which are culturally different. By comparison, the construction of narrative space demands not only legibility in some vague semiotic way, but also that spaces be *didactic*—that we can learn from them or even engage in a dialogue. We are not talking here about what spaces mean to people but rather how they speak to convey messages about progressions of events, context, and associations.

The difference between semiotic and didactic communication in the environment can be illustrated by the example of the medieval Gothic church. The entire form of the building is a symbol of the cross and, by extended reference, an image of the crucified Christ. The priest is located at the head of Christ, in the choir, and the congregation in the body, represented by the nave. Furthermore, the structural forces embodied in the building are expressed by ogives (ribs), even though they are not crucial to the vaulted structure. These are the semiotics of the church.[4] But there is more. The sculptural program surrounding the entrances to a Gothic church and stained glass in the windows carried didactic messages, communicating stories and concepts to people who could not read. The semiotic form of communication has been developed and explored by architects from the beginning—in some ways it *is* architecture. The didactic form of communication in architecture, requiring media to communicate specific messages, remains not much beyond what it was in the medieval Gothic church.

So while the technology of communication has advanced incredibly, its use in conveying narrative content to places remains relatively crude—as can be seen in outdoor advertising, for example. Times Square is filled with messages, as are streets in Hong Kong, Shanghai, and many Asian cities where signs virtually overwhelm the architecture. There are so many conflicting messages that none stand out, and the places are illegible. By and large this is because the media involved are still mainly paintings or photographs—relatively old technologies—in addition to a few "Jumbotrons." But even television has been around now for more than half a century.

■ LESSONS FROM ARCHAEOLOGY

We need to look elsewhere for more interesting uses of technology and media in environments. One promising area is archaeology, a field linked to both architecture and heritage. Archaeology tries to understand and communicate the meaning of material culture through the discovery of physical sites and artifacts from the past. Archaeologists ask, What do the remains of places say about the people who made them? This is the inverse of the question facing designers, who are asking, How do we make places that speak more clearly?

Archaeology, like heritage, is located squarely in the lower right-hand corner of the matrix in figure 10.1. And like heritage, it involves making connections between documented places and documented narratives. Archaeology has sometimes received the same kind of criticism as heritage—that it represents poor history, anthropology, or science.

Nevertheless, some interesting things are happening in archaeology. First of all, archaeologists increasingly have turned to technology to extract more and more information from the remains of people and places. Radiocarbon dating, pollen analysis, trace element analysis, advanced data processing, and other innovations of the physical and biological sciences have revolutionized archaeological analysis. So now when a bone is discovered, we can tell its owner's age, race, health, and place of birth, what the climate was like, where the person lived, and the cause of death. This evidence has led in turn to revised interpretations of written history. So we see in archaeology that the narrative record—produced by literary culture—and the material record are beginning to merge. This is the equivalent of being able to identify and name the person whose bones we discovered.

Second, fueled by new discoveries and knowledge, as well as by movies like *Raiders of the Lost Ark*, the interest in archaeology has grown enormously. Archaeologists increasingly are confronted with the need to present and interpret their findings to other disciplines and to the public, and to make accessible excavations and resources in the ground. This is not so easy to do since, contrary to popular ideas, many of these resources are just crumbling foundations and stains in the dirt.

Archaeologists have struggled with designers to link information from the archaeological and historical record to physical sites and objects to make them more legible. A whole generation of new archaeological interpretive sites, museums, and working digs has been opened to the public. These locales experiment with ways of integrating media, content, and physical environments and are advancing the state of the art in designing narrative places. Examples include:

- *Re-creations.* These involve the construction of replica buildings and landscapes over the original foundations and other archaeological remains in the ground. An example is St. Mary's City in Maryland, where seventeenth-century buildings have been re-created on the exterior; the interiors house contemporary museum spaces and exhibits. Re-creations are often settings for "living history," as at Plimoth Plantation in Massachusetts, where actors in period costumes inhabit a replica town, acting out the lives of seventeenth-century Pilgrims.

- *Remnant landscapes.* These attempt to give the sense of historic places as they once may have existed, without fully re-creating them. Remnant landscapes are like ruins. At Carter's Grove in Virginia, for example, the early site of an Indian massacre is delineated by paths, gates, portions of stockades, and building elements constructed over the archaeological remains below. What is missing in the form is replaced by media, including drawings, a model of the settlement, and on-site audio interpretation, narrated by the archaeologist Ivor Noel Hume.

- *Interpretive landscapes.* These are abstractions that attempt to convey what is actually known about a former place rather than what is conjectured. Typically this might include the scale and shape of forms, but not the tactile details. This approach was pioneered at Independence National Historical Park in Philadelphia, particularly at Franklin Court, where the original home of Benjamin Franklin is outlined as a steel "ghost structure" because its actual appearance is unknown. Words of Franklin, artifacts, and some exposed foundation elements are incorporated into the pavement treatment, providing a sense of the person as well as the place.

- *Site-linked museums.* These attempt to overcome the limitations of interpreting archaeology in an outdoor setting. This is achieved by building a museum structure over exposed archaeological sites to protect them from the weather and to support sophisticated media interpretation. Examples include Jorvik, a Norse town excavated in the center of York, England, where the museum spans an entire block. At Pointe-à-Callière in Montreal, visitors descend through the floor of a historic structure to view the remains of the city's first settlement, walking beneath the streets to emerge in a nearby plaza. At Saint-Romain-en-Gal, France, the museum space is suspended above Roman foundations, and artifacts are interpreted on the floor several feet above the place where they were discovered.

■ TYPOLOGY OF NARRATIVE PLACES

The above examples drawn from archaeology represent only a fraction of the total range of narrative places now emerging in the environment. To these we might add other heritage prototypes: historic marker programs where information is placed on buildings and in guidebooks; heritage routes, like Boston's Freedom Trail, where exemplary structures are preserved, interpreted, and linked into a system; projects that reuse famous public places and buildings, such as Faneuil Hall Marketplace, reintroducing them into the public experience. These examples are motivated primarily by the desire to preserve significant buildings that have stories associated with them, but we could also look at examples that are motivated by the desire to preserve important stories related to specific places. Included in this category are the growing number of traditional festivals and pageants that are being revived in historic settings, for example, as well as reenactments of historical events.

Figure 10.2 attempts to map these various types of narrative places according to the relative importance of the stories versus

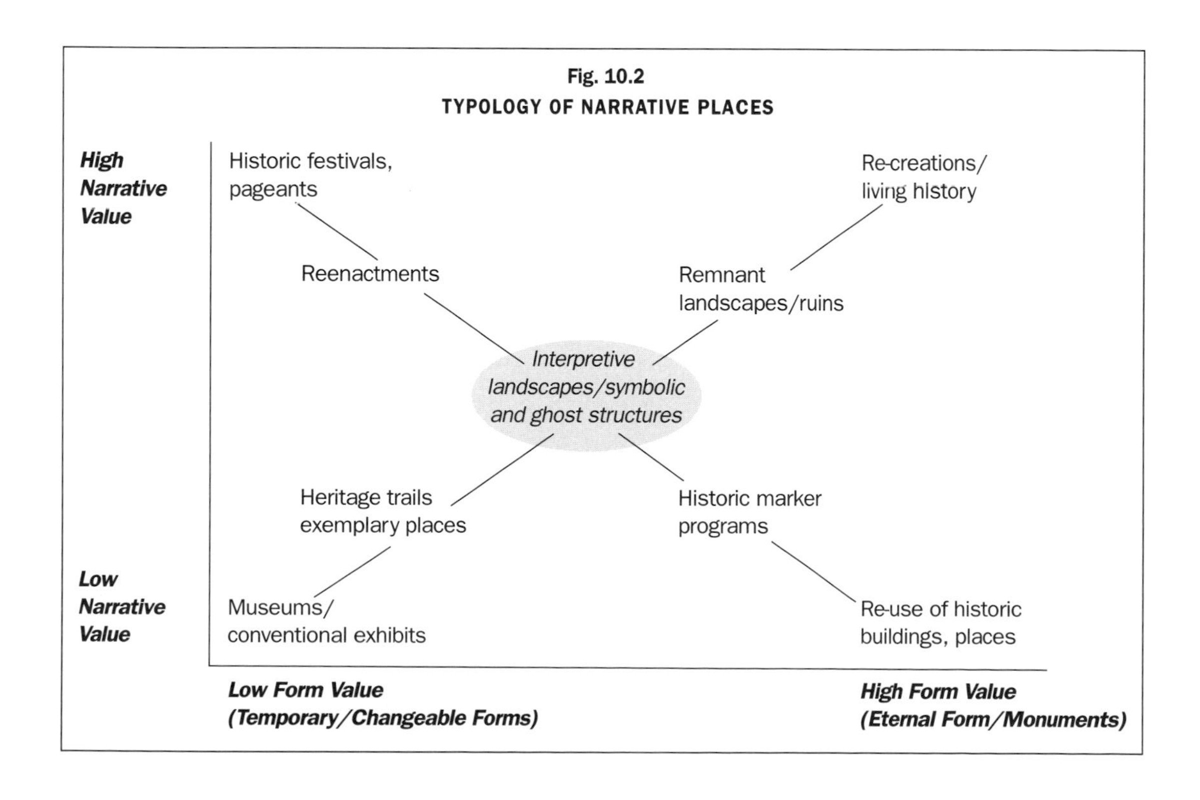

their physical form in creating an experience for their users. While the mapping is subjective, it does serve to highlight some of the common characteristics and differences among narrative places. For example, *re-created environments*—those that provide a setting for living history—are places that have both high form and high narrative content. By contrast, traditional *museums* have low form and low narrative content, because they house collections of artifacts (or even buildings) that are removed from their environment and explained with labels. Figure 10.2 also illustrates the potential for relationships between narrative places that have similar characteristics. Many new museums, for example, are being linked to heritage trails or networks in their communities. Finally, *all* of the types of places that appear in figure 10.2 are being created in cities in great numbers. They are now largely disconnected, but it is easy to see how over time they will merge with one another, along the lines implied by the diagram. The result will be a new city form.

From a city design perspective, the *interpretive landscape* emerges as one of the most interesting types of narrative places, because it lies at the intersection of several forces. Not only museum officials but preservationists, real estate developers, event planners, and educators are all looking for ways to support communication in the environment; it's either learning or marketing, depending upon your point of view. An interpretive landscape can be seen as the matrix for interconnecting and organizing various types of narrative places and events, from recreations to reenactments. The design of environments that meet these multiple information and physical needs in a coherent way is a challenge. Interpretive landscapes like Franklin Court in Philadelphia seek a balance and interplay between narrative content, media, and symbolic form, allowing each message to find its appropriate place without overpowering the others. But Franklin Court is a small installation devoted to the life of one man, Benjamin Franklin. How do we make interpretive landscapes at the urban scale? And how do we make these places meaningful—what messages are they to carry?

TWO CASES

The issues and the design challenges involved in the making of such narrative places can be illustrated in two controversial projects now under way in the United States, involving the hallowed sites of Gettysburg Battlefield in Pennsylvania, setting of the turning point in the American Civil War, and Jamestown, Virginia, the first permanent English settlement in the New World. Both projects have involved the author's firm, ICON architecture, inc., which has been engaged in heritage planning and urban design since the 1970s, together with the National Park Service and a host of other public and private groups.

■ GETTYSBURG

Gettysburg illustrates how the message of a place can shape its use and design. At a site held sacred by many different groups for different reasons, how do we decide what is significant? And how should its narrative be presented? The battle took place from July 1 to July 3 in 1863, ending with a Union victory but at the terrible cost of more than 51,000 lives. The importance of the event was immortalized by Abraham Lincoln in his Gettysburg Address, which is known by every schoolchild in America.

Almost immediately after the battle, states and communities on both sides of the conflict began to mark where their boys fought and fell, and guides began offering battlefield tours, a tradition that continues today. Eventually, more than 1,800 monuments were erected across the rolling hills and farmland in and around Gettysburg (figs. 10.3, 10.4). In 1895, the battlefield was acquired by the United States War Department and redesigned as a park in the City Beautiful tradition, with miles of formal avenues. In 1933, it was transferred to the National Park Service, which in the name of conservation removed some avenues but encouraged tenants to consolidate small fields and use modern farming techniques that even more drastically altered the landscape. A former private museum was acquired as a visitor center, and in the 1960s a new center, the Cyclorama, was opened to

Fig. 10.3 *(above)*: Gettysburg National Military Park: View from Little Round Top.

Fig. 10.4 *(right)*: Gettysburg National Military Park, a landscape of monuments.

Fig. 10.5: The draft plan for the park proposes involving the town of Gettysburg.

house a famous nineteenth-century panorama of Pickett's Charge. The stark, modern building, designed by Richard Neutra, was sited on ground that lay at the very nexus of the battle.

Today Gettysburg National Military Park includes more than 5,700 acres, a palimpsest of landscape treatments layered over the years. At the same time, the interpretive message of the park has remained unchanged for more than a century, a narrative from the Union general's viewpoint of key events that occurred on the second and third days of the battle. Currently, more than 1.8 million visitors each year receive the same message and visit the same sites, mainly by automobile. There are problems with this approach to interpretation. First, by concentrating visitors in just a fraction of the park, these few sites are literally being worn away; at the same time, too many cars, buses, and people can distract from the experience of being there. Second, by focusing on the general's interpretation of the battle, specifically the strategic movement of troops, many other ways of understanding the event are overlooked, such as the soldier's viewpoint, the woman's viewpoint, or even Lincoln's viewpoint; these may be more meaningful to some visitors. Finally, the boundaries of the park as well as the story told include almost nothing of the town of Gettysburg (fig. 10.5). This is astonishing, since the town contains many buildings that stood within sight of the battle and in some ways preserve more of a sense of the period than does the battlefield. Nevertheless, the town of Gettysburg receives few benefits from the park, despite bearing the impacts of traffic and strip development. Visitors pass through historic local streets on their way to the battlefield, but the federal government in the past did little to support local efforts at preservation, interpretation, or visitor management.

To address these issues, a new draft plan for the park considers a different way of telling the Gettysburg story, arguing that the battle should be interpreted from multiple points of view. These would include the global view (outside the United States), the general's view (traditional approach), the soldier's view, the local family's view, Lincoln's view, and the descendant's view (from hometowns across the country). Each would involve its own medium and venues for interpretation. The aim is to make

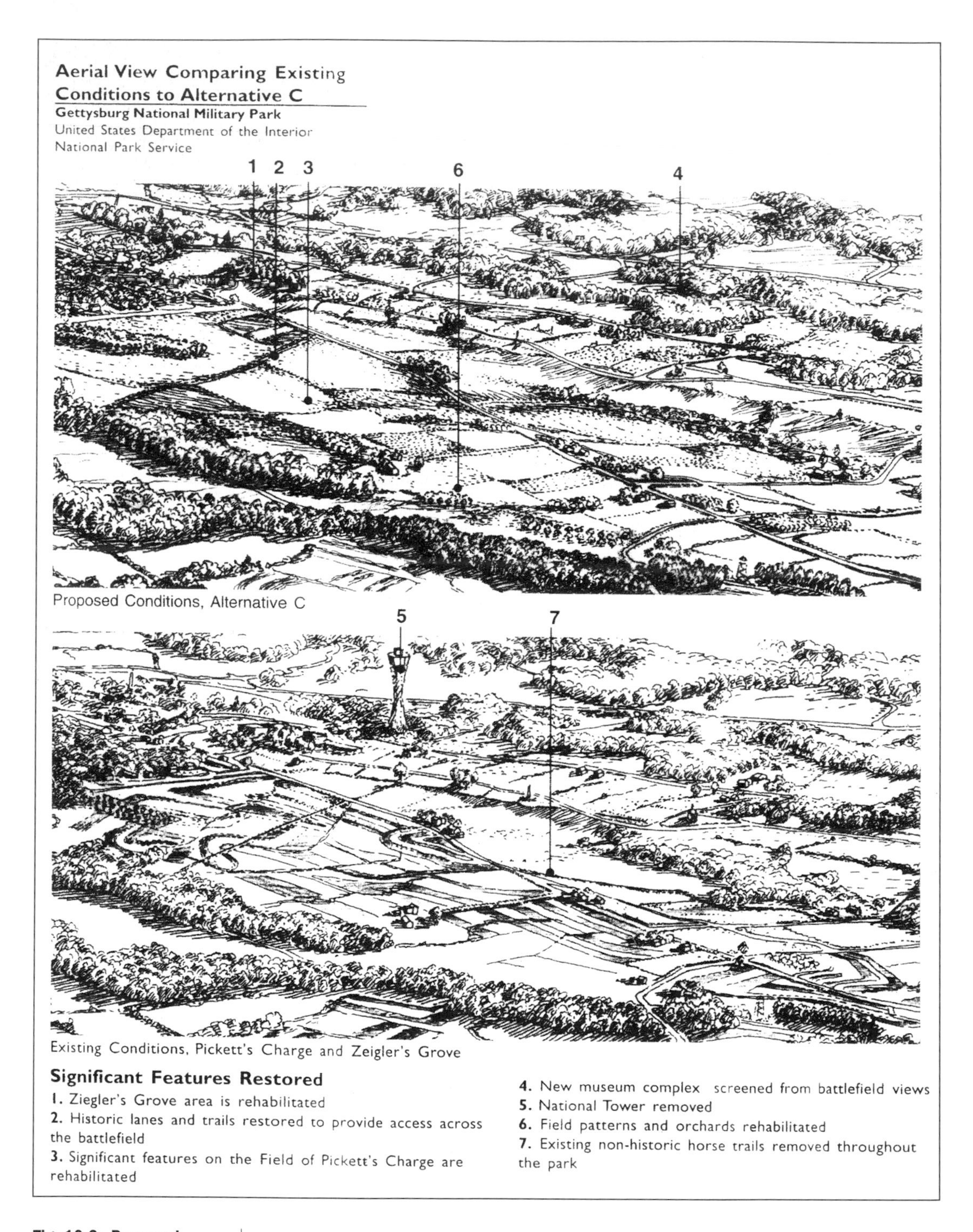

Fig. 10.6: Proposed changes at Gettysburg to interpret the landscape: Views showing proposed changes and existing conditions.

the battle story more relevant to a broader constituency and to engage visitors with more of the resource.

Changing the narrative in this way will necessitate changes in the physical design of the park as well. First, to interpret new stories, new venues within the park are proposed, potentially linked by shuttle buses to reduce the intrusion of cars. Second, to communicate the family view and Lincoln's view, park interpretation may be extended into the town, opening avenues for technical and financial assistance for townspeople and cooperating businesses. Third, to understand the soldier's view, features of the 1863 battlefield may be re-created by replacing small fields and fences and removing woods that have grown up (fig. 10.6). Such treatment would be limited to areas of crucial battle action, providing a more authentic setting for reenactments and living history. Lastly, the draft plan proposed that the current visitor center and Cyclorama building be removed, because they occupy places of key battle action (they are outdated as well) (fig. 10.7). In partnership with a private developer, a new visitor center would be built on a less significant site outside the park boundary.

Fig. 10.7: Gettysburg National Military Park: Cyclorama Building that would be removed under draft plan; the tower has already been demolished.

It should be noted that the proposed changes have brought on a firestorm of criticism—the "Second Battle of Gettysburg," in the words of *USA Today*. The National Park Service has been cast by its critics as poor in planning, insulting to the memory of Civil War veterans, insensitive to the community, and a shill for private developers. The controversy confirms that many people have a lot invested in the traditional story and the way it is told on the site, even if it is one-sided and eroding the resource. Conservative Civil War buffs see the multiple viewpoints as a liberal attempt at diversity that will dilute the "real" story. Existing businesses would rather see visitors stay concentrated where they are—close to the beer and souvenirs. The battlefield guides don't want competition from other forms of interpretation. Local park users want to preserve the woods and keep visitors out of their way. And finally, architectural critics are more concerned with the memory of Richard Neutra than Robert E.

Lee. Nevertheless, the Park Service is pressing ahead with its own plan because, unlike other agendas, it is rooted in the story of the battle.

■ JAMESTOWN

The history of Jamestown, Virginia (fig. 10.8), illustrates issues similar to those of Gettysburg. But at Jamestown, the resource has more than changed; it is largely invisible, existing as archaeological remains under the ground. Even its history has been obscured by centuries of folklore, including the legend of Pocahontas. At such a place, how should the physical environment be designed and what should it communicate? How do we separate myth from knowledge? Jamestown was settled by a company of English men and boys who arrived at the island in three ships, constructing a fort there in the spring of 1607. As the first capital of Virginia, it endured starvation, Indian massacres, fire, and rebellion until it was abandoned almost 100 years later for the new capital of Williamsburg. Farms occupied the island for the next 200 years, as almost all traces of the town

Fig. 10.8: Jamestown Island, Virginia.
Courtesy Jamestown Rediscovery, Association for the Preservation of Virginia Antiquities.

Fig. 10.9: Recent archaeology at Jamestown by the Association for the Preservation of Virginia Antiquities has rediscovered the original 1607 fort.

disappeared. At the end of the nineteenth century, the Association for the Preservation of Virginia Antiquities (APVA) purchased what it believed to be the original town site and began to dig. The process of archaeology has continued on and off ever since, yielding an amazing collection of artifacts. In 1997, the APVA rediscovered the remains of the original James Fort (fig. 10.9). This find garnered worldwide attention, since at the time it was thought that the fort had eroded into the James River centuries earlier.

Commemoration of the founding of Jamestown first took place in 1807. One hundred years later, it was the subject of an international exposition held in Norfolk, Virginia, a few miles down the river. The APVA erected an obelisk on the island and simple buildings to serve a growing number of visitors. In the 1930s the National Park Service acquired the remainder of the island, eventually connecting it into a regional park system that involves the re-created city of Williamsburg and the Yorktown battlefield, where England surrendered in the American Revolution. Linked by the Colonial Parkway, these three sites tell the story of British colonial America.

In 1957, the National Park Service oversaw major improvements at Jamestown to commemorate its 350th anniversary. The parkway was extended to the island, where a visitor center was built. Nearby on the mainland, the Commonwealth of Virginia constructed a living-history museum, featuring a re-creation of the original fort and the three ships, to host celebration activities that were attended by Queen Elizabeth. Now known as Jamestown Settlement, the living-history museum has evolved over the past forty years into a major attraction, while visitation to the island and the original town site has languished (figs. 10.10, 10.11). And it's no wonder since, although the island is beautiful, there is little to do or see there when the visitor arrives.

Fig. 10.10 (*above*): Jamestown Settlement, a re-creation of the early town on an off-island site, sponsored by the Commonwealth of Virginia.

Fig. 10.11 (*below*): In contrast to the re-created Settlement (fig. 10.10), there is little to see at the original town site on the island.

As Jamestown's 400th anniversary in the year 2007 approaches, new plans have been considered. While controversial and therefore unlikely to be implemented, one proposal illustrates the power of a story to change the sense of a place. Unlike the Settlement, which recounts the popular history of Jamestown during its *first* 100 years, the proposal recast the island narrative to emphasize the rediscovery of Jamestown in our own time, in the *last* 100 years. Ironically, this is a story of advances in archaeology, science, experimentation, and discovery, as much oriented to the future as it is to the past. It is also true to the resource, which continues to be an object of research and discovery. Under the proposal, the role of the site was reconceived to facilitate research and to help visitors appreciate how scientific advances are being applied to reveal new things about the past, and in the process to rewrite the Jamestown story. This is dramatized by APVA's rediscovery of the fort, but also by other revelations. For example, research conducted for the National Park Service by Colonial Williamsburg recently revealed that the settlers unwittingly arrived during the worst drought in centuries; no wonder so many starved.

New facilities in an interpretive landscape could communicate this unfolding story. The proposal called for the existing visitor center, which intrudes on the town site, to be replaced by a new Institute of the Seventeenth Century, housing not only collections of artifacts but also space for scholarly research, curator activities, and scientific laboratories. It would have served as a base for archaeology at Jamestown and other seventeenth-century sites. Finally, it would have been an educational center, a place for holding conferences and disseminating information on seventeenth-century America. The public visiting the island would first encounter the institute through media, exhibits, and a virtual collection (also accessible on the Internet). The aim was to show that history is dynamic and to engage visitors in the excitement of discovery.

In the proposal, the island landscape was designed to communicate the current state of knowledge about the fort and the early town. Known building locations, lot lines, streets, and paths were represented by changes in level, plantings, or paving materials, and where no knowledge exists, level grass served to mark unknown territory. The aim was to create a landscape that would have been both a full-scale map of our current knowledge and a garden of great beauty and distinctive design. In one scheme, interpretive stations stood as sculptural elements within the garden, partially underground and earth covered. The stations provided a means to connect the landscape to specific themes and stories while protecting archaeological remains and ongoing excavations (fig. 10.12). Within the stations, sophisticated media would have illustrated the discoveries that were made there and what they revealed about Jamestown.

Fig. 10.12: At Jamestown, on-site media illustrate the relation between archaeology and the original town. Courtesy Jamestown Rediscovery, Association for the Preservation of Virginia Antiquities.

A NEW PRACTICE OF CITY DESIGN

What does this say about the future of cities and the practice of city design?

■ CITY FORM

First and foremost, there will be many more of these kinds of narrative places in the future. The first candidates are the thousands of heritage sites, for which there are a lot of documentation and an economic incentive to make connections between this information and the place. For example, Boston's Freedom Trail began in the 1950s as a simple concept for connecting seven historic sites in the city by a line on the ground. It has become the backbone of an entire information system as the sites develop their messages, employ media, and make links to other historic sites, educational institutions, and businesses. This is having an economic and physical effect; properties on the trail are increasing in value and accessibility. Such networks of places are being built at many scales in the city and regions, and do not involve just heritage. There are recreation, sports, entertainment, conventions, hotels, and other places associated with the new information economy. Each of these is already wired up. Sports fans do more than watch the game; they also watch the scoreboard, learning about activities in other ballparks and gleaning information about the players and the team.

■ A NEW TYPE OF SPACE

These examples represent the emergence of a new type of space that is connected by media to narrative information, other times, and other places—"mediated space." Coupled with the Internet, mediated space can be explored before you get there and experienced in several ways once you've arrived—or after you have left. Right now there are many mediated spaces being developed in the city, but they are disconnected. Perhaps an infrastructure can be built among them by using the medium of virtual cities—a parallel digital world of narrative and graphic information. In Deuxième Monde—a virtual version of Paris discussed by Anne Beamish in chapter 11—each ground-floor commercial space in the city eventually will have its counterpart in digital city accessible on the Net. Mediated spaces will be easy to access in such an environment. And so, as the virtual world expands, I think that we will see mediated spaces emerge at many more locations, including in the public realm.

Such a world will be less linear and more transparent, more mystical, where stories and personalities intermingle with material forms, where past and present are equally accessible, and where more people can be present than are actually in the room. Our world may become more like those of many prehistoric cultures, where all physical objects were imbued with spirits and stories and where the ancestors who had departed continued to live in the space. This was predicted in the 1960s by Lynch's contemporary, Marshall McLuhan. Speculating on the impact of television and global communication, he observed that the segmented, linear thinking fostered by the printed word was giving way to more holistic visual and spatial forms of communication in which distance was irrelevant and the past and the present commingled. The explosion of heritage and efforts to imbue the physical world with content and meaning is evidence that we are arriving at the future he envisioned.

■ A NEW TYPE OF PRACTICE

I think it is clear that to make the city legible, as Lynch encouraged, city designers need to deal with far more than the physical elements of form. We need to know about the past, because heritage has become such an important activity in the city; but we also need to understand how new forms of media and technology will affect activities and functions in the future. And we need to become involved in the content and the messages that are delivered. Perhaps we need to add five elements of a good urban narrative to Lynch's five elements of good urban form. We could ask city dwellers to draw maps of urban stories and meanings and would, I imagine, come up with the same array of overlapping and divergent perceptions as Lynch did. This is because information and heritage in the city are as ubiquitous as physical form. And in an information age, they demand the same attention to legibility that Lynch brought to the physical aspects of the environment forty years ago.

11

The City in Cyberspace

Anne Beamish

■ EDITORS' OVERVIEW

Urbanist Anne Beamish has been following the urban imagery rapidly emerging on the Internet. The amount of spatial material is surprising because the Net is an antispatial invention. Yet human beings, from the moment they first discover their bodies, use space to orient themselves; thus the Net is filled with spatial imagery, some of it produced by organized groups who build whole cybercities. As such cities are designed and visited, they demonstrate another surprising aspect of the digital world: It encourages the formation of specialized communities.

The Internet communities appear in both text and graphic forms. The text-based communities can be a gathering of people with a common interest, such as the interactive mailing lists of urban historians or the newsgroups of people who follow reports on the world's endangered mammals. These specialized interest groups seem to be very much a traditional kind of community, more like research clusters at a professional convention than a gathering of friends in your backyard. The city-building groups represent a more unusual assembly. Here strangers work together over the Net to build or use representations of either real cities like Paris or San Francisco, or imagined urban places.

The virtual cities established so far tend to be oversimplified, rather pale versions of the actual urban realm, and they often suffer

the same blandness that is an objectionable feature of the contemporary landscape. Yet these cities can hardly be called anti-urban, whether dense or spread out, because their builders spend countless hours making them. Maybe they should be viewed in the same light as the elaborate model railroads built by railroad enthusiasts.

At this point in time, both the text associations and the graphic builders seem powerful additions to the community expressions of Americans. City building on the Net is very much in its infancy, so it is difficult to envision its future forms, but urban designers ignore the phenomenon at their peril. Beamish urges them to join the undertaking, both as learners and as teachers.

INTRODUCTION: DIGITAL COMMUNITIES

Computer technology can be much more than a means to retreat from urban life by permitting access to its riches from afar. Paradoxically, perhaps, it can also be employed to recover the very kinds of social interaction, community, and place that the physical city affords. This chapter explores some of the ways the networked computer has been used to create proto-urban environments in cyberspace, with increasingly sophisticated architectural and social components that simulate real-world urbanism.

Historically, we have often taken a profoundly dark view of urban life.[1] Cities have been seen as places from which we escape; they have acted as a backdrop to our worst fears, imagination, and experiences. Our anti-urban feelings are amply reflected in media: Computer games, advertising, and literature all paint a threatening and grim picture of urban life. Associated with this negative outlook is a very long history of lamenting the loss of community.

Thomas Bender notes in *Community and Social Change in America* that the literature offers a picture of a cycle of community breakdowns in the 1650s, 1690s, 1740s, 1780s, 1820s, 1850s, 1880s, 1920s, on up until the present day. The anxiety about community, along with its closely related public life, has continued unabated in what Michael Brill quite accurately calls a "literature of loss." Richard Sennett in *The Fall of Public Man* regrets the loss of public life; Ray Oldenburg in *The Great Good Place* writes about the lack of informal meeting places, or "third places." Robert Putnam in his 1995 essay "Bowling Alone" worries about Americans no longer belonging to groups. In short, at almost any time during the past 350 years, "a rather simple and direct relationship between past and present is assumed: In the past, there was community; in the present it has been (or is being) lost."[2]

Part of the reason we lament the demise of community and the failure of our urban areas must be that we desire it so much. "Community" is a word that has tremendous positive association—a word that "seems never to be used unfavorably."[3] It is a romantic and often sentimental notion that evokes heartwarming images of sitting on the front porch on a warm summer evening with family and neighbors who care about you, sharing happiness as well as grief.

But our images of and ideas about the city and community are full of contradictions. On one hand, we reject urban life, wish to escape it, and fear those unlike us; on the other hand, we romanticize the city as a place of excitement, adventure, and opportunity. Alongside any rejection of urban life runs a contradictory but equally deep vein of bright optimism, confidence, and belief in our need for urban life, public space, and a sense of community as well as our ability to create it. From the New England colonial town to Brasília, our past is full of attempts to reinvent ourselves and the places where we live.

SPACE AND DIGITAL WORLDS[4]

This drive to build new worlds, cities, communities, and public places continues today, and digital technology has given us a new medium with which to experiment and build. No longer are we constrained by the physical; bricks and mortar, water mains, and roads can be replaced by bits.

```
<<< CLEVELAND FREE-NET DIRECTORY >>>

  1 The Administration Building
  2 The Post Office
  3 Public Square
  4 The Courthouse & Government Center
  5 The Arts Building
  6 Science and Technology Center
  7 The Medical Arts Building
  8 The Schoolhouse
  9 The Community Center & Recreation Area
 10 The Business and Industrial Park
 11 The Library
 12 University Circle
 13 The Teleport
 14 The Communications Center
 15 Weather Center
---------------------------------------------
h=Help, x=Exit Free-Net, "go help"=extended help

Your Choice ==>
```

Fig. 11.1 ***(above)*****: Opening screen of the Cleveland Free-Net.**

Fig. 11.2 ***(right)*****: Screen shot of Apple's eWorld®.**

Fig. 11.3 ***(below)*****: Opening screen of The Palace.**

Though one of the principal characteristics of digital technology is that it is "fundamentally and profoundly antispatial,"[5] digital worlds incorporate space, either metaphorically or literally, surprisingly often. They use spatial concepts to organize and categorize information, such as in the opening screen of the Cleveland Free-Net (fig. 11.1). Graphic spatial metaphors help users navigate through a site—often the first view is of a "town's" significant public buildings (fig. 11.2). Spatial images are used to create a backdrop or environment in which users interact (fig. 11.3), and sometimes the city is simply used to evoke an image.

At first glance, the idea of using spatial concepts in an aspatial medium may seem counterintuitive—after all, it is the nonspatial characteristics of digital technology that permit asynchronous and geographically dispersed communication. But our insistence on imposing spatial concepts on a nonspatial world has to be due, at least in part, to the fact that we are spatial creatures. Our social relationships are intertwined with spatial ones, and not only are our physical bodies spatial, but we use spatial concepts figuratively, literally, and metaphorically to structure our thoughts and give meaning to our actions. We bring ourselves to these new worlds and, not surprisingly, with us come our past, our ideas about space, and our images of cities and communities.

The types of virtual worlds are surprisingly similar to those of public space; both are usually categorized either by appearance or by use.[6] With respect to appearance, they can be either text or graphical, with the graphical world subdivided into 2-D and 3-D (fig. 11.4). In terms of use, digital worlds vary in two fundamental ways: Some sites emphasize object building and construction, whereas others focus on social interaction (fig. 11.5). Many worlds have both capabilities but tend to emphasize one aspect over the other.

Fig. 11.4 ***(right)*****: Digital worlds categorized by appearance.**

Fig. 11.5 ***(below)*****: Digital worlds categorized by use.**

DIGITAL WORLDS CATEGORIZED BY APPEARANCE

Text	Graphical
• MUDs • MOOs • Newsgroups • Mailing lists • IRC Chat	• 2D (Palace, WorldsAway) • 3D (AlphaWorld, V-Chat, Worlds Chat)

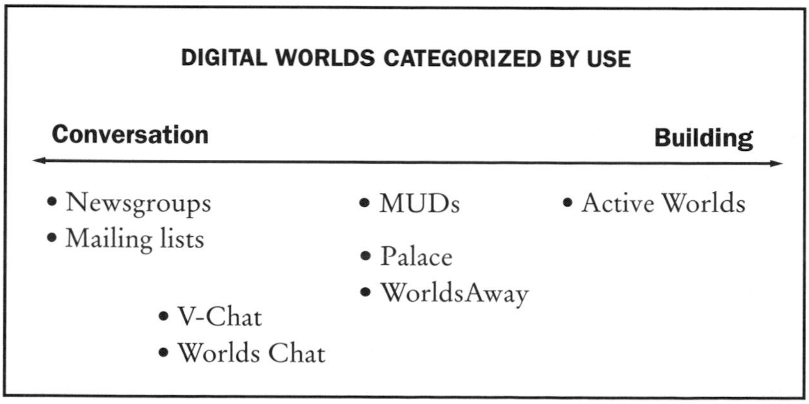

DIGITAL WORLDS CATEGORIZED BY USE

Conversation ←→ **Building**

- Newsgroups
- Mailing lists
- V-Chat
- Worlds Chat
- MUDs
- Palace
- WorldsAway
- Active Worlds

Fig. 11.6 *(right)*: A scene from a VZone from Avaterra.com.
© 2001 Avaterra.com, Inc.

Fig. 11.7 *(below)*: Microsoft's V-Chat.
© Microsoft Corporation. All rights reserved.

How spatial concepts are incorporated also varies with the type of digital world.[7] Mailing lists (to which participants must subscribe if they wish to receive electronic messages) and newsgroups (which are much more public in that anyone with the appropriate software can read the messages posted to any particular group) are asynchronous text-based discussion groups, and though they typically do not use space either metaphorically or literally, many consider themselves to be tight-knit communities. MUDs (the acronym for Multi-User Dungeons, Multi-User Dimension, or Multiple-User Dialogue) and MOOs (a type of MUD that is even more social in nature) are synchronous worlds where text reigns supreme—not only is it used for conversation, but the environment and everything that users "see" in the world is described in text.

Graphical worlds are usually synchronous and combine both text and graphics. While most focus on social interaction, some specialize in providing an environment where participants can build their own buildings and colonize whole territories. Participants are represented by avatars[8] that can take almost any form—often an animal or cartoon character—with speech appearing as text balloons over the speaker's (avatar's) head (fig. 11.6). The Palace and WorldsAway are examples of two-dimensional worlds where avatars move in front of a static flat background, which may or may not depict a three-dimensional scene. Three-dimensional worlds such as Worlds Chat™, Microsoft's V-Chat, and Active Worlds®[9] allow the user's avatar to move in all three dimensions through the space (fig. 11.7).

Other 3D graphical worlds simulate existing real-life cities rather than creating new imaginary ones. Some of these worlds are Planet9™, Deuxième Monde (Paris), Virtual Whitehall (London), and Virtual Los Angeles™ (figs. 11.8, 11.9). Their purposes vary: Users of Deuxième Monde mainly talk with other visitors, but they can also participate in special daily events, create 3D Web pages, and shop online. Deuxième Monde is particularly interesting because the virtual version of Paris is just like the physical version. Commercial

Fig. 11.8 *(right)*: Virtual Los Angeles™.
© Urban Simulation Laboratory, UCLA

Fig. 11.9 *(below)*: Deuxième Monde.
© Canal Numedia

space is available to rent for $30,000 to $80,000 per year, with the most desirable spaces online located in the same places as prime real estate in "real-life" Paris. Planet9 creates virtual worlds and cities for "marketing, advertising, product visualization, training, architectural simulation, data visualization, and entertainment." Virtual Whitehall aims to provide users "with the ability to gain the 'urban experience' of London." And Virtual Los Angeles is a simulation of Los Angeles intended for educational and planning purposes, in particular to "facilitate the modeling, display, and evaluation of alternative proposed environments. It can be used to visualize neighborhoods as they currently exist or how they might appear after built intervention occurs."

There is an intriguing relationship between text, graphics, realism, and sociability in these digital worlds. Proponents of text-based worlds often claim that they have more social interaction, resulting in a greater sense of community; while the more visually realistic worlds, especially the 3D ones, can be less sociable places for several reasons. First, graphical environments can have a greater number of activities and places available to participants, which can distract them from conversing. Second is the issue of density: 3D worlds can be very large (AlphaWorld claims to be more than 400 square kilometers), making it more difficult to find other participants within conversational range. And finally, the ability of avatars to change appearance can also affect the sociability in both text and graphical worlds. Unlike the real world, where humans cannot substantially alter their looks or disappear in an extremely short period of time, avatars can change their physical appearance and location instantaneously. Because one can never be sure that a conversational partner who drastically changes his or her looks (or perhaps disappears only to reappear moments later) is in fact the same person that began the conversation, the dialogue can be rather shallow and repetitious.

Related to the physical attributes of a digital environment and its inhabitants is the issue of time, which turns out to be as much a philosophical as a programming question for designers of digital worlds. In one sense, time in synchronous virtual worlds directly parallels real time. For example, users who visit early in the morning will probably not find many with whom they can converse, but if they return later at night, the site will likely be active and crowded. There is also a second aspect of time—its interaction with the artifacts within the world, called "persistence"—that has begun to be incorporated into some virtual worlds. For example, if an avatar puts an object down on a table, will it (should it) still be there if the user leaves and returns later (assuming no one else has touched it in the meantime)?

THE APPEAL OF DIGITAL WORLDS

For the uninitiated, it is often difficult to understand the attraction of these virtual worlds, because conversation can be superficial, even inane,[10] and the environments can be primitive and crude.[11] In spite of this, many individuals spend countless hours a week building, governing, and participating in their chosen world, and find the experience deeply satisfying and rewarding.[12]

The three main reasons people find these worlds appealing are sociability, creativity, and identity play. Digital worlds can be very sociable places; visitors and inhabitants are more willing to strike up conversations with strangers, since everyone assumes that everyone else is there to socialize. Digital worlds also offer a creative outlet. Users can create their own avatars; many digital worlds allow the building of private rooms, spaces, and objects; others allow users who learn the world's programming language to navigate and express themselves in quite unusual ways. Giving the individual the ability to experiment with identity is an attractive feature of these worlds; participants may alter or hide their gender, personality, or physical looks,[13] a feature that seems to horrify and delight outsiders in equal measure.

There is another important reason these virtual worlds attract people. Participants are not simply consumers of these worlds—they are also their creators, producers, and inhabitants. These digital worlds and communities offer participants the opportunity to create not only public space but *civitas.* And because they are investing their time and energy, users tend to judge their world by its potential and how engaged they are with others, not simply on superficial appearances.

VIEWS OF THE CITY FROM THE DIGITAL WORLD

Because they are so visual, graphical worlds are the most rewarding ones to explore in terms of how they represent and reflect our images of community, public space, and the city.

Simulated cities such as Planet9, Deuxième Monde, Virtual Whitehall, and Virtual Los Angeles represent the city literally. Unlike other digital worlds, these are not imaginary places—their creators have tried to duplicate the physical world, re-creating some of the larger, more exciting cities such as London, Paris, New York, San Francisco, and Los Angeles. Cities such as Tulsa, Springfield, and Newcastle do not seem to spark the creators' imaginations in quite the same way. They also seem to approve of the city's physical environment, because buildings and streets are painstakingly re-created; but unlike the real thing, they are clean and free of crime. Unfortunately, in their efforts to sanitize and secure the city, the creators also succeed in removing much of its life—often there are no people, no cars, no trees, and the streets are eerily empty.

Virtual worlds have not been successful at creating completely safe and detached realms. In many worlds, deceit and evil deeds are introduced by people and are not necessarily related to the physical environment. As a result, regular participants spend many hours developing social rules for their worlds and defining what is acceptable and unacceptable behavior. AlphaWorld has created a police force to help fight anarchy. The literature also describes virtual crimes and misdeeds. Rob Rossney tells about the virtual world of WorldsAway, where headhunters on the streets of Kymer regularly steal the heads of unsuspecting first-time visitors. Two stories have risen to almost mythical heights: Lindsay Van Gelder's essay on "The Strange Case of the Electronic Lover" and Julian Dibbell's story "A Rape in Cyberspace."[14]

Another group of worlds has been created using Active Worlds software, including AlphaWorld, Metatropolis, and Virtual City.[15] Metatropolis is dark and beautiful. Newly arrived visitors see the glittering city in the distance, but as they travel through the world, they realize that they are unable to reach the beckoning lights, which remain just out of grasp on the horizon. In Metatropolis, visitors find themselves stranded in a lonely world of late-night road stops and neon lights (fig. 11.10).

Fig. 11.10: Metatropolis.
© Activeworlds.com

Another Active World, Virtual City, has similar characteristics. Upon arriving in a glass pavilion, visitors see a large modern city of high-rises in the near distance. Teleport booths are provided to take them to various parts of the world: Virtual Park, the industrial park; Parque Del Mar, the theme park; and the Barrio de Tiempo Libre. But there is no way of actually getting to the heart of downtown. All parks and neighborhoods are located equal distance from the downtown, and residents of Virtual City are limited to life in the virtual suburbs; the tantalizing downtown remains just out of reach (fig. 11.11).

Brasília is also created with Active Worlds software, but unlike other virtual cities, it mimics the real-life version, except for its eternally dramatic sunset (fig. 11.12). Most of the inhabitants are Portuguese-speaking, and the buildings in the digital version are in more or less the same position as the originals. Visitors travel by bus rather than teleporting (though the process is the same), and it is one of the few places to have vehicles for the highways that have been created.

Fig. 11.11 ***(below left)*****: Virtual City.**
© Activeworlds.com

Fig. 11.12 ***(below right)*****: Brasília.**
© Activeworlds.com

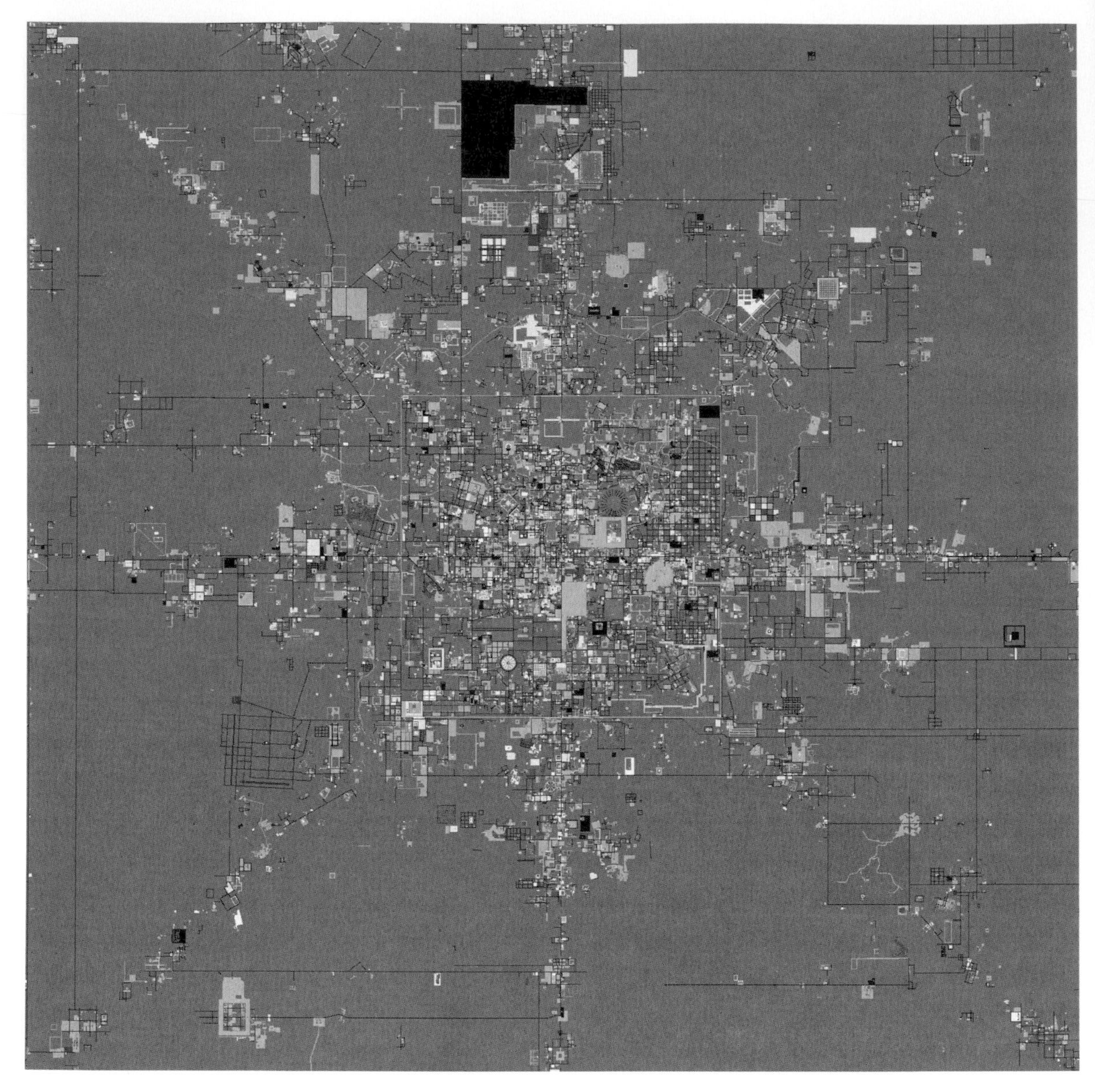

Fig. 11.13: Map of Alpha-World, December 1996.
© Activeworlds.com

AlphaWorld is the largest of the Active Worlds; it grew significantly in the late 1990s (figs. 11.13, 11.14). It, like other worlds, has an odd frontier/suburban feel about it, with disconcerting characteristics such as two-lane highways in a world that has no cars and where residents get around on foot or by teleporting themselves over longer distances. Buildings with sloped roofs and walls are built in a world with no snow, rain, wind, or cold. There are few public buildings and apparently no zoning.

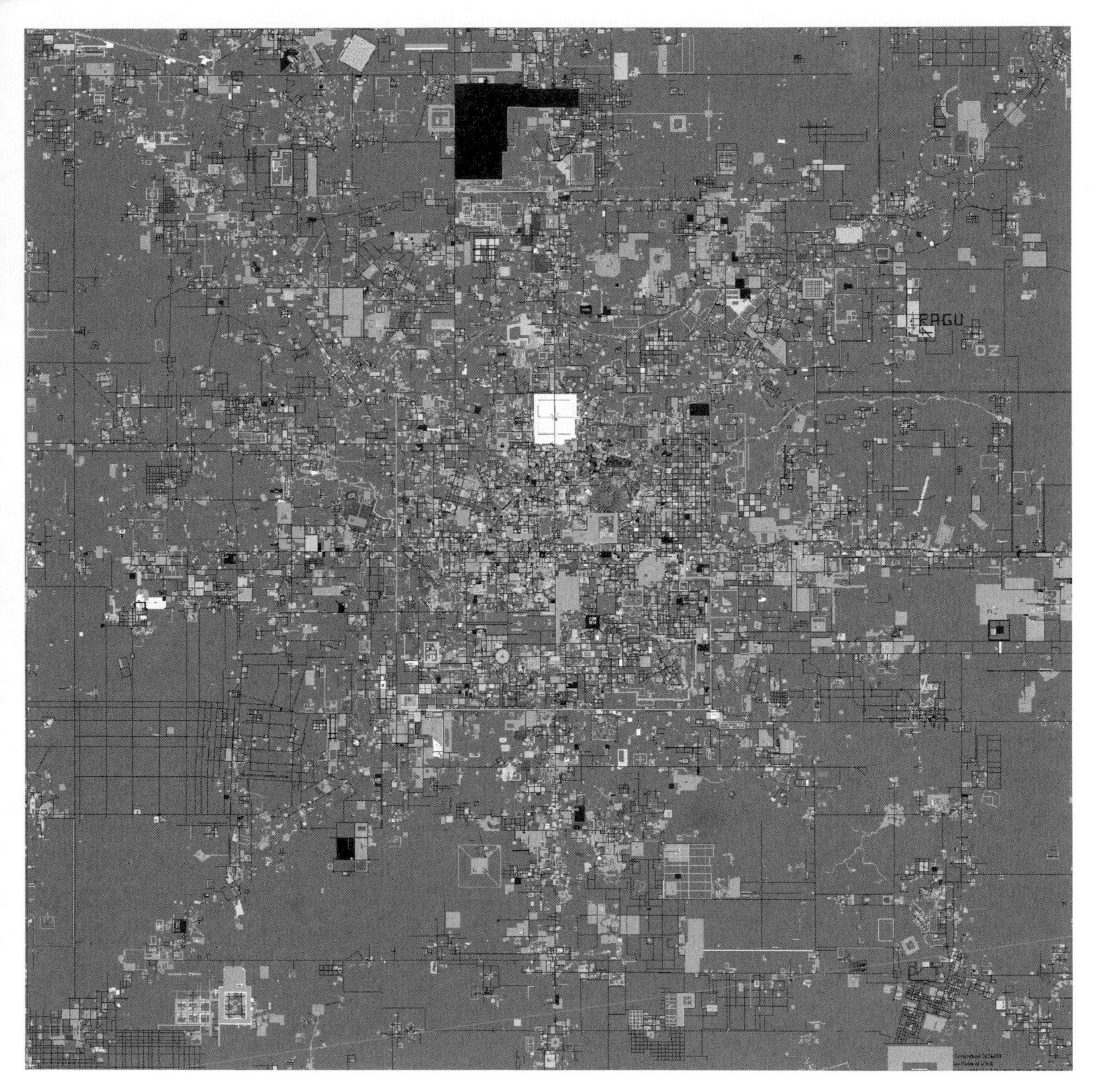

Fig. 11.14: Map of AlphaWorld, December 1998. © Activeworlds.com

There is a building code, however, which can be summed up as follows: Keep it simple, keep it sparse, and keep it spread out.[16]

The 2D worlds created with Palace software are similar to the 3D worlds in that the image of the city is frequently used as the opening screen when the world is entered. Cartoonlike drawings of cities are most common, but photographs are also used. The city analogy soon breaks down, however, and visitors immediately go from a long-distance view of a city or town directly into smaller rooms or spaces; rarely would visitors find midscale public spaces such as streets, plazas, or parks.

What do these digital worlds tell us about the creators' image of the city? When digital urban environments are designed, the downtown is often seen as the Holy Grail—the vivid, exciting, teasing, tantalizing city is held up within sight, but out of reach. The image of the city is used to attract us and to draw us into the world, but it functions mainly as a decoration or marketing technique intended to get the customer in the door. The creators of these virtual worlds appear to take the image of the city literally but superficially, and they generally do not seem to have given much thought to what it is about a city that their visitors would find appealing. They use the image of the city liberally but strip it of meaning.

VIEWS OF DIGITAL CITIES FROM THE PHYSICAL WORLD

If we are to look at the images of physical cities through the lenses of their digital cousins, it is only fair to reverse the view and look at digital cities through the lens of the "real" world. To do so, one must question how successful they are as cities, as public places, and as communities.

Are they able to successfully re-create the urban experience? Too often, rather than mimicking the vitality and excitement of downtown, the digital environment is disconcertingly desolate and empty; the buildings are blandly modern; and it is common to travel around these worlds without meeting another soul.

To be fair, though, the crude and simplistic environment is not always a reflection of the creators' aesthetic taste; it is also a reflection and result of technology, economics, and regulations. The database of Virtual Los Angeles, for example, whose graphics are quite detailed and realistic, is currently hundreds of gigabytes and will soon exceed one terabyte. This much detail requires either massive storage or large amounts of bandwidth to transfer the information. When designers and builders of simulated and imagined cities are forced to choose between speed and detail, the visually interesting details usually lose. Buildings are plain because, as in the real world, complicated, intricate buildings are more expensive and difficult to build. Regulations can also affect the environment. In AlphaWorld, for example, residents are required to pave over land to stake their claim—they may never return to build on it, but it remains out of circulation, resulting in vast paved open areas.

Are these digital worlds public places? Spiro Kostof in *The City Assembled* defines public space as a place that promotes social encounters, ensconces community, and serves the conduct of public affairs. Certainly many other theorists have weighed in with their own definitions: Public space is a stage on which communal life unfolds; a place freely accessible and shaped by its inhabitants; a landscape that reflects us; a world of strangers; a place that hopefully engenders tolerance of diverse interests and behaviors; and a place of social and commercial encounter and exchange.[17] Regardless of which definition is used, many virtual worlds arguably could qualify as public space.

Not only are they public spaces, but many are civic spaces as well, and it is in the realm of promoting *civitas* that these worlds have much to offer. Worlds such as De Digitale Stad (Digital Amsterdam), Municipia, and community networks emphasize civic debate and discussion rather than attempting to duplicate the physical characteristics of a city.[18] With these sites, the boundary between the physical city and the virtual begins to blur,[19] creating a new type of public space.

Are these virtual worlds communities? The verdict is mixed; the answer lies, of course, in how community is defined. Our long history of lamenting the loss of community is probably matched only by our equally long history of not being able to agree on exactly what community is. Definitions of community can include geographic area, common consciousness, shared interests or attitudes, collections of institutions, social interaction, or networks of social relations.[20] We are often unable to separate what we feel it *should* be with what it *is*;[21] we are often unsure whether we're discussing a locality, experience, or relationship; and we aren't always able to distinguish between the familiar community and the nonfamiliar public space.

Howard Rheingold, one of the first and foremost proponents of virtual communities, would certainly argue that they are communities.[22] And those who are active participants in these places, especially the text-based social worlds, would no doubt claim that they are communities and that they play a real and meaningful part in their lives. If we define community as a social network characterized by a kind of human interaction, it becomes possible to take the idea of virtual community seriously.[23] Of course, to those who believe that community must be a physical entity, "virtual community" will always remain an oxymoron.

Benedict Anderson in *Imagined Communities* makes a useful distinction between imaginary and imagined communities.[24] Although the topic he was addressing was nationalism, he made the point that nations are imagined—not imaginary—as limited by geographic boundaries and language, sovereignty, and a community with deep, horizontal comradeship. Even though they are imagined—a creation of their inhabitants—there is nothing false or fabricated about them. This is a very useful way of thinking about digital worlds. Perhaps virtual worlds should be thought of as imaged communities that are conceived, created, sustained, and believed in by their inhabitants.

Virtual communities exist, but to call every group that ever met online a community would be absurd. Not every group whose members get together to talk or write each other is a community, nor should it be. As Thomas Erickson asserts, not every online group has to be a "community" to be useful, or entertaining, or meaningful. Online discourse can be useful and engaging, even if participants form no lasting relationships, share few values, or can't count on one another. What is important is the communication itself, rather than the real or perceived bond. Others also suggest that it may be counterproductive to try and label these groups as communities simply because of the assumptions and cultural baggage that come with this, proposing that these digital worlds are best thought of as a form or extension of social networks rather than a community.[25]

Robert Putnam may claim that virtual worlds are just pale

imitations of "real life," but strangely enough, these worlds have much in common with the bowling leagues he longs for.[26] Perhaps if we put virtual worlds in the same category as bowling leagues—with the associated social network—rather than communities, we would gain not only a refreshing and useful perspective but a better understanding of both their limitations and possibilities.

CONCLUSION: DIGITAL DESIGN

Digital worlds bring design issues to the forefront. Even though the medium has presented us with the opportunity to create the best possible imagined communities and places, we appear to have succeeded only in duplicating some of the worst aspects of the physical world—dark, empty, bland cities and landscapes—the very ones that we wish to escape from in the first place. Part of the problem lies in the creators of these worlds not taking the spatial aspect very seriously. Sometimes they appear to think of the city as a trivial backdrop, consequently treating it rather superficially; perhaps this is because the creators of these worlds are usually computer programmers, not urban designers and architects.[27] And, of course, part of the problem is technical: Because of very real and legitimate technical limitations, extreme simplification is necessary. We simply cannot duplicate the physical world in all its richness with present-day technology.

Our image of the city is ambivalent and conflicted. On one hand, the popular media paint a dark picture of the city as a place to fear; some digital worlds continue this theme, though perhaps not intentionally, creating worlds that are desolate, dreary, and depressing. But digital worlds can also be creative, enjoyable, social, and stimulating places, and the image of the city can be glittering, exciting, intriguing, and bright. After all, the city image can be used as a marketing tool only if it makes the city appear desirable. Digital worlds, in spite of their many drawbacks and failings, still make a positive statement about cities—we try to create them digitally because, in spite of everything, we still think cities are exciting and rewarding places to be.

We should take digital worlds and virtual communities seriously, but not too seriously. We have a long history of creating new worlds, cities, and neighborhoods. These new digital worlds are part of our continuing attempt to create community and public space, but now with a new medium. The medium is young, and we shouldn't be too critical of our first efforts. As William Mitchell said, though virtual worlds may appear trivial and primitive, we should not be fooled by their crudeness. We are exploring the early incarnations of these potentially sophisticated online environments. They are blurring important boundaries and creating new types of public spaces in which urban designers need to be involved.[28]

The design of our environment, whether it be made of bits or atoms, is important and should be taken seriously. Designers of future digital worlds need to remember that what we create online will always be connected to the physical world; virtual worlds can never be completely new because we will always bring our old selves to them. Finally, there are many lessons from city design that can be applied to the new digital worlds. Virtual communities and digital worlds may not be physical, but they are very real.

Urban Images on Children's Television

Lawrence J. Vale and Julia R. Dobrow

■ EDITORS' OVERVIEW

It is possible to find ideas and models for responsive city design in some very unlikely places. Urban design historian Lawrence Vale and media scholar Julia Dobrow examine the role of children's television environments—*Sesame Street,* as well as several recent animated shows—in the production of city images and stereotypes. They observe that these programs emphasize images of childhood independence and unrestricted movement and underplay the violence and mayhem that dominate the adult-oriented television programs set in cities.

These carefully designed environments—which many children visit more frequently than they do real cities—are places of frequent social engagement, where everything and everyone a child could want are located in convenient proximity. Often, interviews suggest, these shows represent nostalgia on the part of the shows' producers and creators for the neighborhoods of their own childhoods. In the simplified cityscapes of children's television, the sensory overload of urban life is minimized; familiar faces far outnumber strangers. In Lynchian terms, they are places characterized by a rich condensation of nodes and landmarks. This is not to suggest that real cities should become more cartoonlike, yet it seems clear that these energetic televisual landscapes revel in the true meaning of animation.

TELEVISION, CITIES, AND CHILDREN

For the past half-century, the burgeoning force of television has profoundly affected the production of city images and stereotypes. Just as television once helped ingrain the mythologies of the American West (supplementing a plethora of films), so newer genres of crime shows, medical dramas, and urban comedies have sent repeated messages about city life into hundreds of millions of homes. It is no mere coincidence that the urbanization of television scenography has precisely paralleled the flight of Americans to suburbia. Urbanist Lewis Mumford noticed a connection more than forty years ago, commenting that most of these new suburbanites may be "settling for just so much of the city as they can take in vicariously through a television set."[1] In the 1950s, however, much suburban living was predicated on a daily commute to the core city, at least for the family's wage earner. Today, given the broad shift of many kinds of jobs toward the outer fringe of cities, the majority of commuting has become suburb to suburb. For many, the city core has become the periphery. This is especially true for America's suburban children. To an increasingly suburban and suburbanizing society, the televisual images of cities may well represent both the first and the dominant exposure many children have to urban places. It therefore seems important to examine what messages they are being sent.

From *Sesame Street* and *Mr. Rogers' Neighborhood* to Arthur-the-Aardvark's Elwood City and the nuclear-powered Springfield of *The Simpsons,* our nation's youngest audiences are presented with repeated exposure to fictional cities and towns. For at least the last three decades, children's television producers have been actively engaged with inventing and developing not just memorable characters but distinctive settings where these characters reside, parallel worlds that children are invited to join. "Can you tell me how to get, How to get to Sesame Street?" "Every day when you're walking down the street, and everybody that you meet has an original point of view." "Won't you be my neighbor?" These are a few of the song lines that accompany the opening credits of popular children's television shows. They entice the viewer to join the adventures and commonplace happenings of characters in the mythical urban televisual landscapes that make up children's TV.

There is no doubt that children are increasingly exposed to images on television. More than 99 percent of all American homes have access to television, a higher percentage than have telephones. In homes with children under the age of 18, well over half have cable television, and even higher proportions have VCRs. Research has shown that the average preschool child watches between twenty-five and twenty-eight hours of television per week; by the time the average American child graduates from high school, she or he will have spent more time watching television than doing anything else, except sleeping.[2]

Although the degree to which television's images might affect children continues to be a source of debate among researchers, educators, politicians, and parents, it does seem clear that cumulative exposure has some effects. Research conducted during the last thirty years by George Gerbner and his associates at the University of Pennsylvania has consistently found that viewers who watch a great deal of television tend to see the world in stereotype to a far greater extent than do lighter viewers. This is of particular concern, since studies also have found the world of children's television to be inequitable in terms of ethnic, racial, and gender distribution.[3] In this chapter, however, we make no claims about effects; our concern is with the production of images.[4]

To be sure, not all children's television is concerned with urban imaging; in fact, paralleling the nonurban skew of the American population, very little of children's television is citylike. Some shows geared to the youngest audiences, such as the self-contained suburban schoolyard of *Barney* or the rolling rural pastels of *Teletubbies,* are overtly nonurban. Other programs, like the currently ubiquitous *Rugrats,* depict the environment from the perspective of infants and toddlers, a world mostly circumscribed by the dimensions of home and yard. More pervasively, the much-maligned world of Saturday morning action-adventure cartoons (now seen on all days and at all times on various channels) is steeped in fantasy violence. These shows present a vast array of animated superheroes and supervillains in battle across a myriad of landscapes, few of which bear much resemblance to the cities and towns of conventional daily life. All that said, there are many children's programs that do attempt to introduce children to seemingly habitable and attractive parallel worlds, and to encourage sustained social involvement with the community lives of their characters, whether human, cartoon, or Muppet.

For this preliminary investigation, we have chosen to look at five televisual environments designed, at least in part, to appeal to children. Our sample is not random; it is chosen to include shows that have consciously emphasized the urbanity of their sets and settings. These are shows, that is, where place-making and community formation constitute a central aspect of the narrative purpose; each episode is not just a story, but part of an ongoing engagement with a place. Within this category of place-oriented shows, we have limited ourselves to examples that are both highly popular and currently being aired. The five programs—*Arthur, Sesame Street, Hey Arnold!, Disney's Doug*, and *The Simpsons*—depict a variety of settings, from small cities to dense city centers, and are oriented to appeal to a wide range of audiences, from preschoolers to adolescents (not to mention adults). All of them feature children (or childlike creatures, in the case of *Sesame Street*'s Big Bird and his colorful associates) as central characters, and the principal narrative focus remains firmly tuned to children's activities.

FIVE CHILDREN'S TELEVISION PROGRAMS

First aired in 1969, *Sesame Street* was the brainchild of educator and activist Joan Ganz Cooney, who brought together a remarkable team of writers, researchers, creative people, and puppeteers to create what has become one of the longest running, and certainly most heavily researched, children's shows of all time. As Cooney puts it, "*Sesame Street* became the most famous street in America in one television season."[5] Over the course of the next thirty years, the PBS show received seventy-one Emmys (more than any show in history) and eight Grammys. Seventy-seven percent of American preschool children watch *Sesame Street* at least once a week; there are an estimated 11 million weekly viewers. Moreover, different versions of the show are produced in nineteen other countries and aired in more than 140. *Sesame Street*'s parent company, Sesame Workshop (formerly Children's Television Workshop), has published more than 600 *Sesame Street* books, oversees six magazines with a readership that exceeds 12 million adults and children, and licenses countless *Sesame Street* products. According to Gerald Lesser, *Sesame Street*'s original director of curriculum, *Sesame Street* was the first show to prove that "television could teach."[6] *Sesame Street*'s stated educational objectives are to teach children symbolic representation, such as letters, numbers, and shapes; cognitive processes, such as developing reasoning and problem-solving skills; physical environment awareness, such as learning about cycles in nature; and social skills—learning about family, home, and community.[7] These objectives are met through an hour-long show that has recurring human and Muppet (the word derives from the combination of puppet and marionette) characters who peacefully coexist on *Sesame Street,* interacting around a particular issue, interspersed with many animated and filmed sequences not specifically tied to the storyline of the day.

Based on the award-winning *Arthur* books by Marc Brown, the animated series *Arthur* went on the air in 1996. It quickly became PBS's most popular children's show, won Emmy awards for outstanding children's animated program in 1998 and 1999, and was the number one–rated children's television program for viewers between the ages of two and eleven in 1998.[8] The stories center on the life of nine-year-old Arthur Read, his family and friends, all of whom are drawn as various animals but whose lives and traits are distinctly human. Arthur resides in Elwood City, described by executive producer Carol Greenwald as a "small city" named after the Pennsylvania town where her grandmother lived and near where Marc Brown grew up.[9]

Doug, launched in 1991, is an animated series that originally aired on Nickelodeon. In 1996, after Nickelodeon failed to exercise its option to order additional new episodes, Disney bought out the *Doug* franchise in a multimillion-dollar deal that followed closely on Disney's decision to purchase ABC. The show quickly became "the cornerstone and highest-rated new program on ABC's Saturday morning lineup" and "a key contributor to making the network No. 1 in Saturday morning ratings."[10] Nickelodeon retained rights to the initial fifty-two episodes, so the show airs both on that channel and on ABC, where it is known as *Disney's Doug.* Set in Bluffington, "bumper sticker capital of the world," the series follows the trials and tribulations of twelve-year-old Doug Funnie and his friends. In 1999, it gained an even greater following due to the success of *Doug's First Movie.* Creator Jim Jinkins comments that the TV show, while not strictly autobiographical, contains some plotlines based on events from his childhood, spent outside Richmond, Virginia, and is "emotionally very accurate."[11]

Hey Arnold!, which airs on Nickelodeon and in Spanish on Telemundo, presents the inner-city urban world of nine-year-old Arnold (a kid with a "football shaped" head) and his fellow fourth-graders from P.S. 118. Designed to target children ages six to twelve, it draws an audience that ranges from two-year-olds to teens. The show takes its name from the various greetings and taunts Arnold receives from his neighbors, which sound forth in the opening sequence of each episode. Arnold's hometown is not named, although producer Craig Bartlett makes clear that it is drawn to recall aspects of Seattle, Portland, and Brooklyn.[12]

First aired in 1987, *The Simpsons*—a creation of cartoonist Matt Groening—was primetime television's first animated series (and is even credited with helping to revive the medium of animation). It quickly gained both critical acclaim and great popularity on the Fox network, garnering an audience ranging from children through adults, airing in more than seventy countries.[13] At the peak of its marketing rampage in 1990, there were a hundred companies licensed to sell Simpsons merchandise. In 1994, Fox went so far as to propose a U.S. postage stamp featuring Bart Simpson's writings (the Postal Service rejected the suggestion).[14] *The Simpsons* focuses on the lives and adventures of the endearingly dysfunctional Simpson family (Homer and Marge and their children: ten-year-old Bart, eight-year-old Lisa, and infant Maggie), as well as a host of oddball characters who interact with them. Set in Springfield, a city somewhere in the United States, the Simpsons' adventures often take them to various places both around town and outside the city limits.

IMAGING THE CITIES OF CHILDREN'S TELEVISION

In order to assess the structure and identity of these five televisual landscapes, we have attempted to analyze them in Lynchian terms. Obviously, we could not actually interview the characters about the imageability of their hometowns, but we could analyze the way these characters are shown to inhabit and move about these places.[15] We wondered how well Lynch's classic quintet of place descriptors—*landmarks, paths, districts, edges,* and *nodes*—would elucidate the urban worlds on children's television. In the Lynchian schema—derived from observations, interviews, and cognitive mapping exercises conducted in Boston, Los Angeles, and Jersey City during the late 1950s—these five elements help to clarify the structure and identity of the most imageable places. For Lynch, *landmarks* refer to certain key visual reference points in the city, ranging from prominent buildings to smaller and more personal objects, such as a sign or even a doorknob. *Paths* connote the networks of streets and sidewalks that structure movement. *Districts* describe the various subsections of cities thought to carry a distinctive shared identity or ambience (such as Chinatown). *Edges,* by contrast, mark the various breaks and separations that occur in cities, caused either by natural features such as waterways or cliffs or by constructed barriers such as walls, highways, and railroad tracks. Lastly, Lynch defined *nodes* as the social focal points of cities, such as parks, where people go to gather with others. In what follows, we attempt to view the cities and towns of children's television through a Lynchian lens.

■ SESAME STREET

On *Sesame Street,* the opening sequence sets the stage for how this show treats the urban environment. Big Bird—who, despite being eight feet two inches tall—is "psychologically written to represent a six-year-old,"[16] walks through New York's Central Park with a racially mixed group of children. The children play in the park; greenery or water fountains are shown in the foreground of all shots, and a few large buildings are shown in the background. The opening montage presents images of Big Bird leading children through safe, clean places in the park or across streets that have parked cars but no moving traffic, juxtaposed with scenes of children jumping in puddles in front of a brownstone or playing without any apparent adult supervision in a park. The entire opening sequence (which has undergone repeated alteration and updating over the years) conveys the sense that even a large city can seem like a small town: Children can play freely and enjoy abundant outdoor space. Even the most urban spaces are shown as intimate, clean, and safe. Still, as Jon Stone, who produced and directed the show for twenty-six years, observed, even a sanitized streetscape was a radical departure for children's television: The creators "didn't want another clubhouse or treasure house or treehouse. . . . My proposal was that this should be a real inner-city street, and we should populate it with real people."[17] A real inner-city street, perhaps, but a single-sided one devoid of motorized traffic, immune from rain or snow, impervious to strangers, wheelchair accessible, and populated by a Technicolor array of Muppets and an equally diverse collection of multigenerational humans. Executive producer Michael Loman sees it all more simply, if no less idealistically: Sesame Street is "an integrated neighborhood with adults watching kids."[18]

In 1993, after nearly twenty-five years, the *Sesame Street* team greatly enlarged the set, augmenting the familiar streetscape with a new section dubbed "around the corner." The expanded set allowed the show to include a whole new set of landmarks and nodes. In addition to long-standing landmarks such as Big Bird's nest, Oscar the Grouch's trash can, the Sesame Street street

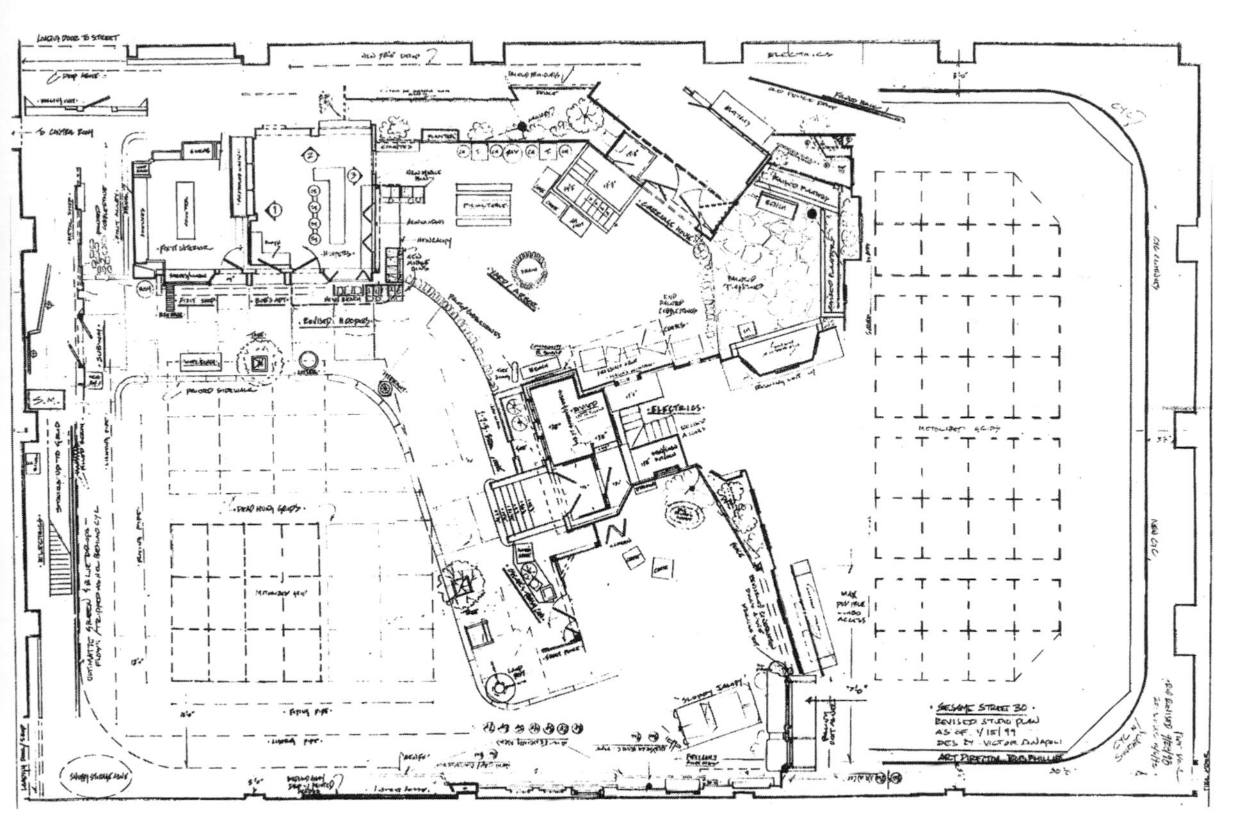

Fig. 12.1: Plan of the *Sesame Street* set, as of January 1999.

sign, the Fix-It Shop, and Hooper's Store, the expanded set incorporated Gina's day care, the Furry Arms Hotel, Celina's dance studio, and a seemingly adjacent urban park. Unfortunately, the change, according to Loman, created new problems: It was "too big" and "confused children" (perhaps, ironically, making *Sesame Street* seem *too* citylike). Eager to return to the focused "neighborhood feeling" of the original set, the producers eliminated the new portion beginning with the 1998–99 season, one act of urban renewal that apparently drew little protest from either humans or Muppets (fig. 12.1). Loman's goal was to reemphasize the sense of "people in a neighborhood" and the intensity of "belonging" that can occur in a place where "diversity is paramount." In a culture that too often preferred to situate children with "cute little bunnies," he commented, *Sesame Street*'s mission remained one that encouraged outreach to the "real urban world" around them. Determined to avoid stereotypes, its producers assembled a racially and ethnically diverse cast but stressed their commonalities as humans just as often as they celebrated culturally specific customs or acknowledged differences. *Sesame Street* researchers and designers toured New York's ethnic neighborhoods, continually searching for ways to update their set to reflect contemporary practices; one result was an expanded sidewalk presence for Hooper's Store.[19]

Ironically, for a place that bills itself as a "street," there appear to be no real *paths* in this neighborhood: Characters are shown going only from one contiguous locale to another. Beyond this, there is no sense of how one gets to anywhere other than Sesame Street (or how one gets to Sesame Street from anywhere else). It is the center of its world. Doors from the subway station, marked by a sign, open into a courtyard filled with all the familiar Sesame Street landmarks. The smooth sidewalk yields to cobblestone at one end, enhancing a feeling of a place somehow set apart from the rest of the urban world, almost an urban cul-de-sac. The only *paths* depicted on the show occur in some of the filmed sequences in which children are shown riding a city bus while doing such things as pointing out landmarks or counting the blocks to school. Similarly, Sesame Street is its own seemingly self-sufficient *district,* suggesting that its denizens can find all they need to live in the city within a short walk. It is not even necessary to acknowledge the existence of other districts. So, too, it is an *edge*-less city. The walls that do exist are there chiefly to make the Muppeteers' presence unobtrusive; they are not used as barriers to separate or divide Sesame Street from less-hospitable domains beyond. On Sesame Street, the only true edge is the television screen itself, marking the border between the highly variable life experiences of its audience and the fantasy city they come to visit daily.

■ HEY ARNOLD!

Like *Sesame Street, Hey Arnold!* is unambiguously set in the heart of a large northern American city. Creator/producer Craig Bartlett grew up in Seattle, went to art school in Portland, and has an abiding love for Brooklyn; all of these predilections come across in the architecture and ambience of *Hey Arnold!* Bartlett chose not to name the city because he wanted "kids to have fun speculating," but made sure that no one would confuse it with Los Angeles, where—as with most other cartoons—the show's production is headquartered. In contrast to the stucco-and-tile houses that pervade the perpetually sunny cartoon landscapes drawn by many Angelinos, *Hey Arnold!*'s unnamed city is a place with frequent rain and clearly defined seasons. The entire animation has a darker and grayer palette than its rivals, as if it were lit to reflect the more subdued climatic conditions of northern cities, and scenes frequently take place at dusk, or even at night. Arnold lives with his grandparents and several of their tenants in a Victorian-era boardinghouse located beneath a highway overpass, in what Bartlett terms "a savage juxtaposition" of old and new.[20] It is a neighborhood that urban renewal seems to have passed by, but just barely, and Arnold himself displays a particular interest in historic preservation.

Since it is an animated show, *Hey Arnold!* does not take place on a set the way *Sesame Street* does, but its producers and

Fig. 12.2: View of *Hey Arnold!*'s Seattle-like setting.

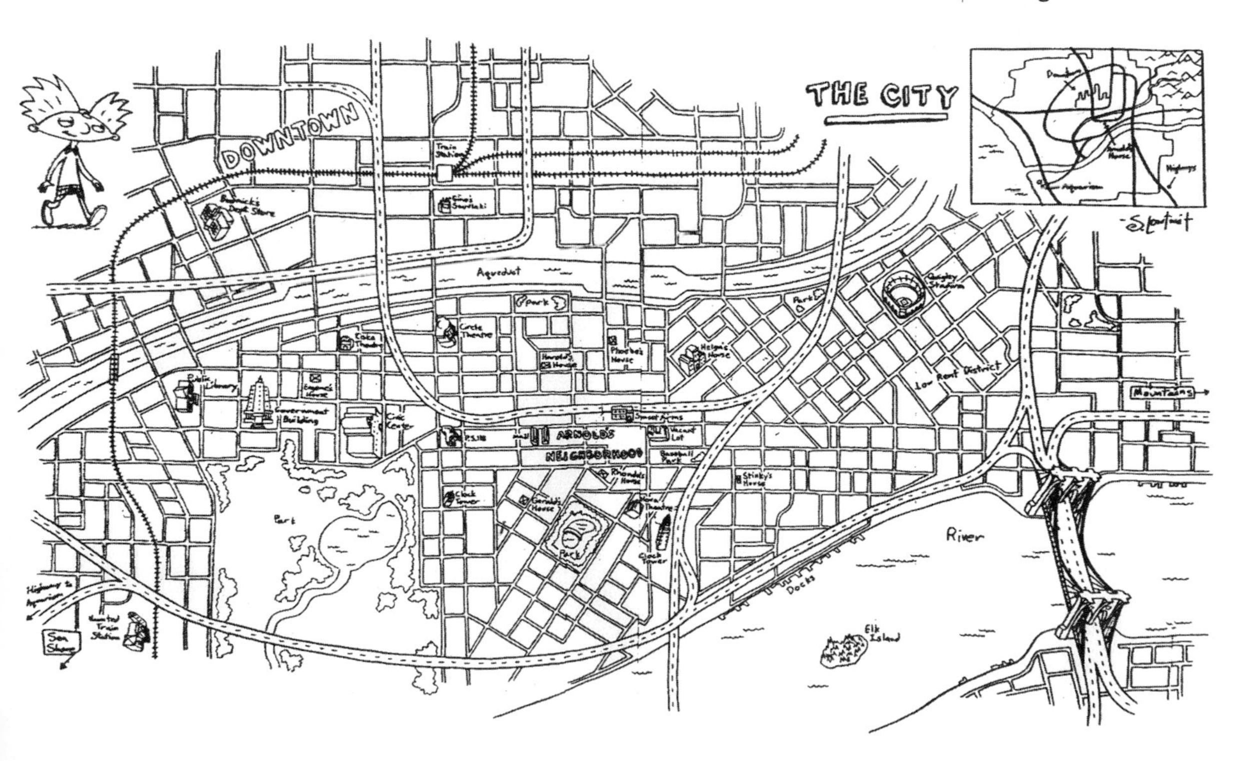

designers do plan episodes with a city schematic—introduced to help with the show's second season—firmly in mind (fig. 12.2). This map determines where the various nodes of activity are located in relation to one another; Bartlett adds that such a base map is also useful for planning future film and interactive CD-ROM ventures.[21]

A lot about this show would appeal to architects and designers, since it features some richly detailed interiors (especially Arnold's house) and takes such obvious pleasure in conveying streetscapes from many different perspectives—for example, rooftop shots and aerial oblique views. Bartlett calls *Hey Arnold!* "a pro-urban, nostalgic, idealistic view of community," one that would be "comforting" to viewers unfamiliar with such places, yet somehow still just potentially dangerous enough to be "alive" and interesting. He explicitly sought to create a nonsuburban image, a place that could be valued for the intensity of its community ties. Bartlett recognizes that he has idealized this place ("it is the community that we all wanted to live in"), but defends its "retro" orientation. It is a world without chain stores, one where contemporary plotlines take place against a backdrop of 1950s automobiles that—unlike in real cities—are treated more as artistic objects than as modes of transportation. The freeway that appears so prominently is devoid of cars, and, as on *Sesame Street* and other shows for children, the automobile is not allowed to impinge upon the primacy of pedestrians and street life.

This idyllic sense of community is perfectly evoked in the show's opening sequence, which is set at dusk in a Victorian-era neighborhood of two- to five-story brick-and-stone walk-ups. The first shot is of girls jumping rope in the glow of a streetlight on the sidewalk. The scene shifts: A girl shouts "Arnold!" as he marches down his granite steps with flashlight in hand, and cats, dogs, and a pig scurry out the door and past him. His grandparents peer lovingly and trustingly from the doorway as he leaves their watch. Arnold shines the light up at Helga (his apparent nemesis, she secretly adores him), who is looking down at him from a window in a building across the street. He strides down the sidewalk, alone and confident, passes Big Al's Tasty Café, all lit up for the evening, and finds his friends playing hoop on a well-lit half-court in a back alley. A grandmotherly figure looks down on them as she shakes out her linens. Two other boys join the basketball players: a gentle bully and another kid who makes a spooky face with his flashlight, prompting a distant scream. Two 1950s cars are parked in the background, and music accompanied by shouts of "Hey Arnold!" fills the air as the boys look up to see Helga yelling down at them. The small gang of boys form a line and stride six abreast down the middle of the street, past two girls playing a clapping game on the sidewalk. The scene then cuts to Arnold, who is standing by some street graffiti that spells out his name in yellow chalk. A bus zooms by. Helga leans out the bus window, tauntingly calling "*Ar*-nold!" In the next instant, Helga meets up with her friends, forming a girl gang that strides toward Arnold's group. The two lines face off in a spotlighted back alley, observed by eight adults looking down from windows above, laundry on the lines spanning the alley. Helga challenges Arnold, saying, "Move it, football head." He graciously allows her to pass, and the camera focuses in on Arnold, alone in the middle of the street. The scene cuts to a blue background superimposed with the show's credits.

In just a few seconds of dense imagery, *Hey Arnold!*'s design team has established the entire feel of the show. The opening evokes aspects of *West Side Story,* rendered here in terms of gender conflict; however, the tension is softened by the comforting presence of watchful adults whose eyes remain fixed on the outdoor rooms of the city. Producer Bartlett describes it as "upbeat and funny and funky and kinda cool," intended to engage viewers immediately with a sense of someone else's distinctive world. Unlike *West Side Story*, however, it is not a stylized world of ethnic and racial conflict or mortal danger; it is a community where racial and ethnic diversity exists without much comment and disputes can be peacefully resolved. *Hey Arnold!* celebrates the street-level independence of kids but acknowledges the presence of adults above the ground plane. As Bartlett observes, "Most kids can't be out after dark, especially in the city, but Arnold can, and so they live vicariously through him."[22]

Like many places on children's television, Arnold's city is dominated by its nodes. Most prominently, since Arnold himself remains at the center of his world, the show centers on his school (P.S. 118, established 1932), his house, and his favorite places for play. The latter take many forms—including park, arcade, bowling alley, and ball field—and seem uniformly easy to reach. Despite the unconstrained access and the predominance of street scenes, it is difficult to get much sense of the *paths* that connect these nodes simply from watching the episodes (although this information can be gleaned by perusing the city map). Paths are omnipresent as infrastructure, but there never seems to be one specific way to go. Arnold's city also has its *landmarks,* ranging from a distant high-rise skyline to the pseudo-Brooklyn Bridge that spans the river to the library, and even Arnold's house seems distinctive enough to qualify. On an even smaller scale, there are numerous locally owned individual businesses—one for produce, another for meat; others selling televisions, art supplies, pets, or skates—whose presence helps to orient the characters and their audience. In short, Arnold's domain is a pre-supermarket, mid-twentieth-century retail landscape of the sort celebrated by Jane Jacobs in *The Death and Life of Great American Cities.*[23] However, in contrast to the worlds that Jacobs extols—epitomized by New York's Lower East Side—Arnold's city is not a place of bustling strangers. Rather, like other cities on children's television, it is a place where the adults (like the moving cars) appear only when they are directly involved in the storyline. Arnold and his fellow fourth-graders are free to play stickball in the middle of the street, sneak into construction sites to play in the mud, and ride independently on city buses; kids are in control. Arnold's city is a place where urbanity breeds familiarity rather than chance encounters with unexpected persons and challenges.

As such, in Lynchian terms, it is a city that lacks hard edges or distinct districts that thrive on their articulated differences. The freeway could be considered an *edge,* but because it is carless and elevated well above and apart from the ground-level street activity, it functions more like a landmark than a barrier.

Similarly, the waterfront certainly functions as an edge but is not a problematical place of transition. In one episode, for instance, nine-year-old Arnold confidently spends fifty cents to hire a fisherman to row him out to an island in search of a recluse author he desperately wants to interview.

Nor is Arnold's city often shown as a place of distinct districts, although in one episode he challenges one of his grandparents' adult boarders to navigate his way across the city in order to demonstrate his newly gained literacy skills. In another episode, Arnold designs a parade float with a "carnival" theme intended to represent the city: "Downtown is a roller coaster since it's exciting and unpredictable, Southside a giant souvlaki stand because of all the great places to eat; a tilt-a-whirl is city hall since it's kinda crooked; and the waterfront is a water slide since there's lots of water. It'll be whirly color, just like the city itself." The whirl of Arnold's world, however diverse, still spins according to his own designs.

■ ARTHUR

In contrast to the big-city urbanism of *Sesame Street* and *Hey Arnold!*, shows such as *Arthur* convey similar child-centered networks in much smaller places. Because the television series emerged from the wildly popular series of books by Marc Brown (26 million copies sold as of 1999),[24] those who adapted *Arthur* for television recognized the need for some continuity yet also wished to make significant changes in Arthur's environment. Executive Producer Carol Greenwald observed that Brown's books drew most of their imagery from his home base in Hingham, Massachusetts (population 20,000) and thought it necessary to move beyond this "pretty tony suburb." She sent crews on photo shoots to a variety of "transitional urban areas" in and around Boston, which helped designers to make parts of Elwood City more genuinely citylike, integrating stores, a bus system, and an industrial area. The televisual *Arthur* that resulted thus includes not just residents in single-family homes of various sizes but major characters who live in an apartment building and a condo complex. This multifamily housing is located nearest to the Main Street businesses but is still only two or three blocks away from Arthur's single-family house. Most of the town's wealthiest residents live just up the hill (past a security post) in Flauntwell Heights. This single-access enclave of looping streets is in distinct contrast to the traditional grid of the rest of Elwood City, yet it is not emphasized as a separate district in the plotlines of the program; rather, the show stresses the possibilities of friendships that bridge class lines, relationships that are facilitated by the proximity of the town's richest and poorest residents (none of whom are actually very poor). Similarly, another high-income area of the town, Upper Downs ("where all the happy rich people live"), is desirably located adjacent to the lakefront, but also only a block away from the pizza parlors and bike shops of Main Street. Epitomized by Ziggy Marley's reggae rendition of the theme song that jauntily urges everyone to "listen to the rhythm, the rhythm of the street," the producers and designers deliberately chose to introduce diversity and to "move away from mainstream white suburban America."[25]

The result of all this is a degree of intimate integration that makes it seem as if the whole of Elwood City is a rich mixture of family-friendly uses, even though discernible microzones exist that are almost exclusively residential, commercial, or even industrial (fig. 12.3). For *Arthur*'s creators, a map of Elwood City became "part of the writers' 'bible,'" and all new places have been fit into this established framework.[26] Rather remarkably, within two or three blocks of Arthur's house are not only his school, the library, and the high school but video and music stores, a cinema, a dry cleaner, and restaurants; two banks, the town hall, and a post office; a ball field, the woods, Puffer's Pond, and a good sledding hill; two churches and a synagogue, plus a community center with pool; two gas stations and an auto body shop; and, also within the same short walk, Food City, Bargain City, and the Mill Creek Mall. Of special importance to Arthur, his grandmother and most of his friends all live within this same narrow radius, and the major social *node* of their daily lives, the Sugar Bowl, is on a corner only half a block away from

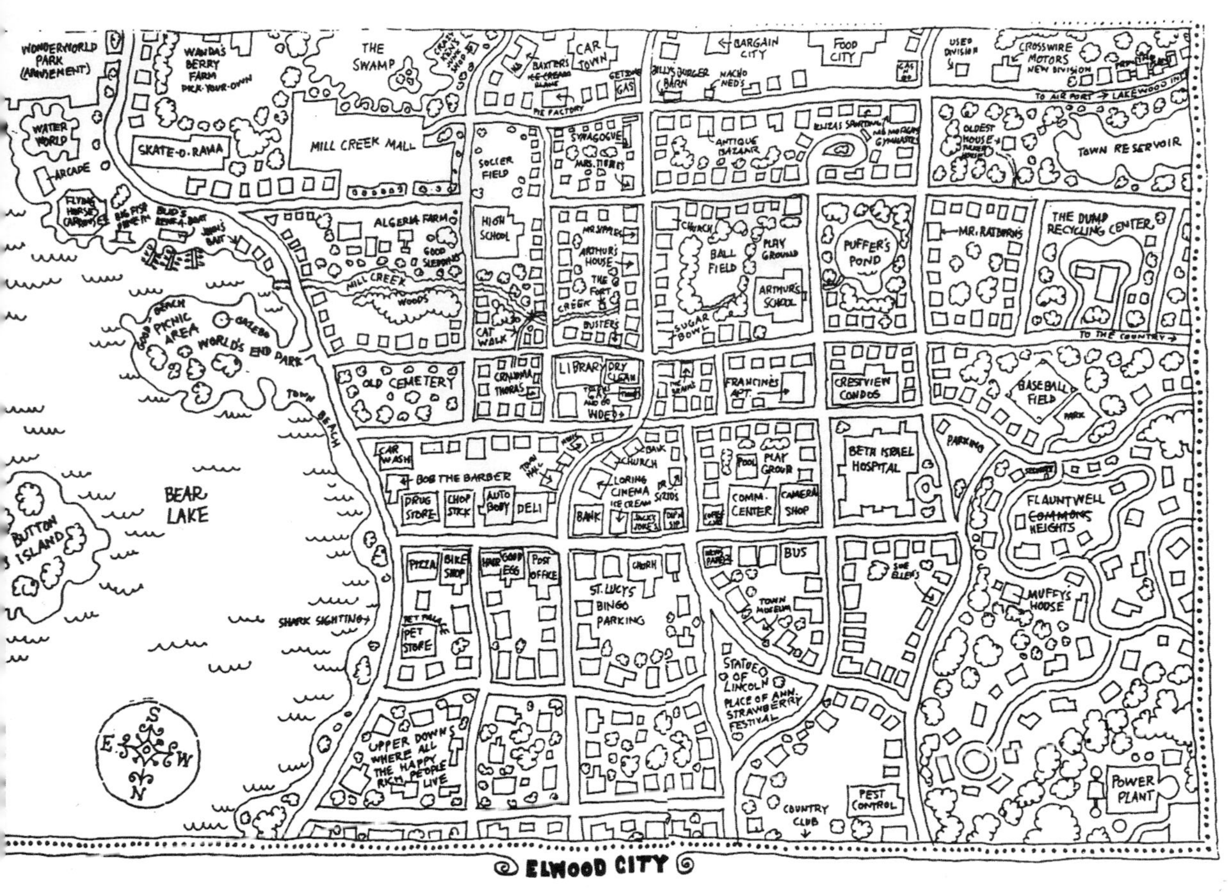

Fig. 12.3: Map of Elwood City, *Arthur's* hometown.

Arthur's house. The result is a density of destinations and institutions that, in a real town, would have to be socially and financially supported by far more than the 200 or so houses shown on the map of Elwood City. Yet there is certainly no evidence that children are bused into town to fill the schools, nor any sign of the vast parking lots that would be needed to service the malls and other institutions (the only off-street parking is for bingo, behind St. Lucy's). Instead, Elwood City is presented as the perfect fit for its protagonists' needs, a place where strangers are few and always friendly, where poverty and violence (random or otherwise) simply do not exist. It is a child-centered distillation of attractions, one that makes a strong appeal to world-wary parents, as well.

Executive Producer Greenwald concedes that the spatial freedom afforded to Arthur and his third-grade friends probably exceeds common social practice by "about two years." In explaining the decision to depict such freedoms, she personalizes her response in a revealing way: "Where and when I grew up you could do it." Younger characters on the show, such as Arthur's four-year-old sister D. W., are more closely supervised by parents or older siblings, but the overall effect is of a neighborhood in which not only friends but key social nodes—the library and the Sugar Bowl hangout—are accessible to all. Shown chiefly from the point of view of ten-year-olds, Elwood City is a space where kids are in control of their environment. The opening montage features Arthur striding purposefully down the sidewalk, shot from below to accent the empowerment of his pose; later in the sequence, he is shown striding atop a rotating globe, quite literally on top of his world. Even in the episode where Arthur nervously boards a public bus (on a day when his mother is unable to drive him to his swim lesson), falls asleep, and wakes to find himself on the unfamiliar, partly industrial outskirts of town, he is quickly comforted by the kindness of everyone he meets. The message is not that he has foolishly crossed an *edge* that should not have been transgressed but that such dangerous *edges* are simply not to be found in Elwood City. (The only other *edges* shown on *Arthur* are even more positively depicted: lakefront amenities such as beaches, picnic areas, and amusement parks.) In the rare cases where an unidentified adult appears on screen, he or she is invariably smiling. On *Arthur*, pedestrian movement and bicycle travel are unimpeded by the threatening presence of unfamiliar cars or people. Although Greenwald attributes the relative paucity of traffic movement and other background activity to "animation issues" regarding "how much action we can afford to do," the net result is an environment edited for safety.[27] Whether due to technical and financial limits or to deliberate underplaying of potential neighborhood and city hazards, the construction of animated life in Elwood City necessarily relies on a limited number of experiential layers. Children's animated television—often created by baby boomers nostalgic for the perceived spatial safety of their own childhoods—builds edited worlds.

■ DOUG

Doug is set in the small town of Bluffington (population 21,001), located between the much larger cities of New Hamster (population 132,000) and Bloatsburg (population 250,000). Like *Arthur*'s Elwood City, which it closely resembles, Bluffington is laid out in a loose interpretation of a traditional grid and is adjacent to water (fig. 12.4a). We are told that, in addition to its preeminence as the bumper sticker capital of the world (fig. 12.4b), it boasts "the second-lowest crime rate in the country." In contrast to usual practice, *Doug*'s creators do not include scenes of Bluffington in their opening montage, which instead features characters moving against a featureless backdrop. More typically, though, they have endowed the town with a thorough mytho-historical foundation: Established in the nineteenth century by Thaddeus Bluff on the site of "a forked tree which had been struck twice by lightning and had moss growing on its south side," the settlement began with a factory that manufactured good-luck charms. Most other townspeople farmed giant beets or worked at the beet-packing plant. The founder's grandson, Hy Bluff, made his fortune with Lucky Bluff Foods, a mail-order gourmet specialty food company. This was later diversified into the conglomerate Bluffco Industries, which currently controls most of the town's commerce. Its companies include Beet Publishing (whose ventures include *Shut Up!—The Magazine with an Attitude*), the Stick 'Em Up Bumper Sticker Company, the Déja Vu Recycling Plant, and the Funkytown theme park ("an archaic paean to the disco era").[28]

The downtown area, comprised mostly of two- and three-story attached buildings, is intended to have "a small-town urban feel to it," according to its creators. With growth, the beet farms on its outskirts have given way to suburban neighborhoods and two shopping malls. The town is home to a variety of businesses, including Sully's Comic Book Nook and the gentrified Chez Honqué (formerly known as the Honker Burger). Bluffington is visually distinguished by several landmarks: a beet-shaped water tower, a domed town hall, and a communications tower. On a

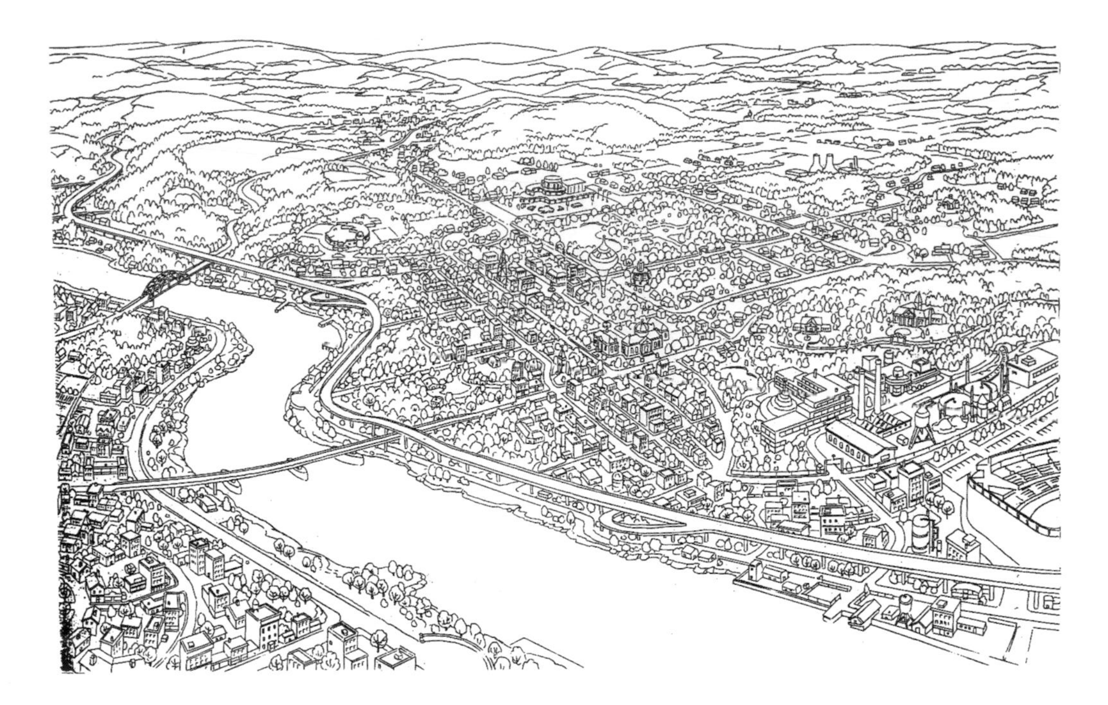

Fig. 12.4a: Bird's-eye view of Bluffington, the setting for *Doug*.

Fig. 12.4b: Detail map of Bluffington, showing *Doug's* major nodes and landmarks.

smaller scale, there is the gateway to Lucky Duck Park, a statue of Thaddeus Bluff, and the tepee-shaped doghouse (which has its own address, mailbox, and satellite dish) of Doug's pet, Porkchop. From the air, the Beebe Bluff Middle School certainly qualifies as a landmark. Bill Bluff (heir to Bluffco Industries) not only put up the money to build the school, he named it after his daughter and had it built in the shape of her head. Doug, Skeeter, Patti, and most of their friends (drawn in various brightly hued skin tones) attend this school, described by the creators as "a typical public school with kids from a wide variety of socioeconomic backgrounds."[29]

Although Doug Funnie's house (in the Lucky Hills section) is at one edge of town, no destination in the whole of Bluffington is more than about a ten-block walk or bicycle ride away. Creator Jim Jinkins insisted early on that all writers work in compliance with a common base map, so that relative distances would be realistic: When Doug goes to school, he walks, but when he goes to Patti's apartment, he rides his bicycle. Most of Doug's friends live closer than Patti, and all are no more than a short walk from the centrally located Lucky Duck Park, which is adjacent to Swirly's ("preteen Bluffingtonians' favorite place to hang out"). As the official *Disney's Doug* Web site explains, "After the Honker Burger was bought by Fat Jack and turned into Chez Honqué, the kids of Bluffington adopted Swirly's as their favorite place to sit, talk, drink Frothy Goats, and eat Tater Twisties." In its attempt to convey the daily life of Doug and his contemporaries, the show also depicts other *nodes*, such as Suicide Mountain skateboard park and the middle school, but everything is skewed by the preferences and pastimes of twelve-year-old Doug. It is as if the entire town were designed for the convenience and enjoyment of this particular age cohort, who pass through it with no cars or strangers to impinge or intrude on their freedom of movement. Especially in the more residential areas of town, Doug regularly stands fearlessly in the middle of the street; as in other children's cartoons, the animators have done little to acknowledge the presence of traffic. Jim Jinkins says he deliberately chose to present Bluffington as an innocent place of intrepid children but notes that the absence of cars in the animation was primarily a technical constraint rather than an artistic choice. Much of *Doug*'s world, he confesses, is a "gentle look backwards" at his own childhood in Virginia: "I could run out as a four-year-old into the woods and play and my mother wouldn't worry and didn't have to; now this would be impossible." Part of the appeal of working on *Doug* is "the dream that this world would be restored." Jinkins yearns for his show to project a hopeful future and to resist the "cynicism of the edge" that prevails elsewhere on television.[30]

Even in Bluffington, though, there are exceptions to all this fearless innocence: In one episode, Doug and his friend break a traffic light, and cars instantly emerge to form a horn-blasting traffic jam; on other occasions, Doug has dreams of monster-filled scary places, rendered as high-density urban environments. In stark contrast to these intrusive moments, however, the streetscapes of everyday Bluffington are peaceful and child-friendly. Bluffington's image is selectively constructed. Unlike real cities, which must serve wildly diverse constituencies and whose shared images are the sum product of many different kinds of preference and experience, the cities of animated children's television can often be marketed more narrowly.

■ THE SIMPSONS

Unlike the fictional towns and cities of *Sesame Street*, *Hey Arnold!*, *Arthur*, and *Disney's Doug*, the animated Springfield of *The Simpsons* is constructed to appeal primarily to older audiences. Although the Simpson children figure prominently in all plotlines, and although Springfield Elementary School is consistently a key *node* of action, this is a show in which an adult urban world overlays the children's world, yielding a concerted satirical edginess that is far more prominent than that found in most programs directly designed for children. Springfield is rendered as a fully dysfunctional city, one presented as comically aware of its many deficiencies ("America's Worst City," says *Time*; "America's Krud Bucket," claims *Newsweek*; "Least Popular City in America, National Survey," and "In Science, Dead Last"). This send-up of the place-rating phenomenon (a subject dealt with more seriously in chapter 15 of this volume) is but one example of the ways that writers for *The Simpsons* use Springfield to satirize urban America. In contrast to the peaceful coexistence that undergirds the other shows discussed in this chapter, *The Simpsons* is riddled with conflicts. In its first nine full seasons, the show featured no fewer than forty-one separate riots and instances of mob violence. At various points, the show has made reference to thirteen different local penal institutions. Home to the accident-prone Springfield Nuclear Power Plant (where Homer obliviously drones as a "safety inspector" for Sector 7G, munching donuts and dozing off), Springfield in the 1990s hosted a multiplicity of explosions and crime sprees, as well as six toxic spills, four major power outages, two earthquakes, two avalanches, two tidal waves, two tornadoes, an alien invasion, and the "world's longest-burning tire-yard fire."[31] The nuclear power plant is Springfield's most imageable *landmark* as well as its major *node* for the show's adult characters (equaled only by Moe's Tavern, perhaps). Other *landmarks* include Springfield Bridge (the only way in or out of town "due to poor civic planning, rampant corruption, and an overly yokelized workforce"); the statue of city founder Jebediah Springfield in Springfield's town square (motto: "A noble spirit embiggens the smallest man"); Springfield War Memorial Stadium (home of the Springfield Isotopes); the Springfield Trade Center (the city's tallest building); Springfield Gorge; Duff Brewery; the Springfield tar pits; the Springfield monorail ruins, which "dot the city with various decaying pieces of elevated rail, dangling chunks of concrete, and rusting passenger cars that hang precariously over heavily trafficked sidewalks"; the Springfield lemon tree, planted by the town's founder ("the very embodiment of Springfield itself" since "it continues to grow despite neglect and poor city management"); the First Church of Springfield; and the Kwik-E-Mart.[32]

In contrast to *landmarks* in a conventional city, however, those in Springfield (with the possible exception of the power plant cooling towers) seem to serve no orientation function, either for residents or for viewers. Unlike the programs discussed previously, there is no underlying city plan for Springfield to regulate the juxtaposition of places. Rather, the various writers and animators seem relatively free to add new landmarks and destinations with little regard for their overall placement in the metropolis. More disconcerting, return visits to a single place, such as Moe's Tavern, do not necessarily show the place in the same urban context in different episodes. In a city that would probably house well over 100,000 people, there is little sense of how any one place relates to any other. Significantly, the frontispieces for Matt Groening's *The Simpsons: Guide to Springfield* simply collect key *landmarks* and *nodes* of the city in a faux-aerial view—as if they were located immediately adjacent to one another—even though the show's animation never represents them in this way (fig. 12.5).[33]

Similarly, those who write *The Simpsons* make occasional passing references to districts (such as Lower East Side, Springfield Heights, Bum Town, Recluse Ranch Estates, Little Newark, and Old Springfield Towne—a for-profit historical park), but such places are neither located in relation to any other place nor (with the exception of the Lower East Side) ever mentioned again. Instead, even as four key *nodes* remain consistent (the Simpsons' house, Bart and Lisa's school, the nuclear power plant, and Moe's Tavern), there is no discernible set of *paths* to link them, and the rest of the city remains in flux. The only time the show explicitly engages the concept of *path* is to satirize it: The "Educational, Nonprofit Foot-trail" is described as "a blue line painted on Springfield's downtown sidewalks that leads visitors to especially boring, underfunded attractions." Similarly, we are told that Noise Land Video Arcade ("Springfield's favorite hangout of perennial kids and sullen teenagers") may be reached from the town square by following "the cacophony of digitized gunfire and death knells."[34]

New places and sites are continually introduced. Individual episodes make reference to such places as the Springfield Museum (home to the "world's largest cubic zirconia"); adult

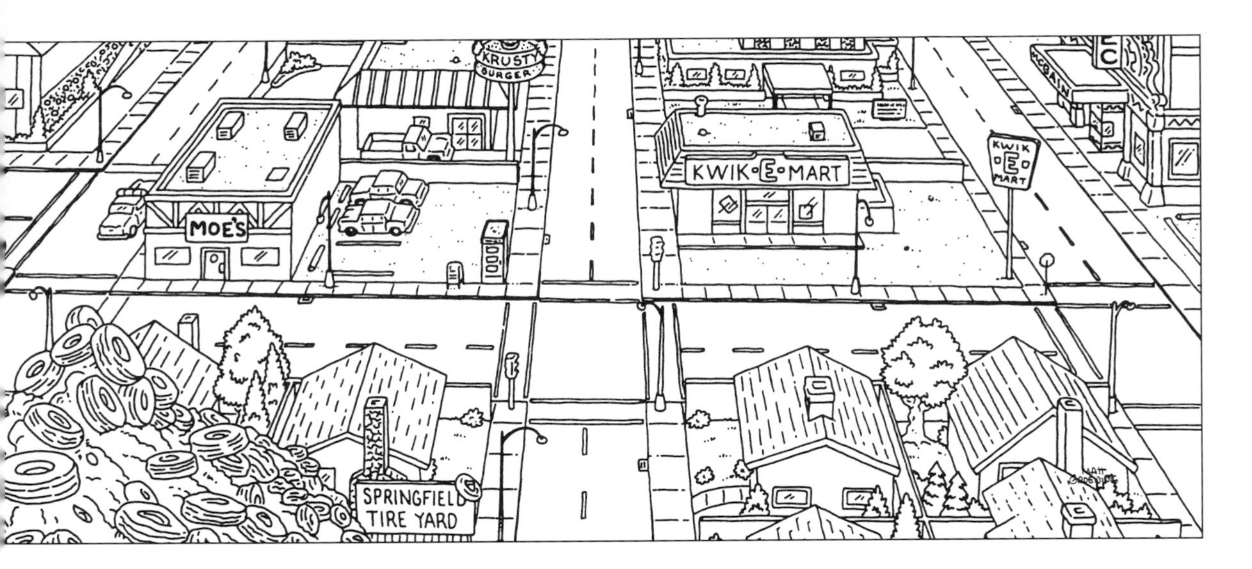

Fig. 12.5: Springfield, USA. On *The Simpsons,* major nodes and landmarks such as Moe's Tavern, Krusty Burger, Kwik-E-Mart, and the Springfield Tire Yard do not occupy fixed places and, in this image, are shown as immediately adjacent to one another.

entertainment destinations like the She-She Lounge, the Hate Box, Shotkickers, Maison Derriere; the Bloodbath and Beyond Gun Shop; and Itchy & Scratchy Land—billed as the "Violentest Place on Earth" (where kids can "frolic at Torture Land, Explosion Land, Searing Gas Pain Land, Unnecessary Surgery Land, and the upcoming Bloodclot Center") and said to feature "the finest amusement-park-run ER and triage center in the state." For those with more upscale tastes, there is also the swanky Springfield Squidport (filled with "trendy, demographically correct stores like Turban Outfitters, Just Rainsticks, It's a Wonderful Knife, and Malaria Zone" that replaced the "once-famous squid gutteries of Springfield Harbor"). The profligacy of cleverly invented places is both entertaining and profoundly disorienting. Much like the destination-oriented entertainment development that has been happening in real cities, there is little to help orient visitors to the whole and much that works to fragment the city. In Lynchian terms, Springfield is all identity and no structure. It is a profusion of clever *landmarks* and wanna-be *nodes.* Springfield is full of restaurants (including the Frying Dutchman, Jittery Joe's Coffee Shop, TacoMat, Planet Hype!, and the Gilded Truffle), but it seems significant that Bart's beloved Krusty Burger is a chain with "dozens and dozens of locations in the Springfield metropolitan area" rather than a unique hangout like Elwood City's Sugar Bowl or Swirly's in Bluffington.[35]

The whirl of life in Springfield is perfectly captured by the show's opening sequence. It shows the Simpson family in frenetic motion, traversing through Springfield in what turns out to be a mad rush home. Marge exits from the supermarket with baby Maggie (who accidentally has been put through the scanner like an item of food) and jumps into her car; Maggie pretends to drive from her infant seat, while the vehicle whizzes past a group of minor characters from the show. Meanwhile, Homer rushes out of the nuclear power plant into the family's other car, a small irradiated rod still stuck in his clothing; Bart flies out of school on his skateboard, careening past seven adults, all of them recognizable from the show; Lisa defies efforts by the school band director to control her idiosyncratic jazz solo and riffs her way out the door of the school. In the scene that follows, there is so much movement that at first it is hard to realize that it all belongs to two cars and one skateboard, rather than to a broader spectrum of urban bustle. Eventually, the two cars intersect at the family's garage, and everyone goes hurtling inside to the famously temperamental red couch, breathlessly eager to do nothing other than watch *The Simpsons* on TV. In just a few seconds of madcap footage, the show's creators and animators manage to accomplish three important things: They focus attention on the show's family-centered *node*, demonstrate the individual empowerment of each child, and concoct a thoroughly disorienting image of Springfield.

WORLDS OF NODES AND LANDMARKS

The opening sequences of the five shows just discussed are all about movement and full of paths, yet it is not clear where such paths will lead us. The answer to the question "Can you tell me how to get, How to get to Sesame Street?" is not given in terms of urban way finding. Rather, as with the other shows, the way that one "gets" to Sesame Street is through repeated viewing and sustained engagement with its televisual community. The important paths are the ones that lead from viewer to setting, not the ones that enable the characters to negotiate their way between *nodes*. The directors rarely waste precious screen time on the journey between places. Similarly, although each show (especially *The Simpsons*) periodically introduces new locales at some undetermined distance from the familiar *landmarks* and social *nodes* of the core settings, these places are seldom identified as *districts*; they are, instead, nascent *nodes*. *Edges*, too, seem quite deemphasized, or, more precisely, they are made nonproblematical. No one seems wary of the missing "other side" of Sesame Street or worries about stepping out into traffic (there isn't any). The edges are simply the edges of the set, or the frame defined by the rectangular image produced by the camera. *Edges*, in these televisual cities, are not defined by physical barriers; they are informally established by the ability of children to walk or bicycle to nearby *nodes*. In this sense, edges do not separate: These shows deliberately avoid all sense of segregation by class, race, or ethnicity that such edges often signal in "real" cities. Significantly, at least in these five shows, there are no places or districts that children are warned to avoid. The temporary unease that Arthur experiences during the "Lost!" episode when displaced to an unfamiliar part of town only reemphasizes the extent to which the cities of children's television are collections of closely spaced *nodes* accessible by foot or bicycle, chock full of reassuring *landmarks*.

One can only imagine the mental maps that Arthur, Doug, Arnold, Bart, or Big Bird would draw of their neighborhoods, of course. Yet, because we get to see them make repeated visits to particular places (which become as familiar to us as they are to them), the voyeurism of television allows us to share in the self-construction of their worlds, to see how and why and where they are circumscribed, and even to imagine the meanings that key places—from Krusty Burger to Big Bird's nest—must hold. The high imageability of children's television is due, in large part, to a single designer's hand producing a distinctive ambience for each setting. It would take no more than a single frame to distinguish a streetscape from *Hey Arnold!* from any place in Bluffington. Similarly, any part of Springfield is instantly distinguishable from any part of Elwood City. Still, the imageability that exists is highly piecemeal. Because the emphasis is on *landmarks* and *nodes*, rather than on *edges*, *districts*, or *paths*, we enter worlds of intense fragments rather than whole, coherent cities.[36]

The animated world of children's television escapes the real-world constraints of city planning at every turn. At base, the entire concept of distance between places becomes a function not of space but of editing. Because there is so little attention paid to paths and way finding, television towns can convey a sense of enhanced adjacency. Moreover, although some of these shows employ town maps as templates to guide their writers and animators, such maps do not show the true sizes of buildings: Even large structures such as schools can be depicted as having a floor area only about five times that of a small house. Image makers who work in the medium of animated television can therefore exaggerate the apparent density of activity by hiding the fact that the true spatial extent of all these neighborhood amenities would sprawl across a much greater area. The trope of the television town permits its creators to construct places that perfectly match the needs of their featured inhabitants, while permitting no extraneous buildings or people. With characters selected to mirror the demographics of their target audiences, TV towns can be imaged to appeal to their intended markets. As Briavel Holcomb suggests in chapter 2, sometimes real cities try to do exactly the same thing.

In other ways, however, the cities and towns of children's television have many advantages over their real-world counterparts. If the conventions of television allow these shows to downplay three of Lynch's five elements of urban imageability, they embrace more wholeheartedly his more holistic notions of good city form. It would be hard to conceive of a better set of descriptors for these environments than Lynch's own set of five "performance dimensions," outlined in *Good City Form*: vitality, sense, fit, access, and control.[37] Moreover, the televisual cities have an important additional advantage: In contrast to the real cities Lynch worried about, these five values never seem to be in conflict with one another, and no class of persons seems victimized by discrimination, so TV cities can evade the need to factor in Lynch's "meta-criteria" of *efficiency* and *justice*.

Certainly, the central message one gets from all of these shows is that children can—and should—take *control* of their environment. The poses and the camera angles combine to show small bodies in charge of large spaces, whether they are striding down sidewalks, playing stickball in the street, or careening on skateboards past more passive adults. Similarly, these are worlds of near-perfect *access*; not only pedestrian-scaled but blessed with the instantaneous adjacency afforded by film editors. Their *fit* with the needs of their inhabitants is always on target, since these are places invented to meet the daily needs of child protagonists. In Lynch's words, there is a supportive correspondence between the "form and capacity" of the place and the "pattern and quantity of actions that people customarily engage in, or want to engage in."[38] These TV cities, although sometimes disorienting as a whole, also earn a high score in the Lynchian dimension of *sense*, since their many nodes and landmarks are so highly legible and match the values of their users. Again, especially in the case of the animated shows, the sensibility of each setting is undergirded by the color palette, line weight, and style of particular designers, yielding images that can be differentiated instantly from all other places. Lastly, the five cities discussed here perform well in terms of *vitality* not only because they are places of vigor and exuberance, but because so much about them is supportive of human biological needs. All are centered around the primary importance of family and kin—often defined very inclusively. All feature easy access to parks and other sources of active and passive recreation. Even Springfield—arguably the very embodiment of serial environmental degradation—is a curiously resilient place, its inhabitants seemingly unaffected by repeated exposure to ecological disaster. Its famous three-eyed mutant fish is treated as more joke than crisis. While one might well prefer the recycling centers that appear prominently in both Bluffington and Elwood City (not to mention *Sesame Street,* where one Muppet's trash is another's treasure) to the environmental vagaries of Springfield, even the Simpsons (through the magical ability of animated television to avoid showing the long-term consequences of violence and destruction) live in an environment that seems capable of sustaining their lives and lifestyles. With Lisa Simpson's vegetarianism and civic-mindedness as a counterpoint, *The Simpsons*—for some viewers at least—may actually enhance awareness of poor health habits and automobile-dependent sprawl through the power of its satire.

Ultimately, the images of cities on children's television present viewers with an appealing diversity of child-centered places. Both *Sesame Street* and *Hey Arnold!* epitomize the eyes-on-the-street urban ideals of Jane Jacobs, revealing the constant energy of a dense cityscape, while *The Simpsons* depicts a large city-region that somehow manages to be sufficiently child-accessible to facilitate neighborhood socialization and permit highly independent lives. By contrast, *Arthur* and *Disney's Doug* cast positive light on smaller towns—the designers of Disney's real town of Celebration, Florida, can only dream of doing as well! At a time when discussion of cities and suburbs often centers on New Urbanism (marked by conscious attempts to reinvent and promote premodernist townscapes through replacement of existing zoning laws with nostalgia-driven architectural and urban building codes), the cities of children's television can help us see that good city plans take many forms. The urban imagery of children's television is facilitated by the special constraints and opportunities of its medium, but it carries an important message for designers who work elsewhere: Real cities also gain from creative editing that enhances performance.

13

URBAN COUNTER-IMAGES

COMMUNITY ACTIVISM MEETS PUBLIC ART

Deborah Karasov

■ EDITORS' OVERVIEW

Advertising and entertainment media continually proffer images of cities, churning up free-floating representations of desire and emotional states. Deborah Karasov, an environmental activist, landscape architect, and former editor of *Public Art Review,* here documents the head-on confrontation of this media wash by urban-focused artists whose goals have been to challenge conventional image representations.

She analyzes several artist movements that seek to combat our current media saturation: conceptual art, contextual practice, community-based imagery, grassroots arts practice, and alternative histories. These are presented in a rough chronology from the 1960s to the present. In general, the trend moves from presenting elements of the city as it is lived to public art that grows out of consultation with residents.

Artists have long been enlisted in, and volunteered for, public campaigns for labor, civil rights, disarmament, wartime patriotism, and antiwar protests. Most often, they contributed in familiar modes: flags, banners, signs, photographs, and films. Beginning in the 1960s, however, artists began to attack the familiar imagery itself. Jenny Holzer wrote slogans of sensible nonsense, and other feminists dramatized a press conference to attack depictions of women as acceptable victims. Hans Haacke and Krzysztof Wodiczko confronted urban stereotypes of street façades and heroic statues by juxtaposing these comfortable, established images with representations of a

slum-managing corporation and homeless New Yorkers. Often, such commentary is tied to community planning practice, as in the London Docklands case where the artists make their work grow from a series of neighborhood consultations.

Karasov reviews many attempts by artists to force onto the public menu of city images representations of the actualities of city living. These artists are heirs to a long tradition from Hogarth and Dutch genre painters onward—artists who brought to the forefront previously invisible members of society.

INTRODUCTION

In early spring 1967, just seven years after the publication of Kevin Lynch's *Image of the City*, a group of some twenty black artists started painting on a semiabandoned two-story building in the center of Chicago's old "black belt" South Side. The city had scheduled the area for demolition to make way for urban renewal. Titling it *The Wall of Respect*, the artists began the mural without fanfare, at first unnoticed by the press, but soon embraced by a festival of the arts for the black community.

Uncommissioned, without patronage or manifestos, the artists intended not to bring aesthetic enlightenment but to publicly express the experience of a people. After much notice in the art and Left press, community artists worldwide recognize the *Wall of Respect* as the beginning of artistic efforts that publicly present a counter-image to that presented by the dominant media.

Concurrently, many artists labeled as avant-garde began work that also challenged mass culture and media. What began as artists wanting to move out from the museums had become, by 1966, everything from antiwar poster groups to feminist media strategists to Dadaist-inspired cartographers of the city. Like a spy behind enemy lines, avant-garde artists, trained in Conceptual art, kept reversing the signposts that mark the crossroads between art and life. These artists imply that the proper answer to "But is it art?" is: "But does it matter?"

Both these artistic precedents, community-based art and Conceptual art, are important for understanding today's critical public art as it relates specifically to imaging the city. On the one hand, community artists like the muralists, scorned as propagandists for the movement or purveyors of vague "cultural pride" images, nonetheless reclaimed public space as an available and accessible site for representation, understandable to a general audience. On the other hand, the avant-garde artists, criticized for seeking an audience not of the community in which a project was sited but of the art world that reviewed it, nonetheless challenged the city structures that mediate our everyday perception of the world. When looked at together, we have a body of powerful public work that asks (1) What politics inform accepted images of the city; and (2) How can we empower individuals and communities to change the conversation?

ART AND CITY IMAGING

After taking in the incessant camera pans of skylines, street façades, and freeway clogs, we may find it hard to truly *see* our city without the visual conventions of the media veiling our eyes. Yet, for all the saturation of images in our lives, critics have advanced very little in analyzing them in comprehensive terms. While scholars have studied city images and stereotypes from the point of view of marketers and city leaders, they have written less on the process of imaging from the grassroots perspective. Further, as the editors say, understanding the dynamic of city imaging requires examining it at many different scales, not just the aerial one.

In contrast to the modest efforts of academicians, artists have explored this dynamic from the scale of the abstract city to particular neighborhoods, and from the imaging process to the final products. They dramatize images that we would sometimes rather not see but that are central to city life, inserting them into the collective memories and democratic discourses of the city itself. They find their impulse in lived experience where others find the tangibility of the world flattened by theory.

We need this work because, truth be said, we do not yet really know what life *is* in a media environment. Los Angeles writer Michael Ventura argues persuasively that:

> We've barely begun a body of thought and art which is focused on what is really *alive* in the ground of a media-saturated daily life. For culture always proceeds from two poles: one is the people of the land and the street; the other is the thinker. . . . The two poles can exist without each other but they cannot be effective without each other."[1]

Artists have provided both street and thought, the local and the conceptual, and planners need to pay attention. When Sam Bass Warner Jr. observes that city dialogue is focused obsessively on economic growth and personal prosperity, we should not overlook the visionary potential of public art. As we shall see, public artists are often able to generate social and communal meaning, even in a media-saturated life.

LEGACY OF CONCEPTUAL ART

Artists who use media manipulation—the exploitation of media coverage and the use of visual imagery designed specifically for media consumption—may be said to have one foot in Conceptualist ideas and the other in the world of political activism and community organizing. We cannot know, of course, the presuppositions of the artists themselves, and it certainly is a convention of art history to place work within the context of others like it. Moreover, from its inception, and continuing to this very day, historians and critics have argued over the antecedents and definitions of Conceptual art. Yet, even if the artists are operating independently, there are enough commonalities to safely call attention to them.

The term "conceptual art" refers to artists considering the idea itself as art. Art historian Alexander Alberro defines it broadly to be "an expanded critique of the cohesiveness and materiality of the art object, a growing wariness toward definitions of artistic practice as purely visual, a fusion of the work with its site and context of display, and an increased emphasis on the possibilities of publicness and distribution."[2] The influential art critic Lucy Lippard features the effect of Conceptual art as a "democratic means of making art ideas cheap and accessible" by replacing the conventional "precious object" with "everyday" or worthless and/or ephemeral mediums such as typed sheets, photocopies, snapshots, booklets, and streetworks.[3]

Over time, conceptualism coincided with the counterculture and the often-academic New Left. A heady measure of anti–Vietnam War sentiment, ideals of cultural revolution, and feminism added to the multiple and opposing practices. Several artists suffered under the derisive charge that they were petit-bourgeois artists with revolutionary sympathies. Some decided to abandon art altogether, while others simply muted the pitch of their militancy.

■ FEMINISM

For their part, feminists of the early 1970s did not abandon aesthetics for activism; they activated aesthetics by drawing upon their own experiences as women. In particular, it was the experience of violence—and glamorized violence in the media—that gave rise to feminist media art. In 1978, Suzanne Lacy and Leslie Labowitz formed Ariadne: A Social Art Network, an exchange between women in the arts, governmental politics, women's politics, and media. Through Ariadne they developed a media strategy on how to manage the media in order to project a feminist viewpoint through its lenses:

> As you begin to look more closely at the media, its effectiveness in generating emotional responses and states of desires will become apparent. Once you have demystified the image-making process—how the messages one gets depend upon the arrangement of color, form, and content—you will be able to respond more objectively and critically to the bombardment of visual media in your daily life.

Fig. 13.1: ***In Mourning and in Rage*** **(1977), a public media event staged by Ariadne on the steps of Los Angeles City Hall.**
Suzanne Lacy and Leslie Labowitz, Ariadne

> Sensitivity to this is important for your analysis; once you pierce the manner in which meaning is conveyed through media, you can begin to generate your own meaning.[4]

Ariadne's media strategy incorporated several different approaches to reach different sectors of the population. Often they juxtaposed two kinds of images within the context of a street, shopping mall, or press conference. The first was an image of social reality as we all know it through television and newspapers. The second was that image seen through a feminist consciousness of a different reality. "The public thus views, through art, information contrary to that which it sees as 'the truth' and views it in a manner sufficiently provocative visually to encourage reconsideration of 'the truth.'" Ariadne was determined to control not only the production of images, but also the way its images were perceived and understood.[5]

In Mourning and in Rage (1977) (fig. 13.1) is an example of a public "media event" staged specifically for the press on the steps of Los Angeles City Hall. The event was in response to the sensationalistic and simplistic news coverage of the so-called Hillside Strangler murders, a case in which ten women were found raped and murdered along populated hillsides in suburban Los Angeles in 1977. Where some in the media seemed to blame the victims, Ariadne designed *In Mourning and in Rage* to project images of strong women taking positive action in defense of themselves.

The event included a funeral motorcade of twenty-two cars filled with women, a chorus of mourners, and ten seven-feet-tall, heavily veiled women making statements that connected the Hillside Strangler murders with the larger social and political issues of violence against women (an analysis missing from the media coverage). The performance fixed media attention by anticipating its journalistic conventions, including the need for bold, simple images (larger-than-life black-and-red-robed women), the repetition of images over and over for maximum press consumption (the mourners speaking ten times, the echoing chorus), the same images set up for every possible camera angle so that the pictures on the nightly news would all show what the artists intended (the resolute delegation of "unified woman-strength"), and the "establishing background shot" (City Hall, which would confer authority upon the performance).

Later women artists—Barbara Kruger, Jenny Holzer, and others—extended this critique of media in order to intervene in

Fig. 13.2: Jenny Holzer, *Truisms* (1977), displayed on theater marquee (42nd Street Art Project).
Photograph © Maggie Hopp

the representation and languages of everyday life. Jenny Holzer's is a "situationist" strategy: She offers a play of words that becomes theater, a bedlam of voices that mocks the certainty of received ideas. The work called *Truisms* (1977) (fig. 13.2), for example, is an alphabetical list of statements that together confound all order and logic. First presented as public information posters on New York City walls (and since then as t-shirts, electronic signs, plaques, and works of art), the *Truisms* place in contradiction certain ideological notions that are usually kept apart.

Barbara Kruger seeks to dispel those media representations in which women are presented as objects of the male gaze. In her panels, posters, and books, Kruger appropriates photographs (mostly of women) from media sources, blows them up and crops them severely, then combines them with short texts. She alternates image and text in a way reminiscent of photo-stories, creates montages in a parody of display ads, and combines them (fig. 13.3). Kruger re-presented various images (e.g., of a woman slumped among fashion magazines or with her hands clasped in prayer) stamped with single words (e.g., "deluded" or "perfect") that rendered them invalid. This "interception" of the stereotype is her principal device. In time, however, Kruger came to believe that rather than questioning the values, image appropriation may, in fact, confirm them.[6]

Fig. 13.3: Barbara Kruger, *Untitled* ("You Thrive on Mistaken Identity"), 1981.

Critic Hal Foster notes that Holzer and Kruger, like their contemporary Krzysztof Wodiczko, separately use many different forms of production and modes of address (photo-text collage, constructed or projected photographs, videotapes, critical texts, appropriated, arranged, or surrogate artworks, and so on). Yet they are alike in this: Each treats the public space, image, or language in which he or she intervenes as both a target and a weapon. This shift in practice entails a shift in position: The artist becomes a manipulator of signs more than a producer of art objects, and the viewer an active reader of messages rather than a passive contemplator of the aesthetic or consumer of the spectacle. This shift is not totally new—Dadaists used photomontage and pop artists used appropriation—yet it remains strategic for seeing artists as entangled in the city systems of imaging and power.

CONTEXTUALIST ART PRACTICE

In addition to deciphering cultural signs, Conceptualist artists taught us that the meaning of an artwork resides not in the autonomous object but in its physical, institutional, social, or conceptual context. Art historians have connected this idea to subsequent developments in the 1970s, including expanded notions of sculpture and public art. Critic Hal Foster calls this "situational aesthetics," but we might simply note its special attention to site, address, and audience.

For example, one contextual question that artist Dan Graham asks is: What is the relevance of history to the images in our everyday life? He notes that "in historicism there is no real past, only an overlay of interpretations of a simulation of the past, [but] in opposition to this notion of history of simulation, there is possible the idea of an actual, although hidden past, mostly eradicated from consciousness but briefly available in moments not obscured by the dominant ideology of newness."[7]

For Graham, history is not a seamless narrative but, like the rough-cut patchwork of his video documentary *Rock My Religion*, a cluster of counter-images and memories that we occasionally glimpse through our everyday life and that secretly undergird our hopes and aspirations. Critics have likened Graham to the German Marxist Walter Benjamin, who hoped to

Fig. 13.4: ***Two Adjacent Pavilions*** by Dan Graham (1978–1981), mirrors viewers' own images as well as the city environment.

break through the collective dream state induced by consumer capitalism and to obliterate official images and narratives. In a similar manner, in his earliest texts and artworks of the 1960s, Graham sought to convey things "as they (simply) appear to be." His writing showed an almost fanatical attention to immediate descriptive detail, and his architectural projects proposed a space in which contradictions can play against one another rather than being resolved in a mythic image.

In recent writings, Graham offered an example of the latter in architect Robert Venturi's 1978 proposal for Transportation Plaza in Washington, D.C. On the ground of this small city park, Venturi wanted to install a marble map of L'Enfant's original plan for the federal city, punctuated with scale models of the major monuments. In this way, Graham believed, the architect evoked the historic "ideal" city amid the reality of the contemporary public sphere. The relation of Washington's past image to the present city is "made accessible to public scrutiny in situ. Placed in a public square, the exhibit was intended to function like a Greek democracy's agora."[8] Venturi's proposal was contemporaneous with Graham himself creating pavilion-like mirror sculptures presented in garden or park sites—works such as *Two Adjacent Pavilions*, 1978 (fig. 13.4), which mirrored the viewers' own images as well as the city environment.

Regrettably, art historians suggest that the highly theoretical aspect of Conceptual art, as demonstrated by the Graham example, was not often commensurate with its democratic philosophy. Despite its ambitions, it remained an exclusive art form. At its worst, the movement was said to lead to artists spinning visual cobwebs and playing in a cul-de-sac of language games. The works of many so-called postmodern artists like Judith Barry have met comparable fates. Their work is different, and yet similar in theorizing dominant cultural representations with little geographic specificity. However, there are other artists who take specific social geographies as their starting point.

■ STRATEGIES OF INTERVENTION

Few people have written so compellingly and rigorously on strategies of intervention in institutional spaces and discourses as critic Rosalyn Deutsche. Nearly single-handedly she has portrayed artists Krzysztof Wodiczko and Hans Haacke as engaged in "critical aesthetic strategies," uncomfortably fitting within art history's norms. With these strategies, the artists do not create self-contained art projects but rather explore the cultural process of meaning production.

One famous work by artist Hans Haacke on New York's real-estate industry, *Shapolsky et al. Manhattan Real Estate Holdings, A Real-Time Social System, as of May 1, 1971* (fig. 13.5), offered an unparalleled opportunity for Deutsche to write about strategies of intervention. In 1971 the Guggenheim Museum cancelled an exhibition of Haacke's works because of this and another real estate piece, which the Guggenheim judged to be incompatible with the functions of a prestigious art institution. "Art may have social and political consequences," the Guggenheim's director Thomas Messer wrote to Haacke, "but these, we believe, are furthered by indirection and by the gener-

214 E 3 St.
Block 385 Lot 11
5 story walk-up old law tenement

Owned by Harpmel Realty Inc., 608 E 11 St., NYC
Contracts signed by Harry J. Shapolsky, President('63)
Martin Shapolsky, President('64)
Principal Harry J. Shapolsky(according to Real Estate
Directory of Manhattan)

Acquired 8-21-1963 from John the Baptist Foundation,
c/o The Bank of New York, 48 Wall St., NYC,
for $237 600.- (also 7 other bldgs.)

$150 000.- mortgage at 6% interest, 8-19-1963, due
8-19-1968, held by The Ministers and Missionaries
Benefit Board of the American Baptist Convention,
475 Riverside Drive, NYC (also on 7 other bldgs.)

Assessed land value $25 000.- , total $75 000.- (including 212 and 216 E 3 St.) (1971)

216 E 3 St.
Block 385 Lot 11
5 story walk-up old law tenement

Owned by Harpmel Realty Inc., 608 E 11 St., NYC
Contracts signed by Harry J. Shapolsky, President('63)
Martin Shapolsky, President('64)
Principal Harry J. Shapolsky(according to Real Estate
Directory of Manhattan)

Acquired 8-21-1963 from John the Baptist Foundation,
c/o The Bank of New York, 48 Wall St., NYC
for $237 600.-(also 7 other bldgs.)

$150 000.- mortgage at 6% interest, 8-19-1963, due
8-19-1968, held by The Ministers and Missionaries
Benefit Board of the American Baptist Convention,
475 Riverside Drive, NYC (also on 7 other bldgs.)

Assessed land value $25 000.-, total $75 000.- (including 212-14 E 3 St.) (1971)

Fig. 13.5: Hans Haacke, *Shapolsky et al. Manhattan Real Estate Holdings, A Real-Time Social System, as of May 1, 1971* (detail), 1971.

alized, exemplary force that works of art may exert upon the environment, not, as you proposed, by using political means to achieve political ends, no matter how desirable these may appear to be in themselves."[9] Because of its specificity, in other words, Haacke's work is "political" in contrast to the "indirect" art, which is "neutral."

The Guggenheim's actions, as well as the work itself, are a crucial development in what Deutsche calls "contextualist art practice," projects that combat the images of prevailing architectural and urban discourse. Haacke's work countered such an important image for the powers that be that the Guggenheim Museum itself felt the need to repress it.

Shapolsky et al. displays the vast slum holdings of the Shapolsky Real Estate Corporation and a myriad of other corporations connected familially through board relations. The piece consists of 142 photos of the tenement façades and vacant lots, numerous property documents such as deeds and mortgage agreements, and a map indicating the location of the properties in Harlem and the Lower East Side. The vast detail and size of the piece visually reinforces the depth of Shapolsky's contribution to the housing crisis in New York. The photographs, shot from street level, looking up at the building, emphatically present the structures as neutral commodities, a striking contrast to the strong ethnic and racial identities of the communities in which the buildings are located. Haacke constructs his narrative by using only publicly available material. His criticism, therefore, is directed not only at overturning the immaculate corporate image but also to show that part of the problem rests in the public's apathy.

Krzysztof Wodiczko entered the arena of New York spatial politics when he mounted an exhibition in a New York art gallery in 1986. The work, called *The Homeless Projection* (fig. 13.6), exists only as a proposal first presented at 49th Parallel, Centre for Contemporary Canadian Art. Consisting of four montaged slide images projected onto the gallery's walls and a written statement by the artist distributed in an accompanying brochure, the proposal outlined a plan for the transformation of

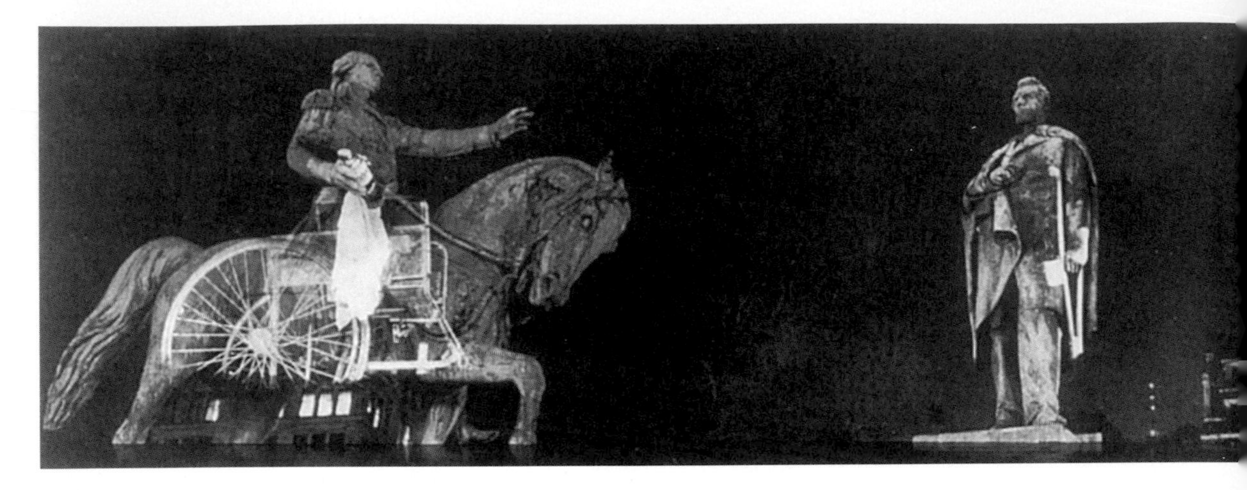

Fig. 13.6: In ***The Homeless Projection*** **(1986), Krzysztof Wodiczko imperceptibly merges images of New York City's homeless population onto the forms of public statues.**

Union Square Park. He proposed to project images onto the surfaces of the four figurative monuments (George Washington, Lafayette, Mother and Child, Abraham Lincoln), which offer "reassuring illusions of a continuous tradition"; these were featured prominently in the marketing displays of the new condominiums surrounding the park. The projected images are of New York's homeless population, the group most noticeably dispossessed by gentrification. Wodiczko seamlessly joined the images with the statues' own forms. For example, he superimposed a photograph of a human hand over a statue's bronze one, so that the projected image merged imperceptibly with the sculpted figure's anatomy.

According to Deutsche, *Homeless Projection* interferes with the "official aesthetic image of revitalization," restoring the viewer's ability to perceive the connections that these images sever or cosmeticize. "Architecture and all symbolic structures of the city often operate as media images, such as postcards and photographs in newspapers," says Wodiczko. "Since the significant context of city events is always city symbolic structures, very often our description of the structure is interconnected with a description of the event. In the case of my projects, the symbolic structure temporarily becomes an urban event itself." His events, he writes, "should also help parents to teach their children to 'think the city' and to measure critically the city's pulse."[10]

Operating independently, artists in addition to Krzysztof Wodiczko, like Dennis Adams (fig. 13.7) and Alfredo Jarr, devised myriad strategies for public address in the 1980s. The range included illuminated light boxes, posters, LED (light-emitting diode) signs, and temporary structures, all of which transmit the artist's message for a given period of time and then disappear.

Fig. 13.7: Dennis Adams, *Bus Shelter II* (1986), Fourteenth Street and Third Avenue, New York. Courtesy of the artist and Kent Gallery, New York

The hit-and-run tactics practiced by Wodiczko and fellow "critical public artists" (called this by critics to distinguish them from artists of public sculpture) are congenerous with the writings of the Situationist Internationale. The Situationists were an underground confederation of politically inclined European artists and writers clustered around the French artist Guy Debord from 1957 until 1972, when the group officially disbanded.[11] They were thoroughly engrossed with urban issues and the psychological impact of the built environment. Debord's 1967 book *The Society of the Spectacle* includes a succession of provocative pronouncements regarding mass consumption and the degradation of everyday life into pure "spectacle":

> In societies where modern conditions of production prevail, all life presents itself as an immense accumulation of spectacles. Everything that was directly lived has moved away into a representation.
>
> The spectacle is not a collection of images, but a social relation among people, mediated by images.
>
> The spectacle within society corresponds to a concrete manufacture of alienation.

> The spectacle . . . is the diplomatic representation of the hierarchic society to itself . . . [it] is the existing order's uninterrupted discourse about itself, its laudatory monologue. It is the self-portrait of power.[12]

Debord's antidote to the authority of the spectacle involved creating "situations"—spontaneous street events and transformations of familiar images, events, and concepts through changes in context—that would serve to awaken passersby from the torpor and alienation imposed by the spectacle. "The construction of situations begins in the ruins of the modern spectacle," Debord wrote. "We must develop a methodical intervention based on the complex factors of two components in perpetual interaction: the material environment of life and the comportments which it gives rise to and which radically transform it."[13]

The Surrealist movement of the 1920s was another precedent known to these critical public artists. The Surrealists turned the spectacle of the city inside out through what some art critics called "counter-memories" and "counter-itineraries." By reclaiming fragments of the past, the Surrealists implicitly figured an alternative future. Their use of displaced imagery to subvert expectations and their sense of play directly affected the Situationists. However, the latter firmly rejected the Surrealist's enthrallment with imagination and the subconscious mind, thinking it a form of decadent self-indulgence. The Surrealist inheritance for today's artists persists, though, when they create seductive yet ambiguous images whose potency can never be fully rationalized.

One of the first times Wodiczko worked with video and sound was for the Bunker Hill Monument Projection in Charlestown, Massachusetts, produced and presented by Boston's Institute of Contemporary Art. For several hours on consecutive evenings, he illuminated the southern face of the Bunker Hill monument in Charlestown with video image projections and sound from a group of mothers of murdered youth, breaking their code of silence. Wodiczko explains:

> Those projections added emotional images of the human face and human gestures and sounds of the human voice to the abstract shape of the obelisk. It became the gigantic human figure of a private citizen, an actual person, a Charlestown or South Boston resident, who speaks freely and boldly of her or his personal experiences and struggles for the pursuit of life, liberty, and the pursuit of happiness and justice for all. This historic monument, dedicated to the heroes of a Revolutionary War battle, became a contemporary memorial to the present-day heroes or heroines who continue another battle on the same sacred ground of Bunker Hill.[14]

For some Charlestown residents, Wodiczko explains—the successful, privileged Charlestowners who defend the monument and the Charlestown image as a real estate venture—the Bunker Hill monument project was negative and wrong. But others said, "When we open it up to the rest of the world and to the city, we produce a positive image of a place that in fact shares its troubles."[15]

COMMUNITY-BASED IMAGERY

■ MURALS

Participation through interpretation—a key strategy of the critical public artists outlined above—is impossible if the images are too ambiguous and obscure to comprehend, however provocative they may be aesthetically and intellectually.

There is, however, one art form with a large audience that cannot be accused of abstruseness even while being provocative. The inner-city mural movement on New York's Lower East Side, Chicago's South Side, and in the barrios of Los Angeles, San Francisco, and Santa Fe, asserts the presence of an invisible population. Varying widely in style, subject, and "quality," they too have an art historical model to which they look—the Mexican mural movement of the 1930s and 1940s.

"Current discussions of public art for the most part omit muralism," critic Lucy Lippard writes, "following the art work patterns of ignoring community-based artists in favor of those who cater to the marketplace."[16] Despite that, no activist art has had more community support and long-term social impact than murals.

Murals are often used as cosmetic "Band-Aids on cancer" to cheer up neglected neighborhoods, or they can be relatively superficial in their images. But if the skilled muralist continues to probe for hidden histories—the underlying tensions of a place and its people—a more profound image begins to emerge, based in lived experiences rather than imposed ideas and stereotypes.

In 1973, New York's Cityarts workshop painted a mural called *Chinatown Today,* a striking two-point perspective showing a Chinatown stripped of clichés. Directed by staff member Alan Okada, the mural illustrates teenagers "trucking" down the street, prostitutes, a caravan of vulgar tourists, and a dead man lying under the spray of gambling cards. Sometimes the choice of site itself is the vehicle to subvert imposed images. For example, the group Artes Guadalupanos de Aztlán in Santa Fe, New Mexico, instantly became the focus of opposition when it proposed a mural for Canyon Road, which is *the* "arts and crafts road" in Santa Fe, known throughout the country as an art colony. The uproar was "an excitement bordering on panic, fired by indignation, and nurtured by the fear that the natives were opening their mouths and were about to expose them—the residents, or occupants, of Canyon Road—for the frauds that they were, and continue to be to this day."[17]

In other instances, the timing of a mural is an affront to the way a city wants to present itself. Estrada Court in Los Angeles has more than eighty murals painted on the walls of its two-story, cracker-box housing units, spanning a wide range of imagery. But in 1984 many outsiders objected to a mural painted with an image of Che Guevara and a large title saying, "We Are Not A Minority." Cuban immigrants defaced the mural, declaring that they did not want such an image to be seen by visitors to Los Angeles for the 1984 Olympics.[18]

Chicana artist Judith Baca, founder of the Citywide Mural Project and later the Social and Public Art Resource Center (SPARC), offered that one of the most controversial murals she organized in the 1970s was a piece that showed, on one side, an idyllic scene in the Venice, California, community done in the style of a Persian miniature; on the other side were bulldozers wiping out the residents, knocking down the small wooden houses on the canals to make room for a plush condo city.[19] In the corner was an illustration of an actual graffiti: "Stop the pigs [greed]. Save Venice." Realtors had the mural nearly painted over before the artists, after a battery of meetings with city officials, saved it.

By taking a small object and transforming it into a giant image, Baca says, you teach people to look at it in a different way. Consider, for example, the effect of four days spent rendering each person being forced on a bus for deportation, standing next to the oversized face of someone who is feeling the agony of that deportation. At the end of that process, the artist will perceive the concept of deportation in a substantially different way.[20] Also, because of the monumentality of showing people in public murals, the depictions offer a respect often lacking in their lives and in other representations of their communities.

In at least this one way, the process of measuring oneself to a larger size echoes Wodiczko's projections. Speaking of the Bunker Hill monument, he says, "Imagining themselves being fifty times taller than we are . . . was part of the project. The project became not only a political or cultural act of speech but an act of psychological development on the part of those who were about to speak."[21]

■ GRASSROOTS ARTS PRACTICE

Murals spread across the nation as part of a general creative outburst accompanying community organizing in the 1960s and 1970s. Community arts overlapped with legal struggles, direct-action movements, self-defense efforts, and rising community militancy.

Fig. 13.8: *Pulp Fiction* (Carole Condé and Karl Beveridge, 1949) chronicles the agitprop history of a pulp and paper mill in northern Ontario.

The media-savvy performances of a number of political and community groups from this period anticipated a grassroots art practice. Carole Condé and Karl Beveridge are two Canadian artists who, feeling a widening gulf between practice and theory, redirected their commitment of a politicized art practice to a more local arena. This couple is significant for their "positive" and didactic portraits of the Canadian labor movement that simultaneously explore the contradictions and conflicts of workers' lives. For instance, seeking to redress women's historical absences from traditional labor representations, Condé and Beveridge worked with the unions to create a series of photo-narratives, using staged settings with photographic inserts, that emphasized women's roles as both behind-the-scenes and frontline organizers.

Pulp Fiction (fig. 13.8), a series of color photographic montages completed in 1993 in collaboration with the Paperworkers Union, chronicles an agitprop history of a pulp and paper mill in northern Ontario. The montages extend the visual logic of hand-painted sets and cutout figures, reminiscent of nineteenth-century working-class graphic and vaudeville stage traditions. The artists were incited by the way in which corporate culture portrays the working class as an obstacle to a "progressive" agenda of change and innovation. Similarly, the Canadian forest industry presents an image where the jobs of unionized workers are pitted against the struggles of environmentalists to preserve natural resources. While not downplaying the tense issues of clear-cutting and acid rain, Condé and Beveridge present in *Pulp Fiction* a counter-narrative to the negative media charge of forest-industry workers as "rednecks" hostile to the environmental movement. They trace the ways in which the pulp and paper union has attempted to work, both historically and in a contemporary context, to protect the environment.

According to writer Dot Tuer, Condé and Beveridge are "battling for image recognition in an increasingly hostile field of representation." Their community-based, class-identified narratives are "one of the few barricades being erected against the onslaught of a cultural corporatism that seeks nothing less than the eradication of class consciousness."[22]

Robert Pincus, art critic of the *San Diego Union-Tribune*, offers another example of the local arena in what he calls "America's biggest border town": San Diego. There, a small and shifting number of artist and community activists have garnered a great deal of attention for their work, including David Avalos, Louis Hock, and Elizabeth Sisco. In 1988 they designed a photomural declaring "Welcome to America's Finest Tourist Plantation" and purchased advertising space for it on one hundred

Fig. 13.9: Photomural by Elizabeth Sisco, Louis Hock, and David Avalos, *Welcome to America's Finest Tourist Plantation* (1988). The image was displayed on 100 buses in the San Diego area in January 1988 to coincide with Super Bowl XXII.

local buses for one month (fig. 13.9). It was the first of seven collaborative projects to dramatize issues central to the civic life of San Diego and its surrounding region, bordering on Mexico. (Artists involved in other projects included Deborah Small, William Weeks, Bartlett Sher, and Cheryl Lindley.) The artists superimposed the words on three images. The central and largest one was of a border patrol agent handcuffing two people, a picture taken by Sisco on a San Diego Transit bus in the affluent seaside community of La Jolla. Flanking this photograph were images of a dishwasher and a chambermaid representing, in the artists' words, "the restaurant and hotel/motel industries."

In this case the artists were working directly against the image of San Diego, a city that had long billed itself as a mecca for tourists, not acknowledging the pervasive presence of illegal immigrants in the economy of the city. By employing public advertising space, as Pincus explains, the trio of artists chose to raise a thorny issue about the reality of civic life just at a moment when city officials didn't want it raised: in the full glare of the national media, gathered in San Diego for the Super Bowl.

One hundred posters became thousands of reproductions when the morning and evening newspapers, as well as the local edition of the *Los Angeles Times*, published front-page stories accompanied by photographs. Commentaries followed (including Pincus's); certain city officials informed the press that they were trying to have the poster removed, and national coverage ensued. Most important, editorials, guest editorials, and letters to the editors of the local papers debated the role of the illegal immigrant in the local economy and the validity of the poster.[23]

Throughout January 1988, the photomural catalyzed a civic debate that few other activist artists have succeeded in generating. Referring to San Diego's boosterish slogan, "America's Finest City," one letter writer to the *San Diego Union* argued, "I think it's time we stop fooling ourselves with Madison Avenue slogans." Indeed, all of the artists' other projects sparked similar controversy even when, in Pincus's opinion, the works themselves had a few "flaws." Every project was different—varying from billboards, bus bench images, and an exhibition of photographs to street theater and performance art.

Pincus suggests that the forms of the work owe something to the Conceptual aesthetic. Like classic Conceptual art (admitting that many say such a thing did not exist), the work was not to have a lasting material existence but would exist only as a catalyst to change and help to deconstruct or to destroy existing material—established icons. In the artists' words, "We believe that the creative act involves not only the artist's initiative but the community response. Our contributions around public issues of local concern insist that community identity is the ongoing creation of a multiplicity of voices. We attempt to play an artful role in the process of community self-definition, forging a truly public vision of our city."[24]

Yet in addition to the Conceptual tradition, their work is just as firmly linked to politically engaged art in San Diego itself, looking to the ideals and practice of civil rights, Chicano, labor, and other social movements in the community. One prominent manifestation of such a tradition can be seen in the city's largest park, Balboa Park. There, community activists and artists demanded the creation of a Chicano cultural center after one artist was asked to leave a city-owned storage space he had been using, with permission, as a studio. Following negotiations, the City offered to convert a former water tank, also located in Balboa Park. Today the round structure is the mural-covered Centro Cultural de la Raza, where the renowned Border Art Workshop/Taller de Arte Fronterizo was established and where David Avalos came of age as an artist. Thus, while classic Conceptual art had its main audience in galleries and art magazines, this work finds a broader audience and participates in producing community-based images.[25]

British artists Loraine Leeson and Peter Dunn, founding artists of The Art of Change (originally named the Docklands Community Poster Project), work and live near a London neighborhood called the Docklands, along the River Thames. They began collaborating with the community to fend off trendy upscale redevelopment which, they believed, threatened homes and livelihoods. Called a "wasteland" by the Thatcher government, the Docklands was home and workplace to more than fifty thousand politically invisible people; it was a working-class district of low-cost family homes, inexpensive artists' spaces, and commercial businesses and warehouses. According to the local groups united in opposition, developers designed luxury flats too expensive for locals, and rather than creating new jobs, caused established firms to relocate, thereby disrupting the workforce.

In a changing set of photomurals on six billboard sites, Leeson and Dunn, an artist team, and the community charted an alternative and local narrative, in opposition to the publicity images for the Canary Wharf development. To the extent that the media described the development corporation in terms like "controversial," the project ruptured the publicity material's illusion of harmony. While referencing labor history, the photomurals were not nostalgic re-creations of past places nor monuments to alternative heroines like those of The Power of Place, the Los Angeles–based organization founded by Dolores Hayden. The series of eight-by-twelve-foot billboards was actually a cycle of images; different sections of the whole picture gradually changed over an extended period, with each change creating a distinct new composite image, unrolling like a "slow-motion animated film." The team sited the billboards for pedestrians who walked by regularly, allowing an argument to unfold through time. Messages included, "What's Going On Behind Our Backs?" "Big Money Is Moving In," "Don't Let It Push Out Local People," and "Our Future Is In The Docklands" (figs. 13.10, 13.11). The group also distributed the images as posters and postcards at meetings and festivals. By garnering media attention, they let the area's struggle be known to the rest of England (and the world). None of this stopped the Docklands redevelopment, however.

The artists set out clear definitions for terms such as "community": "All communities are essentially communities of interest," stating that "the word is often associated with nostalgic or highly romanticized images of 'place.'" To writer Malcolm Miles, "The group developed 'local narratives' against the grand

Fig. 13.10: Photomontage from the *Changing Picture of Docklands* series, as displayed on six billboard sites around the London Docklands, 1981–1990.
© Loraine Leeson, The Art of Change (formerly Docklands Community Poster Project)

Fig. 13.11 : Photomural in situ (1982).
© Loraine Leeson, The Art of Change (formerly Docklands Community Poster Project)

narratives of international modernism and multinational economic interests, defining the specificity of the voices suppressed by mainstream culture."[26]

Dunn and Leeson are dubious about the relationship of their work to the avant-garde art world. They ask: Why does the Left seem so obsessed with media images?

> Each year, millions of words go into print which are devoted to these images: analyzing them, explaining their illusions, demonstrating how they work, and seemingly concluding what most people already know by experience. This is not to devalue such work; on the contrary, it is simply to point out that, in itself, such analysis does not diminish the ideological power that these images possess. It cannot perform a simple (or even a complex) exorcism merely by revealing the process of their construction; neither can it decrease any pleasure derived from their consumption. On the contrary, it serves to enhance this pleasure by adding another dimension to the reading of such images and actually may *create* pleasure, via metadiscourse, even though the original material is regarded as distasteful or offensive on primary impact.[27]

Where, then, does the power of these images lie, and how can the analysis of them be of use in the development of an activist art? Dunn and Leeson propose that it is not enough for an activist art practice to be a "crude mirror image of its capitalist counterparts—a kind of advertising agency for the Left, using easy slogans which gloss over the complexity of the issues." They continue: "The politics of representation is not confined just to what lies within the frame of an image, its decoding and analysis. It concerns the wider questions of a total working process—its structure and context, who it represents and engages, and who—ultimately—it serves."[28]

In practice this means a total inversion of the process. Rather than a billboard imposed from above or permeated with aesthetic, even if avant-garde, conventions, the Docklands billboards began with the community. Local activists and tenants groups decided what was needed, what form the work should take, what visual strategies would be best, even the size and location of the billboards.

While work of this kind is too didactic, agitprop, or "preachy" for some, it nevertheless offers the living ground, in Michael Ventura's words, that so much Conceptual art lacks.

New York–based REPOhistory (repossessing history), a multiethnic collective of artists, writers, performers, and educators, takes the current debates on history, imagery, and multiculturalism into the streets where everybody "can be confronted or provoked or challenged by the information." They call their work "cognitive remapping of the ambient urban environment." Founded in 1989, the group includes many alumni of PAD/D (Political Art Documentation/Distribution), an overtly political group from the 1970s to 1980s, whose goal was to use image-making on behalf of disenfranchised people.

Fig. 13.12: Tess Timothy and Mark O'Brien, *The Meal and Slave Market,* Wall and Water Streets, New York (1992–93). From the series "The Lower Manhattan Sign Project," REPOhistory, New York.

First called the History Project, the collective began as a study group and developed into a proposal (by REPOhistorian Greg Sholette) to "retrieve and relocate absent historical narratives as specific locations in the New York City area through counter-monuments, actions and events."[29] Originally, the collective believed that guerilla art projects would be the only course of action available to groups interested in re-presenting history based on a multicultural reading of class, race, gender, and sexuality. However, they recently created their seventh officially sanctioned, publicly funded, site-specific project.

REPOhistory premiered in 1992 with The Lower Manhattan Sign Project in which more than forty artists, activists, and writers combined efforts toward a history-based re-presenting of thirty-nine sites. One sign was a memorial to those Chinese traders and seamen who, in the 1830s, formed the first Chinese residential community in the United States in the area around what is now the South Street Seaport. Another, called *The Meal and Slave Market* (fig. 13.12), referred to 1746, when nearly one in every five New Yorkers was black, and New York was the country's

Fig. 13.13: ***Native Hosts,*** **Portland, Oregon (1998). Hachivi Edgar Heap of Birds, an artist of Cheyenne/ Arapaho descent, mounted aluminum signs with geographic names in backward letters, followed by "Today Your Host Is Modoc" and the names of other tribes, forcing the viewer to reflect on the history of their places.**

second largest urban slave center. The sign marked the site of a Colonial slave market and recalled the vital role that enslaved Africans played in the city's social and economic growth from the early 1600s until the state abolished slavery in 1827.

As an example of other projects, *Queer Spaces* (1994) commemorated historical sites where gays and lesbians gather. *Entering Buttermilk Bottom* (1994) was a collaboration with artists from Atlanta, Georgia, to reclaim an African-American neighborhood bulldozed in the 1960s to make room for modern Atlanta and the "New South."

There are now perhaps hundreds of artists' projects that reclaim history to counteract official narratives, although not all are "total inversions," as described by Docklands artists Leeson and Dunn. Hachivi Edgar Heap of Birds, an artist of Cheyenne/ Arapaho descent, offers installations that both subvert and convert perceptions of place. In 1988 he mounted aluminum signs reading "New York" in backward letters, followed by "Today Your Host Is Shinnecock," to force viewers, struggling to read the reversed letters, to literally look backwards, thrusting them into a new relationship with "their" state. He mounted a similar sign for Oregon (fig. 13.13). Different tribes whose land was occupied were the subject of signs in different places: Shinnecock, Seneca, Tuscarora, Mohawk, Werpoe, and Manhattan. Another project, *Day/Night* (1991), located in Pioneer Square in so-called high-tech Seattle, picked up the theme of dispossessed Native Americans in the context of homelessness: "Far Away Brothers And Sisters We Still Remember You." Next to a statue of the chief who gave the city its name, the artist wrote, "Chief Seattle Now The Streets Are Our Home" in both English and the local Native American language.

ART AND MEMORY

Heap of Birds demonstrates that today's politically engaged artists are not afraid to insert images of controversial memories into city spaces. Emphatically, of all the implications of media saturation, perhaps the effect on memory is the most insidious. Personal and social, controversial and shared, memory is what we have designed out of postindustrial society and for which "the data banks of cyberspace have become shallow substitutes."[30]

Certainly, urban critics have alerted us for years to the consequences of the domination of media images. For one thing, it has led to an impoverished understanding of the built environment, turning social space into a fetishized abstraction.[31] We have reduced the space of lived experience to a system of visual stereotypes. And with this increasing emphasis on visual perception we have correspondingly reduced other forms of sensory perception, as well as of memory.

As one response, Wodiczko, REPOhistory, Heap of Birds, and others enable the public to repossess the city through the activities of perception, memory, and constructing narratives—all the activities Kevin Lynch implied in his concept of "sense." Most, although not all, activate a skepticism about traditional imagery that city planners (and marketing) do not. Their particular targets, whether monuments, corporate publicity, or advertising, are only examples of structures that cities have long used in order to present beautiful, bedazzling images of themselves. Critic Patricia Phillips warns that if citizens do not identify and project their own images, their own sense of the potential of places, then someone or some organization will set the terms for the future for them.[32]

The work we have shown here involves provocations that are not overtly political (in the sense of ideology) but that have political consequences. The artists' tactics keep alive critical thought and skeptical perspective in a wider public often informed only by mainstream media.

How are we to judge these art works? Noticeably, the philosophical and ethical ambition of the works is at its most intense, if also at its most tenuous, in art that has been placed in the midst of, created especially for, or made in the name of a geographically specific community. Without geographical and community specificity, artists inadvertently perpetuate an abstract theoretical outlook—an outlook that in many ways replicates the distracted engagement with the world that artists criticize.[33]

Looking at a formal product at the end, just as looking only at the good intentions or effectiveness of the work, is certainly not the whole picture. Critic Jeff Kelley states, "You have to have people [critics] who can evaluate the qualities of a process, just as they evaluate the qualities of a product."[34]

"Perhaps, in the end," artist and writer Suzanne Lacy offers, "the merit of a single and particular work in and of itself will not be the sole concern of our criticism."[s] If public artists are envisioning a new form of society—a shared project with others in the community who are not artists—then the artwork must be seen with respect to that vision and assessed in part by its relationship to the collective social proposition to which it subscribes. That is, art becomes one's statement of values as well as a reflection of a mode of seeing—and sensing.

If in these many works, and in this idiosyncratic review of them, we reframe the field within which they operate, then perhaps our understanding of this art, of the potential of place, and of the potential of people to sense these places, will be redirected in a more substantive way.

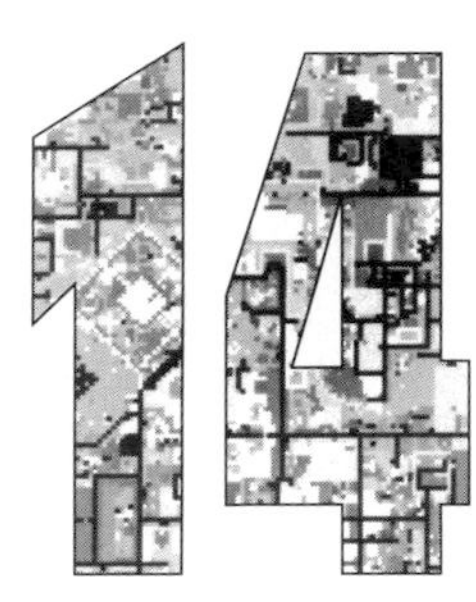

Ephemera, Temporary Urbanism, and Imaging

J. Mark Schuster

■ EDITORS' OVERVIEW

Urban ephemera are organized, momentary, repeated urban public presentations. They include parades, festivals, celebrations, outdoor performances, and rituals of all kinds. Because they impress themselves upon the public images of cities in ways small and large, Mark Schuster, a cultural policy analyst, urges city designers and planners to add ephemera planning to their list of tools.

In the past, critics have viewed these events as grist for tourist promotions, or they have expressed alarm at their possibilities for public pacification. The tourist promoters mistake the shows for real urban life, whereas the social alarmists mistake communal fun for a social drug. Schuster challenges both groups by adding a third unit of analysis to the familiar dichotomy of local images and outside images in the urban image discussion—corporate media. This step makes explicit the assumptions of many of the essays in this book. Schuster asks whether such corporate media images really do so dominate the reputation of cities that city dwellers must accept their portraits. The workings of ephemera reveal the absurdity of such a stance.

With the exceptions of world's fairs and Olympic Games, most ephemera are events where local people play before local audiences. If some of them catch the media's attention, and thereby the public's fancy, they may attract tourists. Surely the Mardi Gras in New Orleans and the Tournament of Roses in Pasadena are such events.

Boston's First Night celebration and the Head of the Charles Regatta are, despite their crowds, not tourist attractions.

Schuster reviews a number of locally significant public events around the world: the long-standing *Las Fallas* festival of Valencia, the newly altered Daimonji Festival in Kyoto, and the new WaterFire spectacle in Providence, Rhode Island. In all three, Schuster stresses the local component. The fact that city residents carry on these events year after year, often as volunteers, is the key to their energy and dynamism. In all cases, the city government offers support, as do local businesses, and the media report and publicize. Thus, like every aspect of urban planning, urban ephemera are mixed affairs, full of possibilities for both local apathy and local conflict.

In his presentation of events, Schuster considers the full range, from local street clubs that perform without anyone's aid to the heavily subsidized Olympics. In the end he makes a persuasive argument that ephemera benefit their cities in important ways, especially by encouraging residents to represent themselves and to come together in ways that make them more fully appreciate their city. For planners, there are all the familiar issues of land-use politics: competition, conflict, and the difficulties of locating and maintaining the public interest. In his review, Schuster confirms the planner's wisdom that an open process is the surest path to enduring success.

INTRODUCTION: EPHEMERA

My topic is ephemera—the ephemera of urban life—the temporary, the occasional, the fleeting. Spectacles, pageants, rituals, celebrations, and events of all sorts will be considered, but I wish to cast my net even more widely to include other, smaller phenomena—the ephemera of daily, weekly, and seasonal life. I will pay particular attention to designed and managed ephemera, ephemera that occur with some identifiable and understood regularity. My belief is all ephemera—large and small—deserve our attention as planners, as urban designers, and as citizens. I will argue that ephemera make an important contribution to the life of the city, as well as to the imaging of the city; I will also argue that ephemera may be components of imaging that actually work their influence more outside the realm of the media than inside that realm.

One does not normally think of ephemera as an important element in planning and urban design. Why? Is it because we feel that something that is ephemeral is fleeting and insubstantial, perhaps frivolous, only to be considered after the more serious matters of urban life are resolved? As planners we are trained to be instrumental, single-minded, and calculatingly rational in our actions, but not to be playful or experimental or to pay attention to emotions and feelings. We have surrendered to the discourse of economics; "value" has taken on a narrow meaning incorporating only costs and benefits that can be readily measured. Yet our memories and images of places, our views of their importance and meaning, and our impressions of their quality and value are shaped by ephemera. Surely we would be remiss not to notice.

As I have considered urban ephemera, I have thought about Olympic Games and world's fairs; about New York ticker tape parades and inaugural pageantry; about holiday festivities and days of mourning. I have also found myself thinking about flea markets and street fairs; about neighborhood festivals and street decorations; about seasonal plantings and temporary kiosks that appear and disappear throughout the year; about electoral campaigns and the arrivals and departures of conventions; about the beacon at the top of the old John Hancock building in Boston, tracking the weather and indicating whether or not the Red Sox game has been canceled. I have found myself intrigued with the Standing the Pillar ceremony held once every seven years at the Kamisuwa and Suwa shrines in Nagano, Japan,[1] as well as with the Passion Play held every ten years in Oberammergau, Germany, fulfilling a vow made to God in 1633 in the hope that the town would be protected from further ravages of the Black Plague.

Linking all of these examples is the desire to create and afford surprise balanced by the expectation of return and routine. The life of the city becomes a bit less predictable, and more becomes possible, if only for a moment. Yet, perhaps paradoxically, in the regularity of these events lies a key to their power. Even the Olympics, which a single city usually gets to host only once in a lifetime, is experienced, I would argue, as a kind of "time-share" ephemera.[2] But an even more important link among them is the contribution they all make to the unique images of the places from which they come.

THE LITERATURES OF EPHEMERA

It is rather difficult to find articles on ephemera in the planning literature (though that is beginning to change). Neither planners nor planning researchers have paid as much attention as they might (indeed, as they should) to these phenomena. Yet, allied literatures have a considerable contribution to make to a planner's understanding of urban ephemera.

One might begin with the literature on festivals, including discussions of everything from Kool-Aid Day in Hastings, Nebraska, the Shrimp and Petroleum Festival in Morgan City, Louisiana, and the Octubafest in Carlisle, Pennsylvania, to the Passion Play in Oberammergau.[3] But to do justice to festivals alone, one must enter the fields of comparative religion, anthropology, sociology, ethnography, cultural studies, geography, and folklore, to name just a few of the disciplines that have focused their attention on one or another aspect of these gatherings. Because of both their visibility (their imageability) and their urban impact, the Olympic Games have attracted considerable scholarly attention. World's fairs, too, have been thoroughly mined for their greater significance.[4]

From an urban planning perspective, two literatures have been predominant. One is the "Livable Cities" literature embodying an idea first promoted by Partners for Livable Places and now formalized in a series of annual conferences. This literature often makes passing mention of ephemera,[5] but to my knowledge it has not yet addressed them systematically. Of more recent vintage is what might be called the "Arts and Urban

Development" literature,[6] a genre that attempts to document the role that arts and culture can play in urban economic development. Deben, Musterd, and van Weesep, who are quite cautious about the evidence concerning the impact of this role, pose a key question: "Is there a new cultural vitality to be witnessed in the cities, and is it based broadly enough to be able to speak of a revival of urban culture? Or does the revival end in superficiality, in organized events where the opposite numbers in urban society can rub shoulders for one day or one night, before returning to their respective places and lives, relieved that once more the feared social explosion did not happen?"[7]

Most literature on the arts and urban development does not concern itself with this question. Rather, it is relentlessly instrumental. The arts and culture are seen as tools for urban revitalization, the central idea being that they can (1) provide the catalyst for physical and environmental renewal, (2) attract tourists and capital investment, (3) enhance a city's image, and (4) create new jobs.[8] While I will ultimately be concerned with the third and, to a lesser extent, the first and second, this literature offers little clue as to why one might encourage ephemera either for their own sake or for their contribution to building and defining community.

I refer to these literatures not because they offer exactly what I would like—there is a huge research agenda here—but because they are what is available. Only one author of whom I am aware organizes her thinking along lines similar to the ones I wish to pursue: Sarah Bonnemaison, in her excellent albeit much too brief paper "City Policies and Cyclical Events," explores a variety of questions pertaining to temporary urbanism.[9] If there is a single foundation other than my own experience upon which the current paper is built, it is this.

■ KEVIN LYNCH ON EPHEMERA

In *What Time Is This Place?* Kevin Lynch extended his work on the image of the city to take account explicitly of the influence of time on that image. This is an excellent place to begin from the urban design perspective. Because he saw planning as the management of change, an emphasis on time was only logical. He calls upon us to notice those things that are temporary yet important in shaping our images and experiences of the city—noises, odors, lighting, events, physical traces of change—and to notice the time-based ebb and flow of these elements. He exhorts planners, designers, and citizens to take note of the dimensions along which the structure of time can vary and, by extension, the richness that comes from variation in the urban environment. The concepts of grain, period, amplitude, rate, synchronization, regularity, and orientation become the building blocks of time-cognizant planning and design: "We take pleasure in distinctive events, as in distinctive places. Important hours should be perceptually remarkable, and then we can find our way in time. Places and events can be designed to enlarge our senses of the present, either by their own vivid characters or as they heighten our perception of the contained activity—setting off the people in a parade, an audience, or a market. Places can be given a particular look at particular times."[10]

As always, Lynch's work is not only rich in theory but overflowing with practical, honest suggestions as to what planners and designers might do to incorporate these ideas into their practice. I attach contemporary examples to his suggestions:

- They might act to imprint change on the physical environment—the use of paving stones to trace the former walls of the Bastille in Place de la Bastille in Paris, or Claes Oldenburg's proposal to place two monumental toilet floats in the Thames to reflect its tides and call attention to its pollution.[11]
- They might encourage special lighting or decoration—the draping of the Reichstag or the Pont Neuf by Christo and Jeanne-Claude or the stunning use of temporary fire in WaterFire by Barnaby Evans in Providence, Rhode Island (more about this later).
- They might lobby for regulations that allow for variation in official closing hours and, more generally, in what is

permitted and what is not—the recognition in Manchester, England, that overly restrictive licensing hours brought all inebriated patrons out into the streets at the same time, exacerbating the problems of nightlife rather than alleviating them.

- They might design or reserve special locales for particular occasions—summer concerts in the waterfront Harborlights Pavilion in Boston.
- Certain areas might be made accessible (or inaccessible) on particular days—the annual commemorative openings of the Catalan Parliament building, the City Hall, and the offices of the regional government in Barcelona; or Sunday closings of Memorial Drive in Cambridge, Massachusetts.
- Temporary memorials might be created, to be replaced later by permanent memorials or removed.[12]
- They should pay attention to seasonal plantings.
- Music and dance should be employed, and action should be encouraged.
- Surprises can be incorporated into the public environment—the use of "Street Surprises" by First Night Boston to herald the coming of the city's New Year's Eve celebration of the arts.[13]
- New rituals of time can be invented—Caixa Catalunya, a bank, commissioning Els Comediants, a renowned Catalan street theater group, to produce a celebration to "deliver" La Pedrera, Gaudi's well-known apartment building, back to the city following its restoration.
- Fireworks can be used as punctuation.
- Temporary uses can, and should, be found for vacant spaces—Gallery 37's use of a vacant city block in the Chicago Loop for its summer arts apprenticeship job training program, or the temporary transformation of Boston's City Hall Plaza into a viewing area, complete with centerfield bleachers, a simulated "Green Monster" wall, and two giant television screens, where the citizens

Fig. 14.1: Temporary installation of a simulated Fenway Park on City Hall Plaza in Boston, Massachusetts, 1999.
Photograph © Carla Osberg

of Boston could gather with the mayor for a free viewing of the 1999 Baseball All-Star Game (fig. 14.1).

Despite the power of these examples, planning agencies (at least American ones) have hardly responded to Lynch's exhortations. Indeed, he was not entirely optimistic:

> [I]n the United States we are rarely willing to transform the public environment in any really striking temporary way. The tinsel hung along the light poles of shopping streets at Christmas is pitiful indeed. The fun and glitter of temporary architecture is a pleasure forgone. We only pretend to it by building elephantine world fairs that last too long.[14]

Halfhearted attempts are one thing, but there are other, more serious critiques that challenge Lynch's optimism. Two of them deserve particular attention.

■ DANIEL BOORSTIN ON EPHEMERA

In 1961, only one year after the publication of Kevin Lynch's *The Image of the City*, another rather different book on the power of image appeared: Daniel Boorstin's *The Image: A Guide to Pseudoevents in America*. Paraphrasing George Will's comments in his afterword to the twenty-fifth anniversary edition of Boorstin, both books changed the way we think because they changed the way we see and listen, but they accomplished this in very different ways with very different analyses. Boorstin's topic was the American image and how increasingly it was being shaped not by the accumulated daily actions of its citizens but by the influence of the media.[15]

Boorstin's challenge to Lynch derives from his much more pessimistic view of society's ability to create the possibilities for spontaneous events; indeed, he would be very hesitant to accept the notion of designing spontaneous events. Boorstin centers his warning on the rise of "pseudoevents," events created for and structured by the media, which in his view increasingly supplant real, spontaneous events. He argues that this is happening because:

- Pseudoevents are more dramatic (since they are planned to be suspenseful).
- Pseudoevents are easier to disseminate and make vivid (since they are planned for dissemination).
- Pseudoevents can be repeated at will, and their impression reinforced.
- Pseudoevents cost money to create; hence someone will have an interest in disseminating, magnifying, advertising, and extolling them as events worth watching or worth believing.
- Pseudoevents are more intelligible (since they are planned for intelligibility) and hence more reassuring.
- Pseudoevents are more sociable, easier to converse about, and more convenient to witness.
- Knowledge of pseudoevents becomes the test for being informed.

- Pseudoevents spawn other pseudoevents in geometric progression.[16]

I have reproduced Boorstin's list of the characteristics of pseudoevents in detail because of the role that "planning" plays in that critique: The particular requirements of the media cause one to plan in order to satisfy those requirements, and one becomes caught up in a cycle of "pseudoness." One can easily imagine Boorstin warning Lynch that planning would have a deadening effect on any innovative initiative with respect to ephemera. One can also imagine that Lynch would not have been fully convinced.[17]

■ DAVID HARVEY ON EPHEMERA

A good deal of the academic literature on the influence of ephemera in modern life is critical, brooding, complaining, and cynical. Very little of it is upbeat or optimistic in the Lynchian style. Much of this work is rooted in or makes reference to the work of David Harvey, whose critique originates in political economy rather than in media studies.

Harvey chronicles the rise of the "entrepreneurial city," which, because of the globalization of capitalism, finds itself engaged in four types of competition:

- Competition for position in the international division of labor
- Competition for position as a center of consumption
- Competition for control and command functions (financial and administrative powers in particular)
- Competition for governmental redistributions

With little else to fall back on, image becomes key: "The production of an urban image through, for example, the organisation of spectacles . . . becomes an important facet of interurban competition at the same time as it becomes a means to rally potentially alienated populations to a common cause."[18]

From here it is only a short step to the conclusion that festivals and urban spectacles are nothing more nor less than instruments of social control in societies inevitably riven by class conflict. Festival marketplaces, professional sports activities, and Olympic Games become symbols of the supposed unity of class-divided and racially segregated cities, although they are actually hegemonic devices by which an elite has its way through placating and deceiving the masses. It is not difficult to imagine Harvey extending this analysis to ephemera more generally.

■ OTHER LITERATURE ON EPHEMERA

Harvey's analysis is powerful and worth heeding. It has been picked up with a vengeance in the literature on public events, festivals, and celebrations. Helen Lenskyj, for example, worries about the difficulties faced by those brave citizens who challenge hegemonic assumptions concerning the value of Olympic sporting competition.[19] But the trap in this approach, of course, is that it suggests that anyone who thinks the Olympics (or, for that matter, ephemera more generally) are a good idea is engaged in hegemonic behavior, either by wishing to exert hegemony or by virtue of having been duped. That does not leave much room for another view.

Rodger Brown takes a slightly different tack on this issue:

> With space defeated by cars, the SST, fiber optics, and the Internet, people react by clinging to place, and the idea of places. But a sense of place can only develop over time, and it is increasingly difficult for people to remain in one space for enough years for it to deeply become a place. . . .
>
> As a replacement for real meaningfulness, we cast the world within a cloud and occupy the shadow geographies, remaking our homes inside imagined communities, accepting appliqué in place of depth. There, traditions are invented and reinvented, produced and reproduced; mythologies of the past are reanimated; themes are colonized. These shadow geographies operate through schemes of desire; they are therapeutic and also imperialist, taking

> over where once was real history; and they are occupied by a type of refugee. Mayberry is a shadow geography in our theme park world. You have to cup your hands around your eyes in order to see. It is a play of light on the land, a flickering in your head that lets you think you see something that really isn't there, like a wish come true.[20]

Thus, for him the "shadow geographies" of ephemera are functional, responding to internal psychological needs rather than imposed from without. Where Harvey is critical, Brown is resigned.

Yet, not every commentator who has taken a look at ephemera has come away critical. In particular, such analyses begin to seem less compelling when one stops to ask citizens themselves about their reaction to these phenomena. Mark Sussman set out to critique the New York City ticker tape parade that welcomed soldiers home from the Gulf War, but he pulled up short when he realized that "None of this quite explains why millions of people turned out with homemade costumes and signs, photographs of loved ones, and messages of patriotism."[21] Harry Hiller seemed genuinely surprised when he discovered the level of residual support and goodwill among the citizens of Calgary for the 1988 Calgary Winter Olympics.[22] Alma Guillermoprieto, Carol Flake, and Abner Cohen all demonstrate how poor, disadvantaged communities (as well as wealthy ones) embrace festival and celebration, investing considerable resources to indulge in class role reversal at Carnival time.[23]

Harvey's views are echoed in Ley and Olds's work on world's fairs. To them the world's fair is a manifestation of the culture industry imposing hegemonic meanings through spectacles onto a depoliticized mass audience. Yet, as they sifted through their evidence, they came to the realization that "a number [of the pavilions] displayed themes which revealed more diversity than a tightly woven view of hegemony might accommodate." They ultimately conclude, "The cultural dupes posed by mass culture theorists are less visible on the ground than they are in nonempirical speculation."[24]

Dupes or not, Harvey's critique is one that informs much of the thinking behind ephemera in cities. Indeed, it may be what keeps planners and urban designers from considering ephemera as part of their urban design/planning tool kit. We need to be aware of this critique and adopt a position with respect to it, but there is no compelling need to succumb to it. Lynch would not have been overly troubled. He would have remained upbeat and optimistic, continually searching for the many counterexamples that could support a different, more positive point of view and provide an alternative understanding.

MEDIA, EPHEMERA, AND IMAGING

It is the claim of much of this volume that the electronic and print media are now the primary agents in imaging cities. And, in many ways, those influences are just as salient with ephemera as with other attributes of the city and its life. One can only assume that any city would be delighted, as Fremantle, Australia, was, with Morley Safer's comments on *60 Minutes* concerning its hosting of the America's Cup: "So unimportant an event as a rather esoteric boat race has meant something to a whole country and given it a focus. . . . The joy of nations is a strange thing. A people with so much wealth and achievement and so much self-doubt become believers in themselves. And all because of a rather useless, ugly and overdone hunk of Victorian silver."[25] And it seems that both Barcelona and Catalunya have good reason to be pleased with the image they projected to the world through the Olympic Games.[26]

The omnivorous quality of the media does present risks for cities bold enough to engage visibly and proudly with ephemera. Charles Rutheiser, in his scathing critique of the redevelopment of Atlanta published just prior to the Olympic Games, captures that risk rather well: "Approximately 15,000 journalists will be descending upon Atlanta in the summer of 1996, an unspecified percentage of whom will have the express purpose not of covering the Games, but of demonstrating how Atlanta is not really what it claims to be."[27] The citizens of Atlanta may now be of mixed mind as to how well the media served the image-building elements of their Olympic project.

Moreover, the media are not merely passive in transmitting an image, positive or negative; they can be active actors in shaping that image. A few anecdotes make the point. Boorstin, in looking at the depictions of places in guidebooks, recounts: "In Berlin, in the days before the First World War, legend tells us that precisely at the stroke of noon, just as the imperial military band would begin its daily concert in front of the Imperial Palace, Kaiser Wilhelm used to interrupt whatever he was doing inside the palace. If he was in a council of state he would say, 'With your kind forbearance, gentlemen, I must excuse myself now to appear in the window. You see, it says in Baedeker that at this hour I always do.'"[28]

Jack Ludwig, in his book on quintessential American events, recounts a more cautionary tale from the 1973 Tournament of Roses Parade:

> [T]he city of Pasadena erected bleacher seats on a 300-foot parkway which, for the preceding twelve years, had been traditionally—and unofficially—occupied by local blacks living in the vicinity of the Rose Bowl. Elderly black people would be set up in seats early and be served food and hot drinks by young community blacks during the parade. The black community had established squatters' rights to that particular spot in 1960. The area they used had grown steadily till the 1972 Rose Bowl Parade, when about seventy people were accommodated.
>
> When the black community protested the disappearance of their seats, the city's defense was that California freeway robbery took away about 10,000 parade seats. To cut that 10,000 by seventy "black community seats" seemed, to white Pasadena, only just and right.

A white policeman offered an alternative explanation:

> Hell, they were killing Pasadena's image. Some TV cameramen showed them last year—messy, wrinkled, old. And

> noisy. Paying no real attention to the parade—just drinking, and eating. Hell, my Daddy told me we *never* had *Tobacco Road* in Pasadena, even during the Depression, so why have it now? Nobody wants to see a bunch of old Negroes bugaloo first thing New Year's morning.[29]

There are more recent examples as well. To manage the images that would appear on television during the Seoul Olympics, organizers constructed walls and barriers to obstruct the cameras' view of slums and poor-quality houses along the torch and marathon routes.[30]

Indicative of the pressures on image are the debates that occur around Olympic cultural festivals. Each Olympics is required by the International Olympic Committee to sponsor a full program of cultural events to parallel the games. One might have expected the cultural program to develop as a way of offsetting the increasingly global nature of the Olympics, acting as a haven in which the local could be showcased. But pressures have moved things in the opposite direction.

Eager to present themselves on the world stage, the organizers of the Sydney Cultural Olympiad found themselves moving away from the opportunity for local expression to plans that, in Deborah Stevenson's view, reinforced existing divisions between high and low cultural expression and provided few opportunities for direct grassroots participation in order to make a statement about Sydney's status as a world-class city and assert Australia's position as a center of cultural and artistic excellence.[31] Tellingly, Olympic organizing committees have tried to deal with this dilemma by creating a strict organizational and perceptual separation between the cultural elements of the opening and closing ceremonies in which local cultural elements are featured, on the one hand, and the Olympics arts festival, on the other.

Thus, the influence of the media is detectable, but a countervailing force that is unwilling to submit entirely to that media influence has developed and even flourished. Ironically, it is the representation of local culture offered up through the opening and closing ceremonies that are broadcast to the world, not the offerings of the Olympics arts festival. To notice that the opening and closing ceremonies of the Olympic Games are presented in such a way and at such a scale that they are broadcast around the world is not the same thing as concluding that the media have created that image.

Clearly there are issues of image at play in each of these examples, but the last example suggests that local, indigenous ephemera indicative of a place have sufficient salience and power that they will see the light of day and may play an important role in the shaping, if not the determination, of that image. If this is so, then one must ask to what extent the image of the city is shaped by hegemonic, externally created ephemera and to what extent it is actually shaped by other, more local, temporary, cyclical manifestations of that place. It may be just possible that ephemera help build that image in a manner that is surprisingly unaffected by the media.

SIGNATURE EPHEMERA

Ephemera do contribute to image—the many examples I have cited so far have made that quite clear—but I want to posit that it is less the ephemera staged for the media ("media events") that accomplish this than those ephemera that remain outside the media's design if not outside its attention. If this is true, an important conclusion follows: The first task of image building is self-image.

For the sake of argument, let us consider the existence of a form of ephemera that I will call "signature ephemera," temporary urban phenomena that are indicative of and native to a particular place. Events and other ephemera that have no evocative place link are not to be considered in this category.[32] Calvin Trillin understands what I have in mind, I think, when he points out that Mardi Gras and New Orleans have become "virtually congruent," adding that there are not many American festivals that could be described as congruent with the city in which they take place.[33] Yet, even though Mardi Gras may define one extreme of signature ephemera, it hardly epitomizes the class.

To clarify the concept of signature ephemera, select a city with which you are familiar and then list, as quickly as possible without undue nit-picking, the essential signature ephemera of that place. By way of example, let me propose two lists for Boston. First, in no particular order, the big six: the Boston Marathon; the swan boats in the Public Garden; the Head of the Charles Regatta (even though it is arguably more a Cambridge phenomenon); First Night Boston; the Walk for Hunger; and the Fourth of July celebration on the Esplanade. Then, because reasonable people are sure to quibble, let me add thirteen more: the Evacuation Day (i.e., St. Patrick's Day) Parade in South Boston (perhaps less of a signature event than it once was); the various saints festivals in the Italian North End; the Beanpot (the four-college ice hockey tournament); the summer season of the Boston Pops (arguably more visible as ephemera than the seasons of other local performing arts organizations); the summer concert season at the Harborlights Pavilion (architecturally as well as programmatically); the fall visit of the Ringling Brothers and Barnum & Bailey Circus (now supplemented, if not supplanted, by the spring visit of the Big Apple Circus—even though the latter qualifies as a New York signature ephemera as well); the ebb and flow of rental trucks in the Back Bay the first weekend in September (to demonstrate that the ecology of the actions of individuals can produce signature ephemera); the *Make Way for Ducklings* parade commemorating Robert McCloskey's beloved children's book; events honoring various moments in the Revolutionary War—the Boston Tea Party, Paul Revere's Ride, the Boston Massacre, and Bunker Hill Day; the spring round of college graduations; the Franklin Park Kite Festival; the Chinese New Year and the Festival of the August Moon; and Haymarket, Boston's outdoor fruit and vegetable market, on Fridays and Saturdays.

I do not claim this as a definitive list; I only claim it as *my* list. What is key here, though, is that I am quite sure that I have evoked an image of Boston for you, an image of what Boston "is" and how it is different from other places. The extent to which I have created that image by suggestion rather than by teasing out your "real" image, at least as that image touches upon ephemera, is unclear. Nevertheless, this exercise demonstrates that ephemera *do* play an important role in image.

But I want to claim something more. Notice that these images, built as they are on signature ephemera, are for the most part not generated for, or particularly shaped by, the media. To be sure, many of these signature ephemera are reported in the media, perhaps even covered live, but they do not have the qualities of true media events.[34] They are shaped by citizens and passed along by local practices, customs, and word of mouth. Many of the most stunning signature ephemera have precious little to do with tourism or chambers of commerce. In fact, the deadening hand of these influences is more likely to lead to similarity rather than differences, to copying rather than to local creativity, and, consequently, away from a distinctive image.

I do not intend to argue here that all local ephemera, even signature ephemera, are always immune from the influences of commercial or political interests. It is all too easy to find examples of such influence (though it is nonetheless worth asking how pervasive they are). Writing on carnivals, Alexander Orloff criticizes "the mundane carnivals that have completely lost touch with their roots and have become lavish show business productions for the entertainment of paying tourists. Not only have all the cult rituals been purged, but the spontaneous participation of the public has also been structured out of these staged celebrations in which the participants are hired to play in front of passive spectators." But he is also quick to point out that this is not the only possible result: "[I]n most carnivals the tourist is a tolerated by-product of the celebration."[35] The serious student of ephemera should take notice of that crucial phrase.

Consider *Las Fallas* of Valencia, Spain, arguably the most signature of signature ephemera.[36] During the city's main festival, the festival of St. Joseph, more than 750 sculptures made of wood and papier-mâché, some of them more than twenty meters tall, are constructed in the city's public squares. Designed by artists and paid for by groups of neighbors who band together to produce each year's local *falla*, these sculptures represent a wide variety of social and political commentary. Finally, toward the end of the festival at midnight on March 19, the sculptures are

Fig. 14.2: ***Falla Na Jordana*, large, outdoor paper-mâché and wood sculpture, one of more than 750 such sculptures burned down at midnight to mark the end of the festival of *Las Fallas*, Valencia, Spain.**
Photograph © J. Mark Schuster

burned down in a sequence of bonfires that light up the entire city (fig. 14.2). One notable element of this festival is the fact that over the centuries the aesthetics of the *fallas* have tended to converge toward a particular exaggerated cartoonlike populist style. At least one commentator attributes this convergence to a conscious attempt to address a broader audience of tourists who previously had found the cryptic, local social commentary difficult to appreciate.[37] Indeed, earlier in the century *Las Fallas* were marketed heavily, with *fallas* trains being chartered from all over Spain and even *fallas* boats arriving from America; one result of this increased attention was that the scale of the entire event was ramped up. Yet, although the aesthetics, the institutional structure, and the scale of *Las Fallas* have all evolved over the centuries, one would still have to agree that they are signature ephemera that make a distinctive contribution to the image of Valencia, among both its residents and its visitors.

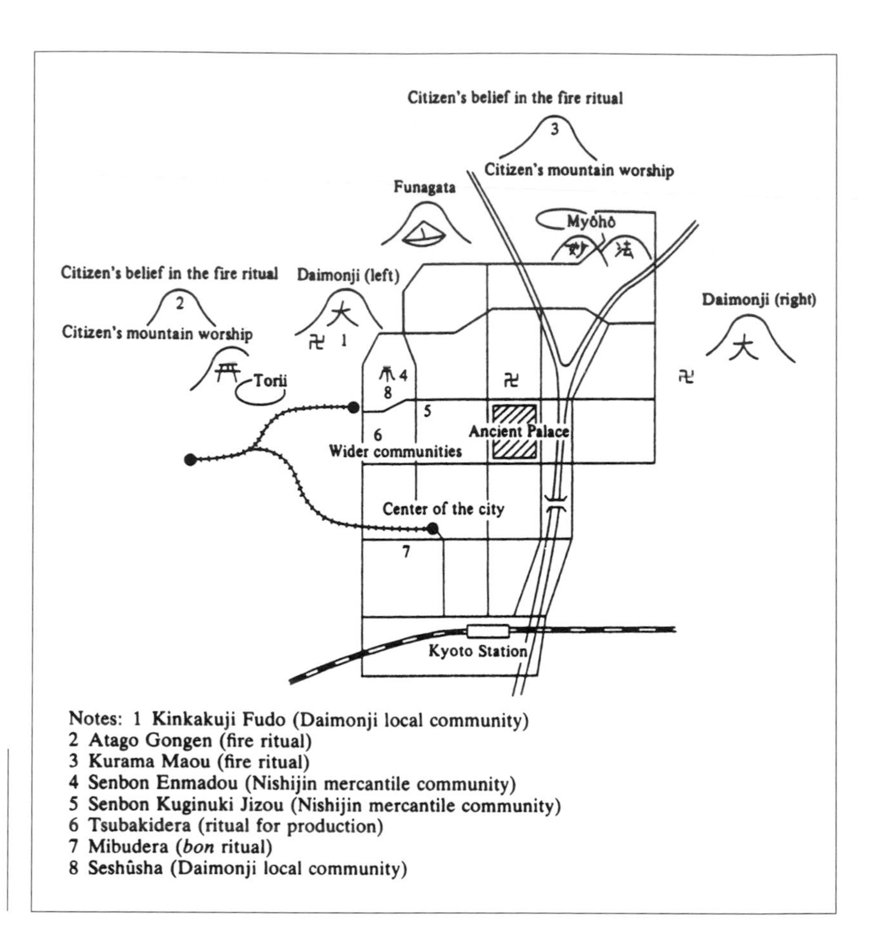

Fig. 14.3: Schematic diagram of the *bon* ritual, Daimonji Festival, Kyoto, Japan.
Courtesy of Edinburgh University Press. Reprinted by permission.

Similarly, the International Alliance of First Night Celebrations, which has overseen and encouraged the growth of some 220 New Year's Eve celebrations of the arts and community, finds itself increasingly concerned about the homogenizing effects that the recent heavier reliance on corporate sponsorship as a source of funding is having on the programming of its member First Nights.[38] The Alliance finds itself asking the question, to what extent is it still possible to create truly unique, locally distinctive ephemera?

The evolution of the Daimonji Festival in Kyoto, Japan, provides yet another fascinating example of locally significant ephemera. For Japanese Buddhists the period from August 13 to August 16 is the occasion of the *bon* ritual, a time during which the ancestral spirits are said to return to earth from heaven to visit and stay with their living relatives. The Daimonji Festival marks the end of the *bon* ritual. Five fires symbolizing respect and farewell are lit on the mountaintops that surround the city of Kyoto, illuminating the path of the ancestral spirits up to the other world (fig. 14.3). Wazaki recounts the external pressures on this festival and the response of the citizenry. He observes that the definite order in which the bonfires on the five mountains are lit is "a late invention," the result of government efforts in the 1960s to make the festival into "a more satisfactory event for tourists." City officials tied their economic assistance to the five Daimonji organizations to compliance with this plan, but, Wazaki observes, "the people of Kyoto did not receive this edict passively. Rather, they reinterpreted the received order of the rituals to create a religious story with the theme of ritual movement from the eastern to the western sides of the city. . . . It is a democratically constructed urban cosmology. . . . Thus the people of Kyoto have successfully reconciled their folk beliefs with the Buddhist doctrine to create a 'Kyoto story.'" Moreover, citizens of Kyoto have begun "to portray their belief in this religious story of progress through the five mountains towards the western paradise as traditional and as deeply rooted in history."[39] In a sense, this example is just as much a tribute to the power of signature ephemera as it is to the power of other forces that might be brought to bear on ephemera.

Recognizing the presence of these pressures and influences, however, is not the same thing as capitulating to David Harvey's analysis and condemnation. Surely such influences must be noticed, considered, and accounted for in any strategy that employs ephemera as an element in building community, but the fact that such influences exist does not mean that the whole ephemeral enterprise must be abandoned. Ephemera, particularly signature ephemera, remain a particularly fruitful focus for detecting the distinctively local contribution to the image of a place.

A stunning recent example of signature ephemera, and one that deservedly has received considerable attention, is WaterFire, an outdoor art installation in downtown Providence, Rhode Island[40] (fig. 14.4). For its tenth anniversary, First Night Providence (Providence's New Year's Eve celebration) commissioned

Fig. 14.4: WaterFire, outdoor fire installation with music, by Barnaby Evans, Providence, Rhode Island. Photograph © J. Mark Schuster

artist Barnaby Evans to create an outdoor installation that would take advantage of the newly opened rivers of downtown Providence. Formerly decked over, they had been uncovered and exquisitely landscaped, but the street life that was expected to return had not. That first year, Evans placed ten braziers in the middle of the river. Fires were lit and kept burning throughout the evening by volunteers in boats. Hauntingly evocative music was played through loudspeakers placed along the rivers. WaterFire was brought back for a second showing during an outdoor art conference, and it became a highly popular event. Since 1997, the fires have been lit every two weeks during the spring, summer, and fall months. Nearly one hundred braziers now line the rivers. It is not unusual for 10,000 people or more to come downtown to experience the smells, the sound, and the ambience of the evening. Providence has adopted WaterFire as its own. There are waiting lists for people who have volunteered to light and replenish the fires. People come, sit, visit, meditate, and linger long after the fires are extinguished and the music is turned off. It is a model of what is possible: an authentic, locally distinctive, shared experience that is all the more striking for its evanescence. WaterFire makes downtown Providence a more interesting place to be, and not only on those evenings when it is ablaze.

In a sense, what I have been asking us to do through my excursion into signature ephemera is to recognize authenticity in the midst of imaging. David Rowe and Deborah Stevenson, in their broad-ranging discussion of the applicability of festival marketplaces to provincial Australian cities, back into this point when they conclude that state authorities prefer "spectacular images of a transformed physical environment. More modest, alternative plans and proposals, such as those based on existing local cultures and facilities, appear tentative and insipid by comparison, although they appear to be much closer to the everyday interests of local populations, much more easily achieved and of greater appeal to tourists seeking 'authenticity.'"[41] Paul Goldberger picks up this theme is his fascinating review of the construction of the Millennium Dome in Greenwich:

> And why should a government even be trying to do what everyone knows Disney can do better? If there is any reason to stage such an event today, it is to do something different; it is related to the notion of the authenticity of public experience. That is the striking paradox of the Millennium Dome. For, while its programming weakly echoes theme parks and world's fairs, the project does contain the promise of bringing people out of their houses for the one experience that the world of technology denies them: that of being in a large public space together with other people.[42]

Indeed, being together in a large public space with other people may be a defining characteristic of signature ephemera—one that should command the planner/urban designer's attention.

Before moving on, have a go at the signature ephemera game yourself. It is both addictive and instructive: Fifth Avenue at

Christmas, the New York Marathon, the Greenwich Village Halloween Parade, Times Square on New Year's Eve, the Big Apple Circus's season in its outdoor tent at Lincoln Center, Shakespeare in the Park, Macy's Thanksgiving Day Parade, ice skating at Rockefeller Center, ticker tape parades, chess matches in Washington Square Park, and any number of neighborhood festivals in Manhattan; inauguration parades and the Cherry Blossom Festival in Washington, D.C.; skating on the Rideau Canal and Winter Carnival in Ottawa; the Blessing of the Fleet in Gloucester, Massachusetts; the Rose Bowl Game and Tournament of Roses Parade in Pasadena; the Hollywood Bowl season and the Oscars in Los Angeles; the Canadian National Exhibition in Toronto; the Iditarod, the Tour de France, and the Giro d'Italia; the Mummers Parade in Philadelphia; Carnival in Venice and many other cities; the Day of the Dead in Mexico; the Sundance Film Festival in Park City, Utah; the "Marching Season" in Belfast; and on and on. Surely, as planners and urban designers we should train ourselves not to miss or dismiss these phenomena; rather, we should learn their lessons.

AN AGENDA FOR PLANNERS AND URBAN DESIGNERS

Sarah Bonnemaison points out that "City planning has traditionally been involved with the permanent urban fabric, with little thought for a cyclical layer."[43] What would it mean to pay attention to a cyclical layer of the urban fabric? What would it mean to adopt a planning and design agenda for temporary urbanism?

One possibility would be to train event-planning specialists. Writing about the forthcoming celebration of the nation's Bicentennial, Lynch noticed, "The conscious design of special events is being practiced again. . . . An event designer would be charged with creating an array of occasions, designing the environment, arranging the details, supporting and suggesting possibilities for the actions themselves. He would be competent in the suitable media. . . . He would be skilled in timing. . . . He would be a temporary environmental manager. . . ."[44] In later writings, he actually called for a new type of urban professional: "Most city events are accepted as if they just happened. Event designers are unsung. Their professional role is precarious, their work ephemeral, and their next job uncertain. If these happenings had a more stable institutional base, and if their composers had more explicit recognition—perhaps if their works, like that of a composer or a dramatist, were repeatedly performed and thus attracted critical judgment—then event design might be a more compelling role."[45] I am sure that he would have agreed to extend this diagnosis to the management and design of ephemera of all types.

At the very least, it is clear that ephemera have spatial implications that planners and designers need to appreciate. Hallmark events are often remembered for their architectural or planning gestures; the Crystal Palace, the Eiffel Tower, the white city of Burnham and Olmsted, the Rome Olympic stadium, the Seattle space needle, the Tokyo Olympics swimming hall, and the Barcelona pavilion, recently reconstructed, are all legacies of such events, as are many others.[46] The subtitle of Paul Goldberger's article on the Millennium Dome—"It's impractical, extravagant, and useless—a great European monument"[47]—was chosen quite seriously with little or no intended irony.

But we do need to be vigilant about window dressing where something more is required. It is not surprising that the Main Street program of the National Trust for Historic Preservation has focused on festivals as an element in their main street revitalization strategies. They have even published a directory of festivals in Main Street towns.[48] The truth, of course, is that in many places such festivals and events occur in front of empty storefronts filled for the occasion with posters, bunting, and children's artwork, a desultory and all too temporary result that calls attention to failure more than success.

In the literature on festivals and parades and their physical manifestations, a distinction is drawn between "parade space" and "carnival space."[49] Parade space fixes the spectator in more or less one location, making the parade into a spectacle, an event to be watched, whereas carnival space breaks down barriers and distinctions, encouraging the mingling of crowd and performer. Sometimes the distinction cannot be drawn so sharply, however. Some parades are processions that encourage participation and demand the attention of planners: "Parades let people reclaim urban spaces not just as a place of work but to renew their relationship with the environment. By animating all senses, parades change people's relation to the city, letting them look at the city in a new way. Parades allow all different groups of people to get together in public in an important way, crossing all political, economic, religious, and ethnic barriers. There are very few events in the city that do that."[50] Parades and processions (and events of all sorts) can be designed to make use of and highlight the city. This has been the genius of many of the First Night celebrations. They endeavor to use the city in new ways, showing it off and arranging it in a series of new and unfamiliar spaces (fig. 14.5).

More broadly, planners and designers must surely be involved in decisions about what Robert McNulty calls the "amenity infrastructure,"[51] capital investments intended to provide recreation, entertainment, and cultural enrichment. He points out that many cities have made no significant new invest-

Fig. 14.5: Projections on the façade of City Hall, part of the city's New Year's Eve festival of the arts, First Night Boston (Boston, Massachusetts). Photograph by Scott Dietrich.

ment in their amenity infrastructure since those amenities were first put in place.

Often, attention to ephemera is a good first step in planning initiatives. Planners in Baltimore "began creating animation—creating happenings, turning the city on to itself, using public programming as a means of bringing people back downtown again. We did it initially for one real reason—school spirit. What we wanted Baltimoreans to do was to begin to feel good about themselves, so that then they would feel good about their city."[52] In a similar vein, consider this description of ephemera planning in pre-Guggenheim Bilbao: "Th[e] participatory approach is complemented by an attempt to inject dynamism into city life, by organising celebrations, festivals and other cultural animation initiatives. There is a clear intention to rediscover for the city the atmosphere of the fiesta and the vibrancy of celebration, and open air performances which help transmit the feeling of urban liveliness. Expenditure on initiatives of this type is becoming more and more significant in Bilbao. Open-air cinema, festivals in parks and carnivals proliferate."[53] Both examples strike jaded Cantabrigian eyes as a bit corny, but they are considerably less expensive than an uncertain capital investment, and may well be necessary as a precursor.

What can planners and designers do to incorporate ephemera into their work? They might endeavor to make ephemera visible. One of the great sights in Los Angeles is the early-morning flower market, where orchids from Hawaii are received in huge quantities during the night. I have seen it featured in only one guidebook, though it is fascinating and absolutely authentic. When I added moving vans in the Back Bay in early September to my list of Boston signature ephemera, it brought to mind a project that placed artists in various New York City departments. Mierle Laderman Ukeles, working in the Department of Sanitation, created a piece of choreography for street-sweeping machines. Imagine Boston welcoming students back with a dance of the moving vans. Occasional looks behind the scenes of the city could be fascinating and instructive—consider the tours of the Paris sewers or industrial plants. Our cities could do much the same.

One could create ephemera. The success of First Night Boston and its spread to some 220 communities in North America, New Zealand, Australia, and England is a case in point. Creation can happen at all scales. One should be sensitive to the ephemera created by citizens and work to nurture and support them.

In an odd sort of way, ephemera can become the reason for actually getting things done in our cities that otherwise would not get done. The visibility and the date-specific nature of many ephemera, particularly hallmark events, give a concrete target to work toward. Speaking of the Millennium Dome once again, Paul Goldberger pointed out that "the one thing a building for the millennium cannot be is late."[54] But it is also because hallmark events have become so large that they present the opportunity to pursue other goals, and this, in turn, can be used to justify the expense.[55] It has been claimed that thirty years of infrastructure investment was made in Barcelona in the six years between its selection by the International Olympic Committee and the opening of the Olympic Games. Lluís Millet i Serra, in a fascinating article on the urbanism of the Barcelona Olympics, asserts that projects associated with the Olympics fared much better than other projects of substantial scale that lacked this association. He makes the telling point that delays in the latter sorts of projects "do not affect overall urban identity," whereas Olympic projects carry special import: "[W]e are not speaking of a stadium more or a stadium less, but the overall activity of the city, the expectation generated by the Olympic project, and the renewed trust in the city's own capacity for administration and transformation. Without the Olympic Project, Barcelona would not have changed in this respect."[56]

Planners need to think, too, about the legacy of ephemera, particularly those ephemera that occur on a regular cycle but in a different place each time. Much of the debate about the impact of Olympic Games or world's fairs is about this legacy.[57] Considerable care must be taken in designing infrastructure and venues that will have a viable life after the event, since the record of these events is invariably mixed in this regard.

However, it is important to expand one's purview beyond the physical and economic legacy of these events. The organizers of the Barcelona Olympics would say that one of the main legacies of the Olympic Games has been the creation of a spirit of volunteerism among the citizens of the city, a spirit that was notably absent before. They would also say—and it is a point that is certainly linked to the first one—that there has been a tremendous improvement in the citizens' image of their own city. Nor is Barcelona the sole positive example. Harry Hiller, in considering the impact of the 1988 Calgary Winter Olympics on the community, concludes that the residents of Calgary transformed the Olympics from an elitist athletic event into an urban festival partly planned and partly spontaneous, providing the pretext for an urban celebration that often made the athletic event less important than what took place in the community.[58] To have accepted the challenge and met it successfully is worth a lot to a city's self-image.

Some events are designed to leave an institutional rather than a physical legacy. Consider the clever model of the National Folk Festival. Established in 1934, this event became America's first multiethnic folk festival. The 1935 festival, held in Chattanooga, featured mountain fiddlers, Cherokee and Kiowa dancers, Mexican balladeers, and local black spiritual choirs. In the 1970s, the National Folk Festival Association became the National Council for the Traditional Arts, and the festival was moved to Wolf Trap Farm, near Washington, D.C., where it was held for eleven years in collaboration with the National Park Service. But then a new model was put in place. Today the National Folk Festival travels around the country, taking up residence in a particular site for three years before moving on. It was located in Lowell, Massachusetts, in 1987, 1988, and 1989. When the festival moved on to a new site, the Lowell Folk Festival was created, a direct legacy of the careful structuring of the National Folk Festival version. Attendance approaches 200,000 each year, and the local organizing committee believes that it has become an important element in the continuing effort to revitalize downtown Lowell.

Fig. 14.6 *(left)*: *Castellers* performing as part of *La Mercé*, the major festival of Barcelona, Spain.
Photograph © J. Mark Schuster

Fig. 14.7 *(right)*: *Nit de Foc* ("Night of Fire"), festival of Sant Joan, midsummer's night, Barcelona, Spain.
Photograph © J. Mark Schuster

In the end, it is the legacy of a change in image that cities are hoping for, whether they pursue megaevents or facilitate more modest ephemera. Bob Scott, chief executive of the Manchester Olympic bid, made this hope manifestly clear while discussing Manchester's Olympic campaign: "As an Olympic city, the old image of Manchester would simply evaporate."[59] While there are many other questions one must address with respect to ephemera, the question of image remains central.

It is not enough to plan ephemera; we must also grapple with how to fund them, at whatever scale. The specter of instrumentality returns at this point. Are we willing to consider public expenditures only if they are clearly in the service of economic development or attracting tourists?[60] Beyond this, do we want to entertain the possibility of mounting only those events that corporate sponsors will support? Or is there a place for "we did it because we wanted to"? Very few of the signature ephemera are, in the end, justified simply because they are instrumental in bringing about other economic and development goals. Such rationales are often voiced, but in the end residents get involved in the most successful ephemera because they want to and they think their lives will be richer as a result. How else can one explain the growth of the traditional elements of citizen participation in, for example, Catalan festivals—the groups of *castellers* building human castles, the creation and display of each city's and each neighborhood's emblematic giants, the involvement of young people in groups of devils to present the *correfoc,* or the creation of floral carpets for the feast of Corpus Christi in Sitges (figs. 14.6, 14.7, 14.8)?

Fig. 14.8: *Catifes Florals* ("Floral Carpets"), feast of Corpus Christi, Sitges, Spain.
Photograph © J. Mark Schuster

It has been suggested that one of the main appeals of hallmark events to planners and city officials is that they offer the opportunity to extract considerable funds from other levels of government. Ley and Olds point out that as part of the preparations for the 1915 Panama-Pacific International Exposition a survey was addressed to San Francisco businessmen, asking if they were in favor of the fair and whether they knew of "any other event likely to occur about that time that would better enable us to secure state and government aid."[61] Many Olympic and world's fair bids are built on the promise of considerable infrastructure investment from a higher level of government.

There are pitfalls, of course. Cities that are reluctant to embrace the messy business of events, festivals, celebrations, or ephemera of whatever stripe might find it attractive to accept the funding that comes attached to offers of prepackaged events created by promoters and sponsors. Davis points out that special events are now an important subindustry of public relations.[62] Corporations "take over a city for a day" to promote their corporate image or their products through one event or another. All costs are covered, all publicity arranged. And if the event is ambitious enough, television networks that are looking for cheap programming are more than happy to jump on board. This phenomenon, which museums have been dealing with for some time in the form of exhibits assembled and curated by corporate sponsors, is becoming more prevalent. The arrival of European-style banners in the streets of our major cities has not been simply because we like the aesthetics of banners flapping in the breeze. Mark Sussman, in discussing the ticker tape parade as a civic ritual, picks up this theme: "[I]t is the mayor's privilege to announce one—and the business community's privilege to step in and fund the festivities."[63] (Of course, someone has to pay for the manufacturing of ersatz ticker tape, which is no longer available free as a by-product of the operations of Wall Street.) Such prepackaged events do, of course, run the risk of being co-opted by corporate values and objectives. They suggest that an image built on ephemera might well be ephemeral, but we should not let the existence of counterexamples distract our attention from other, more organic ephemera, which, if I am right, contribute much more to a place's image.

Alexander Orloff offers the most provocative rejoinder to those who are unwilling to use resources of whatever type to pay for such ephemera: "We are renewed by our extravagance and our disregard for the restraints within ourselves and our society."[64] His reference is to carnival, but would an extension of this idea to other urban ephemera be too out of place?

The other side of this coin, of course, is the prospect of autocratic planning decisions made by a few on behalf of the many. The literature on Olympic bids—even those less scandal-ridden than Salt Lake City's—makes it clear that they are often developed in secret, without input from the citizens whose lives will be most directly impacted, and manipulated by the corporate interests of those who are willing to put up the money.[65] But this is not only true of the Olympic Games. Ephemera, like any other social activity, have the potential for serving certain interests while conveniently ignoring others. Ross Thorne and Margaret Munro-Clark make this point in considering the decisions that led to the construction of the Sydney monorail as part of the Darling Harbour Bicentennial redevelopment. Similarly, Peter Booth and Robin Boyle cite a museum curator who took a rather negative view of Glasgow's selection as European City of Culture: "1990 was a year when an intellectually bankrupt and brutally undemocratic administration projected its mediocre image onto the city and ordered us to adore it."[66] Helen Lenskyj, in comparing the processes followed by Sydney and Toronto in preparing their Olympic bids, argues that even though it lost the bid, Toronto "won" because of its more democratic bid preparation process, which funded community groups to prepare research reports on the predicted social impact of the Olympic Games.[67] The financial politics are exacerbated, of course, when public money is at stake.

It would be a mistake to undertake only those ephemera that were devoid of the possibility of tension and debate. As Deborah Karasov makes clear in chapter 13 of this volume, when artistic inspiration—often deriving from an intent to be provocative and confrontational—is at the heart of what is being proposed and designed, it is not uncommon for that inspiration to come into direct conflict with other forms of decision making. The social criticism on which much of the carnival tradition is based makes it stronger and more salient as a communal activity.

One avenue through which such tensions surface is through countervailing ephemera. The Doo Dah Parade in Pasadena, California, is a humorous case in point.[68] Originating from a community protest against the economic and political forces behind the redevelopment of Old Town Pasadena as well as an artistic vision of a counterstatement to the Tournament of Roses Parade, the Doo Dah Parade sprang up in 1978 when community artists surprised an audience expecting the real parade with a countercultural parody. (The Tournament of Roses Parade occurs on the first of January unless that day falls on a Sunday; 1978 was the exception, and local artists jumped into the breach.)

The St. Paul Winter Carnival has, throughout the years, incorporated countervailing elements into its structure. A Royal Family, representing both the cold of winter and order, is selected to preside over the many activities of Winter Carnival. An ironic counter to the Royal Family is embodied in the Vulcans, who represent warmth and disorder. They appear at public events and lampoon the Royal Family; they have license to commit mischief (coating their faces with soot so that when they pursue women and give them a kiss they will smudge their faces). The inevitable annual victory of the Vulcans over the Royal Family symbolizes the defeat of winter and the coming of spring.[69] When the ordinary is turned on its head, all sorts of unexpected, wonderful, and challenging things can (and do) happen. Of course, this attribute of festive ephemera, particularly events in the carnival tradition, is what makes them even more challenging for public officials.

Under pressure from the Catholic church, historically the target of much of the social and political commentary embodied

Fig. 14.9: Statue of the *Virgen de los Desamparados* ("Our Lady of the Helpless"), decorated with flowers brought in tribute during the *Ofrenda de Flores* ("Offering of Flowers"), festival of *Las Fallas*, Valencia, Spain. Photograph © J. Mark Schuster

in *Las Fallas* of Valencia, Franco (who had been reluctant to crack down on the ephemeral social commentary that lasted only several days in the streets of Valencia) finally ordered the creation of a countervailing element in that festival, the *Ofrenda de Flores* (Offering of Flowers). During a two-day period, nearly 150,000 people parade through the square in front of the Basilica to pay tribute to the *Virgen de los Desamparados* (Our Lady of the Helpless). Women and men in traditional dress carry more than 40,000 bouquets and baskets of flowers into the square. These flowers are then used to form the dress of the fourteen-meter-high figure of the Virgin (fig. 14.9) and to adorn the façade of the Basilica.

As Alexander Orloff puts it, "Carnival and revolution have never mixed well, the one too serious, the other too frivolous to see that their goals are identical."[70] One wonders how David Harvey might react.

The design and management of public space for the purpose of facilitating ephemera is hardly an apolitical act, particularly when decisions are made that privilege one voice over another. Which client is the ephemera planner to represent? Yet this is not a reason to steer away from ephemera; planners and urban designers working for and with public clients ought to be used to such give-and-take. Ephemera are like any other planning and public policy action in this regard. Here, though, the saving grace is that the expression of these voices will be temporary and modulated by the expression of other such voices (if one is a responsible curator and broker of ephemera). The fact that they are fraught with pitfalls and uncertainty is no reason to leave ephemera out of the planner's tool kit nor out of the urban designer's palette.

IN CONCLUSION

While writing this essay, I worried a lot about the penchant of academics to quibble, to criticize, and to belittle. It is one thing to sit back and level a critique (as many of the articles that I have cited do), but it is quite another to go out and try to change the way things are (as many of the movers and shakers behind the ephemera I have discussed have done). Lynch, Bonnemaison, and many of the others I have cited help point the way, but there is a lot more work to do before the value and potential of ephemera are fully understood.

I was fortunate to be able to spend a 1992–93 sabbatical year in post–Olympics Barcelona, where my attention was drawn to the rich menu of official and unofficial urban festivals, celebrations, and traditions as well as to the rich street life. While by most accounts Barcelona has enjoyed an enviable improvement in its international image since the success of the Barcelona Olympics, my Catalan friends have taught me that it is the citizens' image of their own city that is the most crucial, and if that image is positive, the image that others have of that place will surely follow.

Are Olympic bids or proposals for world's fair designation the only moments in which we will allow ourselves to have a vision that is out of the ordinary for our cities and our lives in those cities? I sincerely hope not. The question is not *whether* planners and city designers should become involved in the impractical, the extravagant, the extraordinary, the useless, and the ephemeral—but *how*. We need to pay attention to variation, change, cycles, because they are what make urban life vital; if the role of a planner is to build community in both senses of that concept, we must remember to pay attention to activity as well as setting.

Victor Turner describes festivals as society in its subjunctive mood.[71] Ephemera highlight differences, offer experiments, depart from the "normal." If planners and city designers cannot ask "What if?" then who can? If we do not see, encourage, and perhaps even act to create these elements of our communal urban life, we impoverish our cities and ourselves.

15

RATING PLACE-RATINGS

John de Monchaux

■ EDITORS' OVERVIEW

For the past decade or so, magazine and guidebook publishers have extended the popular American pastime of compiling sports statistics to the ranking of American cities. These tabulations have shaped urban reputations, allowing those with little firsthand knowledge to form images of distant places. John de Monchaux, an urban designer, takes this new phenomenon seriously. His concern is not so much that cities use the rankings for promotional purposes but that the shortcomings of these place-rankings include an important planning deficit: At present, planners lack any reliable way to assess the consequences of their interventions, save the grossest measures such as traffic movement, housing units, acres of open space, and the like.

Aside from any literary descriptions, the rankings are simply reworkings of United States Census and published marketing data. The variables chosen are those that might crop up in general conversation: the weather, the cost of living, crime, education, house prices, and transportation. The audience for these compilations is imagined to be the millions of Americans who are about to move to a new place. Some compendia are arranged so that readers can make profiles of what they value, enabling them to match their preferences to particular cities. Most listings, however, combine measures according to the author's personal recipe. No theory lies behind the weighting of the variables as they come together to form an overall rank.

The data most commonly reported are metropolitan-wide conditions, because the greatest variety of data is available at this scale. Such a practice, of course, ill serves a relocating family wanting to

know how one part of a city differs from another. Moreover, these year-to-year snapshots lack both consequences and dynamics. Did a city with a high score for schools attract more families with children than one with a low score? Atlanta reports a very high crime rate, yet it is growing lustily. Planners, especially, require a dynamic report. Change is their concern.

De Monchaux's central attack focuses on the essential, but frustratingly vague, measures of the quality of life. Improved quality of life has long been a basic planning goal. He reminds us that quality of place and quality of life are not synonymous. Some of the failings of ordinary measures, he points out, could be mended by shifting the research focus from external images to those generated by the experiences of residents. Residents are, after all, the planner's principal clients. In their urban lives, objective criteria and subjective images meet in ways that are central to the planning enterprise. De Monchaux argues that the new research agenda lies in the joining together of image and actuality.

INTRODUCTION: RATING PLACES AND RATING PLANNERS

Recent years have seen the proliferation of reports that rate towns and cities according to qualities and conditions believed to be of interest or value to some particular constituency. This could be people facing a necessary or desired move, whether required or elective, or those simply seeking the information that a "snapshot" image of a place can offer. That such ratings are intended to influence or inform decisions about place, and therefore implicitly address matters of value upon which such decisions are made, is of interest for at least two reasons. First, these ratings tell us about the attributes of the city considered to be of value in operating terms—these may or may not be exactly congruent with the dimensions we address in urban planning—and secondly, they tell us something about the role of the media in constructing or affirming the images we have of places.

All planners share a common imperative—to improve the quality of life, however defined, for those in the areas that they plan. Since many of the rankings and ratings of towns and cities are associated with place and based on attributes often used to measure or indicate quality of life, can we as planners learn anything from these ratings in terms of both the theory and the practice of planning?

Planners perhaps share only with teachers the long-term premises and aspirations of these professions, and feedback on our effectiveness is often anecdotal and sometimes politically distorted. Often we have to be satisfied with surrogate measures that are methodologically questionable. Yet we do need to understand where we have been successful in achieving the intended outcomes of the actions we recommend and to develop our professional competence through this knowledge. It is true that we might understand that traffic circulation has improved, for example, or that open space is more available and more intensively used—but without specific behavioral research at every turn, we cannot easily know how much "happier" these changes have made people. It is no surprise, therefore, that we might look to the ratings literature for some sense of how we are doing, and in the context of this book, ask how much this material might contribute to our imaging of places, particularly those that are otherwise unfamiliar to us.

So what do we find when we look to the ratings with this in mind?

THE RATINGS PHENOMENON

The growth in ratings activity has been so dramatic that one writer remarks that it can be thought of as a "national pastime."[1] Another, writing recently in an airline magazine, suggests that rating places is a peculiarly American pastime "that caters to two cherished American values. The first is faith in the new frontier," and the second is "an unending fascination with statistics."[2] As Lawrence Vale and Julia Dobrow note in chapter 12, it has even become the subject of entrenched parody on television shows such as *The Simpsons*. But though the ratings phenomenon may seem fairly recent, it does in fact reach into the past with a long if rather thin line. Documents existing as far back as the seventeenth century can be seen to fulfill this purpose,[3] and in chapter 1 of this volume, Julian Beinart draws our attention to the role of praise books in the Middle Ages as booster-style and comparative descriptions of pilgrimage destinations. In 1931, a memorable piece of place rating was done by Angoff and Mencken in their *American Mercury* article comparing the then forty-eight states across a wide range of measures.[4]

The more recent proliferation of place-rating guides may be attributed to a number of factors, most of them associated with the need for information and feedback on actions taken or being considered. They include, first, the exercise by state and federal government of controls on spending and their interest in more accountability with respect to aid and grant expenditures, which translates into the greater availability of comparative data: a "supply-side" explanation. A second explanation may lie in the increased mobility of populations: It is reported that more than 7 million Americans move every year and that three times that number express an interest in moving. A third explanation may lie in our competitive leanings. Undoubtedly, the competitive format of place-ratings, conveying as it generally does "worst to best" or "winners and losers," plays a part in sustaining interest. Even if we have nothing to do with the dynamics or are not among the constituency upon which a particular rating is focused, we cannot help but note where our town falls and be pleased if it is rated highly for some positive attribute. For example, the city of Boston recently published a pamphlet reporting Boston's rank in no less than thirty-four different ratings and boasted that most had Boston "topping the charts"![5] And a fourth possible explanation may be related to the current popularity of easily accessible expert judgments—for example, the use of numbers of stars to rate films or restaurants.

Ranking and rating endeavors are undertaken for a variety of purposes. They vary widely in terms of their focus, the seriousness of their approach, and the stringency of their methodology, with relatively few meeting what might be described as exacting academic standards. According to one of the few serious examinations of the ratings phenomenon, they serve to "booster" particular places. "In the U.S.," writes Susan Cutter, "place boosterism is not an idle pastime but part of an important industry that entices tourists, fosters municipal growth and public investment and attracts industrial location decisions."[6]

At the more analytical end of the spectrum, the ratings (or place comparisons based on specific attributes) tend to be more associated with an effort to devise and use social indicators as a part of planning practice.[7] Examples of these efforts can also be found in the annual reports on human development prepared by the United Nations Development Program and the World Bank and in publications that render comparative socioeconomic or attitudinal data in lucid graphic form, such as *The Atlas of American Society* or *Latitudes & Attitudes, An Atlas of American Tastes, Trends, Politics and Passions*.[8] I do not include these social indicator or atlas variety comparisons in this review as they constitute comparisons along a single dimension only and do not attempt to convey aggregate evaluations or overall performance measures for a given place.

The place-rating guides that are the subject of this review are available in many forms and, in general, seek to compare places across aggregate measures of general and popular interest. These encompass diverse sorts of publications, ranging from those that include a wide variety of numerically expressed measures for a single place and often also aggregate all measures to derive an "overall" rating, to those that focus on a numerical comparison of a particular attribute, such as the quality of local fishing, to those that are nonnumerical, and very often literary, comparisons of the affective properties of place.

Thus, for purposes of this review, place-rating publications tend to fall into three broad categories, which I am calling "location and moving guides," "do-it-yourself guides," and simply "good reading."

■ LOCATION AND MOVING GUIDES

Perhaps the most widely recognized location and moving guide is the *Places Rated Almanac* compiled by David Savageau with Richard Boyer originally, and now with Geoffrey Loftus; it focuses on the attributes of North American cities and city-regions. It has been published in successive editions in 1981, 1985, 1988, 1993, and 1998. Since 1981, this publication has reportedly sold more than 750,000 copies—a major publishing accomplishment. It rates and ranks 343 metropolitan areas "on 10 factors," it says, "that greatly influence the quality of place: cost of living, job outlook, housing, transportation, education, health care, crime, the arts, recreation and climate."[9]

These rankings are devised in relation to very specific indicators in order to assist potential movers or answer the questions of people who ask, "Where can I find a good place for *x*?"—*x* being some particular interest, such as proximity to outdoor recreation, or need, such as child care. Often, of course, people must move without the option of studied choice—so to many the rankings are of theoretical value only. It is only for those who are financially able to move wherever they wish that the rankings have any real value. Often these rankings are for those to whom the style "breezy" might apply.

Some of the rankings in this category address particular sets of needs and interests. For example, the magazine *Working Mother* ranks selected cities with respect to child care, and *Fortune* magazine regularly ranks cities with respect to the opportunities for knowledge workers. Supplementing statistical data with local interviews, John Villani has compiled an unranked list of the best small art towns in America, and Norman Crampton has identified, but not ranked, a listing of the 100 best small towns in the forty-eight contiguous states.[10] (It would be of interest to understand more fully why only five towns—Kalispell, Montana; Lebanon, New Hampshire; Silver City, New Mexico; Newport, Oregon; and Brattleboro, Vermont—appear on both lists.)

A recent and potentially disturbing publication is the *Rating Guide to Environmentally Healthy Metro Areas*. It offers comparisons of 317 U.S. metropolitan areas across ten sensibly distinct environmental or functional attributes—such as air quality, drinking water quality, number of manufacturers, population density—but then provides an overall result derived from an unweighted addition of all attributes.[11]

In a rather different vein, Mark Cramer's recent book, *Funky-Towns USA*, purports to be a guide to "the best alternative, eclectic, irreverent and visionary places" in the country. Of special interest is the explicit consideration, with narrative evidence, of three physical attributes in his longer and weighted list of criteria for inclusion as a funky town. These are the existence of "public hangouts," whether a place is "pedestrian friendly," and whether "different activities are not segregated into bland single function neighborhoods."[12]

■ "DO-IT-YOURSELF" GUIDES

Do-it-yourself guides have a more "popular" and interactive flavor. They allow the reader to fill in accompanying forms or questionnaires that, through self-analysis or send-in services, provide an indication of the compatibility of particular places with perceived needs and interests. One such service is available through the Web site of *Money Magazine*, which, on the basis of such a personal profile, identifies a "best fit" against data embodied in its own ratings. With the proper "urban quality indicators," it becomes possible to "inventory your neighborhood or city, compare it to other places, and set your own community goals."[13]

The *Places Rated Almanac* also offers a preference profile that you can use to score and match a particular place to your needs or wishes; it even includes advice on how to make choices and what factors to take into account. Perhaps indicative of the fantasies embodied in some of these exercises, *Harper's* magazine published a guide you could use to identify "utopia by computer."[14]

■ GOOD READING

"Good reading" publications offer a comparative guide to places in essay form and resemble travel literature. One of the most engaging examples of this genre is Terry Pindell's essay collection *A Guide to Good Places to Live,* which describes, in an intimate and thoughtful way, fourteen cities or regions in America.[15]

SHORTCOMINGS

Before we consider these ratings in terms of anything they might contribute to city design and development, or to the imaging of places from a planner's point of view, it is worth asking how well they serve their own declared purposes. Perhaps they may do this satisfactorily, and perhaps it might be asking too much that they extend their relevance to planning. In order to reasonably assess what help ratings might be to planners and designers, it is necessary to understand some of their inherent shortcomings.

First, it is important to understand the fallibility of the ratings themselves before we ask more of them. The literature is full of cautions,[16] and the principal shortcomings may be summarized as follows.

■ QUALITY-OF-LIFE INDICATORS

Although the usual suspects tend to appear on almost all the general lists of indicators—crime, health, education, transportation, and so on—no definitive list of indicators exists that can comprehensively cover a broad concept such as "quality of life," particularly on a comparative scale. Though the indicators used in some reports are based on—or at least tested through—social inquiry, most are simply assumed or declared by the authors to represent factors important to people in assessing their environments and thought to impinge on their perceived quality of life.[17]

■ CONGRUENCE ACROSS RATINGS

Even in cases where different authors are addressing the same or similar issues, there is often little congruence in the ratings outcomes. One study of four examples of city ratings showed little overlap of the lists, even though the major factors addressed were the same. No city appeared on all four lists, and in each case the top-ranking city was different.[18]

■ THE MEASURES USED

The theoretical basis of many of the measures used is often nonexistent or debatable. The ratings tend to use surrogate measures for intangible or hard-to-measure qualities (crime statistics as a measure of security, or life expectancy statistics as a measure of health, for example). A measure is often used because it is available rather than because it adequately measures a particular attribute.

■ THE STATISTICAL BASIS OF THE RATINGS

The rankings have been described as "marvels of data collection, manipulation and synthesis," but it has also been pointed out that they are not based on "any meaningful fieldwork."[19] On the whole, they use statistical data collected for other purposes by other agents—often relying on government census figures—that include limited or no perceptual, behavioral, or experiential data.

Researchers and compilers of these rankings may attempt to deal with many of the methodological problems of measurement by employing a variety of techniques, from simple weighting procedures to complex statistical recalculations, and results may be skewed by those techniques. In at least one case, a city challenged a rating and, using a different statistical calculation, the city moved to an "improved" position on the particular scale.[20]

■ AGGREGATING THE DATA

Because the areas across which rankings are made are determined by the availability of data, which are largely drawn from secondary sources, they aggregate across areas for which the degree of internal variations cannot be accounted for and which may—if known—represent wide and significant variations. The possibility that some footloose mover may use the broad area rankings as a guide to where to relocate does not validate the use of area averages. Savageau and Boyer make a virtue out of a necessity, defending their use of the metropolitan area on the basis that it is the smallest unit for which there is a large amount of data and that local areas are less relevant today when people work in one area, live in another, recreate in another, and so forth.[21] But this defense draws attention to the social implications of such a claim—namely, that the ability to sample the full range of offerings across a metropolitan area belongs only to the more affluent residents of that area. Thus, these ratings encode a potential class bias. Or, seen another way, the metropolitan aggregation of data for rating purposes masks the often severe inequalities within a city-region. To take just one example, the aggregate Los Angeles data will surely mean something very different depending on whether you are relocating to Brentwood or to Watts. In this regard, Moser and Scott understandably regret the absence of data relating to small areas and the consequent need to confine their work to areas for which census data exists.[22]

■ THE BALANCE AND WEIGHTING OF ATTRIBUTES

The indicators themselves are hard to balance collectively in terms of influence, accuracy, and meaning. It is difficult, for example, to evaluate indicators on weather and temperature against indicators of crime or residential density. Quite apart from the conceptual and weighting problems of adding specific rating scores in order to achieve overall ranking scores, there is an additional problem for policymakers. Many of the component ratings—such as those involving weather or climate—are not open to intervention, yet they may have contributed to a judgment about a particular place that in fact appears to call for intervention of some kind.

■ LACK OF LONGITUDINAL COMPARISONS

Most rankings represent a single moment in time. On the whole, there are no systematic rankings that compare areas on the same scales over time, and the few repeat studies that do exist rarely constitute longitudinal studies, since the rating factors are often redefined, as are the boundaries of the areas being rated. While this may prove to be of little concern to someone moving at that moment, in the absence of some time dynamic it is hard even to hypothesize—as planners must do—about the possible effect of intermediate interventions and change decisions. As but one illustration of the intentional variability of data between one year and the next, *Money Magazine* recalibrates its ratings each year based on a sample survey of its readers' priorities. Needless to say, this practice builds in a measure of obsolescence to each year's ratings, no doubt helping to contribute to extra sales.

THE MEANING AND INTERPRETATION OF INDICATORS

It is not always clear what a particular indicator in the rating scale is assumed to indicate. For example, a large number of library books purchased per thousand population may be used to indicate a quality-of-life issue related to municipal services. But it may also, and not necessarily compatibly, indicate a civic priority on education or the success of a particularly vocal and aggressive library administration—and even then it is meaningless without comparative data from within the same town and in relation to other towns. Furthermore, high rankings on so-called quality-of-life indicators do not, as might otherwise be implied, necessarily indicate the absence of negative or urban stress factors. Levine examined places highly rated by Savageau and Boyer in 1985 and found little relationship between the indicators, even identifying some places where positive quality-of-life ratings accompanied high levels of stress indices.[23]

This array of eight types of shortcomings certainly suggests a sobering view of the place-rating hype. Beyond these, however, there are three additional deficiencies that particularly affect the value these ratings can have for planners: their virtually uniform absence of reliance on user perception, their limited engagement with the physical aspects of place, and their inability to advance causal explanations.

PERCEPTION AND ATTITUDES

Decisions about place are often affected by factors that cannot be fully captured by statistical indicators, or perhaps even by social inquiry. Pindell, for example, noted that those who search for a good place to live care not only about low crime, low taxes, and low traffic, but frequently refer to issues of community, political pluralism, and social life—matters that seem recognizable enough but are often too elusive and slippery to define.[24]

Popular or user perceptions and opinions of quality of life in towns and cities are rarely sought for the ratings and may or may not be congruent with the ratings themselves.[25] Some suggestion of such a gap between the perception and the rating is found in the indignation in residents' reactions when their city receives low ratings—though this may be complicated by a tendency to defend one's own territory, particularly when it is under implicit attack and when one has no choice but to stay there. And while the statistical data on which the ratings are based may well be implicitly accorded a greater level of objectivity, perceptions and opinions are fundamentally important to the identity of often intangible attributes of place. The overall image of a place may well be comprised of factors not picked up in the statistics. However effectively the planner solves systematic and design problems in a particular place, it is the perception and experience of their having done so that ultimately tests or confirms their creativity.

Ratings often carry political consequences, and this complicates the interaction between statistical rating and subjective perceptions. The degree to which a particular ranking is reinforced or challenged may depend on what spin particular groups wish to give it.[26] Thus, a low ranking on a particular indicator may imply candidature for federal or state help—whether for a new airport or an improved central area—but at the same time may be politically unwelcome in the immediate terms of attracting business. Potential damage to city image must always be balanced against potential new opportunity for city funding.

Anecdotal evidence suggests that ratings can be taken very seriously, particularly when they are poor. For example, Cutter reports that the city of Tulsa and the Tulsa Metropolitan Chamber of Commerce once filed a $26 million lawsuit against a researcher who admitted errors in ranking the city's quality of life.[27] (The suit was eventually dropped.)

■ PHYSICAL ATTRIBUTES

Other than in what I have termed the "good reading" forms of place comparison, the physical features of towns and cities are not included in the ratings—and even in the "good reading" literature, material tends to be anecdotal and judgmental rather than systematic. The physical attributes of towns and cities are admittedly hard to measure and compare, but without some understanding of the way in which quality-of-life issues relate to physical infrastructure and setting, the serious value that can be attached to the rating and ranking of those towns and cities remains limited. In their early British study, Moser and Scott, for example, had hoped to include physical features in their account of British towns but found it infeasible in the absence of suitable indicators—let alone the existence of data for such attributes as pollution or sprawl.[28] Others point to a need to understand the relationship between quality of life and quality of place—which they add are not necessarily the same thing, nor are they necessarily related to one another.[29] That the physical attributes of towns and cities clearly play a part in our judgments and images of them—think of Paris, Venice, or Singapore—only adds to the frustration of not being able to systematize this process in some useful way—particularly in relation to the more modest towns and cities in which the majority of people make their lives. And the people who make their lives there may well perceive those towns' physical attributes differently from the stranger or the visitor.

■ CAUSALITY

This last ratings shortcoming is perhaps the most critical, particularly—if not exclusively—to planners. It is that the rankings embody no causal theories or propositions. They offer no explanatory or causal relationships between indicators themselves or between indicators and particular urban conditions or policies (although, misleadingly, they sometimes imply such a relationship). Some more analytical studies[30] do attempt to identify variables that relate to one another in some way (such as poverty, infant mortality, and social class), but most rating systems do not, and indeed do not intend to, present data in ways that would allow consumers or researchers at least to make inferences about correlation, if not causality.

In fact, many of the rankings are likely to have complex explanations that, if used as the basis for action, will almost inevitably call for equally complex policy responses. But even rankings that are intended simply to serve as guides for personal moving decisions warrant some further explanation or elaboration. A potential mover to Washington, D.C., for example, might be more than a little interested in understanding how and to what possible personal effect its high ranking for clean air, good water, low property taxes, and good health care should be considered in light of its high crime rating. To the extent that the planner's task is to devise solutions for problems in which interventions can be designed that at the very least increase the probability of certain kinds of changes or improvements, ratings with no causality factor embodied in them can be of little value.

APPLICATION TO PLANNING

Given this rather formidable list of doubts, what, if anything, can we, might we, or should we do with these ratings?

One slightly flippant way is to view them—particularly the more popular and commercial rankings—as a version of *Cliffs-Notes*™ that give some notion of what to expect, provide some buzzwords that sum up the city in a recognizable way, and offer a general broad picture of what a particular town or city might seem like if you were to visit it. But we can be forgiven for expecting more from these ratings.

To the extent that lower ratings imply apparent deficiencies or shortfalls, ratings may influence locational and development decisions, especially those of a speculative nature by change agents such as developers, industrialists, or business interests. Where they do influence action by these agents, obviously they can be important—if not altogether willingly complicit—adjuncts to development policy. Unfortunately, and significantly, we have little data about how rankings influence decisions of this kind, though there is evidence to suggest that planning officials, at least, do not in fact use the rankings in any significant way in their decision making.[31]

In trying to glean some operational value to planners from the ratings, there are a number of important points to take into account. The first is that where rankings deal with issues that clearly do have serious quality-of-life implications, they may well carry policy imperatives. However, these policy imperatives need to be carefully framed in terms of the way the data are presented. Thus, given a ranking that endorses fifteen cities where child-care provision seems especially good, the policy imperative to improve facilities in lower-rated places becomes far more compelling than the implied directive for mothers to move. And the identification of cities with high urban stress indices (such as alcoholism, suicide, or divorce) carries imperatives for social and support policies and the expenditure of resources; such data should not just be seen as a directive to move to cities that are rated more positively.

Related to this first point is a second one, perhaps obvious but certainly important: These cities, even if the rankings say they have certain favorable qualities, cannot dispense those qualities at will to prospective newcomers, though that implication undergirds many of the more commercial rankings that purport to offer matching services. Thus, a city known for its slower pace of life will not guarantee such a slower pace of life to people who move there—particularly if they are predisposed to a faster pace. Nor can a particular individual count on the availability of good child-care services, however high in the rankings a city may be on that scale. Such rankings suggest probabilities only, which are, in turn, nonrandomly skewed across a metropolitan area.

Third, positive ratings on the same quality-of-life indicators across a number of cities do not in any way suggest that the same events or influences in each of those cities operated cumulatively to produce that similar result. Indeed, as mentioned above, there is little if any explanatory power in the ratings themselves.

Fourth, cited earlier, is the lack of relationship between the evidence of a city's high rating on a variety of quality-of-life indicators and that city's performance in terms of urban stress factors.[32] This lack of a necessary relationship between the quality-of-life indicators and the absence of urban stress factors reflects more the complexity of urban life and urban dynamics than any direct relationship between the good life and mental health. Fast cities may well attract fast-paced people rather than make them more so; people in distress and needing support may be drawn to places where remedial services are inexpensive, of high quality, and available.

Finally, there is the point—one of particular significance to urban planners and designers—that quality of life does not necessarily equate with quality of place.[33] The literature points to the need to understand where the two ideas intersect, particularly in terms of whether public policy can bring about change and improvement. It is true that certain quality-of-life indicators, such as open space and good housing, may sometimes act as surrogate measures for quality of place because they are more likely to be present where there is quality of place; however, they do not do so reliably enough to act as policy imperatives by themselves.

If we look to the ratings as some kind of an aid to planning and find them wanting in the ways I have described, how can we find what it is that we want the ratings to tell us? If planners want the kind of help that rankings promise but do not deliver, then what are they to do? Various writers make suggestions. Swanson and Vogel, for example, propose that, rather than depend on rankings that tend to be undertaken by outsiders with little concern or interest in actually helping communities, those towns and cities should develop their own accounting systems that relate to their own interests and needs.[34] Individual towns and cities can also best deal with the need to collect material on a finer-grained basis and can deliberately seek information on policy-relevant factors that are otherwise hard to obtain and measure. Rapid advancements in geographic information systems (GIS) technology can facilitate this sort of inquiry.

Susan Cutter argues that efforts to improve quality-of-life studies should ensure that indicators do, in fact, measure the attribute or condition they rate; that social, perceptual, and environmental factors, and both subjective and objective appraisals, be included; and that the scale be specified. In other words, she asks that most of the limitations I have described be corrected. But it is hard to imagine the ratings authors dealing seriously with these issues or committing resources to the investigations that they call for. Tellingly, in light of the content of most ratings, Cutter also cautions against statistical overkill and adds that there will always be people who disagree with the rankings. Even horrid places have their admirers. She concludes with the following qualification: "No matter how empirically defined the quality of life of places becomes, there will always be a very personal element that will defy measurement. Just as beauty is in the eye of the beholder so may be the place's quality of life."[35] It is a powerful thought, but a skeptic could say that it is also romantic—coming just as efforts are being made to disassemble notions of beauty into Darwinian meanings, "quality of life" might also become susceptible to measurement. In the end, the only real options open to planners are to try to influence existing place-raters to improve their rating systems—a difficult task given the interests involved—or to support their own studies intended to improve the value of the ratings. The whole field is rich in research topics—both theoretical and practical—and we should encourage greater inquiry wherever and whenever we can.

IMAGING PLACES

Let me turn now to the ways that these rankings and ratings might affect the imaging of place. Swanson and Vogel suggest that one effect of rankings is that they, directly and indirectly, shape "the images held by persons and businesses of particular cities and desirability of locating in them."[36]

As human beings, one of the ways we deal with the unknowns of the world is to imagine what things might be like and how we might experience them. We inform what we imagine with as much information as we have, and we supplement that with anecdotes, stories, pictures, and the experience of others to put together what such an unknown might be like if we were to experience it for ourselves. We do this with everything from bungee-jumping to walking on the moon. When it comes to imagining places, we do much the same thing, however unconsciously. We put together all the bits and pieces we have access to and "image" the place to reflect them. Some of the bits and pieces are more reliable than others, but we do not always depend on the most reliable sources. The experience of a friend who was mugged in one place, for example, may well lead us to regard it as dangerous, even though it may have "ranked" in someone's analysis as relatively free of crime.

In all this, the media are particularly powerful. Articles in the popular press describing "hot cities" appear from time to time and may have a telling effect on our perceptions of a city, even contributing to that city's mythology about itself.[37] Cutter describes this in the following terms: "Everyone has images about real and imaginary places. These images influence, to some degree, our subjective assessments of place and ultimately quality of life. There are a number of factors which influence our individual images of place. These include individual factors such as personality, learning, knowledge and experience. These internal factors are influenced by a number of exogenous factors such as culture, mass communication and the use of symbols to represent places."[38]

It is daunting to imagine how each of these factors might be identified, measured, related to one another, and aggregated to represent anything approximating a "general image," and yet we continue to speak in those terms and unwittingly fall into simplifications, stereotypes, and what Cutter describes as "geographic chauvinism."[39]

The reflex to image is powerful. Mention Venice or Paris or Berlin, and images appear in the mind. They may be memories or they may simply be pictures—and reproductions at that—of printed images we have picked up through the media. And they may not convey everything we know or that can be known about the city—crime, housing problems, ease of securing a job, and so forth. But it is difficult to mention the place names without the mental pictures appearing.

The farther away we go from towns we know anything about, the more we have to depend on information, reports, and anecdotes to imagine them, and the less consistent our images are likely to be. We have a lot of material if we want to use it. Travel books, chamber of commerce reports, media stories, news reports, and—in the case of American towns and cities, at least—all of the material I have been referring to so far. But across a given population, the composite images held by different individuals may vary widely. This is because the images that emerge also reflect idiosyncratic material such as the experience of our friends, or the opinions of people we trust, as well as our interpretations of news and media reports that may themselves be slanted from a particular perspective, and because the image is projected through our own frameworks of values and needs. If we want anything like a general image of a particular place, we will have to be satisfied with those that represent what "people on the whole" seem to hold as an image, that is, the image lying at the middle of the bell curve. Even then, questions remain. Do all people's opinions matter equally? How were they asked to describe the image of the place? What, if any, useful meaning can be attached to such a general image?

If we want to analyze the particular image of a town or city, it is possible to deconstruct it according to a variety of factors that contribute to that image. And many of these factors—often at a more subjective, experiential level—reflect the many factors used in the rankings I discussed earlier. However, if we begin with those factors and try—in some sort of blind test—to reconstruct the particular town or city to which they applied, we almost certainly will not end up with the particular town in question. It is more likely that we will define a "class" of places for which the particular place might qualify. Thus, if we had all the rankings and some nonidentifying anecdotal material about Boston, while some clever Sherlock Holmes might detect Boston in the pattern, the material itself would not construct itself into Boston. A little like painting by numbers—starting with the numbered spaces, you can end up with something that looks like Van Gogh's sunflowers, but it is not an artist's image. Theoretically, you can break down the elements that are deemed to make a great work of art a great work of art, but reassembling those in the abstract will not re-create that great work of art.

Virtually all of the factors used by raters and rankers to analyze towns and cities are individually "imageable," at least in a behavioral sense—good health services, good schools, high crime, and so on—but the images cannot be easily "fused" and become the single image of place. Yet we do often seek this "fused" image, if only as a shorthand way of conveying opportunity or apprehension. Thus, New York is described as "hectic," Boston as "historic," and Los Angeles as "sprawling." Curiously, these one-word characterizations of ambience or pace may be derived more from the physical image—conveyed perhaps on postcards or television or from the accounts of friends—than from any aggregation or fusing of the rankings offered in place-rating guides. This question provides an interesting link to Judith Martin and Sam Bass Warner's investigation of the ways that metropolitan areas are "imaged" by reference to specific submetropolitan places or streets (see chapter 6).

The lists of factors chosen by rankers and raters give planners and designers an implicit, general sense of how cities and towns are expected to perform and which conditions in them are likely to be valued (good housing opportunities, health services, transportation, and the like). But on the whole, such information is already part of the value and knowledge bases of these professions; it is not news.

Clearly, the rankings enter the media and political discourse because they make for good headlines. They prompt challenges and reactions for a variety of reasons. Thumbnail descriptions suffice to encapsulate the vast complexity of single towns and cities, classifying places in simplistic terms. *Newsweek* describes the American search for "cities that are manageable enough to avoid urban blight, yet large enough to be economically and culturally alive."[40] It would take another essay to examine, let alone begin to understand, the reality of such a place.

If we take the rated factors as the basis for planning and policy imperatives—insisting that whatever is being planned should seek the highest ranking possible on all relevant measures—we are really only putting a different set of words around the search for a best possible planning solution, which is the imperative of the profession in any event.

Towns and cities are dynamic; they change in spite of rankings and ratings. One way in which they might change *because* of rankings and ratings deserves further exploration. We should consider the extent to which publicity about positive rankings can alter the very conditions that merited this distinction. Has any town identified as an outstanding place for its isolation and gentle pace of life, for example, been inundated with footloose newcomers who have changed the very attribute that attracted them?[41] Have cities and towns with highly ranked school systems been overwhelmed by newcomers whose children have so added to the numbers that school standards have been compromised? We should try to get answers.

CONCLUSIONS

Planning on the whole has a long-term focus, and rankings and ratings are too immediate to be significant without a clear and persuasive account of cause and effect, which is critical to the determination of possible planning interventions. These measures are of limited assistance to planners in policy terms, particularly over the long haul, but they may well have effects and influences on the very dynamics and conditions to which planners apply their skills. Rankings and ratings are part of the often vast and detailed information that planners assess when analyzing problems and when designing and defending what they propose. Planners deal in policy variables and need to make professional judgments about the likely future effects of alternative interventions. These cannot be reliably informed by ranking and rating material that deals only with existing conditions, at a very coarse grain, for a given moment in time. And, given the focus of many of the ratings, I should add that city designers do not simply deal with matters that will attract movers; they must also deal with the circumstances and conditions of those who do not move—and who may well have quite a different perspective.

Ultimately, planners and designers need to learn about the effectiveness and success of planning actions. They need to know whether their intentions have been realized and how their work has altered the "quality of life" in places they care about. This means planners should not depend on flawed data but must develop far more sophisticated, systematic, and reliable measures. The field is rich with possibilities and is a research challenge to us all.

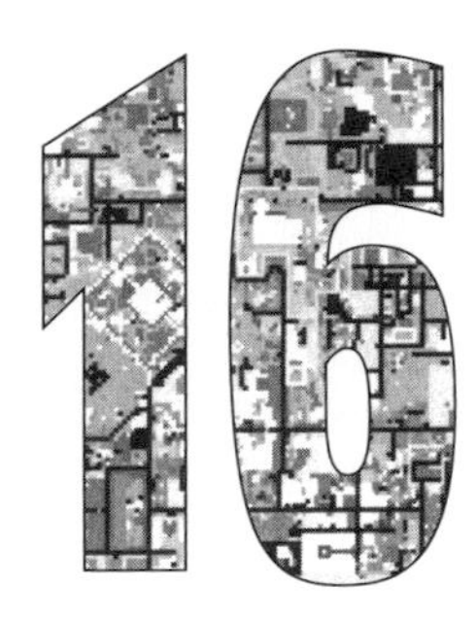

New Public Realms: Re-imaging the City-Region

Lawrence J. Vale

■ EDITORS' OVERVIEW

Whereas most of the essays in this volume focus on the imaging or re-imaging of a particular place, this last chapter suggests that one of the most powerful ways to change the image of a place is to invent a new cross-jurisdictional way to perceive it. Urbanist Lawrence Vale argues that those who lament the decline of public space in cities are looking much too narrowly, focusing chiefly on private corporate plazas or festival marketplaces. Beyond these, he argues, there are several emergent types of new public realms that are worth watching and nurturing.

Vale categorizes these nascent place-types as *corridors, traces, watches*, and *ways*. Corridors (such as rails-to-trails conversions) take advantage of image-making opportunities made possible by transportation routes across and between city-regions, while traces allow disparate places to be conceptually linked according to the thematic interests of each citizen. Watches encourage citizens to take shared interest in the fate of large urban and regional ecosystems, and ways are constructed pathways that lead pedestrians through landscapes, help to clarify their history, and work to create new economic value. Each of these new kinds of public realm gains imageability and recognition from powerful use of media, and each offers a method to break down destructive barriers between cities and suburbs. By working with a disparate coalition of individuals,

institutions, and interest groups, planners and city designers can design new public places, support new activities, and promote new images for city-regions.

INTRODUCTION: THE DEATH AND LIFE OF URBAN PUBLIC SPACE

Contemporary critics lament the decline of the public realm, caused by radical shifts in the way we perceive space, time, information, and community identity. Frequently, what passes for public life in cities takes place in privately owned and privately managed places, under the wary eye of surveillance cameras and private security forces. In some cities, entire protected enclaves (such as Baltimore's Harborplace) have been designed to serve tourists and conventioneers—who are perceived to be otherwise too wary to chance an urban visit. Other American cities (such as Boston, San Francisco, or Seattle) have for the most part managed to evade the trend toward spatially distinct "tourist bubbles" and have absorbed visitors more seamlessly, allowing them to partake in a broader citywide ambience in a manner more characteristic of cities in Europe.[1] Both kinds of cities—those praised for their ambience and those touted for their specialized attractions—are rendered as composite images by the media. They are relentlessly marketed for outsiders even as they are packaged for consumption by long-term residents and ambivalent suburbanites.

Yet the promise of media-driven urbanism can be seen as more than a compendium of depersonalized threats and manipulated experiences. At the heart of Kevin Lynch's line of inquiry is a commitment to the centrality of the public voice, a belief in the duty of city planners of all stripes and titles to be responsive as well as directive. The expanding reach of media can serve such ends, and this chapter explores some of the ways that designers and planners are working to re-image public life at the scale of the city-region.

During the last three-quarters of the twentieth century, urban design was hampered by the mental construct of zoning—which views cities and suburbs as mosaics of single-purpose districts. With new construction sorted into residential, industrial, and commercial zones, whereby not only the type but the intensity of land use could be regulated, the rapid and automobile-focused growth of American metropolitan regions suffered from enhanced fragmentation. In a world built to conform to the tenets of "one function" zoning, designers and developers tried vainly to insert new public space into districts that were single use, bounded, centered, product oriented, efficiency driven, and almost always resistant to change. Urban designers tended to accept this districting as axiomatic and to use such districts as a unit of analysis. These districts formed convenient boundaries for implementing discrete design interventions and policies, often meant to enhance the particular character of each place. The result has been a series of disconnected set pieces of single-image locales, whether comprising suburban subdivisions or downtown malls. Zoning theory presumed that the "cleaner" the definition and organization of districts, the better the resultant quality of life. Districts in zoning were not only descriptive, capturing the essence of what existed, but predictive, aiming to achieve conformance in future development toward an ideal end. Thus, one object of urban design practice became the pursuit of the ideal district—jurisdictions where environment and behavior were organized by a single overriding purpose: housing developments to raise children, industrial parks to produce goods, retail malls to support consumption.

However, the greater our success in building ideal districts of this kind in practice, the more critical we have become about the sterile environments and public life that they promote. In the effort to build powerful place images that could be clearly differentiated from their surroundings, we ended up with a landscape dominated by functional types. Even as efforts arose in recent decades to design projects that would be deliberately mixed use, such as office/retail complexes, the results often reverted to new kinds of predictable types, epitomized by auto-dependent edge cities.

The situation is made worse by the metropolitan scale of many contemporary lives and lifestyles. As more and more of us have come to operate at the regional scale, as commuters and as consumers, the old Lynchian categories have become attenuated and depersonalized. Lynch's classic quintet—districts, landmarks, paths, nodes, and edges—still resonate as concepts, but, rooted in pedestrian-centered images, they are no more than a partial representation of current metropolitan structure, identity, and meaning.

In today's city-regions, especially those in the United States, our "districts" have become both disparate and distant, a scattering of disconnected destinations. Similarly, our "landmarks" are more likely to be the logo-festooned tips of distant private towers or the highway sign that signals a crucial exit ramp, rather than the intimate detail of a distinctive neighborhood doorknob so beloved by Lynch's sensuous pedestrians. The window shopping and casual encounters along our "paths" have long since been scaled upward and outward into billboard carscapes; our "nodes" are urban and exurban malls and office complexes instead of corner stores; and our "edges" have become even edgier.

FROM PATCHWORK DISTRICTS TO CONNECTIVE PUBLIC REALMS

Yet this dark view of the narrow patchwork metropolis must be seen to coexist with a much more encouraging set of alternatives. A new designed public realm seems to be emerging. Citizens groups and elected officials across the country are recognizing the need for a neo-Lynchian approach to urban design, a construct that, instead of premiating efficiency and rigid divisions, is more value-laden and more meaningful to the people who live and work within individual communities and interconnected regions.

Unlike traditional land use and zoning districts, which defined and regulated activities within discrete boundaries, these new public realms are designed as connectives to link places across physical and social boundaries. The old Lynchian elements of districts, landmarks, paths, nodes, and edges are not simply the dated descriptors of an outmoded pedestrian city, but can—and indeed already do—form the basis for a more progressive public realm that connects across former edges and nurtures new kinds of nodes, landmarks, paths, and districts.

This transformed concept of a connective public realm represents a profound shift in thinking about city design and development; it requires a new set of design, planning, and political principles. Instead of simply accommodating its users, the public realm can change, educate, and empower its constituents. By acknowledging and responding to our information-based society, which has become more complex and disaggregated, the public realm can generate or restore a rich sense of place and belonging. The metropolitan complexity of contemporary city-regions can be turned from a seeming liability into a set of new opportunities. Part of this challenge is captured by the title of Charles Little's book, *Greenways for America*,[2] but the emergence of new public realms is more than a matter of connective green space. Rather, what matters most is the artful recombination of open space and built space, brought together by a complex interpretive framework. It becomes possible to envision a new public realm that is multiple use, unbounded, decentralized, organized around information and ideas, more inclusive in its efficiencies, differentially imageable, and expected to change.

CORRIDORS, TRACES, WATCHES, AND WAYS

A group of colleagues at the Massachusetts Institute of Technology[3] has identified four types of emerging urban and regional public realms, each of which gains imageability and recognition from powerful use of the media. We call these four types *corridors*, *traces*, *watches*, and *ways*.

■ CORRIDORS

Corridors are organized around transportation routes, including canals, roads, rivers, and railroads. The routes provide a vehicle for the interpretation of a region's multiple pasts and presents and a locus for organizing diverse resources. The unique linear form of a corridor enables the creation of an interlocking system of natural, cultural, and recreational landscapes, with the potential to enhance area economic development, tourism, and educational opportunities (fig. 16.1).

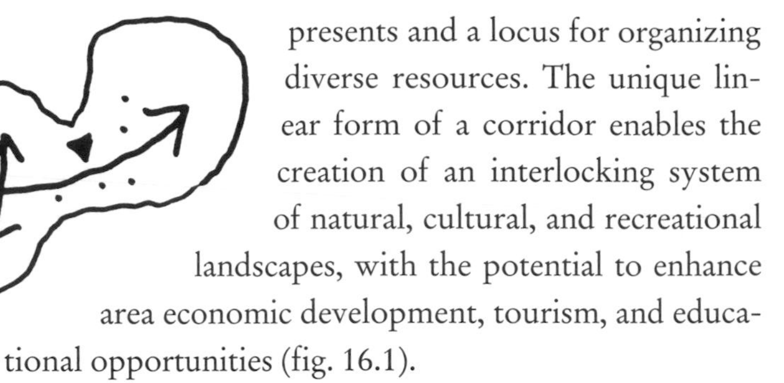

Fig. 16.1: Corridors.

Corridors not only provide the means to move through or across a regional landscape but also permit passersby to pause and partake of a variety of opportunities en route. In many cases, contemporary use of these corridors represents a reinvigoration of a disused and underappreciated resource.

Canal Corridors

This is most obvious in the case of canal corridors. Several of these early-nineteenth-century transportation routes have been designated by Congress as National Heritage Corridors since 1986, intended to promote awareness, preservation, recreation, and development along such once-famous routes. These corridors include the Ohio and Erie Canal (built to connect Lake Erie to the Ohio River, providing the nation's first waterway linkage between the Great Lakes and the Gulf of Mexico); the Illinois and Michigan Canal (similarly built to link Chicago/Lake Michigan to the Illinois River and beyond); and the Chesapeake and Ohio Canal (used to bring coal from western Maryland to Washington, D.C.). Canals, however, are much less ubiquitous than other types of corridors, which were organized around roads, rivers, or rail lines.

Road Corridors

This type of corridor draws on earlier concepts of parkways and greenways, which date back to the work of Frederick Law Olmsted and others in the nineteenth century. In recent years, the notion of road corridors has begun to return to its metropolitan roots. The national network of "scenic byways" has been expanded to encompass more than just corridors located in rural areas of great natural beauty. In 1996 the Selma to Montgomery March Byway—the route of Martin Luther King Jr.'s famous civil rights trek through Alabama—was designated an All-American Road. Another byway, the Minneapolis Grand Rounds—a system of trails, paths, and roadways located in an urban setting—gained status as a National Scenic Byway in 1998. Other road corridors, such as the Lewis and Clark National Historic Trail (which begins near St. Louis and extends all the way to Oregon), the Lincoln Highway (the country's first transcontinental highway, from New York to San Francisco), the National Road (stretching from Maryland to Illinois), and Route 66 (from Chicago to Los Angeles), all have urban components.[4] The National Park Service is involved in many of these projects and has enacted legislation to help guide such efforts nationwide.

Even major interstate highways sometimes have corridor-type constituencies. In western Washington, for instance, the Mountains to Sound Greenway Trust, an organization devoted to preserving and enhancing views along the I-90 corridor, joined with the King County government and private corporations to sponsor the planting of 200,000 trees along the highway during the year 2000.[5]

Another unusual road corridor is Los Caminos del Rio (The Roads of the River), a nonprofit public–private partnership bridging two countries along a 200-mile stretch of the U.S.–Mexico border. This project, which parallels the Rio Grande between Laredo/Nuevo Laredo and Brownsville/Matamoros, connects nearly 250 heritage sites, including eighteenth-century colonial towns, ranches, historic forts, and battlefields. Los Caminos del Rio has attracted well over $10 million in public and private investment and gained a high profile following an award-winning book and an Emmy-nominated PBS documentary. According to Mario L. Sanchez, an architect with the Texas Historical Commission who first conceived the project, local residents were particularly affected by the production of an interpretive map of their region, since they had tired of seeing it portrayed only as a source of drugs, pollution, poverty, and corruption: "Those issues are all there, but through history we are able to present another face of the border."[6] Los Caminos del Rio, though unusual because of its international dimension, is only one of many corridors based on the path of a river.

River Corridors

Rivers are an important organizational force in corridor development throughout the United States and beyond. New York's Hudson River Valley Greenway, for instance, is a ten-county regional framework for cooperation, stretching 130 miles north from New York City along both sides of the river. Established in 1991, it is a voluntary partnership between local governments and the state to encourage economic development while also preserving the natural environment of the area.[7]

The Blackstone River Valley National Heritage Corridor, designated by Congress in 1986, attempts to tell the stories of the American Industrial Revolution by identifying, mapping, and coordinating a series of working landscapes that connect twenty-two towns linking two of New England's largest cities—Worcester, Massachusetts, and Providence, Rhode Island. Instead of viewing these towns and cities as separate destinations in different states, the corridor concept re-images them as part of a single shared industrial heritage, a regional approach that makes clear the intrinsic ties between industrializing America and its rural hinterland. As one local official proudly put it, once a unified system of informational signs showing the corridor's distinctive graphic image had been installed all over the valley, "It felt different, more like we were a bigger place."[8]

Although frequently sanctioned, most of the land in such corridors remains in private ownership, and most visitor attractions are managed and staffed by public and private partners, rather than by the federal government.

Rail Corridors

Some corridors are established along the path of historically significant railway lines, such as the Allegheny Ridge Corridor, which follows the route of the Pennsylvania Railroad in southwestern Pennsylvania. Even more pervasive is the vast and multiplying network of rails-to-trails conversions—the adaptive reuse of abandoned railroad corridors into biking and hiking routes. According to the Rails-to-Trails Conservancy, there are more than 1,000 such trails now open nationwide, totaling over 11,000 linear miles and traversing all fifty states; more than 1,200 more trail projects collectively spanning 18,000 miles are currently in the works. The Rails-to-Trails Conservancy—with its newsletter, Web site, and nationally distributed field staff—sees its mission not simply in transportation terms but as "enrich[ing] America's communities and countryside":

> [Rail-trails] recycle the landscape that was once home to rail cars and reinvent an old connection between neighboring areas. When they are well conceived and crafted, rail-trails can turn around economically depressed towns and transform an eyesore into the pride of the community. They accommodate diverse groups in harmony, while serving environmental functions such as acting as buffer zones for pollution from fields and highways. At their best they can do all these things and simultaneously advance transportation, recreation and appreciation for nature and history.[9]

The rails-to-trails movement is but one example of the kind of innovative institution building that characterizes the development of the new corridor-type public realms.

Throughout the 1980s and 1990s, many cities instituted bicycle-oriented corridors, sometimes part of rail-trail conversions, but often—as in Minneapolis and Indianapolis—located independently.[10] All across the country there are ongoing efforts to construct long cross-jurisdictional trails, primarily for pedestrians. The contemporary heirs to the Appalachian Trail and the Pacific Crest Trail include the Ice Age Trail, which follows the edge of the last glacier for 1,000 miles through thirty-one counties in Wisconsin, and the Iditarod Trail, which marks the Alaskan gold rush route from Anchorage to Nome.[11] At the scale of the city-region, such pedestrian-oriented corridors include the Brooklyn-Queens Greenway (traversing two densely populated

New York boroughs to connect the Coney Island Boardwalk with Long Island Sound through a network of Olmsted parks and Moses parkways) and the ongoing efforts in Massachusetts to establish the Bay Circuit, an interconnected outer necklace of open space around Boston.[12]

Corridors that connect across jurisdictions can help to reconceptualize city-regions, but this is not the only way to re-image such places. Increasingly, the connecting links do not need to take the form of a linear corridor. Rather, the new public realm can appear more as a network of linked places, in which the links are defined not by linear proximity but by the particular shape of individual or group interests. The result is not a corridor but a kind of metropolitan palimpsest, a trace.

■ TRACES

Traces organize multiple places, buildings, and activities around a concept or a constituency, creating a cognitive link among locations that have no actual physical contiguity (fig. 16.2). These are districts of the mind, where an idea is the key connective force, where selective recognition by constituencies, and not universal recognition, is the key to definition. Trace-makers design and manage themes rather than theme parks.

Pieces of a trace may be temporary, such as the festivals or public art installations described in the chapters by Mark Schuster and Deborah Karasov, or they may be permanent; in either event the resonances that remain transform public perceptions of a place. The Chattahoochee Trace of Alabama and Georgia, an interstate compact signed in 1978, supports economic development and historic preservation in an eighteen-county region by organizing tourism according to a series of suggested themes, ranging from peanut research to antebellum architecture. Even more long-standing are traces that connect as sites associated with Civil War battles. Yet even these have experienced recent

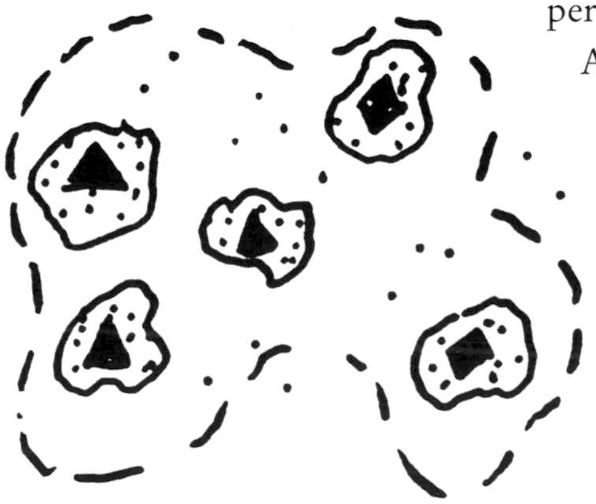

Fig. 16.2: Traces.

transformations intended to give greater structure and imageability to regional themes, epitomized by the designation of the Lee vs. Grant trail in Virginia.[13] Since 1984, when the National Register of Historic Places program introduced a "multiple property documentation form," proposals to designate broad-based themes have become increasingly popular.[14]

In recent years, the trace phenomenon has diversified and intensified. Many traces, especially those supported by congressional initiatives, are oriented toward organizing the interpretation of American industrialization. Instead of visiting a single museum in a single city, these traces organize disparately located "primary source" sites, tracing themes across a variety of cultural landscapes. Southwestern Pennsylvania established an Industrial Heritage Route (known as the Path of Progress) in 1988. America's Agricultural Heritage Partnership (known as Silos and Smokestacks), established in 1996, traces "the story of how American agriculture fused with industry to feed the world" in a seventeen-county rural and urban area of northeast Iowa. AmeriCorps volunteers assigned to Silos and Smokestacks worked with a local public radio station to produce a highly acclaimed driving guide and set of interpretive audiotapes. In the process of celebrating the achievements of local agriculture, these tapes—which have sold out several editions—help both visitors and locals to understand the "taken-for-granted 'ordinary' landscape."[15]

Other heritage traces established in 1996 include the National Coal Heritage Area, developed across the eleven-county Appalachian region of West Virginia, which interprets the regional culture, coal industry, and the organization of trade unions, and the Steel Industry American Heritage Area (known as Rivers of Steel) in a seven-county area of Pennsylvania that includes Pittsburgh. In 1998, not to be left out, an Automobile National Heritage Area was established in Michigan. Run by a nonprofit partnership of political, industry, and university leaders, it aims to highlight the industry's history, encourage tourism, and promote economic development.[16]

In addition to the spate of interest in industrial-era heritage traces, there has been a burgeoning commitment to the facilitation of other interest-based traces, often led by state or local groups. The women's rights movement, for instance, has been conceptualized as a new kind of trace. In addition to the Women's Rights National Park in Seneca Falls and Waterloo, New York, planners in New York have come up with a much broader trace, called "Where Women Made History," that maps and links eighty-three sites in more than three dozen disparately located counties statewide.[17] This "women's history" trace is sponsored by the New York State Department of Economic Development; visits to any of the eighty-three sites rapidly translate into economic gain for the neighborhoods around them. It would be easy to imagine this trace extended to national or international scales, as well.

A National Park Service project, "Our Shared History: Celebrating African American History and Culture," provides visitors with a "travel itinerary" linking "the historic places of the civil rights movement." The journey ranges across forty-one sites listed on the National Register in all corners of the United States—from Mississippi to Massachusetts, from North Carolina to Nevada. The intent of this, the Park Service says, is to demonstrate two key facets of the civil rights movement: It was "designed, led, organized, and manned by African Americans," and it was "not led by one or two men" but by "a dispersed, grassroots campaign that attacked segregation in many different places using many different tactics." Here, through the process of mapping, the civil rights struggle is spatially re-imaged. Urban and rural locations and events are combined to tell a more truly national story.[18]

The international dimension of traces is especially compelling. There are many new ways to organize visits to the United States by foreigners. These visits are designed to showcase more than just a series of standard cities or recreational opportunities; they provide a specialized analysis of conceptually linked sites that carry special significance for the relationship between the United States and the visitor's home country. The "Japan trace," for instance, is a diverse assortment of sites in New England that conveys aspects of Japanese-American relations since the nineteenth century and forms the common itinerary for hundreds if not thousands of visitors annually. Japanese visitors are disproportionately attracted to such destinations as Commodore Perry's home in Newport, Rhode Island. Similarly, Japanese visitors flock to the Alcott House in Concord, Massachusetts, because Japanese schoolchildren all read *Little Women*.[19]

Specialized traces operate within large cities, as well. In Los Angeles, a project by Dolores Hayden and her colleagues called "The Power of Place" attempts to narrate and expand the understanding of the city's economic history by identifying locations that clarify the everyday lives and economic contributions of ordinary individuals from diverse ethnic and racial groups. "The map and historical vignettes we present make these overlapping work histories into a set of memories located in the physical city. . . . The sum of all the sites could be a network of new public places designed for the preservation and interpretation of Los Angeles's unique social history." Despite the distance between sites, Hayden hoped that "the sense of a journey on an historic path, or even the sense of a pilgrimage can be cultivated here, planned and designed. Special paving linking sites and a 'Power of Place' van or trolley could one day unify the itinerary."[20]

Traces compel their followers to find echoes of their particular interests in many unexpected places. A trace, for instance, would narrate the history of rock and roll not through the single-object setting of Cleveland's Hall of Fame, but as played out in the streets and clubs of New York City. One could imagine a similar "blues trace" in Chicago, or a "jazz trace" in New Orleans or Kansas City. Whether intended as a way to facilitate specialized forms of tourism or as a means to encourage local people to view their own region in a personally responsive way, traces use narrowcast media and imaging to build positive connectivity. In every case, constructing a trace requires innovative communication tools and marketing techniques, greatly facilitated by the emergence of the Internet and by the corresponding temptation to sort one's life by keyword searches. For each trace, however, the interest group transcends its cybercommunity to create a new and visitable public landscape that reconceives and recombines scattered pieces.

Some kinds of corridors and traces (though certainly not all) may seem designed for single visits rather than repeated exposure, but there is a third kind of new public realm—watches—that demands sustained vigilance rather than rapid passage between linked places.

■ WATCHES

Watches are districts defined by the *eye*; the boundary is the viewshed around a valued community asset (fig. 16.3). Watches are created by the interested parties, who assume responsibility for ensuring the stewardship of a resource. The maintenance of this protected district depends on the shared vigilance of a diverse—usually "unofficial"—group of citizens linked by a common concern. The district may or may not be formalized by public action and resulting policies. In any case, a watch is a new public realm with a purpose that goes beyond mere recreation. Like most corridors and traces, watches have an educational component. They are concerned not only with protecting shared space, but with demonstrating that protection of common resources is in the public interest.

In the United States, the notion of watches seems to have emerged out of a much earlier citizens' concern over the stewardship of particular single buildings, such as George Washington's Mount Vernon. By the mid–twentieth century, however, the locus of concern was expanding to encompass entire urban districts, from antebellum central Charleston to art deco Miami Beach. Spurred by passage of the National Historic Preservation Act of 1966, planners increasingly have viewed preservation in terms of larger areas, such as historic corridors or thematic traces.[21] More recently, watchers have set their sights not on architecture and dis-

Fig. 16.3: Watches.

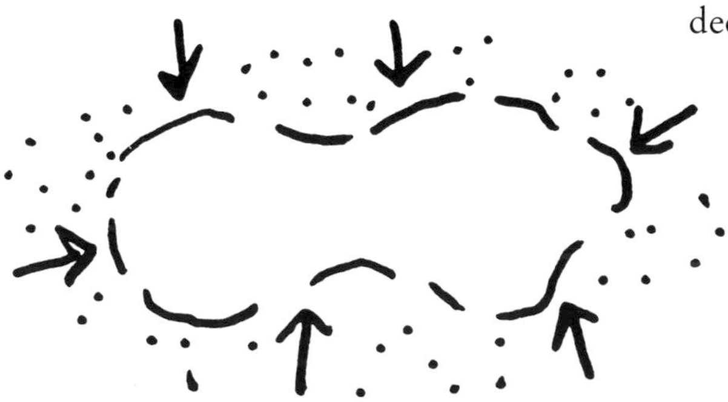

tricts but on broader regional aspects of urban ecology.[22] Some cities have started to post signs in heavily urbanized areas, pointing out to pedestrians and motorists that they have just entered the watershed of a particular river or creek. Although the particular water feature may have been long since buried or otherwise marginalized by urban development, there is increased realization that these forces do not always flow away quietly. Often, buried floodplains threaten the homes that were ill-advisedly built upon them, contributing to subsidence, abandonment, and neighborhood disinvestment.[23] Sometimes, more proactively, city leaders will decide to reembrace their neglected or buried waterways, as has been done to such celebrated effect in Providence. Similarly, as city, state, and federal agencies reconsider the effects of such infrastructural shortcomings as combined-sewer overflows, there is increased consciousness about the relationship between upstream actions and downstream consequences. In each case, infrastructure crisis and ecological threat can be re-imaged as a city design opportunity.

Examples of this type of emergent public realm abound. To cite just a few, there is the Charles River Watershed Association in Massachusetts (joined recently by the Clean Charles 2005 coalition, a consortium of five universities and area businesses) and the Friends of Walden Pond and the Walden Woods Project in Concord/Lincoln, Massachusetts.[24] In the Middle Atlantic, there is New Jersey's Delaware and Raritan Canal Watch. Near Atlanta, the Tri-County River Watch, Inc., was formed to fight landfills.[25] In the late 1990s, the Archdiocese of Detroit began a River of Life program, described as "a crusade to help clean up the Clinton River and other area streams."[26] The Southwest Florida Water Management District (otherwise known as Swiftmud) established the Citrus County River Watch to monitor water quality, one of many such efforts nationwide. Not all watches are wholly successful. In the Florida case, for instance, a local developer soon appropriated the River Watch moniker as the name for a new suburban subdivision.[27] Other watches, such as one to nurture the Tijuana River Valley that traverses the

U.S.-Mexican border between San Diego and Tijuana, have yet to be suitably established at all.[28]

The concept of watches has caught on in many countries. In Malaysia, the Sungei Penchala River Watch Committee initiated a campaign of "civic consciousness" among riverfront residents to curtail the disposal of rubbish into the water, part of a nationwide "Love Our River Campaign" that covers more than 160 rivers.[29] Most watches—in the United States and elsewhere—remain focused on the ecology, but some—drawing a parallel with the concept of "neighborhood watch"—have been conceived mostly as crime-prevention strategies. In Scotland, the Salmon Fishery Board established a River Watch along the Dee, described as a "pioneering partnership" aimed at "cracking down on crime, including poaching, on one of Scotland's main salmon fishing rivers."[30] Similarly, the Niagara River Watch, on the U.S.-Canadian border near Buffalo, was launched to assist the United States Coast Guard in identifying "suspicious activity."[31]

Many watches focus on threatened inland ecosystems; increasingly, they also nurture larger bodies of water, such as lakes or even ocean coastlines. In conjunction with its massive harbor cleanup project, Boston has developed an award-winning comprehensive plan for restoration of its beaches and beachfront amenities. Here, as with other sorts of watches, the emphasis is on the common resource that is shared by diverse communities. Similarly, many cities along the Great Lakes—notably Cleveland and Toronto—are re-imaging themselves as water-oriented places.[32] Even Chicago, long the gold standard for urban waterfront public space, has increased its investment in lakefront recreational and educational opportunities. Often, what begins with a disconnected set of citizen-activists and nonprofit organizations, each targeting a small section of a large resource, is transformed into a broad public–private coalition that discovers its commonalities and can act in concert. The result can be a re-imaging of the resource itself. What was once one riverfront town's problem is reconceptualized as a regional ecological challenge.

Whatever their scale, watches are constructed by groups to

identify, enhance, and protect urban and regional assets. In contrast to traces—which are often accompanied (or even characterized) by efforts at niche marketing—watches seek to nurture a more wholly inclusive public realm, one that is relatively immune to conventional consumerism.

Finally, there is a fourth kind of burgeoning public realm, ways, which are concerned not with the imageability of natural resources and transportation corridors, but with the design of the city dweller and city visitor's pedestrian experience.

WAYS

Ways are pedestrian in nature and allow exploration of places via constructed pathways revealed through a system of way-finding aids, including maps, guides, signs, and markers of all sorts. They may be open-ended, allowing users to join or leave the path as they wish. As a result, value is created on either side of the way, encouraging nodes of educational and economic development opportunities (fig. 16.4).

To a great extent, a way is a walkable trace. In a relatively small area, it facilitates a particular thematic vision of a place. Whereas traces exist over wide and disconnected terrain, however, the spatial concentration of a way permits a focus on the connectivity among points, not just a consideration of the commonality of the points themselves. A way is a planned path that helps visitors extract a coordinated partial slice from the overwhelming sensory overload of a city. It is a tool to nurture focus but need not—and should not—control interpretation of what is seen. Like corridors, traces, and watches, ways carry an agenda-setting function: They do not suggest what to think, but they do suggest what to think *about*.

Fig. 16.4: Ways.

Some ways, such as Jerusalem's Stations of the Cross, have existed for centuries (though these, too, were invented and designed at some point). Most cities offer many self-guided walking tours, often organized by theme as well as by district.

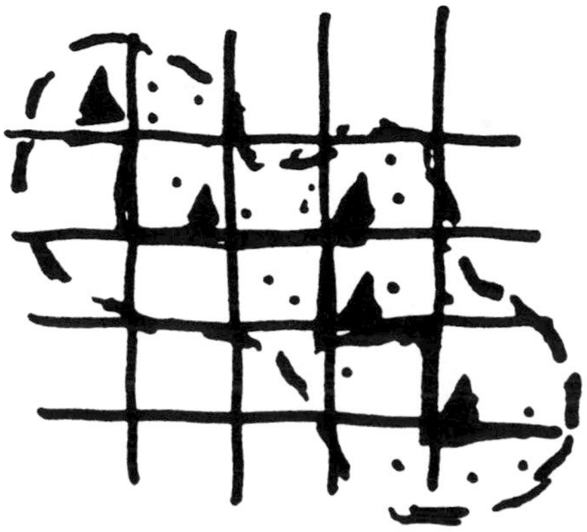

Some ways, such as San Antonio's River Walk, Denver's Platte River Greenway, and Chattanooga's Riverwalk, follow the course of a waterway, while others are completely independent of any single organizational device.

The most famous recently constructed American way is Boston's Freedom Trail, first conceptualized in 1951. This thin red line marks out a route through the oldest parts of the colonial city. Although it certainly does not permit visitors to successfully screen out the sights, sounds, and smells of the contemporary city, it does invite attempts at such temporal editing. No one following this way will be able to reconstruct an overall image of Revolution-era Boston, but even a partial re-imaging of a city can be powerful. Even for nontourists, the presence of the Freedom Trail provides an organizing force, a periodic reminder that parts of the twenty-first-century city have been superimposed upon a seventeenth-century street pattern and were once home to seminal events in the nascent nation's development. At the same time, because the physical presence of the line encourages a particular pattern and flow of movement—at least among tourists—the line itself creates economic value by generating support for adjacent businesses (arguably the earliest sort of "online" commerce!).

More recently, Bostonians have developed a second downtown way, the Black Heritage Trail, a path through the back side of Beacon Hill that highlights the early achievements of the city's African Americans, while also making clear that the events celebrated by the nearby Freedom Trail did not immediately guarantee equal liberties to all. Other places offer parallel kinds of ways, such as Washington, D.C.'s Black Georgetown Journey, or Savannah, Georgia's Negro Heritage Trail Tour.

All of the above examples—whether corridors, traces, watches, or ways—share similar characteristics as designed public places. Each is a programmed and managed piece of the environment. Each has enough constraint and direction to permit its jurisdiction to gain a new structure, identity, and set of meanings. While their elements can be defined, they may not be defined intuitively in the landscape; therefore, they do not necessarily have strong physical limits and may be discontinuous. But they are all made up of linked places, unique resources tied together by a common abstract idea based as much on mediated information as on form.

RE-IMAGING THE CITY-REGION

The imaging and re-imaging of such places is accomplished through the ways in which they are portrayed, marketed, and developed. A city-region becomes a vastly different place, for instance, if it is re-imaged as a set of multijurisdictional watersheds within which diverse constituencies share commonly vested interests. Similarly, the boundary between city and suburb loses some of its hard edge if it is blurred by networks of bicycle corridors or pedestrian trails, linking and locating newly discovered shared amenities. Such places are inherently mixed in use, often reuniting land previously segregated into residential, industrial, and commercial parcels. Most important, these places are generated and sustained by a variety of overlapping interest groups. Because they are the products of negotiation between otherwise discordant or disconnected parties, these places can become environments that heal. Even as we may lament the substitution of media-scripted environments for direct sense experience of neighborhood and community ties, there seems ample evidence that city designers can still help citizens image the cities and regions they desire. It is time to design a new set of public realms.

City Imaging: A Bibliographic Essay

Lawrence J. Vale

CITY IMAGE AND CITY PERFORMANCE

Following publication of *The Image of the City* in 1960, Kevin Lynch's next twenty-five years of writing and practice demonstrated that what he initially termed "imageability" is only one aspect of what makes for high-quality urban form. To attain environmental quality, one must also incorporate other elusive principles. In his last major book, *Good City Form,*[1] Lynch identified five "performance dimensions"—*vitality, sense, fit, access,* and *control*—and showed how each is affected by metacriteria of *efficiency* and *justice.* In this later formulation, the early ideas of imageability and legibility are largely subsumed under the single category of *sense,* which Lynch defined as "the degree to which the settlement can be clearly perceived and mentally differentiated and structured in time and space by its residents and the degree to which that mental structure connects with their values and concepts." The other performance dimensions address the ability of spatial settings to sustain human biological needs (*vitality*), support human behaviors (*fit*), connect to other persons and opportunities (*access*), and permit those who use, work, or reside in such settings to create, repair, modify, and manage them (*control*). All of Lynch's performance dimensions are user-centered and premised on the desirability of human agency. Yet, as Lynch's inclusion of the "metacriteria" of justice and efficiency implies, the user-centered paradigm is subject to contestation by larger structural forces and principles.

Oddly, and perhaps tragically, Lynch's more full-bodied later work—with its focus on the relationship between form and action—remains eclipsed by the power of his 1960 contribution, still regarded as a classic of the planning literature. This notion of image—even though the concept has mutated dramatically during the last four decades—remains an especially salient term for interpreting the production, design, and appearance of cities.

MEDIATED EXPERIENCES

Lynch's early work emphasized the perceptual characteristics of the urban environment, stressing the ways that individuals mentally organize their own sensory experience of cities. Increasingly, however, city imaging is supplemented and constructed by exposure to visual media rather than by direct sense experience of urban realms. In the "hyper-visual"[2] contemporary city, the whole question of city image and city imaging warrants renewed scrutiny. Lynch's 1960 study deliberately deemphasized the *meanings* that places hold for their inhabitants, yet this aspect remains central.[3] City images are not static but subject to continual revision and manipulation by media-savvy individuals and institutions.

Although humans have always lived vicariously through the tales of others and have found ways to construct images that promote or denigrate particular places, the availability of new media has enabled this image construction to become more self-conscious and ubiquitous. Most obviously, this takes the form of advertising which, no longer limited to signs and billboards on the outdoor cityscape, has covered almost every available surface. Corporations from TWA to Qualcomm have paid tens of millions of dollars for football stadium–naming rights while other companies pay to append their names to the events that take place inside;[4] city buses have become transformed into three-dimensional mobile logos; sections of public highways have their roadside maintenance sponsored by companies delighted to have a sign erected to attest to their civic-mindedness; even grocery store and ATM receipts carry advertising messages. Advertising long ago permeated our homes, most notably through the audiovisual reach of television. More recently, with the widespread commercialization of the Internet, our computer screens, too, are framed with flashy enticements to further consumption. For urban designers, who seek to nurture the public realms of cities and regions, physical plans now are paired with public relations plans. In recent years, urban designers (and others) have invoked city image proactively—seeking innovative ways to alter perceptions of urban, suburban, and regional areas. As the title of a late–1990s television show put it succinctly, we are building *Spin City.*

IMAGING TECHNOLOGIES AND THE PRACTICE OF CITY DESIGN

Pioneers of urban simulation like Peter Bosselmann invariably plead for neutrality and fairness in the representation of places.[5] Most images, though, are not constructed by "neutral" university-based labs but are deliberately skewed to sell a proposal, flatter a specific design, depict (and thereby delimit) an intended clientele, and convey a particular mood. Other city planning researchers, concerned about the imbalance in informational resources between well-heeled project proponents and less technologically sophisticated community groups, have developed techniques linking geographic information systems (GIS) to other multimedia applications, such as video. By sharing such resources among all parties in a way that makes them accessible not only at community meetings but at many times and in many different places, it becomes possible to establish a commonly understood and accessible body of information and images. Ideally, such shared data can facilitate a consensus-building process.[6]

More broadly, increased use and reliance on GIS may fundamentally alter the ways that cities are imaged. Because such systems allow diverse kinds of spatially encoded data (such as income, race, location of hazardous facilities, and incidence of health problems) to be mapped together, these media not only facilitate urban database management but permit researchers to perform a wide variety of visualization, spatial analysis, and spatial modeling.[7] Such studies can be used for a range of purposes, from finding optimal solutions for facility location and transport routes to identifying profound instances of environmental inequity. Researchers are only now beginning to explore the role of media in debates over "environmental justice" and to discuss the potential of GIS as a proactive tool, yet such issues are surely important to a larger understanding of how media and city development have become linked.

IMAGES AND IMAGING

Kenneth Boulding's book, *The Image: Knowledge in Life and Society*, published in 1956, was the first of three significant volumes featuring the concept of "image" to appear in rather rapid succession. Lynch's *The Image of the City* was published four years later, followed in 1961 by Daniel Boorstin's *The Image: A Guide to Pseudo-events in America*.[8] Oddly enough, none of these books makes any reference to the earlier works. Taken together, however, they attest to the growing concern with this topic within the uneasy prosperity of Cold War America.

Boulding looked at images more broadly than Lynch did, exploring how individuals construct images based on their life experiences. Ranging widely across the social and biological sciences, he argued that the study of images and their impact on social, economic, and political processes could form the basis of a new scientific discipline. His book has little to say about the images of places, however, and remains centered on analysis of organizational and institutional behavior. Even so, in many ways Boulding's volume is the missing theoretical foundation for *The Image of the City*, and it is unfortunate that Lynch did not know of this parallel work at the time of his own study.

The premise of Boorstin's book is tangential to Lynch's but

diverges in important directions. It explicitly connects images to media in ways that Lynch ignored but, like Boulding's opus, does not focus on cities. Instead, Boorstin stresses the "pervasiveness of image-thinking," part of what he dubbed the "Graphic Revolution." His book was perhaps the first to detect and dissect a collective societal preference for images over reality, and echoed Boulding's concern over the growing import of the emerging concept of "public image." "By our very use of the term," Boorstin commented, "we imply that something can be done to it: the image can always be more or less successfully synthesized, doctored, repaired, refurbished, and improved, quite apart from (though not entirely independent of) the spontaneous original of which the image is a public portrait."[9]

In the decades since this triple flurry of image books, image-making has become more pervasive, but books about the phenomenon have become more narrowly specialized. Examining the spate of volumes that purport to deal with *image*, one finds scores of books that obsess over the psychological effects of body image, many that examine theological questions about the relationship between God and man or explore sociological questions about the images of marginalized groups, and a slew of others that focus on techniques of advertising, public relations, and mass communication of all kinds. A notable outlier is Lloyd Rodwin and Robert Hollister's *Cities of the Mind: Images and Themes of the City in the Social Sciences*,[10] which draws explicitly on Boulding and even contains one of Kevin Lynch's last essays, in which he reconsiders the origins and effects of *The Image of the City*. Although it deals centrally with images and with cities, *Cities of the Mind*[11] is more concerned with mental concepts than with designed images and, like two of its distinguished predecessors in the literature, says little about how media contribute to image construction. The present volume thus attempts to find and till the common ground that underlies the three germinative books of Boulding, Lynch, and Boorstin by nurturing the hybrid growth of images, media, and cities.

Environmental costs and benefits are not distributed equally among persons, nor are they distributed in accordance with a single set of values. As Lynch put it, we must always ask "1) What is the cost . . . of achieving [the desired] degree of vitality, sense, fit, access, or control? and 2) Who is getting how much of it?" Many of those who conducted studies inspired by *The Image of the City* have emphasized ways that city images vary not only among individuals but also from one subgroup to another, tied closely to questions of class, race, ethnicity, and gender—while others have stressed, as Lynch originally did, just how much about environmental perception and preference is widely shared. These Lynch-inspired studies are described in Jack L. Nasar's *The Evaluative Image of the City*.[12] In coming to terms with the continual battles over images in city design and development, it is important to remember the links between *image* and the other performance dimensions outlined by Lynch. To do so means analyzing images of cities in terms of the distribution of costs and benefits to the places and people they promote. The "Imaging the City" phenomenon is neither wholly positive nor wholly negative, just wholly pervasive.

Image-building efforts encompass not only changes to the built environment but also encode broad conceptual orientations. Image-making is about finding new ways (and new technologies) to represent and promote cleaner environments, better communities, and socioeconomic progress, yet images may also serve to mask or perpetuate existing inequalities (or to highlight them as a deliberate means of provocation). Images may be promoted in service of some broad "public good," but they are also subject to extreme manipulation by market forces that resist any such wider efforts to plan. In a world of decentralized planning and rapid economic change, urban designers and media professionals share many opportunities to alter public attitudes toward urban places.

NEW MEDIA CHALLENGES

In a frequently quoted passage from *The Hunchback of Notre Dame*, Victor Hugo challenged us to consider whether the fifteenth-century advent of the printed book meant the death of architecture. In the second half of the twentieth century, new modes for mediated representations of place proliferated—from television shows to cyberspace—adding further challenges to the traditional role of buildings as the arbiter and index of power. Just as monumental architecture has coped with the advent of mass-produced literature, so too it will continue to survive the interpretive onslaught of other media. Even as it does so, however, architecture and city design gain new layers of meaning. Increasingly, the built environment is the setting for widely publicized, orchestrated events. What was once a local parade or festival is often now a carefully marketed and scripted celebration of heritage, aimed outward as well as inward. Architecture and urban design have long been central to the production of what Eric Hobsbawm has called "invented traditions,"[13] but production of new ways of marking and marketing heritage seems to be proliferating. Often, what David Lowenthal has decried as the "heritage crusade"[14] does indeed consist of trivialization and manipulation of history for narrow, present-minded purposes.

In other places, however, invented traditions have more positively led to productive reuse and revaluing of long-neglected places. Throughout Europe and the United States, for instance, urban designers have attempted to find contemporary value for seemingly obsolete nineteenth-century industrial landscapes and, more generally, efforts at historic preservation and conservation have gained ground—often giving enhanced visual pleasure to places that lacked it in their grimy prime. In the best cases, the museumizing impulse has been paired with honest reappraisal of both past glories and past infamies and has included forward-looking efforts to restore these places as centers of employment, whether industrial or service related. Elsewhere, over the last two decades, there has been a national and international spread of ephemeral "First Night®" festivals on New Year's Eve. Similarly, the global publicity afforded to temporary public art installations such as the Wrapped Reichstag attests to the collaborative power of planners and artists to transform the meanings of monuments and urban spaces. Many urban public artists have literally erected or projected alternative images of the city onto and into the spaces of city streets and squares, using a wide array of new and traditional media to critical advantage. Together with a new generation of media-oriented and image-conscious architects, they have provoked us to think about how present-day cities hold different visual values and pose issues different from those raised before the advent of television.

CONSTRUCTING URBAN IDENTITY

In recent years, there has been a growing acknowledgment of the ways that media and the built environment work together to shape and alter public perceptions of places.[15] For decades, urban sociologists like Morris Janowitz and Gerald Suttles have noted how community identity is socially constructed not only by local residents but also by a wide variety of outsiders, including newspaper reporters and editors, civic boosters, developers, real estate professionals, marketing firms, and city officials.[16] Such castings and portrayals can have both positive and negative connotations. Sometimes, as is vividly conveyed in Mike Davis's account of the contradictions of twentieth-century Los Angeles in *City of Quartz*, the myth-making of the boosters has its own darker counterpart vying to capture the public imagination.[17] While some critics, such as Michael Sorkin, may regard Los Angeles as ". . . the most mediated town in America, nearly unviewable save through the fictive eyes of its mythologizers,"[18] Los Angeles is hardly alone. All cities, and the neighborhoods within them, are constructed and interpreted by many forces. We learn about places not only from the people who live in them but also from the built environment in which social life takes place and from the media environment (including the reportage of "pseudo-events"[19]) that serves to edit and alter our perceptions.

Television, film, and digital media constitute a sprawling realm of constructed vicarious experience. The globally disseminated vision of *Dallas*—televised in more than ninety countries from Algeria to Hong Kong[20]—portrayed an image of a suburb-less world comprised entirely of a glittering high-rise downtown and spacious cattle ranches. A more recent show, *Providence*, depicts Rhode Island's capital "bathed in a golden light as a locale of romance and drama." Each Friday night, more than thirteen million viewers are transported to a city that seems to be undergoing a renaissance. The real city's colorful mayor, Vincent (Buddy) Cianci, was only too pleased to appear in an episode playing himself, eager to shake the city's persistent reputation as a hotbed of corruption. As *Providence*'s creator and executive producer, John Masius, explained it, "I told the mayor that we were going to shoot postcards of the city, make it as beautiful as possible. . . . The city is one of the characters in the show." Co-executive producer Bob DeLaurentis noted that "It stands for that semimythical place we all feel we miss, where families are still close and people still look out for each other." Buddy Cianci tells the story of his conversation with Baltimore's mayor Kurt Schmoke, who reportedly praised the show and commented: "Boy, the skyline looks terrific, with a good storyline about a woman coming home, helping her family, contributing to the community." According to Cianci, the mayor then ruefully added, "I've got a show too on television. It's called *Homicide*."[21]

From *The Streets of San Francisco* to *L.A. Law* and *L.A. Doctors*; from *WKRP in Cincinnati* to the Boston of *Cheers*; from *NYPD Blue* and *Brooklyn South* to *Chicago Hope* and *ER*—decades of repeated exposure to place-specific television narratives have established visual and social stereotypes about many, perhaps most, large American cities. The most popular television dramas focus on inner-city crime fighting or chronicle the incoming wounded of urban emergency rooms. Even the 1990s spate of urban TV comedies about groups of single friends living in city apartments, epitomized by the nine-year run of *Seinfeld*, tended to confirm stereotypes of what one critic called "a vibrant city that is quirky and diverse but not very nice."[22] In other cases, such as MTV's *The Real World*, where producers annually seek out urban settings intended to forge the very definition of what's fashionably "cool," television has served to restore a certain cachet to urban life. Sometimes, as with

Providence, the televisual attention coincides with discernible progress in the city's physical fabric and economic well-being. More often, however, these TV settings cast unwanted aspersions on troubled neighborhoods and institutions. Whatever the specifics of the message, more people construct their perceptions of cities on the basis of television images than actually live in those cities or visit them.

The film medium perpetuates the same phenomenon. Film portrayals, like urban development ventures, inherently judge the human capital worth and potential of people and the places they inhabit. Hollywood producers and directors seek out distressed urban settings from South Central Los Angeles to Detroit to darken the usually grim portrayals of inner-city life—images that reinforce and perpetuate negative stereotypes. For some frequently depicted cities, though, there is a broader range of viewpoints to adopt. Hundreds of feature films have taken New York as their setting (if not always as their subject), making it nearly impossible to retain a neutral impression about the city regardless of whether an actual visit has been made. Moreover, since films often feature sights less familiar than the expected tourist destinations and business venues (and are often actually filmed in a city other than the one they purport to represent), films enter into consciousness as counterpoints and contradictions rather than confirmations of direct sensory experience.

The metro–media nexus occurs not only within the realms of film and television; increasingly, urban images are conveyed through newer digital media. Popular computer-based games such as SimCity 3000 allow participants to direct the development of a metropolis and encode a myriad of assumptions about how cities can be structured. Other alternative cyberworlds use physical cities as metaphors for creating new interactive social realms that permit those with computers to experience analogous rooms, sidewalks, squares, and office water coolers.

Books have provided similar entry ports into other worlds for centuries, but film, television, and digital media have made places ever more visually accessible and mass marketed. In the past, we usually experienced the ambience of unvisited places through the mediated lenses of great (or less-than-great) writers, musicians, and artists. In fiction and poetry, in the visual and performing arts, just as in social science research, men and women have sought to interpret, critique, and re-image cities.[23] For the few who most insistently filter and position their own vicarious exposures to evade the sights and sounds of contemporary mass media, such older outlets may remain dominant. Even for many who are more wholly immersed in the hypermedia whirl of advertising, public relations, radio, television, film, and computers, older media still help generate powerful urban images. It remains almost impossible to imagine nineteenth-century London without invoking Dickens. Other city–sensibility pairings also persist: Joyce's Dublin, Whitman's New York, Baudelaire's Paris, Dreiser's Chicago, Calvino's Venice, to name just a few. Similarly, we can still hear Gershwin's "American in Paris" or Rogers and Hammerstein's corny "Oklahoma"; and we can still see Canaletto's Venetian horizons, the smoke and steam of Monet's Gare Saint-Lazare, Riis's photos of the desperate "Other Half," Hopper's lonely diners. The production and reproduction of such images continues. Yet, even as contemporary novelists, poets, artists, and composers persist in attempts to convey the energies and contradictions of cities, they do so within a cultural landscape dominated by mass markets.

Facilitated by the gradual privatization of planning and development functions and by the need of many cities to alter their economic base, the intersections of media that comprise "city marketing" are thriving. City leaders seek not only to capitalize on existing resources that appeal to potential investors, visitors, and tenuously connected suburbanites but also to build new facilities with these constituencies centrally in mind. New monumental facilities—especially convention centers, sports stadia, and museums—are conceived and built to be omnipresent and exportable visual icons.

This is hardly a new phenomenon, of course. Some would contend that the marketing of cities can be traced to the competition among medieval Italian city–states or to the civic boosterism of the Hanseatic League, or—as Julian Beinart argues in chapter 1 of this volume—even as far back as the earliest efforts to extol the merits of Christian pilgrimage sites. Still, whatever the depth of its history, it is a phenomenon that seems to be accelerating. Even Stephen Ward's recent attempt to construct a longer history for the place-selling phenomenon commences with the comment that "the last quarter of a century has seen a massive worldwide growth in the practice of place marketing and promotion."[24] We have come a long way in a short time from the pilgrim's travelogue to the Luxembourg-based company that markets a "Virtual Pilgrimage to the Holy Land" through its Web site: www.Jesus2000.com.[25]

CITY IMAGING AND CITY DESIGNERS

Even as new communications technologies mediate the experience of the city through the creation of parallel fictional cyberworlds—urbanism-at-a-distance—city-imaging efforts also continue to thrive in the built world of urban real estate development. Because of this, city designers and planners face new challenges. The traditional wisdom of "location, location, location" still drives urban redevelopment initiatives but, more than ever, locational values are not self-evident: They depend on the marketing efforts of media-industry partners. Increasingly, flagship development projects take on the trappings of staged ventures in which image-building is at the head of the agenda and the flagship risks losing sight of the fleet.

The emerging directions for city imaging therefore seem to bridge the concerns of physical planners, media professionals, and city developers in ways that affect planning practice throughout the United States and elsewhere. If the imaging (and re-imaging) of districts, cities, and regions is indeed at the heart of contemporary urban development practice, it is essential that urban designers and planners understand the phenomenon. Only then will they be able to work more effectively within its constraints or to devise alternative frameworks.

IMAGING TECHNIQUES

The imaging and re-imaging of places entails a variety of techniques and occurs at a variety of scales. Some of these techniques are old, some are new, but all are deployed in novel combinations. Often, in the effort to shift and lift public (or investor) confidence, places are named or renamed to convey future hopes—as with Detroit's Renaissance Center—or to imbue them with a more upscale or pastoral image. This is not a new phenomenon, but it is one that seems to be diversifying and accelerating. In the middle of the twentieth century, tenements and slums were replaced by public housing projects with names like "Orchard Park" and "Elm Haven"; in the late 1990s, many failed housing projects were themselves being torn down and rebuilt as New Urbanist mixed-income communities, again with new identities and new names (not to mention glossy brochures and promotional videos). Baltimore's notorious Lafayette Courts project is re-imaged as Pleasant View Gardens; Atlanta replaces Techwood Homes with Centennial Place; Chicago tries to bury the infamy of Cabrini-Green in a billion-dollar new neighborhood.[26] Similar re-imaging occurs in other parts of American cities: Now-seedy areas are recast as Arts Districts, and abandoned nineteenth-century industrial landscapes become resuscitated as centers of Heritage Interpretation, Historic Preservation, and (it is hoped) Economic Development.

In thc 1980s, Indianapolis Mayor William Hudnut's staff launched a major marketing campaign on behalf of the city, replete with videos produced for executives at Fortune 500 companies and a successful bid to attract a professional football franchise. In Boston, city officials and civic leaders not only launched bids to host the Olympics and the Democratic National Convention but, in 1997, went beyond the usual tourism and economic development marketing to try to convince suburbanites to return to the city. With the slogan "Boston—It's all right here," the City of Boston sponsored a series of television ads (using services donated by a major ad agency and free commercial air time on local stations) that attempted to promote homeownership in the city, stop suburban flight, and allay fears about crime and the city's school system. In the first set of ads, intended to play up the city's advantages over "boring" suburbs, city dwellers and suburbanites were asked to cope with a series of challenges: "Find a mariachi band"; "Find neighbors to help you move your couch"; "Commute to work on in-line skates." The message? City dwellers can do such things easily, whereas suburbanites must struggle for sociability and convenience. As Mayor Thomas Menino put it, "We want to change the perception that a city is just a place to work, and a suburb is a place to live." Charles Royer, a former mayor of Seattle, adds, "If advertising can sell potato chips and beer, why not a city?"[27] Such marketing and place-branding is now becoming pervasive. From Times Square to the Las Vegas strip, entrepreneurial mayors have tried to turn their cities into "family-friendly" destinations.[28]

RE-IMAGING AT NEIGHBORHOOD, CITY, REGIONAL, AND NATIONAL SCALES

The artful re-imaging of places has always proceeded unevenly, however. Often, many critics have charged, efforts at tourist promotion and regeneration of historic areas have fostered further inequalities. Twenty-five years ago, Kevin Lynch called on designers and planners to help city officials and city dwellers develop a clearer sense of the passage of time in urban areas. Now, however, his intriguing question, "What Time is This Place?"[29] is often answered by calculated efforts to select and highlight certain past eras of the city's culture and ambience while bypassing less-marketable elements, periods, and persons.[30] Everything from the streetscape and the architecture of new and renovated facilities to the typeface of tourist brochures and signage attempts to recapture a lost piece of heritage in a way intended to portend a new, postindustrial economic viability. Redevelopers of Tampa's Ybor City, for example, seek to attract tourists and reinvestment dollars by harkening back to the late-nineteenth-century days when the neighborhood marked the global center of cigar manufacturing and served as a nexus for Italian, Cuban, and Spanish immigrant culture—even though the neighborhood is now home to a predominantly African-American population.

Re-imaging also occurs at the level of the city as a whole. Places such as Pittsburgh and Cleveland—not long ago widely stereotyped as the epitome of Rust Belt decline—are now reinterpreted as the poster children of Rust Belt renaissance. To accomplish this image change, city leaders have long recognized that tangible evidence of economic growth is necessary but not sufficient; what matters is both high profile physical redevelopment and the skillful marketing of such efforts at visible change. The Cleveland Tomorrow effort, for instance, seems premised on equal doses of urban development and public relations campaigns.[31] Other cities in the United States and elsewhere stage elaborate promotional ventures in an attempt to attract national and international events like major conventions or the Olympic Games.[32]

In many places, the process of image-making has extended beyond city limits to encompass the broader regions in which metropolitan homes and workplaces are increasingly found. In Lynch's terms, this is about "managing the sense of a region" in ways that enable residents to identify—and to identify with—a wider set of jurisdictions.[33] Progress on regional image-making has been sporadic and slow, especially in areas of high racial and ethnic spatial polarity between inner-city and outer suburbs. For every vague notion of "Chicagoland," there are many cities where personal identification ends strictly at the city line. Still, there are more promising countertrends, from Portland Metro—where regional government and ecologically sensitive management seem to have made significant gains—to the burgeoning rails-to-trails open space networks that cut across political jurisdictions in regions throughout the United States.[34]

At the still broader locus of nations and nationalism, too, architecture and urban design have regularly been used in the service of promoting the preferred self-image of powerful persons and institutions. Whether through efforts to consolidate colonial rule or through postcolonial attempts to forge group-based identities through the design and construction of new capital cities and parliamentary districts, image-making has been a central aspect of city-making.[35]

ASSESSING THE IMAGES AND THE IMAGE-MAKERS

Most of those who have begun the assessment of re-imaging efforts have attacked them as superficial and divisive, yielding Disneyfied cities that are more racially and economically polarized than ever before. Such critics—typified by those who contributed to Michael Sorkin's edited collection of essays entitled *Variations on a Theme Park*—have bemoaned what they consider the "privatization of public space," a trend seen as permitting enhanced surveillance and fortress-like urban design.[36]

Cultural geographers in Britain and Europe (with limited participation by American colleagues) have contributed recent volumes with titles such as *Selling the City: Marketing Approaches in Public Sector Urban Planning; Selling Places: The City as Cultural Capital, Past and Present*; *Place Promotion: The Use of Publicity and Marketing to Sell Towns and Regions*; *Marketing the City: The Role of Flagship Developments in Urban Regeneration*; *Selling Places: The Marketing and Promotion of Towns and Cities 1850–2000*; and—perhaps most provocative-sounding—*Reimaging the Pariah City: Urban Development in Belfast and Detroit*. Dennis Judd and Susan Fainstein's edited collection, *The Tourist City*, is more even-handed and therefore less wholly despairing.[37]

Still, at all scales—from the local to the international—the image-making process seems ubiquitous and often oversimplistic. Most academic critics have tended to see all such efforts as uniformly nefarious: *Selling* anything is equivalent to *selling out*. They see these attempts at constructing new group identities as serving the interests of dominant groups while further marginalizing all others. Yet, it is far from clear that the broad-brush critique yields a wholly satisfactory picture. If "imaging the city" is indeed the ascendant mode of design and development we have, then it behooves designers, planners, and city leaders to understand how it works, and how it can be improved or, if necessary, superseded.

NOTES

INTRODUCTION. Sam Bass Warner Jr. and Lawrence J. Vale

1. Lynch, K. 1984. Reconsidering *The image of the city.* In L. Rodwin and R. Hollister, eds. 1984. *Cities of the mind: Images and themes of the city in the social sciences.* New York, NY: Plenum.

2. Boulding, K. 1956. *The image: Knowledge in life and society.* Ann Arbor, MI: University of Michigan Press.

3. We are grateful to Gary Hack for calling attention to this example.

4. Lynch, K. 1960. *The image of the city.* Cambridge, MA: MIT Press.

5. Lynch, K. 1981. *Good city form.* Cambridge, MA: MIT Press. *See also* discussion of *Good city form* in the appendix to the present volume.

6. Lynch, K. *The image of the city.*

7. Morris, W. 1891. *News from nowhere.* Reprint ed. 1972. New York, NY: Routledge; Dreiser, T. 1900. *Sister Carrie.* Reprint ed. 2000. New York, NY: Dutton/Signet; Howells, W. D. 1890. *A hazard of new fortunes.* Reprint ed. 1995. New York, NY: Penguin/New American Library; Wells, H. G. 1898. *The war of the worlds.* Reprint ed. 1981. Mattituck, NY: Amereon Ltd.

1. Julian Beinart

1. Lopez, S. 1998. Greetings from America's secret capitals. *Time* 13: 46–61.

2. Ellul, J. 1970. *The meaning of the city.* Grand Rapids, MI: William B. Eerdmans, 32.

3. Gruppo D'Impegno Di Citta' Alta. n.d. *Cognoscere Bergamo, Guida Turistica di Controinformazione.*

4. Hyde, J. K. 1966. Medieval descriptions of cities. *Bulletin of the John Rylands Library Manchester* 48, 2.

5. *Crazy People.* 1990. Directed by T. Hill. Paramount Pictures. Videocassette, 91 min.

6. Beinart, J. 1990. From Olympia to Barcelona: Themes of permanence and transition. *Space and Society/Spazio e Societa'* 50.

7. Report of the Conference. 1988. *Hosting the Olympics: The long-term impact.* Seoul, Korea.

8. Ferrariae, Hercules Dux. 1492. Letter to the Secretary of the Duke of Genoa, 20 November. In *Revue des etudes juives*. 1980. Translated by Paolo Ceccarelli.

9. Ceccarelli, Paolo. 1998. Letter to Julian Beinart. 30 July.

10. Frugoni, C. 1991. *A distant city*. Princeton, NJ: Princeton University Press, 135.

11. Frugoni, *A distant city*, 169.

12. Mumford, L. 1961. *The city in history*. London, UK: Secker and Warburg, 9, 10.

13. von Simson, O. 1967. *The Gothic cathedral*. New York, NY: Harper, 6–7.

14. Peters, F. E. 1986. *Jerusalem and Mecca: The typology of the Holy City in the Near East*. New York, NY: New York University Press, 31–2.

15. Pirenne, H. 1925. *Medieval cities*. Garden City, NY: Doubleday Anchor, 84.

16. Brantl, R., ed. 1966. *Medieval culture*. New York, NY: George Braziller, 227–8.

17. Atiya, A. S. 1962. *Crusade, commerce and culture*. Bloomington, IN: Indiana University Press, 45.

18. Peters, *Jerusalem and Mecca*, 47.

19. Elon, A. 1989. *Jerusalem, city of mirrors*. Boston, MA: Little Brown, 120.

20. Peters, *Jerusalem and Mecca*, 27.

21. Peters, *Jerusalem and Mecca*, 229–30.

22. Elon, *Jerusalem, city of mirrors*, 119.

23. Brantl, *Medieval culture*, 227.

24. Elon, *Jerusalem, city of mirrors*, 29, 34.

25. Turner, V., and E. Turner. 1978. *Image and pilgrimage in Christian culture*. New York, NY: Columbia University Press, 188.

26. Brown, P. 1981. *The Cult of the Saints*. Chicago, IL: University of Chicago Press, 88.

27. Melczer, W. 1993. *The pilgrim's guide to Santiago de Compostela*. New York, NY: Italica Press, 2–3.

28. Wharton, A. J. 1995. *Refiguring the post-classical city*. Cambridge, UK: Cambridge University Press, 92.

29. Runciman, S. 1955. The pilgrimages to Palestine before 1095. In K. M. Setton, ed., *A history of the Crusades*. vol. 1. In Series *The first hundred years*. Series editor M. W. Baldwin. Philadelphia, PA: University of Pennsylvania Press, 71.

30. Peters, *Jerusalem and Mecca*, 20.

31. Elon, *Jerusalem, city of mirrors*, 128.

32. Starkie, W. 1957. *The road to Santiago*. New York, NY: E. P. Dutton, 62.

33. Brantl, *Medieval culture*, 249.

34. Starkie, *The road to Santiago*, 47.

35. Savage, H. L. 1969. Pilgrimages and pilgrim shrines in Palestine and Syria after 1095. In H. W. Hazard, ed., *The art and architecture of the Crusader States*. Vol. IV in K. M. Setton, ed., *A History of the Crusades*. Madison, WI: University of Wisconsin Press, 38.

36. Brown, *The Cult of the Saints*, 437, 143.

37. Christian, W. A. 1996. *Visionaries*. Berkeley, CA: University of California Press.

38. Haffert, J. M. 1950. *Russia will be converted*. London, UK: International Press.

39. Starkie, *The road to Santiago*, 68–9.

40. Atiya, *Crusade, commerce and* culture, 46–7.

41. Wilkinson, J. 1977. *Jerusalem pilgrims*. Warminster, UK: Aris and Phillips, 1, 10.

42. Wilkinson, *Jerusalem pilgrims*, 5.

43. Dajani-Shakeel, H. 1986. Al-Quds: Jerusalem in the consciousness of the counter Crusader. In V. P. Gross, ed., *The meeting of two worlds: cultural exchange between East and*

West during the period of the Crusades. Kalamazoo, MI: Medieval Institute Publications, Western Michigan University.

44. Peters, *Jerusalem and Mecca*, 79.

45. Adler, E. N. 1966. *Jewish travelers*. New York: Hermon Press, xvii.

46. Wilkinson, *Jerusalem pilgrims*, 10.

47. Peters, F. E. 1985. *Jerusalem*. Princeton, NJ: Princeton University Press, 170.

48. Rosenau, H. 1979. *Vision of the temple*. London, UK: Oresko, 44–5.

49. Anderson, S. A. 1995. Memory in architecture. *Daedalus* 58 (December): 22–37.

50. McClung, W. A. 1983. *The architecture of paradise*. Berkeley, CA: University of California Press, 71.

51. Elon, *Jerusalem, city of mirrors*, 31.

52. Frugoni, *A distant city*, 76.

53. Frugoni, *A distant city*, 75.

54. Hyde, Medieval descriptions of cities, 313, 322.

55. Nichols, F. M. 1986. *The marvels of Rome*. New York, NY: Italica Press, 67.

56. Hyde, Medieval descriptions of cities, 322.

57. Baron, H. 1966. *The crisis of the early Italian renaissance*. Princeton, NJ: Princeton University Press, 198.

58. Dajani-Shakeel, Al-Quds: Jerusalem in the consciousness of the counter Crusader, 211.

59. Dajani-Shakeel, Al-Quds: Jerusalem in the consciousness of the counter Crusader, 204.

60. Sivan, E. 1971. The beginnings of the *Fada'il Al-Quds* Literature. *Israel Oriental Studies* 1: 278.

61. Melczer, *The pilgrim's guide to Santiago de Compostela,* 15.

62. Melczer, *The pilgrim's guide*, 31–2.

63. Starkie, *The road to Santiago*, 40–1.

64. Starkie, *The road to Santiago*, 44.

65. Stone, S. 1927. *The Cult of Santiago*. New York, NY: Longmans Green, 253.

66. Thurston, H. 1900. *The golden year of the Jubilee*. St. Louis, MO: B. Herder, 346.

67. Lea, H. C. 1896. *A history of Auricular confession and indulgences in the Latin Church*. Philadelphia, PA: Lea Brothers, 201.

68. Boase, T. S. R. 1933. *Boniface VIII*. London, UK: Constable, 235.

69. Little, L. K. 1978. *Religious poverty and the profit economy in medieval Europe*. Ithaca, NY: Cornell University Press, 32.

70. Atiya, *Crusade, commerce and* culture, 192.

71. Egane, A. 1673. *The book of rates now used in the sin custom-house of the Church of Rome*. London, UK: Benjamin Southwood, 8–11.

72. Rabbat, N. 1998. Architects and artists in Mamluk society: The perspective of the sources. *Journal of Architectural Education* 52, 1.

73. di Giovanni, G. *Agrigento*. Agrigento: di Giovanni.

74. Lynch, K. 1960. *The image of the city*. Cambridge, MA: MIT Press.

75. See W. L. Porter, remarks made at the Boston Architectural Creativity Symposium, April 1998.

2. Briavel Holcomb

1. Hall, T., and P. Hubbard. 1998. *The entrepreneurial city: Geographies of politics, regime and representation.* Chichester, UK: Wiley, 7.

2. Boulding, K. 1956. *The image: knowledge in life and society*. Ann Arbor, MI: University of Michigan Press; Lynch, K. 1960. *The image of the city*. Cambridge, MA: MIT Press.

3. U.S. Bureau of the Census. 1996. *Statistical Abstract of the United States.* 115th ed. Washington, DC: U.S. Government Printing Office.

4. Ward, S. V. 1998. *Selling places: The marketing and promotion of towns and cities, 1850–2000*. London, UK: E & FN Spon.

5. Hall and Hubbard, *The entrepreneurial city*.

6. Holcomb, B. 1990. Purveying places: past and present. CUPR Working Paper No. 7. New Brunswick, NJ: Center for Urban Policy Research; Ward, *Selling places.*

7. Jones, H. M. 1946. The colonial impulse: An analysis of the promotion literature of colonization. *Proceedings of the American Philosophical Society* 90: 132.

8. Bingham, R., and R. Mier, eds. 1997. *Dilemmas of urban economic development. Urban Affairs Annual Reviews* 47. Thousand Oaks, CA: Sage; Boorstin, D. 1965. *The Americans: The national experience.* London, UK: Weidenfeld and Nicholson; Boyle, M. R. 1990. An economic development education agenda for the 1990s. *Economic Development Quarterly* 4: 92–100.

9. Levy, J. 1990. What local economic developers actually do: Location quotients versus press releases. *Journal of the American Planning Association* (Spring): 153.

10. Boyle, M., and G. Hughes. 1994. The politics of urban entrepreneurialism in Glasgow. *Geoforum* 25, 4: 453–70; Deakin, N., and J. Edwards. 1993. *The enterprise culture and the inner city.* London, UK: Routledge; Duffy, H. 1995. *Competitive cities: Succeeding in the global economy.* London, UK: Spon; Eisenschitz, A., and J. Gough. 1996. The conditions of neo-Keynesian local economic strategy. *Review of International Political Economy* 3: 434–59; Harvey, D. 1989. From managerialism to entrepreneurialism: the transformation of government in late capitalism. *Geografiska Annaler* 71B: 3–17; Jessop, B. 1997. The entrepreneurial city: Re-imaging localities, redesigning economic governance, or restructuring capital? In N. Jewson and S. Macgregor, *Realising cities: new spatial divisions and social transformation.* London, UK: Routledge; Savitch, H., and P. Kantor. 1995. City business: An international perspective on marketplace politics. *International Journal of Urban and Regional Studies* 19: 495–512.

11. Squires, G., ed. 1989. *Unequal partnerships: The political economy of urban redevelopment in postwar America.* New Brunswick, NJ: Rutgers University Press.

12. Eisenschitz and Gough, The conditions of neo-Keynesian local economic strategy.

13. Archer, K. 1996. Packaging the place: Development strategies in Tampa and Orlando, Florida. In C. Demaziere and P. Wilson, *Local economic development in Europe and the Americas.* London, UK: Manwell; Boyle, M., and G. Hughes. 1991. The politics of the representation of the "real": Discourses from the Left on Glasgow's role as city of culture, 1990. *Area* 23: 217–28; Hubbard, P. 1996. Re-imaging the city: the transformation of Birmingham's urban landscape. *Geography* 81: 26–36; Hubbard, P. 1996. Urban design and city regeneration: Social representations of entrepreneurial landscapes. *Urban Studies* 33: 1441–61; Hula, R. 1990. The two Baltimores. In *Leadership and urban regeneration: Cities in North America and Europe.* vol. 37. *Urban Affairs Annual Reviews*. Newbury Park, CA: Sage, 191-215; Loftman, P., and B. Nevin. 1996. Going for growth: Prestige projects in three British cities. *Urban Studies* 33: 991–1019; Neill, W. J. V., D. Fitzsimons, and B. Murtagh. 1995. *Reimaging the pariah city: Urban development in Belfast and Detroit*. Brookfield, VT: Ashgate Publishing Company; Rutheiser, Charles. 1996. *Imagineering Atlanta: The politics of place in the city of dreams.* London, UK: Verso.

14. Morgan, N., and A. Pritchard. 1998. *Tourism promotion and power: Creating images, creating identities.* Chichester, UK: John Wiley.

15. Hall and Hubbard, *The entrepreneurial city*, 28.

16. Downs, R., and D. Stea. 1973. *Image and environment: Cognitive mapping and spatial behavior.* Chicago, IL: Aldine; Holcomb, B. 1972. The influence of culture on perception of the urban environment. Ph.D. dissertation, University of Colorado; Lynch, *The image of the city.*

17. Baudrillard, J. 1983. *Simulations.* New York, NY: Semiotext; Giddens, A. 1990. *The consequences of modernity.* Cambridge, UK: Polity.

18. See, for example, chapters by Holcomb and others in the collections by J. R. Gold and S. V. Ward, eds., *Place promotion: The use of publicity and marketing to sell towns and regions* (Chichester, UK: John Wiley, 1994); D. Judd and S. Fainstein, eds., *The tourist city* (New Haven, CT: Yale University Press, 1999); and G. Kearns and C. Philo, eds., *Selling places: The city as cultural capital, past and present* (Oxford, UK: Pergamon, 1993). See also Morgan and Pritchard, *Tourism promotion and power,* and Ward, *Selling places.*

19. Ward, *Selling places,* 185.

20. Ward, *Selling places,* 188.

21. Lynch, K. 1972. *What time is this place?* Cambridge, MA: MIT Press, 1.

22. Ward, *Selling places.*

23. Millennium Commission. 1999. World Wide Web site of The Millennium Commission, London, UK, at www.millennium.gov.uk (retrieved June 1999).

24. Holcomb, B. 1998. Landscapes of the millennium. Poster presented at the Annual Meetings of the Association of American Geographers. Boston (March).

25. *New York Times.* 1998. Editorial, Tony Blair's millennium dome. March 5, A28.

26. Segedy, J. 1997. How important is "quality of life" in location decisions and local economic development? In *Dilemmas of Urban Economic Development. Urban Affairs Annual Reviews* 47. Thousand Oaks, CA: Sage.

27. Weber, B. 1997. Cities are fostering the arts as a way to save downtown. *New York Times* (November 18): A1, 24.

28. Wade, D. ed. 2000. Renaissance Britain. *Sunday Times Magazine.* London, UK. April 30.

29. Bagli, C. 1998. Investors bet on revival for troubled Newark. *New York Times* (July 5): A1, 18.

30. Bianchini, F., and M. Parkinson. 1993. *Cultural policy and urban regeneration.* Manchester, UK: Manchester University Press; Boyle and Hughes, The politics of the representation of the "real"; Damer, S. 1990. *Glasgow: Going for a song.* London, UK: Lawrence and Wishart.

31. Quoted in Boyle and Hughes, The politics of the representation of the "real," 220.

32. Boyle and Hughes, The politics of the representation of the "real," 220, 221.

33. Boyle and Hughes, The politics of urban entrepreneurialism in Glasgow.

34. Kantor, P. 2000. Can regionalism save poor cities? Politics, institutions, and interests in Glasgow. *Urban Affairs Review* 34, 6: 794–820.

35. Noll, R., and A. Zimbalist, eds. 1997. *Sports, jobs and taxes: The economic impact of sports teams and stadiums.* Washington, DC: The Brookings Institution.

36. McMenemy, T. 1991. The old shell game. *In These Times* (May 1–7).

37. Miller, T. 1998. Sports venues bring economic energy back downtown. *Urban Land* 57, 2: 53–5.

38. Holcomb, B. 1999. Marketing cities for tourism. In D. Judd and S. Fainstein, eds., *The tourist city.* New Haven: Yale University Press, 107–23.

39. Law, C. 1994. *Urban tourism: Attracting visitors to large cities.* London, UK: Mansell, 101.

40. Rutheiser, *Imagineering Atlanta.*

41. Bryson, B. 2000. Sydney. *National Geographic* 98, 2 (August): 2–25; McGuigan, C. 2000. The good, the bad, the boring. *Newsweek* (June 5): 58–60.

42. Holcomb, B., and M. Luongo. 1996. Gay tourism in the United States. *Annals of Tourism Research* 23, 3: 711–3.

43. Cramb, G. 1998. Gay Games prove commercial success. *Financial Times* (August 1, 2): A2; Johnson, K. 1998. Event founded to fight bias is accused of it. *New York Times* (August 1): A1, C2.

44. Hughes, H. 1998. Sexuality, tourism and space: the case of gay visitors to Amsterdam. In D. Tyler, Y. Guerrier, and M. Robertson, eds., *Managing tourism in cities: Policy, process and practice.* Chichester, UK: Wiley; Morgan, N., and A. Pritchard, *Tourism promotion and power.*

45. Hall and Hubbard, *The entrepreneurial city*, 29.

46. Hannigan, J. 1998. *Fantasy city: Pleasure and profit in the postmodern metropolis.* New York, NY: Routledge.

47. Levin, A. 1986. Building names for themselves. *Trenton Times* (October 5): C1.

48. Huxtable, A. L. 1979. Selling cities like soap. *New York Times* (January 16): A28.

49. Williams, R. 1977. Facelift for Detroit. *Saturday Review* 4 (May 14): 6–11.

50. See, for example, Berry, M., and M. Huxley. 1992. Big build: Property capital, the state and urban change in Australia. *International Journal of Urban and Regional Research* 16: 35–59; Loftman and Nevin, Going for growth; Neill, Fitzsimons and Murtagh, *Reimaging the pariah city*; Short, J. R. 1998. Urban imagineers: Boosterism and the representation of cities, in A. Jonas and D. Wilson, eds., *The Urban Growth Machine.* Albany, NY: SUNY Press; and Smyth, H. 1994. *Marketing the city: The role of flagship developments in urban regeneration.* London, UK: E & FN Spon.

51. http://www.newbrunswick.com (viewed June 1999).

52. Ward, *Selling places*, 228.

53. Mitchell, K. 1996. Visions of Vancouver: Ideology, democracy, and the future of urban development. *Urban Geography* 17, 6: 495.

54. Short, J., and Y. Kim. 1998. Urban crisis/urban representations: Selling the city in difficult times. In T. Hall and P. Hubbard, eds., *The entrepreneurial city: Geographies of politics, regime and representation.* Chichester, UK: Wiley, 55.

55. Lynch, *The image of the city.*

56. Kenny, J. T. 1995. Making Milwaukee famous: Cultural capital, urban image and the politics of place. *Urban Geography* 16: 440–58.

57. Croucher, S. 1997. Constructing the image of ethnic harmony in Toronto, Canada: The politics of problem definition and nondefinition. *Urban Affairs Review* 32, 3: 319–47.

58. Deakin and Edwards, *The enterprise culture and the inner city*, 3, 4.

3. Eugenie Ladner Birch

1. Bowman, C. 1998. Interview by Eugenie Birch with C. Bowman, Center for Community Partnerships, University of Pennsylvania, Philadelphia, PA. October 12; Morton, J. 1998. Interview by Eugenie Birch with J. Morton, Morton-Jennings, New York City, NY. October 15.

2. Bronx Overall Economic Development Corporation (OEDC). n.d. Folder.

3. Bagli, C. 1998. In Yankee bleachers, triumph and troubles, Bronx offers stadium plan for keeping team. *New York Times* (September 28): B1, B3; Beyer Blinder Belle Architects and Planners. 1998. Safe at home, Yankee Stadium in the Bronx. Office of the Bronx Borough President. September.

4. Hall, T. 1999. A South Bronx very different from the cliché. *New York Times* (February 14): 11-1.

5. Community Board Three. 1993. *Partnership for the future.* New York, NY: Community Board Three.

6. New York City Department of City Planning. 1993. Briefing sheet (November 10), 2; New York City Department of City Planning, New York City Department of Environmental Protection. 1994. *Melrose Commons URA, final environmental impact statement.* New York. April.

7. Bronx OEDC (n.d.).

8. This chapter builds on T. A. Reiner and M. Hindery, City planning: Images of the ideal and existing city. In L. Rodwin and R. M. Hollister, eds. 1984. *Cities of the mind: Images and themes of the city in the social sciences.* New York: Plenum, 133–47.

9. Burrows, E. G., and M. Wallace. 1999. *Gotham: A history of New York City to 1898.* New York: Oxford, 743, 1054.

10. Hermalyn and Ultan observe: "By 1934 housing in the borough had many more times the amenities than that of the other boroughs: almost 99 percent of the residences had private bathrooms; about 95 percent, central heating; and more than 97 percent, hot water." Hermalyn, G. D., and L. Ultan. 1995. Bronx. In Kenneth T. Jackson, ed. 1995. *The encyclopedia of New York City.* New Haven: Yale University Press, 142–6.

11. Ultan, L., and G. Hermalyn. 1988. *Beautiful Bronx: 1920–1950.* New York, NY: Crown.

12. New York City Housing Authority. 1991. Project data. New York: NYCHA Office of Program Planning.

13. Salins, P. D. 1980. *The ecology of housing destruction*. New York: New York University Press; Schwartz, J. 1995. Rent regulation. In Jackson, *The encyclopedia of New York City*, 998.

14. Women's City Club. 1977. *With love and affection: A study of building abandonment.* New York.

15. Caro, R. A. 1974. *The power broker*. New York: Knopf, 890–4.

16. New York City Planning Commission. 1969b. *Plan for New York City, 2: The Bronx*. New York: Planning Commission.

17. Committee on Housing Statistics. 1967. *Housing statistics handbook*. New York: Committee on Housing Statistics, 45; Stegman, M.A. 1985. *Housing in New York City: Study of a city, 1984*. New York: Department of Housing Preservation and Development, 29.

18. New York City Planning Commission, *Plan for New York City, 2: The Bronx*, 18–20; Stegman, *Housing in New York City,* passim; Women's City Club, *With love and affection*, 22.

19. New York City Planning Commission. 1969a, 1969b. *Plan for New York City.* vols. 2 (*The Bronx*) and 4. New York: City Planning Commission.

20. Plan for New York City. 1971. *New York Planning Review* 17, 1 (Summer): 1–27.

21. Spatt, B. M. 1969. Dissenting report of Commissioner Spatt. In *Plan for New York City, 1: Critical Issues.* New York: City Planning Commission.

22. Barnett, J. 1998. Interview by Eugenie Birch with J. Barnett, Professor of City Planning, University of Pennsylvania, and former member of the New York City Department of City Planning, Urban Design Group. October 15.

23. See, for example, National Advisory Commission on Civil Disorders (Kerner Commission). 1968. *Report.* New York: Dutton.

24. Hyman, H. 1998. Interview by Eugenie Birch with Herbert Hyman, former head of New York City Model Cities program for East Harlem. October 10; Mittenthal, S. J. 1969. Citizen participation and Model Cities. Unpublished Ph.D. dissertation, Columbia University, New York; Spiegel, H. B. C. 1998. Interview by Eugenie Birch with H. B. C. Spiegel, Professor Emeritus, Hunter College, New York. October 10.

25. New York City Planning Commission, *Plan for New York City, 2: The Bronx.*

26. New York City Planning Commission, *Plan for New York City, 2: The Bronx.*

27. Rooney, J. 1995. *Organizing the South Bronx.* Albany: State University of New York Press, 56.

28. Rooney, *Organizing the South Bronx*, 58.

29. After passage of Local Law 45 (1977) allowing for city foreclosures on tax-delinquent properties after one year as an effort to forestall further deterioration or arson, the city would be even more besieged. At the peak, the city owned more than one hundred thousand units, about half in occupied buildings and the remainder, vacant abandoned buildings. Between 1984 and 1991 the Bronx had 30 to 40 percent of the city's total occupied stock (Stegman, M. A. 1988. *Housing and vacancy report, New York City 1987.* New York: Department of Housing Preservation and Development, 206; Stegman, M. A. 1993. *Housing and vacancy report, New York City 1991.* New York: Department of Housing Preservation and Development, 77–81).

30. By 1984, Stegman reports that the city owned 25 percent of the housing stock in the South Bronx, about half in public housing and half in tax-delinquent buildings for which the city had taken title in response to Local Law 45, the "fast foreclosure" law (Stegman, *Housing in New York City*; Fried, J. P. "City's housing administrator proposes 'planned shrinkage' of some slums." *New York Times* (February 3, 1976): 35; DeRienzo, H. 1989. Planning shrinkage: The final phase. *City Limits* (April): 10–11.

31. Yardley, J. 1997. Clinton praises Bronx renewal as U.S. model. *New York Times* (December 11): 1, B10.

32. Wolfe, T. 1987. *The bonfire of the vanities.* New York, NY: Farrar, Straus and Giroux.

33. Wolfe, *The bonfire of the vanities*, 37–8.

34. Lee, R. 1984. The affordable option: Charlotte Street manufactured housing. In E. L. Birch, ed., *The unsheltered woman: Housing issues of the eighties.* New Brunswick, NJ: Center for Urban Policy Research, 277–82.

35. Schwartz, A. 1999. New York City and subsidized housing: Impacts and lessons of the City's $5 billion capital budget housing plan. *Housing Policy Debate* 10, 4: 839–78.

36. Blakely, E. J. 1994. *Planning local economic development, theory and practice.* Thousand Oaks, CA: Sage Publications; Wilson, W. J. 1996. *When work disappears: The world of the new urban poor.* New York: Random House.

37. It should be remembered that Charlotte Street represented a remarkable achievement: new, middle-income housing in an area few believed would ever see such construction ever again.

38. Commission on Homelessness. 1992. *The way home: A new direction in social policy.* New York (February), 66.

39. Manhattan Borough President David N. Dinkins's Task Force on Housing for Homeless Families. 1987. *A city is not a home.* New York; Mayor's Task Force on Homelessness. 1987. *Toward a comprehensive policy on homelessness.* New York.

40. Commission on Homelessness, 67–8.

41. The commission did not succeed in developing a general plan for the city until 1969. See "City planning urged by art group" (*New York Times*, February 24, 1936); "Riegelman urges 50-year city plan" (*New York Times*, March 18, 1936); "Thacher appeals for City Planning Board under proposed charter; would prevent waste" (*New York Times*, May 3, 1936); "Mayor scores foes of city planning" (*New York Times*, May 5, 1936); "City 'master plan' put before the public" (*New York Times*, February 24, 1941); "Master plan ideas 'silly,' says Moses" (*New York Times*, December 12, 1941).

42. Passow, S. 1986. The legacy of city planning. *New York Affairs* 9, 4 (Fall): 77–89; Summary provisions of the city's new charter. 1936. *New York Times.* November 5.

43. New York City Planning Department. 1989. *The challenge ahead—50th anniversary conference proceedings*. New York.

44. Birch, E. L. 1996. Planning in a world city: New York and its communities. *Journal of the American Planning Association* 62, 4 (Autumn): 442–59; Bressi, T., ed. 1993. *Planning and zoning New York City: Yesterday, today and tomorrow.* New Brunswick, NJ: Center for Urban Policy Research; The long march to charter revision: An historical review. 1990. *The Charter Revision Review* 3, 3 (Winter): 6–10; New York City Department of City Planning. 1991. *Planning New York City, 1991–1992*. New York.

45. See H. Gans, *The urban villagers* (New York: Free Press, 1962) and P. Davidoff, Advocacy and pluralism in planning. *Journal of the Institute of Planners* 21, 4 (November 1965).

46. *New directions for the Bronx: Toward a more beautiful Bronx—Ecology, education, better waterfront usage, and historic preservation. Report of the Bronx Development Council.* Report distributed as a newspaper supplement (*Daily News*, February 22, 1990): 1–17.

47. Birch, Planning in a world city.

48. Bronx Center Steering Committee. 1993. *Bronx Center*, 16.

49. Community Board Three, *Partnership for the future*.

50. New York City Department of City Planning/Bronx Office. 1989. *162st Street study. Melrose Commons: A redevelopment plan for the South Bronx.* New York. October.

51. *Melrose Commons URA, final environmental impact statement* (note 5), 3.3-15 to 3.3–25.

52. Rothstein, M. 1994. A renewal plan in the Bronx advances. *New York Times* (July 10): 9-1, 8.

53. Office of the President of the Borough of the Bronx, Bureau of Planning and Development. 1992. *The Bronx Center land use and urban design study*. April; Ferrer, F. 1994. Statement of the Borough President. Attachment B, Department of City Planning Briefing Sheet for Melrose Commons. February 23.

54. *Bronx Center land use and urban design study*; Ferrer, Statement of the Borough President.

55. Rothstein, A renewal plan in the Bronx advances, 8.

56. Ferrer, Statement of the Borough President.

57. Cary, C., P. Stand, and L. Weintraub. 1993. We stay: How Melrose hopes to build its future. *The Liveable City* 16, 2.

58. Alvarez, L. 1996. City plans to auction off a Bronx group's dream. *New York Times*. September 29; The courthouse of last resort. 1996. *Village Voice* (July 30): 12; Kappstatter, B. 1996a. Courthouse sale hits bump. *New York Daily News* (October 2); Kappstatter, B. 1996b. Rudy asked to stop courthouse sale. *New York Daily News* (October 21).

59. Nos Quedamos. 1994. Outline for proposed Melrose Commons standards and draft guidelines. January; Nos Quedamos. n.d. Statement of planning principles (Advisory, not part of urban renewal plan).

60. Kwartler, M. 1998. Interview by Eugenie Birch with Michael Kwartler, Environmental Simulation Lab. October 16; Moed, A. 1998. Neighborhood. *Metropolis* (Jan./Feb.): 62.

61. Moed, Neighborhood, 62.

62. Cary et al., We stay: How Melrose hopes to build its future.

63. Nos Quedamos, Statement of planning principles.

64. Robbins, I. D. 1994. Letter to Joseph Rose, Chairman, New York City Planning Commission. March 9.

65. Wright, D. 1994. Commissioner, Department of Housing Preservation and Development. Letter to Joseph Rose, Chairman, New York City Planning Commission. April 22.

66. The author's notes at the time of the vote record the high level of sentiment involved. She recorded that although the commission as a whole wanted to assure passage of the plan, which all agreed was excellent, a large minority objected to the modifying language, believing that it weakened the plan. She also observed: "The vote is a significant challenge to who is boss, the city agencies against the borough president and community groups." Special meeting of the New York City Planning Commission, April 25, 1994.

67. Alvarez, City plans to auction off a Bronx group's dream; The courthouse of last resort; Kappstatter, Courthouse sale hits bump; Zimmerman, B. 1995. Memorandum to Richard Kahan. June 13.

68. The courthouse of last resort, 12.

69. Cole, D. V. 1997. Letter to Fernando Ferrer, Borough President, and Genevieve Brooks, Deputy Borough President. October 22; Ferrer, F. 1998. Letter to Teresa Bainton, Acting Director of Multi-family Housing, U.S. Department of Housing and Urban Development. June 18; Kappstatter, Courthouse sale hits bump; Proposed agenda for meeting with Commissioner Richard Roberts. n.d.

70. Named after the biblical rebuilder of Jerusalem, the Nehemiah housing program began with the much heralded success of SBC's sister group, East Brooklyn Churches (EBC). EBC built fifteen hundred units in Brownsville and East New York, leading the U.S. Department of Housing and Urban Development to champion such programs nationally (Glaser, L. 1989. The powers to be. *City Limits* [October]: 24-28).

71. Stuart, L. 1999. Come let us rebuild the walls of Jerusalem. In Robert D. Carle and Louis A. Decaro, eds., *Signs of hope in the city: Ministries of community renewal.* Valley Forge, PA: Judson Press.

72. Stuart, Come let us rebuild the walls of Jerusalem, 133.

73. Stuart, Come let us rebuild the walls of Jerusalem, 130.

74. Rosenbloom, Salama, Shill and Upham. n.d. Land use, housing and community development in New York City (a case study of alternative development models for construction of affordable housing in the South Bronx).

75. Rosenbloom, Salama, Shill, and Upham, Land use, housing, and community development.

76. Glaser, The powers to be; Rosenbloom, Salama, Shill, and Upham, Land use, housing, and community development; Stuart, Come let us rebuild the walls of Jerusalem.

77. Stuart, Come let us rebuild the walls of Jerusalem, 137.

4. Patricia Burgess, Ruth Durack, and Edward W. Hill

1. An earlier version of this chapter was presented at the "Imaging the City Colloquium" of the Department of Urban Studies and Planning at the Massachusetts Institute of Technology on November 2, 1998. Between January and September of 1999 it was substantially revised and refocused in response to discussion generated at the initial presentation. We thank several people for their close readings and comments on the paper. These include Robert Jaquay, Larry Ledebur, Richard Shatten, Ken Silliman, and Steve Strnisha. Not all agree with our interpretations and comments, but all were very helpful in correcting factual mistakes and in challenging our assertions. We also benefited from the comments of the participants in the seminar session at MIT, especially Larry Vale.

2. Hill, Edward W. 1995. The Cleveland economy: A case study of economic restructuring. In W. Dennis Keating, Norman Krumholz, and David Perry, eds. 1995. *Cleveland: A metropolitan reader.* Kent, OH: Kent State University Press; W. Dennis Keating, Norman Krumholz, and David Perry. 1995b. The ninety-year war over public power in Cleveland. In Keating et al.,

Cleveland: A metropolitan reader; Magnet, Myron. 1995. How business bosses saved a sick city (reprinted from *Fortune* [1989]). In Keating et al., *A metropolitan reader.*

3. Magnet, How businesses bosses saved a sick city; NBC Nightly News, November 4, 1994.

4. Austin, J. E., and A. L. Strimling. 1996. The Cleveland turnaround (a): Responding to the crisis (1978–1988). Boston, MA: Harvard Business School Publishing. Rev. November 30, 1996. Case Number 9-769-151; Austin, J. E., and A. L. Strimling. 1996. The Cleveland turnaround (b): Building on progress (1989–1996). Boston, MA: Harvard Business School Publishing. Rev. November 30, 1996. Case Number 9-769-152; Magnet, How business bosses saved a sick city.

5. Adams, B. 1997. Cleveland: The partnership city. In Bruce Adams and John Parr, eds. 1997. *Boundary crossers: Case studies of how America's metropolitan regions work.* College Park, MD: Academy of Leadership Press; Peirce, Neal, and Curtis Johnson, eds. 1997. *Boundary crossers: Community leadership for a global age.* College Park, MD: Academy of Leadership Press; Purdy, Janis. 1995. Revitalizing Cleveland: Organizing citizens to respond to the challenge. *National Civic Review* (Fall): 340–7.

6. Swanstrom, Todd. 1995. Urban populism, fiscal crisis, and the new political economy. In Keating et al., *Cleveland: A metropolitan reader*; Bartimole, Roldo. 1995. Who governs the corporate hand? In Keating et al., *Cleveland: A metropolitan reader.*

7. Hill, Edward W. 1995. The Cleveland economy: A case study of economic restructuring. In Keating et al. 1995, *Cleveland: A metropolitan reader,* op. cit.

8. This appears to be the case in other large cities as well. Robert Mier, reflecting on his time as Chicago's development director, said: "The question [of economic development] is, "How does an agenda and operating ad hoc go hand in hand?" Mier's quote is found in Norman Krumholz and Pierre Clavel, *Reinventing cities: Equity planners tell their stories* (Philadelphia, PA: Temple University Press, 1994, p. 79) and in Robert Giloth and Wim Wiewel, Equity development in Chicago: Robert Mier's ideas and practice, *Economic Development Quarterly* 10, 3: 204–16.

9. Hill, Edward W. 1997. Revitalizing Cleveland, not comeback Cleveland: Local and federal forces that rebuilt a region. In Bennett Harrison and Marcus Weiss, 1997. *Rethinking national economic development policy.* Washington, DC: Economic Development Administration.

10. Jaquay, Robert. 1991. Civic Vision: participatory city planning in Cleveland in the 1980s. Case study prepared for the Kennedy School of Government Case Program, Harvard College, Boston, Massachusetts; W. Dennis Keating, Norman Krumholz, and David Perry. 1995b. The ninety-year war over public power in Cleveland. In Keating et al., *Cleveland: A metropolitan reader.*

11. The first was by McKinsey & Co. (1981), completed at the request of Cleveland Tomorrow. Although it was not part of the strategy's evolution as such, suggestions in a 1982 study by Rand Corporation that the region develop policy research capacity played into the implementation (*The Cleveland metropolitan economy.* Santa Monica, CA: Rand Corporation). This, in turn, led to the foundation of Regional Economic Issues, which eventually became part of the Weatherhead School of Business at Case Western Reserve University. The other two documents that trace the strategy's evolution are reports issued by Cleveland Tomorrow itself (*Cleveland Tomorrow: Building on a new foundation.* Cleveland, OH: Cleveland Tomorrow, 1988; *Investing in the future: Cleveland Tomorrow's strategic picture for the 90s.* Cleveland, OH: Cleveland Tomorrow, January 1993).

12. Shatten, Richard. 1995. *Cleveland Tomorrow: A practicing model of new roles and processes for corporate leadership in cities.* In Keating et al., *Cleveland: A metropolitan reader*; Hill, Edward W. 1997. Policy lessons from Cleveland's economic restructuring; and accompanying case study. The Urban Center, Cleveland State University, Cleveland, Ohio.

13. Cleveland Tomorrow. 1988. *Cleveland Tomorrow: Building on a new foundation.* Cleveland, OH: Cleveland Tomorrow; Cleveland Tomorrow. 1993. *Investing in the future: Cleveland Tomorrow's strategic picture for the 90s.* Cleveland, OH: Cleveland Tomorrow. January.

14. Jaquay, Civic Vision.

15. City of Cleveland, Department of Economic Development (DED). 1983 (approx.). Summary of mission, goals, policies, and strategies. Cleveland, Ohio: DED. Unpublished mimeo.

16. Jaquay, Civic Vision; Hill, Policy lessons from Cleveland's economic restructuring.

17. Cleveland Tomorrow, *Cleveland Tomorrow: Building on a new foundation,* 25.

18. During this time, discussions about a new stadium for the Cleveland Browns football team—whether to replace the existing one in the same location or at a different site—were under way. The Browns were then moved by their owner to Baltimore, where they became the Baltimore Ravens; a new Browns franchise began playing in a new Browns Stadium at North Coast Harbor in the fall of 1999.

19. Keating, W. Dennis, Norman Krumholz, and John Metzger. 1995. Postpopulist public–private partnerships. In Keating et al., *Cleveland: A metropolitan reader.*

20. Bingham, R. D., and Veronica Z. Kalich. 1996. Blest be the tie that binds: Suburbs and the dependence hypothesis. *Journal of Urban Affairs* 18, 2: 153–72.

21. Hill, Policy lessons from Cleveland's economic restructuring.

22. Steven Strnisha, at an April 2, 1995, forum at Cleveland State University, said that "upwards to 70 percent of the income taxes paid are actually paid by suburbanites." The City of Cleveland gets almost 60 percent of its operating budget from the wage tax. The suburban share (70 percent) of the wage tax's share of the operating budget (60 percent) is 42 percent of the operating budget. *See* Bingham and Kalich, Blest be the tie that binds, for the full quote.

23. Cleveland Tomorrow, *Building on a new foundation*; Cleveland Tomorrow, *Investing in the future.*

24. Deloitte & Touche. 1994. *Convention and visitors assessment and planning study, Phase I.* Cleveland, OH: Convention and Visitors Bureau of Greater Cleveland; Iannone, Donald T. 1994. *Northeast Ohio's visitor industry: Development prospects and competitive advantage.* Cleveland, OH: The Urban Center, Cleveland State University; Regional Economic Issues. 1992. *Visitors and the economy of Northeast Ohio.* Case Western Reserve University, Cleveland, Ohio.

25. Cleveland Tomorrow, *Building on a new foundation*, 21; Cleveland Tomorrow, *Investing in the future,* 9, 19–20.

26. *See* Bingham and Kalich, Blest be the tie that binds.

27. Richard Shatten provided us with a list of fourteen intermediaries that were either begun, or assisted, by Cleveland Tomorrow. The following are devoted to non-downtown neighborhood development: Shorebank; Enterprise Development, Inc.; Cleveland Housing Network; and Neighborhood Progress, Inc. The Cleveland Advanced Manufacturing Program; Work in Northeast Ohio; Akron's EPIC (an intermediary devoted to the polymer industry); Cleveland's Edison Biotech Institute; University Technology, Inc.; and the Technology Leadership Council are devoted to regional business development and innovation. Primus Capital Fund, the Ohio Innovation Fund, and North Coast Capital Fund are all capital market instruments. Health Quality Choice was founded to respond to the business community's concern over rising health-care costs in the early 1990s. This list does not include place-based development organizations such as Gateway's or Playhouse Square's development organizations.

28. Hill, Policy lessons from Cleveland's economic restructuring. The neighborhood development corporations have adopted housing development as a key product. This is partially due

to their funding relationships with the two major community foundations and the role played by Neighborhood Progress, Inc., as the wholesaler and development consultant to these projects, with leverage provided by a combination of the Local Initiatives Support Corporation (LISC), Enterprise Development, Inc., Shorebank, Cleveland's development fund, and Cleveland's residential property tax abatement program.

29. Jaquay, Civic Vision.

30. *See* Shatten, *Cleveland Tomorrow: A practicing model.*

31. Jaquay, Civic Vision.

32. Ibid.

33. Ibid.

34. Fagen, Jocelyn, and Ziona Austrian. 1997. Downtown Cleveland's economic base, 1989–1996. The Urban Center, Cleveland State University, Cleveland, Ohio (May 2), 5.

35. Hill, Edward W., and John Brennan. Forthcoming. Employment specialization within Ohio's metropolitan areas. In John Brennan and Edward W. Hill, eds., *Where is the renaissance?* Washington, DC: The Brookings Institution.

36. *Civic Vision 2000: Downtown plan* (1989); *Civic Vision 2000: Citywide plan* (1991). Cleveland, OH: City Planning Commission.

37. *Civic Vision 2000 and beyond:* Vol. I, an overview; *Civic Vision 2000 and beyond:* Vol. II. 1998. Cleveland, OH: Cleveland Tomorrow.

38. Roman, J. K. 1998. Keynote address to the Great Lakes Economic Development Conference. Federal Reserve Bank of Cleveland, Cleveland, Ohio. October 15; Strnisha, S. 1998. Talk to students in the Sixth Year Urban Design Studio of the School of Architecture and Environmental Design, Kent State University, Ohio. September 11.

39. Jaquay, Civic Vision.

40. Lubinger, Bill. 1996. Updating plan for Cleveland: Community leaders taking a fresh look at development issues. *Plain Dealer* (December 6); Lubinger, Bill. 1997. Public input sought at forum on downtown development. *Plain Dealer* (October 5); Lubinger, Bill. 1998. Vision for city's lakefront unveiled. *Plain Dealer* (February 6); Litt, Steven. 1997. Revival and relief on Euclid. *Plain Dealer* (December 21); Litt, Steven. 1998. City planning a private affair. *Plain Dealer* (May 3); Litt, Steven. 1998. Lakefront plan lacks stirring vision. *Plain Dealer* (February 15); Litt, Steven. 1998. Public asked to review "Civic Vision" of downtown Cleveland. *Plain Dealer* (June 30).

41. Litt, City planning a private affair; Litt, Lakefront plan lacks stirring vision; Litt, Public asked to review "Civic Vision" of downtown Cleveland; Lubinger, Vision for city's lakefront unveiled.

42. Litt, Steven. 1999. Public space sacrificed in new lakefront proposals. *Plain Dealer* (June 30); Lubinger, Bill. 1999. Visions for the North Coast. *Plain Dealer* (June 27).

43. Lubinger, Visions for the North Coast.

44. Litt, Steven. 1999. The meaning behind Disney's designs. *Plain Dealer* (July 25).

45. Hannigan, John. 1998. *Fantasy city: Pleasure and profit in the postmodern metropolis.* New York, NY: Routledge.

5. Larry R. Ford

1. Castells, M. 1989. *The informational city.* Oxford, UK: Blackwell; King, A., ed. 1991. *Culture, globalization and the world-system.* London, UK: Macmillan; Leaf, M. 1996. Building the road for the BMW: Culture, vision, and the extended metropolitan region of Jakarta. *Environment and Planning A*, 28: 1617–35; Mueller, G. 1992. Watching global real estate mar-

kets. *Urban Land* (March): 30–2; Murphy, R. 1980. *The fading of the Maoist vision: City and country in China's development.* Andover, MA: Methuen; Sassen, S. 1991. *The global city.* Princeton, NJ: Princeton University Press; Sassen, S. 1994. *Cities in a world economy*. Thousand Oaks, CA: Pine Forge Press; Thrift, N. 1992. Muddling through: World orders and civilization. *The Professional Geographer* 44, 1: 3–7; Zukin, S. 1992. The city as a landscape of power: London and New York as global financial capitals. In L. Budd and S. Whimser, eds., *Global finance and urban living.* Andover, MA: Routledge, 195–223.

2. Olds, K. 1995. Globalization and the production of new urban spaces: Pacific Rim megaprojects in the late 20th century. *Environment and Planning A*, 27: 1713–43; Olds, K. 1997. Globalizing Shanghai: the "global intelligence corps" and the building of Pudong. *Cities* 14, 2: 109–23.

3. *Architecture*. 1998. Special issue: American exports; Is Asia's boom over?; Shanghai rising; and American architecture: The view from abroad. January; *Asiaweek.* 1998. The great Asian sale. February 20: 28–51; *World Architecture*. 1997a. Top 250. 52: 11–6; *World Architecture*. 1997b. Country focus: Japan; and Profile: The Stubbins Associates. 61: 26–55 and 56–79; *Asian Business*. 1998. Property blues: Facing the music, by Laura O'Shea, 31, 1: 12–9; Mitchell, W. 1997. Do we still need skyscrapers? *Scientific American* (December): 112–3.

4. Chen, N. 1998. Interview by the author with N. Chen, president of the Hong Kong Institute of Architects; Marshall, R. 1998. Interview by the author with R. Marshall, architect with Bagot Woods, Kuala Lumpur; Olds, Globalization and the production of new urban spaces; Olds, Globalizing Shanghai.

5. Chen, Interview.

6. Olds, Globalizing Shanghai.

7. Chong, F. 1997. Asia: Where to now? *Property Magazine* 12, 4: 12–5.

8. Pacelle, M. 1996. Asia major: Hot market, big egos draw top architects to tall buildings. *Chicago Tribune*, April 14: 3Q.

9. Ford, L. 1994. *Cities and buildings: skyscrapers, skidrows, and suburbs.* Baltimore, MD: Johns Hopkins University Press.

10. Gottmann, J. 1966. Why the skyscraper? *Geographical Review* 56: 190–212.

11. Urban Redevelopment Authority. 1996. *New downtown: Ideas for the city of tomorrow.* Singapore: Urban Redevelopment Authority.

12. Pelli, C., C. Thornton, and L. Joseph. 1997. The world's tallest buildings. *Scientific American* (December): 92c–101.

13. Murphy, *The fading of the Maoist vision*; Olds, Globalizing Shanghai.

14. Garreau, J. 1991. *Edge city: Life on the new frontier.* New York, NY: Doubleday.

15. Urban Redevelopment Authority. 1995. *Downtown core planning report.* Singapore: Urban Redevelopment Authority.

16. Melvin, J. 1996. I want one like that. *World Architecture* 52: 63–7; Pacelle, Asia major.

17. Coxe, W., and M. Hayden. 1993. Report from East Asia. *UIA project work group: Trends in private practice*. Rocky Hill, NJ: International Union of Architects; *World Architecture*, Top 250.

18. *World Architecture*, Top 250.

19. Lynch, K. 1960. *The image of the city.* Cambridge, MA: MIT Press.

6. Judith A. Martin and Sam Bass Warner Jr.

1. Lynch, K. 1960. *The image of the city*. Cambridge, MA: MIT Press.

2. For accounts of such vernacular landscapes, *see*: Kuntsler, W. 1993. *The geography of*

nowhere. New York, NY: Touchstone; Langdon, P., 1994. *A better place to live*. Amherst, MA: University of Massachusetts Press; Lynch K. *The image of the city*; Lynch, K. 1976. *Managing the sense of a region*. Cambridge, MA: MIT Press; Lynch, K., D. Appleyard, and J. R. Myer. 1964. *The view from the road*. Cambridge, MA: MIT Press; Martin, J. A., and D. Lanegran. 1983. *Where we live*. Minneapolis, MN: University of Minnesota Press. Meinig, D. W., ed. 1979. *The interpretation of ordinary landscapes*. New York, NY: Oxford University Press; Sudjic, D. 1992. *The 100-mile city*. London: A Deutsch; Warner, Sam Bass Jr., 1983. The management of multiple urban images, in Derek Fraser and Anthony Sutcliffe, eds., *The pursuit of urban history*. London, UK: Edward Arnold.

3. Lynch, *The image of the city*, 112.

7. Henry Jenkins

1. Lynch, K. 1960. *The image of the city.* Cambridge, MA: MIT Press, 1.

2. Baudrillard, J. 1988. *America*. Translated by C. Turner. London, UK: Verso Books, 56.

3. Barbera, A., S. Cortellazo, and D.Tomasi, eds. 1997. New York, New York: La citta, il mito, il cinema. Cited in Chinese boxes and Russian dolls: Tracking the elusive cinematic city by C. McArthur. In David B. Clarke, ed., *The cinematic city*. London, UK: Routledge, 42. Allen's more recent *Manhattan Murder Mystery* (1993) amplifies this impression of New York as a cinematic city, combining location shooting with quotations of films ranging from *Lady from Shanghai* (1948) to Alfred Hitchcock's *Rear Window* (1954), suggesting that the characters inhabit a world already colonized by the movies.

4. There are, of course, many different ways one could explore the role of cinema in the construction of city images. One could, for example, follow Lynch's own lead, interviewing everyday citizens about their own mental maps of urban spaces, though in this case, looking at their recall of previous cinematic representations of the city. One could construct a statistical sample of all the Hollywood films produced that are set in a particular city or look only at those representations of the city that have been most commercially successful. Each of these projects would yield somewhat different insights into our core question: How has the cinema shaped our image of New York City? The core assumption behind this essay is that there may be something especially revealing about the ways that significant filmmakers from throughout the twentieth century struggled to reconcile the conflicting goal of telling a particular story and representing the diversity of urban life. I have purposely chosen films representing different periods and genres and posing alternative models for reconciling these aesthetic and ideological goals. What all of these films share is that they take the city as their theme and not simply their setting, and as a result, they tell us something of the process by which our mental images of the city are given aesthetic form and put into broader cultural circulation.

5. Lynch, *The image of the city,* 8–9.

6. de Certeau, M. 1988. Spatial stories. In *The practice of everyday life*. Translated by S. Rendall. Berkeley, CA: University of California Press, 115–30.

7. Singer, B. 1995. Modernity, hyperstimulus, and the rise of popular sensationalism. In L. Charney and V. R. Schwartz, eds., *Cinema and the invention of modern life*. Berkeley, CA: University of California Press, 95.

8. For discussions of the urban dominance of the economics of film exhibition, see Balio, T., ed., 1985, *The American film industry*. Madison, WI: University of Wisconsin. For discussions of film exhibition in small towns, see Fuller, K., 1996, *At the picture show: Small-town audiences and the creation of movie fan culture.* Washington, DC: Smithsonian Institution.

9. Cohen, M. 1995. Panoramic literature and the invention of every genres. In L. Charney

and V. R. Schwartz, eds., *Cinema and the invention of modern life.* Berkeley, CA: University of California Press, 231.

10. More recent examples of such panoramic films would be *New York Stories* (1989, Woody Allen, Francis Ford Coppola, Martin Scorsese) and *Four Rooms* (1995, Allison Anders, Alexandre Rockwell, Robert Rodriguez, Quentin Tarantino).

11. de Certeau 1988, 91.

12. de Certeau 1988, 92.

13. Boyarsky, A. 1996. Chicago à la carte. In R. Middleton, ed., *The idea of the city.* Cambridge, MA: MIT Press, 10–48. Boyarsky's emphasis on the continuity and consistency of these images across historical periods or geographically distinct cities parallels my own claim that there are strong continuities throughout the twentieth century in our cinematic representations of the city and especially in the kinds of aesthetic and ideological problems that surround the artistic goal of telling the story of the city.

14. de Certeau 1988, 97.

15. de Certeau 1988, 97.

16. Lynch's own focus on the ways cities are experienced and remembered by the people who live there, rather than on the abstract maps and architectural plans that dominated earlier generations of urban scholarship, might well satisfy de Certeau's desire for a more particularized account of moving through the city.

17. Lefebvre, H. 1996. Seen from the window. In E. Koffman and E. Lebas, editors and translators, *Writings on cities.* London, UK: Blackwell, 219.

18. Lefebvre 1996, 227.

19. Lynch himself drew upon analogies between urban form and musical structure to express his desire for a more sensuous and legible city space.

20. Kasinitz, P. 1995. Metropolis: Centre and symbol for our times. Cited in Something more than night: tales of the noir city by F. Krutnik. In D. B. Clarke, ed., *The cinematic city.* London, UK: Routledge, 11.

21. Tonnies, F. 1957. *Community and society (Gemeinschaft and Gesellschaft).* Translated by C. P. Loomis. East Lansing, MI: Michigan State University.

22. Lynch, *The image of the city*, 115.

8. Sandy Isenstadt

1. Mitchell, W. J. T. 1994. *Picture theory: Essays on verbal and visual representation.* Chicago: University of Chicago Press.

2. Culot, M., and L. Krier. 1978. The only path for architecture. *Oppositions: A Journal for Ideas and Criticism in Architecture* 14 (Fall): 39–53; Koolhaas, R. 1978. *Delirious New York: A retroactive manifesto for Manhattan.* New York, NY: Oxford University Press; Rowe, C., and F. Koetter. 1978. *Collage city*. Cambridge, MA: MIT Press.

3. Culot and Krier, The only path for architecture, 41.

4. Koolhaas, *Delirious New York*, 6, 74.

5. Krier, L. 1980. *Drawings, 1967–1980.* Brussels, Belgium: Archives d'Architecture Moderne.

6. *The Charlottesville Tapes*. 1985. Transcripts of the Conference Held at the University of Virginia School of Architecture, Charlottesville, Virginia, November 12 and 13, 1982. New York, NY: Rizzoli, 9–11, 22–36.

7. Koolhaas, *Delirious New York*, 162.

8. Koolhaas, R., and B. Mau. 1995. *S, M, L, XL.* New York, NY: Monicelli Press, 894–939.

9. Castells, M. 1989. *The informational city: Informational technology, economic restructuring, and the urban–regional process.* Oxford, UK: Blackwell.

10. Sennett, R. 1998. Process and form, work and place. Paper presented at the Imaging the City Colloquium, Massachusetts Institute of Technology, Cambridge. September.

11. Culot and Krier, The only path for architecture, 40.

12. Kentlands, Gaithersburg, Maryland. n.d. Promotional brochure from Kentlands Information Center, Gaithersburg, Maryland.

13. Koolhaas and Mau, *S, M, L, XL*, 170.

14. Koolhaas and Mau, *S, M, L, XL*, 1156–1209.

9. Thomas J. Campanella

1. Sorkin, M., ed. 1992. *Variations on a theme park: The new American city and the end of public space.* New York, NY: Noonday, xi.

2. White, M., and L. White. 1969. The American intellectual versus the American city. In Alexander B. Callow, ed., *American urban history*. New York, NY: Oxford University Press, 353.

3. Rourke, F. 1969. Urbanism and American democracy. In Alexander B. Callow, ed., *American Urban History*. New York, NY: Oxford University Press, 374.

4. Jefferson, T. 1784 [1972]. Notes on the State of Virginia. In A. Koch and W. Peden, eds., *The life and selected writings of Thomas Jefferson*. New York, NY: The Modern Library (1972), 280.

5. Cited in Rourke, *Urbanism and American democracy*, 374.

6. Marx, L. 1964. *The machine in the garden.* New York, NY: Oxford University Press, 5–11.

7. White and White, *The American intellectual,* 356; Wilson, H. F. 1936. *The hill country of northern New England.* New York, NY: Oxford University Press.

8. Belasco, W. J. 1979. *Americans on the road: From autocamp to motel, 1910–1945.* Cambridge, MA: MIT Press.

9. Campanella, T. J. 1997a. American curves: Gilmore D. Clarke and the modern civic landscape. *Harvard Design Magazine*. Summer.

10. Crosby, Stills, Nash, and Young. 1970. "Woodstock." From the album *Déjà Vu.* Atlantic 19118.

11. Campanella, T. J. 1997b. The rugged steed: Mythologies of the sport utility vehicle. *Harvard Design Magazine*. Fall.

12. Davis, M. 1990. *City of quartz.* New York, NY: Verso Books; Ellin, N. 1997. *Architecture of fear*. New York, NY: Princeton Architectural Press; Sorkin, *Variations on a theme park*.

13. Ellin, *Architecture of fear*, 32.

14. Webber, M. M. 1964. The urban place and the nonplace urban realm. In M. Webber, et al., eds., *Explorations into urban structure*. Philadelphia, PA: University of Pennsylvania Press, 79–89. Webber suggested that "urbanity" could be "more profitably conceived as a property of the amount and the variety of one's participation in the cultural life of a world of creative specialists, *of the amount and the variety of the information received* [emphasis added]," rather than a function of physical location and urban space. With new means of communication and access to information, urbanity—"the essence of urbanness"—is "no longer the exclusive trait of the urban dweller . . . increasingly the farmers themselves are participating in the urban life of the world."

15. Mitchell, W. J. 1995. *City of bits: Space, place, and the infobahn.* Cambridge, MA: MIT Press, 8.

16. Mumford, L. 1963. *Technics and civilization*. New York, NY: Harcourt, Brace & World, Inc., 239.

17. Emerging technologies such as low earth orbit (LEO) satellites, ubiquitous broadband cable service, and inexpensive access to wireless data networks will further dissolve the geo-spatial component of information access. The Iridium LEO satellite network enables telephony from nearly any point on earth, no matter how geographically remote.

18. Webber, M. M. 1968. The post-city age. *Daedalus* 97.

19. By employing "packet switching technology," data was broken into bundles (packets) and routed over parallel circuits simultaneously, assuring passage even if several routes were blocked.

20. Benedetti, P., and N. DeHart, eds. 1996. *Forward through rear-view mirror.* Cambridge, MA: MIT Press, 39, 51, 66.

21. Toffler, A. 1981. *The third wave.* New York, NY: Bantam Books, 200–4.

22. Action at a distance. 1914. *Scientific American* 77: 39.

23. Marx, *The machine in the garden*, 3.

24. Examples of positive city-imaging in interactive games include Shigeru Miyagawa's Star Festival, Rhinestone Publishing's Zero Zero, and SimCity.

25. Udell, S. 1998. Tribal rage. *Computer Games* 88 (March): 28.

26. *Computer Games*. 1998. 88 (February), 60, 94–5.

27. McLuhan, M. 1967. *Verbi-voco-visual explorations.* New York, NY: Something Else Press. Item 14.

28. The Playboy interview: Marshall McLuhan. 1969. *Playboy*. March.

29. Gilder, G. 1995. *Forbes ASAP* (February 27): 56; Moss, M., and A. Townsend. 1998. How telecommunications is transforming urban spaces. New York, NY: Taub Urban Research Center, New York University. Retrieved at *http://urban.nyu.edu/research/telecom-urban-spaces/*; Toffler, *The third wave*, 194, 203.

30. Gibson, W. 1993. *Virtual light*. New York, NY: Bantam Books, 14–63.

31. Stephenson, N. 1992. *Snow crash*. New York, NY: Bantam Books, 3–32.

32. Acronym for "the end of the world as we know it."

33. Feder, B. J., and A. Pollack. 1998. Computers and 2000: Race for security. *New York Times,* December 27: 1, 22–3.

34. Feder and Pollack, *Computers and 2000*, 22; McCullagh, D. 1998. Crunch time for Y2K suppliers. *Wired News.* November 5; Struckman, R. 1999. Bulk food sellers reap benefits from millenial movement. *Billings Gazette,* January 31; Struckman, Robert. 1999. Millennium fever. *Billings Gazette,* January 31.

35. Poulsen, K. 1998. The Y2K solution: Run for your life! *Wired* 6 (August): 122–5, 164–7.

10. Dennis Frenchman

1. Lynch, K. 1960. *The image of the city*. Cambridge, MA: MIT Press, 6.

2. See Judd, D. R., and S. S. Fainstein. 1999. *The tourist city.* New Haven, CT: Yale University Press.

3. Lynch, *The image of the city*, 71.

4. Eco, U. 1980. Function and sign: the semiotics of architecture. In G. Broadbent et al., eds., *Signs, symbols and architecture.* New York, NY: Wiley.

11. Anne Beamish

The author would like to thank William J. Mitchell and Dulcy Anderson for their thoughtful comments on this paper.

1. See T. J. Campanella, chapter 9 of this volume.

2. Bender, T. 1978. *Community and social change in America*. New Brunswick, NJ: Rutgers University Press, 51, 4; Brill, M. 1989. Transformation, nostalgia, and illusion in public life and public place. In I. Altman and E. H. Zube, eds., *Public places and spaces*. New York, NY: Plenum Press, 7–29; Oldenburg, R. 1989. *The great good place: Cafés, coffee shops, community centers, beauty parlors, general stores, bars, hangouts, and how they get you through the day.* New York, NY: Paragon House; Putnam, R. D. 1995. Bowling alone: America's declining social capital. *Journal of Democracy* 6 (January): 65–78; Sennett, R. 1977. *The fall of public man*. New York, NY: Knopf.

3. Williams, R. 1976. *Keywords: A vocabulary of culture and society*. New York, NY: Oxford University Press, 66.

4. Digital or virtual worlds are interactive, online, multi-user environments that emphasize social interaction or discussion, let participants decide on self-representation, and permit users to create objects within the world. Each world offers a distinctive flavor, purpose, and capabilities to participants. The boundary of what constitutes a virtual world or digital community is somewhat permeable, but the main types are newsgroups, mailing lists, chat, MUDs, and graphical worlds. There are some games that meet many but not all of these criteria—for example, Quake, which is interactive and multi-user, although its primary objective is to win (any social interaction is strictly secondary), and SimCity, which is intended for a single user, though it recently created a Web site that lets participants play a Java version of the original game with the added capability of chatting with other users.

5. Mitchell, W. 1995. *City of bits: Space, place, and the infobahn*. Cambridge, MA: MIT Press.

6. *See* Kostof, S., 1992, *The city assembled: The elements of urban form through history,* Boston, MA: Little, Brown and Company, 144–61, for a typology of public space.

7. The URLs for the sites discussed in this chapter are as follows:

Active Worlds: *http://www.activeworlds.com/*
Cleveland Free-Net: *http://cnswww.cns.cwru.edu/net/easy/fn/*
(no longer active)
De Digitale Stad: *http://www.dds.nl*
Deuxième Monde (Virtual Paris): *http://www.2nd* –world.fr/
Municipia: *http://www.municipia.org*
Palace: *http://www.thepalace.com*
(no longer supported)
Planet9: *http://www.planet9.com/*
Quake: *http://www.planetquake.com/*
http://www.idsoftware.com/quake/
SimCity: *http://simcity.ea.com/us/guide*
V-Chat: *http://www.microsoft.com/ie/chat*
Virtual Los Angeles: *http://www.aud.ucla.edu/~bill/ACM97.html*
Virtual Whitehall: *http://www.casa.ucl.ac.uk/vuis/*
Worlds Chat: *http://www.worlds.com/ns.html*
WorldsAway: *http://*www.avaterra.com

8. The word *avatar* comes from Hindu mythology and means the earthly manifestation of a god.

9. Active Worlds are 3D worlds that use software owned by Activeworlds.com, Inc. AlphaWorld is the largest and best known of the group.

10. Thomas Erickson said the talk in many virtual worlds "resembles a cross between a cocktail party and cruising zone with its anonymity, superficial conversation, and the ephemer-

al nature of the interactions." (Erickson, T. 1997. Social interaction on the Net: Virtual community as participatory genre. In J. F. Nunamaker Jr. and R. H Sprague Jr., eds., *Proceedings of the Thirtieth Hawaii International Conference on System Sciences.* Los Alamitos, CA: IEEE Computer Society Press, 23–30.)

11. The crude graphics and primitive environment are certainly off-putting to many, but today's graphics are much improved over those of even three years ago, and the quality and sophistication of graphics will only improve.

12. Digital worlds certainly appeal to many, but it is difficult to know exactly who they are, or how many there are. Demographic information is scarce, and although owners of worlds frequently claim large populations, it often seems more for the benefit of advertisers and potential users than for the sake of accuracy. AlphaWorld, for example, claims a population of 300,000, yet it is not uncommon to visit the site and find less than a dozen people spread over many square miles.

13. See Turkle, S., 1995, *Life on the screen: Identity in the age of the Internet*, New York, NY: Simon and Schuster, for an in-depth look at issues of identity online.

14. Dibbell, J. 1993. A rape in cyberspace or how an evil clown, a Haitian trickster spirit, two wizards, and a cast of dozens turned a database into a society. *Village Voice* (December 21): 36–42; Rossney, R. 1996. Metaworlds. *Wired* 4, 6: 141; Van Gelder, L. 1996. The strange case of the electronic lover. In R. Kling, ed., *Computerization and controversy: Value conflicts and social choices.* 2nd ed. San Diego, CA: Academic Press, 533–46.

15. There are currently almost 300 worlds created with Active Worlds software, and certainly not all of them are created in the image of the city. Landscapes with white-capped mountains and green plains are at least as popular as smaller-scale built environments such as palaces, buildings, and bars.

16. An Active Worlds Web site includes the following building tips: "This is *the most important* and overlooked aspect of building: To claim land you must *completely* cover it with objects. You must cover every inch of land you own. Don't leave any gaps! Be sure to claim as much land as you will need. If you don't cover it, you don't own it, and people are free to build on any empty spaces you leave. Don't count on others to be polite and honor your borders. If you don't want others building there, cover it. Using large flat pieces (such as walks) is the easiest and most efficient way to cover your land. Far too many people fail to do this and simply spread trees and fences around their house, leaving the yard open."

17. Brill, Transformation, nostalgia, and illusion; Carr, S., M. Francis, L. G. Rivlin, et al. 1992. *Public space*. Cambridge, MA: Cambridge University Press; Francis, M. 1989. Control as a dimension of public-space quality. In I. Altman and E. H. Zube, eds., *Public places and spaces.* New York, NY: Plenum Press, 147–72; Jacobs, A. B. 1993. *Great streets.* Cambridge, MA: MIT Press; Kostof, *The city assembled*, 123–4. Franck and Paxson (Franck, K., and L. Paxson, 1989, Women and urban public space, in I. Altman and E. H. Zube, eds., *Public places and spaces*, New York, NY: Plenum Press, 121–46) also remind us that all users do not experience public space in the same way, and in particular, public space may have different meanings to women.

18. Though these sites may claim to encourage civic debate, discussion is often disappointingly limited.

19. Digital Amsterdam's citizens were originally intended to be residents of the physical city, but the site's organizers have discovered that their residents are spread throughout the world.

20. See chapter 2 of Bell, C., and H. Newby, 1974, *Community studies: An introduction to the sociology of the local community*, New York, NY: Praeger Publishers, Inc., for a review of community theory and definitions.

21. Bell and Newby, *Community studies*, 21.

22. Rheingold, H. 1993. *The virtual community: Homesteading on the electronic frontier.* Reading, MA: Addison-Wesley. One could also certainly argue that many virtual communities and digital worlds are, in a sense, gated communities in that users must have special software, equipment, and knowledge, good connections, and time—all of which are not equally available to everyone.

23. Bender, *Community and social change*, 11.

24. Anderson, B. 1983. *Imagined communities: Reflections on the origin and spread of nationalism.* London, UK: Verso, 15–6.

25. Erickson, Social interaction on the Net; Wellman, B., J. Salaff, D. Dimitroval, et al. 1996. Computer networks as social networks: Collaborative work, telework, and virtual community. *Annual Review of Sociology* 22: 213–38.

26. Putnam, Bowling alone, 231.

27. For example, in the three volumes of manuals for the Palace software, a program that lets users build their own graphical world, and which comes with default background graphics, there is no mention of what might be appropriate graphics, layouts, or backgrounds for the environment.

28. Mitchell, W. 1998. Commentary at the "Imaging the City" session on "The City in Cyberspace." Massachusetts Institute of Technology. October.

12. Lawrence J. Vale and Julia R. Dobrow

1. Bauer, C. 1957. Do Americans hate cities? *Journal of the American Institute of Planners* 23 (Winter).

2. Levin, D. E. 1998. *Remote control childhood?* Washington, DC: National Association for the Education of Young Children; Potter, W. J. 1998. *Media literacy.* Newbury Park, CA: Sage; Stranger, J. 1997. *Television in the home: The 1997 survey of parents and children.* Annenberg Public Policy Center Series, number 2. Philadelphia, PA: University of Pennsylvania.

3. Barcus, E. B. 1983. *Images of life on children's television.* New York, NY: Praeger; Dobrow, J., and C. Gidney. 1998. The good, the bad, and the foreign: The use of dialect in children's television. In A. B. Jordan and K. H. Jamieson, eds., *The Annals of the American Academy of Political and Social Science* 557: 105–19; Gerbner, G., and L. Gross. 1976. Living with television: The violence profile, *Journal of Communication* 26, 2: 172–99; Gerbner, G., et al. 1993. Growing up with television: The cultivation perspective. In J. Bryant and D. Zillman, eds., *Media effects: Advances in theory and research* (Hillsdale, NJ: Lawrence Earlbaum Associates); Greenberg, B. S., and J. F. Brand. 1993. Cultural diversity on Saturday morning television. In G. Berry and J. K. Asamen, eds., *Children and television: Images in a changing sociocultural world.* Newbury Park, CA: Sage.

4. It is expected that the next phase of this research will entail examination of the effects of children's programming set in urban locales on the images children hold of cities. We gratefully acknowledge the support received for this project from the MIT Provost's Fund for Humanities, Arts, and Social Sciences.

5. Borgenicht, D. 1998. *Sesame Street unpaved: Scripts, stories, secrets, and songs.* New York, NY: Hyperion, 9

6. Borgenicht, *Sesame Street unpaved*, 15.

7. Borgenicht, *Sesame Street unpaved.*

8. The Nielsen Company. 1998.The Nielsen Television Index.

9. Greenwald, C. 1999. Interview by the authors with Carol Greenwald, executive producer of *Arthur.*

10. Eller, C. 1999. With 'Doug,' Nickelodeon's loss may be Disney's gain. *Los Angeles Times*, March 9: C1.

11. Jinkins, J. 1999. Interview by the authors with Jim Jinkins, creator of *Disney's Doug.*

12. Bartlett, C. 1999. Interview by the authors with Craig Bartlett, producer of *Hey Arnold!.*

13. Whittell, G. 1999. Future looks scarily like The Simpsons. *The Times* (London), January 23.

14. Clarifications. 1997. *Minneapolis Star Tribune*, May 29; Matzer, M. 1997. Company town; Simpsons' sales: Halving a cow. *Los Angeles Times*, September 25: D1.

15. The authors are grateful for the assistance of T. Luke Young, Tia Kaul, and Karen Leavitt, who helped us code the content of numerous episodes of each show into Lynchian categories. We also appreciate the comments offered by three of our children: Mira, Aaron, and Jeremy.

16. Borgenicht, *Sesame Street unpaved*, 34.

17. Borgenicht, *Sesame Street unpaved*, 15.

18. Loman, M. 1999. Interview by the authors with Michael Loman, executive producer of *Sesame Street.*

19. Loman. 1999. Interview.

20. Bartlett. 1999. Interview.

21. Bartlett. 1999. Interview.

22. Bartlett. 1999. Interview.

23. Jacobs, J. 1961. *The death and life of great American cities*. New York, NY: Random House.

24. Book sales increased exponentially after the television version premiered. In twenty years of publishing prior to the show, Marc Brown sold an impressive five million books; in the first three years after *Arthur* went on television, Brown sold twenty-one million more. During the same years, librarians also reported a marked increase in requests for *Arthur* books (including demand from "previously unmotivated children tied to the television series"), much to the delight of folks at PBS (Greenwald 1999).

25. Greenwald. 1999. Interview.

26. Greenwald. 1999. Interview.

27. Greenwald. 1999. Interview.

28. Jumbo Pictures, Inc. 1996. Welcome to Bluffington. In *Disney's Doug Production Guide.*

29. Jumbo Pictures, Inc. 1996.

30. Jinkins. 1999. Interview.

31. The Simpsons Archive. 1999. *http://www.snpp.com/guides/city.profile.html.*

32. Groening, M. 1997. *The Simpsons: A complete guide to our favorite family*. R. Richmond and A. Coffman, eds. New York, NY: HarperCollins; Groening, M. 1998. *The Simpsons: Guide to Springfield*. New York, NY: HarperCollins.

33. Groening, *The Simpsons: Guide to Springfield.*

34. Groening, *The Simpsons: Guide to Springfield.*

35. Groening, *The Simpsons: A complete guide*; *The Simpsons: Guide to Springfield.*

36. The lack of emphasis on the journey on children's television shows runs parallel to adult behavior in the automobile-dependent realms of new city-regions. There, too, it is *nodes*—home, office, mall—that are featured. The commute between them, by contrast, is something to be willfully ignored if possible; or, if not, something to curse. Cars are marketed in ways that stress their ability to tune out the sensory experience of the city. Salespersons emphasize a "quiet ride" (rendered largely irrelevant by the corresponding demand for a powerful stereo) and sophisticated "climate control" systems, not to mention privacy-enhancing tinted glass. Car

design is an attempt to turn *paths* into mobile pseudo-*nodes*, a process that—because of its individuation—strips both the driver and the streetscape of sociability.

37. Lynch, K. 1960. *The image of the city*. Cambridge, MA: MIT Press. For a brief discussion of these performance dimensions, see the Appendix.

38. Lynch, *The image of the city*, 118.

13. Deborah Karasov

1. Ventura, Michael. 1988. Report from El Dorado. In Rick Simonson and Scott Walker, eds., *Multi-cultural literacy.* Saint Paul, MN: Graywolf Press, 188.

2. Alberro, Alexander. 1999. Reconsidering Conceptual art, 1966–1977. In Alexander Alberro and Blake Stimson, eds., *Conceptual art: A critical anthology.* Cambridge, MA: MIT Press.

3. Lippard, Lucy. 1991. Hot potatoes: Art and politics in 1980. In Howard Smagula, ed., *Re-Visions: New perspectives of art criticism.* Englewood Cliffs, NJ: Prentice Hall, 37.

4. Lacy, Suzanne, and Leslie Labowitz. 1985. Feminist media strategies for political performance. In Douglas Kahn and Diane Neumaier, eds., *Cultures in contention.* Seattle, WA: Real Comet Press, 126.

5. Lacy and Labowitz, Feminist media strategies.

6. Foster, Hal. 1985. *Recodings: Art, spectacle, cultural politics.* Port Townsend, WA: Bay Press, 112.

7. Graham, Dan. 1988. Video in relation to architecture. In Doug Hall and Sally Jo Fifer, eds., *Illuminating video.* New York, NY: Aperture; San Francisco, CA: Bay Area Video, 187–8.

8. Graham, Dan. 1993. *Rock my religion: Writings and art projects 1965–1990.* Brian Wallis, ed. Cambridge, MA: MIT Press, 301.

9. Deutsche, Rosalyn. 1996. *Evictions: Art and spatial politics.* Cambridge, MA: MIT Press, 165.

10. Wodiczko, Krzysztof. 1999. *Critical vehicles: Writings, projects, interviews/Krzysztof Wodiczko.* Cambridge, MA: MIT Press, 171–2, 59.

11. Boswell, Peter. 1992. Krzysztof Wodiczko: Art and the public domain. In *Public address: Krzysztof Wodiczko* (exhibition catalog). Minneapolis, MN: Walker Art Center.

12. Debord, Guy. 1983 [originally published 1967]. *The society of the spectacle.* Revised English edition (unpaginated). Detroit, MI: Black & Red. Also published by Zone Books (New York, 1994), trans. Donald Nicholson-Smith.

13. Debord, Guy. 1981. Report on the construction of situations and on the International Situationist Tendency's conditions of organization and action. In Ken Knabb, ed., *Situationist International anthology*. Berkeley, CA: Bureau of Public Secrets, 22, 25.

14. Wodiczko, Krzysztof. 1998. Presentation to the Imaging the City Faculty Colloquium, Massachusetts Institute of Technology, Cambridge, MA. October 5.

15. Wodiczko, Presentation.

16. Lippard, Lucy. 1998 (revised edition). Foreword to the 1998 edition. In Eva Cockcroft, John Pitman Weber, and James Cockcroft, eds., *Toward a people's art: The contemporary mural movement.* Albuquerque, NM: University of New Mexico Press, xi.

17. Garduño, Geronimo. 1998. Artes Guadalupanos de Aztlán. In Eva Cockcroft, John Pitman Weber, and James Cockcroft, eds., *Toward a people's art: The contemporary mural movement.* Albuquerque, NM: University of New Mexico Press, 208.

18. Drescher, Timothy. 1998. Afterword: The next two decades. In Eva Cockcroft, John Pitman Weber, and James Cockcroft, eds., *Toward a People's Art: The contemporary mural movement.* Albuquerque, NM: University of New Mexico Press, 302.

19. Baca, Judith. 1985. Our people are the internal exiles. In Douglas Kahn and Diane Neumaier, eds., *Cultures of contention.* Seattle, WA: Real Comet Press, 68.

20. Baca, Our people are the internal exiles.

21. Wodiczko, Presentation.

22. Tuer, Dot. 1995. Is it still privileged art? The politics of class and collaboration in the art practice of Carole Condé and Karl Beveridge. In Nina Felshin, ed., *But is it art? The spirit of art as activism.* Seattle, WA: Bay Press, 220.

23. Pincus, Robert. 1995. The invisible town square: Artists' collaborations and media dramas in America's biggest border town. In Nina Felshin, ed., *But is it art? The spirit of art as activism.* Seattle, WA: Bay Press, 33.

24. Pincus, The invisible town square.

25. Pincus, The invisible town square.

26. Miles, Malcolm. 1997. *Art, space, and the city: Public art and urban futures.* New York, NY: Routledge, 179.

27. Dunn, Peter, and Loraine Leeson. 1985. The art of change. In Douglas Kahn and Diane Neumaier, eds., *Cultures in contention.* Seattle, WA: Real Comet Press, 17.

28. Dunn and Leeson, The art of change, 18.

29. REPOhistory. 1992. The Lower Manhattan sign project. Unpublished exhibition brochure. New York, NY, 4.

30. Kelley, Jeff. 1995. Common work. In Suzanne Lacy, ed. *Mapping the terrain: New genre public art.* Seattle, WA: Bay Press, 143.

31. Leach, Neil. 1999. *The anaesthetics of architecture.* Cambridge, MA: MIT Press, 10.

32. Phillips, Patricia. 1992. Images of repossession. In *Public address: Krzysztof Wodiczko* (exhibition catalog). Minneapolis, MN: Walker Art Center, 52.

33. Leach, *The anaesthetics of architecture*, 87.

34. Quoted in Lacy, Suzanne, ed. 1995. *Mapping the terrain: New genre public art.* Seattle, WA: Bay Press, 45.

35. Lacy, *Mapping the terrain*, 46.

14. J. Mark Schuster

1. Haga, H. 1970. *Japanese folk festivals illustrated.* Tokyo, Japan: Miura Printing Company, 35.

2. I am indebted to Larry Vale and Sam Bass Warner for commending to my attention the power of cyclicality and its contribution to image, a contribution that is much less salient with one-off sorts of events.

3. Lexington. 1998. Nebraska's Kool-Aid test. *The Economist* 348, 8082: 24; West, A. B. 1998. *Main Street festivals: Traditional and unique events on America's Main Streets.* New York, NY: John Wiley & Sons.

4. Huntoon, L., and M. Wilson. 1998. Footprints in the sands of time or gone with the wind: Do ephemeral events have long-term impacts on urban development? Paper delivered at the conference of the Association of Collegiate Schools of Planning, Pasadena, California; Ley, D., and K. Olds. 1988. Landscape as spectacle: World's fairs and the culture of heroic consumption. *Environment and Planning D: Society and Space* 6, 2: 191–212.

5. Green, K. W., ed. 1983. *The city as a stage: Strategies for the arts in urban economics.* Washington, DC: Partners for Livable Places; Lennard, S., and H. Lennard. 1984. *Public life in urban places.* Southampton, NY: Gondolier Press; Lennard, S., and H. Lennard. 1987. *Livable cities—people and places: Social and design principles for the future of the city.* Southampton, NY:

Gondolier Press; Lennard, S., and H. Lennard. 1995. *Livable cities observed: A source book of images and ideas for city officials, community leaders, architects, planners and all others committed to making their cities livable*. Carmel, CA: Gondolier Press; McNulty, R., D. Jacobson, and R. L. Penne. 1985. *The economics of amenity: Community futures and quality of life*. Washington, DC: Partners for Livable Places; Taylor, L., ed. 1981. *Urban open spaces*. New York, NY: Rizzoli; Taylor, L., ed. 1982. *Cities: The forces that shape them*. New York, NY: Rizzoli.

6. Bianchini, F., and M. Parkinson, eds. 1993. *Cultural policy and urban regeneration: The West European experience*. Manchester, UK: Manchester University Press.

7. Deben, L., S. Musterd, and J. van Weesep. 1992. Urban revitalization and the revival of urban culture. *Built Environment* 18, 2: 85.

8. Lim, H. 1993. Cultural strategies for revitalizing the city: A review and evaluation. *Regional Studies* 27, 6: 589–95.

9. Bonnemaison, S. 1990. City policies and cyclical events. *Design Quarterly* 147: 24–32.

10. Lynch, K. 1972. *What time is this place?* Cambridge, MA: MIT Press, 83.

11. Lynch, *What time is this place?*, 183.

12. A recent interesting article (Ross, C., 1998, Roadside memorials: Public policy v. private expression, *American City & County* 113, 5: 51–3) explores the phenomenon of roadside memorials—temporary memorials to accident victims raised by friends and family at the side of the road—and discusses how official policies with respect to these memorials vary widely.

13. Schuster, J. M. 1995. Two urban festivals: La Mercé and First Night. *Planning Practice and Research* 10, 2: 173–87.

14. Lynch, *What time is this place?*, 176–7.

15. Lynch, K. 1960. *The image of the city*. Cambridge, MA: MIT Press; Boorstin, D. 1992 [orig. ed. 1961]. *The image: A guide to pseudo-events in America*, 25th anniversary edition. New York, NY: Vintage Press, 317.

16. Boorstin, *The image*, 39–40.

17. MacCannell (1973, Staged authenticity: Arrangements of social space in tourist settings, *American Journal of Sociology* 79, 3: 589–603), writing in the literature on the sociology of tourism, offers one way out of this polarized debate concerning image. He applies and partially rejects Boorstin's ideas as they play out in the field of tourism, arguing that there are a number of interesting examples of accommodations being made between the real and the pseudo, particularly as they involve what he calls the "back regions" of the places tourists visit because these regions are associated with intimacy of relations and authenticity of experiences. In the end, he is much more generous to tourists than Boorstin, lamenting that the word "tourist" has increasingly come to be used to indicate someone who seems content with his obviously inauthentic experiences.

18. Harvey, D. 1989. *The urban experience*. Oxford, UK: Basil Blackwell, 233.

19. Lenskyj, H. 1996. When winners are losers: Toronto and Sydney bid for the Summer Olympics. *Journal of Sport & Social Issues* 24: 392–410.

20. Brown, R. 1997. *Ghost dancing on the cracker circuit: The culture of festivals in the American South*. Jackson, MS: University of Mississippi Press, 185.

21. Sussman, M. 1995. Celebrating the new world order: Festival and war in New York. *The Drama Review* 39, 2: 147–75.

22. Hiller, H. 1989. Impact and image: The convergence of urban factors in preparing for the 1988 Calgary Winter Olympics. In G. Syme, B. Shaw, D. Fenton, and W. Mueller, eds., *The planning and evaluation of hallmark events*. Aldershot, UK: Avebury; Hiller, H. 1990. The urban transformation of a landmark event: The 1988 Calgary Winter Olympics. *Urban Affairs Quarterly* 26, 1: 118–37.

23. Cohen, A. 1993. *Masquerade politics: Explorations in the structure of urban cultural movements.* Oxford, UK: Berg Publishers Limited; Flake, C. 1994. *New Orleans: Behind the masks of America's most exotic city*. New York, NY: Grove Press; Guillermoprieto, A. 1990. *Samba*. New York, NY: Vintage Books. Manning (1989, Carnival in the city: The Caribbeanization of urban landscapes, *Urban Resources* 5, 3: 3–8+), however, fears a trend toward increasingly expensive, and therefore socially exclusive, productions in carnivals.

24. Ley and Olds, Landscape as spectacle, 203, 209.

25. Quoted in Newman, P. 1989. The impact of the America's Cup on Fremantle—An insider's view. In G. Syme, B. Shaw, D. Fenton, and W. Mueller, eds., *The planning and evaluation of hallmark events*. Aldershot, UK: Avebury.

26. De Moragas Spà, M., N. Rivenburgh, and N. García. 1995. Television and the construction of identity: Barcelona, Olympic host. In M. de Moragas and M. Botella, eds., *The keys to success: The social, sporting, economic and communications impact of Barcelona '92*. Barcelona, Spain: Centre d'Estudis Olímpics i de l'Esport, Universitat Autònoma de Barcelona; Ladrón de Guevara, M., X. Cóller, and D. Romaní. 1995. The image of Barcelona '92 in the international press. In de Moragas and Botella, eds., *The keys to success*; Tomlinson, A. 1996. Olympic spectacle: Opening ceremonies and some paradoxes of globalization. *Media, Culture & Society* 18, 4: 583–602.

27. Rutheiser, C. 1996. *Imagineering Atlanta: The politics of place in the city of dreams.* London, UK: Verso.

28. Boorstin, *The image*, 103–4.

29. Ludwig, J. 1976. *The great American spectaculars: The Kentucky Derby, Mardi Gras, and other days of celebration.* Garden City, NY: Doubleday & Company, 169.

30. Essex, S., and B. Chalkley. 1998. Olympic Games: Catalyst of urban change. *Leisure Studies* 17, 3: 187–206.

31. Stevenson, D. 1997. Olympic arts: Sydney 2000 and the cultural Olympiad. *International Review for the Sociology of Sport* 32, 3: 227–38.

32. Of course, one could have a very interesting debate as to what constitutes "place linked." There are countless examples of festivals that are linked by name to the places in which they are located—the Edinburgh Festival, the Avignon Festival, and the like—but despite their fame, many of these festivals could take place almost anywhere without doing damage to the event. What I have in mind is events and other ephemera that are hard to imagine happening elsewhere, at least with the same salience. For this reason, I disqualify the seasons of professional sports teams, though they too are seasonal and endowed with the name of a place.

33. Trillin, C. 1998. New Orleans unmasked. *The New Yorker* 73, 45: 38+.

34. Sussman (Celebrating the new world order, 153) cites Katz's definition of a "media event" as (1) being preplanned, (2) being for live transmission, (3) framed in time and space, (4) featuring a heroic personality or group, (5) having high dramatic or ritual significance, and (6) having the force of a social norm that makes viewing mandatory.

35. Orloff, A. 1981. *Carnival: Myth and cult*. Wörgl, Austria: Perlinger.

36. Lawrence, D. 1992. Transcendence of place: The role of *La Placeta* in Valencia's *Las Fallas*. In I. Altman and S. Low, eds., *Place attachment*. New York, NY: Plenum Press.

37. Bayarri Llobat, V. 1994. *Asi son Las Fallas*, 4th edition. Valencia, Spain: Bayarri Communicación.

38. Schuster, Two urban festivals.

39. Wazaki, H. 1993. The urban festival and social identity. In A. Cohen and K. Fukui, eds., *Humanising the city? Social contexts of urban life at the turn of the millennium.* Edinburgh, Scotland: Edinburgh University Press, 137–8.

40. Schroeder, J. 1999. WaterFire Providence: A case study of art's role in urban revitaliza-

tion. Unpublished paper presented at the 5th International Conference on Arts and Cultural Management, Helsinki, Finland.

41. Rowe, D., and D. Stevenson. 1994. "Provincial paradise": Urban tourism and city imaging outside the metropolis. *Australian and New Zealand Journal of Sociology* 30, 2: 178–93. Note that at least some of the authors collected here do not tar all tourists with the same brush of searching for familiarity and comfort and the predictable.

42. Goldberger, P. 1998. The big top. *The New Yorker* 74, 10: 152–9.

43. Bonnemaison, City policies, 31.

44. Lynch, *What time is this place?*, 88.

45. Lynch, K. 1984. The immature arts of city design. *Places* 1, 3: 10–21. Reprinted in T. Banerjee and M. Southworth, eds., *City sense and city design: Writings and projects of Kevin Lynch.* Cambridge, MA: MIT Press.

46. Kelly, I. 1989. The architecture and town planning associated with a hallmark event. In G. Syme, B. Shaw, D. M. Fenton, and W. Mueller, eds., *The planning and evaluation of hallmark events*. Aldershot, UK: Avebury.

47. Goldberger, The big top.

48. West, Main Street festivals.

49. Sussman, Celebrating the new world order.

50. Kugelmass, J. 1994. Wishes come true: Designing the Greenwich Village Halloween parade. In J. Santino, ed., *Halloween and other festivals of death and life*. Knoxville, TN: University of Tennessee Press, 202. Sussman (Celebrating the new world order, 157) cites Mary Ryan, who offers a different take on parades: "The genius of the parade was that it allowed the many contending constituencies of the city to line up and move through the streets without ever encountering one another face to face, much less stopping to play specified roles in one coordinated pageant."

51. McNulty et al., *The economics of amenity.*

52. Hillman, S. 1983. Leveraging prosperity in Baltimore. In K. Green, ed., *The city as a stage: Strategies for the arts in urban economics.* Washington, DC: Partners for Livable Places.

53. Gonzalez, J. M. 1993. Bilbao: Culture, citizenship, and quality of life. In F. Bianchini and M. Parkinson, eds., *Cultural policy and urban regeneration: The West European experience.* Manchester, UK: Manchester University Press, 78–9.

54. Goldberger, The big top.

55. Yet, the recent experience of the Atlanta Olympics seems to suggest that this is highly context specific. Based on the Atlanta experience, French and Disher (1997, Atlanta and the Olympics: A one-year retrospective, *Journal of the American Planning Association* 63, 3: 379–92), conclude: "The Olympics and other large-scale events can generate large new financial resources, but it is difficult to direct those resources toward the most pressing urban problems." Rutheiser would argue that there was never any real intent or attempt to do so (Rutheiser, C. 1996. How Atlanta lost the Olympics, *New Statesman* 125, 4293: 28–99; Rutheiser, C., *Imagineering Atlanta*).

56. Millet i Serra, L. 1995. The games of the city. In M. de Moragas and M. Botella, eds., *The keys to success*, 200.

57. De Moragas, M., and M. Botella, eds. 1995. *The keys to success: The social, sporting, economic and communications impact of Barcelona '92*. Barcelona, Spain: Centre d'Estudis Olímpics i de l'Esport, Universitat Autònoma de Barcelona; Roche, M. 1992. Mega-events and micro-modernization: On the sociology of the new urban tourism. *The British Journal of Sociology* 43, 4: 563–600; Syme, G., B. Shaw, D. M. Fenton, and W. Mueller. 1989. *The planning and evaluation of hallmark events*. Aldershot, UK: Avebury.

58. Hiller, The urban transformation.

59. Hill, C. R. 1994. The politics of Manchester's Olympic bid. *Parliamentary Affairs* 47, 3: 343.

60. I was astonished to discover in the course of my research that the Scopes trial—*State of Tennessee v. John Thomas Scopes*—which most schoolchildren know as having pitted creationism versus evolution in an epic battle between Clarence Darrow and William Jennings Bryan, was actually conceived as an economic development scheme for the town of Dayton, Tennessee. When the ACLU announced that it was looking for a case to test the Butler Law banning the teaching of evolution in state-funded schools, two local residents decided that if they could get the trial to happen in Dayton they would attract the world's attention and perhaps bring in outside investment. They convinced Scopes, a substitute teacher, to say that he had taught evolution in order to force the trial. "It was all a stunt, a staged spectacle, cultural performance in the service of capital investment" (Brown, Ghost dancing on the cracker circuit). It seems doubtful that the trial had its desired effect, but a dramatic version of the trial transcript is still performed each year in the original courtroom as part of the Scopes Trial Play and Festival.

61. Ley and Olds, Landscape as spectacle, 198.

62. Davis, S. G. 1988. "Set your mood to patriotic": History as televised special event. *Radical History Review* 42: 122–43.

63. Sussman, Celebrating the new world order.

64. Orloff, *Carnival: Myth and cult*, 94.

65. Cochrane, A., J. Peck, and A. Tickell. 1996. Manchester plays games: Exploring the local politics of globalisation. *Urban Studies* 33, 8: 1319–36; Hill, The politics of Manchester's Olympic bid; Kitchen, T. 1996. Cities and the "world events" process. *Town & Country Planning* 65, 11: 314–6; Law, C. 1994. Manchester's bid for the Millennium Olympic Games. *Geography* 79, 3: 222–31; Lenskyj, When winners are losers; McGeoch, R., with G. Korporaal. 1994. *The bid: How Australia won the 2000 Games*. Port Melbourne, Australia: William Heinemann Australia; Simson, V., and A. Jennings. 1992. *The lords of the rings: Power, money, and drugs in the modern Olympics*. London, UK: Simon & Schuster; Socher, K. 1997. How not to get Olympic Games: Destination managers instead of strategists. *The Tourist Review* 52, 2: 41–7.

66. Booth, P., and R. Boyle. 1993. See Glasgow, see culture. In F. Bianchini and M. Parkinson, eds., *Cultural policy and urban regeneration: The West European experience*. Manchester, UK: Manchester University Press, 22; Thorne, R., and M. Munro-Clark. 1989. Hallmark events as an excuse for autocracy in urban planning: A case history. In Syme et al., eds., *The planning and evaluation of hallmark events*. The European City of Culture program is an example of what might be called "designated years," in which a central agency provides designation by selecting from among competing bidders. The Arts Council of England's Arts 2000 program in which eight cities and regions have been selected to host various arts years (e.g., 1992 Year of Music in Birmingham, 1997 Year of Opera and Musical Theatre in the East of England), concluded with the nationwide Year of the Artist in 2000. Such programs, which seem to be growing, have received limited research attention to date (Bilic, P. 1996. Bringing home the cultural bacon. *New Statesman & Society* 9, 386: 31; Booth and Boyle, See Glasgow, see culture; Boyle, M., and G. Hughes. 1991. The politics of the representation of "the real": Discourses from the left on Glasgow's role as European city of culture, 1990. *Area* 23, 3: 217–28; Lim, Cultural strategies for revitalizing a city; Myerscough, J. 1992. Measuring the impact of the arts: The Glasgow 1990 experience. *Journal of the Market Research Society* 34, 4: 323–35) and deserve more.

67. Lenskyj, When winners are losers.

68. Lawrence, D. L. 1987. Rules of misrule: Notes on the Doo Dah Parade in Pasadena. In

A. Falassi, ed., *Time out of time: Essays on the festival.* Albuquerque, NM: University of New Mexico Press.

69. Lavenda, R. H. 1992. Festivals and the creation of public culture: Whose voice(s)? In I. Karp, C. Kreamer, and S. Lavine, eds., *Museums and communities: The politics of public culture.* Washington, DC: Smithsonian Institution Press; Lavenda, R. H. 1997. *Corn fests and water carnivals: Celebrating community in Minnesota.* Washington, DC: Smithsonian Institution Press. Unfortunately, it has become necessary to curtail some of the participatory events traditionally associated with Winter Carnival because insurance companies were reluctant to write liability insurance. Indeed, many of the traditional elements of European festivals, particularly those involving fire, would be impossible in the United States for this reason.

70. Orloff, *Carnival: Myth and culture*, 45.

71. Turner, V. 1987. Carnival, ritual, and play in Rio de Janeiro. In A. Falassi, ed., *Time out of time: Essays on the festival.*

15. John de Monchaux

1. Cutter, S. L. 1985. *Rating places: A geographer's view on the quality of life.* Washington, D.C.: Resource Publications in Geography.

2. Edmondson, B. 1998. The place-rating game. *U.S. Airways Attaché* (November): 72–8.

3. Levine, R. 1988. City stress index: 25 best, 25 worst. *Psychology Today* 22 (November): 52–8.

4. Angoff, C., and H. L. Mencken. 1931. The worst American state. *American Mercury* xxiv (93, 94, 95): 1–16, 175–188, 355–371.

5. Boston Redevelopment Authority. 1998. *Boston topping the charts.*

6. Cutter, *Rating places.*

7. Moser, C. A., and W. Scott. 1961. *British towns: A statistical study of their social and economic differences.* Edinburgh, Scotland: Oliver and Boyd.

8. Andrews, A. C., and J. W. Fonseca. 1995. *The atlas of American society.* New York, NY: New York University Press; Weiss, M. J. 1994. *Latitudes and attitudes: An atlas of American tastes, trends, politics and passions.* Boston, MA: Little, Brown, and Co.

9. Savageau, D., and R. Boyer. 1993. *Places rated almanac: Your guide to the best places to live in North America.* New York, NY: Prentice Hall Travel.

10. Crampton, N. 1993. *The 100 best small towns in America.* New York, NY: Prentice Hall; Labich, K. 1993. The best cities for knowledge workers. *Fortune* 128 (November): 50–2; Summers, A. 1991. 15 best cities for child care. *Working Mother* 14 (February): 66–70; Villani, J. 1994. *The 100 best small art towns in America. Where to discover fresh air, creative people, and affordable living.* Santa Fe, NM: John Muir Publications.

11. Weinhold, R. S. 1997. *Rating guide to environmentally healthy metropolitan areas.* Durango, CO: Animas Press.

12. Cramer, M. 1995. *FunkyTowns USA.* Annapolis, MD: TBS Publishing.

13. *Money* Online. 1998. http://cgi.pathfinder.com/cgi-bin/Money/cgi.citypages.

14. Savageau and Boyer, *Places rated almanac*; Utopia by computer. 1987. *Harper's* 275 (September): 28.

15. Pindell, T. 1995. *A good place to live: America's last migration.* New York, NY: Henry Holt and Company.

16. See, for example, Walters 1995 (Why nice cities finish last. *Governing* 8, September: 18–22) and Cutter, *Rating places.*

17. Savageau and Boyer 1993.

18. Wiens, J. 1994. The ten best places to live. *Earth Journal* 6 (January/February): 47–8.

19. Landis, J. D., and D. S. Sawicki. 1988. A planner's guide to the *Places rated almanac. APA Journal* (Summer): 336–46.

20. Loftus, G. R. 1985. Say it ain't Pittsburgh. *Psychology Today* 23 (October): 42–8.

21. Savageau and Boyer, *Places rated almanac.*

22. Moser and Scott, *British towns: A statistical study.*

23. Levine, *City stress index.*

24. Pindell, *A good place to live.*

25. Landis and Sawicki, A planner's guide to the *Places rated almanac.*

26. Swanson, B. E., and R. K. Vogel. 1986. Rating American cities: Credit risk, urban distress, and the quality of life. *Journal of Urban Affairs* 8 (Spring): 67–84.

27. Cutter, *Rating places.*

28. Moser and Scott, *British towns: A statistical study.*

29. Landis and Sawicki, A planner's guide to the *Places rated almanac.*

30. Moser and Scott, *British towns: A statistical study.*

31. Landis and Sawicki, A planner's guide to the *Places rated almanac.*

32. Levine, *City stress index.*

33. Landis and Sawicki, A planner's guide to the *Places rated almanac.*

34. Swanson and Vogel, *Rating American cities.*

35. Cutter, *Rating places.*

36. Swanson and Vogel, *Rating American cities.*

37. America's hot cities. 1989. *Newsweek* (February 6): 42–9; Levy, S. 1998. The hot new tech cities. *Newsweek* (November 9): 44–50.

38. Cutter, *Rating places.*

39. Cutter, *Rating places.*

40. America's hot cities.

41. Crampton, *The 100 best small towns in America.*

16. Lawrence J. Vale

1. Judd, D. 1999. The tourist bubble. In Judd, D. R., and S. S. Fainstein, eds., *The tourist city.* New Haven, CT: Yale University Press, 35–53.

2. Little, C. E. 1990. *Greenways for America.* Baltimore, MD: Johns Hopkins University Press.

3. The origins of this typology of new public realms may be traced to a series of faculty seminars held at MIT during the early 1990s that culminated in an unpublished paper from which some of the following discussion is adapted. (Frenchman, D.; L. Vale; M. Schuster; and L. Craig. 1992. Designing a new public realm. Unpublished paper. Department of Urban Studies and Planning, Massachusetts Institute of Technology. December.)

4. Cleeland, T. A. 1993. Route 66 revisited. *CRM* 11: 15–8; Gaines, D., and A. Gomez. 1993. Perspectives on Route 66. *CRM* 11: 21–3; Kanamine, L. 1996. Commemorating the rugged road to civil rights. *USA Today*, October 17: 14D; Kelly, L. 1993. The national road: A story with many facets—a road with many resources. *CRM* 11: 50–3; Scenic byways: All-American roads and national scenic byways. 2000. www. byways.org/pages/designated_byways.html.

5. Workers to plant 200,000 trees along the Interstate 90 corridor. 1999. *Seattle Times*, September 3: B3.

6. Jones, K. 1997. Slipping in and out of Mexico. *New York Times*, January 26: Sec. 5, 15; Miller, L. 1998. Border browsing. *Texas Magazine*, January 11; Sanchez, M. L., and K. A.

Henderson. 1997. Los Caminos del Rio: A bi-national heritage project along the lower Rio Grande. *CRM* 11: 13.

7. Sampson, D. S. 1993. Hudson River Valley Greenway. *CRM* 11: 45–6.

8. Cited in Means, M. 1999. Happy trails. *Planning* 65, 8: 4–9.

9. Reinventing the wheel. 1998. *Trailblazer* (Rails-to-Trails Conservancy News) (July–September): 1; www.TrailLink.com.

10. Brandt, S. 1999. Midtown greenway won't be done again this year; but Minneapolis path project should be open next summer. *Minneapolis Star Tribune*, December 21: 1B; McClaren, G. 1999. Official envisions using pathways to tie city together. *Indianapolis Star*, August 16: A1; McCleery, B. 2000. Greenways to remain priority under new city administration. *Indianapolis Star*, January 5: B3.

11. McCann, D. 1999. Stepping into the Ice Age clears the mind. *Milwaukee Journal Sentinel*, November 10: Cue 1.

12. Hiss, T. 1990. *The experience of place*. New York, NY: Knopf; Little, *Greenways for America*.

13. Ruth, D., and M. Andrus. 1997. Lee vs. Grant: Battlefields and tourism in Virginia. *CRM* 5: 28–31.

14. McClelland, L. F. 1994. Connecting history with historic places: The multiple property approach. *CRM* 2: 8–9.

15. Giant leap forward: National Heritage Areas legislation passes as 104th Congress adjourns. 1996. *Heritage Links: News from the National Center for Heritage Development* 3, 3 (November): 2, 6; Means, Happy trails.

16. Giant leap forward 1996; King, R. J. 1999. New promotion highlights area's automotive heritage. *Detroit News*, December 2: B1.

17. Where women made history. 1998. New York State Department of Economic Development. Map and pamphlet.

18. National Park Service. 1999. Our shared history: Celebrating African American history and culture. www.cr.nps.gov/aahistory. The National Register has also produced a number of itineraries that focus on cultural resources associated with Hispanic heritage; Pope, S. D. 1997. Hispanic history in the National Register of Historic Places. *CRM* 11: 10–2.

19. Joroff, M. 1992. The Japan trace. Unpublished manuscript. MIT School of Architecture and Planning.

20. Hayden, D., G. Dubrow, and C. Flynn. n.d. The power of place: Los Angeles. Map and pamphlet; Hayden, D. 1995. *The power of place: Urban landscape as public history*. Cambridge, MA: MIT Press.

21. Liebs, C. H. 1993. Reconnecting people with place: The potential of Heritage Transportation Corridors. *CRM* 11: 9–11.

22. Spirn, A. W. 1984. *The granite garden: Urban nature and human design*. New York, NY: Basic Books.

23. Spirn, A. W. 1998. *The language of landscape*. New Haven, CT: Yale University Press.

24. Allen, S. 1999. Thoreau's place. *Boston Globe*, November 23: B1; Carlock, M. 1992. Hopes rise for Charles River pathway. *Boston Globe*, October 4: West 11; Howe, P. J. 1999. EPA raises Charles River's cleanliness grade: Seeks businesses for cleanup group. *Boston Globe*, April 14: B2.

25. Kent, P. 1997. Dump foes to savor success at party. *Atlanta Journal and Constitution*, March 21: 1J.

26. Schabath, G. 1999. Church shift: Prayer to preservation. *Detroit News*, October 5: D5.

27. Homebuilder to develop River Watch subdivision. 1996. *St. Petersburg Times*, April 28: 10; Tomlin, J. 1992. Kings Bay residents test water themselves. *St. Petersburg Times*, August 17: 1.

28. Apigian, M. 2000. Landscapes of convergence. Master of Architecture/Master in City Planning thesis, Massachusetts Institute of Technology.

29. Hussin, K. 1995. River watch campaign begins to show results. *New Straits Times* (Malaysia), April 19: 1; Love our rivers campaign pays off. 1997. *New Straits Times* (Malaysia), October 4: 9.

30. Urquart, F. 1994. Crime crackdown aims to net salmon poachers. *The Scotsman*, August 9.

31. Sheriff's department launches Niagara River watch. 1998. *Buffalo News*, May 14: 5B.

32. Pepper, J. 1999. Detroit should learn from Toronto how to use waterfront. *Detroit News*, November 5: B1.

APPENDIX. Lawrence J. Vale

1. Lynch, K. 1960. *The image of the city.* Cambridge, MA: MIT Press; Lynch, K. 1981. *Good city form.* Cambridge, MA: MIT Press.

2. Boyer, M. C. 1996. *CyberCities: Visual perception in the age of electronic communication.* New York, NY: Princeton Architectural Press, 138–50.

3. In an essay written near the end of his life that reflected on the strengths and weaknesses of *The Image of the City*, Lynch observed that "the original study set the meaning of places aside and dealt only with their identity and their structuring into larger wholes." Yet, as he candidly notes, "It did not succeed, of course. Meaning always crept in, in every sketch and comment. People could not help connecting their surroundings with the rest of their lives. But wherever possible, those meanings were brushed off the replies, because we thought that a study of meaning would be far more complicated than a study of mere identity." Lynch, K. 1984. Reconsidering *The image of the city.* In L. Rodwin and R. Hollister, eds. 1984. *Cities of the mind: Images and themes of the city in the social sciences.* New York, NY: Plenum, 151–61.

4. Krupa, G. 1999. The name game: Little-known N.H. firm hopes Super Bowl at Pro Player Stadium will bring it fame. *Boston Globe* (January 26), D1, D17.

5. Bosselmann, P. 1998. *Representation of places: Reality and realism in city design.* Berkeley, CA: University of California Press.

6. Shiffer, M. J. 1998. Managing public discourse: Towards the augmentation of GIS with multimedia. In P. A. Longley, M. F. Goodchild, D. J. Maguire, and D. W. Rhind, eds., *Geographical information systems.* Vol. 2, Management issues and applications, 2d ed. New York, NY: John Wiley and Sons, 723–32.

7. Yeh, A. G.-O. 1998. Urban planning and GIS. In P. A. Longley et al., *Geographical information systems,* 877–8.

8. Boorstin, D. 1961 [reissued 1992, Vintage Books]. *The image: A guide to pseudo-events in America.* New York, NY: Vintage Books; Boulding, K. 1956. *The image: Knowledge in life and society.* Ann Arbor, MI: University of Michigan Press; Lynch, K. 1960. *The image of the city.*

9. D. Boorstin, *The image,* 86–7.

10. L. Rodwin and R. Hollister, *Cities of the mind.*

11. Lynch, K. 1984. Reconsidering *The image of the city.* In L. Rodwin and R. M. Hollister, *Cities of the mind.*

12. Nasar, J. L. 1998. *The evaluative image of the city.* Thousand Oaks, CA: Sage, 6–16.

13. Hobsbawm, E. 1983. Introduction: Inventing traditions. In E. Hobsbawm and T. Ranger, eds. 1983. *The invention of tradition.* New York, NY: Cambridge University Press, 1–14.

14. Lowenthal, D. 1997. *The heritage crusade and the spoils of history.* Cambridge, UK: Cambridge University Press.

15. For a somewhat different account of this relationship, focusing on its implications for public housing redevelopment, see Lawrence J. Vale (1995). The imaging of the city: Public housing and communication. *Communication Research* 22, 2.

16. Janowitz, M. 1952. *The community press in an urban setting.* Chicago, IL: University of Chicago Press; Suttles, G. D. 1972. *The social construction of communities.* Chicago, IL: University of Chicago Press. *See also* Weiss, M.A. 1987. *The rise of the community builders.* New York, NY: Columbia University Press.

17. Davis, M. 1992. *City of quartz: Excavating the future in Los Angeles.* New York, NY: Vintage.

18. Cited in M. Davis, *City of quartz*, 20.

19. The pseudo-event concept, coined by D. Boorstin (*The Image,* 11–2) and discussed in chapter 14 of the present volume, refers to a happening that is 1) "not spontaneous, but comes about because someone has planned, planted, or incited it," 2) is "planted primarily (not always exclusively) for the immediate purpose of being reported or reproduced," 3) has an "ambiguous . . . relation to the underlying reality of the situation," and 4) is usually "intended to be a self-fulfilling prophecy."

20. Liebes, T., and E. Katz. 1990. *The export of meaning: Cross-cultural readings of Dallas.* New York, NY: Oxford University Press; Ang, Ien. 1985. *Watching Dallas: Soap opera and the melodramatic imagination.* Translation by Della Couling. London, UK: Methuen, 1.

21. Aucoin, D. 1999. Namesake show strikes chord in Providence. *Boston Globe* (April 16), A1, B20; Latour, F. 1999. Shadow cast on Providence revival: New scandal resurrects memories of old troubles. *Boston Globe* (April 30), B1, B7.

22. Grunwald, M. 1997. America's living rooms lose a laugh: Quirky TV show epitomized NYC, yadda, yadda, yadda. *Boston Globe* (December 27), A1.

23. Pike, B. 1981. *The image of the city in modern literature.* Princeton, NJ: Princeton University Press; L. Rodwin and R. Hollister, *Cities of the mind*; Sharpe, W., and L. Wallock. 1987. *Visions of the modern city: Essays in history, art, and literature.* Baltimore, MD: Johns Hopkins University Press; Caws, M. A., ed. 1991. *City images: Perspectives from literature, philosophy, and film.* New York, NY: Gordon and Breach.

24. Ward, S.V. 1998. *Selling places: The marketing and promotion of towns and cities, 1850–2000.* London, UK: E & FN Spon.

25. A virtual pilgrimage is complete with souvenirs. 1998. *New York Times* (December 31), G3.

26. These public housing transformations are being carried out with support from the U.S. Department of Housing and Urban Development's HOPE VI program.

27. Reidy, C. 1997. Putting a spin on life in the Hub. *Boston Globe* (January), C1, C7.

28. Parker, R. D. 1999. *Las Vegas: Casino gambling and local culture.* In Judd, D. R., and S. S. Fainstein, eds., *The tourist city.* New Haven, CT: Yale University Press, 107–23; Sassen, S., and F. Roost. 1999. The city: Strategic site for the global entertainment industry. In Judd and Fainstein, *The tourist city*.

29. Lynch, K. 1972. *What time is this place?* Cambridge, MA: MIT Press.

30. At the same time, however, countervailing efforts seek to highlight the contributions of previously marginalized groups. *See,* for example, Hayden, D. 1995. *The power of place: Urban landscapes as public history.* Cambridge, MA: MIT Press.

31. *See* chapter 4 of this volume by Patricia Burgess, Ruth Durack, and Edward W. Hill, Reimaging the Rust Belt: Can Cleveland sustain the renaissance?

32. Holcomb, B. 1999. Marketing cities for tourism. In D. Judd and S. Fainstein, *The tourist city*, 59–61.

33. Lynch, K. 1976. *Managing the sense of a region.* Cambridge, MA: MIT Press.

34. Abbott, C. 1997. The Portland region: Where city and suburbs talk to each other—and often agree. *Housing Policy Debate* 8, 1: 11–51; Vale, Lawrence J., chapter 16 of this volume.

35. Alsayyad, N., ed. 1992. *Forms of dominance: On the architecture and urbanism of the colonial enterprise.* Aldershot, UK: Avebury; Vale, L. J. 1992. *Architecture, power, and national identity.* New Haven, CT: Yale University Press; Wright, G. 1991. *The politics of design in French colonial urbanism.* Chicago, IL: University of Chicago Press.

36. Sorkin, M., ed. 1992. *Variations on a theme park: The new American city and the end of public space.* New York, NY: Noonday.

37. Ashworth, G. J., and H. Voogd. 1990. *Selling the city: Marketing approaches in public sector urban planning.* London, UK: Belhaven Press; Kearns, G., and C. Philo, eds. 1993. *Selling places: The city as cultural capital, past and present.* Oxford, UK: Pergamon; Gold, J. R., and S. V. Ward, eds. *Place promotion: The use of publicity and marketing to sell towns and regions.* Chichester, UK: John Wiley; Smyth, H. 1994. *Marketing the city: The role of flagship developments in urban regeneration.* London, UK: E & FN Spon; Ward, S. V. 1998. *Selling places: The marketing and promotion of towns and cities 1850–2000.* London, UK: E & FN Spon; Neil, W. J. V., D. Fitzsimons, and B. Murtagh. 1995. *Reimaging the pariah city: Urban development in Belfast and Detroit.* Brookfield, VT: Ashgate; Judd, D. R., and S. S. Fainstein, eds., *The tourist city. See also* Jackson, K. T., ed. 1995. *The encyclopedia of New York City.* New Haven, CT: Yale University Press; and Paddison, R. 1993. City marketing, image reconstruction, and urban regeneration. *Urban Studies* 30, 2.

While the Anglo-European literature has taken a decidedly critical tone, the origins of the place-promotion literature are largely American, dating back to a 1938 volume entitled *How to Promote Community and Industrial Development* (F. H. McDonald. New York: Harper and Row). Such work focuses on how to market successfully, rather than on the more complex cultural questions about what such place-marketing means.

CREDITS

The authors and publisher have made extensive efforts to contact and credit copyright holders of the illustrations reprinted in this book. If copyright proprietorship can be established for any illustration not specifically attributed in the Credits, please contact Editor, Center for Urban Policy Research. Omissions will be corrected in reprinted editions.

The publisher wishes to express special thanks to Activeworlds.com, Inc., of Newburyport, Massachusetts, for use of a portion of its AlphaWorld map (© Activeworlds.com) on the cover of this book, as a design element throughout the book, and in chapter 11.

CHAPTER 1

Fig. 1.1: *Guida Turistica di Controinformazione* (Conoscere Bergamo, Citta Alta), 1973. Publicity poster issued by Bergamo, Italy.

Figs. 1.2, 1.3: From F. Hartt, *Art: A History of Painting, Sculpture, Architecture,* 3rd ed. (New York, NY: Harry Abrams, 1989). Original frescoes photographed by Studio Canali, Capriolo (Brescia), Italy.

Fig. 1.4: From Walter Starkie, *The Road to Santiago: Pilgrims of St. James* (New York, NY: E. P. Dutton, 1957).

Figs. 1.5a–d: From John Wilkinson, *Jerusalem Pilgrims* (Warminster, Wiltshire, UK: Aris & Phillips Ltd.), Plates 1, 2, 3, 5. Used with permission.

Fig. 1.6: From John Wilkinson, *Jerusalem Pilgrims* (Warminster, Wiltshire, UK: Aris & Phillips Ltd.), p. 31. Used with permission.

Fig. 1.7: From Helen Rosenau, *Vision of the Temple: The Image of the Temple of Jerusalem in Judaism and Christianity* (London, UK: Oresko Books, 1979, p. 48). Left, Maimonides, *Mishnah Commentary* (Oxford, Bodleian Library). Right, Maimonides, *Mishneh Torah* (New York, Jewish Theological Seminary).

Fig. 1.8: From Chiara Frugoni, *A Distant City: Images of Urban Experience in the Medieval World* (Princeton, NJ: Princeton University Press, 1991). Translation by William McCuaig. Photograph by Eugenio Roncaglia, Modena, Italy.

Fig. 1.9: From Walter Starkie, *The Road to Santiago: Pilgrims of St. James* (New York, NY: E. P. Dutton, 1957) (anonymous Spanish painter). Original in the Museo del Prado, Madrid.

Fig. 1.10: From Walter Starkie, *The Road to Santiago: Pilgrims of St. James* (New York, NY: E. P. Dutton, 1957).

Fig. 1.11: From Walter Starkie, *The Road to Santiago: Pilgrims of St. James* (New York, NY: E. P. Dutton, 1957). Original in the Museo del Prado, Madrid.

Fig. 1.12: From T. S. R. Boase, *Boniface VIII* (London, UK: Constable Publishers, 1933), p. 235.

Fig. 1.13: From Herbert Thurston, *The Golden Year of the Jubilee* (St. Louis, MO: B. Herder, 1900), p. 359.

Fig. 1.14: "Roman Holiday: In Celebration of the Millennium, a Long-Forgotten Tradition is Due for a (Second) Renaissance," by Andrew Santella. From the *New York Times Magazine*, March 14, 1999. Used with permission of Andrew Santella and *The New York Times*.

Fig. 1.15: © 2001 Wm. Hoest Enterprises, Inc., Lloyd Harbor, New York. Reprinted courtesy of Bunny Hoest and *Parade* magazine.

Fig. 1.16: From William Melczer, *The Pilgrim's Guide to Santiago de Compostela* (New York, NY: Italica Press), p. xxi. Courtesy Tourist Office of Spain.

Fig. 1.17: © Chip Simons.

CHAPTER 2

Fig. 2.1: Briavel Holcomb.

Fig. 2.2: New Brunswick Development Company, New Brunswick, New Jersey.

Fig. 2.3a, b: (a) New Brunswick Development Corporation. (b) Briavel Holcomb.

Fig. 2.4: From Barrie Evans, "The Dome Experience," Construction Study. *The Architect's Journal* (November 27, 1997). Photograph © Chorley Handford/Hayes Davidson.

Fig. 2.5: From promotional brochure for New Jersey Performing Arts Center, Newark, New Jersey.

CHAPTER 3

Figs. 3.1a, b: Courtesy of the American Broadcasting Company.

Fig. 3.2: Cover of "Safe at Home: Yankee Stadium in the Bronx," prepared by Beyer Blender Belle Architects and Planners for the Office of the Bronx Borough President.

Fig. 3.3: Photograph by Camillo Vegara. Courtesy of Office of the Borough President, Bronx, New York.

Fig. 3.7: Courtesy Jimmy Carter Library.

Figs. 3.8a, b: Photographs by E. L. Birch.

Figs. 3.9a, b: Photographs by E. L. Birch.

Figs. 3.10a, b: Photographs by Camillo Vegara. Courtesy of Office of the Borough President, Bronx, New York.

Figs. 3.11a, b: Photographs by Camillo Vegara. Courtesy of Office of the Borough President, Bronx, New York.

Figs. 3.18a, b: Photographs by E. L. Birch.

CHAPTER 5

Figs. 5.1–5.5a, 5.6, 5.7: Larry Ford.

Fig. 5.5b: Illustration by Nina Veregge.

CHAPTER 6

Figs. 6.1, 6.3, 6.7, 6.8, 6.13, 6.17, 6.20, 6.25, 6.26, 6.29, 6.33: Judith A. Martin.

Fig. 6.2: "Tempo of the City" (1938). From Berenice Abbott, *New York in the Thirties*. New York, NY: Dover Publications, 1973. © 1939 by The Guilds' Committee for Federal Writers' Publications, Inc. Copyright renewed 1967 by Berenice Abbott.

Figs.6.4, 6.5, 6.16, 6.24: University of Minnesota, Cartography Lab.

Figs.6.6, 6.9–6.12, 6.14, 6.15, 6.18, 6.19, 6.21–6.23, 6.27, 6.28, 6.30–6.32, 6.34–6.36: Paula R. Pentel.

CHAPTER 7

Fig. 7.1: *Manhattan*, © 1979 United Artists Corporation.

Figs.7.2, 7.3: *West Side Story*, © 1989 (1961 orig.) United Artists Pictures, Inc.

Fig. 7.4: *Sidewalk Stories*, © 1989 Palm Pictures.

Figs.7.5, 7.6: *Koyaanisqatsi*, © 1982 Institute for Regional Education.

Fig. 7.7: *On the Town*, © 1976 Metro-Goldwyn-Mayer, Inc.

Fig. 7.8: *Sunrise*, © 1954 Twentieth Century Fox Film, Inc.

Fig. 7.9: *The Out-of-Towners*, © 1969 Paramount Pictures Co., JALEM Productions, Inc.

Figs.7.10, 7.11: *Street Scene*, © United Artists.

Fig. 7.12: *Do the Right Thing*, © 1989 Universal City Studios, Inc.

Figs.7.13, 7.14: *The Clock*, © 1972 Metro-Goldwyn-Mayer, Inc.

Fig. 7.15: *After Hours*, © 1985 Geffen Film Co.

Figs.7.16, 7.17: *Taxi Driver*, © 1976 Columbia Pictures Industries, Inc.

Fig. 7.18: *Dark City*, © 1998 New Line Cinema, Inc.

CHAPTER 8

Fig. 8.1: Maurice Culot and Leon Krier, "The Only Path for Architecture, *Oppositions* 14 (Fall 1978): 49. Reprinted with permission of MIT Press.

Figs.8.2–8.6: Richard Economakis, ed., *Leon Krier: Architecture and Urban Design, 1967–1992* (London, UK: Academy Editions, 1992). Fig. 8.2, pp. 16–17; Fig. 8.3, p. 21; Fig. 8.4, p. 23; Fig. 8.5, p. 43; Fig. 8.6, p. 224. © John Wiley & Sons Limited. Reproduced with permission.

Fig. 8.7: Reprinted from Rem Koolhaas, *Delirious New York: A Retroactive Manifesto for Manhattan* (New York, NY: Oxford University Press, 1978): 72.

Fig. 8.8: Reprinted from Rem Koolhaas, *Delirious New York* (New York, NY: Oxford University Press, 1978): 295. © Office for Metropolitan Architecture (OMA)/Rem Koolhaas. Used with permission.

Figs.8.9, 8.10: Reprinted from Rem Koolhaas and Bruce Mau, *S, M, L, XL* (New York, NY: Monacelli Press, 1995). Fig. 8.9, p. 933; Fig. 8.10, p. 1201. © Office for Metropolitan Architecture (OMA)/Rem Koolhaas. Used with permission.

CHAPTER 9

Fig. 9.1: Screen capture of television commercial (1997) produced by Young & Rubicam, Inc., for AT&T's Universal Master Card.

Figs.9.2–9.4: Screen capture of television commercial (1996) produced by M&C Saatchi for Packard Bell.

CHAPTER 10

Figs 10.1, 10.2: Dennis Frenchman.

Figs 10.3, 10.4, 10.7: National Park Service.

Figs 10.5, 10.9–10.11: Icon architecture, inc.

Fig. 10.6: Gettysburg National Military Park, *Final General Management Plan and Environmental Impact Statement, Volume 1.* U.S. National Park Service, June 1999. Drawn by Richard Segars.

Figs.10.8, 10.12: Courtesy Jamestown Rediscovery, Association for the Preservation of Virginia Antiquities.

CHAPTER 11

Fig. 11.1: *Note:* The Cleveland Free-Net discontinued operation on October 1, 1999.

Fig. 11.2: © Apple Computer, Inc.

Fig. 11.3: *Note:* The Palace (formerly at Communities.com) is no longer operational.

Figs.11.4, 11.5: © Anne Beamish.

Fig. 11.6: © 2000 Avaterra.com, Inc.

Fig. 11.7: Copyright © 2001 Microsoft Corporation, One Microsoft Way, Redmond, Washington 98052-6399 U.S.A. All rights reserved.

Fig. 11.8: © Urban Simulation Laboratory, UCLA, Los Angeles.

Fig. 11.9: © Canal Numedia.

Figs.11.10–11.14: © Activeworlds.com

CHAPTER 12

Fig. 12.1: Sesame Street, the Street Sign and the set design are trademarks and service marks of Sesame Workshop. All rights reserved.

Fig. 12.2: "The City" from Nickelodeon's *Hey, Arnold!*. Used by permission.

Fig. 12.3: Courtesy of WGBH and CINAR from ARTHUR on PBS.

Fig. 12.4a, b: © Jumbo Pictures, Inc.

Fig. 12.5: Reprinted from *The Simpsons: Guide to Springfield,* published by HarperCollins, ©1998 Bongo Entertainment, Inc. & Matt Groening Productions, Inc. All Rights Reserved. The Simpsons © and ™ Twentieth Century Fox Film Corporation. All Rights Reserved.

CHAPTER 13

Fig. 13.1: Suzanne Lacy and Leslie Labowitz, *In Mourning and in Rage.* © Ariadne, 1977.

Fig. 13.2: Photo: © Maggie Hopp. Jenny Holzer, Various texts. Theater marquee, *Truisms, 42nd Street Art Project.* Time, New York, 7/93–3/94.

Fig. 13.3: Barbara Kruger, *Untitled* ("You Thrive on Mistaken Identity") 60" x 40"—Photograph, 1981. MBG#909, Mary Boone Gallery, 745 Fifth Avenue, New York, New York 10151.

Fig. 13.4: Dan Graham, *Two Adjacent Pavilions,* 1978–1981. Two-way mirror, transparent glass, steel. Two units 98¾" x 73¼" x 73¼" each. Collection of Kröller-Müller Museum. Courtesy Marian Goodman Gallery, New York.

Fig. 13.5: Hans Haacke, *Shapolsky et al. Manhattan Real Estate Holdings, A Real-Time Social System, as of May 1, 1971* (detail), 1971. © 2001 Artists Rights Society (ARS), New York / VG Bild-Kunst, Bonn. Photo: Fred Scruton.

Fig. 13.6: © Krzysztof Wodiczko, *The Homeless Projection* (1986).

Fig. 13.7: Dennis Adams, *Bus Shelter II* (1986). 14th Street and Third Avenue, New York. 243.8 x 349.3 x 245.1 cm., aluminum, wood, enamel, stainless steel hardware, plexiglas, fluorescent light, duratrans. Image courtesy of the artist and Kent Gallery, New York.

Fig. 13.8: *Pulp Fiction* (1949). Carole Condé and Karl Beveridge. © 1993. Medium: Cibachrome.

Fig. 13.9: © Elizabeth Sisco, Louis Hock, and David Avalos. *Welcome to America's Finest Tourist Plantation* (1988). Photomural, silkscreen on paper, 50" x 20".

Fig. 13.10: © Loraine Leeson 1982, The Art of Change (formerly Docklands Community Poster Project). Photomontage, 18" x 12".

Fig. 13.11: Photomural in situ (1982). © Loraine Leeson, The Art of Change (formerly Docklands Community Poster Project).

Fig. 13.12: Tess Timothy and Mark O'Brien, *The Meal and Slave Market,* Wall and Water Streets, New York (1992–93). From the series "The Lower Manhattan Sign Project," REPOhistory, New York. © REPOhistory. Photo © Tom Klem.

Fig. 13.13: *Native Hosts*, Portland, Oregon. © Edgar Heap of Birds, 1998.

CHAPTER 14

Fig. 14.1: Photograph © Carla Osberg.

Fig. 14.2: Photograph © J. Mark Schuster.

Fig. 14.3: From Haruka Wazaki, "The Urban Festival and Urban Identity," in Anthony P. Cohen and Katsuyoshi Fukui, eds., *Humanising the City: Social Contexts of Urban Life at the Turn of the Millennium* (Edinburgh, Scotland: Edinburgh University Press, 1993), p. 141. Reprinted by permission.

Fig. 14.5: Photograph by Scott Dietrich.

Figs. 14.4, 14.6–14.9: Photographs © J. Mark Schuster.

CHAPTER 16

Figs. 16.1–16.4: Courtesy of Dennis Frenchman.

CONTRIBUTORS

ANNE BEAMISH is an assistant professor in the Community and Regional Planning program in the School of Architecture, University of Texas at Austin. Her research interests center on the spatial and social aspects of information technology, virtual and physical communities, and the design of online environments. For the past two years, she has been managing editor of *ArchNet*, an online community of architects, planners, designers, and scholars with a special focus on the Islamic world. She received her Ph.D. from the Department of Urban Studies and Planning at the Massachusetts Institute of Technology and holds professional degrees in architecture and urban planning.

JULIAN BEINART is Professor of Architecture at the Massachusetts Institute of Technology, where he teaches classes on the theory of city form as well as urban design studios. His projects and writing have been published widely. Recent writings have focused on a new plan for Chandigarh (India), proposed at the fiftieth anniversary of the city; the Olympic Games and city form; the form of urban grids; and methods of application of economic instruments in the nineteenth century. He practices as an architect and urban designer in many parts of the world. He is collaborating with architect Charles Correa in work on the new neurosciences center at MIT.

EUGENIE LADNER BIRCH, FAICP, RTPI (honorary), is professor and chair of the Department of City and Regional Planning at the University of Pennsylvania. A former member of the New York City Planning Commission, she has also served as editor of the *Journal of the American Planning Association* and is coeditor of *Planning Theory and Practice*. Her current research, funded by the Fannie Mae Foundation and the Lincoln Institute of Land Policy, focuses on downtown living in forty U.S. cities.

PATRICIA BURGESS, historian and city planner, has published work on land use, land-use controls, and urban development. After teaching at the University of Texas–Arlington and at Iowa State University, she served as director of Planning and Urban Design Services at the Urban Center in Cleveland State University's Maxine Goodman Levin College of Urban Affairs. She is presently enrolled at Case Western University School of Law, where she will complete her Juris Doctor degree in May 2002.

THOMAS J. CAMPANELLA is an urbanist and historian of the built environment. He holds a Ph.D. from the Massachusetts Institute of Technology and was a Fulbright Fellow at the Chinese University of Hong Kong. His writing has appeared in a variety of publications, including *Salon, Metropolis, Architectural Record,* and the *Harvard Architecture Review.* Campanella is a contributing writer for *Wired* magazine and a lecturer in the Department of Urban Studies and Planning at MIT.

JOHN DE MONCHAUX is Professor of Architecture and Planning at the Massachusetts Institute of Technology. After twenty years of international practice as an urban designer and planner, he came to MIT in 1981 as dean of the School of Architecture and Planning, stepping down in 1992 when he became general manager of The Aga Khan Trust for Culture in Geneva. Returning to MIT on a full-time basis in 1996, he teaches in the school's city design and development group. His interests include urban planning and conservation in the developing world, urban design, and the implementation and outcomes of urban plans and policies.

JULIA R. DOBROW is acting director of the Communications and Media Studies program at Tufts University, where she also teaches in the Department of Child Development. Her research focuses on the effects of ethnic and gender representations in media and on the ways in which animated children's programming portrays race, ethnicity, and gender. She holds a doctorate from the University of Pennsylvania.

RUTH DURACK is director of Kent State University's Urban Design Center, which offers design assistance, research, and public education programs to community organizations and government agencies throughout northeastern Ohio. She teaches seminars and studios in the graduate program in urban design at the university's Architecture School. Prior to moving to Ohio, she practiced urban design at Wallace Roberts & Todd in Philadelphia and San Francisco. She holds degrees in architecture and city planning from the University of Western Australia, the University of California at Berkeley, and the University of Pennsylvania, and has taught urban design at Temple, Drexel, and the University of Pennsylvania.

LARRY R. FORD is Professor of Geography at San Diego State University, where he teaches a variety of courses on cities, including one focusing on globalization and comparative urbanization. He has carried out research in urban areas in North America, Europe, Latin America, and East and Southeast Asia. In 1991, he taught at the University of Indonesia in Jakarta on a Fulbright scholarship. His books include *Cities and Buildings* and *The Spaces between Buildings*, and he has just completed a manuscript for a book on American downtowns. His main interest in all cultural contexts is the relationship between urban landscape change and the spatial structure of cities.

DENNIS FRENCHMAN is Professor of the Practice of Urban Design at the Massachusetts Institute of Technology, where he directs the City Design and Development group and is chair of the Master's in City Planning program. He is a registered architect and founding principal of ICON architecture, inc., located in Boston, with an international practice in architecture, urban design, and planning. His work has focused on the transformation of older, underutilized areas of cities, including many nationally significant historic places. He has a particular interest in the redevelopment of former industrial resources and has prepared plans for the renewal of textile mill towns, canals, rail corridors, steels mills, coal and oil fields, shipyards, and ports. His work in these areas has been cited as the most outstanding in the United States on three occasions by the American Planning Association.

EDWARD W. (NED) HILL is Distinguished Professor of Economic Development at the Maxine Goodman Levin College of Urban Affairs of Cleveland State University and Nonresident Senior Fellow of The Brookings Institution, where he is affiliated with the Center on Urban and Metropolitan Policy. He writes on economic development and urban public policy and is editor of the journal *Economic Development Quarterly*. His most recent book is *Ohio's Competitive Advantage: Manufacturing Productivity* (2001). He holds a Ph.D. in urban and regional planning and economics from MIT.

BRIAVEL HOLCOMB is a professor at the Edward J. Bloustein School of Planning and Public Policy at Rutgers, The State University of New Jersey. Three decades ago, her doctoral dissertation used Kevin Lynch's ideas to explore cultural differences in urban imagery. Since then, she has published on urban revitalization, women and development, and urban economic development. Her recent research focuses on aspects of tourism, primarily in Latin America and the Mediterranean. She holds a Ph.D. in geography from the University of Colorado.

SANDY ISENSTADT teaches architectural history and design at the University of Kentucky's College of Architecture. His writings have focused on the spectacularization of everyday life, a topic approached variously through real estate appraisal, refrigerator design, picture windows, and themed environments. He is currently preparing a history of spatial illusions in American house design for Cambridge University Press. Professor Isenstadt, who holds a doctorate in architectural history from the Massachusetts Institute of Technology, will join the Department of the History of Art at Yale University in 2002.

HENRY JENKINS, director of the Comparative Media Studies program at the Massachusetts Institute of Technology, has spent his career studying media and the way people incorporate it into their lives. He has published articles on a diverse range of topics relating to popular culture, including work on *Star Trek*, WWF Wrestling, Nintendo games, and Dr. Seuss. In 1999, he testified before the U.S. Senate during the hearings on media violence that followed the Littleton (Colorado) shootings and served as cochair of Pop!Tech, the Camden Technology Conference. Jenkins has published six books and more than fifty essays on popular culture. His books include *From Barbie to Mortal Kombat: Gender and Computer Games*; *The Children's Cultural Reader*; *What Made Pistachio Nuts? Early Sound Comedy and the Vaudeville Aesthetic*; *Classical Hollywood Comedy*; *Textual Poachers: Television Fans and Participatory Culture*; and *The Politics and Pleasures of Popular Culture* (forthcoming). Jenkins holds a Ph.D. in communication arts from the University of Wisconsin at Madison and an M.A. in communication studies from the University of Iowa.

DEBORAH KARASOV is codirector of the Institute for Public Art and Design at the Minneapolis College of Art and Design and a consultant for the environmental group Great River Greening. As a landscape architect and cultural geographer, she works with artists, designers, and ecologists in collaborative projects in Minneapolis and Saint Paul. She has held positions at the Walker Art Center, the Design Arts Program of the National Endowment for the Arts, the University of Minnesota, the American Academy in Rome, and at *Public Art Review*. She holds a Ph.D. from the University of Minnesota and an MLA from Harvard University.

JUDITH A. MARTIN is Professor of Geography and director of Urban Studies at the University of Minnesota, where she has taught in six departments in three different colleges over twenty-five years. Her publications have addressed diverse urban concerns such as planning and development, historic preservation, urban renewal, metropolitan governance, and urban design. Martin is general editor of the University of Pennsylvania Press Metropolitan Portraits book series. She has served on the Minneapolis Planning Commission for a decade and has been active in regional policy efforts. Martin is a Fellow of the Lincoln Institute of Land Policy and has served on Fannie Mae's Housing Impact Advisory Committee. She is currently also chair of the Urban Affairs Association.

J. MARK SCHUSTER is professor of Urban Cultural Policy in the Department of Urban Studies and Planning at MIT. He specializes in the analysis of government policies and programs with respect to the arts, culture, and urban design. He has served as a consultant to many organizations in the cultural field, including the Arts Council of Great Britain, the UNESCO World Commission on Culture and Development, the National Endowment for the Arts, the Hungarian Ministry of Culture, the Canada Council, the Council of Europe, and National Public Radio. He is the author of *The Geography of Participation in the Arts and Culture*, *The Audience for American Art Museums*, *Preserving the Built Heritage—Tools for Implementation* (with John de Monchaux), and *Patrons Despite Themselves: Taxpayers and Arts Policy* (with Alan Feld and Michael O'Hare), among numerous other books, articles, and reports. He is currently serving as joint editor of the *Journal of Cultural Economics* and as chairman of the International Alliance of First Night Celebrations. He received his A.B. in applied mathematics from Harvard College and his Ph.D. in urban studies and planning from the Massachusetts Institute of Technology.

INDEX

Note: Italicized page numbers refer to tables, figures, and illustrations.

C

D

I